encyclopedia of
religion, communication, and media

ROUTLEDGE ENCYCLOPEDIAS OF RELIGION AND SOCIETY

David Levinson, *Series Editor*

The Encyclopedia of Millennialism and Millennial Movements

Richard A. Landes, *Editor*

The Encyclopedia of African and African-American Religions

Stephen D. Glazier, *Editor*

The Encyclopedia of Fundamentalism

Brenda E. Brasher, *Editor*

The Encyclopedia of Religious Freedom

Catharine Cookson, *Editor*

The Encyclopedia of Religion and War

Gabriel Palmer-Fernandez, *Editor*

The Encyclopedia of Religious Rites, Rituals, and Festivals

Frank A. Salamone, *Editor*

The Encyclopedia of Pentecostal and Charismatic Christianity

Stanley M. Burgess, *Editor*

The Encyclopedia of Religion, Communication, and Media

Daniel A. Stout, *Editor*

encyclopedia of
religion, communication, and media

Daniel A. Stout, Editor

Religion and Society
A Berkshire Reference Work

ROUTLEDGE
New York   London

Published in 2006 by

Routledge
270 Madison Avenue
New York, NY 10016
www.routledge-ny.com

Published in Great Britain by Routledge
2 Square Park
Milton Park, Abingdon
Oxon OX14 4RN
www.routledge.uk.com

A Berkshire Reference Work
Routledge is an imprint of Taylor & Francis Group.

10 9 8 7 6 5 4 3 2 1

Library of Congress Cataloging-in-Publication Data

Encyclopedia of religion, communication, and media /
Daniel A. Stout, editor.
     p. cm. — (Routledge encyclopedias of religion and society)
  "A Berkshire Reference work."
  Includes bibliographical references and index.
   ISBN 0-415-96946-8
  1. Communication—Religious aspects. I. Stout, Daniel A. II. Series.
P94.E48 2006
201'.6—dc222006012600

Contents

Editorial Advisory Board

List of Entries

List of Entries

List of Abbreviations

KJV	King James Version
NAB	New American Bible
NASB	New American Standard Bible
NIV	New International Version
NJB	New Jerusalem Bible
NRSV	New Revised Standard Version
OEB	Oxford English Bible
RSV	Revised Standard Version

Introduction

Communication is the sine qua non of religion; it is the essence of prayer, sermons, ritual, and congregational fellowship. Unfortunately, the academic study of religion and communication has occurred in disparate fields, with few epistemological bridges between them. Scholars in the communication disciplines, from rhetoric to mass communication, have little to say about religion. Conversely, few anthropologists, psychologists, or sociologists draw from communication theory in their studies of religion. Consequently, no single field provides a deep and thorough exploration of the religion-communication interface. This situation has resulted in new efforts to venture beyond disciplinary borders in order to better understand religion in the current age. *The Encyclopedia of Religion, Communication, and Media (ERCM)* aims to stimulate fresh dialogue and research on this important topic.

This volume breaks down disciplinary walls in numerous ways. First, it combines information about the intrapersonal, interpersonal, group, and societal levels of communication into a single resource. At the *intrapersonal* level, new issues are raised about communication between individuals and deity:

- Why is religious experience difficult to explain in rational terms?

- Why is silence more sacred than spoken prayer in some religious communities?

- What is the nature of "thought communication" in religious meditation?

- Why is the use of profanity justified in some religious circles?

- How does idolatry reinforce religious customs and values?

- Why was chanting one of the first forms of religious communication?

Religious information is also exchanged *between* individuals at the level of *interpersonal communication*. This volume identifies rituals that have not been adequately analyzed in terms of communication aspects:

- Why do some sects require public confession?

- Why is body decoration an acceptable form of worship in some religious groups, but not in others?

- How does dance communicate the sacred through metaphoric movement?

- What are the multiple forms of communication with the dead?

- Why are feasts a form of religious worship in all major religions?

- How does the study of organizational communication apply to religion?

This volume also aids study of *mediated* communication to larger groups both inside and outside religious denominations. Throughout history, technology has simultaneously aided and impeded communication processes; this also applies to religious culture:

- How did religion change during the historical transition from orality to literacy?

- How did printing contribute to the diffusion of religious values in the world?

- Why have religious novels grown in popularity?

- Is television considered a religious medium?

- How has the Internet affected religious congregations and communities?

- What is religious media literacy?

These are only a few of the questions addressed by this encyclopedia. Articles also deal with (1) *concepts* such as information, communication, and censorship, (2) *denominations* which exhibit different communication practices, and (3) the various *media* used in religious worship.

Entries were contributed by scholars from various disciplines, including religious studies, communication, anthropology, sociology, ancient studies, religion and modern culture, theology, and many others.

The *Encyclopedia of Religion, Communication, and Media* benefits a number of audiences. University students will find timely and relevant topics for research and literature reviews. Journalists, on the other hand, are gatekeepers of information; a comprehensive source like this helps assure that facts are accurate. And, lastly, there are the theorists, or those seeking a deeper more thorough examination of religion and communication. For their work to be conceptually grounded, this volume is an essential resource.

A Resource for Theory Building

Emerging fields require new research questions and theory building. This encyclopedia provides foundational information for the systematic study of a phenomenon that has not been examined adequately, and it comes in response to a number of societal developments such as the rise of information technology, emerging forms of worship, and new uses of mass media within denominations. These changes stimulate ideas about the nature of the religion–communication interface; this volume is a means of further analyzing them. Following are some examples of how specific entries might be used to do this, as well as themes covered in the *Encyclopedia*.

The Information Society

How the "Information Society" ultimately shapes religious worship is an open question. In this late period of capitalism, individuals are increasingly interconnected and dependent on information technology for the accomplishment of everyday activities. According to Schement and Stephenson (1996) the information society presents both "tendencies and tensions" for religious groups. Do opportunities for information access extend to everyone in the congregation? Will social networks on the Internet strengthen or weaken religious communities?

Those pursuing such questions will find helpful information in this volume. The entry "Information" argues that religious messages are increasingly sold as a commodity, creating a proliferation of religious information products. In the entry "Information Society," we learn that communication on the Internet is primarily about specialized religious topics. According to the entry "Internet and Cyber-environments," many conventional rituals are now performed online such as cyberpilgrimages, cyberseders, and online prayer groups. The *Encyclopedia* explains how denominations are using new media and summarizes relevant research on the subject.

The Rise of the Religious Marketplace

Perhaps more than at any other time, individuals draw from more than one religious tradition in religious worship. According to Roof (1999, 4), "boundaries separating one faith tradition from another that once seemed fixed are now often blurred; religion identities are malleable and multifaceted, often overlapping several traditions." In the entry "Religious Marketplace" we read about growing personal autonomy in religious worship and how mass media often supplement traditional forms of worship. The entry "Interpretive Community" argues that religious audiences use media texts according to goals for personal growth or efforts to better understand teachings of the institutional church. Entries "Material Culture" and "Youth Culture" explain some of the ways people combine beliefs from several religions into a single personalized form of religious worship.

The Emergence of Postmodern or "Cultural Religion"

Not only are individuals sampling different religious cultures, but nontraditional religious communities are also emerging. This development has a number of communication dimensions. Sylvan (2002, 3) asserts that: "...the religious impulse has simply migrated to another sector of the culture, a sector in which religious sensibilities have flourished and made an enormous impact on a large portion of the population." Ritual, semiological, and communal aspects of religion are now found in media of popular culture such as rock music, television, and film. Religious experiences have been described by teen Internet users (Beaudoin 1998), devotees of popular music (Sylvan 2002), and fans of Elvis Presley (Doss 1999).

This type of religion is postmodern in that it is rarely connected with institutions and is practiced outside of traditional houses of worship. These practices are similar to what is described as popular religion (Long 1987), vernacular religion (Primiano 1995) and cultural religion (Albanese 1996). The point is, these developments demand new definitions of "religion" and "communication." Toward that end, several entries in this volume provide historical, cultural, and economic contexts for cultural religion. In the entry "Numinous," readers learn how certain experiences come to be holy and why activities like listening to music are often described in spiritual terms. The entries "Novels," "Music Video," and "Sports" describe how spirituality is manifesting itself in new places in cultural life.

The Religious Media Literacy Movement

Much conjecture exists about the secularizing influence of mass media: do they strengthen or undermine faith? This is one of the most compelling dilemmas for contemporary denominations, as demonstrated by the Southern Baptist boycott of Disney entertainment (Warren 2001) and the Islamic fatwa on popular novelist Salman Rushdie (Palmer and Gallab, 2001). As seen in "Media Activism," religions often issue guidelines for media use and sometimes organize boycotts. In the entry "Media Literacy" we learn an alternative to activism: teaching members critical skills for using media in optimal ways. Hess (2001), for example, explores how movies and television programs can be used to teach religious values. For those seeking a deeper understanding of media literacy, several entries in the *Encyclopedia of Religion, Communication, and Media* should be helpful. An important step in studying this phenomenon is observing what religious leaders teach their members about media use, and subsequently, how church members actually use the media. Entries on various denominations, as well as those on particular media, should be helpful to researchers.

Beyond Browsing: An Encyclopedia for the Research Imagination

Research on the information society, religious marketplace, cultural religion, and the media literacy movement will be aided by the entries in this encyclopedia. However, it is also hoped that the *Encyclopedia of Religion, Communication, and Media* will stimulate what Hart (1998) calls the "research imagination," or the process of combining pieces of information into fresh questions for future research. Such questions are vital to a developing field such as religion and communication. In his seminal book, *The Sociological Imagination* C. Wright Mills elaborates on the need to bring previously disconnected ideas together (1978, 232):

> The sociological imagination, I remind you, in considerable part consists of the capacity to shift from one perspective to another, and in the process to build up an adequate view of a total society and of its components. It is this imagination, of course, that sets off the social scientist from the mere technician.

At the technical level, the *Encyclopedia of Religion, Communication, and Media* is an excellent resource for fact-finding and browsing. However, it will accomplish more in the hands of imaginative researchers willing to synthesize ideas across disciplines such as communication, anthropology, sociology, psychology, and religious studies. The *Encyclopedia* combines entries from these and other fields into the first comprehensive collection of its kind. Whether it is used to select a topic for future study or strengthen a literature review, this work is an effort to better understand the relationship between religion and communication. The extent of that understanding, however, depends on the imagination of the researcher.

The volume contains one hundred twenty-four articles covering five broad topics—Alternative Religious Movements, Forms of Communication and Media, Historical Periods, Key Concepts, and Religious Traditions. The articles are supplemented by dozens of photos and sidebars and an extensive index.

DANIEL A. STOUT

Further Reading

Albanese, C. L. (1996). Religion and American popular culture: An introductory reader. *Journal of the American Academy of Religion* 59(4). 733-742.

Beaudoin, T. (1998). *Virtual faith: The irreverent spiritual quest of generation X.* San Francisco: Jossey-Bass.

Doss, E. (1999). *Elvis culture: Fans, faith, & image.* Lawrence, KS: University Press of Kansas.

Hart, C. (1998). *Doing a literature review: Releasing the social science research imagination.* London: Sage.

Hess, M. (2001). Media literacy as a support for the development of a responsible imagination in religious community. In D. A. Stout & J. M. Buddenbaum (Eds.)

Religion and popular culture: Studies on the interaction of worldviews (pp. 289–311). Ames: Iowa State University Press.

Long, C. H. (1987). Popular religion. In M. Eliade et al. (Eds.) *The encyclopedia of religion,* Vol. 11 (pp. 442–452). New York: Macmillan.

Mills, C. W. (1978). *The sociological imagination.* Oxford: Oxford University Press.

Palmer, A. & Gallab, A. (2001). Islam and western culture: Navigating terra incognita. In D. A. Stout & J. M. Buddenbaum (Eds.) *Religion and popular culture: Studies on the interaction of worldviews* (pp. 109–124). Ames: Iowa State University Press.

Primiano, L.N. (1995). Vernacular religion and the search for method in religious folklife. *Western Folklore 54,* 37-56.

Roof, W. C. (1999). *Spiritual marketplace: Baby boomers and the remaking of American religion.* Princeton, NJ: Princeton University Press.

Schement, J. & Stephenson, H. (1996). Religion and the information society. In D. Stout & M. Buddenbaum (Eds.) *Religion and mass media: Audiences and Adaptations* (pp. 261–289). Thousand Oaks, CA: Sage. .

Sylvan, R. (2002). *Traces of the spirit: The religious dimensions of popular music.* New York: New York University Press.

Warren, H. (2001). Southern Baptists as audience and public: A cultural analysis of the Disney Boycott. In D. Stout & J. Buddenbaum (Eds.) *Religion and popular culture: Studies on the interaction of worldviews* (pp. 169–186). Ames: Iowa State University Press.

List of Contributors

Armentrout, Don
Sewanee University
Altars

Armstrong, Rick
Wichita State University
Televangelism

Badaracco, Claire M.
Marquette University
Literature
Religious Poetry

Baker, Sherry
Brigham Young University
Mormonism

Bishop, Kyle
Southern Utah University
Profanity (Taboo)

Bliese, Richard H.
Luther Theological Seminary
Sermons

Borden, Anne L.
Emory University
Bookstores

Bossius, Thomas
Göteborg University
Youth Culture

Bryant, Jennings
University of Alabama
Pornography

Buddenbaum, Judith M.
Indianapolis, IN
Journalism

Campbell, Heidi
Texas A&M University
Internet and Cyber Environments

Carstarphen, Meta
University of Oklahoma
Native American Religion

Casey, Eric
Sweet Briar College
Commemoration

Christians, Clifford
University of Illinois, Urbana-Champaign
Technology

Clanton, Dan W.
University of Denver
Apocrypha

Claussen, Dane
Point Park University
Censorship

Cohen, Yoel
Netanya Academic College
Judaism

Craigo-Snell, Shannon
Yale University
Silence

List of Contributors

Cressman, Dale
Brigham Young University
Satellite Communication

Crowther, Edward
Adams State College
Middle Ages

Dokupil, Susanna
Houston, TX
Bells

Draney, Dan W.
Fuller Theological Seminary
Encyclicals

Drumheller, Matthew
Abilene, TX
Profane Communication

Duncan, Dean W.
Brigham Young University
Film

Ferre, John
University of Louisville
Protestantism, Mainline

Fitzsimmons, James
University of South Dakota
Relics

Fortner, Robert
Calvin College
Political Communication

Frasca, Ralph
Marymount University
Books
Feasts
Priests

Fullmer, Glen T.
Baha'i National Center
Bahai

Gibson, Twyla
University of Toronto
Orality

Gillum, Gary
Brigham Young University
Choirs
Libraries

Gold, Malcolm
Malone College
Stereotyping

Golden, Anne
University of Utah
Apparel
Material Culture

Graham, Mark
College of Wooster
Literature, Secular

Gray, Campbell B.
Brigham Young University
Museums

Gring, Mark A.
Texas Tech University
Knowledge

Gutierrez, Cathy
Sweet Briar College
Dead (Communication with)

Hager, Andreas
Abo Akademi University
Music Video
Youth Culture

Hammann, Louis J.
Gettysburg College
Tolerance

Hammond, Scott C.
Utah Valley State College
Organizational Communication

Harrison, Milmon F.
University of California, Davis
Black Spiritual Churches

Hassner, Ron E.
Harvard University
Temples

Hatcher, Anthony
Elon University
Magazines

Hedquist, Valerie
University of Montana
Paintings
Sculpture

Hess, Mary E.
Luther Seminary
Media Literacy

Holmes, Cecile S.
University of South Carolina
Buddhism
Newspapers

Hoover, Stewart
University of Colorado, Boulder
Media
Religious Marketplace

Howard, Robert Glenn
University of Wisconsin, Madison
Fundamentalism

Hutchinson, Dawn L.
Florida State University
Miracles

Hwang Chen, Chiung
Brigham Young University, Hawaii
Daoism

Isbell, Charles David
Louisiana State University
Confession

Juss, Satvinder Singh
King's College, London
Meditation
Sikhism

Kashyap, Rina
Lady Shri Ram College
Jihad

Kelso, Anthony
Iona College
Advertising

Kent, Stephen
University of Alberta
Scientology

Klaus, Byron D.
Assemblies of God Theological Seminary
Charisma

Kornegay, Van
University of South Carolina
Art

Lamoureux, Edward L.
Bradley University
Medium Theory

La'Porte, Victoria
Melbourne, Australia
Defamation

Larsen, David L.
Trinity Evangelical Divinity School
Cross, The
Persuasion

Lateju, T.F.
Obafemi Awolowo University
Mosques

Leach, Robert T.
Ogden Dunes Community Church
Epistemology

Levinson, David
Berkshire Publishing Group
Wicca

Lewis, Todd V.
Biola University
Entertainment

Lindlof, Thomas R.
University of Kentucky
Interpretive Community

Luft, Shanny
University of North Carolina, Chapel Hill
Boycotts

Magdalinski, Tara
University of the Sunshine Coast
Sports

Mahan, Jeffrey H.
Illif School of Theology
Myths

Mahony, Diana
Brigham Young University, Hawaii
Humor and Laughter

Maresco, Peter A.
Sacred Heart University
Signage

Mattson, Craig
Trinity Christian College
Media Activism
Sacred Communication
Symbolism (Semiotics)

McCloud, Sean
University of North Carolina, Charlotte
Popular Culture

McGuckin, John A.
Union Theological Seminary
Angels
Orthodoxy

Mendieta, Eduardo
State University of New York, Stony Brook
Enlightenment, The

List of Contributors

Mitchell, Jolyon
University of Edinburgh
Radio

Moore, Rick
Boise State University
Culture Wars

Morgan, David
Valparaiso University
Pamphlets

Nadeau, Kathleen
California State University
Confucianism

Neumann, Caryn E.
Ohio State University
Chanting
Shaman

Ogungbile, David O.
Obafemi Awolowo University
Body Decoration

Ojo, Matthews A.
Obafemi Awolowo University
Idolatry
Prophets

Palmer, Allen
Brigham Young University
Islam

Peters, John Durham
University of Iowa
Calendar
Clock
Communication

Petersen, Todd
Southern Utah University
Novels

Peterson, Dan W.
Southwestern Missouri State University
Organizational Communication

Rajagopal, Arvind
New York University
Hinduism

Rytting, Bryce
Utah Valley State College
Music

Samuelsen, Eric
Brigham Young University
Drama

Sautter, Cia
United Theological Seminary of the Twin Cities
Dance

Scott, David
University of South Carolina
Free Speech

Seales, Chad
University of North Carolina, Chapel Hill
Congregations

Shusko, Christa
Syracuse University
Numinous

Smith, Michael R
Campbell University
Proseletyzing
Protestantism, Conservative

Stout, Daniel
University of South Carolina
Audience
Information
Information Society

Strayer, Kerry
Otterbein College
Anabaptists

Sturgill, Amanda
Baylor University
Evangelicalism

Tilson, Donn
University of Miami
Public Relations

Vance-Trembath, Sally M.
University of San Francisco
Canonization
Catholicism

Wansink, Craig
Virginia Wesleyan College
Papyrus
Translation

Warren, Hilary
Otterbein College
Television

Williams, Julie K.H.
Samford University
Puritanism

Yelle, Robert A.
University of Toronto
Mantra

Advertising

Advertising's relationship to religion can be approached from several different directions. The most apparent connection concerns the use of advertising to promote faith or attendance at a place of worship. Its impact in this area has probably been minimal compared to the role of family and cultural traditions in shaping religious beliefs and practices. Some critics would assert, however, that incorporating advertising and related activities into the realm of spirituality tends to coarsen religion by mixing commercial and sacred elements. Other scholars depict a more debatable link between the two institutions, claiming that advertising itself serves as a kind of religion or has even partially supplanted religion in its alleged ability to guide people on how they should think and behave in a fully industrialized society. If this argument is accepted, then advertising's influence on religion has been more profound. Still another site of intersection involves the development of advertising campaigns to encourage the consumption of both nonreligious and religious goods and services by market segments classified according to their religious affiliations.

As in many academic fields, definitions of *advertising* abound, depending on the perspective of the authority viewing the field. From the standpoint of a business procedure, it can be put simply: advertising is "paid communications with one's market" (Laird 1998, 15). Advertising, within this context, is but one element of the marketing process, which consists of myriad strategies and tactics that relate to creating, defining, and packaging a product; determining how it should be priced; deciding on places of distribution; and devising promotional methods—of which advertising is but one option. Yet such a practical definition reveals little about advertising's noneconomic interaction with society and culture, including religion. To investigate advertising from this angle, several scholars offer definitions that attempt to go further in assessing advertising's social impact beyond its obvious promotional task. For example, James B. Twitchell contends that advertising is "*ubiquitous, anonymous, syncretic, symbiotic, profane*, and especially, *magical*" (Twitchell 1996, 16)—ubiquitous because, as various researchers estimate, a person living in one of the highly technologically advanced societies is likely to be exposed daily to thousands of advertisements; anonymous because the author writing on behalf of the sponsor of an advertisement is rarely identified; symbiotic because advertising connects to other trends in a given culture; profane because it directly pitches ephemeral goods and services; and magical because it often infuses products with symbolic meaning and implies that these wares can deliver quick solutions to complex problems. Both economically oriented and socially or culturally oriented definitions of advertising have implications in terms of the subject of religion.

Advertising's Origins

Rudimentary forms of advertising can be traced to antiquity in places such as Egypt, Greece, and Rome. For thousands of years, people involved in trade employed public criers and pictorial signs to attract attention to products as varied as spices and rugs. During the medieval period in Europe, merchants hung visual storefront signs indicating what type of items customers could purchase within—a baker might be identified, for instance, by a depiction of a sheaf of wheat. Yet modern advertising as it is understood today did not emerge until the nineteenth century. A number of factors—especially industrialization and the ability of manufacturers to produce more goods than the existing market could consume—provided the impetus for creating more sophisticated means of advertising to stir demand.

Although modern advertising developed simultaneously in both Europe—particularly England—and the United States, it flourished in the New World as chieftains of business displayed more positive attitudes toward the promotional tool than their counterparts in England, who often dismissed it as crass or "puffery." During its origin, modern advertising acquired a dubious reputation due, in part, to the fact that makers of patent medicines—medically unsound panaceas that promised relief from a host of ills—were among the leaders in foreshadowing the rise of national, brand-name marketing and advertising. Advertisements for these tonics often appeared in religious weekly periodicals, which were vastly popular in the United States and were among the first publications to accept advertising in general as a way to reduce the prices customers must pay. Patent medicines sometimes appropriated the discourse of religion to build credibility. The inventor of Radway's Ready Relief, for instance, stated in an advertisement that his healing solution had been "revealed to him in a providential manner" (Presbrey 1929, 291). Occasionally, ministers provided testimony in advertisements for popular nostrums.

In the United States, a number of renowned early practitioners were either sons of ministers, former ministers themselves, or had contemplated ministry before arriving at their careers in advertising. In the 1880s, Artemas Ward, the son of an Episcopal clergyman, for example, was one of the most celebrated early architects of modern advertising, helping to make Sapolio, a scouring soap, perhaps the most recognized brand of its time. The successful copywriter Claude C. Hopkins came from a long line of clergymen and was, for a short while, a preacher himself before channeling his energy toward selling goods and services. Various scholars point out that many of the men who established advertising as a profession in the United States had a tendency to conflate Protestant virtues with the benefits of business.

Advertising as a Method of Advocating Faith

Although the use of advertising to promote religious belief or gathering at worship services is most associated with Christian Evangelical denominations, many influential members of other religious faiths and institutions also employ the tool in various ways. For example, rabbis and Jewish officials have initiated advertising campaigns to persuade unaffiliated Jews to attend synagogue and practice their religion. In India, religious pay television, targeted mostly to the majority Hindu population, seeks advertisers to offset the cost of its programs to viewers. As a means not of encouraging the adoption of a particular religious belief system but of trying to gain greater tolerance toward its adherents, Muslim organizations launched educational advertising campaigns after the 11 September 2001 terrorist attacks in the United States because those accused of participating in the suicide mission were all self-proclaimed Muslims—the groups hoped to explain that most branches of Islam do not endorse mass violence. Appearances around the world by well-known spiritual teachers who aim to communicate various Buddhist principles, such as the Dalai Lama of Tibet and Thich Nhat Hanh, are announced through advertising. To help pay for trips for speaking engagements, Pope John Paul II secured corporate sponsorship from firms, allowing some companies to affix his image on packages for products.

Engaging in marketing and advertising activities to promote religion has a particularly rich history in the United States. The historian Nathan O. Hatch explains that, during the early 1800s and throughout the century, because the young nation, unlike its European predecessors, inscribed in its founding documents the separation of church and state and the rejection of an established faith, the free practice of religion led to vigorous sectarianism. Consequently, evangelists—mostly of various Christian denominations—found themselves in a competitive environment and needed to implement strategies for drawing people to their respective congregations. In essence, a type of spiritual marketplace arose. Popular religious revival meetings, for example, frequently blended preaching and worship with commercial activities to create a somewhat carnival-like atmosphere. The tradition of mixing marketing and advertising with faith has continued until the present day. Bumper stickers and clothing with religious slogans; commercials for churches that can accommodate thousands of people and feature, for instance, fast-food courts, multimedia presentations, and dozens of self-improvement programs; advertisements for congregations that adopt irreverent techniques commonly found in consumer-goods campaigns; provocative billboard displays—these are just a few of the tactics that have been deployed to further the cause of religion. Some particularly savvy religious marketers utilize some of the same terminology, research and strategical methods, and standards of execution as their counterparts in the consumer-goods field. Today, such advanced religious marketing and advertising endeavors are a worldwide phenomenon and extend to numerous faiths and denominations, many of which are not generally thought of as Evangelical.

Using marketing and advertising to promote faith is a contentious issue for a portion of religious adherents. Proponents contend that churches and other religious institutions must adapt to a contemporary marketing and media-saturated environment if they hope to both preserve the allegiance of existing believers and recruit new participants. Those critical of the techniques often postulate that advertising religion in the same manner as other products diminishes or trivializes faith and threatens to reduce its sacred aura by attaching it to the secular realm.

Advertising as Religion

An even more controversial topic among scholars of both media and religion centers on whether advertising functions as a type of religion in highly industrialized societies or has even largely replaced it in providing people with socially sanctioned ways of thinking and behaving. One argument holds that advertising expresses a similar didacticism and employs the same rhetorical patterns as religion. Instead of giving substantial information about products and services, much of advertising offers moral lessons about everyday life and a type of secular salvation. A typical commercial for a shampoo, for example, might show a consumer who is initially socially ostracized but later, after purchasing and using the advertised product, is nearly instantaneously transformed into someone with a dramatically improved sense of self-esteem that results in a passionate relationship with an especially attractive person. Those who subscribe to this perspective do not claim that one advertisement can deeply affect the worldview of the viewers exposed to it. Rather, they maintain, people's outlook on life and sense of values are bound to be shaped by the cumulative impact of the literally thousands of similarly themed advertisements that they are sure to encounter year after year.

Other theorists propose a different line of reasoning, contending that advertising derives its strength by filling goods with symbolic properties to provide meaning—a task commonly attributed to religion—in a technological environment, by supplying a sense of hope or therapeutic promise, or by adding magic or a renewed sense of the sacred to a supposedly secularized milieu. For instance, partly because of its successful advertising campaigns developed over many decades, Coca Cola is not perceived by those who drink it as merely an artificially colored, carbonated water containing a high quantity of sugar, but, at least on an unconscious level, as a cultural icon that stands for wholesome pleasure and represents a magical instrument for bringing people from around the world together. The beverage carries so much resonance that when the company once attempted to replace it with "New Coke" there was considerable public protest because the audience realized that the manufacturer was not only altering the taste of the product but, more importantly, was tampering with everything it had come to signify. Today, there is an entire museum devoted to the display of Coca Cola memorabilia. Coke represents a particularly striking example of a product attaining near mythological status. But one of the main tasks of advertising is to transform countless commodities into brands with figurative associations so that they acquire more meaning than they would if they were recognized only for the utilitarian purposes they serve. For each of the allegations made by the critics who suggest that advertising has somewhat usurped the role of religion in communicating meaning, however, there are counterclaims that identify advertising as but one message system among a diversity of others; within the context of family, education, interaction with peer groups, and a still-powerful structure of religious institutions, advertising cannot be assumed to mimic or to have significantly replaced the role of religion in people's day-to-day experience.

Religious Rhetoric of Advertising Practitioners

Several historians have illustrated that from the late nineteenth century through the 1920s, a number of advertising agents—particularly in the United States—through their use of language commonly linked with religion, displayed a tendency to position their industry as though it were satisfying an almost sacred mission. A practitioner in Atlanta declared in 1911, for instance, "There is no higher calling, ministers not excepted, in America or any other country than ours" (Pope 1973, 317). Earnest Elmo Calkins, a prominent member of the First Baptist Church who later entered the field of advertising, stated that the businessman should call upon the advertising professional "for advice—for prophecy almost, as Belshazzar turned to David" (Calkins 1928, 229–30). Members of the industry sometimes entered churches to deliver sermons, entitled, for example, "The Religion of Advertising" and "Advertising and Righteousness" (Pope 1973, 321). Bruce Barton, a cofounder of the eventual transnational agency Batten, Barton, Durstine, and Osborn (BBDO), was even more forceful in drawing upon the domain of religion to discuss his profession. The son of a liberal Protestant minister, Barton nearly became a clergyman himself. In the 1920s, he gained fame with *The Man Nobody Knows: A Discovery of the Real Jesus*, which became the best-selling nonfiction book in the United States in 1925. In the work, Barton portrayed Christ as the founder of modern business and an advertiser deserving of emulation, writing, for example, "Take any one of the parables, no matter which—you will find that it exemplifies all the principles on which advertising text books are written" (Barton 1925, 143).

Although religious-sounding rhetoric among advertising professionals has ebbed and flowed throughout the field's history and has never been widespread, such language is still expressed. Internal publications within large international agencies, for example, assert that advertising, through its ability to create symbolic meaning for brands, can inject spirituality into the lives of people who no longer find profound fulfillment through long-established institutions, including places of worship or prayer. Sal Randazzo, a specialist in advertising research, maintains that it is "fitting that advertising should come to play a role in creating and reinforcing the mythologies that shape our lives. The Greeks had their pantheon of gods; Americans have brands" (Randazzo 1993, 49).

The Appropriation of Religious Symbols and Themes in Advertising

A related way in which the advertising industry has blended religious expression with the promotion of goods and services, according to various researchers, is by imbuing advertisements with traditionally religious symbols or themes. Roland Marchand argues that creators of print advertisements in the 1920s and 1930s often appropriated religious iconography and employed techniques that mirrored the patterns of religious parables. Contemporary advertisers, on occasion, take the same approach—for example, a nineteenth-century Shaker hymn has been used to promote a car, Adam and Eve have appeared in advertisements for cosmetics, and Catholic nuns have been depicted in a commercial for a computer. Nor are religious symbols and motifs in advertising co-opted only from Christian

faiths. Eastern monks or mystics have been represented in various commercials, Zen Buddhist–like concepts have been utilized to advertise a variety of products, and Orthodox Jews have been pictured in a campaign for a computer online service.

Advertising to Religious Markets

Another area of overlap between religion and advertising focuses on the use of advertising to promote nonreligious goods and services to markets defined according to religious demographics. As advertising has evolved with the help of more rigorous research and the development of increasingly sophisticated methods, most advertisers realize they cannot appeal to everyone in the same way and, instead, segment an audience according to varied characteristics. They then decide which markets to target and how they should attempt to successfully address each one. Accordingly, some advertisers have shown interest in reaching, for example, the Christian Evangelical market or the Jewish market. To accomplish the goal requires sensitivity to the faiths of people classified within each market. Advertisers that endeavor to sell their products worldwide are faced with particular challenges, because they must adapt to, for instance, a Judeo-Christian sensibility throughout most of the Western nations; the Muslim faith honored in much of the Middle East and Africa, and parts of Asia; and the Eastern sacred principles, including tenets from Buddhism and Confucianism, held by many Asian citizens. Although advertising is regulated around the world, in some countries these restrictions are influenced by religious beliefs and practices. For example, in Saudi Arabia, in compliance with its interpretation of Islam, government agencies have mandated that advertisers observe strict taboos. In many other instances, limits are not formalized in law but suggested by religious leaders or followed by advertisers that are attuned to their audiences' religious perceptions and wish to avoid offending them. As a case in point, in 1997, the Vatican issued an encyclical regarding its views on the ethics of advertising—although the document is not legally binding, advertisers are free to consider it when targeting a heavily Catholic population. Numerous advertisements have been protested by various religious believers because they found the materials to be an affront to their convictions. For instance, a Muslim minister decried a commercial created by the Miller Brewing Company that portrayed three angels drinking beer in heaven. Often, companies have retracted the unfavorably received materials if their marketing staffs felt that the negative publicity could hurt their businesses' reputations or sales. In France, for example, an advertising agency dropped and issued an apology for an ad that presented a satirical version of Leonardo Da Vinci's painting, *The Last Supper*.

At the same time, many organizations target religious audiences with advertising for religious goods and services. Recent decades have witnessed the growth of religious product marketing and the specialty retail outlets that house the featured items, including "What Would Jesus Do" (WWJD) jewelry and clothing; religious CDs and posters; coffee mugs, coasters, and other articles etched with religious images or expressions; new translations of the Bible designed to reach young adults with packaging that incorporates the conventions of popular teen magazines; and a host of other religious merchandise. Advertising for religious products and stores can commonly be found in magazines and on television networks devoted to serving people of faith.

The Future

All of these issues regarding the interplay of advertising and religion are likely to be further debated and deliberated on in the future. One area of research that is lacking, however, is to what extent audiences find religious meanings in nonreligious forms of advertising.

Anthony Kelso

See also Persuasion; Public Relations; Religious Marketplace; Signage

Further Reading

Al-Olayan, F. S., & Karande, K. (2000). A content analysis of magazine advertisements from the United States and the Arab world. *Journal of Advertising, 29*(3), 69–82.

Arens, W. F. (2004). *Contemporary advertising* (9th ed.). Boston: McGraw-Hill Irwin.

Barton, B. (1925). *The man nobody knows: A discovery of the real Jesus.* Indianapolis, IN: Bobbs-Merrill.

Calkins, E. E. (1928). *Business the civilizer.* Boston: Atlantic Monthly Press.

Fox, S. (1984). *The mirror makers: A history of American advertising and its creators.* New York: William Morrow.

Hatch, N. O. (1989). *The democratization of American Christianity.* New Haven, CT: Yale University Press.

Hindley, D., & Hindley, G. (1972). *Advertising in Victorian England, 1837–1901.* London: Wayland.

Jhally, S. (1990). *The codes of advertising: Fetishism and the political economy of meaning in the consumer society.* New York: Routledge.

Laird, P. W. (1998). *Advertising progress: American business and the rise of consumer marketing.* Baltimore: Johns Hopkins University Press.

Lears, J. (1982). From salvation to self-realization: Advertising and the therapeutic roots of the consumer culture, 1880–1930. In R. W. Fox & T. J. Lears (Eds.), *The culture of consumption: Critical essays in American history, 1880–1980* (pp. 3–38). New York: Pantheon.

Lears, J. (1994). *Fables of abundance: A cultural history of advertising in America.* New York: Basic.

Marchand, R. (1985). *Advertising the American dream: Making way for modernity, 1920–1940.* Berkeley: University of California Press.

McDaniel, S. W. (1989). The use of marketing techniques by churches: A national survey. *Review of Religious Research, 31*(2), 175–182.

McDaniel, S. W., & Burnett, J. J. (1991). Targeting the evangelical market segment. *Journal of Advertising Research, 31*(4), 26–33.

Moore, R. L. (1994). *Selling God: American religion in the marketplace of culture.* New York: Oxford University Press.

Pope, D. A. (1973). The development of national advertising, 1865–1920 (Doctoral dissertation, Columbia University, 1973). *Dissertation Abstracts International, 34* (06), 3318.

Presbrey, F. (1929). *The history and development of advertising.* Garden City, NY: Doubleday, Doran.

Randazzo, S. (1993). *Mythmaking on Madison Avenue: How advertisers apply the power of myth and symbolism to create leadership brands.* Chicago: Probus.

Spitzer, L. (1962). American advertising explained as popular art. In A. Hatcher (Ed.), *Essays on English and American literature* (pp. 248–277). Princeton, NJ: Princeton University Press.

Twitchell, J. B. (1996). *Adcult USA: The triumph of advertising in American culture.* New York: Columbia University Press.

Altars

Altar is a translation of a Hebrew word that means "place of sacrifice," "to slaughter," or "to slaughter and cut up for the purpose of sacrifice." An altar is usually a raised structure, but it can be any structure or place on which sacrifices are offered, incense is burned, or gifts are presented in worship of a deity or deities, and sometimes of an ancestor. In Christian churches, a structure of wood or stone, sometimes called a communion table, holds the Eucharistic elements of bread and wine for consecration in the Mass or Lord's Supper. In the Judeo-Christian tradition, an altar is a place of communication between God and humanity.

Old Testament

There are over four hundred references to altars in the Old Testament. The first occurs in Genesis in the story of Noah's ark. When all the people and animals left the ark after the flood, "Noah built an altar to the Lord" and offered burnt offerings of animals and birds on the altar (Genesis 8:20, RSV). This would have been an offering of thanksgiving. In the book of Exodus, the commandment to offer sacrifices to God upon an altar was given at the same time the Ten Commandments were given to Moses. "An altar of earth you shall make for me and sacrifice on it your burnt offerings and your peace offerings, your sheep and your oxen; in every place where I cause my name to be remembered I will come to you and bless you. And if you make me an altar of stone, you shall not build it of hewn stones; for if you wield your tool upon it you profane it. And you shall not go up by steps to my altar, that your nakedness be not exposed on it" (Exodus 20:24–26). Therefore, an altar was to be made of earth or uncut stone, natural materials that had not been profaned by human construction. Furthermore, the altar was not to have any steps so that the officiating priest would not be exposed. Because altars of earth could easily be destroyed, stone altars were preferred.

Exodus 27:2 provides information about a very important part of the altar: "And you shall make horns for it [altar] on its four corners; its horns shall be of one piece with it." While the precise significance of the horns is unclear, these horns were believed to symbolize the power and strength of God. On the Day of Atonement these horns were sprinkled with blood. Because the altar was sacred, a person grasping the horns of the altar could not be killed, thus the horns provided a kind of sanctuary or refuge.

New Testament

Altars are not nearly as important in the New Testament as they are in the Old Testament. The Scripture stating that Jesus Christ "offered for all time a single sacrifice for sins" (Hebrews 10:12) could be interpreted as putting an end to sacrificial worship and consequently any need for altars. Probably the only direct reference to a Christian altar is in the metaphor in Hebrews 13:10: "We have an altar from which those who serve the tent have no right to eat." What this altar refers to is greatly debated. Some say it refers to the cross, others to the communion table, and still others say that it means Christ is our altar.

The book of Hebrews in the New Testament notes the correspondence between the Old Testament sacrificial system and the death of Jesus Christ on the cross. Hebrews 7:29 stresses that Jesus is the high priest of the new covenant who has sacrificed his own body.

There are only twenty-four references to altars in the New Testament. Eight allusions to altars are in Revelation. Six references are made by Jesus in Matthew 5:21–26, where Jesus is giving an illustration of the true understanding of the law. The heart of the passage is verse 23: "So if you are offering your gift at the altar, and there remember that your brother has something against you, leave your gift there before the altar and go; first be reconciled to your brother, and then come and offer your gift." The higher righteousness is reconciliation with the brother, not offering one's gift on the altar.

In the Pauline epistles there are six references to altars, the most significant being the observation he made at Athens in Acts 17:23–24: "So Paul, standing in the middle of the Areopagus, said: 'Men of Athens, I perceive that you are very religious. For as I passed along, and observed the objects of your worship, I found also an altar with this inscription, 'To an unknown god.' What therefore you worship as unknown, this I proclaim to you." Paul makes clear that this unknown God has been revealed in Jesus Christ, and does not now dwell in shrines made by man.

Early Church

The Early Christians replaced the Jewish altar with the Eucharistic table; they substituted the Eucharist for Old Testament sacrifices and used tables similar to that used for the Last Supper Jesus ate with his disciples in the upper room on Maundy Thursday. Some early Christian writers insisted that the true altar was the heart of the Christian.

In the first two centuries, Christians met in homes for their worship, what we might call "house churches." In these places they did not have altars, but had a simple, wooden table, *mensa* in Latin. It served the functional purpose of providing a place to set the bread and wine for Holy Communion. So until about 250 CE, communion was administered from a moveable wooden

A statue of the Buddha at an altar in China. *Courtesy of Tomasz Resiak/ istockphoto.com.*

table, possibly a single step above the rest of the floor. Gradually in the Western church this place of celebration was called an altar, and in the Eastern Church it was called a holy table or the "table of the Lord," based on 1 Corinthians 10:21. Thus "altar" and "table" have been used interchangeably, with the resultant confusion that the Eucharist has been viewed as a sacrifice (altar) or meal (table). During the Middle Ages, "altar" replaced "table," and the Eucharist was regarded as a "bloodless sacrifice" of Christ offered by the priest.

Pope Felix I (269–274) decreed that "mass should be celebrated above the tombs of martyrs," an observance probably based on Revelation 6:9: "I saw under the altar the souls of those who had been slain for the word of God and for the witness they had borne." Therefore Christians erected altars over the burial places of martyrs. This practice developed into the medieval custom that no altar could be consecrated unless it contained a relic or relics of a martyr. Later entire churches were built over the tombs of martyrs, the most significant being St. Peter's Basilica in Rome.

In the early church the altar/table was freestanding, rather than against a wall. The clergy who were participating in the liturgy and the bishop, who was the main celebrant, sat behind the altar facing the congregation. Eventually, the church in the West moved the altar against the wall and the celebrant presided at the Eucharist with his back to the people.

Medieval Church

With the end of persecution and the beginning of closer relations between the church and the Roman Empire, church architecture, furniture, and ritual became more elaborate. For example, a canopy, called a ciborium or baldachin, was hung over the altar. Today the ciborium contains the bread for the Eucharist. In the early church one altar for one church was the rule. During the Middle Ages, the multiplication of masses required additional altars, ending the patristic principle and practice of one altar about which the people of God gathered each Lord's Day. These side altars were usually dedicated to certain saints, and private masses were held there for the repose of the soul of the founder. When a church or cathedral had more than one altar, the principal one was called the high altar.

Additionally, in this medieval period, more and more altars were made from stone than from wood. As the material changed from wood to stone, so the shape changed from table to tomb, and the meaning changed from meal to sacrifice.

Reformation

At the time of the sixteenth-century Reformation, Protestants and Anglicans dropped the word "altar" and replaced it with "table." This stated the new theological understanding that the Eucharist was not the sacrifice of the Mass, but the Lord's Supper, and a supper should be eaten at a table. The cultic significance of the altar was challenged and changed by the Reformation. Many reformers promoted the destruction of stone altars, which seemed to imply a tomb, and replaced them with wooden tables, which obviously implied a meal. Retaining an altar was a sign of unreformed doctrine. Calvinists were much more opposed to altars than were the Lutherans. In England the word "altar" was retained in the 1549 *Book of Common Prayer*, known as the First Prayerbook of Edward VI. However, the 1552 *Book of Common Prayer*, the Second Edwardean Prayerbook, did not have the word "altar." Altars were replaced by moveable wooden tables, known sometimes as "God's board." A moveable table could actually be moved into the midst of the worshipping congregation.

Today

The liturgical movement of the twentieth century has had an impact on a number of Protestant denominations. This movement has stressed the centrality of the Eucharist at each Sunday worship service. This means that the Sunday service will have a sermon and the Lord's Supper or Eucharist. Also, the significance of baptism has been regained. This means that the foci of Christian worship are the font, the pulpit or ambo, and the table. The table has replaced the altar and it has been moved out from up against the wall. The officiant presides from the back of the table facing the congregation, thus emphasizing a communal meal. The table is less highly decorated than the older altars used to be. Basically all a table needs is a tablecloth.

The Second Vatican Council (1962–1965) encouraged Roman Catholics to regain the concept of the Eucharist as a meal. While the element of sacrifice is retained, the Roman Catholic Eucharist now is more like a meal in which the communicants receive both the bread and the wine. The *Catechism of the Catholic Church* (1994) teaches that the altar of the New Covenant is the Lord's cross from which the sacrament of the Paschal mystery flows. The altar is the center of the church, and on that altar the sacrifice of the cross is made present under the sacramental signs of bread and wine. The altar is also the table of the Lord, to which the people of God are invited.

The altar should not have items on it not related to the Eucharistic celebration, such as flowers. It should be freestanding, centrally located, and each member of the worshipping congregation should be able to see it and to hear what is being said at it.

In Roman Catholic churches, altars are consecrated by a bishop. The most essential part of the consecration is the anointing with chrism, to indicate the richness of grace, and the placing of relics in the repository. The 1979 *Book of Common Prayer* of the Episcopal Church has a liturgy for "The Dedication and Consecration of a Church." Within that liturgy is a dedication of the altar.

Donald S. Armentrout

Further Reading

Aharoni, Y. (1979). The horned altar of Beersheba. *Biblical Archaeologist, 37,* 2–6.

Catechism of the Catholic Church. (1994). Mahwah, NJ: Paulist Press.

De Vaux, R. (1961). Altars. In *Ancient Israel*. New York: McGraw-Hill.

Haran, M. (1970). *Temples and temple service in Ancient Israel.* Oxford, UK: Clarendon Press.

Humfrey, P., & Kemp, M. (Eds.). (1990). *The altarpiece in the Renaissance.* New York: Cambridge University Press.

LaRocca-Pitts, E. C. (2001). *Of wood and stone: The significance of Israelite cultic items in the Bible and its early interpreters.* Winona Lake, IN: Eisenbraun.

Pocknee, C. E. (1963). *The Christian altar in history and today.* London: A. R. Mowbray.

Anabaptists

Economic, social, and political factors combined to lead early-sixteenth-century Europe into the Protestant Reformation. The invention of the press by Gutenberg in 1445 helped this movement by enabling reformists to reach large numbers of the public—who were increasingly educated and able to read—through the dissemination of popular pamphlets. With a growing awareness of social inequities, a general spirit of resentment rose against the Catholic Church, culminating in a major religious revival at a time when the church was least able to provide moral and ethical leadership. A conciliatory movement calling for a "reformation of the head and members" of the church rose from within its own ranks and quickly spread to the laity. The "Reformation," so designated by the agents of change themselves, was conceived to alter the existing order and to create theological change in the church.

Historians date the symbolic beginning of the Protestant Reformation to 31 October 1517, when Martin Luther nailed ninety-five theses to the church door in Wittenberg, beginning a counter-theology that would become Lutheranism—profoundly religious, pessimistic about perfecting society, insistent that Christians should not withdraw but should lend a hand in the maintenance of order. On a more practical level, one of Luther's requests was for the Mass, performed in Latin, to be delivered in the native tongue of participants.

Uniqueness of the Anabaptists

Other major theological reform movements agreed with Luther's critique of Rome but parted ways with him on other theological issues. The Reformed Churches of Germany and French Switzerland, led by Ulrich Zwingli and John Calvin, believed instead in the possibility of creating the Kingdom of God on Earth among the elect. A third, and uniquely sectarian, theological reform movement was the Anabaptists, or "rebaptizers," so called because of their practice of "believer baptism," the baptism of adult believers rather than infants. This "third wave" of theological reform, known as the Radical Reformation, sought to complete the reforms begun by Luther and Zwingli, searching the Scriptures to recover the patterns of the early church, including a more egalitarian relationship among believers and less ritualistic, more participative worship experience.

The general baptism of infants, Anabaptists believed, filled the church with nonbelievers and improperly conflated church and culture. Thus rejecting the cultural practices of the day, Anabaptists sought to create a true church composed only of true believers. Achieving and maintaining the purity of such a church would require separation, not only of church and state but of the church from larger society itself.

Early Anabaptists were eclectic in their philosophical and theological precepts. The Renaissance tradition of humanism, and the advent of printing, had led to the rediscovery of many ancient writers and a flowering of philosophical thought. From Martin Luther they adopted the position of salvation by grace at the same time as they rejected his continued acceptance of church sacraments and hierarchy, agreeing (in part) on these latter issues with Andreas Karlstadt, who advocated equality among the membership. Many Anabaptist leaders initially followed Ulrich Zwingli; advocating "ad fonts" faith (returning to the source), he encouraged his followers to go directly to the Bible for guidance. From Thomas Muntzer, Anabaptists adopted a critique of existing social and economic systems; they admired Erasmus's treatise on the freedom of the will, as well as his profound devotion to pacifism.

While scholars through most of the twentieth century agreed that Anabaptism had originated in Zurich, more recent scholars have revised this claim, arguing that the movement was polygenetic in origin, with three relatively independent starting points: the Swiss Brethren, South German Anabaptism, and the Melchiorites (North German and Dutch).

Swiss Brethren

The Swiss Brethren were the closest followers of Ulrich Zwingli; however, when Zwingli aligned himself with the Zurich City Council in 1523, betraying, in the opinion of the Brethren, many of his original positions, they began to distance from him. In January 1525, when the Council resolved a debate on infant baptism by demanding that all Anabaptists baptize their babies in the next eight days or face expulsion from the city, the Brethren broke away from Zwingli, who had sided with the Council. The date 21 January 1525 is generally recognized as the formal beginning of the Anabaptist movement; following a meal together, a number of Anabaptist leaders performed the first adult baptism on each other.

Because infant baptism was the means by which the government kept count of its citizens (in essence an early census), the Anabaptist movement was dangerous to the authority of the state; because the reformers rejected the doctrine of original sin, the movement was dangerous to the authority of the church. Perhaps inevitably, the Anabaptists provoked extensive opposition and persecution, resulting in the violent deaths of many members. Most of the first generation of leaders were in their twenties when the movement started; few died naturally or lived past thirty.

One early leader, priest-turned-Anabaptist Michael Sattler, drafted one of the first systematic statements of the early movement. He gathered with other leaders in Schleitheim, Switzerland, to outline a document on unity—the Schleitheim Confession. The Confession consisted of seven articles setting forth the Anabaptists' doctrine concerning baptism, the ban (sanctions against straying members), the Lord's Supper, separation of the church from the larger society, the pastor's role, use of the sword (pacifism), and prohibition of the oath (promises of fealty to the state) to believers. Printed and circulated widely, the Confession provoked written responses from both Zwingli and Calvin, who urged moderation and counseled against so radical a stance. But the Schleitheim Confession only grew in influence; it established a common doctrinal foundation for the growing Anabaptist movement and has continued to influence contemporary Anabaptists, such as the Mennonite Church, through the present day.

South German Anabaptism

Anabaptism in South Germany was more mystical in tone than that of the Swiss Brethren, emphasizing inward spirituality and preaching apocalyptic visions. Though this group left little in the way of an institutional legacy, its influence was in its leaders' contributions to a series of meetings held in the Bavarian city of Augsburg to discuss the future of Anabaptism. Often called the "Martyr's Synod" because so many of those present were killed soon afterward, the meetings brought together a wide range of perspectives in a rich discussion of theology.

Another contribution of South German Anabaptism was the work of Pilgram Marpeck, who came to the city of Strassburg in 1528 to join the Anabaptists. Marpeck, who may have been spared because of his work as a city engineer, wrote extensively on theological issues; his writings on the Scripture helped unify the second generation of Anabaptists.

Melchiorites

Anabaptism spread throughout sixteenth-century Northern Europe and the Netherlands, which were experiencing both general religious tolerance and a strong sacramentarian movement. Leaders like Melchior Hoffman preached to and baptized hundreds of people in the Low Countries. Combining his own apocalyptic vision with a positive view of government and the Christian's role in government, Hoffman urged his followers to help bring the new Jerusalem, which he believed would be Strassburg, to fruition. Some of Hoffman's more radical followers led an armed takeover of Munster, Germany, claiming it as the New Jerusalem; after the city was retaken by Bishop Waldeck, terrible persecution and general discrediting of the Anabaptist movement followed.

On a more positive note, another priest who left to join the movement was Menno Simons. Through twenty-five years of extensive travel and writing as an Anabaptist leader—from 1536 until his death in 1561—Simons established "a measure of uniformity over the Melchiorite movement" (Weaver 1987, 103); by the middle of the century, people had begun to refer to the movement by Menno's own name (Mennonists, now Mennonites).

The Anabaptist Experience in Europe and Beyond

At the end of the first century of the Anabaptist movement, two distinct groups of Mennonites survived: the Swiss Brethren, who strictly followed the articles of Schleitheim, and the Melchiorites, who shared the more pacifistic interpretations of Menno Simons. Although these two groups remained in contact over the early years, they were to follow different paths of emigration. During the next two-and-a-half centuries in Europe for the Mennonites (as they became known), their story is characterized by periods of tolerance, followed by renewed persecution. When persecution occurred, the Mennonites moved on. In time, this included leaving Europe to seek safer quarters.

Those who originated primarily in Switzerland and South Germany came to North America starting in 1683 and over the next seventy years. Settling predominantly in the eastern United States and Ontario, Canada, this group included Amish Mennonites (a group that split off around 1700 to follow Jacob Ammann, who proposed a stricter church discipline) and Mennonites (labeling themselves "Old Mennonites" sometime around 1800, this group eventually formed itself, in 1875, into the Mennonite Church).

The group that had originated in northern Germany and Holland followed a more circuitous route, moving east to Poland as early as 1530 and into Russia on the invitation of Catherine II in 1762, before most of the group left eastern Europe for North and South America, beginning with a first wave from 1874 to 1880 and in a second wave in the 1920s and '30s. Since many of these Mennonites had extensive farming experience, they chose to settle in the central United States in the Plains states and up into the central and western Canadian provinces. These immigrants drew together the Russian Mennonites and several smaller diverse groups, to form the General Conference Mennonite Church in 1896.

As a note, these two largest Mennonite denominations in the United States and Canada voted to merge in 1995, forming the Mennonite Church USA, with 110,000 members, and the Mennonite Church Canada, with 60,000 members. Currently, there are nearly twenty formally organized Mennonite groups in North America, numbering approximately 323,000 in the United States and 128,000 in Canada. Worldwide, there are over 1.3 million Mennonites in sixty-five countries.

The South German strain of Anabaptism all but died out in Europe; although it thrived in the second half of the sixteenth century, renewed persecution at the turn of the century left few save for a small group of Hutterites. Begun in 1528 by Jacob Wiederman, and under the continuing leadership of Jacob Hutter, descendants also eventually migrated to the New World; today there are approximately 23,000 Hutterites in the United States and Canada, with one colony in Japan.

Contemporary Anabaptists

The most well-known descendents of Anabaptists today are the Mennonites and the Amish. These groups vary widely in practice, from the Amish, who use the horse and buggy for transportation, do not use electricity in their homes, and wear distinctive plain dress, to Conservative Mennonites, who wear modest dress and often do not participate in voting or other political activity, to the more progressive Mennonite groups such as the members of the Mennonite Church USA and Canada, most of whom would be indistinguishable from their Protestant counterparts in dress and daily life. However, most of these groups still follow many of the tenets of their Anabaptist forebears, including Believer's Baptism, pacifism, and a Christ-centered, Bible-based theology leading to discipleship.

The Hutterites continue the Melchiorite traditions of communal living and community of goods (material possessions owned by the church and shared by all). This groups also dresses distinctively, in a more colorful version of the Amish plain dress.

While contemporary Mennonites embrace communication technologies, producing a denominational magazine and newspaper, websites, and films, more conservative Mennonites and Amish have struggled over the choice to adopt various technologies. Discussions over television ownership among Mennonites in the 1950s and whether it would have a "worldly influence" on the group were followed by struggles and debates over the necessity of telephones within Amish communities in the 1970s and '80s. As the amount of available farmland has receded, many in the Amish community have gone to work in factories or producing goods for the tourist trade. The necessity of maintaining websites and phone access to sell cheese, furniture, and other Amish goods has produced the curious phenomena of phone booths on the edges of Amish farms and computers powered by generators in Amish barns.

At the end of a circuitous five-hundred-year path from the Protestant Reformation, Mennonites and Amish today follow many of the same theological precepts as those of their forebears; contemporary Anabaptists continue to spread their beliefs in Jesus Christ, discipleship, pacifism, and service around the globe.

KERRY L. STRAYER

Further Reading

Anabaptists today. (2000). Retrieved December 14, 2005, from http://www.anabaptistchurch.org/anabaptists_today.htm

Bainton, R. H. (1952). *The Reformation of the sixteenth century.* Boston: Beacon Press.

Bender, H. S. (1944). The Anabaptist vision. *Church History 13*, 3–24.

Durnbaugh, D. F. (1985). *The believers' church: The history and character of radical Protestantism.* Scottdale, PA: Herald Press.

Dyck, C. J. (Ed.). (1981). *An introduction to Mennonite history: A popular history of the Anabaptists and the Mennonites* (2nd ed.). Scottdale, PA: Herald Press.

Dyck, C. J., & Martin, D. D. (Eds.). (1990). *The Mennonite encyclopedia: A comprehensive reference work on the Anabaptist-Mennonite movement, Volume V, A-Z.* Scottdale, PA: Herald Press.

Hillerbrand, H. J. (1968). *The Protestant Reformation.* New York: Harper & Row.

Juhnke, J. C. (1989). *Vision, doctrine, war: Mennonite identity and organization in America, 1890–1930.* Scottdale, PA: Herald Press.

Kauffman, J. H., & Driedger, L. (1991). *The Mennonite mosaic: Identity and modernization.* Scottdale, PA: Herald Press.

Kauffman, J. H., & Harder, L. (1975). *Anabaptists four centuries later: A profile of five Mennonite and brethren in Christ denominations.* Scottdale, PA: Herald Press.

Klaassen, W. (1973). *Anabaptism: Neither Catholic nor Protestant.* Waterloo, Ontario, Canada: Conrad Press.

Klaassen, W. (Ed.). (1981). *Anabaptism in outline: Selected primary sources.* Scottdale, PA: Herald Press.

MacMaster, R. K. (1985). *Land, piety, peoplehood: The establishment of Mennonite communities in America, 1683–1790.* Scottdale, PA: Herald Press.

Mennonite Church USA. (2005). Retrieved December 14, 2005, from http://www.mennoniteusa.org

Pannebecker, S. F. (1975). *Open doors: The history of the general conference Mennonite church.* Newton, KS: Faith and Life Press.

Redekop, C. (1989). *Mennonite society.* Baltimore: The Johns Hopkins University Press.

Schlabach, T. (1988). *Peace, faith, nation: Mennonites and Amish in nineteenth-century America.* Scottdale, PA: Herald Press.

Smith, C. H. (1950). *The story of the Mennonites* (3rd ed.). Newton, KS: Mennonite Publication Office.

Stayer, J. M., Packull, W. O., & Depperman, K. (1975). From monogenesis to polygenesis: The historical discussion of Anabaptist origins. *The Mennonite Quarterly Review 49*, 83–121.

Toews, J. B. (1982). *Czars, Soviets & Mennonites.* Newton, KS: Faith and Life Press.

Weaver, J. D. (1987). *Becoming Anabaptist: The origin and significance of sixteenth-century Anabaptism.* Scottdale, PA: Herald Press.

Who are the Mennonites? (n.d.). Retrieved December 14, 2005, from http://www.mennoniteusa.org

Williams, G. (1962). *The radical Reformation.* Philadelphia: Westminster Press.

Angels

Angels are, in a sense, a supreme symbol of the liaison between religion and media, between worship and announcement—for such is their name and office in all Jewish and Christian thought. The word "angel" derives from the Greek term for "messenger" (*angelos*), the name that was used to translate the Hebrew term (*malakh*) in the Greek version of the Hebrew Bible known as the Septuagint that became authoritative for the early Christian communities. In most of the many scriptural references to God's angels (e.g., Genesis 16:7; Genesis 32:1; Judges 6:11; Daniel 7:10), they appear as the intermediaries who serve God's will by mediating with humankind. They are especially the deliverers of revelation and, as such, play a large role in the New Testament accounts of the Annunciation and the Birth of the Messiah (Matthew 1:20; 2:13; Luke 1:26–38) and the Resurrection (Matthew 28:2–7; John 20:12).

Early biblical Judaism shared a belief in angels as inhabitants of the heavenly court of the supreme God (considered a celestial King) with many of the religions of the Near Eastern nations (1 Kings 22:19). Our popular conception of angels as winged beings is a direct borrowing of the Israelite tradition from the concept of the lesser gods of the Ancient Near Middle East. No-

where can this be seen more clearly than in the description of the Ark of the Covenant (Leviticus 37:1–9) with the winged cherubim (high angels) kneeling down as the footstool of the invisible High God and stretching out their wings to overshadow the mercy seat where His holy presence was believed to dwell.

Of course, even in the borrowings there were significant changes. Israelite belief, rising over the centuries from Henotheism (that only our God is significant) to Monotheism (that there can only be one God), developed its angelology distinct from the other Near Eastern religions, by marking an ever greater gap between the High God and the angelic servants of God (who in many other religious systems were conceived of simply as lesser deities). The function of the heavenly angels in Israel's understanding was to sing the praises of God, much like earthly courtiers around an ancient high king, and to fulfill His missions. The Israelites developed the role of angels more than many other ancient religions precisely because of their exalted concept of the High God, whose face could never be seen by mortals.

All earthly divine intervention in the Hebrew Bible became increasingly mediated, in order to preserve the divine transcendence, through angelic operations. One of the frequent titles of the angels in the Psalms was the "Sons of God," a term that even appears in the Old Testament literature as a synonym for God. In late rabbinic thought even the accounts of God's direct appearances (such as to Moses on Mount Sinai when he gave the Torah) become reworked as an appearance not of God as such but of the "Great Angel of the Covenant" to Moses.

In some parts of Jewish thought (such as the philosopher-theologian Philo in the first century BCE) this great angel of God became identified as the Logos. This was one of the matrix ideas of Hellenistic religious and philosophical culture (the Logos as the rational substructure of all the cosmos in Stoic thought and as the spirit of intellective insight in Platonic reflection). The Christians seized on the whole notion in a very early phase of the Gospel writing, and by their seeing Jesus as the historical incarnation of the great Logos, such texts as the Gospel of John were produced that explained the earthly career of Jesus in terms of a great sweep of God's timeless activity working for the salvation of mortals on earth. As a result of this Jesus-Logos theology, the early Christian angelology was extensive.

At first the Logos was seen as the highest of all the angels of God, but then in later texts, after the third century CE, the angelic aspect faded away, and more and more exclusive attention was paid to the relationship of the Logos with the divine Father (the roots of the Christian doctrine of the Trinity). Even so, the traces of the concept of Jesus as a descended angel, who suffered and then returned on high in triumph, after defeating the earthly invisible powers, can be witnessed in many places in the New Testament literature (cf. John 1:1; 1:52; Colossians 1:15–20; Colossians 2:14–15; 1 Timothy 3:16; Hebrews 1:1–14).

In several parts of the Scriptures, angels are depicted as more warlike than merciful and especially used by God to exact punishment among the wicked (2 Samuel 24:16). The Four Horsemen of the Apocalypse (Revelation 6:1–8) are angelic figures that bring calamity and disaster more than relief, for their task is one of purification and does not bring any message of comfort to the world. Jesus himself referred to angels on several occasions during his ministry, teaching that they always enjoyed the presence and vision of the Father (Matthew 18:10) and that they would form the accompanying army of God that would return with the Son of Man at the Parousia at the end of time (Matthew 16:27). His apparent requirement of celibacy from his disciples ("eunuchs for the sake of the Kingdom") has been interpreted by some scholars as a deliberate attempt to mirror the life of the angels of God on earth in his "new community of the Kingdom" and, so far as this symbolically brings about the "impossible" condition of the angelic life of the Next Age, within this Present Age, has in turn been seen as an attempt to cause the irruption of the apocalyptic Kingdom (the End Time), which was expected by many of the radical Jews in the first century and often described as the advent of the Kingdom of God.

From about 200 BCE onward, Jewish religious thought renewed its interest in the concept of the heavenly court of God and the functions of the angels who inhabited the "Kingdom." It was at this era that the genre of apocalyptic thought was born, as can be witnessed in parts of Ezekiel, throughout the book of Daniel, and in most of the apocryphal, intertestamental literature. In the apocalyptic books angels are an explanation of how God's providence breaks in to the flow of world history. Here the Hebraic belief in Providence was asserted over and against the Greco-Roman view of earthly affairs as being under the doom of a fickle Fate (Fortuna), and so the literature speaks extensively about how the angels of God intervene on earth to protect the elect saints of God, or to avenge them. The book of Revelation, the last book of the New Testament, is the only full-scale example of this genre in the Christian canon, and it offers many vivid word-pictures of the throne room of God and how the angels

A marble statue of an angel in a cemetery in Croatia.
Courtesy of Tina Rencelj/istockphoto.com.

and elect saints (whose destiny is to be caught up among the angels) represent the perfect world of the true Kingdom, after the many false kingdoms that have set themselves up in opposition to God within world history.

After the biblical era, the belief in angels continued as a lively element of Jewish and Christian theology, but it lost much of its original stature. Christian theologians of the second century CE, such as Irenaeus of Lyons, insisted that the angels were distinct creatures of God (not a system of divine emanations as Gnostic Hellenism often imagined) and, like humanity, they had a destiny to serve and worship the deity (Irenaeus. *Adversus* Haereses 2. 30. 6–9). Origen, one of the greatest of all Christian thinkers, writing in the third century CE, greatly extended the patristic understanding of the angelic orders, with his doctrine of the preexistence of souls. The angels, in Origen's scheme, were the original souls created by God before the making of the world, who retained their heavenly dignity and ethereal status. Humanity had once been angelic but had fallen into corporeality because of premundane sins, although one day the faithful soul could ascend again to become transfigured into angelic glory. It was Origen who brought the widespread belief in individual guardian angels into church life, with his teaching that God had appointed some angels to watch over the destiny of nations (Deuteronomy 32:8) but also others to care for the safe journey of each soul on Earth, until it returned back to its original heavenly family.

The Origenian scheme of preexistence was highly attractive to the Christian mystics, such as Evagrius, but was never accepted by the larger church. In the fourth century CE Gregory of Nazianzus rescued the doctrine of angels from the implication of Origenian preexistence doctrine and laid out a system that would become authoritative for the wider tradition. God, Gregory argued, had made three creations. The first was the angelic order. The second was the material and animal creation, and the third was humanity. The first two creations were simple and coherent in their ontology, spiritual and fleshy respectively. Mankind alone was a "mixed creation" (flesh and spirit). By faithful obedience and a constant "ascent" of soul, human beings could attain to the glory of angelic status in the afterlife (Gregory of Nazianzus, *Carmina* 1:1:7).

Two scriptural passages caught the imagination of the early church, in which the "ranks" of the angels were described with some differences (Colossians 1:16; Ephesians 1:21). The early patristic writers, putting them together, came up with an enumeration of five different ranks. Dionysius the Areopagite, a sixth-century writer, added to that list of five the separate ranks of angel, archangel, seraph and cherubim and thus set out the definitive list of the nine orders of the angels, which would form the basic understanding of the Christian churches ever after: angels, archangels, principalities, powers, virtues, dominions, thrones, cherubim, and seraphim. The seraphim occupied the seventh heaven alongside God, and their proximity to the Divine Presence resulted in their eruption into pure fire (in such a way are they always depicted in iconography). In postbiblical Jewish writing the names of individual angels were more extensively given than in Christian literature, and they were often used in Kabala as sources of power. Among the Orthodox churches four great angels (archangels) are referred to as Taxiarchs (commanders of the armies of heaven). They are: Michael (Daniel 10:21), Gabriel (Daniel 8:16), Raphael (Tobias 3:17), and Uriel (Sibylline, Oracles 2:214–215). Other archangels are also referred to (Salathiel, Jegudiel or Jekuthiel, Barachiel, Jeremiel or Remiel), and in the Coptic Church there is devotion to the archangels Surael, Sakakael, Sarathael, and Ananael.

Much of the Jewish and Christian interest in angels passed also into Islam, which accepted most of the biblical references as well as other lesser traditions. In particular, Muhammad was said to have received the Qur'an from the angel Gabriel (Gibril). Islam developed on the notion of guardian angels, teaching that each soul has two angels accompanying it: one to record the good deeds, the other recording all the evil of a person's life. In Islamic culture Gabriel and Michael are the greatest of the angels, but others also perform specific functions: Ishrael is the angel of death; Israfil is the angel who blows the trumpet to announce the day of Resurrection, and Ash Shaitay is Satan.

The angels were seen to be endowed with almost infinite mobility and vast powers. In early Christian understanding they also attended the liturgy of the church whenever it was celebrated on Earth. In the Byzantine liturgy the ordained deacons often assumed a role of symbolizing the angelic orders, and the imperial eunuchs (sexless, as Jesus had said the angels were in heaven: cf. Mark 12:25) had the special task of singing the cherubic hymn at the time of the Great Entrance. The words of this are as follows: "We who in a mystery represent the Cherubim, and sing the thrice holy hymn to the life-creating trinity, now lay aside all earthly cares, that we may receive the King of all who comes escorted by the ranks of unseen angels." In Byzantine times this was sung in eerie castrato, to produce a frisson among those who heard it. Even today it is a solemn part of the Eastern Orthodox liturgical ceremonies that is meant to remind those attending church that they are in the awesome company of angelic beings, those whom the Syrian Christians called "The Watchers."

JOHN ANTHONY McGUCKIN

See also Miracles

Further Reading

Burke, A. G. (1991). *Glories of Saint Michael the Archangel.* Geneva, NE: St. George Press.

Daniélou, J. (1988). *The angels and their mission according to the fathers of the church.* Dublin, Ireland: Four Courts Press.

Frank, K. S. (1964). *Angelikos bios.* Munster, Germany: Graumann.

Godwin, M. (1990). *Angels: An endangered species.* New York: Simon and Schuster.

Keck, D. (1998). *Angels and angelology in the Middle Ages.* New York: Oxford University Press.

Marshall, G. J. (1999). *Angels: An indexed and partially annotated bibliography of over 4,300 scholarly books and articles since the 7th century B.C.* Jefferson, NC: McFarland Publishing.

Peterson, E. (1964). *The angels and the liturgy.* London: Darton, Longman and Todd.

Apocrypha

The term "Apocrypha" stems from the Greek word *apokrypha*, meaning "hidden." It has been used historically to denote certain religious writings, particularly in Judaism and Christianity, that, although not accepted into various official lists of canonical sacred writings, were thought to be inspired and therefore important for both worship and doctrine. One of the main ways in which these and other religions have attempted to construct a concrete identity for themselves is to hold up certain writings as authoritative, and to include them in their canons. Apocryphal writings, therefore, often represent alternative views of religious identity expressed through narrative, history, poetry, and other genres. Although excluded from the canon, these writings were, and still are, important for both a well-rounded historical understanding of the development of Judaism and Christianity, as well as for various faith communities as they reflect on their relationship to the sacred.

Old Testament Apocrypha

The writings commonly referred to as the Old Testament Apocrypha were mostly composed in a Semitic language (in this case Hebrew or Aramaic) in Palestine and stem from a discrete time period (c. 300 BCE–70 CE). This period, which falls into the time in Jewish history known as the Second Temple Period (c. 515 BCE–70 CE), was a tumultuous one. The Second Temple was rebuilt in approximately 515 BCE, and almost immediately various groups began to posit different understandings of the identity a "restored Israel" should embody. As Joseph Blenkinsopp has shown, one of the main ways Jews in this period constructed their identity was through the creation of literary interpretations of preexisting sacred texts. Some of these views are included in the canon of the Hebrew Bible, namely, Ezra-Nehemiah, Ruth, Jonah, and the latter prophetic books of Haggai and Zechariah. The debate over identity represented by these texts intensified when, in 332 BCE, Greek forces under the command of Alexander the Great conquered Palestine, bringing with them not only technological advances in material culture, but also a new worldview we now call Hellenism. The fact that all Jews living in Palestine now had to become at least partly acculturated to the new ideology of Hellenism, along with the subsequent presence of the Romans beginning in 63 BCE, increased the urgency with which ancient authors attempted to argue for various understandings of Jewish identity in written works.

The Old Testament Apocrypha consists of thirteen main works with a variety of genres. There are historical works that purport to tell the story of Hellenism's encroachment into the land, and how one family (the Maccabees) revolted against this new worldview and eventually established an independent monarchy (1, 2 Maccabees). Also included are narrative works that are most likely popular and/or folkloric in origin, but also contain messages emphasizing piety, faith in God, and even female initiative (Judith, Tobit). Works dealing with wisdom, such as the Wisdom of Solomon and Sirach, are also found in this corpus, as are additions to canonical texts such as Esther and Daniel (the Prayer of Azariah and Song of the Three Young Men; Susanna; and Bel and the Dragon). There are also apocalyptic works, namely 1 and 2 Esdras, as well as shorter pieces such as Baruch, the Letter of Jeremiah, and the Prayer of Manasseh.

Even though these works stem from disparate communities and historical contexts, they are all involved in the creating of Jewish identity during the Second Temple Period. For example, the short story of Susanna, one of the additions to the Book of Daniel, is set in Babylon during the sixth century BCE. It tells the tale of a beautiful, pious woman named Susanna who resists the rape attempt of two elders of the community. Instead of acquiescing, she cries to God, and a young Daniel saves her by cross-examining the elders separately from one another. When their conflicting stories reveal their guilt, they are executed, Susanna returns to her family, and Daniel is lauded. Thus, this story serves as an internal call to Jewish communities to strengthen themselves so that they might not be as vulnerable to foreign powers. On the other hand, the book of Sirach "shows a basic openness to the larger Hellenistic world," and thus praises piety at the same time it advocates a widening of the parameters of Jewish identity (Murphy 2002, 120). One of the most interesting

Selection from *The Life of the Great Martyr Thecla of Iconium, Equal to the Apostles*, as recorded in the *Acts of Paul and Thecla*

This text—considered New Testament Apocrypha—emphasizes the importance of women in early Christianity. It was probably translated by Jeremiah Jones (1693–1724).

Chapter 2

1. While Paul was preaching this sermon in the church which was in the house of Onesiphorus, a certain virgin named Thecla (whose mother's name was Theocleia, and who was betrothed to a man named Thamyris) sat at a certain window in her house.

2. From where, by the advantage of a window in the house where Paul was, she both night and day heard Paul's sermons concerning God, concerning charity, concerning faith in Christ, and concerning prayer.

3. Nor would she depart from the window till with exceeding joy she was subdued to the doctrines of faith.

4. At length, when she saw many women and virgins going in to Paul, she earnestly desired that she might be thought worthy to appear in his presence and hear the word of Christ; for she had not yet seen Paul's person, but only heard his sermons.

5. But when she would not be prevailed upon to depart from the window, her mother sent to Thamyris, who came with the greatest pleasure, as he hoped now to marry her. Accordingly he said to Theocleia, Where is my Thecla?

6. Theocleia replied, Thamyris, I have something very strange to tell you. Thecla, for the space of three days, will not move from the window not so much as to eat or drink, but is so intent in hearing the artful and delusive discourses of a certain foreigner, that I am completely astonished, Thamyris, that a young woman of her known modesty will suffer herself to be so prevailed upon.

7. For that man has disturbed the whole city of Iconium, and even your Thecla, among others. All the women and young men flock to him to receive his doctrine; who, besides all the rest, tells them that there is but one God who alone is to be worshipped, and that we ought to live in chastity.

components of expressing Jewish identity in this literature is the depiction of female characters. Scholars have examined not only the story of Susanna, but also the stories of Judith and Esther, the characters of Anna and Sarah in Tobit, the portrayals of women in Sirach, and the characterization of Wisdom as female in the Wisdom of Solomon to determine what these characterizations reveal about ideals and prescriptions regarding gender during the Second Temple Period.

Many of the writings that have survived from the latter Second Temple Period have been classified as Apocryphal. The reasons for this classification are threefold. First, scholars have determined that "by the second century BCE, there is clear evidence of an awareness of a three-part set of sacred, authoritative writings," namely, the Law, the Prophets, and the other writings (deSilva 2002, 30). As such, these newer writings would have been looked upon with suspicion, and as a result perhaps not all of them were even consid-

ered for inclusion in the canon. Second, there seems to have been a consensus among Jewish writers by the second century BCE that prophecy had ceased with the death of Ezra. Thus, these works could not claim prophetic inspiration and thus had less of a claim to canonical status. Third, most of these writings were preserved and transmitted in Greek. When Jerome made his translation of the Bible into Latin in the fourth century CE, he used only the Hebrew works, and thus relegated the Greek works to "apocryphal" status. Augustine, on the other hand, supported the inclusion of these works in the canon without reservation. In the sixteenth century, the status of these texts was again raised, when Protestant Reformers such as Karlstadt (Andreas Bodenstein) and Martin Luther followed Jerome's lead by declaring Apocryphal works *nützlich*, that is, "useful" for instilling piety, but denying them the same status as the canonical writings. Jean Calvin rejected them outright, while the Council of Trent took

Selection from *The Life of the Great Martyr Thecla of Iconium, Equal to the Apostles*, as recorded in the *Acts of Paul and Thecla (continued)*

8. Notwithstanding this, my daughter Thecla, like a spider's web fastened to the window, is captivated by the discourses of Paul, and attends upon them with prodigious eagerness and vast delight; and thus, by attending to what he says, the young woman is seduced. Now you go and speak to her, for she is betrothed to you.

9. Accordingly Thamyris went, and saluted her with care not to surprise her, and said, Thecla, my spouse, why are you sitting in this melancholy posture? What strange impressions are made upon you? Turn to Thamyris, and blush.

10. Her mother also spoke to her after the same manner and said, Child, why do you sit so melancholy, like one astonished, and make no reply?

11. Then they wept exceedingly: Thamyris, that he had lost his future spouse; Theocleia, that she had lost her daughter; and the maids, that they had lost their mistress; and there was universal mourning in the family.

12. But all these things made no impression on Thecla to incline her so much as to turn and take notice of them, for she continued to contemplate on the discourses of Paul.

13. Then Thamyris ran into the street to observe who they were who went in to Paul and came out from him; and he saw two men engaged in a very warm dispute, and said to them;

14. Sirs, what business have you here? And who is that man within, belonging to you, who deludes the minds of men, both young men and virgins, persuading them that they ought not to marry but continue as they are?

15. I promise to give you a considerable sum if you will give me a just account of him, for I am the chief person of this city.

16. Demas and Hermogenes replied, We cannot so exactly tell who he is, but we know that he deprives young men of their intended wives, and virgins of their intended husbands, by teaching there can be no future resurrection, unless you continue in chastity and do not defile your flesh.

---

the opposite position: it declared all of the Apocryphal writings to be inspired, and thus canonical, even though it termed them the "Deuterocanonical" works, that is, works of a "second canon." Finally, as David A. deSilva notes, "The tendency in modern Greek Orthodox churches is to view the books as canonical" (2002, 39). Thus, in both Catholicism and the Greek Orthodox Church, these writings are afforded the same status as other canonical texts, even though their presence in modern Protestant communities is marginal. Even so, the influence of these writings in the religious history of Judaism and Christianity, not to mention art, literature, and music, has been immense.

New Testament Apocrypha

The religious tradition we now designate as Christianity originated as a sect of Second Temple Judaism, and as such the earliest followers of Jesus were Jews who were involved in the same matrix of identity formation through textual interpretation and creation as other Jews of the period. Unlike the Old Testament Apocrypha, many of the texts now classified as apocryphal New Testament writings were composed during the same time period the canonical texts were being written (c. 50–125 CE) or shortly thereafter. This was a turbulent period for the early followers of Jesus, as they searched the Hebrew Scriptures in order to understand Jesus' life, teachings, and, most importantly, His death. The religious and geographical disparity among early Christian communities led to quite different understandings of Jesus' significance, and many of these disparate views have been included in the canon; for example, Matthew and Luke's Jesus are very different, as is the Jesus of the authentic Pauline letters and that of Hebrews. As the Jesus movement spread throughout the Mediterranean region, various theological understandings began to mature, and we find texts exhibiting more metaphysical speculation on the nature of Jesus. By the early second century, these movements began to homogenize, and a moderate, or proto-ortho-dox center began to emerge between the more conser-vative Jewish and more liberal Hellenistic positions. The Pastoral Epistles and other deutero-Pauline literature best exemplify this proto-orthodox position, the main characteristics of which are an advocation of a specific ecclesiastical hierarchy, a certain view of Scripture, and the notion that the Christian movement would have to adapt to Roman society if it were to survive. It was this proto-orthodox position that eventually defined the New Testament canon as it now exists, most likely in re-sponse to alternative canonical lists by interpreters like Marcion, as well as other theological movements that did not adhere to the majority view of theology and so-ciety. Texts produced by these and other communities, as well as texts that were not widely used by various communities, were not included in the formation of the canon, probably begun in the late second century and fi-nalized in the late fourth century.

In his work, Stephen J. Patterson organizes the vast amount of texts in the New Testament Apocrypha ac-cording to genre. He includes six different genres: Gospels and Related Forms, Treatises, Apocalypses, Acts, Letters, and Liturgical Materials. Unlike the Old Testament Apocrypha, this collection is much more varied, both in terms of form and content.

These texts demonstrate the theological vitality of the early followers of Jesus, both in their literary and theological creativity. They bear witness to the hetero-geneity and complexity of Christianity from the late first century to the fourth century. For example, one of the most important discoveries in the collection of Gnostic texts found at Nag Hammadi in Egypt is the Gospel of Thomas. A sayings source containing 114 sayings (logia) of Jesus, the Gospel of Thomas is now usually dated to the late first century, and as such pro-vides scholars with a very different portrait of Jesus than the ones presented in the Gospels. In the Gospel of Thomas, Jesus sounds very much like a Jewish sage, and His sayings reveal many themes not found in the canonical texts, for example, a focus on the secret, inner knowledge embedded in the human self that will ulti-mately free humans, and an antiapocalyptic emphasis on the Reign of God as being present both temporally and spatially, but only for those who possess the knowledge to discern it, that is, a recognition of their identity as "Children of God," and not as worldly people. Because this text has both an early date and such a different picture of Jesus, many scholars now routinely utilize it in their reconstructions of Jesus'

teachings. Another important apocryphal text is the Acts of Paul and Thecla. This text provides us with not only an interesting view of Paul, but also an insight into women's participation in early Christian evangel-izing efforts. The date of the text is unsure, but stories about Thecla were known as early as the late second century, and by the fourth century not only was the text being circulated and used, some groups even con-sidered it canonical. This story tells of a young woman named Thecla who was enraptured by Paul's preach-ing, and wanted to be baptized and travel with him. Paul is hesitant to allow her to do so, but Thecla per-sists. After being thrown to the lions, she baptizes her-self, dresses as a man, and seeks out Paul, who finally gives her his permission to preach and teach. This story is important for two main reasons. First, it gives us a glimpse into a tradition of female participation in the early Christian movement, as well as the starting point for a devotional movement attached to Thecla. Second, D. R. MacDonald has argued persuasively that the Pastoral Epistles were written in response to stories like that of Thecla, and as such the Acts of Paul and Thecla, may represent one of the positions against which the proto-orthodox position of early Christian-ity formed itself. Even though writings like these were not included in the New Testament canon, they have had a large impact on popular devotion, not to men-tion art and literature.

Implications

These writings have enormous importance for our understanding of both the "official" trajectories of Judaism and Christianity, and the theological and de-votional movements that were considered either unim-portant or dangerous. They represent the "other side" of canonical texts in that they offer the reader alterna-tive views of religious identity, but at the same time they use the same genres, texts, and conceptual cate-gories as the canonical writings do. Therefore, in order to appreciate the textual traditions of both Judaism and Christianity, serious stock must be taken of these rich and enjoyable texts.

DAN W. CLANTON, JR.

Further Reading

Blenkinsopp, J. (1981). Interpretation and the tendency to sectarianism: An aspect of Second Temple History. In E. P. Sanders, et al, (Eds.), Jewish and Christian self-definition, volume 2: Aspects of Judaism in the Graeco-Roman period (pp. 1–26). Philadelphia: Fortress Press.

Cartlidge, D. R. and Elliott, J. K. (2001). *Art and the Christian Apocrypha*. New York and London: Routledge.

Charlesworth, J. H. (1992). Old Testament Apocrypha. In D. N. Freedman, et al, (Eds.), *The Anchor Bible dictionary* (pp. 292–294 in vol. 1). New York: Doubleday.

Clanton, D. W., Jr. (2002). *The good, the bold, and the beautiful: The story of Susanna and its Renaissance interpretations*. Doctoral Dissertation, Iliff School of Theology & University of Denver.

Davis, S. J. (2001). *The cult of St. Thecla: A tradition of women's piety in late antiquity*. Oxford: Oxford University Press.

deSilva, D. A. (2002). *Introducing the Apocrypha: Message, context, and significance*. Grand Rapids, MI: Baker.

Gruen, E. S. (1998). *Heritage and Hellenism: The reinvention of Jewish tradition*. Hellenistic Culture and Society Series, Vol. XXX. Berkeley: University of California Press.

Harrington, D. J. & Harrington S. J. (1999). *Invitation to the Apocrypha*. Grand Rapids, MI: William B. Eerdmans.

Lapham, F. (2003). *Introduction to the New Testament apocrypha (Understanding the Bible and its world)*. New York: Continuum.

MacDonald, D. R. (1983). *The legend and the apostle: The battle for Paul in story and canon*. Philadelphia: Westminster.

Murphy, F. J. (2002). *Early Judaism: The exile to the time of Jesus*. Peabody, MA: Hendrickson.

Newsom, C. A. and Ringe, S. H. (Eds.). (1998). *The women's Bible commentary*. Expanded Edition, with Apocrypha. Louisville, KY: Westminster/John Knox Press.

Patterson, S. J. (1992). New Testament Apocrypha. In D. N. Freedman, et al, (Eds.), *The Anchor Bible dictionary: Vol. 1.* (pp. 294–297). New York: Doubleday.

Segal, A. F. (1986). *Rebecca's children: Judaism and Christianity in the Roman world*. Cambridge & London: Harvard University Press.

VanderKam, J. C. (2001). *An introduction to early Judaism*. Grand Rapids, MI: William B. Eerdmans.

Apparel

The word *apparel* typically connotes the clothing and adornment worn by individuals. In a religious context, it signifies the religious clothing, hair styles, accessories, jewelry, makeup, and body decoration that communicate an individual's religious or spiritual values and beliefs.

Apparel as Religious Communication

Consumer behavior researchers observe that individuals choose clothes to define and describe themselves. Some researchers have even debated about whether clothing can be seen as a communicative device with its own grammar, syntax, and codes. The communication of apparel takes place as part of the individual transmitting a message through clothing and the viewer interpreting the message that has been sent. Individuals use apparel to form a sense of community with others of their faith by dressing in similar ways or by wearing similar religious items.

A communicative process happens when individuals interact with their religious apparel to create meaning and construct their sense of reality and significance. This constructivist view holds that reality is created in the interaction between the religious object and the individual who is wearing the object and interpreting its meaning. This also portrays the values of individuals, because the more important a social role is to the individual meaning-maker, the greater importance he or she places on dressing for it.

The apparel a religious individual chooses to wear can be a confirmation of an inner change or it can initiate change in the individual. The clothing is a reflection of an inner value system that has been encoded and made manifest. The apparel an individual chooses to wear is a reflection of that person's religious consumption, identity, and values. An example of this would be when individuals choose apparel that sends a traditional religious message, such as when they dress in a way that reflects the Protestant ethic stressing modesty and simplicity. Alternatively, individuals can dress in a way that sends a more trendy and outspoken religious message, which occurs when they wear shirts with slogans such as "Jesus Is My Homeboy."

Controversies arise in this communicative process when one individual communicates through clothing and a viewer desires to silence the message and, similar to free speech controversies, seeks to censor the religious communication of the individual. One example of this involves head scarves for Muslim girls in French schools, where the school authorities have mandated that Muslim girls remove their headscarves at the entrance of the school. This is due to the educational establishment's enforced code of secularism and nationalism within the school boundaries. However, some of the Muslim girls have sought to overturn the rule as a part of their religious observance. In a communicative context, this act by the Muslim girls can be seen as an act that seeks to preserve their voices and beliefs (as manifested through their apparel) in the religious communicative sphere.

Clothing can be seen as a system of signs, similar to verbal messages that individuals communicate to each other. In this light, religious clothing can send a formal and highly ritualized message, or it can send a much more casual message. The clothing of a priest is highly formalized and ritualized, while current trends such as the "What Would Jesus Do?" (WWJD) shirts are more informal and communicate a religious message in a manner similar to slang. These slang choices in apparel can be seen in pop culture settings, with trendy Christians wearing shirts with Christian slogans or buying jewelry, memorabilia, and other items that have been labeled as "Christian Kitsch." Like their religious forebears, these new Christians feel that their religion is a way of life that includes the clothes they wear and the jewelry or other accessories that symbolize their inner beliefs.

Individuals can also communicate a religious message through their clothing by wearing an entire religious outfit or uniform, which in a communicative context is similar to transmitting an entire sentence holistically. Alternatively, they can wear religious adornments that enhance nonreligious outfits, which in a communicative context would be similar to adjectives or adverbs, with the adornments acting as modifiers to the communicative message.

However, some Christians have expressed concern with the idea of wearing religious apparel that sends strong messages. They wonder if their viewers would perceive their messages favorably or unfavorably and feel that their behavior should signal their religiosity and not be portrayed by what is stated on their shirts. Others worry that if religiosity becomes a fad, with its own clubs, slogans, and pop culture, than the deeper meaning can fade, just as many fads do over time.

Primitive Societies

The use of religious apparel as a form of communication and consumption has existed throughout the history of mankind, with anthropologists observing that in certain primitive societies, individuals used to adorn themselves with paint as part of their religious observance. Often this was thought to have a magical effect that could attract positive powers and guard against evil influence. At times, this can have such an intense sense of meaning for the individuals in their culture that it can comprise their entire outfit. One example of this can be seen in the religious observance of modern Australian bushmen, who may spend extended periods of time adorning themselves and their relatives with body designs painted with colored clay, and then may wear little else except for an amulet.

Ritual Dress

Individuals have also communicated through ritual dress, designing and wearing special clothing that signaled the passages and major events of life such as christenings, weddings, and funerals. These items of clothing have communicated powerful messages, including the purity and innocence of a white wedding gown and the black mourning outfit, which signaled grief at a funeral.

Some of the apparel choices can communicate complex multiple messages, such as those communicated through the christening gown that parents place on their infant as part of the christening ritual. Alison Lurie (1981) observes that the infant's christening gown is usually much longer than the baby that wears it, sometimes extending up to six feet long. This could possibly connote the parents' unconscious desire to design the gown to fit the adult that the child may become. In this sense, it also may become a communicative device reflecting the parents' desire that the child grow to adulthood. This may have grown from the unease in past centuries concerning the illnesses and tragedies that could abbreviate children's lives. The gown also has other symbolic qualities, indicated by its traditional whiteness, which symbolizes purity and innocence, and the fineness of its materials.

Religious Uniforms

Scholars have also observed that the religious uniform, such as the priest's robe or the nun's habit, are often intentionally symbolic. It identifies its wearer as a member of a particular group and often locates him or her within a hierarchy. At times, the religious uniform can also give information about the wearer's achievements.

Religious uniforms create a sense of community and signal the inner convictions of the individual. They may also have the effect of transforming someone's actions. There are multiple symbolic interpretations of the uniforms that are worn by different religions. The uniforms can be a reflection of religious consumption and lifestyle and can also send messages concerning the level of implicit or explicit power held by the individual. The long robes worn by religious leaders have often sent a message of eminence and temporal or spiritual power. This message sent by the religious apparel has also been adopted in the ritual dress of other professions, such as academia and law.

Current Trends

Religious communication as signaled through apparel has evolved radically in the past few years, as pop culture religious trends have emerged and been embraced by growing numbers of individuals. Some examples of this new communication have been the "What Would Jesus Do?" shirts and the growing market for Christian clothing and jewelry. As the market, consumption, and negotiation of meanings over the new apparel has evolved, so have the new controversies, which involve the differing interpretations of the messages sent by the innovative apparel. Some religious individuals have embraced the new apparel, while others have felt uncomfortable about the message. Those who were uncomfortable have asked, Should you wear your religion on your shirt?

In spite of the hesitations, the market has grown exponentially for the new religious apparel. The ABC News program *World News Tonight* reported (5 May 2005) that sales of religious-themed apparel have taken off, observing that in the past year Christian booksellers sold $84 million worth of clothing and accessories, which did not include the religious gear sold at concerts, festivals, and in non-Christian stores. Some of these have included shirts and hats featuring the slogan "Jesus Is My Homeboy" and "Mary Is My Homegirl." Teenage Millionaire, the clothing company that produced this apparel, has sold more than a million of these shirts in the past few years. Their sales were initially driven by trend-setting celebrities who were seen sporting the message on their shirts. In addition, other Christian retailers, such as Extreme Christian Clothing, have produced shirts with slogans such as "Satan Sucks."

Controversies

There have also been controversies concerning religious apparel within the realm of freedom of speech and expression. These have involved a clashing of message interpretations as institutions debated what level of allowance they would extend to those who wished to communicate religious messages through their apparel within nonreligious contexts or institutions.

In France, controversies have involved Muslim girls who were not allowed to wear head scarves in school.

This was a battle of the school system's nationalistic values versus the religious practices of some of the students. In a similar vein, controversies in the United States have concerned the wearing of religious head scarves in schools. When the schools originally banned the head scarves, they were seeking to target the headscarves worn by gang members as part of their uniforms and membership identification. Separating out the prohibition of gang head scarves while permitting religious head scarves has been a complex undertaking because both types of scarves serve as an indicator of values, community building, and consumption, but they collide with each other in the school system. If the schools try to keep a uniform enforcement of the same clothing code, then by trying to silence one form of symbolic communication, they mute the other form of symbolic communication and religious voice as manifested through apparel.

This has also been an issue in the United States Armed Services, as religious individuals and defense administrators have had conflicts over the religious identification and apparel desired by religious individuals versus the uniformity of dress required in the armed services. The First Amendment Center observed that a controversy involving ordained rabbi S. Simcha Goldman of the U.S. Air Force in the early 1980s involved freedom of expression involving religious apparel.

Goldman, who had been wearing his yarmulke while serving in the Air Force for several years, was suddenly ordered to stop wearing it after he gave testimony as a witness for the defense at a court martial. A yarmulke is a small head covering, primarily worn by males in the Orthodox Jewish faith. The prosecutor in the case filed a complaint against Goldman because of his yarmulke. A colonel then ordered Goldman to stop wearing this piece of apparel. The Air Force's position was that it needed to maintain a rigid uniform requirement to maintain esprit de corps and teamwork. Goldman observed that the yarmulke was an important piece of religious apparel that held tremendous significance for him and was a valuable part of his identity.

Goldman filed a federal lawsuit, stating that the Air Force had violated his First Amendment rights under the free-exercise clause. The case was heard by the Supreme Court in 1986, where Goldman narrowly lost in a 5–4 vote. However, the next year Congress passed a provision that has been termed the Religious Apparel Amendment, which stated that a member of the armed forces could wear an item of religious apparel while in uniform.

Messages Sent

Apparel as a form of religious communication involves both the individual who wears the religious commodity and the viewer of the religious message that is being sent. The communicative process can take place between the individual and the article of apparel, as the individual constructs a sense of meaning and purpose from the article of clothing or accessory. Multiple purposes and meanings are communicated through the differing forms of religious apparel, which can signal either holistic or partial messages to society. In current society, individuals can communicate traditional religious messages through their dress or trendy or slang messages through their apparel. However, as a message medium, apparel as a form of communication is imperfect and is prone to misinterpretation and mixed readings by the receivers and viewers of the message.

ANNE V. GOLDEN

Further Reading

Goffman, E. (1959). *The presentation of self in everyday life*. Garden City, NY: Anchor Books.

Lurie, A. (1981). *The language of clothes*. New York: Vintage Books.

McCracken, G. (1988). *Culture and consumption: New approaches to the symbolic character of consumer goods and activities*. Bloomington: Indiana University Press.

Rubinstein, R. P. (1995). *Dress codes, meanings and messages in American culture*. Boulder, CO: Westview Press.

Stout, D. A., & Buddenbaum, J. M., (Eds.). (1996). *Religion and mass media: Audience and adaptations*. Thousand Oaks, CA: Sage.

Stout, D. A., & Buddenbaum, J. M., (Eds.). (2001). *Religion and popular culture: Studies on the interaction of worldviews*. Ames: Iowa State University Press.

Art

Whether it be a statue of the Virgin Mary, a decorative passage of calligraphy from the Qur'an, or mass-produced plastic figurines of Hindu gods, visual expression is a central element in virtually every religious belief system.

Religious adherents are guided by traditions and doctrines that govern the role of art in worship. Those whose belief systems restrict or ban images are known as iconoclasts, while those who freely embrace images are known as iconodules.

It would be impractical and unwieldy to catalog all of the visual forms of religious expression among the world's faiths. Instead, this analysis will identify the basic uses of religious art and examine how the doctrines of five of the world's major faiths shape visual expression in worship.

Roles of Religious Art

At the most basic level all religious art serves a decorative function. It is used to aggrandize or adorn some surface, usually in the context of a place of worship, in order to set a tone of reverence, tranquility, or awe. It may also be applied to vestments and regalia to identify and set apart those with a ceremonial role in worship. Increasingly, religious imagery, usually combined with song lyrics or liturgical text, is used as a fleeting decoration during worship in Protestant churches by being electronically projected onto a screen in front of worshippers.

Another function of religious art is to represent the central historical narrative of the faith. A Catholic crucifix with the figure of Christ on the cross, a statue of a saint, or a Jewish memorial in a museum serve as historical markers of actual persons and events.

Other religious art serves a more symbolic role as a physical representation of spiritual ideas and concepts. A Buddhist landscape garden uses arrangements of vegetation, rocks, and sand to point to concepts about the spiritual harmony of nature. A simple, stylized Protestant cross is missing the body of Christ in order to symbolize His Resurrection and victory over death.

In addition to serving as a literal re-presentation of the past, some faiths believe religious art can serve as a container or vessel that embodies an innate spiritual quality, power, or connection to the spiritual world. Hindus, for example, believe an important part of worship is to face or "see" one of the many anthropomorphic idols that serve as containers or vessels for a wide variety of Hindu deities.

Some faiths also use art as a transformative or experiential element in meditation or worship. The Buddhist landscape garden is designed to inspire meditation and pursuit of enlightenment. But the act of cultivating the garden is also thought to cultivate or shape the spiritual life of the gardener.

Art and Christianity: Striving for Balance

Christian doctrines related to the use of images attempt to reconcile the temporal and spiritual aspects of the faith. To the Christian, God is an omniscient spirit,

The Last Supper on stained glass. *Courtesy Greg Wolkins/istockphoto.com.*

something difficult to visually represent. However, He is also found in the person of Jesus Christ, a man fully human and fully divine and therefore capable of being represented.

Perhaps because of this spiritual/temporal duality Christians have often struggled with the proper role of art in worship. Disputes over the use of images were among the key issues that led to the first major schism in Christianity in 1054 CE between the Eastern Orthodox and the Western Latin Church. In the sixteenth century the role of the image in worship was a central focus of the Reformation.

Role of Iconic Images

In both of these disputes iconoclasts believed images were idolatrous when worshippers treated them as if they served as a proxy for the invisible God or as a conduit for a visitation from the spiritual realm. Iconodules, predominantly from the Eastern Orthodox Church, believed that images could serve as a physical manifestation of the spiritual world and that the sacred was actually present in the image.

The legacy of these controversies is still evident today. In general the Eastern Orthodox and Catholic churches are adorned with icons, crucifixes, paintings, and sculptures that depict Christ, the Virgin Mary, the

apostles, and the saints. These images may be integrated into some element of worship and worshippers may face or kneel before these images while they pray. The vestments of priests are colorful and richly decorated with embroidered symbols and patterns.

In contrast, images are mostly symbolic or decorative in Western Protestant churches. Crosses are stylized and the figure of Christ is absent. Sculptures or paintings of actual figures are rare, and if they are present, they are rarely integrated into the worship service. Clergy wear black or white robes with little or no decorative embellishment, and in some denominations they wear no ceremonial attire at all.

Modern Uses of Imagery

While traditional iconography is often shunned in Protestant churches there has been a rapid growth and adoption of new media technologies for projecting text, graphics, photography, and video. Several studies indicate these devices may be present in up to half of all Protestant churches. Ironically, these same studies have shown that Eastern Orthodox and Catholic churches almost universally reject the use of these imaging technologies during worship.

From the early days of Christianity until the twentieth century, religious art was a ubiquitous and accepted part of the visual culture in the Western world. However, in contemporary society religious art has often generated as much controversy as it has cultural agreement. Museum exhibits, popular movies, paintings, even the display of Nativity scenes at Christmas have sparked clashes about the perceived denigration of sacred symbols and the proper role of religious art in public life.

However, contemporary religious art has not lost its ability to inspire reverence and even unite people of different faith communities. The movie *The Passion of the Christ* was a hit among broad cross-sections of Christian denominations, especially Catholics and evangelicals. The 1940 portrait of Jesus, *Head of Christ*, by former advertising executive Warner Sallman, was printed and distributed to troops during World War II and has since become so ubiquitous that is considered to be one of the most definitive and recognizable images of Christ to many Western Christians.

Alternatives to the Image

The impulse to communicate visually among people of faith is strong, even among those whose doctrines ban the use of certain imagery or where spiritual concepts are abstract and difficult to represent with concrete symbolism.

Islam, Calligraphy and Ornamentation

Due to prohibitions in the Qur'an, Muslims normally avoid depictions of animate objects, and consequently Islamic art is dominated by calligraphic writing and art that is geometric or ornamental in nature.

The Qur'an teaches that writing is the chief means by which God sends his message to humans. As a result of this veneration of the written word, Muslims have developed a quite ornate and decorative style of writing.

In Islamic history, those who perfected the art of writing Qur'anic verse were revered. Arabic letters have become an icon or badge of cultural identity for Muslims. This common cultural tie has extended into the secular world and is found in manuscripts, inscriptions on palaces and public buildings, and writing applied to metalwork, pottery, and textiles.

As noted above, Islam generally frowns upon images that depict animate figures of humans or animals; hence, the abundance of religious images of patterns composed of geometric or vegetal ornamentation. Yet, these patterns also have a symbolic message in that their repetitive application suggests the infinite nature of God.

Because of its chiefly decorative nature, Islamic art is most often applied on textiles, carpets, ceramics, carved wood and stone, and architecture, not, as with other faiths, sculpture or painting. This may explain why most Islamic artists, with the exception of a few famous calligraphers, remain anonymous. Few signatures are found on Islamic works of art.

Buddhism and the Transformational Space of the Garden

Nature plays a major role in much of Buddhist art and a central role in Buddhist beliefs, which diverge from Western ideas about art as a means to represent or even embody the spiritual world. Instead, all of nature is thought to house spirits, or *hami*, that live within the rocks, water, trees, and mountains. Man interacts with nature, and nature in turn shapes the mind and body of man. The goal of this interaction is a state of satori, or enlightenment.

One of the most visible aesthetic expressions that embodies Buddhist principles is the landscape garden. Such gardens serve a representational role to Buddhists in providing glimpses of the world to come.

Shinto, one of the earliest forms of Buddhism, used nature shrines that incorporated rocks, small lakes, and waterfalls both to represent nature on a smaller scale and to play a representational role in pointing to an otherworldly beauty. A later form of Buddhism, Zen, embraced the idea of gardens as a link to the spiritual world but in a more abstract way. For example, the presence of water might only be represented by rocks or moss with arrangements that could suggest a riverbed.

For the Buddhist, gardens embody a number of spiritual truths. One of them is the belief that life is constantly in a state of flux or change. To express this idea most landscape gardens feature an irregular design with an asymmetrical arrangement of elements of rocks and plants. Borders and pathways are usually curved rather than straight and squared off.

The landscape garden is a cultivated space, yet the pattern is purposefully subtle. Buddhists believe this irregular, incomplete aesthetic invites the observer to meditatively complete the design and thus be transformed by active participation and interaction with the garden.

Hinduism and the Practice of Seeing

Visual imagery is at the core of Hindu worship of multiple gods and goddesses. Hindus use art as a vehicle in which their deities are embodied in human forms depicted in statues, posters, plastic models, and even by actors on serialized television shows.

These forms also play an experiential or transformative role in worship, since Hindus believe that the idol actually sees them as they worship before it. A frequently used Hindu term for going to worship is to go to the *darshan*, or "seeing" of the deity. So important is this act of seeing that when a Hindu idol is created the last act is a ceremonial one that gives the figure eyes, either through the stroke of a paintbrush or by placing porcelain orbs into the sockets.

Hindus have shown a willingness to readily embrace seeing and interacting with religious images outside places of worship, even images that come through the mass media. A serialized television program called *Ramayan*, a story based on an ancient religious epic, premiered on India's government-run television network, Doordashran, in 1987 and created a nationwide sensation. In many Indian homes watching *Ramayan* became a religious ritual, with viewers burning incense in front of the screen and adorning the television set with garlands. When the series concluded a year and a half later, it had become the most popular program ever shown on Indian television.

Judaism: Art and Remembrance

Judaism is often considered to be an iconoclastic faith due to the second of the Ten Commandments, which prohibits making graven images. However, this prohibition only pertained to images used in idol worship. In fact, the Old Testament elevates the role of decorative artistic expression as central to Jewish religious life.

Starting in chapter 25 of the book of Exodus, there is an exhaustive description of how the Ark of the Covenant containing the Ten Commandments and the Tabernacle used for worship were to be lavishly adorned with fine woods, precious metals, stones, and colored fabrics. Exodus 31 names an "artist in residence," Bezalel, who was endowed with skill in all kinds of crafts and charged with making artistic designs using metals, stone, and wood.

The impulse for visual expression has been an important part of the narrative throughout Jewish history. However, while the religious art of other faiths has often incubated in the crucible of a specific culture, the Jews have endured conquest and exile in foreign countries since the end of King Solomon's reign in 922 BCE. As result, Jewish art adopted many of the artistic styles and forms of the cultures where they settled, and it is hard to identify a single stylistic thread that runs through Jewish visual expression.

However, the idea of remembrance is an important theme for Jews, and it finds its expression in the artifacts and ceremonial objects, known as Judaica, that have been gathered in memorials and museums worldwide. These repositories of cultural memory sprung up in Europe with growing frequency in the late eighteenth and early nineteenth centuries at a time when Jews were moving out of isolated enclaves and integrating more fully into the larger culture.

From the synagogues and into public spaces came Torah shields, circumcision benches, paintings, and ceremonial objects that served to help establish Jewish identity among the many ethnic identities of Europe. These public repositories aren't synagogues, and in this setting these objects are not used in a religious context. But they do serve a representational function for Jews and could be considered a transformational part of their religious identity. For Jews these memorials aren't merely static monuments but spaces and objects that represent who they were in the past and affirm who they are in contemporary life.

Keeping Pace with Religious Practice

Among the world's five major religions, all have developed visual vocabularies to communicate the tenets, practices, and historical record of the world of faith. Under the influence of new image-making technologies and the mass media, these vocabularies and doctrines that govern them are still evolving.

VAN KORNEGAY

See also Body Decoration; Culture Wars; Idolatry; Paintings; Sculpture

Further Reading

Cohen, R. (1998). *Jewish Icons: Art and society in modern Europe.* Berkeley: University of California Press.

Eck, D. (1998). *Darshan: Seeing the divine image in India.* New York: Columbia University Press.

Elgood, H. (1999). *Hinduism and the religious arts.* London: Cassell.

Gibson, D. (2004, February 21). What did Jesus really look like? *The New York Times*, Section B, Page 7.

Miles, M. (1985). *Image as Insight: Visual understanding in Western Christianity and secular culture.* Boston: Beacon Press.

Morgan, D. (1999). *Protestants and pictures: Religion, visual culture, and the age of American mass production.* New York: Oxford University Press.

Pilgrim, R. (1993). *Buddhism and the arts of Japan.* Chambersburg, PA: Anima Books.

Plate, S. (2002). *Religion, art, and visual culture.* New York: Palgrave.

Schimmel, A. (1984). *Calligraphy and Islamic culture.* New York: New York University Press.

Audience

Parishioners gather for religious worship (i.e., sermons, public prayers, ordinances, etc.) in what are generally referred to as "congregations." When they use secular media such as television or film, they become a religious "audience." How members of religious audiences experience popular culture is an important question in media studies; it broadens understanding of how church members interact with the secular world. Audience behavior varies significantly across denominations, ranging from the Amish, who abstain from television, to Unitarians, who occasionally incorporate actual programs into worship services. Some audience members are activists, such as Southern Baptists boycotting Disney products or Muslims protesting the publication of Salman Rushdie's novel, *The Satanic Verses.* Clergy often encourage "religious media literacy," or the use of mass media within the context of one's spiritual goals and values.

History of Religious Audiences

The religious audience is not a new phenomenon and is exemplified by the Romantic period, during which Christian patrons enjoyed spiritual themes in the secular works of Shakespeare as well as the inspirational plays of Victor Hugo and Friedrich Schiller. By the 1870s, the lyceum and Chautauqua adult-education movements in the United States were attracting church members to secular plays, poetry readings, and lectures. The transition from congregation to audience was an uneasy one, however, and church members were ambivalent about the appropriateness of pure entertainment. Consequently, late-nineteenth-century lyceums presented secular entertainment in churches along with theological instruction (Cravens 2005).

With the advent of radio and television, religious audiences have expanded both in number and complexity. In the current information society, the Internet, interactive television, and satellite communication have created opportunities as well as challenges for religious communities.

Audience Diversity

Religious audiences are comprised of smaller "interpretive communities" (Lindlof 2002) and are rarely homogenous in terms of media use and interpretation. Within the highly literate culture of Judaism, for example, the ultraOrthodox Haredim have been known to forbid secular television viewing, while TV shows and movies are enjoyed by many Reformed Jewish families. Similar diversity exists within Islam. Despite shared skepticism of some Western values, American Muslims are more likely to view Hollywood-produced movies than Shiite Muslims in the Middle East, who have greater disdain for secular media of the West. Muslim resistance to Western media is illustrated by Yusuf Islam/Cat Stevens, the popular rock musician who converted to Islam, sold his musical instruments, and refrained from performing many of his songs (Palmer and Gallab 2001).

When Luthra (2001) compared a small Hindu *satsangh* (a devotional study group) with a larger community of Internet newsgroup users, she found that audience members varied dramatically in their attitudes about media. The smaller group used entertainment media sparingly, mostly when it promoted spiritual growth. Hindu newsgroup members, however, were more familiar with mainstream U.S. media and were more likely to engage in antidefamation activity when Hindus were depicted negatively.

Christian Audience Diversity

Audience diversity also exists within Christianity. Conservative Protestants in the Evangelical tradition (e.g., Southern Baptists, Pentecostals, Nazarenes) are more likely to assess secular media as antithetical to Christian values (Schultze 1996) than mainline Protestants (e.g., Methodists, Presbyterians, Lutherans), who often praise TV news and educational programming for raising awareness about drug abuse, poverty, and other social issues (Buddenbaum 1996). Audience behaviors often change, as in the case of the Nazarenes, who once abstained from going to movies but now use a wider range of media (Lepter and Lindlof 2001).

Catholic approaches to media have also evolved considerably. In the 1950s, Catholics looked to the National Legion of Decency and National Office of Decent Literature for direction in selecting media. Since the 1993 writings of Pope John Paul II, however, media use is becoming a matter of individual conscience (Jelen 1996). Diversity in the Mormon community is illustrated by avoidance of R-rated movies but sharp disagreement about whether television can play a positive role in family life (Valenti and Stout 1996).

Using Secular Media in Religious Worship

A major dilemma for religious audiences is whether to resist or embrace media of secular culture. Dualistic "culture wars" rhetoric fails to capture the complex ways religions interface with media of popular culture; genres that were once condemned are now used for spiritual purposes. Among conservative Protestants, such media as religious novels, TV talk shows, and rock music have emerged as new hybrid genres. Programs such as *The 700 Club* and *Hour of Power* combine the format of TV news and entertainment programs with elements of traditional church meetings. Many Southern Baptists protested against *The Last Temptation of Christ* but mostly praised *The Passion of Christ*, showing the film in church buildings. Some Baptist churches also use the 1960s TV sitcom *The Andy Griffith Show* to teach moral principles in Sunday School classes.

Beyond conservative Protestantism, a more general theory is emerging about how media use is affecting the growth of religious institutions. Based on a national survey and over four hundred interviews, Wuthnow (2003) concludes that interest in art and music is revitalizing a number of denominations. The religious audience, he argues, is bringing secular art and entertainment back into the church, sponsoring art exhibits, concerts, dramas, and even artists-in-residence. According to the data, parishioners look to media for reinforcement of religious belief. These essential yearnings for inspiration have resulted in audience members organizing dance performances, art festivals, and reading groups within the walls of the church.

Secularization

Research is inconclusive on the question of secularization, or the assumption that religious commitment weakens through exposure to mass media. Secularization, however, is a controversial theory that does not hold up in all cases. For example, Stout (2004) found that a sample of Mormons in the entertainment city of Las Vegas remained devout despite considerable exposure to media considered deleterious. Similarly, Lepter and Lindlof (2001) observed that as members of the Church of the Nazarene expanded their media use, they continued to express strong commitments to their faith. And Warren (2001) found that the boycott of Disney by Southern Baptists resulted in stronger group cohesion, suggesting that the ultimate effect of secular media is difficult to predict. Researchers agree that loss of religious commitment is a complex process and not easily attributed to a single factor such as media. More study is needed, however, to determine which situations are most likely to result in secularization among various audiences.

The Future

New lines of inquiry have emerged in religious audience research. Hess (2001), for example, is exploring religious media literacy and the extent to which secular media can be used in the teaching of values. Another interesting area is the religious consumer audience. Haley, White, and Cunningham (2001) found that audience members are divided on the question of whether marketing communication should be used to promote religious brands of products (e.g., jewelry or clothing). And Campbell (2004) is examining whether audience members' Internet behavior serves to strengthen or weaken religious communities.

DANIEL STOUT

See also Charisma; Congregations

Further Reading

Buddenbaum, J. M. (1996). Christian perspectives on mass media. In D. A. Stout & J. M. Buddenbaum (Eds.), *Religion and mass media: Audiences and adaptations* (pp. 81–94). Thousand Oaks, CA: Sage.

Campbell, H. (2004). Challenges created by online religious networks. *Journal of Media and Religion, 3*(2), 81–99.

Cravens, M. (2005). *Lyceum, Chautauqua, and magic*. Retrieved February 19, 2005 from http://www.floraco.com/lyceum/

Haley, E., White, C., & Cunningham, A. (2001). Branding religion: Christian consumers' understandings of Christian products. In D. A. Stout & J. M. Buddenbaum (Eds.), *Religion and popular culture: Studies on the interaction of worldviews* (pp. 269–288). Ames: Iowa State University Press.

Hess, M. (2001). Media literacy as a support for the development of a responsible imagination in religious community. In D. A. Stout & J. M. Buddenbaum (Eds.), *Religion and popular culture: Studies on the interaction of worldviews* (pp. 289–311). Ames: Iowa State University Press.

Jelen, T. (1996). Catholicism, conscience, and censorship. In D. A. Stout & J. M. Buddenbaum (Eds.), *Religion and mass media: Audiences and adaptations* (pp. 39–50). Thousand Oaks, CA: Sage.

Lepter, J., & Lindlof, T. (2001). Coming out of abstinence: A root-metaphor study of Nazarenes' relation to movies and media. In D. A. Stout & J. M. Buddenbaum (Eds.), *Religion and popular culture: Studies on the interaction of worldviews* (pp. 217–234). Ames: Iowa State University Press.

Lindlof, T. (2002). Interpretive community: An approach to media and religion. *Journal of Media and Religion 1*(1), 61–74.

Luthra, R. (2001). The formation of interpretive communities in the Hindu diaspora. In D. A. Stout & J. M. Buddenbaum (Eds.), *Religion and popular culture: Studies on the interaction of worldviews* (pp. 125–139). Ames: Iowa State University Press.

Palmer, A., & Gallab, A. (2001). Islam and Western culture: Navigating terra incognita. In D. A. Stout & J. M. Buddenbaum (Eds.), *Religion and popular culture: Studies on the interaction of worldviews* (pp. 109–124). Ames: Iowa State University Press.

Schement, J., & Stephenson, H. (1996). Religion and the information society. In D. A. Stout & J. M. Buddenbaum (Eds.), *Religion and mass media: Audiences and adaptations* (pp. 261–289). Thousand Oaks, CA: Sage.

Schultze, Q. (1996). Evangelicals' uneasy alliance with the media. In D. A. Stout & J. M. Buddenbaum (Eds.), *Religion and mass media: Audiences and adaptations* (pp. 61–73). Thousand Oaks, CA: Sage.

Stout, D. A. (2004). Secularization and the religious audience: A study of Mormons and Las Vegas media. *Mass communication and society 7*(1), 61–75.

Valenti, J., & Stout, D. (1996). Diversity from within: An analysis of the impact of religious culture on media use and effective communication to women. In D. A. Stout & J. M. Buddenbaum (Eds.), *Religion and mass media: Audiences and adaptations* (pp. 183–196). Thousand Oaks, CA: Sage.

Warren, H. (2001). Southern Baptists as audience and public: A cultural analysis of the Disney boycott. In D. A. Stout & J. M. Buddenbaum (Eds.), *Religion and popular culture: Studies on the interaction of worldviews* (pp. 169–186). Ames: Iowa State University Press.

Wuthnow, R. (2003). *All in sync: How music and art are revitalizing American religion.* Berkeley: University of California Press.

B

Baha'i

The Baha'i Faith, the youngest of the world's independent religions, was born in Persia (present-day Iran) in 1844, the year Samuel F. B. Morse inaugurated the age of telecommunications by telegraphing the phrase "What hath God wrought?" from Washington, D.C., to Baltimore, Maryland. Advances in communications technology have paralleled and facilitated the Baha'i Faith's emergence as a truly global religion and lent credence to the Faith's central tenet that humanity is now reaching its long-awaited stage of maturity, when its unity will be recognized and established on a global scale.

The Baha'i Faith was founded by Mirza Husayn Ali (1817–1892), a Persian nobleman who adopted the title Baha'u'llah (The Glory of God). The teachings of Baha'u'llah revolve around the theme of oneness: There is only one God, absolutely transcendent and unknowable. There is only one religion, revealed progressively from age to age through the agency of unique and peerless individuals, known as Manifestations of God, the founders of the world's major religions. Baha'u'llah claimed to be the Manifestation of God for this age, the latest in a series of messengers from God that includes Moses, the Buddha, Zoroaster, Jesus Christ, and Muhammad. He said there is only one human race, carrying forward an ever-advancing civilization destined to recognize its oneness and firmly establish a just and global social order.

Baha'u'llah's universal message quickly attracted converts from Muslim, Christian, Jewish, Zoroastrian, Hindu, Buddhist, and other backgrounds, all of whom recognized in him the fulfillment of the prophetic expectations contained in their respective scriptures. The Baha'i community now has more than 5 million members and represents a cross-section of humanity, including men and women from more than two thousand ethnic and tribal backgrounds. Baha'i communities are established in more than 230 countries and dependent territories, with elected national administrative institutions in 182 countries. According to the 2001 *World Christian Encyclopedia*, the Baha'i Faith is the second-most geographically widespread religion, after Christianity.

A survey of Baha'i communications reveals the existence of several qualitatively different types of communication, each occupying its own unique position within the life of the religious community. In broad terms, these types include communications from God to humankind; from the Faith's authoritative leadership to the community of believers; among the community of believers; and from the community of believers to the general public. In each of these categories, the Baha'i Faith has employed a variety of communications media, and the choice of media has also evolved as the Baha'i Faith developed through several clearly demarcated historical periods, namely, the ministries of Baha'u'llah (1852–1892); His son, Abdu'l-Baha (1892–1921); and His great-grandson, Shoghi Effendi (1921–1957); and the current period under the leadership of an elected governing body, the Universal House of Justice, which was first formed in 1963.

Ministry of Baha'u'llah (1852–1892)

In Baha'i theology, Manifestations of God—the Founders of the worlds major religions—are considered the *Word made flesh*, the perfect embodiments and conduits of God's attributes, such as grace, power, knowledge, and will. The utterances and writings of the Manifestations are considered the revealed Word of God, endowed with a transcendent and creative potency. For Baha'is, the only completely authenticated repositories of the Word of God are the writings of Baha'u'llah; the writings of his herald, the Báb (Siyyid Ali Muhammad, 1819–1850); and the Qur'an. During a nearly forty-year ministry, Baha'u'llah authored more than fifteen thousand books, tablets, and letters that today comprise the sacred scripture of the Baha'i Faith. A unique feature of the revelation of Baha'u'llah is the authenticity of its scripture. Unlike the teachings of Christ, for example, which were written down by others decades after they were uttered, the words of Baha'u'llah were recorded and authenticated at the time they were composed.

Baha'u'llah spent the nearly forty years of his ministry as a prisoner and exile under the Ottoman authorities. Exiled from his native Persia in 1852, he was banished to Baghdad, Istanbul, Adrianople, and finally to Akka, then a prison-city in Ottoman Palestine. Communication with His followers was achieved through written correspondence, and these letters were delivered by couriers who traveled, often on foot and under conditions of extraordinary hardship, throughout Persia and the Middle East. Baha'u'llah also wrote tablets to the kings and rulers of his day, including Queen Victoria, Napoleon III, Kaiser Wilhelm, Czar Nicholas Alexander, Sultan Abdul-Aziz, and Nasiri'd-Din Shah.

The original manuscripts of Baha'u'llah's writings, some in his own hand and others meticulously transcribed by his personal secretaries, are today kept at the Baha'i World Center in Haifa, Israel. Researchers at the Baha'i World Center are charged with organizing and indexing the thousands of documents in the collection and producing translations, compilations, and commentaries. Only a small portion of Baha'u'llah's voluminous writings has been translated from the original Persian and Arabic into other languages. The work of translation into English was given a major impetus by Shoghi Effendi, Baha'u'llah's great-grandson, who headed the Baha'i Faith from 1921 to 1957 and who produced authoritative translations of several major doctrinal, mystical, and devotional works. Selections from Baha'u'llah's writings have been translated into more than eight hundred languages.

In his writings, Baha'u'llah addressed the powerful role of mass communications and the moral responsibility it entails:

> In this Day the secrets of the earth are laid bare before the eyes of men. The pages of swiftly appearing newspapers are indeed the mirror of the world.

They reflect the deeds and the pursuits of divers peoples and kindreds. They both reflect them and make them known. They are a mirror endowed with hearing, sight and speech. This is an amazing and potent phenomenon. However, it behoveth the writers thereof to be purged from the promptings of evil passions and desires and to be attired with the raiment of justice and equity. They should enquire into situations as much as possible and ascertain the facts, then set them down in writing. (Baha'u'llah, *Tablets of Baha'u'llah*, 39)

Ministries of Abdu'l-Baha and Shoghi Effendi (1892–1957)

A unique feature of the Baha'i Faith is a clear line of succession and explicit teachings on the organization and leadership of the Baha'i community, which have preserved the Baha'i Faith from major schisms. Baha'u'llah left a written will appointing His eldest son, Abdu'l-Baha (1844–1921), as the Head of the Faith and authoritative interpreter of His Teachings. Baha'u'llah also forbade the formation of a clerical class and ordained a system of elected lay councils to administer the affairs of the faith. Abdu'l-Baha in turn designated His eldest grandson, Shoghi Effendi (1897–1957), as His successor and conferred upon him the title of Guardian of the Baha'i Faith. With the passing of Shoghi Effendi in 1957, the line of hereditary leaders of the Baha'i Faith came to an end. In 1963, following provisions established by Baha'u'llah, a nine-member council known as the Universal House of Justice was elected to direct the spiritual and administrative affairs of the worldwide Baha'i community. Baha'u'llah endowed this body with authority to legislate on all matters not specifically laid down in the Baha'i scriptures.

Communications that originate from these leaders of the Faith fulfill the unique functions of providing authoritative guidance, interpretation, legislation, and plans for the expansion and consolidation of the Faith. During the ministries of Abdu'l-Baha (1892–1921) and Shoghi Effendi (1921–1957), the principal form of communication from the head of the Faith to the community of believers was in the form of written correspondence addressed mainly to individual believers, to elected national and local Baha'i spiritual assemblies, and generally to the community of believers in a particular country or region. Many volumes of these letters have been compiled and published.

During Abdu'l-Baha's ministry, nascent Baha'i communities in Europe, North America, Australia, and the Far East began to publish regular Baha'i news periodi-

Excerpt from *The World Order of Baha'u'llah* by Shoghi Effendi

Shoghi Effendi, head of the Baha'i Faith from 1921 to 1957, saw the rapid evolution of communications technology as both a symbol of and a means to achieving the unification of the human race in an organic global society. In 1936, in an essay describing Baha'u'llah's vision of the emerging world order, he wrote:

> The unity of the human race, as envisaged by Baha'u'llah, implies the establishment of a world commonwealth in which all nations, races, creeds and classes are closely and permanently united, and in which the autonomy of its state members and the personal freedom and initiative of the individuals that compose them are definitely and completely safeguarded... A mechanism of world intercommunication will be devised, embracing the whole planet, freed from national hindrances and restrictions, and functioning with marvellous swiftness and perfect regularity... A world language will either be invented or chosen from among the existing languages and will be taught in the schools of all the federated nations as an auxiliary to their mother tongue. A world script, a world literature, a uniform and universal system of currency, of weights and measures, will simplify and facilitate intercourse and understanding among the nations and races of mankind... The press will, under such a system, while giving full scope to the expression of the diversified views and convictions of mankind, cease to be mischievously manipulated by vested interests, whether private or public, and will be liberated from the influence of contending governments and peoples...

Source: Effendi, S. (1936). *The world order of Baha'u'llah.*
Baha'i Publishing Trust, Wilmette, IL.

cals to inspire, inform, and nurture their communities. North American Baha'is published *Star of the West*, the first international Baha'i news periodical, from 1910 to 1935. It is considered an important source of first-hand historical data on the early development of the faith. At present, most National Spiritual Assemblies, and many local Assemblies, publish regular news periodicals in some form, ranging from glossy magazines to full-length newspapers to simple mimeographed bulletins and community calendars.

In the first decade of the twentieth century, the first Baha'i publishing agencies were formed to make available the Faith's primary and secondary literature. Today more than thirty publishing trusts are operated by National Spiritual Assemblies around the world, providing Baha'i scripture and other books about the religion in most major languages. The United States Baha'i Publishing Trust was established in 1955, and in 2000 the Trust launched Baha'i Publishing, a trade paper imprint producing books for adult readers interested in Baha'i religion and spirituality.

While the Baha'i Faith forbids aggressive proselytizing—including any form of psychological pressure or material inducements to effect conversion—efforts to share the Faith with the general public and attract receptive populations have been a focus of Baha'i activity from the Faith's inception. During the time of Baha'u'llah, this was achieved primarily by word of mouth and through the agency of itinerant traveling teachers. Abdu'l-Baha undertook a series of historic missionary journeys through Europe and North America in the evening of his life, and hundreds of his public addresses have been compiled and published.

Shoghi Effendi pioneered the use of a variety of communications channels to reach government, academic, media, and other influential circles. He established the Baha'i International Community (BIC) as a registered nongovernmental organization to serve as the Faith's diplomatic and public information arm, and it has had consultative status at the United Nations since 1948. In 1925, he initiated the periodic publication of *The Baha'i World*, a comprehensive international survey of the Baha'i Faith and its activities. It was published in twenty volumes between 1925 and 1991, and relaunched as a yearbook series in 1992. Shoghi Effendi also encouraged Baha'is around the world to undertake systematic publicity and advertising campaigns employing the press and radio.

Current Developments

In recent decades, the size and demographic profile of the worldwide Baha'i community have changed dramatically. In the early 1950s, Baha'is numbered about two hundred thousand, and most of them lived in Iran. There were probably fewer than ten thousand Baha'is in the West and no more than three thousand Baha'is in the Third World, mostly in India. In 2005, more than 5 million Baha'is reside in nearly every nation and territory on earth. About 90 percent of the Baha'i population resides in developing countries in Latin America, Africa, and South and East Asia. Western Baha'is comprise only 4 percent of the total, and Middle Easterners (mostly Iranians) about 6 percent. The range and complexity of Baha'i communications has correspondingly increased.

At the international level, the Baha'i International Community (BIC) continues to function as the Faith's diplomatic and public information arm, maintaining a United Nations Office in New York with a branch office in Geneva. These offices represent the interests and concerns of Baha'is throughout the world, both at the United Nations and in other international forums. They also stimulate and coordinate relevant efforts by local and national Baha'i communities.

The BIC Office of Public Information, based at the Baha'i World Center in Haifa, Israel, with a branch office in Paris, communicates with the public, the news media, and nongovernmental organizations. In addition to *The Baha'i World* yearbook series, the Office publishes *One Country* (www.onecountry.org), an award-winning quarterly newsletter first published in English in 1989. It now has a circulation of about forty thousand, in six languages and 174 countries. It offers a Baha'i perspective on current events and trends in such areas as sustainable development, the advancement of women, and human rights, focusing on the emergence of consensus in the world community.

In 1996, the BIC Office of Public Information launched the *Baha'i World* website, www.bahai.org, as the Faith's official presence on the World Wide Web, offering in-depth information about the history, teachings, and activities of the worldwide Baha'i community. It is the centerpiece of a rapidly expanding Baha'i presence on the Internet. The *Baha'i World News Service*, news.bahai.org, was launched in 2000 as a source of news reports and photographs that can be picked up by the news media and by Baha'i magazines and news periodicals around the world. Many of the 182 National Spiritual Assemblies around the world have their own national Baha'i websites, and thousands of other websites feature Baha'i content, ranging from personal and local community sites, to sites created by youth workshops, publishers, bookstores, directories, and Baha'i schools.

In 2001, the BIC launched the Baha'i International Radio Service with the primary mandate of dissipating misinformation about the Baha'i Faith in Iran, where the Faith continues to suffer intense persecution. Its programs are heard in Iran on shortwave radio as well as on the Internet at www.bahairadio.org.

National Baha'i communities around the world use a range of media suitable to their means and circumstances. For example, in rural areas of Latin America and Africa where the Faith has experienced large-scale growth, low-power radio stations have become an increasingly valuable tool for creating Baha'i community identity and serving the social and economic development needs of largely indigenous populations. At present, there are six Baha'i radio stations, five in Latin America and one in North America.

In the United States, where the Baha'i community currently numbers about 150,000, the National Spiritual Assembly publishes a newspaper, *The American Baha'i*, distributed free of charge to every Baha'i household ten times per year, as well as a video newsreel highlighting the latest Baha'i events and activities, which is distributed to the community several times per year in VHS format. The National Assembly also publishes *World Order*, an award-winning quarterly journal of analysis and opinion. A scholarly journal, the *Journal of Baha'i Studies*, is published quarterly by the Association for Baha'i Studies of North America.

In recent years, the U.S. Baha'i community has experimented with various forms of mass media outreach to raise the level of public awareness and understanding about the Baha'i Faith. Surveys conducted periodically since 2000 indicate that about one third of the adult U.S. population is aware of the Baha'i Faith and a substantial portion has a positive and accurate perception of the Faith. To broaden this level of awareness, the National Assembly has produced a series of half-hour documentary-style video programs highlighting the Faith's teachings on race unity, gender equality, world unity, the power of prayer, the family as the fundamental unit of society, and other subjects. These have been broadcast on national cable and broadcast networks, as well as on local public access cable and at public informational gatherings. A number of thirty- and sixty-second TV spots have been produced and broadcast in local media markets where the Baha'i community offers children's classes, adult study circles, and devotional programs to the general public.

Other public information campaigns have focused on Baha'i perspectives on social issues and current events. For example, in the aftermath of the September 11, 2001, terrorist attacks in New York, the National Assembly published a full-page statement in *The New York Times* on "The Destiny of America and the Promise of World Peace." The statement became the centerpiece of a campaign that included banner advertising on the Web, publication of the statement and related news articles and editorials in dozens of major newspapers, public meetings, and other forms of outreach. A similar publicity effort was launched in September 2004 with a statement titled "Cultural Cleansing: Destroying a Community, Erasing Memory," issued in response to the Iranian government's demolition of several sites of great historical value and spiritual significance to Baha'is.

GLEN T. FULLMER

Further Reading

Abdu'l-Baha. (1982). *The promulgation of universal peace: Talks delivered by Abdu'l-Baha during His visit to the United States and Canada in 1912.* Wilmette, IL: Baha'i Publishing Trust.

Abdu'l-Baha. (1984). *Some answered questions.* Wilmette, IL: Baha'i Publishing Trust.

Baha'u'llah. (1983a). *Gleanings from the writings of Baha'u'llah.* Wilmette, IL: Baha'i Publishing Trust.

Baha'u'llah. (1983b). *Tablets of Baha'u'llah.* Wilmette, IL: Baha'i Publishing Trust.

Baha'u'llah. (1993). *The Kitab-i-Aqdas: The most holy book.* Wilmette, IL: Baha'i Publishing Trust.

Baha'u'llah, the Báb, and Abdu'l-Baha. (2002). *Baha'i prayers: A selection of prayers revealed by Baha'u'llah, the Báb, and Abdu'l-Baha.* Wilmette, IL: Baha'i Publishing Trust.

Baha'u'llah. (2003). *The Kitab-i-Iqan: The book of certitude.* Wilmette, IL: Baha'i Publishing Trust.

Barrett, D. B., Kurian, G. T., & Johnson, T. M. (Eds.). (2001). *World Christian encyclopedia.* Oxford, UK: Oxford University Press.

Bowers, K. E. (2004). *God speaks again.* Wilmette, IL: Baha'i Publishing Trust.

Esslemont, J. E. (1980). *Baha'u'llah and the new era: An introduction to the Baha'i Faith.* Wilmette, IL: Baha'i Publishing Trust.

Hatcher, W. S., & Martin, J. D. (2002). *The Baha'i Faith: The emerging global religion.* Wilmette, IL: Baha'i Publishing Trust.

Hein, K. J. (1988). *Radio Baha'i Ecuador.* Oxford, UK: George Ronald.

Shoghi Effendi. (1974). *God passes by.* Wilmette, IL: Baha'i Publishing Trust.

Shoghi Effendi. (1993). *The world order of Baha'u'llah.* Wilmette, IL: Baha'i Publishing Trust.

The Baha'i world: An international record, 2000–2001. Haifa, Israel: Baha'i World Centre.

Universal House of Justice. (1985). *The promise of world peace: To the peoples of the world.* Wilmette, IL: Baha'i Publishing Trust.

Universal House of Justice. (2001). *The century of light.* Haifa, Israel: Baha'i World Centre.

Universal House of Justice. (2002). *To the world's religious leaders.* Wilmette, IL: Baha'i Publishing Trust.

Bells

The use of bells in religious rites dates back to ancient times. Bells take a variety of shapes, generally falling under one of two forms: the open-mouthed bell or the *crotal* ("jingle bell"). The open-mouthed bell may be struck or shaken, depending on whether it has an internal or external clapper. The crotal is almost fully enclosed with a pellet in the middle to produce the ringing sound. Although both types have had religious and secular uses throughout history, this article will confine its discussion to the religious uses.

Asia

The earliest development of the open-mouthed bell was probably in China, between 1500 and 1000 BCE. The distinctive "fish mouth" shape of the Chinese bells probably imitated a grain scoop. Confucian music employed rows of these bells tuned to different tones and struck with a hammer. When Confucianism spread to Japan, the Chinese rows of twelve tuned bells were incorporated into the emperor's ritual animal sacrifices. Ancestor worship also required a bell for the home altar, rung daily to attract the ancestors' attention.

The earliest bells in Japan, called *dotaka*, have been found buried at crossroads, on hilltops, and in other sacred spots, sometimes in assemblages. Burying *dotaka* was a part of the ancient agrarian society's interaction with nature. The bell itself was likely an object of reverence and sometimes decorated with scenes from daily life.

In India, the open-mouthed bell did not appear until the fifth century BCE, but the use of crotals in jewelry dates back to 3000 BCE. By the fourth century, Hindu deities regularly appear carrying crotals or open-mouthed bells. In Hinduism, the bell manifested a spiritual force. The shape of the bell was also a sacred symbol representing a circle, a hemisphere, and a lotus. This is the same shape that later appeared in Christian

bells two thousand years later. Hindu worshippers rang bells or used their images to ward off evil spirits. When entering or leaving a temple, the worshipper would also ring a bell to announce his presence.

As Buddhism gained popularity in China, Japan, Korea, and India, so did the presence of large bells in temples. During the Ming dynasty (1368–1644 CE) in China, each city had one large bell, typically inscribed with Buddhist scriptures. The large bells also signaled the time for worshippers to assemble. Large bells had a particular significance because their tones simulated the sacred sound *om*. Buddhist priests used hand-held bells in ceremonies as an important part of the liturgy, as well as to ward off evil or attract a god's attention.

Wind bells decorate the eaves of pagodas, both as ornaments and as talismans against evil spirits. In India, wind bells also protect sacred spots, such as the burial places of saints' relics. Crotals also hang on the statues of beasts that protect the temple.

Ancient Near East

Bells appear in many ancient Mesopotamian cultures. Israelite priests wore bells on the hems of their garments. Archaeologists have evidence that Assyrian priests used bells in worship. In Egypt, the *crotal* appeared in prehistoric times, and *crotals* may have adorned temple

dancers or highlighted parts of processions. Archaeologists have discovered bells with heads of Egyptian gods, possibly imitating the shape of a funerary urn. Egyptians also buried bells with their dead.

In the Middle East today, Islam is the dominant religion. Muslims do not use bells in worship, favoring the sound of the human voice to call the faithful to prayer.

Europe and Christian Near East

The early church used boards knocked together as the call to worship. While Christians were persecuted, the quieter boards made more sense than bells. In Eastern European churches this tradition persisted in the form of large resonant boards, called *semantron*, struck with a hammer. When tower bells did take hold, they were hung stationary and rung with a string pulling the clapper. This method not only kept the custom of knocking, but also permitted much heavier bells than the Western bell towers.

In the Western Christian Church, Celtic missionaries popularized the open-mouthed bell in the fifth to ninth centuries. The faithful accorded these iron handbells great reverence. By the sixth century, Benedictine monks in Italy began casting bells. These cast bells gradually replaced the forged iron ones and grew larger, evolving into the bells we know today. Western churches mounted the large bells such that they ring by swinging back and forth like a pendulum or in a full circle, perhaps hearkening back to the handbell-ringing tradition.

In Christian churches, bells are typically rung to announce the beginning of the worship service, other religious occasions, weddings, and deaths. Churches use different bells in various combinations to convey different announcements. Some churches, for example, ring the largest bell shortly before the sermon.

Catholic churches do not allow the ringing of church bells until they have been consecrated through elaborate baptism and dedication ceremonies. Bells form an integral part of the Catholic liturgy, and the time and manner of ringing them is prescribed by custom and tradition. The Catholic liturgy excludes carillons from the sacred liturgy, although many churches have them for ringing out melodies on festive occasions.

Many church bells bear ornamentation and inscriptions. The decorations may reflect religious themes or just aesthetic design. The inscriptions may proclaim the maker or donor of the bell, or they may reflect the church bell's higher calling. Scriptures and dedications to the Virgin Mary or various saints or apostles appear frequently. By the eighteenth century, some inscriptions were more lighthearted, such as "Pull on brave boys, I'm metal to the back, but I'll be hanged before I crack."

The Future

People in many parts of the world and at many points in history have considered bells to have special properties. It is therefore unsurprising that as religion has evolved, bells have been retained to mark worship, solemnize occasions, and send public messages. Perhaps the emphasis on the magic of bells has diminished with time, but their majestic tones continue to form an important part of religious practice.

SUSANNA DOKUPIL

Further Reading

Corbin, A. (1998). *Village bells: Sound and meaning in the 19th-century French countryside* (M. Thom, Trans.). New York: Columbia University Press.

Dunkin, E. (1878). *The church bells of Cornwall*. London: Bemrose.

Gatty, A. (1848). *The bell: Its origin, history, and uses*. London: George Bell.

Instruction on Sacred Music and Liturgy (1958). In *Adoremus Bulletin*. Retrieved July 6, 2005, from www.adoremus.org/1958Intro-sac-mus.html#anchor36297672

Lefevre, K. (1942). Bells in religion. *Religion in Life, 11*(2), 257–268.

Macy, L. (Ed.). Bell. *Grove Music Online*. Retrieved July 6, 2005, from www.grovemusic.com.ezproxy.baylor.edu

Price, P. (1983). *Bells and man*. Oxford, UK: Oxford University Press.

Raven, J. J. (1906). *The bells of England*. London: Methuen.

Von Falkenhausen, L. (1993). *Suspended music: Chime-bells in the culture of Bronze Age China*. Berkeley: University of California Press.

Walters, H. B. (1908). *Church bells*. London: Mowbray.

Black Spiritual Churches

Spiritualism is an alternative religious movement; its followers believe some individuals have the power to communicate with spirit beings. Black Spiritual churches are the institutional embodiment of this widely divergent religious tradition sharing common ideological origins with other Spiritualist groups.

Modern Spiritualist Movement in America

Spiritualism's origins go back to the nineteenth century. Based on the eighteenth-century writings of Swedish scientist Emanuel Swedenborg, the movement began to gain popularity in the United States in 1848, when the first mediums and proponents of what came to be known as "modern" Spiritualism, sisters Catherine and Margaretta Fox, moved with their parents into a house in Hydesville, New York, that locals thought was haunted. There they heard rapping sounds throughout the house and eventually worked out a type of language in which a certain number of raps signified "yes," "no," or a particular letter of the alphabet. Their system allowed them to communicate with the spirit of a man who had been murdered in the house by the previous owner. When news of these paranormal communications became public, large numbers of people came to the house to witness them for themselves. Other spirits began to communicate with the sisters, and they eventually began touring and promoting spiritualism, leading others to become mediums. In 1853 the first Spiritualist church was founded, and in 1893, after several state associations of Spiritualist congregations had already been formed, the movement developed further institutionally by establishing the first national association, the National Spiritual Association (of Churches).

Core Beliefs

The central tenet of Spiritualism is the belief that at death the spirit of the deceased continues to live and crosses over into a spirit world that overlaps with the material world. Certain individuals—mediums—have the gift or power to communicate with the spirits of the deceased or angels, spirit guides, and other spirit beings who might be interested or actively engaged in the affairs of the living. God is seen as Spirit (rather than as an old man or judge) as well as Infinite Intelligence, Infinite Spirit, and Perfect Love, among other things. Through the belief and practice of mediumship, prophecies or messages from the spirit world are given to help or warn the living. Also through mediumship, those individuals with this type of spiritual gift or power become the literal media, or means, of communication between two realms of existence, the world of the spirits and the world of the material.

Other beliefs include the concept that heaven and hell do not exist but are projections of the human mind; like God, humans are spirit clothed in matter; and that there was no Fall (and Eve, a woman, was not to blame for humanity's "sinful" condition). In general women have found (or created) places within the Spiritualist movement in a variety of positions of spiritual and church authority. The brotherhood and sisterhood of humanity is affirmed, and the development of one's soul through service and good works are also part of the Spiritualist belief system inherited from its Swedenborgian roots. Individuals are believed to be assisted, or given special insight, to develop or improve their soul's condition as it progresses toward God through the practice of communicating with personal "guides," angels, or other spirit beings through a medium or "channeler." Healing of the physical body and mind are also part of the benefits of communion with or channeling the energy inherent in beings from the spirit world.

Emergence of the Black Spiritual Church

Like other religious movements at various times in American history, the Spiritualist movement initially welcomed the membership of African-Americans into their congregations and associations, and many were accepted and sought after as talented and powerful mediums. Once the initial fervor began to subside, however, white Spiritualists capitulated to the racism that marked the times, and African-Americans were affiliated with the National Spiritualist Association primarily through auxiliary organizations. The first Black Spiritualist Association was founded in 1913 in Chicago, and with the emergence in 1925 of the National Colored Spiritualist Association of Churches—the direct institutional response of blacks to whites in the National Spiritualist Association having forced them to leave the former association—the process of differentiation along racial lines in the Spiritualist movement became institutionalized. Spiritualism continued to grow among African-Americans during this period. It was particularly appealing to those blacks who had recently undergone the Great Migration from the rural South to northern urban industrial centers like Detroit, Chicago, and New York as well as to southern cities like Kansas City and New Orleans.

From the 1920s through the 1940s, a number of new congregations, denominations, fraternal organizations, and faith-based social-services agencies were added to the ranks of the Black Spiritualists as the movement spread to black communities from the Midwest to the South, East, and the West Coast. It was also during this period of racial differentiation and growth in the movement that many blacks began to refer to themselves and their churches as "Spiritual" as opposed to "Spiritualist," as a way of marking themselves, their congregations, and national associations as distinct from those of their white counterparts in the modern Spiritualist movement. At least in the case of African-Americans, Spiritualism seems to be largely an urban, twentieth-century phenomenon arising out of and accompanying the mass population shift, the migration of millions of blacks from the South to the North and to urban centers. It also tends to be fused in some form or another with a Judeo-Christian orientation including use of the Bible.

Important Figures and Organizations

Among the most important figures in the development of Black Spiritual churches was Mother Leafy Anderson, founder of the Eternal Life Christian Spiritualist Association. Around 1920 she organized New Orleans's first Spiritualist congregation among the blacks there in her new home. This church became the twelfth congregation in the Association and signaled the beginning of Black Spiritualism in New Orleans. Students of Anderson included Mother Catherine Seals and Thomas Watson, both of whom founded Spiritualist organizations in the black community in New Orleans in 1929, two years after her death. Mother Seal's church was the Temple of the Innocent Blood, and Watson founded the St. Joseph

Helping Hand Church in Algiers, a suburb across the Mississippi River from New Orleans. In 1934 Watson organized several other emerging Spiritual congregations into the St. Joseph Helping Hand Missionary Association. This organization would develop into the Divine Spiritual Churches of the Southwest in 1936.

In other places around the country Black Spiritual churches were also being founded, some of which are still in existence today. In Detroit, George Willie Hurley founded Universal Hagar's Spiritual Church (1923); in Kansas City, William Frank Taylor and Leviticus L. Boswell founded the Metropolitan Spiritual Churches of Christ, Missouri (1925), and Derk Field founded the Church of God in David, which later became the Spiritual Israel Church and Its Army at around the same time (1925), although the exact date remains obscure. Others include King Louis H. Narcisse, who founded the Mt. Zion Spiritual Temple in 1943 (incorporated into an association in 1945), with an "International Headquarters" in Oakland, California, and an "East Coast Headquarters" in Detroit, as well as other temples in cities like Sacramento, Richmond (California), Houston, Orlando, New York City, and Washington, D.C.

As the Black Spiritual movement continued to develop and grow, tensions erupted and schisms ensued. One of interest here concerned the role of women as the institutionalization of the movement developed. Bessie S. Johnson was named Junior Bishop, under Thomas Watson in the hierarchical organizational structure of the Divine Spiritual Churches of the Southwest that was put into place in 1936. In 1940 Watson demoted Johnson to Reverend Mother Superior, as a result of his changed views concerning women in the bishopric. This move brought about the organization's first major schism. In 1942 the Divine Spiritual Churches of the Southwest merged with the Metropolitan Spiritual Churches of Christ. This new entity became one of the nation's largest associations of Spiritual believers with Thomas Watson as its first national president. A power struggle ensued between Watson and Clarence H. Cobbs, and in 1945 another schism left Cobbs as the leader of the Metropolitan Spiritual Churches of Christ (headquartered in Chicago) until his death in 1979, while Watson remained the leader of the United Metropolitan Spiritual Churches of Christ (headquarters in New Orleans) until his death in 1985. His son, Bishop Aubrey Watson, succeeded him.

Distinctive Elements of Worship

Although Black Spiritual churches share a common origin with those of their white counterparts, they developed along a different trajectory as a result of both their African cultural heritage and the subsequent experience of African descendents in the Americas. For this reason, Black Spiritualism (like other forms of black religion) should not be seen as just a "black" version of the white Spiritualist traditions but as having its own sensibility and history.

The Black Sacred Cosmos

The "Black Sacred Cosmos" refers to the traditional African religious worldview adapted in the context of slavery in the Americas. This particular part of their cultural heritage contains many elements that can be found in the forms of religious expression created by or finding an audience with African-Americans throughout their history. This religious worldview includes (but is not limited to): the belief in one God, the Creator of all; belief in a pantheon of lower level beings, i.e., spirits who devotees seek guidance or assistance from, worship, and indulge in a variety of ways respective to the concerns of particular spirits who, it is believed, engage with and participate in the affairs of humans (the spirits also include those of the ancestors); the belief and practice of ritual dancing, drumming, and feasting; and one of the most important, spirit possession.

Chief among the characteristics of the Black Sacred Cosmos is the adaptability that has allowed for the combining of elements from a wide variety of religious traditions into a number of new versions that differ from their origins in marked ways. Out of the Western slave experience and the adaptability of traditional African beliefs come such religious traditions as Santería and Orisha (Cuba and Puerto Rico), Candomblé and Macumba (Brazil), Shango (Trinidad), and Vodoun (Haiti). Each of these African-based religious traditions has adapted traditional African beliefs, practices, and worship styles to Euro-American religious traditions.

General Characteristics

Two of the most important characteristics of Black Spiritual churches are the eclectic nature of its manifestation across individual congregations, and the belief system's emphasis on changing one's present circumstances through certain "magico-religious" practices (Baer 1984; Baer and Singer 2002). Black Spiritual churches do not conform to any one religious tradition or set of practices but are highly syncretistic, blending elements from any number of traditions. For example, in New Orleans where there is a significant black Catholic history and presence, many of the Black Spiritualist churches include elements of the liturgy and sacraments borrowed from Catholicism. Black Spiritual churches also include aspects of traditional African religions as well as traditions like voodoo and "hoodoo," a popular form of conjure adapted from the more complex religious system of Haitian Vodoun. Respectability is an important factor in whether some churches incorporated elements of folk religion voodoo, or hoodoo (as did Mother Seals in New Orleans). Mother Anderson strictly disavowed any connection with the belief system so popular among blacks in the region, denouncing it (although she did incorporate jazz music into her services at a time when it was still considered the "devil's music"). Anderson's student, Mother Catherine Seals, readily accepted and incorporated elements of hoodoo fused with Catholicism into her Temple of the Innocent Blood and emphasized healing over the communication of messages from the spirit world.

Depending on the background of the particular ministers leading the congregations, Black Spiritual churches can resemble any number of other religions present in the African-American community. Concepts are borrowed from other religions like Catholicism, astrology, African-American Protestantism—especially in its Holiness-Pentecostal iterations, which emphasize dancing "in the spirit" and religious ecstasy and speaking in tongues as part of worship—as well as black Judaism, among other traditions. Some of these churches also model their ecclesiastical structure or liturgy on those found in Catholic or Protestant denominational bodies like the Methodists.

Another distinguishing characteristic of Black Spiritual churches concerns their clientele. Unlike white Spiritualists, who have historically tended to be middle class or affluent, the principle clientele of Black Spiritualist churches has been lower class and female. For this segment of the African-American religious community, as it has been since the movement's earliest days, the focus of the system of belief and practice is not solely on the afterlife but on how followers' communication and interaction with the spirit world can improve their present situation. According to Baer, for blacks the Spiritual movement is a thaumaturgic movement, representing a protest against the systematic barriers placed in their way in a racially, economically, and sexually stratified social structure. This less powerful segment of society resonates so strongly because the movement promises that they can manipulate magico-religious rituals to get their needs met when they cannot get them met through other, mainstream channels.

Male Dominance

One final characteristic of Black Spiritual churches that bears mentioning here is the issue of gender discrimination in the distribution of power within the church. Although women figure prominently in many local congregations and state and national associations of the Black Spiritual Church, the tendency toward male dominance as the movement has developed institutionally mirrors that found in most other forms of African-American religion. This represents, at least in part, the adaptation of cultural patterns forged in Africa but reshaped in a Western patriarchal context.

Their African cultural heritage included the official recognition of women as shamans, priestesses, and other types of spiritual authority figures. But in the context of the Americas where blacks could not participate fully and equally in the mainstream avenues for achieving and exercising power, black males seized upon their churches as a primary means of achieving respectability in their communities. So the black church has been seen as an important vehicle for the affirmation and exercise of black manhood and respectability, but paradoxically it was done at the expense of the masses of black women who make up the majority of its clientele and workforce. As was the case with black and white Spiritualists at the beginning of the movement, the spiritual power of women and their authority was respected and recognized. So the power of women in alternative religions may be greater than in mainstream ones, but that power is limited as the movement becomes more successful and develops along the road to more organizational complexity and takes on a more hierarchical structure. Also women's spiritual power rarely equates into structural power, either within the movement or denomination or within the larger society, a situation against which alternative religions usually form in protest. As with other alternative religions, at the beginning of the new sect the women had preeminence, just the way that whites included blacks at the beginning of the movement in general. But as time goes by, and the process of institutionalization gets under way, the men wrest control from the women and take it over for themselves. In the process, the women are demoted from their previously held titles (as in the case of Bessie Johnson) or the use of them as mediums in the context of the séance becomes supplanted (co-opted) by the public worship services during which the prophecies are given and the spirits are invoked. The special healing and prophecy, or "bless" services, during which the lights might be dimmed or turned off completely and the spirits welcomed, have become the primary means by which many Black Spiritual churches enact their belief in communication with the prophecies to the assembly as a body or to certain individuals within it. This change was part of the process by which women as mediums were stripped of the spiritual authority they once had in the movement.

But in some of the Black Spiritual churches in New Orleans, an affirmation of women's spiritual power and authority has been built into the ritual structure. This affirmation is accomplished in the context of public worship rituals in New Orleans Black Spiritual churches, so that they affirm women's power and their claim to leadership (according to Estes, 1993). These rituals are: (1) the annual memorial services for Mother Anderson in which her story of struggle as a black, female Spiritualist is retold and her spirit is welcomed or evoked (this ritual communion with Mother Anderson's spirit encourages contemporary female church leaders to continue her work and struggle in their present day ministries); (2) the spiritual power of women is honored and affirmed through the ritual feasts in honor of the Blessed Mother or of Queen Esther of the Old Testament; and (3) women's spiritual leadership is validated through ordination services in which women ordain other women as ministers and leaders in Black Spiritual churches.

Black Spiritual Churches Today

In the decades after World War II, Black Spiritual churches have come to exhibit some of the same signs of decline as many other forms of American religion prior to it. Although some of the churches and associations continue to exist and operate today, the number of followers has declined since the days of its greatest popularity, during the period from the 1920s through the 1940s. In certain cities, like New Orleans, however, contemporary followers of Mother Anderson and Mother Seals remain active, and Black Spiritual churches like Israelite Divine, Calvary Temple, and St. Daniel's Spiritual Churches continue along with other religious offerings available to seekers. Outside of New Orleans, churches like the Universal Hagar's Spiritual Church are still in existence today. Although its membership has fluctuated since its original establishment, today the church claims to have twenty-nine temples and seventeen missions in fifteen states, most of which are concentrated in the Midwest, the East, and the South.

MILMON F. HARRISON

Further Reading

Baer, H. A. (1984). *The Black Spiritual movement: A religious response to racism*. Knoxville: University of Tennessee Press.
Baer, H. A. (1993). The limited empowerment of women in Black Spiritual churches: An alternative vehicle to religious leadership. *Sociology of Religion, 54*(1), 65–82.
Baer, H. A., & Singer, M. (2002). *African American religion: Varieties of protest and accommodation* (2nd ed.). Knoxville: University of Tennessee Press.
Estes, D. C. (1993). Ritual validations of clergywomen's authority in the African American spiritual churches in New Orleans. In C. Wessinger (Ed.), *Women's leadership in marginal religions: Explorations outside the mainstream*. Chicago: University of Illinois Press.
Jacobs, C. F., & Kaslow, A. J. (1991). *The spiritual churches of New Orleans: Origins, beliefs, and rituals of an African American religion*. Knoxville: University of Tennessee Press.
Lincoln, C. E., & Mamiya, L. H. (1990). *The Black Church in the African American experience*. Durham, NC: Duke University Press.
Murphy, L. G., Gordon Melton, J., & Ward, G. L. (Eds.). (1993). *Encyclopedia of African American religions*. New York: Garland.

Body Decoration

Body decoration is the customization and modification of the appearance of the human body through manipulation and alteration in the flesh (skin) and hair, or the use of costumes, with the purpose and goal of creating distinct and specific effects within social and communal contexts. Body decoration is a phenomenon that is as old as the beginning of human culture. Customization of the appearance exists in every society as a reflection of individual human artistry and creativity and reflects a people's culture that is derived mainly from religious beliefs, customs, or sociopolitical settings.

Different communities, indigenous and nonindigenous, develop body decorations in response to their notion of what they consider normal, acceptable, attractive, and distinct within the larger world. It is a basic religious activity for indigenous peoples, just as it is an essentially social and aesthetic activity for the modern person. The importance of body decoration as a channel and mode of communication lies in the huge and powerful influence, both positive and negative, of religion on human beings globally.

General Characteristics

There are general and specific features in body decoration, which could be viewed from the perspectives of both the religious and nonreligious. Body decoration that is religious appears to be more enduring, since it defines several levels of identities and human relationships: identities in relation to religious affirmation and denomination, status, power, roles, and gender; relationships of different peoples of religious traditions with spiritual beings; relationships with religious specialists; relationships among different religious persons. Indigenous religious traditions such as those of Africa and Australia attach a great deal of importance to primordial myths—these are often dramatized in ritual, showing some intrinsic meanings of the body and its different parts; hence, its special and stylized decoration. Meanwhile, historic religions such as Judaism, Christianity, and Islam (Abrahamic faiths) draw on prescriptions by the supreme being and religious leaders (including priests and prophets) in their holy texts. Thus, body decoration represents the worldview of many different peoples.

Body decoration may be permanent or transient. Body decoration focuses directly on the human skin and the use of costumes. Beautification through nurturing of such parts of the body as the hair and the use of costumes features prominently in most religious traditions, including the Abrahamic faiths, and alteration and manipulation of the foreskin are common to indigenous religions. Body decoration that is done on the skin represents a permanent type while the use of costumes is usually transient.

Connection with a Deity

Personal and communal spiritual beliefs are expressed in body decoration to establish some connection between the human being and spiritual beings. In this way, body decoration represents a primordial connection to, or spiritual experience of, a deity (or the image of the deity), which the founder of a particular religion prescribes to the followers. Body decoration hence institutes an identity of a people with a religion. It reflects cultural invention and individual artistry within a religiocultural community.

Establishing Identity

Body decoration characterizes gender constructions. Most known cultures have special treatment of the body in relation to male and female sexes. It is a commonplace global practice, for instance, for females to do ear piercing; West African Fulani women and Australian men do nose piercing; and rings are usually inserted into the pierced ears and noses. Most African and recently immigrated African-American women braid and weave their hair.

Body decoration alters a person's real identity and produces another identity that typifies or reflects an essential character that a person decides to exhibit. It signals demonstration of loyalty through initiation into a religious cult. This kind of alteration involves self-mutilation as evinced in cases of membership of secret cults or transitioning into adulthood in indigenous communities.

Forms and Patterns

Body decoration takes different forms according to the messages that are intended by different religious traditions, social statuses or political settings. The most common forms of body decoration are (a) piercing: ear, nose, lip; (b) painting and dyeing: face, leg, nail, palm, eye-penciling; (c) tattooing: chest, hand, thigh, (d) scarification or cicatrization: cheeks; (e) incision of necklaces into the skin of the neck, chest, and torso, particularly at puberty; (f) masking: head, face, body; (g) hairdressing: braiding and plaiting; head-tie; stylized barbing (decorative cuts) and head shaving; beard shaving and beard nurturing; wig wearing; (h) body adornment: wearing of wrist and ankle bangles and jewelry, bracelets, and necklaces, bead wearing; (i) attachment and fixing: of feathers, shells, flowers, leaves, bones, or ornaments made of metals or some other materials on their bodies; (j) circumcision and clitoridectomy (k) tooth filing, chiseling, and removal.

Significance

Body decoration and adornment play important roles in exposing religious attitudes and behaviors, defining religious identity, functions, and locations. It evokes religious ideologies and serves to transform human conditions.

Religious Ideas and Ideals

Body decoration provides powerful channels and modes of communicating religious ideas and ideals in implicit and explicit ways. It has strong and enduring religious prescriptions and implications. Body decoration communicates different forms of religious expressions within the diverse religious traditions. The different levels, degrees, and intensity of body decoration within any given community hinge upon cultural interactions, borrowings, and bonding and ties in time and space/place. As body decoration modifies the physical appearance of the human being, it communicates as much as it affects religious expression. Religious persons express a moment of awesomeness and mystery at the image of a deity with which a religious specialist adorns himself or herself. This is a common practice in African religions.

In some religious movements body decoration is regarded as an expression of extreme piety. Examples can be drawn from the nurturing of the beard by Muslim men and use of *hijab* by Muslim women, the use of head covering by Catholic nuns, the shaving of the head with some dome left at the center by Buddhist men, and the compulsion placed on head covering by women among some Evangelicals and Pentecostals in Africa.

Body decoration has a potency and effect not only on the person wearing the paraphernalia of a particular religious tradition but also on others within a wide range of situations and circumstances. It has great and lasting, and sometimes permanent, effect on the meaning, essence, identity, and role of an individual within religious, sociocultural, and political contexts, as well as in economic and legal issues. These communicative effects constantly reveal the different values of the past and the present as they express some appreciation through personal or communal creativity.

Different kinds of hairstyles can symbolize religious ethics in women. The rich aesthetic culture of the Africans places importance on human essence, particularly the question of destiny, which is intrinsically linked to the head, which is conceived as spiritual. As in other African societies, women in Nigeria have different names for hairstyles with certain structures. Among some devotees in Yorùbáland, hairstyles convey the spirituality of devotees of the female deities Òsun and Oya and male deities (for example, Sàngo) whose essence is tied to their female counterparts in their worldview. Some of these devotees, who are placed under ethical rules (such as preserving their virginity), plait their hair to depict the purity of such deities.

Identity and Relationships

From the earliest times to the contemporary world, it has been noted that body decoration involves the confirmation of identity and further preserves the status quo. It also signifies different levels of relationships (of

A hand marked with red dye in preparation for a Hindu wedding ceremony. *Courtesy of istockphoto.com.*

power and identity), within the social, political, and religious spheres. Social relationship is created in indigenous communities, as body decoration (such as tattoos, scars, and piercing) is permanently inscribed. Tribal marks have become a means of identifying a person or community. This significance is evident in different forms in most religious and historic traditions (e.g., Judaism, Christianity, Islam), indigenous religious traditions (African religions, Australian aboriginal religions, Native American religions), and Asian religions (Buddhism, Hinduism). Wearing of crucifixes by some Christian denominations (Roman Catholic and others) indicates some bonding with the order.

While some historic religious traditions detest body alteration, indigenous traditions extol it as a necessary symbol of religious discipline and dedication. This distinction is explained through the different worldviews of these traditions. For example, indigenous religions hold that the sacred and the profane are inseparable. The tenacity of indigenous tradition in practicing body decoration does not allow a change in the practice. Indigenous traditions make use of the meaning of body decoration in several ways. Thus, body decorations that would be treated in historic traditions as social, aesthetic, or political would carry religious symbolism in indigenous religions.

Vestments

The use of vestments in body decoration perpetuates, institutionalizes, and confers power on the bodies that are so decorated. The wearer of the "new" body represents and presents the essence of the divine in many ways. Priests in all religious traditions, their bodies having been decorated, wear the image of the divine they represent.

Robes for priests are prescribed in Judaism. Among present-day Christians, prescribed vestments depict different ranks, statuses, and roles within each denomination. Among the Muslim Hausa and Fulani, the spiritual leaders wear turbans, which reflect a uniquely Muslim identity. The multiplicity of religious traditions among Africans and Australian aborigines explains the different types of paraphernalia that depict their varying religious traditions; examples can be found among the Yorùbá and Igbo peoples of Nigeria.

The history of religious dress or vestment has a strong connection with religion. It has been noted universally that many religious traditions are grouped together by clothing style. The Catholics, Anglicans, and Lutherans use vestments similar to each other, while the Eastern Orthodox is grouped in similarity with the Byzantine Catholics.

Body Decoration in Ritual Contexts

The ritual significance of body decoration is immense and cuts across most cultures and religions. Such bodily adornments carry both symbolic and practical effects in spiritual healing. In times of crisis, different religious traditions prescribe certain patterns of body decoration to ward off malignant spiritual forces. Among the indigenous peoples of Nigeria, Australia, and Native America, where situations that defy scientific explanation arise, such as mysterious deaths, sicknesses with undiscovered causes, and incessant communal crises, priests and priestesses of certain deities are employed to proffer solutions to such problems by invoking spiritual powers. These individuals have specific ritual costumes, which communicate their mission to the townspeople. The ritual process may also involve scarification and other forms of body mutilation. In this situation, everything ordinary about the ritual specialist is transformed, making him or her capable of invoking spiritual powers to ward off evil from the society.

Rites of Passage

Body alteration or modification establishes networks of sociocultural relationships, which symbolize human transition from one stage of life to another, technically termed *rites of passage* (birth, puberty, marriage, and death). Both Arnold van Gennep (1960) and Victor Turner (1969) focus on the rituals that are performed on the body as the center of ritual transition in separation, liminality, and incorporation. Until recently, circumcision and clitoridectomy were performed as rituals among the indigenous peoples of Africa and Australia; as a mark of identity, puberty rites represent the survival of a tribe or family when young women or men are declared to be moving into adulthood, the age of reproduction, and sociopolitical responsibility. To give a lady a "proper" body shape and induce her transition into puberty, she is given bodily treatment, decoration, adornment, scarification, and clitoridectomy, most of which performed by ritual specialists. In this form, she is dead to her former state of existence and enters into a "rebirth," a more qualitative state of the human life cycle.

Some good examples are found among the Poro and Sande societies of Sierra Leone in Africa. For boys, body alteration can take the form of rigorous training that is meant to change the shape of the body. Tattooing, scratching, or cutting the skin to create a pattern of scars is also performed. Mutilation of the labia in girls is performed, especially among the Kikuyu in Kenya; the Tswana in Botswana; and the Yorùbá, Igbo, Tiv, and Ibibio peoples of Nigeria.

Painting with ritual paint and wearing special clothing typify bodily ritual decoration. Paints drawn from some trees, white clay, and sweet-smelling herbs and oils are used to paint the body. Among the Akan and Ga people of Ghana, the hair of the armpits and pubic areas of girls is shaved. In most cases, such ritual practices, which usher boys and girls into adulthood, are claimed to typify certain mythic heroes or heroines of the culture.

Marriage Ceremonies

Marriage ceremonies also stipulate certain body adornments, but these can differ from culture to culture among various indigenous peoples. Body decoration in marriage may include special traditional clothing, beads on the neck and around the waist, bangles on wrists and ankles, etc.

Festival Drama and Costumes

The use of costumes as seen in the wearing of masks and other ornaments transforms the human body into specific social and political identities, signaling the person's rank, status, and roles within a particular religious tradition in the society. Worshippers of deities in whose honor annual celebrations are performed wear festival costumes. Traditions, both ancient and modern, have found masks to be important, as paraphernalia of religious identity and objects of religious entertainment. Most communities of Africa and Papua New Guinea have one form or another of festivals for their traditional deities.

The wearing of masks by masqueraders is common among indigenous peoples. A masquerader is a representation of divine beings or ancestors of the family or tribe and is believed to possess the power and authority of the deity or ancestors he or she personifies. Masqueraders negotiate power between humans and spiritual beings; during annual and occasional festivals, people solicit their divine protection and providence in such states. Among the Yorùbá people of Western Nigeria, Egungun (masquerade) of various types populate their universe.

Body decoration informs indigenous peoples of the status and roles of divine leadership. In some African communities, the king or queen who carries the symbol of the community has court costumes that may include royal garments, beads of office, a beaded crown, shoes, staff, necklaces, wrist and ankle bangles, a large umbrella, and a scepter.

The Body of the Dead

The different patterns and forms of the decoration of the body of the dead often communicate the essence and praxis of religious traditions. All religious traditions engage in special treatment of the bodies of their dead. In Buddhism, the body is washed and the head shaved after death. After the chanting and burning of incense by the priests, the body is taken in a procession to the crematorium or to the burial ground. The belief in the bodily resurrection of the dead in the world to come by Orthodox Jews explains their respectful burial of the dead. As Jewish law forbids embalming, the body is immediately washed thoroughly and dressed in a white shroud before being lowered into the grave.

In Islam, the face of the dead is turned in the direction of Mecca, given purificatory washing, and perfumed. It is then wrapped in a simple cotton blanket resembling the Pilgrimage *ihram* garment. At the cemetery, the body is placed in a grave with a niche carved out on one side, and the face is placed so it faces Mecca. In Hinduism, the body of the dead is washed immediately after death, then clothed. The eldest son leads a procession of relatives and friends to the cremation grounds. Among the indigenous peoples of Africa, devotees of different religious traditions decorate the body of their dead in specific ways. The head of the dead is thoroughly shaved and the body washed. It is wrapped with white clothing material, before being lowered into the grave with face turned upward.

Contemporary Forms and Expressions

Body decoration, as a powerful nonverbal and visual means of communication, is not static. Due to the effect of intercultural exchanges made possible by globalization, there is cross-cultural transfer and imitation of body decoration. The practice of weaving and braiding, for example, has moved outside the continent of Africa to the Americas, where African-American women and a few men now cherish it as a means of cultural renaissance. A few men in Africa are also now found to weave and braid their hair.

Along with the emergence of a new expression of religious drama in the production of home videos and stage dramas, there is the portrayal of inter- and intra-religious contestations among indigenous religion, Islam, and Christianity in African countries. These religious dramas vividly express such conflicts through the costumes that depict different religious traditions.

Costumes used in Christian commemorative religious ceremonies, such as the Father Christmas costume worn in some countries on 25 December each year, communicate a global awareness of the person of Jesus Christ and his lessons of peace and tranquility. The use of costumes is becoming more pronounced among indigenous peoples, who create new variations of indigenous festivals and festivities. In Western societies, the costumes worn in celebration of Halloween now express to some a feeling beyond the social to sacred engagement.

The adoption of certain practices from Western cultures, such as the use of wedding gowns, veils, and engagement rings by Muslims and Christians in African countries for their marriage ceremonies, demonstrates certain currents in intercultural exchanges. This adoption of Western attire may sometimes be in addition to traditional marriage practices, in which the use of traditional attire in body decoration typifies an age-long tradition of Africans.

In recent times, body decoration has engendered conflict as men and women now venture into what some communities regard as restricted territory for each gender. The use of costumes and vestments as an important aspect of body decoration has been found to invoke, incite, and instigate tension, conflicts, crisis, and riots among different religious traditions. Physical anthropologists, historians of religion, and art historians have found the phenomenon of body decoration informative in writing about the culture and living experiences of peoples, both indigenous and modern.

DAVID O. ÒGÚNGBÍLÉ

See also Art

Further Reading

Burke, K. (1966). *Language as symbolic action.* Berkeley: University of California Press.

De Negri, E. (1976). *Nigerian body adornment.* Lagos: Nigeria Magazine.

Galford, E. (2003). *Religious costumes: Twentieth-century developments in fashion and costume.* Broomall, PA: Mason Crest Publishers.

Gillison, G. (1993) *Between culture and fantasy: A New Guinea highlands mythology.* Chicago: The University of Chicago Press.

Herdt, G., & Stephen, M. (Eds.). (1989). *The religious imagination in New Guinea.* New Brunswick, NJ: Rutgers University Press,

Hewitt, K. (1997). *Mutilating the body: Identity in blood and ink.* Bowling Green, OH: Bowling Green State University Popular Press.

Johnson, K. K., & Lennon, S. J. (Eds.). (1999). *Appearance and power: Dress, body, culture.* Oxford, UK: Berg Publishers, Inc.

Lawal, B. (1996). *The Gelede spectacle.* Seattle: University of Washington Press.

Leach, E. (1995). *Culture and communication: The logic by which symbols are connected.* Cambridge, UK: Cambridge University Press.

Ludwig, T. M. (1989). *The sacred paths: Understanding the religions of the world.* New York: Macmillan Publishing Co.

Makinde, I. O. (1985). *Non-verbal communication in counselling therapy* (Inaugural Lecture Series 73). Ile-Ife, Nigeria: Obafemi Awolowo University Press.

Matthews, W. (1991). *World religions.* St. Paul, MN: West Publishing Co.

Morgan, D. H. J. (1996). *Family connections: An introduction to family studies.* Cambridge, UK: Polity Press.

Olajubu, O. (2003). *Women in the Yoruba religious sphere.* Albany: State University of New York Press.

Olupona, J. K. (1991). *Kingship, religion, and rituals in a Nigerian community.* Stockholm: Almqvist and Wiksell International.

Polhemus, T. (1996). *The customised body.* New York: The Serpent's Tail.

Sullivan, L. E. (1988). *Icanchu's drum: An orientation to meaning in South American religions.* New York: Macmillan Publishing Co.

Turner, V. (1969). *The ritual process.* Chicago: Aldine.

Vale, V., & Juno, A. (Eds.). (1989). *Modern primitive: An investigation of contemporary adornment.* San Francisco: Research Publications.

Van Gennep, A. (1960). *The rites of passage.* Chicago: University of Chicago Press.

Books

Books have been integral to numerous religions throughout history. After Moses held the staff of God aloft all day, helping the Israelites defeat the attacking Amalekites, God instructed him, "Write this down in a book to commemorate it" (Exodus 17:14, NJB). Centuries later, God told the exiled Christian apostle John, "Write down in a book all that you see," just before John received the Revelation (Revelation 1:11). Even God has a book, which he mentioned to Moses: "Those who have sinned against me are the ones I shall blot out of my book" (Exodus 32:33).

Books have served the vital purpose of preserving knowledge and religious teaching in organized religions. For centuries, this process was arduous and expensive. Before the dawn of printing, books were produced by hand copying Bibles and religious tracts, one manuscript at a time. The scribe's work of hand copying was time consuming and tedious, creating the possibility of errors being introduced into various copies of the manuscript.

Emergence of Printing

The invention of the printing press virtually eliminated the inconsistency of scribal work, reduced factual errors in books, and began to freeze the spelling and syntax of the various nations' languages in place. Although there is some controversy over who invented printing, most scholars credit Johann Gutenberg with

Forbidden Books

Some writers whose works have appeared on the "Index of Forbidden Books":

Erasmus	Immanuel Kant	Jean-Jacques Rousseau
Niccolo Machiavelli	Thomas Hobbes	Blaise Pascal
John Calvin	René Descartes	Giovanni Casanova
John Milton	Francis Bacon	John Stuart Mill
John Locke	Michel de Montaigne	Henri Bergson
David Hume	Baruch (Benedict) Spinoza	Jean-Paul Sartre
Daniel Defoe	Victor Hugo	
Jonathan Swift	Emanuel Swedenborg	

creating movable type in 1450, making alterations to a screw-driven wine press, and commencing work on printing a Bible at his shop in Mainz, Germany. The earliest printing presses consisted of a bed of stone with a smooth and level face on which the printing surface rested, and a flat piece of wood or metal called the "platen" that could be pressed down by a screw onto a piece of paper resting on the inked type. The type was held together in a frame for uniformity. This is the type of printing press Gutenberg and his contemporaries used, and the printing press remained largely unchanged for 350 years.

The art of printing spread rapidly throughout Europe, and by 1500 every major European city had at least one printer. Most of their work comprised Bibles, sermons, and other religious books. Through printing, churches were able to standardize worship and doctrines, and spread knowledge of their faiths to the masses, more economically than had ever before been possible.

Some early printers of religious books felt compelled to explain this new art to their readers. "This volume of the Psalms, adorned with a magnificence of capital letters and clearly divided by rubrics, has been fashioned by a mechanical process of printing and producing characters, without use of a pen," German printers Johann Fust and Peter Schoeffer informed readers of the *Mainz Psalter* in 1457. Three years later, an unknown German printer saw God's providence in the invention of the printing press. "By the aid of the most High, at whose nod the tongues of the dumb are made eloquent, and who ofttimes revealeth to children what He hides from the wise…this book, The Catholicon, was printed and completed not by the use of reed,

stylus, or quill, but by a wonderful agreement, conformity, and precision of patrices and forms" (Butler 1940, 91–92).

Printing also accelerated the Protestant revolt against the Catholic Church. After University of Wittenburg theology professor Martin Luther nailed his "Ninety-Five Theses" denouncing Catholicism to the door of the university church in 1517, he had the document published in book form and distributed throughout Germany. Luther used the new technology to spread his beliefs and create a schism in Christianity. The division of Europe into Catholic and Protestant during the sixteenth century prompted efforts by each faction to control dissemination of the opponents' religious books through censorship and customs inspections of imported books.

In 1564, the Catholic hierarchy issued the *Tridentine Index*, a list of prohibited books. In addition to the works of Luther and others who challenged the Catholic faith, the index prohibited books about pornography, magic, demonology, and other subjects that advocated immorality. One prominent early example was Niccolo Machiavelli's *The Prince*, which recommended government authorities use any means they wanted to accomplish their aims rather than accepted standards of moral behavior.

Monarchical Controls

These religious efforts to regulate reading and publishing were often aided by civil governments (in both Protestant and Catholic regions) seeking to maintain political and religious orthodoxy. In the English-speaking world, Henry VII was the first monarch to recognize the challenge the printing press represented to an authoritarian government. During his reign as the first of the Tudor monarchs, 1485 to 1509, he commenced a system of licensing printers and created the Court of the Star Chamber, which punished printers and others who challenged royal authority. His successor, Henry VIII, imposed further press strictures after he failed to secure papal consent to his divorce from Catherine of Aragon in 1529. Henry married Anne Boleyn in 1533, resulting in his excommunication by Pope Clement VII, and the following year decreed the Act of Supremacy, making himself head of the Church of England.

Henry VIII punished many dissident Catholics, including St. Thomas More, who died as a martyr in 1535 defending papal primacy. Ironically, More had helped Henry VIII write *The Defense of the Seven Sacraments* in 1521, a book repudiating Protestantism that earned Henry the title "Defender of the Faith" from Pope Leo X. "[W]hen we learned that the pest of Martin Luther's heresy had appeared in Germany and was raging everywhere," Henry VIII wrote to the pope, "we bent all our thoughts and energies on uprooting in every possible way, this cockle, this heresy from the Lord's flock" (Monti 1997, 128).

Another Tudor monarch, Elizabeth I, controlled the presses during her reign from 1558 to 1603 through the Stationers Company, a governmental agency devoted to censorship. It licensed printers and forbade unauthorized publishing of books, particularly banning any religious books that presented a Catholic or Hebrew perspective. This forced unlicensed printers into hiding, and secret books and pamphlets flourished in seventeenth-century London. As one printer of the era described the process:

> There had long lurked in the garrets of London a class of printers who worked steadily at their calling with precautions resembling those employed by coiners and forgers. Women were on the watch to give the alarm by their screams if an officer appeared near the workshop. The press was immediately pushed into a closet behind the bed; the types were flung into the coal-hole and covered with cinders; the compositor disappeared through a trapdoor in the roof, and made off over the tiles of the neighboring houses. In these dens were manufactured treasonable works of all classes and sizes, from half-penny broadsides of doggerel verse up to massy quartos filled with Hebrew quotations. (Jackson 1885, 176–77)

Some unlicensed printers were caught, though. For them, publishing unlicensed books sometimes meant death. William Carter was tortured and hanged 11 January 1584 for publishing a book expressing the supremacy of the Catholic faith. After his bookbinder betrayed him, Catholic book publisher James Duckett suffered the same fate 19 April 1602. Both printers have been beatified by the Catholic Church.

The American Experience

In the American colonies, religious books were published after a printing press was established at Harvard College by Stephen Daye in 1639. Harvard had been founded three years earlier for the purpose of training Puritan ministers. In addition to Bibles, the Harvard press published sermons, psalm books, and almanacs. English officials viewed these materials as subversive, as they did not conform to the Anglican *Book of Common Prayer*. However, King Charles I did little about dissident religious books across the Atlantic Ocean. These books fueled a widening rift between the established church in Great Britain and the Puritans, who sought to undermine it. Thousands of Puritans immigrated to New England in the seventeenth century, seeking religious freedom and liberty of the press. However, this meant only freedom to publicize their views. Other religious teachings were worthy of censure, Puritans believed, because they represented a threat to their beliefs. As Puritan leaders in Massachusetts noted, censoring religious books was necessary. "For prevention of irregularities and abuse to the authority of this country by the printing press, it is ordered, that henceforth no copie shall be printed but by the allowance first had and obtained under the hands of Capt. Daniel Gookin and Mr. Jonathan Mitchel," they decreed (Duniway 1906, 41–42).

Spurred by waves of immigration, religious book publishing in the United States greatly expanded in the nineteenth century. In 1854, Bloch Publishing Company commenced operations in New York as the country's first producer of Jewish books. The nation's first Catholic book publisher, Ave Maria Press, was founded on the campus of Notre Dame University in 1865.

The Satanic Verses

Despite these signs of religious liberty, intolerance of other religious beliefs has manifested itself throughout both American history and world history, particularly when those beliefs are expressed in print. Salman Rushdie experienced this upon publication of his 1988 book *The Satanic Verses*. The book begins as the two main characters, Gabreel and Saladin, are falling through the air, victims of a terrorist bombing of an airplane. Miraculously, they survive. Gabreel, who entertains doubts about Islam, develops a halo and resembles an angel. Saladin, who remains faithful to Islam, sprouts horns, hooves, and a tail and looks like Satan. Eventually, Gabreel loses his faith and commits suicide, while Saladin returns to his native India.

Faithful Muslims offended by its content staged protests and book burnings. Iran's Ayatollah Khomeini added fuel to the fire when he proclaimed the book blasphemous and condemned Rushdie to death for insulting Islam and the Qur'an. Rushdie claimed his work was more about migration and the change of lifestyle and belief accompanying a change of culture. However, Iranian Muslims placed a $2.5 million bounty on his head and forced him into hiding. The book was banned in India, Japan, Poland, South Africa, Venezuela, and a dozen other countries. In the United States, two bookstores in Berkeley, California were firebombed.

The Status of Religious Books

Although many have predicted the digital age will cause the demise of books, the book-publishing industry remains healthy. The electronic revolution of the 1990s has turned modern bookstores—both religious and secular—into multimedia information and entertainment centers. Audio books, CD-ROMs, music CDs, and videos are common staples of today's bookstore. The most popular nonprint book is the audio book, which is a billion-dollar-a-year industry. The printing of books themselves is evolving. Digital printing presses and computer-to-plate production systems make it possible to produce books to order. The customer can order the book unpublished over the computer, and a copy is produced on point of order. This will eliminate large inventories of unsold books that bookstores return to publishers.

More book titles are published today than ever before. Religious works remain among the most popular categories of books. There are currently almost three hundred publishers of religious books in the United States. More than two hundred of these are Christian, with others specializing in Buddhism, Islam, Judaism, and other faiths.

Religion-themed books have spread beyond the confines of religious publishers. Pastor Rick Warren's *The Purpose-Driven Life* was the best-selling nonfiction book of 2003, and the ninth installment of the *Left Behind* series—a fictional account of Jesus' second coming—was the top-selling novel worldwide in 2001. Books classified as "religious" amassed sales of nearly

$338 million in 2003, an increase of 36 percent over the previous year. Such books include the enduring favorites, Bibles and hymnals, plus Bible-study aids and inspirational works, as well as religion-themed novels and self-help books with a Christian perspective. These books are no longer the exclusive province of Christian and other religious bookstores; many religious titles generate large sales through mass retailers such as Wal-Mart and Barnes & Noble.

The Future

Books have endured throughout the history of organized religion, serving an integral role in transmitting information and beliefs through the ages, and will continue to do so—in whatever form they take as the twenty-first century unfolds.

RALPH FRASCA

See also Censorship; Free Speech; Libraries; Novels; Pamphlets; Pornography; Translation

Further Reading

Bennett, H. S. (1952). *English books and readers, 1475 to 1557.* Cambridge, UK: University of Cambridge Press.
Blum, A. (1940). *The origins of printing and engraving.* New York: Scribner's.
Butler, P. (1940). *The origin of printing in Europe.* Chicago: University of Chicago Press.
Chappell, W. (1970). *A short history of the printed word.* New York: Alfred A. Knopf.
Duniway, C. A. (1906). *The development of freedom of the press in Massachusetts.* Cambridge, MA: Harvard University Press.
Eisenstein, E. L. (1979). *The printing press as an agent of change: Communications and cultural transformations in early modern Europe* (2 vols.). Cambridge, UK: Cambridge University Press.
Febvre, L., & Martin, H.J. (1976). *The coming of the book.* London: Verso.
Handover, P. M. (1940). *Printing in London from 1476 to modern times.* London: Oxford University Press.
Hindman, S. (Ed.). (1991). *Printing the written word: The social history of books, circa 1450–1520.* Ithaca, NY: Cornell University Press.
Jackson, M. (1885). *The pictorial press: Its origin and progress.* London: Hurst & Blackett.
Jones, L. (Ed.). (2004). *The encyclopedia of religion.* New York: Macmillan.
Kapr, A. (1996). *Johann Gutenberg.* Brookfield, VT: Scolar.
McGrath, A. (2001). *In the beginning: The story of the King James Bible and how it changed a nation, a language, and a culture.* New York: Doubleday.

McMurtrie, D. C. (1943). *The book: The story of printing and bookmaking* (3rd ed.). New York: Oxford University Press.

Merrick, M. M. (1947). *James Duckett*. London: Douglas Organ.

Monti, J. (1997). *The King's good servant but God's first: The life and writings of St. Thomas More.* San Francisco: Ignatius.

Tyson, G. P., & Wagonheim, S. S. (1986). *Essays on the advent of printing in Europe*. Newark: University of Delaware Press.

Bookstores

Religious bookstores have several functions for both the individual consumer and religious leaders. They serve as places where individuals buy sacred texts, music, and gifts to mark the life events of loved ones (e.g., baptisms, bar mitzvahs, and weddings). Also, bookstores provide a place for both seekers and scholars to receive guidance from bookstore personnel and to purchase educational reading material. Finally, bookstores serve as meeting places for events, such as book signings, Bible studies, and concerts. In addition to serving the individual customer, religious bookstores serve the needs of leaders of religious organizations, who rely on bookstores for their supplies, including everything from educational materials for children to candles required during services. For the most part, this entry will focus on Christian Protestant bookstores in the United States, but it should be noted that religious bookstores in some form exist for virtually all religions, with the largest numbers of non-Protestant bookstores serving the Catholic, Jewish, and Islamic faiths.

History of Protestant Bookstores

Social and cultural factors after World War II—such as a growing middle class, population shifts, and increased transportation and technology—led to the emergence of "mom-and-pop" Protestant bookstores as a primary means of distributing Christian reading materials. In 1950, the Christian Booksellers Association (CBA) was founded by Ken Taylor and Bill Moore, both of Moody Press, and John Fish, manager of Scripture Press Store in Chicago. CBA was formed with the goals of (1) encouraging wide distribution of Bibles and church supplies; (2) supplying members with merchandising suggestions and assistance; and (3) providing a liaison among bookstore owners, publishers, and suppliers. The founders of the CBA began the organization in an attempt to help struggling bookstore owners who were rich in faith but lacking in business know-how.

The first CBA convention took place in September 1950. Forty-eight publishers and distributors attended, along with representatives from one hundred two bookstores. In 1952, the CBA began publication of *CBA Advance*, a newsletter for Protestant booksellers providing information on topics such as best-selling books and how to best display merchandise. Both the *CBA Advance* and trade association meetings served as a means of uniting booksellers with information and resources.

Dramatic Growth of CBA

The CBA has seen dramatic growth over the past five decades. There were approximately fifteen hundred attendees at their convention in 1960, including suppliers (e.g., publishers as well as retailers); two thousand in 1970; seven thousand in 1980; eleven thousand in 1990; and fourteen thousand in 1998. Changes in the economy brought attendance down a bit in 2004 to approximately eleven thousand. Presently, there are more than twenty-five hundred Christian bookstores in the United States, and Christian merchandise comprises a $4.2 billion industry. The CBA continues to have an annual meeting and trade show and publishes a revamped version of *CBA Advance*—a glossy monthly trade journal entitled *CBA Marketplace*. Due to their value system, conservative Protestants reject much of secular entertainment as sinful. In response, the Christian media industry supplies them with products that are deemed "safe" (i.e., no violence, no sex, no bad language). These Christian alternatives to secular media, such as children's videos and Christian rock albums, are largely distributed through Christian bookstores.

Types of Christian Bookstores

The typical Christian bookstore is a family-run small business, usually located in a strip mall. Often a husband-and-wife team with a deep commitment to both Christianity and books runs these small businesses, and most are lay people, rather than ordained pastors. Christian bookstores are largely characterized by a lack of denominational affiliation. Retailers strive to reach the widest possible audience and commonly carry merchandise that appeals across Protestant denominations. Christian bookstores are also almost always for-profit organizations.

Chains and Franchises

Some exceptions to the typical bookstore described above include Christian chains and franchises. The Christian bookstore landscape includes several Christian chains. The largest chains are Family Christian Stores (320 stores), Lifeway Christian Stores (120 stores), Cokesbury Stores (70 stores) and Berean Christian stores (17 stores). Along with these large chains, there are two Christian franchises. (Franchises differ from chains in that the person who runs the store also puts forth the capital to start the business. Franchises differ from independent stores in that they are often more successful because the storeowner has the benefits of participating in a large marketing and buying group.) Lemstone Christian Stores (36 stores) is the oldest Christian franchise, founded in 1981. Parable Christian Stores (230 stores) is a marketing and buying group that recently provided franchise opportunities to its members.

Both Cokesbury stores and Lifeway Christian stores provide an exception to the nondenominational and for-profit status of the typical Christian bookstore. Cokesbury stores are a division of the United Methodist Publishing House, and Lifeway Christian Stores are a division of the Southern Baptist Convention. Both chains operate as not-for-profits and both downplay their denominational affiliations. Lifeway Christian Stores changed their name from Baptist Bookstores in 1999, both to appeal to customers of all denominations and to reflect their growing product lines.

Diversity of Products

The growing diversity of products is common throughout Christian bookstores. In the 1950s Christian bookstores primarily carried books, print materials for churches (e.g., Sunday School materials), and church supplies (e.g., candles). Christian bookstores began to be transformed from bookstores to "department stores" in the late 1960s. The advent of the "Jesus Movement" brought T-shirts, bumper stickers, and jewelry into Christian bookstores.

Contemporary Christian bookstores often are organized into departments, including a children's department complete with both books and toys. In some stores, consumers will have to make their way to the back of the store in order to find scholarly books. Figures from CBA indicate that sales in Christian stores are distributed as follows: 11 percent of total Christian store sales are for Bibles, 25 percent for books, 16 per-

cent for music, 3 percent for church supplies, and the remaining 45 percent for gift merchandise, cards, videos, and other items such as jewelry.

Confronting Competition

Books and gifts sold in independent Christian bookstores are also available in Christian chains, secular chain bookstores (e.g., Barnes & Noble), online secular bookstores (e.g., amazon.com), and discount department stores (e.g., Wal-Mart). Popular titles, including the bestseller *The Purpose-Driven Life* may be deeply discounted at other stores, causing the typical independent Christian retail establishment to struggle (not unlike the struggle of secular independent bookstores that face competition from chains). Christian retailers confront these challenges with a number of strategies.

Some retailers have found that forming alliances with church leaders, such as pastors and directors of Christian education, is a lucrative strategy. Churches may order materials for Bible study groups and Sunday School classes through the store, thereby boosting sales. CBA has encouraged member stores to build relationships with church leaders and has included "how to" articles in *CBA Marketplace* on the topic. Another strategy is to open a small store that is actually situated in a church. Lemstone has begun to encourage franchisees to open satellite church stores in order to reach more customers. There are presently four Lemstone church stores. The management and inventory are operated through the main store, and the church stores are open only twenty hours a week, making them less expensive to run. Stores located in churches have direct access to those interested in buying Christian books and gifts, thereby both generating profit and serving their niche market.

Other retailers face competition by relying on the knowledge that they provide customer service that surpasses the service shoppers will receive at "big-box" stores such as Wal-Mart. They build relationships with customers and depend on customer loyalty for their success. Many booksellers emphasize the fact that customers can "trust" the items that they find on their shelves. Owners of small Christian stores are knowledgeable about the products and can provide recommendations to individual customers. They can assure customers that everything in the store has passed the owners' scrutiny.

The final strategy for facing competition involves creating an environment that appeals to customers. Some Christian booksellers have followed the trend that is popular in larger secular chain bookstores (e.g.,

Barnes & Noble) of offering coffee in the store. However, the average small Christian bookseller has neither the space nor the staff to run a full coffee bar. Many simply keep a pot of coffee brewing and offer a free cup to browsers. Other owners recreate their stores as a destination for an evening out. Events such as book signings by popular authors or concerts by contemporary Christian musicians draw crowds that otherwise may not shop at the store.

Bookstores for Other Religions

Exact numbers of religious bookstores in the United States are difficult to ascertain, given the fact that most are independent, family-owned stores unaffiliated with a trade association. Given this, it is likely that the following numbers underestimate the prevalence of religious bookstores. There are at least three hundred independent Catholic bookstores and one Catholic chain (Pauline Book and Media, with seventeen stores). Many CBA member stores carry books and gifts that are popular with Catholics as well. There are more than fifty-five Judaica stores, the majority of which are located in New York City. Judaica stores usually carry a variety of items from yarmulkes to menorahs to scholarly texts. There are at least forty Islamic stores located in large cities throughout the United States, including New York, Chicago, and Atlanta, and there are many mail-order catalogs and Internet stores for Muslim books as well.

The Future

In recent years, there has been a dramatic growth in Internet bookstores, both secular and religious. Internet stores enable booksellers to cater to a specific religion and reach out to a large audience without depending on a nearby community of those who share that faith, as brick-and-mortar stores must. The future of religious bookstores will depend on their survival strategies as they face competition from large secular retailers (including amazon.com) who presently carry a variety of religious books.

ANNE L. BORDEN

See also Religious Marketplace

Further Reading

CBA. (2005). Retrieved June 3, 2005, from cbaonline.org
Hendershot, H. (2004). *Shaking the world for Jesus: Media and conservative evangelical culture*. Chicago: University of Chicago Press.
McDannell, C. (1995). *Material Christianity: Religion and popular culture in America*. New Haven, CT: Yale University Press.

Boycotts

The term *boycott* typically describes the actions of an organized party that refrains from economic exchange with another party in order to punish or persuade them to change a course of action. While boycotts have occurred throughout history, the term itself dates to Ireland in 1880, when tenants of Captain Charles Cunningham Boycott protested their low pay and rising rent by cutting social and economic ties to the landowner. Newspapers quickly adopted the term, and it attained common usage across Europe before the captain's death in 1897.

Varying Tactics

Boycotts today involve a range of tactics and come in various forms, including national boycotts, political boycotts, labor boycotts, consumer boycotts, and moral boycotts. Nations engage in boycotts when they cut off trade with another country, such as the Arab League's effort in 1948 to boycott all companies connected with the state of Israel. The Arab League boycott exacerbated military tensions in the region, but most boycotts in the nineteenth and twentieth century have been embraced as nonmilitary forms of protest. In the early twentieth century, Mohandas Gandhi brought together Muslims, Hindus, and Sikhs with calls for nonviolent civil disobedience and boycotts of British-made goods, in an attempt to gain national independence.

Consumer Boycotts

In addition to political goals, modern consumer boycotts have attempted to force companies to improve labor conditions, such as the table-grape boycott, led by Cesar Chavez in 1965, which helped improve working conditions and raise pay for U.S. farm workers. Further, boycotts have been employed in the cause of social equality, such as when the National Negro Convention called for a boycott of slave-made goods in the 1830s. These political, consumer, and moral boycotts suggest the range of organizations, techniques, and historical events that triggered boycotts during the nineteenth and twentieth centuries.

The Southern Baptist Convention's "Disney" Resolution, 12 June 1996

WHEREAS, Southern Baptists and their children have for many decades enjoyed and trusted the Disney Co.'s television programming, feature-length films and theme parks which have reinforced basic American virtues and values; and

WHEREAS, The virtues promoted by Disney have contributed to the development of a generation of Americans who have come to expect and demand high levels of moral and virtuous leadership from the Disney Co.; and

WHEREAS, In recent years, the Disney Co. has given the appearance that the promotion of homosexuality is more important than its historic commitment to traditional family values and has taken a direction which is contrary to its previous commitment; and

WHEREAS, In recent years, we have watched the world's largest family entertainment company with growing disappointment as Disney Co.'s moral leadership has been eroded by a variety of corporate decisions, which have included but are not limited to:

Establishing of an employee policy which accepts and embraces homosexual relationships for the purpose of insurance benefits;

Hosting of homosexual and lesbian theme nights at its parks;

Choosing of a convicted child molester to direct the Disney movie *Powder* through its subsidiary Miramax Productions;

Publishing of a book aimed at teenage homosexuals entitled *Growing Up Gay: From Left Out to Coming Out* through its subsidiary Hyperion, connecting Disney to the promotion of the homosexual agenda;

Producing, through its subsidiary corporations, objectionable material such as the film *Priest* which disparages Christian values and depicts Christian leaders as morally defective;

WHEREAS, These and other corporate decisions and actions represent a significant departure from Disney's family-values image, and a gratuitous insult to Christians and others who have long supported Disney and contributed to its corporate profits; and

WHEREAS, Previous efforts to communicate these concerns to the Disney Co. have been fruitless; and

WHEREAS, Boycotts are a legitimate method for communicating moral convictions;

Now, therefore,

BE IT RESOLVED, We as Southern Baptist messengers meeting in annual session on June 11-13, 1996, go on record expressing our deep disappointments for these corporate actions by the Disney Co.; and

BE IT FURTHER RESOLVED, That we affirm the employees of the Disney Co. who embrace and share our concerns; and

BE IT FURTHER RESOLVED, That we encourage Southern Baptists to give serious and prayerful reconsideration to their purchase and support of Disney products and to boycott the Disney theme parks and stores if they continue this anti-Christian and anti-family trend;

BE IT FURTHER RESOLVED, That we encourage the *Christian Life Commission* to monitor Disney's progress in returning to its previous philosophy of producing enriching family entertainment; and

BE IT FURTHER RESOLVED, That we encourage state Baptist papers and national Southern Baptist publications to assist in informing the Southern Baptist family of these issues; and

FINALLY, BE IT RESOLVED, That the Convention requests the Executive Committee to send a copy of this resolution to Michael Eisner, CEO of the Disney Co., and to encourage the Southern Baptist family to support this resolution with our purchasing power, letters and influence.

Source: Text of the Southern Baptist Convention's "Disney Resolution."
Retrieved December 14, 2005, from http://www.religioustolerance.org/new1_966.htm

Confluence and Conflict

Boycotts interface with religion and media in several respects. First, for boycotts to succeed in affecting change, they typically require broad adoption in society. Religious organizations have been instrumental in organizing large-scale boycotts, often relying on established church organization to organize and facilitate the boycott. Second, conservative Protestant movements in the United States, particularly since the 1970s, have frequently targeted media corporations in their boycott efforts. These religious boycotts frequently charged media corporations with disseminating programs and images that they deemed offensive to public tastes. Two well-known examples of such boycotts are the Montgomery bus boycott and the Southern Baptist boycott of the Walt Disney Company.

In December 1955, a cohort of African-Americans in Montgomery, Alabama, organized a protest against segregated public transit in the city. Led by Martin Luther King, Jr., and organized by a coterie of local black ministers and civil-rights leaders, local blacks boycotted public busses for over a year in an attempt to force the city to end segregated transit. The protest was well organized and responded creatively to a variety of setbacks. Ministers spread word of the boycott through Sunday sermons and updated parishioners on legal developments. As the boycotters held out, some churches invested in station wagons, known as "rolling churches," to taxi men and women to jobs. Ultimately, the Supreme Court intervened and declared segregated busing unconstitutional in November 1956. This victory inspired many African-Americans, and ministers from across the South soon formed the Southern Christian Leadership Conference to organize nonviolent protests to fight for civil rights.

In the bus boycott, religion played a significant role in the spirit as well as the organization of the protest. Reflecting on the events of Montgomery several years later, Martin Luther King, Jr., wrote that "it was Jesus of Nazareth that stirred the Negroes to protest with the creative weapon of love." King acknowledged the inspiration of Gandhi's nonviolent methods but felt that "Christ furnished the spirit and motivation." The Montgomery bus boycott also exemplifies how religious organizations can aide the practical challenges posed to a unified boycott, as black churches dispersed essential information and organized community-support services.

The Southern Baptist boycott of the Walt Disney Company also made use of its strong organizational arm, but instead of civil rights being the driving issue, the boycott attempted to punish the media conglomerate for business practices the Southern Baptists deemed morally unacceptable. In 1997, the Southern Baptist Convention, representing the largest Protestant denomination in the United States, passed a resolution discouraging Baptists from patronizing Disney or any company that "promotes immoral ideologies." The resolution specifically criticized Disney for what the Baptists deemed a "pro-gay agenda," such as the company's decision to extend health benefits to domestic partners of gay employees and broadcasting the television sitcom *Ellen*, which starred a lesbian lead character. Southern Baptists also criticized media products from Disney holdings, such as Miramax Films and Hollywood Records. Several other denominations and politically conservative organizations joined with the Southern Baptists, including the Presbyterian Church in America, the Wesleyan Church, Concerned Women for America, and Focus on the Family. For its part, Disney responded by reaffirming its commitment to family programming and distinguishing the family-friendly Disney label from other holdings. Nevertheless, the corporation distanced itself from the Miramax release *Dogma* in 1999, which Roman Catholic and Evangelical groups protested months before its release.

The Southern Baptist boycott stands out because of what it succeeded, and failed, to accomplish. Despite the national press that the boycott received, the Walt Disney Company saw little economic disruption due to the boycott. From the beginning, some Southern Baptists suggested that their goal was not ultimately to change Disney but to "affirm to us and the world that we love Jesus more than we love entertainment." Thus, while the boycott failed to force Disney to modify its corporate positions, it may have succeeded in organizing a broad coalition of conservative media critics. The Disney boycott is evidence of the restructuring of religious institutions since the mid-twentieth century.

Shift in Strategy

There has been little scholarship of boycotts through the paradigm of religion and media. Yet the Montgomery bus boycott and the Southern Baptist Disney boycott reveal some of the ways contemporary religion works in the public and private sphere with regard to media and culture. In their institutional role, religious bodies can frame the debate in order to organize a community for political or social causes.

On the other hand, individual members within a religious community make use of these messages in a variety of ways. The millions of Southern Baptists encouraged to boycott Disney interpreted this call to suit their personal welfare, and the end result might have had more to do with the construction of identity than with the desire to enact public pressure. Southern Baptists might see the Disney boycott mainly as a personal choice to separate themselves from certain cultural influences rather than effect change in the Disney corporation. This suggests a historical shift in the strategy of boycotting, from mainly public engagement to a significantly private posture.

SHANNY LUFT

See also Free Speech

Further Reading

Hare, A. P., & Blumberg, H. H. (Eds.). (1968). *Nonviolent direct action: American cases: Social-psychological analyses.* Washington, DC: Corpus Books.

King, M. L., Jr. (1958). *Stride toward freedom: The Montgomery story.* New York: Harper.

Laidler, M. W. (1913). *Boycotts and the labor struggle: Economic and legal aspects.* New York: John Lane Company.

Smith, N. C. (1990). *Morality and the market: Consumer pressure for corporate accountability.* London: Routledge.

Warren, H. (2001). Southern Baptists as audience and public: A cultural analysis of the Disney boycott. In D. A. Stout & J. M. Buddenbaum (Eds.), *Religion and popular culture: Studies on the interaction of worldviews* (pp. 169–185). Ames: Iowa State University Press.

Buddhism

Begin with the Buddha

Scholar Huston Smith points to the first step of understanding Buddhism. He writes that to understand the religion, "it is of utmost importance to gain some sense of the impact of Buddha's life on those who came within its orbit." As with Hinduism and other faiths, Buddhism is a vast and rich tradition dating back so many centuries that its origin—like its founder—is swathed in legend. What emerges from the mists of history is the Buddha, a figure notable for both his warmth and his reason, among so many other attributes.

In the past half-century, many Americans have embraced Buddhism as a spiritual path. Electronic media have had a global impact on Buddhism, evidenced by such things as cyber temples, online rituals, electronic publications, and virtual communities. The United States is especially useful in studying these trends

given its cultural pluralism and openness to experimentation with new media. Buddhism in America keeps growing. With an estimated 1.5 million adherents in this country, it ranks as the nation's fourth largest religion. In this country Buddhism is a religion and a philosophy of life as it is lived out in the lives Asian immigrants and western converts.

For some, Buddhism is something they take on in addition to another religious practice, but for many, it is the central means by which they make sense of the world around them and of their life experience. Particularly challenging to grasping the reach of Buddhism in America is an understanding not only of Buddhism's Eastern roots but also of the specific character of the United States' unique religious history and practice. In a nation like this where there is no established church, diversity in religion—and even within the same faith—flourishes. Religions transplanted to this continent follow some similar patterns. They retain the essential truths of centuries but adapt their forms and sometimes their practices to a new culture.

Buddhists Online and Buddhist Media

When a faith as ancient as Buddhism comes to the United States, it follows a mixture of patterns: It keeps what is necessary for its integrity and it also Americanizes. Americanizing includes making use of available media to explain and explore the faith's tenets. The American magazines, journals and other print media published by Buddhists and designed for Buddhist audiences illustrate this pattern. In America today, Buddhists and scholars of Buddhism are just beginning to explore the tensions produced by the diversity of Buddhists and Buddhist practice in this country. While there are many approaches to Buddhism and many centers where it may be studied and practiced, discussions of the tradition's future and shape in the West can also be found in popular books and periodicals, including *Tricycle: The Buddhist Review* and *Shambhala Sun*. Other periodicals such as the *Journal of Buddhist Ethics* and the *Journal of Global Buddhism* are even more specialized, usually attracting a scholarly audience.

Tips for reporters on covering Buddhism from the Religion Newswriters Association's project, *Religion-Link*, call attention to the faith's online presence. WZEN offers a webcast from the Mountains and Rivers order, along with Cybermonk, through which a senior monk will answer online questions about dharma. In addition, there is the Buddhist Channel, offering online Buddhist news and features, and Urban

Statue of Buddha at Golden Gate Park in San Francisco, CA. *Courtesy of Judy Watt/istockphoto.com.*

Dharma, a website with articles and essays on, and photographs of Buddhism in America.

A Rich History

Buddhism has a rich, varied history in this country, dating back at least to the first Japanese Americans who immigrated to the United States in the 1870s. More than 100 years ago, those early immigrants established the Buddhist Churches of America. The oldest Buddhist association in the nation, it has been joined by many other variations of the faith. Many of those forms of Buddhism arrived here with the Asian immigrants who moved to the United States in the twentieth century. Like religious people of many types who immigrated here, the Asians who came soon established temples, communities, study centers, and other associations in which they could practice their beliefs, keep their faith and cultures alive, and school their children in their heritage, languages, and traditions.

In the twentieth and twenty-first centuries, Buddhism has blossomed in America in two ways: through immigrants committed to it as a way of life and among native-born Americans fascinated by Buddhism's traditions and practices. The nation's pluralism has been enriched by the addition of major Buddhist schools such as Zen and Michener (brought by Japanese transplants), Vajaranyan, which came with Tibetans, Ch'an from China, and various versions of the Theravadan tradition from Southeast Asia.

Buddhism has grown in America in recent decades, gaining many new devotees. A City College of New York survey showed that the number of Americans identifying themselves as Buddhists increased more than 120 percent from 1990 to 2001. Those gains raise the estimated number of Buddhists in the United States from around 400,000 to just over 1 million. Other estimates place the number of adherents at 1.5 million.

Early American Buddhists

The first U.S. residents deeply interested in Buddhism hailed from the transcendental movement and the theosophical societies, which became so popular during the later nineteenth century. By the 1950s, with the flourishing of Zen teachers including D. T. Suzuki and Alan Watts, members of the beat generation were turning to Buddhism. Its meditation practices and experiential aspects appealed widely to the country's growing counterculture. That trend has continued into the twenty-first century. Buddhist centers, which once proliferated primarily in large cities, became more and more common in smaller locales and in the Southeast. For example, Pat Phelan was installed as abbess, head of the Red Cedar Zen Temple in Chapel Hill, North Carolina, a university town and popular haven for people eager to explore diverse spiritual traditions.

In the second half of the twentieth century, one of the century's most popular world religious leaders, the Dalai Lama, focused international attention on Buddhism, especially in the United States and Canada. He attracted many followers to Buddhism. Some came in response to his leadership of the Free Tibet movement. Others were attracted by his charisma. Still others wondered about Buddhism after its well-publicized appeal to such Hollywood moguls and megastars as Richard Gere, Martin Scorsese, and Steven Seagal.

Many native-born Americans turn to Buddhism after years of searching for meaning and explanations of life's purpose in other more familiar paths. Others embrace Buddhism as an additional spiritual practice, studying various forms of meditation to bring a greater sense of focus and inner peace to their lives. At least in one sense, however, the U.S.-born practitioners of Buddhism approach it from a completely different perspective. Both their understanding of religion and their sense of self usually are quite different from those of Asian-American Buddhists.

Historic Patterns, American Culture

As a psychotherapist and Buddhist teacher, Harvey Aronson notes in his book *Buddhist Practice on Western Ground* that American society's strong emphasis on the external and on individuality contrasts with traditional Buddhist teachings.

Buddhism was traditionally taught in cultures where practitioners were linked with the larger society through an understanding of mutual relatedness. Many North American practitioners are embedded in their sense that it is good and right to realize and express individual selfhood. They often use Buddhism to promote their individual health and welfare, to heighten awareness of their own feelings, and to allow for more successful individual engagement. When seen from the holistic worldview of traditional Buddhism, such as approach ignores the tradition's rich interpersonal vision of individuality.

As in the East, women generally held few leadership roles in the early stages of Buddhism's development in the United States. That slowly and surely is changing early in the twenty-first century. A new generation of Buddhist thinkers, authors, and writers came into vogue among American Buddhists, with the growing influence of the women's movement on practitioners of the faith and the climb to prestige and influence of a number of American women Buddhist leaders. In addition, popular books focused on Buddhism, but reflecting the West's preoccupation with relationships and self-fulfillment, have proliferated. The July 2005 issue of *Shambhala Sun* featured multiple advertisements for Buddhist books of that type and a cover story entitled, "Women of Wisdom: American Women are Teaching the Dharma and Changing the Face of Buddhism."

A Complex Future

Buddhism tends to adopt the tone of the country in which it is located. In America where there often are wide variations within the same religious group, Buddhism is growing in multiple directions, producing some tensions between different groups. Yet Buddhism's greatest impact on American culture in the long run may come from the impact of its practices on issues ranging from the environment to consumerism. Because the faith emphasizes mindfulness and social action, it is not unusual to move from Buddhist practice to what many call "engaged Buddhism."

CECILE S. HOLMES

Further Reading

Aronson, H. (2004). *Buddhist practice on western ground: Reconciling eastern ideals and western psychology*. Boston: Shambhala.

Batchelor, S. (1998). *Buddhism without beliefs: A contemporary guide to awakening*. New York: Penguin.

Gyatso, G. K. (2001). *Introduction to Buddhism: An explanation of the Buddhist way of life*. Cumbria, England: Tharpa Publications.

Keown, D. (2000). *Buddhism: A very short introduction*. New York: Oxford University Press.

Keown, D. (2000). *Contemporary Buddhist ethics*. London: Taylor & Francis, Inc.

Maguire, J. H. (2001). *Essential Buddhism: A complete guide to beliefs and practices*. New York: Simon & Schuster Adult Publishing Group.

Neusner, J. & Chilton, B. D. (Eds.). (2005). *Altruism in world religions*. Washington, DC: Georgetown University Press.

Singh, R. (2005). *The path of the Buddha: Writings on contemporary Buddhism*. New York: Penguin.

Walbert, D. J. (2003). *Buddhism in the modern world: Adaptations of an ancient tradition*. New York: Oxford University Press.

C

Calendar

Calendars are logistical media—abstract devices of cognitive, social, political, and religious organization. Calendars are among the most basic of human sense-making devices. On a humbler scale, they are like science and religion in rendering the cosmos intelligible for human use. Calendars coordinate periodic astronomical events (years, solstices, months, days, etc.) with periodic human events (holidays, commemorations, anniversaries, etc.). The double job of calendars—to bind earthly history with celestial time—gives them their particular potency as media of communication.

As time-keepers, calendars resemble clocks in some ways. In a sense, clocks are fast calendars and calendars are slow clocks. Calendars model time on a macro scale, starting with the day, and aggregate upward to weeks, months, seasons, years, decades, centuries, and indefinitely larger units (the Hindu *kalpa*, perhaps the largest cycle in human calendars, takes 4,320,000,000 solar years); clocks model time on a micro scale, starting with the day, and subdivide downward to hours, minutes, seconds, milliseconds, and indefinitely smaller units (a yoctosecond is one septillionth of a second). The two are also quite different. Clocks have pointers and indicate the immediate moment in time but lack memory or foresight. They simply repeat the same thing over and over again. Calendars, in contrast, require users first to locate themselves on the grid, but store data, thanks to their linear quality. Calendars are eventful, but clocks are relatively barren, their intelligence being used up every moment. Calendars preserve past and future time.

Determining Days and Years

Humans have been avid calendar makers for all of recorded history and probably long before. Calendars require advanced knowledge of astronomy and are key ingredients of civilization along with writing, mathematics, the division of labor, and centralized religious or state power. Two natural facts—the diurnal rotation of the earth and the annual orbit of the earth about the sun—shape all calendrical systems; the monthly cycle of the moon is also widely used. Everything besides the day and the year—holidays, weeks, decades—results from human choice and culture. Clearly much of the motivation of early calendar making was the desire to synchronize earthly life to the motions of the celestial spheres, a desire both religious and political.

Though all calendars have the day and the year, determining each precisely turns out to be deceptively difficult. Most people think it takes the earth 24 hours to rotate on its axis. Not so. The sun does take 24 hours to return to a point intersecting the meridian, an imaginary north-south line that bisects the sky into eastern and western halves. Yet for the sun to make a complete circuit, the earth must actually rotate about 361 degrees to catch up to where it was yesterday with respect to the sun, which takes about an extra four minutes on average (but with a much wider range than that). The absolute rotation of the earth takes 23 hours, 56 minutes, and 4.09 seconds. The earth's spin is slowing gradually, and 500 million years ago there may have been more than 400 days per year according to evidence from growth rings in fossilized mollusks and coral (dinosaurs would have had very different calendars than we do).

Determining the length of the year is even more complicated. The Babylonians reckoned the year around 360 days and thus chose 360 as the number of degrees in a circle (thanks also to its easy divisibility by 2, 3, 4, 5, and their multiples). Our symbol for *degree*, a raised *o*, comes from the Babylonian symbol for *sun*. Over two thousand years ago in Egypt, Babylon, China, and Greece it was known that the year takes 365 days and a fraction. The calendar implemented in the reign of Julius Caesar (named Julian in his honor) introduced a leap year every four years, putting 365.25 days in the year. The Julian calendar was good to within 11 minutes per year (in fact the earth takes 365.24219 mean solar days to orbit the sun), but small differences add up, and the Julian calendar loses a day about every 128 years. By 1582, when Pope Gregory XIII introduced the Gregorian calendar, which omits three leap years every four hundred years, the Julian calendar was about 12 days off. Protestant countries resisted the change for predictable religious and political reasons. England finally made the switch in 1752; the nation went to bed on Saturday 2 September and woke up on Thursday 14 September. Russia (like Greece and Turkey) did not switch until the twentieth century, with the result that the October Revolution of 1917 took place in what we now call November.

Calendars and Religion

Every religion has a calendar. Jews, Buddhists, Jains, Muslims, Hindus, and Baha'is each have their own calendar. Christianity has at least three, and Roman Catholics, Eastern Orthodox, and Armenian Orthodox can still end up celebrating Christmas on different dates. The chief motive of Gregory's reforms was to regularize the date of Easter, the most important of the Christian "moveable feasts." In contrast to Christmas, which always falls on 25 December, Easter's date varies widely from year to year, being defined as the first Sunday after the first full moon after the vernal equinox. This definition was set in the Council at Nicea in 325 CE after schisms about Easter's proper date among early Christians. Calendar systems are never neutral maps: people signal their religious allegiance and identity by the holidays (holy days) they observe.

For the Jews, the calendar is of central religious significance. Their scripture starts with an account of the creation of the world in which one of the very first items created was the day itself—which was characteristically defined in the Hebrew style as extending from the evening to the next day (Genesis 1:5). (Indeed, the bounds of the day can be defined in many ways—from sunrise to sunrise, noon to noon, sunset to sunset or more artificially, from midnight to midnight). Moreover, the book of Genesis gives divine sanction to the seven-day week, culminating in the Sabbath, or day of rest. Sabbath observance has always been one of the key markers of Jewish identity, as are high holidays such as Yom Kippur (Day of Atonement), Pesach (Passover), and Rosh Hashanah (New Year's), which are also considered Sabbaths, though they may fall on other days of the week besides the seventh. Sabbath observance is perhaps the most intense form of calendrical religiosity. Seventh-day Adventists make an interpretation of the calendar into an article of faith.

The Jews borrowed a lunisolar calendar from the Babylonians, and after diverse refinements, have a calendar that slips about 6 minutes per year, or one day every 216 years. A lunisolar calendar uses both the phases of the moon and the sun. The lunisolar dating of Easter noted above is a legacy from the Jewish calendar, and many early Christians observed Easter on the same day as Passover, the 14th of Nisan. The Muslim calendar, in contrast, is strictly lunar, with a year of either 354 or 355 days made of 12 lunar months. It makes one complete rotation through all the seasons once every 32 Muslim years. Its first year is 622 CE and it uses the abbreviation AH (*anno hegirae*, in the year of the *hegira*). Since the Muslim year goes faster, one cannot calculate its equivalent in the Gregorian calendar by subtracting 622. 2005 CE, for instance, is 1425–1426 AH.

One other historical feature of the Jewish calendar is of general relevance: its governance by central authority. After the destruction of the Second Temple in 70 CE, the diaspora calendar was sent by signal flares and messengers from Jerusalem, which had monopoly control on sighting the new moon and thus declaring the start of the new month. In the era before electricity, the slow movement of such time-sensitive data was a major inconvenience, and Hillel II ended Jerusalem's monopoly in 356 CE, allowing each Jewish community to determine the new moon, doubtless much to their relief. A clear principle in the history of calendar making is that those in power make the calendar—and vice versa. Astrological prognostications have often served as ideological supports for the ruling classes. Among the Aztecs, for instance, a priestly class maintained a complex dual calendar nested within 52-year cycles. Indeed, calendars have always been under the control of priestly classes who serve power; today we call them scientists. A key sign of sovereignty is the power to declare a holiday.

Calendars and Resistance

Every calendar invites resistance. The Qumran sectaries of the Dead Scrolls, for instance, hated the lunisolar calendar imposed by their Greek conquerors and observed instead the "true calendar." Observing the Sabbath has always been a form of resistance to state and market power. Celebrating the Sabbath on the eighth instead of the seventh day may have been partly a political gambit to distinguish early Christians from Jews. Contemporary Jews in turn sometimes resist the Christianity of the dominant calendar by using BCE (before the common era) instead of BC (before Christ) and CE (the common era) instead of AD (*anno domini*, in the year of the Lord). Quakers traditionally called the days of the week by ordinal numbers (e.g., Sunday is first day) to avoid honoring the pagan gods whose names we inherit from the Roman calendar, which tied days of the week to the seven moving heavenly bodies—Sun, Moon, Mars, Mercury, Jupiter, Venus, and Saturn. Ordinal numbers are a common way to name weekdays. In modern Greek, for instance, Sunday is the Lord's Day, Monday is second day, and Tuesday is third day; in Russian, Sunday is resurrection day, Monday is the day after not working, and Tuesday is second day. Obviously the Greeks and Russians start counting in a different place. Indeed, when the week ends and starts is as arbitrary as when the day does. The Jews may have made Saturday the last day to avenge their Egyptian captors, who venerated Saturday as the first day. Our weekend is a composite of the seventh and the first day, though many of us feel like Monday is the first day of the week. Months have a similar arbitrary quality: How many of us readily remember which months have 30 days and which have 31?

Most calendars possess a deep cultural conservatism—appropriately enough for media that store time. Our calendar has roots from millennia ago. Quirks of the Roman world live on in the twenty-first century. July and August, formerly Quintilis (fifth) and Sextilis (sixth), owe their names to the vanity of two men dead for nearly two thousand years, Julius Caesar and Caesar Augustus. We call our ninth, tenth, eleventh, and twelfth months September, October, November, and December, which of course mean seventh, eighth, ninth, and tenth. The calendar gods have a sense of humor—the explanation of this mismatch seems that the Romans once started their year with the vernal (spring) equinox. The idea that the calendar has a middle point, with a negative direction (before Christ) and a positive one (after his birth), is obviously of Christian origin. The modern world operates on top of an ancient calendrical infrastructure.

Modern reformers sometimes sought to strip away the calendar's ancient religious content. The French Revolution tried to institute a 10-day week (like that of the ancient Greeks); the decimal zeal that led to the metric system of weights and measures extended to the calendar itself. The revolutionaries wanted to weaken the grip of religious holidays and the Sabbath (with little success). In a similar spirit, the Russian revolution experimented with a five-day week for about a decade and then gave up. One thing neither revolution could change was the grip of the seven-day cycle. Every religion may have its calendar, but every calendar probably has its religion as well, if even the religion of secular reason. As constructs that synchronize earth and heaven, culture and nature, and the periodic events of history and astronomy, calendars remain among the oldest and most important of all religious media of communication.

John Durham Peters

Further Reading

Richards, E. G. (1999). *Mapping time: The calendar and its history*. Oxford, UK: Oxford University Press.

Steel, D. (2000). *Marking time: The epic quest to invent the perfect calendar*. New York: Wiley.

Zerubavel, E. (1985). *The seven day circle: The history and meaning of the week*. New York: Free Press.

Canonization

Canonization as a communication tool serves to emphasize and give prominence to religious messages, symbols, and even personalities. Canonization is the process by which the Catholic Church declares a person to be a "saint," that is a holy one, a model of holiness. Traditionally saints are recognized either because they have been martyred or because they have displayed "heroic virtue," which is the exemplary practice of Christian love and service so that the person becomes a model of discipleship. Canonization recognizes that they now have a face-to-face experience of God, that is they share in the beatific vision, (the direct knowing and loving of God after death), and the Church officially sanctions and promotes their veneration by the community. The veneration of saints is a distinctively Catholic practice that finds its starting point in Jesus' Resurrection and is a development of reflection upon the meaning of resurrection and life after death.

The first people to be called "saints" were martyrs, or people who were killed for their faith. A martyr is a person who died because he or she refused to renounce his or her faith. The word "martyr" comes from the Greek for "witness" and is used for one whose death testified to his or her faithfulness to Jesus. Like most Christian practices, the veneration of martyrs is rooted in Hebrew Scriptures. In 2 Maccabees, Eleazar and a woman with seven sons refuse to comply with anti-Jewish laws and are tortured and killed as a result. Their "witness" inspires the application of that term in the Christian book of Revelation (c. 95 CE) and in later texts. A martyr's death was seen as rewarded by an immediate transition into eternal life. "Holy" comes from the Greek *hagios,* which describes a person who participates in the life of God. Holiness was ascribed to Jesus' disciples when they were alive and active. Its Christian application is built upon Hebrew Scriptures where God calls upon the people to "Be holy, for I, the Lord, your God, am holy" (Leviticus 19:2, NAB). In the New Testament, Paul addresses the people to whom he writes as "holy ones" (Romans 1:7; 1 Corinthians 1:2; 2 Corinthians 1:1; Ephesians 1:1; Philippians 1:1). The "holy ones" eventually are referred to as "saints." In the first millennium there was no formal process but rather cults of individuals arose in local communities in spontaneous recognition of the person's holy life. Venerating saints has been a part of the life of the Christian Church since the death of the first martyr, Stephen, whose feast is celebrated on 26 December. By the fourth century CE the category of confessor emerged to describe those who suffered for the faith but were not executed.

Cult

The importance of saints was communicated in several ways by the various cults that developed in order to venerate them. The cults developed from the stories of the saint's death and their passion experiences, describing the suffering they endured. The ritual and devotional activity that became the cult of the saints has its earliest mention in the *Martyrdom of Polycarp* (c. 157 CE). This text describes a memorial cult at the resting place of the bones of a martyr. There are two types of accounts of martyrs' deaths: narrative, or "passion," accounts of their suffering, as in the *Passion of Perpetua and Felicitas* (c. 203 CE) and the *Martyrdom of Polycarp* mentioned above, and accounts that describe the trial, sentence, and execution, as in the *Acts of Justin Martyr* (c. 165 CE). Another early text, the *Letter of the Churches of Lyons and Vienne* (c. 177 CE), indicates a form of cultic activity. The letter was probably meant to be read in a liturgical setting and was circulated to other churches. The veneration involved a celebration of the Eucharist at the martyr's tomb on the anniversary of the death. This led to the designation of Feast Days in the Christian liturgical calendar; the practice of feast days for martyrs was stabilized as early as the third century in Rome.

In addition to the cultic memorials at burial sites, saints began to be adopted as patrons of churches or towns, a practice that is displayed today in the vast number of churches, cities, and towns in many parts of the world that are named for saints. People also began very early to believe that the saints' holiness and their status in eternal life gave them power to perform miracles on behalf of the living and thus led to prayers to saints to intercede for personal intentions of the living faithful.

When Christianity became the official religion of the empire, sainthood was identified less with martyrs than with those who were steadfast in faith and in service to God, such as those ascetics who led lives of denial, those who were regarded as excellent and wise teachers, and those who served the poor and marginalized. Augustine (354–430 CE) warned of the tendency towards superstition with regard to the cult of the saints and instead recommended that the saints be honored as models to be imitated. The invocation of saints was a common devotional practice in Augustine's time.

By the eighth century, a cult of relics had emerged and was popular and was also an important aspect of feudal society. More and more liturgical forms emerged and became elaborate, especially the pious devotion to the founders of monasteries and religious orders. Pilgrimages to shrines of individual saints became popular and developed into sources of pride and profit in local places. Relics were traded and the cycle of feast days in the liturgical calendar became more elaborate. These cultic developments led to an increasing concern to suppress the superstitious and magical aspects that can emerge in cultic behavior and the papacy eventually intervened to forestall and curtail such abuses.

History

The canonization of saints served to communicate how Christian life should be lived. This recognition provided various models of Christian behavior that could be

Canonization of Josemaría Escrivá De Balaguer

On 20 December 2001, Pope John Paul II approved the decree issued by the Congregation for the Causes of Saints on a miraculous cure attributed to the intercession of Blessed Josemaria Escriva. The miracle was the cure of Dr. Manuel Nevado from cancerous chronic radiodermatitis, an incurable disease, which took place in November 1992. The decree opened the doors for the canonization of Blessed Josemaria.

Radiodermatitis

Radiodermatitis is a typical skin disease of medical professionals who have been repeatedly exposed to radiation from X-ray machines over a long period of time. The disease is progressive and evolves inexorably, causing the appearance of skin cancers. Radiodermatitis has no cure. The only known treatments are surgical interventions: skin grafts, or amputation of the affected parts of the hand. To date, no case of a spontaneous cure from cancerous chronic radiodermatitis has ever been recorded in medical literature.

The Cure

Dr. Manuel Nevado Rey was born in Spain in 1932. A specialist in orthopedic surgery, he operated on fractures and other injuries for nearly 15 years with frequent exposure of his hands to X-rays. The first symptoms of radiodermatitis began to appear in 1962, and the disease continued to worsen. By 1984, he had to limit his activities to minor operations because his hands were gravely affected. He stopped operating completely in the summer of 1992, but did not undergo any treatment.

In November 1992, Dr. Nevado met Luis Eugenio Bernardo Carrascal, an agricultural engineer working for the Spanish government. On hearing about his disease, Luis Eugenio offered him a prayer card [Josemaria Escrivá De Balaquer] of the Founder of Opus Dei who had been beatified on May 17 that year, and invited him to pray for the cure of his radiodermatitis.

The Intercession of Blessed Josemaria

Dr. Nevado began praying for a cure through the intercession of Blessed Josemaria. A few days after that meeting, he traveled to Vienna with his wife in order to attend a medical conference. They visited several churches and came across prayer cards of Blessed Josemaria. "This impressed me," explained Dr. Nevado, "and it encouraged me to pray more for my cure." From the day that he began to entrust his cure to the intercession of Blessed Josemaria, his hands began to improve. Within a fortnight the lesions had completely disappeared and the cure was complete. By January 1993, Dr. Nevado had returned to perform surgical operations without any problems.

The Canonical Process

The canonical process on this miracle took place in the archdiocese of Badajoz where Dr. Nevado lives, and was concluded in 1994. On July 10, 1997, the Medical Committee of the Congregation for the Causes of Saints unanimously established the following diagnosis: *a cancerous state of chronic radiodermatitis in its third and irreversible stage*; therefore with certain prognosis of *infaust* (without hope of cure). The complete cure of the lesions, confirmed by the objective examinations carried out on Dr. Nevado in 1992, 1994 and 1997, was declared by the Medical Committee to be *very rapid, complete, lasting, and scientifically inexplicable*.

On January 9, 1998, the Committee of Theologian Consultants gave its unanimous approval for attributing the miracle to Blessed Josemaria. The Congregation of the Causes of Saints confirmed these conclusions on September 21, 2001.

Source: *The Vatican's compilation of documents, images and films concerning his canonization.* Retrieved November 9, 2005, from http://www.vatican.va/news_services/liturgy/saints/ns_lit_doc_20021006_index_escriva_en.html

learned and applied to the entire Christian community, and these models challenged all Christians to communicate their beliefs through actions and behaviors. The earliest canonization was by Pope John XV (993 CE) in recognizing the sainthood of Ulrich of Augsburg. The movement towards papal ratification of sainthood is solidified in a letter sent around 1170 CE to the King of Sweden by Pope Alexander III asserting that no one ought to be venerated as a saint except by the authority of the Church of Rome. This letter eventually was included in the *Decretals* of Gregory IX in 1234 and thus became part of the general law of the Church in the West, which is the Roman Church.

Over time and because of various social, intellectual, and cultural developments, Christians became more and more preoccupied with the questions surrounding life after death. As the Church had come to control the recognition of saints, it came to be seen as controlling the merits that the saints possessed and could thus dispense those merits to the faithful. These merits could be used to remedy punishment for sins. This led to the creation of indulgences, which were the remission of temporal punishment that was a result of sin by way of prayers and good works. A bull (a document stamped with the lead seal of the pope) was issued by Clement VI that described a "treasury of merits" that belong to the saints but that the Church has the authority to bestow. The quantification of the saints' merits was a distortion of the notion of holiness that led in part to the Reformation. By the Second Vatican Council (1962–1965) the theological issues raised by the notion of indulgences were sufficiently developed and the Council requested a reformulation. Pope Paul VI wrote a more theologically coherent description of their meaning called *Indulgentiarum Doctrina*.

Process of Canonization

As the process became more complex, it began to communicate the deeper theological reflection that lies behind the recognition of sainthood. Following the first steps towards formal codification of the process of canonization that began with Pope Alexander's letter and Pope Gregory's *Decretals*, the Avignon popes (1309–1377 CE) put more detailed procedures in place. A petition was made on behalf of a candidate for sainthood by an official procurator, or prosecutor of the cause of that person. The popular title of "Devil's Advocate" emerged for the curial official who represented the pope in the cause; this official was called the "Promoter of the Faith." The process became patterned after a legal proceeding and required letters from bishops, temporal

leaders and other important figures requesting that a process of canonization be initiated. This formalization of the process initially led to the decline in the number of saints who were named. However, the cult of the saints was quite strong and models of faithfulness continued to be venerated in local communities.

New legislation was formulated to deal with this spontaneous devotion and those who had not been canonized were called the "blessed" or in Latin the *beati*. In 1634, Pope Urban VIII formalized the distinction between beatification and canonization and instituted the process for each. Between 1734 and 1738, a canonist for the Congregation of Rites and the future Pope Benedict XIV wrote a work called *On the Beatification of the Servants of God and the Canonization of the Blessed*. This text clarified the theology and the practice of canonization. The practices laid down in this text were in effect until 1983 when Pope John Paul II modified the process with the text *The Divine Master of Perfection*. This process puts the primary responsibility for bringing a cause for canonization in the hands of the local bishop in the diocese where the candidate died. That bishop will consult with other bishops as expected by the Catholic notion of collegiality and will gather evidence for the cause. That bishop appoints a Postulator who gathers accurate information about the candidate and develops the argument to move the cause forward. The bishop or someone delegated by the bishop inspects the tomb of the candidate and the place where he or she died and any other places where there might be indications of any cult in the candidate's honor. The bishop must testify in writing that no cult exists that violates the early decree of Urban VIII that no person be publicly venerated without the approval of the Roman Church. The bishop must also affirm the validity of all witnesses and the process. The Congregation then accepts the cause and a Relator is appointed. Along with the Relator's appointed collaborators he prepares the *positio* or argument in favor of the candidate. The argument must show that the person demonstrated heroic virtue or was actually martyred. The document is reviewed by the Promoter of the Faith and another official called the Prelate Theologian before it is presented to the Congregation for the Causes of Saints. One particular Relator is assigned to prepare an argument with regard to miracles; this is done in consultation with a board of medical professionals and theologians.

Two miracles are required: one for beatification and one for canonization, except in the case of a martyr in which only one miracle is required. The Congregation for the Cause of Saints makes a judgment, and if it is in favor of the candidate it is reported to the pope. The pope is the only one who can officially declare that a public cult of sainthood may be developed for this "Servant of God," which is the juridical designation for a saint. At a ceremony declaring the person a saint, the pope says: "We solemnly decide and define that [name] is a saint and inscribe him [or her] in the catalog of saints, stating that his [or her] memory shall be kept with pious devotion by the universal Church." The process of canonization is intended for the greater good of the whole Christian community by recognizing heroic models of Christian love and service and encouraging a similar way of life among Christians. The public cult of the saints is intended to nourish the Christian life and a Christian's own relationship with God. By canonizing signal individuals, the Church mediates just one of the myriad ways in which it enables the human and divine encounter.

SALLY VANCE-TREMBATH

Further Reading

Burns, P. (Ed.). (1998–2000). *Butler's lives of the saints*. Collegeville, MN: Liturgical Press.

Cunningham, L. S., & Egan, K. J. (1996). *Christian spirituality: Themes from the tradition*. New York: Paulist Press.

Farmer, D. (1997). *The Oxford dictionary of saints*. Oxford, UK: Oxford University Press.

Glazier, M., & Hellwig, M. K. (1994). *The modern Catholic encyclopedia*. Collegeville, MN: Liturgical Press.

Johnson, E. A. (1998). *Friends of God and prophets: A feminist theological reading of the communion of saints*. New York: Continuum.

McBrien, R. P. (1994). *Catholicism: Completely revised and edited*. San Francisco: Harper-Collins.

McBrien, R. P. (Ed.). (1995). *The HarperCollins encyclopedia of Catholicism*. San Francisco: HarperCollins.

McBrien, R. P. (2001). *Lives of the saints: From Mary and St. Francis of Assisi to John XXIII and Mother Teresa*. San Francisco: Harper-SanFrancisco.

Richardson, A., & Bowden, J. (1983). *Westminster Dictionary of Christian Theology*. Philadelphia: Westminster Press.

Wilson, S. (1983). *Saints and their cults: Studies in religious sociology, folklore and history*. Cambridge, UK: Cambridge University Press.

Catholicism

Catholicism is intrinsically friendly to communication and the media because its self-understanding is rooted in the essential relationship between the human and the divine (human persons and God). Catholicism is one of the denominations in the Christian tradition that takes its name from the Greek adverbial phrase *kath' holou*, which means "on the whole" and from *katholikos*, meaning "universal." Catholicism's approach to communication is guided by its foundational insight that all of creation is saturated with the presence of God. This insight is displayed in the ancient principle of *lex orandi: lex credendi* (the law of praying is the law of believing), which describes the connection between the conceptual aspects of Catholicism and their public transmission and expressions. Because it is possible for God's presence to be found in every aspect of human life, the desire to communicate such an understanding has been emphasized from Catholicism's earliest beginnings. The first examples of this emphasis upon communication are recorded in the *Acts of the Apostles* in Christian Scripture. The early leaders frequently preached in public places; for example, Paul the Apostle told the story of Jesus Christ in Athens as well as in other centers of activity throughout the region. Both Paul and Peter also preached in Rome, which was the communication center of the known-world. In addition to this form of communication, rituals that transmitted Catholic Christian teaching emerged very quickly. These rituals involved simple activities as well as short explanations (creeds) that communicated the central truth/claims of Christianity. As Christianity developed and split into different denominations, Catholicism retained this emphasis upon the community expression while others focused more on the internal, private relationship with God through the person of Jesus Christ. The essentially Catholic principle of sacramentality (the idea that God is available through all reality; the human and the divine are constitutively linked) has shaped this tradition's understanding and use of communication.

The earliest forms of communication were oral ones that were later written down. The Gospel (that is, "good news") was a new genre in communication that combined theological claims (critical reflection about the divine) with the story of the historical person, Jesus of Nazareth. This combination of theology and story is also displayed in paintings, statuary, and in architecture. Many of the earliest medieval manuscripts were crafted to communicate Christian theology and practice and the first book produced on movable type was the Gutenberg Bible. In more recent history, a radio station was established at the Vatican in 1931 and one of the first messages transmitted by the American communications satellite *Telstar* was a plea for peace by Pope John XXIII during the Cuban Missile Crisis (October 1962).

The Catholic Church has a written tradition about communication as well. The first letter by a pope (encyclical) regarding Catholic teaching on the media was about motion pictures; *Vigilanti Cura* was issued in 1936. In 1957, the encyclical *Miranda Prorsus* described the pope's concerns about radio and television. The Second Vatican Council (the most authoritative teaching body of the Catholic Church, 1962–1965) issued *Inter Mirifica* (The Decree on the Instruments of Social Communication). While calling upon local bishops to oversee media communication, the document teaches that human persons have the right to information to answer a basic human need for "the enlargement and enrichment of human minds" (Flannery 1996, 284). In 1964, the Pontifical Commission for Social Communication was established as an office of the Roman Curia in the Apostolic Letter *In fructibus multis*. These teachings were continued in 1971 in the pastoral instruction *Communio et Progressio* and in *Aetatis Novae* in 1992. These documents recognize that the media are agents of progress and they call for equal access to all forms of communication in order that all human persons are treated justly.

A primary form of communication for Catholics is the press. In the United Kingdom, the weekly publication *The Tablet* was first published in 1840; the Netherlands's Catholic daily *De Tijd* began in 1845; *L'Osservatore Romano* began in the Vatican in 1861, and in France *La Croix* was first published in 1883. Catholic Press Association was established in 1911 in the United States. *The National Catholic Reporter* is a widely read publication and most dioceses have a Catholic newspaper. The United States also established the Catholic Television Network of America.

Definitive Principles

Catholicism is informed and animated by the notion of sacramentality and its adjacent theological principles: mediation and communion. These principles display Catholicism's stance towards communication and the media. *Mediation* describes the insight that God acts and is present through secondary causes and not directly. *Communion* refers to the insight that while God is personally present to each human being, the divine-human encounter is fundamentally communal; it is mediated by the experience of community and not simply as an individual or private experience. While these may be present to some degree in other denominations, Catholicism is marked by the insistence on attention to all three and its various configurations of them. There are several concepts that flow from these principles that guide Catholicism's relationship to communica-

tion and the media. The Catholic understanding of the conscience as the point of contact between the human and the divine displays a positive understanding of the human mind and of human freedom. The human mind and will are seen as intense locations of God's presence and thus can be trusted; even though this concept has many times been ignored or de-emphasized in Catholic history, the Catholic Church has confidence that the search for knowledge is fundamentally good. Free expression and respectful questioning are both valued. The concept of the natural law also displays a positive understanding of human communication. This concept describes human beings as "naturally" fitted for a relationship with the divine and thus the "natural" or "human" tendencies of questioning, discourse, and dialogue that are all essential for communication are also privileged. The signal document that expresses Catholicism's stance is *Dignitatis humanae* (Flannery, 1996, 799).

Definitions and Distinctions

The Catholic Church is numerically the largest Christian denomination, or church, (there are approximately one billion Catholics), and is the largest distinct religious community in the world. A church is "the whole body, or congregation, of persons who are called by God the Father to acknowledge the Lordship of Jesus, the Son, in word, sacrament, in witness, and in service, and, through the power of the Holy Spirit, to collaborate with Jesus' historic mission for the sake of the Kingdom of God" (McBrien 1994, 723). Catholicism is the worldwide church that recognizes the unifying ministry of the Bishop of Rome, the pope, "as the perpetual and visible source and foundation of the unity of the bishops and of the multitude of the faithful" (Flannery 1996, 31). The term *Catholicism* has slightly different meanings for those who are members of the Catholic Church and for those who are not. Members of the Catholic Church see themselves as rooted in the founding Christian community and thus see the Catholic Church as the original Christian community because all Christians were Catholic until the authority of the Bishop or Rome, the pope, led to the disconnection between the East and Western Churches. Again in the sixteenth century this same issue (the authority of the pope) led to the Protestant Reformation that yielded many of the Christian denominations we have today. Within broader Christianity there are those who would claim that when the Catholic Church became involved with the political structures, as a result of the conversion of the Emperor Constantine, it became more of an institution and power structure and less a community of gathered followers of Jesus. *Constantinianism* is the pejorative term that refers to the development when the church was officially recognized and no longer persecuted and thus eventually achieved privileged status. Catholicism itself refutes this analysis and, using its central principle of sacramentality (the idea that God is available through all reality), claims that God's activity and presence is imbued in all things, including organizational and governmental structures.

Catholicism commonly refers to the Roman Catholic Church, which is governed by the institutional bureaucracy that is located in Rome, Italy. Catholicism also refers to a communion of local churches. There are eight distinct Catholic traditions: Armenian, Byzantine, Coptic, Ethiopian, East Syrian (Chaldean), Maronite, Roman, and West Syrian. Catholicism adopted many of the forms of the Roman Empire; it came to identify Rome as its center instead of its founding place in Jerusalem, and it still uses Roman law (canon law) and terminology. For example, *diocese* is a Roman term; it refers to the geographical or territorial Catholic community that is unified by the bishop. Parishes are the next subdivision of a diocese. Priests who are in communion with the bishop lead parishes. The bishop has jurisdiction over all the priests in his diocese.

The identification of Catholicism with Roman Catholicism leads to a confusion of terms that requires clarification. The word *catholic* also refers to the impulse towards unifying geographically and culturally distinct communities under a cohesive, institutional, doctrinal (teaching), sacramental (worship and devotional), and moral framework. There are several Christian communities that affirm such a framework and thus identify themselves as catholic, often referring to themselves as "small c" catholic. Another source of confusion is the common misunderstanding that Protestant is the opposite of Catholic. The more accurate opposite of Catholicism is sectarianism that privileges distinctions among human persons and between the human and the divine. Catholicism not only displays an attempt to find unity among human communities and persons but also between the human, historical world and God. Sectarianism privileges exclusivity, whereas Catholicism privileges inclusivity. Another aspect of Catholicism is its positive stance toward the created world and human history. In contrast, Protestantism refers broadly to the movement that began in the sixteenth century, which rejects the institutional authority of the Bishop of Rome, the pope. As Catholicism is marked by the impulse for unification, Protestantism is marked by the impulse for independ-

A cross on the top of a Barcelona, Spain, cathedral. *Courtesy of Lynn Chealander/istockphoto.com.*

ence. Even though in the twentieth century many Protestant denominations participated in the ecumenical movement, a movement towards greater unity among denominations, the primary orientation of Protestantism is independence and an emphasis upon the local church community. Catholicism displays openness to all human persons and communities, as can be seen in its missionary activity that directed great energy towards proclaiming the message of Jesus in all human contexts, cultures, and historical situations.

Catholicity also describes the desire to create unity in difference thus preserving the various distinctive traditions that are a result of serious recognition of and attention to the characteristics resulting from geographical, historical, and cultural factors. These traditions are seen as gifts that enrich Catholicism without undermining its global unity. A notion of the unity of humanity underlies this unity in diversity; all human persons share in the unity between the human and the divine that was disclosed in Jesus' historic mission, death, and Resurrection. The Catholic community, that is, Church, is committed to the proclamation and instantiation of this claim about God's relationship to the human community. Therefore, it is marked by its openness to all humanity in all its myriad cultural manifestations.

Components and Characteristics

Catholicism has the following essential components: the proclamation of the Gospel, or message, of Jesus; a baptismal rite for initiation into the community; regular celebration of a meal of remembrance; and various charisms (gifts) and ministries (works of care). These components are instantiated in Catholicism's way of life as guided by several characteristically "catholic" frameworks. First is the emphasis upon the freedom of conscience that encourages a dialogic relationship between the individual believer, the teaching authority of the Church, and the community. Freedom of conscience also emphasizes the notion of mystery, that is, those areas of human life about which persons can never come to understand fully because they serve as glimpses of the human and divine encounter. The mysterious character of existence is played out as Catholics discern their response to doctrinal and moral teaching and sacramental activity. The basic framework for their response is attention to unity in diversity. With regard to communication, there are Catholic writings and practices that emphasize the intellect and those that emphasize the affective realm of human existence. This is yet another expression of its universal character in that it attempts to include all facets of human existence. Instead of viewing reality as sets of competing realms, Catholicism emphasizes the compatibility of nature and grace, faith and reason, authority and freedom, faith and works. Its value for the human can be seen in Catholicism's recognition of the provisional aspect of the Church's existence. The Church is not identical with the Kingdom of God (the divine reality) but is rather "a mystery; a reality imbued with the hidden presence of God, and for that reason, is ever susceptible of new and deeper investigation. The Kingdom of God is the future realization of the human and the divine encounter where all persons enter into a new life in the Resurrection of the Body; the Church is the present community that construes reality as the beginning of this future realization" (Anderson 1965, 144). Mystery also refers to the human situation whereby we are both united to God and yet distinct from God. The Church will always fall short of being everything it is intended to be because it is a human community.

With regard to its liturgical life (that is, worship or sacramental activities) Catholicism emphasizes seven sacraments, or ritual encounters with God. These are the primary ways in which Catholicism communicates its teaching and identity. This sacramental expression displays essential Catholic principles by attending to God's presence in all things, persons, and objects; indeed the entire cosmos bears the presence of God.

SALLY VANCE-TREMBATH

See also Cross; Orthodoxy; Priests

Further Reading

Anderson, F. (Ed.). (1965). *Council daybook: Vatican II*. Washington DC: National Catholic Welfare Conference.

Bokenkotter, T. (1990). *A concise history of the Catholic Church*. Garden City, NY: Image Books.

Cunningham, L. (1987). *The Catholic faith: An introduction*. New York: Paulist Press.

Cwiekowski, F. J. (1988). *The beginnings of the church*. New York: Paulist Press.

de Lubac, H. (1958). *Catholicism: A study of the corporate destiny of mankind* (L. Sheppard, Trans.). New York: Sheed and Ward.

Flannery, A. (Gen. Ed.). (1996) *Vatican Council II: The Conciliar and Postconciliar Documents*. Northport, NY and Dublin, Ireland: Costello Publishing.

Glazier, M., & Hellwig, M. K. (1994). *The modern Catholic encyclopedia*. Collegeville, MN: Liturgical Press.

Happel, S., & Tracy, D. (1984). *A Catholic vision*. Philadelphia: Fortress Press.

Küng, H. (2001). *The Catholic Church: A short history* (J. Bowden, Trans.). London: Weidenfeld and Nicolson.

McBrien, R. P. (1994). *Catholicism: Completely revised and edited*. San Francisco: Harper-Collins.

Richardson, A., & Bowden, J. (1983). *Westminster dictionary of Christian theology*. Philadelphia: Westminster Press.

Sullivan, F. (1988). *The church we believe in: One, holy, Catholic and apostolic*. New York: Paulist Press.

Censorship

Throughout history, governments and other powerful elites have often worked to prevent the dissemination of certain spoken or written texts—especially those with religious or political content—and punished those associated with them. Independent thinkers have been persecuted since the ancient Greeks—for example, Xenophanes (c. 570–470 BCE), Thomas Hobbes (1588–1679), René Descartes (1596–1650), Baron d'Holbach (1723–1789), and the English-American pamphleteer

Thomas Paine (1737–1809). In the twentieth century, Communist governments censored religious texts.

Only since the advent of books and other written materials, first hand-copied and then printed in quantities from dozens to hundreds of thousands, has organized, systematic censorship been possible. Primitive censorship was refined after the 1450s, when the modern European printing press with movable, reusable type conclusively demonstrated the written word's power. This prompted the most severe censorship because of the written word's indispensable role in the Protestant Reformation.

Censorship in Christianity was historically justified by numerous injunctions in both the Old and New Testaments against disobeying God, supporting polytheism, worshipping graven images, practicing blasphemy, or embracing heresy; Acts 19:19 even appears to approve public book burning. The prosecution of heresy by Christians started early, no later than Marcion's excommunication (160), thus turning a persecuted religion into a persecuting one. The first *Index,* a list of books off-limits to faithful Christians, was probably *Decretum Gelasianum* (494).

The Christian Bible has been censored, and not only in non-Christian countries. From the thirteenth to the sixteenth centuries, Bibles in languages other than Latin were prohibited in most of Europe. (A cornerstone of Protestantism was making the Bible available in many native tongues.) In sixteenth century England, unapproved books and translations were prohibited and their publishers were prosecuted, policies made official by Henry VIII's own *Index* (1526) and the licensing of printing after 1539. Licensing collapsed with the Civil Wars, but was reintroduced between 1655 and 1679 and again between 1685 and 1695.

Licensing then ceased, but British censorship continued through common law and Parliamentary acts. The Blasphemy Act (1698) resulted in prosecutions of Deists Thomas Woolston (1725–1728), Peter Annet (1761; he had been publishing controversial material since 1737), and Thomas Ilive (1753–1757). In 1818, Thomas Bowdler ("bowdlerization") released *The Family Shakespeare,* with all sexual innuendos omitted. The Indecent Advertisements Act was passed in 1889, and starting in 1857, the Obscene Publications Act was applied on religious grounds to novels and sometimes medical literature; even libraries began segregating and locking up suspect materials. Later in the century, Victorian morality run amok resulted in the Bible's own sex-related passages being either removed or altered. Such acts were supported by the Society for the Suppression of Vice (founded in 1802), and the later National Vigilance Association and the National Council of Public Morals, with only the Obscene Publications Act of 1959 providing partial liberalization.

In 1977, Britain's *Gay News* was convicted of blasphemy for "The Love That Dares to Speak Its Name," a homoerotic poem about Jesus. Even today, the British Board of Film Classification, flowing from 1909's Cinematograph Act, controls film content more tightly than nearly every other Western country, despite the 1977 extension of the 1959 act to cover film. However, the Video Recordings Act of 1984 is Britain's only true censorship law.

Implementing the Inquisition from the twelfth to the sixteenth centuries, Catholic nations used censorship to control the spread of Protestantism. Holy Roman Emperor Charles V banned Martin Luther's works in Spain (1521) and then everywhere (1526), and made a general attack on heresy later (1532). Spain's Phillip II in 1558 instituted censorship both before and after printing—Europe's most tyrannical policy. In France, vernacular Bibles were widely burned in the 1540s and 1550s, and they were placed on Catholic Spain's *Index* of prohibited books in 1551. Before the seventeenth century, books were banned by local clergy and university theologians, and after that time censorship was generally government-controlled.

The Catholic Church's most notorious list, *Index Librorum Prohibitorum,* was issued by the Council of Trent (1564) and updated every thirty or fifty years until 1966. Among its victims were many of the modern West's most important political and scientific thinkers and best novelists; for instance, Galileo Galilei, who was persecuted beginning in 1632 and finally received an apology from Pope John Paul II in 1979. The *Index* was also widely evaded, and its effectiveness declined continuously after the late eighteenth century, although it controlled Irish publishing from the 1920s until the 1970s. Even today, Catholics around the world are still advised by the Church about what films (and sometimes other arts and entertainment) can be seen by all Catholics, only adult Catholics, or no Catholics. Protestant countries have also persecuted Catholic writings and schools of thought: for example, Germany in the 1870s and the United States during some periods in the nineteenth and twentieth centuries.

In Britain's North American colonies, religion-motivated prepublication censorship was almost unknown, but banishing a heretic (such as Anne Hutchinson) was not. The U.S. First Amendment, with its two-pronged approach to religion (freedom of worship and separation of church and state), has made formal censorship of or by religion essentially impossible.

But throughout the nineteenth century, U.S. religious organizations successfully prevented or discouraged Sunday newspapers, and managed to implement U.S. Post Office regulations prohibiting the mailing of publications and other goods considered immoral.

The New York Society for the Suppression of Vice, founded in 1873 by the Young Men's Christian Association and Anthony Comstock, successfully advocated the so-called Comstock Act, the federal statute regulating U.S. mail that, modified, remains in effect. In 1879, U.S. courts adopted (and retained for more than fifty years) the obscenity standard outlined in Britain's 1868 *Regina v. Hicklin*: A work is obscene if it can corrupt someone who is corruptible. By Comstock's death in 1915, he had claimed responsibility for 2,700 criminal convictions and the seizure of millions of pictures, postcards, birth control devices, newspapers, magazines, and books. Other procensorship groups, such as Watch and Ward Society (1891) and Clean Books League (1923), were also founded during this time. Novelists such as James Joyce could not use literary merit as a defense to an obscenity charge until 1933.

In the early twentieth century, fundamentalist Protestants succeeded in banning the teaching of evolution in four states, resulting in the 1925 Scopes "Monkey Trial." Following the formation of the National Board of (film) Censorship and a U.S. Supreme Court ruling that films were not protected by the First Amendment, both in 1915, the Motion Picture Producers and Distributors of America (founded in 1922) implemented the production code of Will Hays, a Presbyterian elder. This code would control U.S. film content (and influence U.S. television) for the next forty years. Catholic leaders wrote the moralistic Motion Picture Code (1929), took over the Production Code Administration (1934), and founded the Legion of Decency (1933) and its National Organization for Decent Literature (1938). All were dedicated to enforcing Catholic moral codes in films, magazines, comic books, and other works. From the 1930s until the 1960s, religion-driven local censorship boards nationwide banned various movies, and arguably U.S. films contained more sexual innuendo and sacrilegious content in 1915 than they did fifty years later.

But in 1952, the U.S. Supreme Court granted First Amendment protection to movies, and finally in 1968, the Production Code was dropped and replaced by ratings. Prosecutions of pornography accelerated, particularly in the 1950s and 1960s, until U.S. Supreme Court decisions had permitted homosexual pornography (1957), established "variable obscenity"—what's obscene for minors isn't necessarily obscene for adults (1968), and allowed for variable local (interpreted as state statutes) obscenity standards (*Miller v. California*, 1973). George W. Bush's administration's efforts, driven by evangelical Protestant officials and constituents, to turn back the clock on obscenity law have not been successful.

Although broadcast television and radio content is subject to the Federal Communications Commission's "safe harbor" rules (driven by conservative Christian moral claims) that ban "indecency" between 6 a.m. and 10 p.m., the FCC has not been willing to similarly regulate cable or satellite television, or the Internet. Successive efforts by religious conservatives to extend "indecency" regulations to the Internet through the Communications Decency Act of 1996 and other legislation have been almost entirely unsuccessful. Religious conservatives have succeeded only in requiring certain new television sets to carry "V-chips" (use is optional; few bother), stepping up (temporarily) FCC "indecency" fines, prompting ratings or other labels on television programs and certain entertainment products (the latter in a few states), banning the sale of pornographic magazines on military bases, and classifying as "child pornography" family photos of one's own naked children.

Religious organizations, individuals, and publications all suffered greatly under twentieth-century Communism. Churches and religious publications were shut down or severely limited throughout Eastern Europe in the late 1940s. Religious publications were never completely banned, but governments often allowed the printing or importing of a few hundred Bibles or other books while demand was estimated at tens or even hundreds of thousands. Effects and responses varied; underground religious and political publications known as samizdat (whether handwritten, typed, photocopied, or somehow printed) emerged to greater or lesser degrees in all Communist-occupied countries; Czechoslovak Catholics were among the most prolific and successful. Today the remaining Communist countries all remain officially atheist; even the People's Republic of China's 1982 constitution, which states "citizens ... enjoy freedom of religious belief," contains other clauses (loopholes) that still allow religious persecution.

Muslim cultures have been particularly unyielding on censorship. Islam has about 1 billion adherents, divided into Shiite and Sunni, and many smaller sects. The Baha'i Faith, for instance, developed from the Shiite, but its literature has been barred or limited in many Muslim countries; ironically, the movement practices formal and informal self-censorship. Literature, movies, art, and other works questioning or ignoring state-endorsed Islam are banned or prosecuted in Muslim countries, although in Tunisia, for instance, Arab and Muslim women cannot be seen nude in movies while other women can be. Movies, mailings, and advertisements in India generally have had to satisfy both Muslim and Hindu morals, resulting in kissing being omitted in the world's most prolific movie industry. Muslims generally are said to self-censor rather than censor, but many exceptions can be found; for instance, post-revolution Iran banned movie production for four years, the Taliban in Afghanistan smashed television sets and videotapes, and arguably only Qatar has a free press among Arab Muslim countries.

Among other major world religions, European Christians burned large amounts of Hebrew works starting in the thirteenth century, Jewish publications were widely suppressed in the Holy Roman Empire starting in the sixteenth century, and both Jews and European governments widely banned and destroyed Hasidic books, particularly from the late eighteenth century to the middle of the nineteenth century (Jews did not persecute heresy until the seventeenth century). In the nineteenth and twentieth centuries, Jewish books, movies, and other works have been widely suppressed, especially in Nazi Germany, Imperial and Stalinist Russia, and Muslim nations. In modern times, Buddhists have been persecuted only in Cambodia and Laos, while Hindus have suffered primarily from sometimes violent clashes with Muslims in India; both Buddhists and Hindus practice obvious self-censorship and in modern times have little record of censoring others.

In the twentieth century, advertisements also have been rejected (censored) by media companies because they would either violate government policies or offend religious consumers. For instance, a poster for the film *The People vs. Larry Flynt* was not used in France, Ireland, and certain parts of the United States because it pictured a Christ-like man in a U.S.-flag-patterned loincloth against a woman's bikini-clad abdomen.

Finally, censorship has often been practiced by the paranoid, the unqualified, and the unethical careerist—resulting in censors "seeing" something offensive that a work's creator did not intend and that few (if any) others would spot. American comic book publishers in the 1950s were not only forced to reflect mainstream political and cultural values, but were also coerced by Cold Warriors to add Batwoman, Kathy Kane, and the dog Ace into the stories of Batman and Robin, in order to limit speculation that the dynamic duo was a gay couple. Overtly homosexual content in media has been censored for religious reasons throughout modern history and worldwide until only recently—and in many countries it still is.

DANE S. CLAUSSEN

See also Free Speech; Media Activism; Puritanism

Further Reading

Bald, M. (1998). *Literature suppressed on religious grounds.* New York: Facts on File.
Carmilly-Weinberger, M. (1997). *Censorship and freedom of expression in Jewish history.* New York: Sepher-Hermon Press.
Collins, R. K. L. & Skover, D. M. (2002). *The trials of Lenny Bruce: The fall and rise of an American icon.* Naperville, IL: Sourcebooks MediaFusion.
Foerstel, H. N. (2002). *Banned in the U.S.A.: A reference guide to book censorship in schools and public libraries, revised and expanded edition.* Westport, CT: Greenwood Press.
Green, J., & Karolides N. J. (2005). *The encyclopedia of censorship, revised edition.* New York: Facts On File.
Heins, M. (1993). *Sex, sin, and blasphemy: A guide to America's censorship wars.* New York: New Press.
Heins, M. (2002). *Not in front of the children: "Indecency," censorship, and the innocence of youth.* New York: Hill and Wang.
Jones, D. (Ed.). (2001). *Censorship: A world encyclopedia.* Chicago: Fitzroy Dearborn Publishers.
Mostyn, T. (2002). *Censorship in Islamic societies.* London: Saqi.
Nelson, J. (1974). *Captive voices: The report of the commission of inquiry into high school journalism.* New York: Schocken Books.
Rasmussen, R. K. (Ed.). (1997). *Censorship (Vol. 1–3).* Pasadena, CA: Salem Press.

Chanting

Chanting is a type of sung speech that is used to quiet the mind and body or to aid in memorization. The book-focused religions of Christianity, Judaism, and Islam include chanting as part of worship, but the practice is more heavily used in animistic and Eastern religions, especially Buddhism.

Chanting is the repetitive use of names, words, and syllables, including nonsensical ones. However, employing the name of a god or gods is almost universally considered to make the strongest chants. Chanting is typically done in accompaniment to drumming, hand clapping, rattling, and other musical noises that are believed to enhance emotional excitation. When chanting is used in meditation, it is frequently accompanied by the use of rosary beads. Material learned by chanting is cognitively processed as songs and are recalled in the same easy manner. For this reason, chanting is preferred by many religions as the best method for rote memorization.

Early Uses

Chanting may have been one of the first types of religious communication. Prehistoric peoples relied upon shamans to mediate between the visible and spirit worlds. Shamans, who could be male or female, chanted to enter a mystical state. The first record of chanting for religious purposes comes from ancient Greece, where women shamans howled chants in an effort to use strong vibrations to increase their magical powers. Neo-pagans and Wiccans continue this ancient tradition by chanting names of deities. The objective of these chants is to achieve an altered state of consciousness and create psychic energy. Like the ancient pagans, modern-day pagans occasionally use chants for magical purposes.

Native American Chanting

Contemporary religions that rely upon shamans, such as Native American belief systems, use chanting for the same purposes as the ancients. Chants are an integral part of such activities and ceremonies as healing, hunting, battles, controlling weather, rites of initiation, and funerals. The Navajos put great emphasis on curative chants, which are interwoven with myths telling how supernatural beings first performed the chants. The chanters must chant the prescribed texts correctly, in the original manner, or else they will be stricken with the disease that the chant was to nullify. Navajo chants can continue for many days. If a chanter of great esteem makes no mistakes but fails to cure the diseased person or persons, then witchcraft is usually blamed.

Use by Eastern Religions

Buddhism, reflecting its ancient roots, has incorporated chanting into everyday religious practice more so than modern religions. Worshippers may sit on the floor barefoot while facing an image of Buddha and chanting. They will listen to monks chanting from religious texts, perhaps accompanied by instruments, and take part in prayers. Buddhists typically repeat the word *Om*, which represents the Buddha. To Buddhists, chanting is the expression of the harmony of the community within the community. The sound is more important than any intellectual meaning because sound unites voices from many mouths, thereby joining the community in one voice. Chanting is as much speech as it is an encouragement to listen closely to other Buddhists.

Followers of Islam also use chanting, typically as a method of learning the Qur'an or as a way to become infused with religious spirit. Followers of Islam chant the ninety-nine names of Allah, called "the Beautiful Names." Sufis or Rifa'im, a fraternity of Muslim mystics from Egypt, Syria, and Turkey who are commonly known as Howling or Whirling Dervishes in the West, chant as a main technique for approaching *melboos*, a mystical state of ecstasy. Using rhythmical timing, they chant "Al-lab" until each of the participants begins to chant the name of Allah. This ritual prayer, known as *dhikr*, is followed with a frantic dance, during which the Sufis howl in a unison rhythm while using hot implements to engage in self-mortification.

Hindus also employ the practice of chanting. According to the Vedic scriptures, the chanting of the name of the Lord is the one way to increase spiritual progress in the Kali Yuga age of quarrel and hypocrisy that began five thousand years ago and that is supposed to continue for thousands of years into the future. Evangelical Hindus, commonly known as Hare Krishnas, believe that chanting will awaken the soul. To supplant the material consciousness with an awareness of God, they believe that a person needs only to prayerfully and frequently chant the name of Krishna. Devotees perform sixteen rounds of *sankirtana* (the chanting of "Hare Krishna") on a 108-bead rosary that is given to each member upon initiation.

Chanting in the West

The most familiar Christian chant is the Gregorian chant. The traditional music of the Catholic Church, it has its roots in the medieval Frankish kingdom of Charlemagne. This plainsong repertory is known as "Old Roman," and it is believed to be related to the Roman tradition from which cantors in the Frankish kingdom learned the Roman chant. This "Old Roman" version continued to be used in Rome for some centuries before being replaced by the "Frankish-Roman" or "Gregorian" version. The Frankish chant is thought to have received the name "Gregorian" after Pope Gregory, in order to give it greater authority and to ease its reception in the Frankish Kingdom. In Gregorian chants, the individual note and the individual word are of little importance. Only the whole sentence with its cadence makes a musical unit.

Protestants have also developed plainsong chants. Like the Protestant Church, Protestant chant has its roots in Rome. Over the long period of its development from the fifteenth century, Anglican chant changed from the Latin rite into its present form. The Evangelical wing of the Church of England supported congregational chanting as part of a program to encourage a greater congregational role in a liturgy made more accessible, both technically and musically, to the ordinary layperson. Many of the Episcopal chants are now sung by trained choirs, who harmonize several texts of the liturgy in four vocal parts with or without organ accompaniment.

Chanting is universally revered as a method of religious communication. It encourages devotion by bringing people closer to one another and to their god or gods of choice.

CARYN E. NEUMANN

See also Music

Further Reading

Gade, A. M. (2004). *Perfection makes practice: Learning, emotion, and the recited Qur'an in Indonesia.* Honolulu: University of Hawai'i Press.

The Gregorian Association. Retrieved December 22, 2004, from http://www.beaufort.demon.co.uk/chant.htm#Latin

Kelly, C. (2003). *Gregorian chant intonations and the role of rhetoric.* Lewiston, NY: The Edwin Mellen Press.

Staal, J. F. (1961). *Nambudir Veda recitation.* The Hague, Netherlands: Mouton de Gruyter.

Strauss, C. (1984). Beyond "formal" and "informal" education: Uses of psychoanalytic theory in anthropological research. *Ethos, 2*(3), 195–222.

Wilson, R. M. (1996). *Anglican chant and chanting in England, Scotland, and America 1660 to 1820.* Oxford, UK: Clarendon Press.

Charisma

Charisma is a key element in establishing the credibility of a communicator/leader, particularly in an intercultural setting. Charisma as an element in the communication/leadership process occurs when a leader's extraordinary claim is present to remedy a distressful situation and when responsibility for resolving that stress situation is accepted by the communicator/leader. When people believe that a person has special gifts or power to lead them out of a crisis, the potential for charismatic leadership is present.

Seminal Research on Charisma by Max Weber

During the mid-twentieth century the work of Max Weber provided the seminal research on the concept of charisma that remains valid to the present. Weber described the effectiveness of a leader/communicator not in terms of rules, traditions, or position, but from the extraordinary characteristics of an individual person. Weber defined charisma as:

> a certain quality of an individual personality by virtue of which he is considered extraordinary and treated as endowed with supernatural, superhuman or at least specifically exceptional powers or qualities. These are such as not accessible to the ordinary person, but are regarded as of divine origin or as exemplary and on the basis of them the individual concerned is treated as a leader.... What alone is important is how the individual is actually regarded by those subject to charismatic authority by his followers or disciples. (Weber 1947, 358–359)

Weber's view of charisma, as present in the dynamics of leadership and communication, was contrasted with rational and traditional authority. *Rational* authority was viewed as impersonal formalized bodies of rules found in bureaucratic organizations and *traditional* authority was viewed as legitimized leadership through established custom found primarily in feudal and preindustrial traditions.

Weber believed that the legitimacy of charisma was based on two major conditions: (1) There would be a need, aspiration, or goal among followers that remained unfulfilled by an existing social order; and (2) there would be a leader to whom followers would submit based on their belief in his or her possession of qualities that fulfilled their expectations. Simply stated, charisma emerges most vividly when people in crisis want a leader.

Weber affirmed that the rise of bureaucracies moved people in society away from personal freedom and creativity toward an ever-increasing depersonalization and routinization. So the foundation of the charismatic leader/communicator was to oppose the status quo and process of routinization. Communicator/leaders who exhibit a vibrant expression of charisma do not gain prominence through influence from institutional position or traditional authority. They are highly regarded by followers and therein lies the foundation for their effectiveness.

Charisma as It Functions in Social Structures

Charisma that emerges within any social structure will exemplify some generally predictable expressions. Usually, there is very little delegation of power and authority by a leader to the followers in the organization. Followers are directly accountable to leaders and this absolute type of relationship means that leaders who function with a high level of charisma hold complete control over the allocation of positions and responsibilities of followers in the social structure. Because charismatic leaders emerge when there is dissatisfaction with the status quo, the resulting organization under the influence of the charismatic leader has few formal rules and procedures. All judgments are made by the charismatic leader on a case-by-case basis as proclaimed in decrees that carry authority that is not to be questioned. As long as the followers continue to believe and support the leader's charisma, the whole of the structure can be changed by the decree of the leader. But, in reality, charismatic leadership can be a temporary and unstable phenomenon, always contingent upon the leader's ability to prove his or her charismatic powers to followers. The continued effectiveness of charismatic leadership in any social structure also assumes certain attitudes in those leaders. For example, there is usually an expression of extreme self-confidence, high expectation for followers, a strong need for power and a deep conviction in the validity of the personal beliefs held. Usually the themes of loyalty and "facing the enemy" provide a symbiosis of motivation between the leader and followers.

Charisma: More than a Function of Context?

The degree to which charisma may be at work in a social structure may be determined by considering some of the following indicators:

- The followers' trust in the correctness of the leader's beliefs

- The similarity between the followers' beliefs and those of the leader

- The unquestioning acceptance of the leader by the followers

- The followers' personal affection for the leader

- The willing obedience to the leader by the followers

- The emotional involvement of the followers in the mission of the organization

- The heightened performance goals of followers due to the influence of the leader

- The continuing belief by the followers that they are able to contribute to the success of the group's mission

Leaders who exhibit high levels of charisma frequently have a strong need for power. Self-confidence and strong convictions by the leader of an organization usually result in the followers' trust in that leader being increasingly strong. The continued credibility of a leader who exhibits strong charisma is predicated on a strong impression by followers that the leader is competent and successful.

The continued effectiveness of the charismatic leader also necessitates the articulation of ideological goals related to the mission of the group or organization being led. Inspiring enthusiasm and raising hopes and engendering vision in the followers are crucial to the maintenance of effectiveness in leaders who rely heavily on charisma. Charismatic leaders in religious contexts often have characteristic styles of rhetoric that brand them as unique. Trademark gestures and even clothing may "brand" a charismatic leader.

The tendency of most charismatic leaders is to act in accordance with the motives supportive to the group's mission. This serves to set an example for followers to imitate. Research on the "Pygmalion effect" and "self-fulfilling prophecy" indicates that followers perform better when the leaders model the behaviors and attitudes that the organization values and then commends followers for their imitation of those attributes. These characteristics then comprise an emphasis on being the best, which serves the continued effectiveness of the organization and the continued influence of the charismatic leader.

Charisma and Transformation

Recent research has begun focusing on the overlapping qualities of charisma and transformation as applied to the study of leadership in organizations. While some researchers now tend to use the two terms interchangeably, others have moved to differentiate between the two concepts. The research that is distinguishing between the two concepts inevitably sees transformation as a broader term for long-term influence of people and social structures. Charisma is seen as a necessary ingredient of transformational leadership, but by itself is not adequate to account for the transformation or change process in a social structure or organization. For example, rock stars, movie stars, and professional athletes may have charisma, but may not have a systemic transformational influence on a social structure. Transformation as a quality expressed in leaders of organizations is not just about clear identification between leaders and followers. Transformational leaders usually include a promise of tangible benefits for followers that add value to the ideological elements that are mutually affirmed. Transformation as a dynamic in the discussion of leaders in organizations creates a sense of destiny for all participants in the organization's mission. There is a sense by most participants that "I was made for this purpose or task." Identification with a mission and its complementary provision of positive personal identity for participants is crucial. Such identification is a significant reinforcement to belonging to the organization and potentially strengthens support of the charismatic leader by organizational participants.

Charisma as Applied to Media Influence

The dynamic nature of charisma in social structure takes on unique characteristics when placed in close proximity to mass media. Media have the capability to create awareness of situations in which charisma may be exhibited by those being observed and reported on. News events, sports figures, economic developments, or political realities, when highlighted repeatedly, can create awareness in which charismatic figures are prone to be highlighted. Because media also have the capability to set agendas, the charismatic figures being focused on can become larger than life. Whether they are movie stars, athletes, politicians, or religious leaders the reality is that they are being created in "the eye of the beholder," receiving from media an accelerated exposure and a resulting breadth of influence. The broad exposure of the media can accelerate the image of the "star" such that the influence of the bearer of charisma enhanced by media exposure creates a virtual reality of relationship between leader/star and follower/admirer. When the leader/star and follower/admirer do connect, for example, in a rock concert, music video, or motion picture, the relationship between the two is a function not only of charisma but of the capability of media to accentuate the factor of charisma exponentially. Billy Graham serves as an ex-

ample of a Christian leader whose influence has broadened due to the enhancement of media. In addition, U2's lead singer Bono and his consciousness-raising about the global AIDS crisis is a further example of how the combination of media influence and charisma can facilitate the expression of powerful opinions on significance issues.

The Dark Side of Charisma

The study of great historical leaders will yield both the positive and negative aspects of charisma. Franklin D. Roosevelt led the United States out of a serious financial depression and implemented major social programs that still have influence in American life more than a half century after their start. Yet at the same time the dark side of charisma was reflected in the charismatic leadership of both Adolf Hitler and Josef Stalin.

Power that accompanies the dynamic of charismatic leadership is a two-edged sword. Power's potential for influence can be used to create a significant betterment of a culture or organization. But the temptation of that power can also be used by some leaders who seek to dominate and subjugate followers by keeping them weak and dependent and the position of the leader impenetrable and protected. Religious cult leaders can use rewards and punishments to manipulate and control followers. When information is restricted and decision making is centralized, the dark side of charisma can be displayed. Here is where the dissonance of extreme narcissism in a leader may be accompanied by considerable skill in communicating the "cause" to a needy constituency. Such a combination can be lethal and create the possibility of organizational and personal dysfunction.

Charismatic leaders rise naturally in incipient stages of religious movements for renewal. However, time usually sees the inevitability of organizational maturation. Institutional authority and its accompanying leadership can replace charismatic leadership. Routine and pragmatism stem the continuing free flow of charisma. It is in the inevitable transition from incipient vibrancy to expected legitimacy that the charismatic leader can wander into the dark side of charisma. The natural tendency to want to preserve the advances of the incipient episodes of the religious renewal can yield leaders who protect the center they now represent and defend with fear against loss of identity and purpose. The religious leader, falling prey to the traps for success in public roles, can easily forget to nurture those dimensions of personal life which keep mission and purpose externally rather than internally focused.

Continued Need for Serious Reflection

Charisma is a quality that is doubled-edged and hence requires continual reflection upon its utility and value. If charisma is perceptual on the part of followers, then it is incumbent upon leader and followers alike to critically evaluate credibility that may or may not exist in the relationship. If charisma is contextual and charisma is most obvious in times of crisis, then charisma must rise above politics to the realm of morality and spirituality to have lasting influence that refuses the downward spiral to self-serving leaders and organizations. If charisma is unstable over time then the long-term good of charisma must be understood in terms of character and not skill alone. Research on charisma must move beyond descriptive reports to prescriptive assertion regarding the long-term benefit of charisma in organizations and social structures.

BYRON D. KLAUS

See also Proseletyzing

Further Reading

Avilio, B. L., & Yammarino, F. J. (2002). *Transformational and charismatic leadership.* Burlington, MA: Elsevier Science & Technology Books.

Bass, B. (1987). *Leadership and performance beyond expectations.* New York: Free.

Bates, D. A. (2003). *Executive charisma.* Boston: McGraw-Hill.

Bradley, R. (1987). *Charisma and social structure.* New York: Paragon House.

Conger, J. A. (1989). *The charismatic leader: Behind the mystique of exceptional leadership.* San Francisco: Jossey-Bass.

Conger, J. A., & Kanungo, R. N. (1989). *Charismatic leadership: The elusive factor in organizational effectiveness.* San Francisco: Jossey-Bass.

Conger, J. A., & Kanungo, R. N. (1998). *Charismatic leadership in organizations.* Thousand Oaks, CA: Sage.

Dodd, C. (1998). *Dynamics of intercultural communication* (5th edition). Boston: McGraw-Hill.

McIntosh, G., & Rima, S. (1997). *Overcoming the dark side of leadership: The paradox of personal dysfunction.* Grand Rapids, MI: Baker.

O'Roark, A. M. (2001). *The quest for executive effectiveness: Turning vision inside-out: Charismatic-participatory leadership.* Nevada City, CA: Blue Dolphin.

Weber, M. (1947). *The theory of social and economic organization.* New York: Free.

Weber, M. (1952). *On charisma and institution building.* Chicago: University of Chicago Press.

Willner, A. R. *The spell binders: Charismatic political leadership.* New Haven, CT: Yale University Press.

Winter, D. G. (1973). *The Power Motive.* New York: Free.

Yukl, G. (1984). *Leadership in organizations.* Englewood Cliffs, NJ: Prentice Hall.

Choirs

A choir is a community that uses its voices to sing texts, both religious and secular, with the hope of edifying not only themselves but those who are listening. The synergy of personalities in harmony can be a spiritual experience, even when the music and the words are secular in nature.

Description

There is much more to a choir than the physics of acoustics and harmonics multiplied by however many sopranos, altos, tenors, or basses there are. (Some choirs have no human voices at all: American Sign Language choirs, brass choirs, and hand-bell choirs.) Choirs can sing either with instruments (orchestra, organ, or piano) or a cappella. As a choir sings, it does so both in time (melodies) and space (chords), reflecting not only the music of the spheres but also a portion of the divinity that exists in every human mind. Voices vary in their timbre, pitch, and quality, from "shimmering light to molten velvet," as soprano Jessye Norman once put it. If the German writer Goethe is correct when he calls architecture "solidified music," then choirs represent ethereal cathedrals; together, the singers create an aural edifice out of their spiritual, mental, and emotional experiences.

Origins

Music was most likely the first human language—and the human voice was probably the first instrument—with as simple a beginning as children imitating the songs of birds or coyotes, the whistling of the wind, the bellowing of a whale, the spitting or roaring of a fire, or the cascading of water down a swiftly-moving mountain stream. Sounds, and therefore music, lie at the very foundations of our existence on this planet. Music has a life all its own, as if it were a living being or a natural phenomenon descending from the music

The Tabernacle at Temple Square, Salt Lake, Utah. *Courtesy of Sathish V. J./ istockphoto.com.*

of the spheres (or from the speech of angels and atoms—the laws of perfect music—according to Philo of Alexandria).

Groups of people eventually joined together more formally (in "choirs") to give harmonic voice to joy, sorrow, contemplation, and praise—sometimes in protest (like black Americans singing "We Shall Overcome"), but seldom in anger and hostility (unless it be Krzysztof Penderecki's "Auschwitz Oratorio"). According to Johann Sebastian Bach, "True music is music that pursues as its ultimate end or final goal the honor of God and the recreation of the soul."

Development

Ancient humans sang in unison and in parallel fourths and fifths, their voices high-pitched with throaty tones. Forest dwellers, because of the complexity of their culture, reflected the myriad noises in the forest by singing polyphonic music. Desert inhabitants typically used but one instrument (or voice) and performed monophonic music because of the sparseness of natural sounds. Mountain people reflected the peaks and valleys of their surroundings by singing in rich bass tones and high frequencies, made easier by the atmospheric pressure on the inner ear and voice. Children learned about their forebears through songs and tribal chants.

Music handed down from one generation to another preserved ancient religions.

In Sumerian temples music was sung for mountain deities or personifications of heavenly bodies, while in Egypt music was considered an important science of divine origin and was studied by priests. The association of music with worship among the ancient Hebrews is mentioned in countless Old Testament passages—the Hebrew word *ruach* means not only the divine spirit of the Creator hovering over the newly created earth, but also the breath of God. Greek philosophers Aristotle and Lucretius believed that music grew out of the human desire to imitate sounds in nature.

Music and religion were divinely intertwined in ancient Greece, and Orpheus is still an important figure in both religion *and* music in Greece. An essential feature of dramatic performances was the chorus (Greek *choro*) that commented on the action, as in Sophocles' *Oedipus Rex* or *The Clouds* by Aristophanes. Bards, minnesingers, and troubadours continued to play this dramatic role throughout the Middle Ages. It sometime happened that secular music became religious, as with the German drinking song "O Sacred Head Now Wounded," which is still known in hymnbooks and congregations throughout Christendom.

Through the work of Hildegard von Bingen, Palestrina, Monteverdi, and Bach, soul-affecting music continued to be composed. Choral music became an effective way to preach the Christian Gospel and as an outlet for the oppressed. African-American spirituals and folk songs expressed temporary joys and the awareness of love despite hardship. Sometimes called "the lighter side of divinity," these spirituals were a major milestone in the development of many aspects of choral music. And it was not only religious people who recognized the power of music. Before the iron curtain fell, a communist functionary was heard to say that "Handel, Bach, and Beethoven ... will surely be played and loved even after nobody on earth believes in God anymore. A true materialist can certainly hear a good concert of classical music in a church without losing his materialist virginity."

Importance

Praising and glorifying deity is the reason why even those who cannot carry a tune often want to sing in a church choir. But while worshiping may be the primary reward of singing in a choir, there are other pleasures as well:

- Providing comfort to those who are mourning

- Improving your musical talents and sharing them

- Disciplining and training your moral values

- Instilling a harmonious balance in souls that have become out of kilter

- Changing your body's metabolism, muscular energy, blood pressure, and digestion

- Sharing a sense of enjoyment and well-being with others

The nineteenth-century German philosopher Arthur Schopenhauer described a composer as someone "who reveals the inner nature of the world, and expresses the deepest wisdom in a language which his reason does not understand" (1909, 336).

Examples

Throughout the world, souls are being uplifted by African-American spirituals, Hungarian gypsy music, Polynesian and Hawaiian singing, Zen Buddhist chanting, the haunting tones of the muezzin from mosques, shamanic drumming, the calm sublimity of Gregorian chant, and the enthusiasm of a Bach cantata or a Wesley anthem. In Hungary, folk music education through the use of choirs is thriving, partly the result of efforts by composers Zoltan Kodály and Bela Bartok. Numerous choral organizations are proliferating throughout the world: the Vienna and Texas boys choirs, the Israel Kibbutz Chorus, the Bach Collegium of Japan, the Mormon Tabernacle Choir, the Eisteddfod (Wales) choral festivals, and the Berliner Singakademie.

In the twenty-first century people sing not only in cathedrals, concert halls, and churches, but spontaneously. Humans everywhere are discovering their unique voice and "becoming one with it as we blend with other songs, rhythms, and instruments in the eternal symphony of life" (Campbell 1997, 219).

Achievement

For centuries choirs have influenced, inspired, and enriched the life and soul of mankind. As one observer eloquently put it:

> Music is the audible manifestation of the well-regulated soul. By living our lives as balanced and directed toward God as are the melodies and concords of music, we produce the "Musica Humana," the music of humanity, which in turn is an echo of that "Musica Mundana," the music of the spheres, which was the force of creation, the moving word of God that made order of chaos, and lit the heavens when the morning stars sang together. Heard music is the spirit audible. (Sartin 1965, 11)

As we strive for unity in a world of dissonance, the importance of choral singing cannot be overestimated. Working together to become one voice, a chorus enables listeners to be caught up in the transcendent beauty of the music and its accompanying spirit, rather than in the individual voices. These are enlightened and highly civilized aims, both of true religion and of true communication.

Gary Gillum

Further Reading

Campbell, D. (1997). *The Mozart effect: Tapping the power of music to heal the body, strengthen the mind, and unlock the creative spirit.* New York: Avon Books.

Mendl, R. W. S. (1957). *The divine quest in music.* London: Salisbury Square.

Norman, J. (2003, June). Music that changed my life. *BBC Music Magazine.*

Nuechterlein, L. G. (1963). *The church choir: The form of a servant.* Minneapolis, MN: Augsburg Publishing House.

Portnoy, J. (1963). *Music in the life of man.* New York: Holt, Rinehart and Winston.

Roustit, A. (1975). *Prophecy in music*. Paris: Albert Roustit.

Sartin, N. E. (1965). *Toward a musician's theology*. N. P. Response VII.

Schopenhauer, A. (1909). *The world as will and idea*. London: Routledge and Kegan Paul.

Smith, J. G., & Young, P. M. (1980). Chorus. In S. Sadie (Ed.), *The new grove dictionary of music and musicians* (pp. 341–357). London: Macmillan.

Wolff, C. (2000). *Johann Sebastian Bach: The learned musician*. New York. Norton.

Clock

What is time, asked St. Augustine. He rightly considered this to be one of the great religious questions. He did not provide a complete answer—but then, neither has anyone else. Whatever time is, clocks measure, control, and constitute it for the modern world. Clocks, like calendars, organize time—the day and the year, respectively. Both devices have rich religious and communicative implications. They are logistical media, at once modes of representation *and* instruments of intervention. They model the periodic cycles of the cosmos and provide human societies means to coordinate collective action. The clock mimics the diurnal rotation of the earth as the calendar models the earth's annual orbit around the sun—neither with complete precision. Clocks and calendars model the heavens and earth and, even in a secular world, thus fulfill the classic religious function of providing a meaningful orientation to the universe. Timekeeping devices are so fundamental that we sometimes overlook them as communications media.

The clock is relatively recent among historical timekeeping devices. The hourglass, for instance, is ancient: Long used at sea, it lives on in board games. Clepsydrae (water-clocks) were in use in Egypt and Babylon by 1600 BCE. These devices are containers with holes that, when filled with water, take a set time to drain. The sundial is also ancient, but it traces a longer time span (all daylight) than either the hourglass or the clepsydra and has direct legacies for the clock. One is clockwise rotation: In the northern hemisphere, the shadow on a sundial moves from west to north to east, and this motion was retained for the hands on mechanical clocks. Another is the dial itself: From the Latin word *dies* (day), a dial is a readout divided into twelve hours, a division of the day that started in ancient Egypt around 2100 BCE. (An even remoter legacy may be the twelve-fold touchtone telephone dial today.) It has long

been customary to adorn sundials with lapidary mottos such as *ultima multis* (the last day for many) or *lente hora, celeriter anni* (slowly the hour, quickly the years), so they have an association with melancholy reflection about the fleetingness of time. All timekeeping devices implicate questions of time and eternity.

The word *clock* derives from the Latin *cloca* and is related to the French *cloche* and the German *glocke*, all of which mean *bell*, and the clock as we know it first emerged in late medieval clock towers. Bells started to be used throughout Europe in the twelfth century, and as large mechanical clocks developed around the fourteenth century, they took their place in church towers, creating a communications center at the heart of many towns. Bells were not mere timekeepers; they were among the central media of religious and civic communication in late medieval and early modern Europe. Bells alerted townspeople to holidays and religious services; announced births, weddings, and deaths; sounded alarms; and served in an intangible way to mark the bounds of a community. Bells were located in either church steeples or municipally owned towers, and a truism in the history of timekeeping is that whoever sets the time controls the society. Bells in late medieval and modern Europe were controlled largely by the church. (Today, in contrast, most timekeeping is in the hands of governments, or to be more precise, the military, as in the U.S. Naval Observatory, which sets the official time in the United States.)

To be sure, bells are a specifically Christian institution, and Longfellow's phrase "the belfries of all Christendom" has sound comparative religious footing. The Muslim rulers of the Ottoman empire prohibited the ringing of church bells in conquered areas, for instance, properly recognizing the great communicative and mobilizing force these media can hold for Christians. Judaism also has no tradition of bell-ringing for religious or chronometric purposes (horns are used for ushering in the new year). Bells continue their symbolic hold on modern timekeeping; the BBC, for instance, long used the chimes of Big Ben to mark the hours on its radio programming.

The modern clock is distinct from previous timekeepers in that it has both a counter and a periodic motion or oscillator. Clocks are data processors. Unlike a metronome, which has a regular beat but says nothing cumulative, clocks interpret the time. The clock is one of the most essential media in the modern world. As clocks have grown smaller and more personal, they have become ubiquitous on wrists, telephones, computers, cars, and ovens, among many other devices. Though the transition from the medieval bell to the modern wrist watch was a loss of an explicit ceremonial function for timekeeping, clocks remain the grid on which our world operates. The clock, argued Lewis Mumford, was the key technological invention of industrial society, much more than the steam engine. The clock is a power machine whose achievement is not principally in tracking minutes and hours but in coordinating the actions of people. The clock, unlike the sundial, ticks away regardless of sun or cloud, human want or need. Instead of the old pattern, in which the twelve hours of the day vary in length depending on the season, the clock institutes a new abstract order of equal hours (whence our saying "o'clock" to indicate use of clock time rather than astronomical time).

The historical process by which timekeeping shifted its focus from the natural world to a more abstract system of mathematical constants has continued in the twentieth century. For thousands of years, astronomers set the time. In the mid-twentieth century timekeeping duties shifted to physicists, completing the long slow abstraction of time from the natural cycles, anchoring time instead in the oscillations of cesium atoms. What the French Revolution began with weights and measures—the creation of a universal invariant standard—science eventually achieved for time. A universal measure of mass and length (the gram and the meter) was more or less settled by 1800; one for the second had to wait until the 1950s.

The clock's origins in Europe were largely religious: the need of monks to observe (in both senses) the canonical hours of prayer. In eleventh century China, in contrast, where horology was much more advanced than in Europe and the first mechanical (water-powered) clocks were developed, the main context for timekeeping was political. The emperor's power was bound up with his declaration of holidays and calendars since he was supposed to operate in tune with nature according to the "mandate of heaven." For debated historical reasons, advancements in Chinese clock technology soon reached a standstill, and Europe became the world leader in clock technology from the late thirteenth century onward.

In modern times, the clock's chief motive is economic, as in Ben Franklin's saying, "Time is money." Critics of industrial capitalism ranging from Karl Marx to Charlie Chaplin have found in the clock's strict time-discipline a cruel distortion of human existence. Deists in the eighteenth century found in the clock's indifferent but constant mechanism a model for the regular cycles of the universe itself: God had wound it up in the beginning and now was letting it run down without further supervision. The minute hand, which started to be used in the sixteenth century, only became practical after Huygens perfected the pendulum in 1656, and the second hand followed soon by the end of the seventeenth century. It is difficult for most modern men and women to imagine life without a minute or second hand. In Olympic sports, hundredths of seconds are routinely used for scoring performances, and much scientific investigation would be impossible without increasingly fine subdivisions of time (for all units less than seconds the decimal system of base 10 replaces the sexagesimal system of base 60). All units of time from milliseconds down to attoseconds (10 to the minus 18th power of a second) and beyond are now being colonized by science.

The clock also played an important role in integrating the modern world spatially. Standard time is a necessity of global transportation and communication. The synchronization of remote clocks answered the problem of calculating the longitude: British clockmaker John Harrison, by creating a clock so accurate that one could know the time in England even on a ship in the middle of the Atlantic, made it possible to reckon one's precise location on an east-west axis. "Minutes" and "seconds," of course, are not only intervals of time but angular measurements and thus measurements of distances on the surface of the earth. In navigation, aided by trigonometry, the clock observes the earth's place in the universe and one's place on the earth. The need for a common time between distant places first emerged at sea.

On land, prior to the railroad and telegraph, every town set its time typically by the shortest shadow (noon). It did not matter if Dover, Brighton, Portsmouth, Plymouth, and Penzance, for instance, stretching from east to west along the southern coast of England, each had a successively later noon hour. By the mid-nineteenth century, the crazy quilt of local times in industrializing countries was causing serious problems in railroad traffic, and diverse nation-states sought to synchronize to a single clock. England is an instructive example. At the Greenwich Observatory in 1833, a leather ball was first dropped down a pole at 1:00 p.m. to serve as a visual signal to ships on the River Thames to set their watches by Greenwich mean time (GMT). GMT was first distributed by telegraph in England in 1852, and by the late 1850s, the country was covered with a network of time balls, cannons, bells, and needles to spread the news of when exactly 1:00 p.m. was (though GMT did not become the official national time until 1880). By 1848 Dickens had already observed the drift away from natural sources of time-keeping: "There was even railway time observed in clocks, as if the sun itself had given in." In 1924 the

BBC started its six-pip signal on the hour, followed in 1936 by a speaking clock service, and radio and television programming remain intensely gridded into time schedules today.

Internationally, the current grid of time zones, centered on Greenwich, was determined in 1884, though wrinkles and local exceptions remain (China, a country with a huge east-west spread, has a single time zone; Iran, Afghanistan, and India start on the half hour, and Nepal on the three-quarter hour, etc.). International standard time is a sine qua non for global communication and coordination today, and the Swiss clock company Swatch has even proposed a new integrated system of Internet time that dispenses with time zones and uses a base 10 system (at this point it seems more a marketing ploy than a viable system; the new meridian passes, with suspicious convenience, through Swatch headquarters in Switzerland).

An earlier, and more profound, examination of standard time took place in Switzerland. In 1905, a young patent clerk named Albert Einstein discovered his principle of special relativity while pondering a problem that daily crossed his desk as he examined proposals for telegraphically coordinated time: How can remote clocks be synchronized? Taking this question farther than anyone before, Einstein asked, in essence, if such a thing as standard time is possible on a cosmic scale. Noting the finite speed of light, he concluded that there can be no universal clock, a revolutionary insight whose consequences range from quantum mechanics to cosmology, art to theology. Time, as Augustine noted, may seem obvious until you ask what it is, and it has always been at the center of both religious inquiries into ultimate things and communicative efforts to design media that manage people's everyday lives.

JOHN DURHAM PETERS

Further Reading

Carey, J. W. (1989). Technology and ideology: The case of the telegraph. In *Communication as Culture* (pp. 201–230). Boston: Unwin Hyman.

Corbin, A. (1998). *Village bells*. New York: Columbia University Press.

Dohrn-van Rossum, G. (1996). *History of the hour*. Chicago: University of Chicago Press.

Galison, P. (2003). *Einstein's clocks, Poincaré's maps*. New York: Norton.

Howse, D. (1980). *Greenwich time*. London: Oxford.

Jones, T. (2000). *Splitting the second: The story of atomic time*. Bristol: Institute of Physics.

Landes, D. (2000). *Revolution in time: Clocks and the making of the modern world*. Cambridge, MA: Harvard University Press.

Mumford, L. (1962). *Technics and civilization*. New York: Harcourt, Brace, Jovanovich.

Peters, J. D. (2003). Space, time, and communication theory. *Canadian Journal of Communication, 28*, 397–411.

Sobel, D. (1995). *Longitude*. New York: Walker.

Thompson, E. P. (1967). Time, work-discipline, and industrial capitalism. *Past and Present, 38*, 56–97.

Commemoration

Commemoration preserves a culture's shared memories and provides specific times, places, and rituals that will evoke events or individuals from the past with a view to shaping group identity in the present. The word itself derives from a Latin verb (*commemorare*) meaning "to remember together," and commemoration does indeed function as a complex interplay between individual memories and historical moments that a culture understands as being formative or pivotal. Commemoration is a form of communication that unites people in the present and links them across generations through the use of various communicative strategies. Just as different people recollect public events with a variety of reactions and emphases, so too do different religions and cultures find themselves frequently in conflict over the significance of a shared object of commemoration. Even though commemoration serves to maintain group identity across generations, it also can become a locus of social anxiety and a catalyst for change.

Two Forms

Religious commemoration takes two primary forms, one consisting of sacred places and objects and the other being the repetition of history or myth in rituals. The locations of events deemed significant to a culture often become sacralized, although there was no initial expectation or understanding that such a transformation would occur. On the other hand, many objects such as statues and monuments are expressly created for the purpose of stimulating commemoration, particularly those associated with funerary or nationalistic contexts. Memory can also be triggered through the contemplation of portable commemorative tokens such as reliquaries, coins, texts, and images. Such objects are often collected and arranged for viewing at public

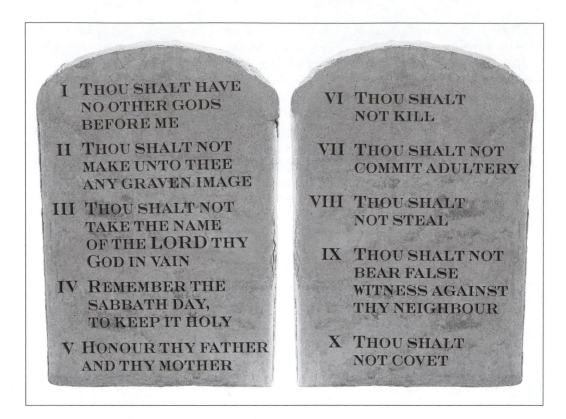

The Ten Command-
ments from the
King James Version
of the Bible.
*Courtesy of
istockphotot.com.*

forums such as museums, libraries, and churches, where their presentations are carefully crafted so as to present a particular image of the past, another culture, or one's own.

The selection of particular commemorative events is very revealing of a culture's self-identity; but the origins of these choices often get obscured over time, making them appear central or essential to the culture and stripping them of any sense of being contingent or accidental. Commemoration of certain political events can constitute an expression of civil religion or a symbolic system that governs national identity in much the same way that religion regulates and promulgates the relationship of the human and the divine. Most nations choose to remember their official founding, as well as the birthdays of select leaders and the winning of various wars and skirmishes. Events generally thought to be indicative of national character are frequently chosen to be commemorated over others that ultimately have more historical import. While American schoolchildren are taught to envision the colorful spectacle of Bostonians tossing tea into the sea, other cultural markers such as the Louisiana Purchase are overlooked.

Civic religion creates a pantheon of secular heroes collectively revered and holidays collectively celebrated. It also can serve to mediate the continuing presence of certain traumatic or infamous events such as

wars or genocides. Commemoration serves to mend cultural rifts by creating a shared legacy in the wake of divisive events. Civil War battlefields or the Vietnam War Memorial exemplify this particular function of commemoration. Some commemorative sites are deliberately created with the intention of preventing future atrocities by publicly memorializing past ones. The preservation of Holocaust death camps, the creation of museums that recount particular genocides such as those of Native Americans or Cambodians, and the evocations of the atrocities of slavery all serve this function.

Rituals

Collective memory is also implicated, preserved, and produced through the use of temporally ordered rituals. Unlike rituals that focus on the individual in the stages of his or her life (birth, puberty, and marriage), commemorative ritual focuses instead on those moments that are understood to be of equal importance to all participants. There are repetitions of primary religious events such as the weekly celebration of the Last Supper at Christian services or annual rituals such as Passover or Independence Day. Rituals generally function to provide a form of commemoration grounded in the reenactment of the past in a highly symbolic and controlled manner. The re-creation of the past effectively serves to collapse time so that believers in the present may participate in foundational religious or cultural events. The presence of important people or historical moments is thereby experienced directly and not merely contemplated.

Ways of Reenacting the Past

The degree to which these reenactments are mediated varies greatly. In some cases, cultures experience direct encounters with the past through visitations by spirits, ancestors, or demons; a common manifestation of this may be seen in religious possession by the gods or the dead. The untimely dead and violently killed are almost universally feared, as can be seen in such disparate geographies as ancient Greece and contemporary Sri Lanka. Both cultures fear the reanimation of the dead in the form of vengeful ghosts and believe that malevolent necromancers can summon up such souls for nefarious purposes.

In other cases, the past is brought into the present less concretely by deploying culturally specific symbols that evoke a common memory. For example, the Jewish seder, a meal that commemorates the Israelites' escape from Egyptian slavery, uses various foods to underscore participation in this event. In the course of retelling the story, believers experience the past through the consumption of the same foods at the same junctures as the protagonists.

Monuments

In many cultures there is an alliance between grand architectural programs and the memory and glory of gods and kings. The great Egyptian pyramids were originally commissioned by pharaohs and today still stand as monuments to the grandeur of what many consider to be the pinnacle of ancient civilization. The pyramids remain the largest stone structures ever constructed, and while the particular commemorative intent of the pharaohs is still disputed among scholars, they commemorate for the world the whole of Egyptian culture and not merely the reputation of the individual rulers. The creation of such massive and immovable monuments as the pyramids, the Sphinx, and the temples of Karnak and Luxor permanently sacralize the geography and effectively merge national and religious histories in a single memory landscape.

Whereas many sacred landscapes are found in nature, and thought to be alive with the presence of gods and ancestors, manmade monuments represent a self-conscious attempt to create sacredness and to commu-

nicate that fact across great distances. As important as commemoration can be for the lasting reputation of an individual, its denial can constitute a dire social punishment, as meted out in such practices as the ancient Roman *damnatio memoriae* in which a name was stricken from the public record and all associated images were defaced.

Gain in Significance through Time

Monuments can gain commemorative significance through time, coming to represent the ethos of an entire culture and not the more limited and practical purpose intended by the original builders. The famous Colosseum in Rome began life as an amphitheater created specifically by the emperors of the Flavian dynasty. Over the centuries, it became one of the most instantly recognizable symbols of the Roman Empire and the bloody spectacle of gladiatorial combat. The Eiffel Tower has undergone a similar metamorphosis for modern France in that it was initially constructed for a world's fair but now represents Paris the world over.

Contested Geography

In some instances, monumental structures can become contested spaces that signify radically different meanings for different religions or groups. The Temple Mount in Jerusalem is perhaps the most famous case, with the remains of the Jewish temple serving as the Wailing Wall for the Jewish population and the top of the mount, containing al Aqsa mosque and the Dome of the Rock, being sacred to the Muslim population. This holy geography has been the cause of legislation, war, and ongoing security concerns in terms of who has access to which part of the shared sacred site and what dangers that division might present to the surrounding area. Religious conflict over the interpretation of sacred geography is an intractable problem, as is evident, for instance, throughout all of Israel and also on the subcontinent, where Hindus and Muslims coexist with varying degrees of religious tension.

Effect of Colonial Hegemony

In cases of colonial hegemony, where one culture appears to have co-opted or destroyed the monuments of the indigenous peoples, those buildings or geographies can continue to be commemorative of the indigenous past, but this is often done in secret. For instance, the Spanish Catholics of the sixteenth century built churches and shrines on top of sites that were already sacred to the native population, but there is ample evidence that the native peoples continued to find the new churches to be commemorative of their own primary gods and goddesses.

Use of Deception

Deception and disguise in commemorative monuments have characterized those in power as well as those on the margins of a society. In second-century Rome, the emperor Trajan may well have perpetrated a deception on his own people by disguising his own future funerary monument as a massive column ostensibly commemorating his military victories. In a probable attempt to liken himself to the great leaders of the past such as Julius Caesar, Trajan appears to have arranged for himself to be buried within the city walls. Since the honor of being thus buried was no longer a current practice and even frowned upon, Trajan used the public commemoration of his victories as a way to conceal his own desire for this type of burial. In this case, an individual seems aware of the transformative capabilities of commemorative monuments and expects the focus of memory to shift rapidly and incontrovertibly from a victorious nation to a glorious ruler.

Commemorating the Dead

Commemoration also functions on community and domestic levels in the nearly universal practice of commemorating the dead. Funerary practices range from the building of massive necropolises and mausoleums to individual tombstones and statuary. The evocation of the memory of the dead serves simultaneously to assure deceased relatives of their family's continued concern and appreciation and to assure the living relatives that the dead are pleased by their efforts.

The dead are frequently credited with great powers that can be harnessed for prophetic or vengeful purposes, and the propitiation of the dead is in large part determined by proper burial and commemoration. In many cultures, the living do not merely observe the departure of the dead but also help them on their way to the next existence. Both the Tibetan and Egyptian Books of the Dead are famous exempla of death as an ongoing process wherein the living are expected to guide the dead on their journey. The death of the body is thus a distinct matter from the death of the individual that can happen over the space of months or even years. The interaction between the living and the dead maintains kinship ties and reinforces for both parties that they remain connected.

In cases where proper burial is impossible due to the destruction or loss of the body, empty funerary monuments (cenotaphs) are used in many cultures as substitutes for graves. In an analogous practice, tombs to unknown soldiers stand in for all those lost in war by posing the possibility that the particular anonymous body could be that of any of the missing and serve for all of them at the same time. As a form of intensified remembering, commemoration thus embodies a paradox in that while seeming to honor the passing of a person, its production of memory effectively ensures that the dead will remain alive in the minds of the living. In "remembering together," the family and the community bring the past into the present by keeping memories of the dead alive.

The Future

In the recent past, the body of scholarship on memory and mnemonic practices has been a burgeoning intellectual field. The importance and cultivation of individual memory in the West from antiquity through the Renaissance has been ably demonstrated, and its centrality to these cultures has been acknowledged. Simultaneously, the academic exploration of funerary practices has long been a subject of study for anthropologists and cultural historians alike. The place of commemoration as a social and collective activity, while beginning to be examined, is still relatively unexplored. The manipulation of multiple interpretations of public memory and the social ramifications for competing memory claims will constitute an important strand of future scholarship. Choosing to cherish certain memories as collective ones both mirrors and changes the culture that creates them.

ERIC S. CASEY

Further Reading

Carruthers, M. (1990). *The book of memory: A study of memory in medieval culture.* Cambridge, UK: Cambridge University Press.

Casey, E. (2000). *Remembering: A phenomenological study.* Bloomington: Indiana University Press.

Chambert-Loir, H., & Reid, A. (Eds.). (2002). *The potent dead: Ancestors, saints, and heroes in contemporary Indonesia.* Honolulu: Allen & Unwin and University of Hawai'i Press.

Davies, P. J. E. (2004). *Death and the emperor: Roman imperial funerary monuments from Augustus to Marcus Aurelius.* Austin: University of Texas Press.

Garland, R. (2001). *The Greek way of death.* Ithaca, NY: Cornell University Press.

Geary, P. J. (1996). *Phantoms of remembrance: Memory and oblivion at the end of the first millennium*. Princeton, NJ: Princeton University Press.

Hallam, E., & Hockey, J. (2001). *Death, memory, and material culture*. New York: Berg Press.

Johnston, S. I. (1999). *Restless dead: Encounters between the living and dead in ancient Greece*. Princeton, NJ: Princeton University Press.

Kuchler, S., & Melion, W. (1991). *Images of memory: On remembering and representation*. Washington, DC: Smithsonian Institution Press.

Matsuda, M. K. (1996). *The memory of the modern*. New York: Oxford University Press.

Mendels, D. (2004). *Memory in Jewish, pagan and Christian societies of the Graeco-Roman world*. New York: T&T Clark International.

Parry, J. K., & Ryan, A. S. (Eds.). (1995). *A cross-cultural look at death, dying, and religion*. Chicago: Nelson-Hall Publishers.

Schwarcz, V. (1998). *Bridge across broken time: Chinese and Jewish cultural memory*. New Haven, CT: Yale University Press.

Wilson, L. (Ed.). (2003). *The living and the dead: Social dimensions of death in South Asian religions*. Albany: State University of New York Press.

Communication

It is obvious that religion has always had a lot to do with communication. What would the religions of the world be without the voice, the word, the text, and all their associated arts? Religious practice and thought have always employed a great variety of communicative practices. Something less often noted is that communication also has much to do with religion, at least in the development of the concept. Communication is a concept notoriously difficult to define, and the widespread consensus that it is one of the chief problems of the modern world has done little to clarify exactly what we mean by it. (The confusion in defining it is an ironic comment on the ideal that communication is often held to represent: indisputable and clear meaning.) The term suggests a jumble of ideas and aspirations about topics as diverse as marriage and mass media, teaching and telephones, computers and communities. This article explores five main conceptions of communication, each of them owing something to religious sources: (1) telepathy, (2) the bridging of space and time, (3) dialogue, (4) dissemination, and (5) ritual.

Telepathy

Probably the most common conception sees communication as the sending and receiving of information. Here communication is measured in terms of the success of transmitting messages. The word *communication* first came to be used for this practice in the nineteenth century with the rise of the electrical telegraph and the other means of distant signaling that followed in its wake, such as the telephone, radio, television, and Internet. Prior to the nineteenth century, *communication* referred to intangible physical processes such as heat, gravity, and magnetism that seemed to work at a distance, and electrical telecommunications followed directly in this tradition. Following on the heels of the telegraph and the telephone, a new concept was coined in 1882: *telepathy*, meaning the transference of thoughts from one person to another without any visible connection. Popular ideas about communication today sound similar: communication means sharing thoughts and feelings without any interference of language, body, space or time. If the criterion of effective communication is the transmission of meaning without noise or distortion, then telepathy represents the culmination of this vision. Dreams of perfect communication have a long religious history. Thomas Aquinas, to take one key example, argued that angels have bodies that are transparent signs, bearing a readily intelligible and unmistakable freight of meaning. St. Thomas considered angelic communication to be a normative model of interaction—one we embodied, language-using humans could never attain. The pathos of this conception— the longing for a transparent and mutual unveiling of souls versus the reality of language and embodiment— continues to haunt thinking about communication today. The dream of communication as telepathic or obstacle-free communion breeds its opposite, the nightmare of breakdown and blockage.

Bridging of Space and Time

A second, related, conception also grows out of the practice of sending messages at a distance. Whereas telepathy focuses on the perfection of reception, the bridging of space and time conceives of communication in a less desperate way. Its interest is more in the possibilities of connection than the actualities of delivery, though life, death, and profit can sometimes hang on successful transmission. As long as humans have lived in complex societies, there has been a need for the carriage of messages over distance. The Chinese, Inca, Roman, and Persian empires, for instance, all had elaborate postal systems (the latter was immortalized in Herodotus's words that are still used as the motto of the U.S. Postal Service). People who carry news by letter or word of mouth have always helped foster distant social connection, whether they are official messengers or freelance travelers. (Our word *angel* descends from the Greek word *angelos*, meaning messenger.) Fast communication across distance has always been crucial for strategic—i.e., military and economic—interests. The Rothschild family's banking empire in early nineteenth-century Europe rested on a communication network of couriers and carrier pigeons that allowed them to get critical financial news faster than their rivals. Napoleon likewise took advantage of the optical telegraph—which used line-of-sight semaphore signals—in his military adventures of the same period. (By midcentury both systems were made obsolete by the electrical telegraph.) The history of warfare and trade is largely the history of the arts and techniques of communication at a distance. Today much of our everyday world of communication—cellular phone, personal computer, transistor radio, television—owes its development to military techniques and technologies.

Fast communication over space usually gets the lion's share of theoretical and popular attention, but equally important is slow communication over time. Transmission can occur across time as well as across space: "cultural transmission" means the passing of values down the generations. Societies need continuity and preservation as much as coordination and extension. Monuments, libraries, museums, and cemeteries are institutions that connect people across time. Religious institutions have exploited the spatial aspect of communication (most notably in missionary work and outreach media of various sorts) as well as the temporal (in Scripture, tradition, codified rules of conduct). Writing is of course humankind's chief form of transcending (or preserving) time, supplemented in the past two centuries by new forms of inscription such as photography and sound-recording. When one reads the Hebrew Bible, New Testament, or Qur'an, for instance, one receives a message sent, as it were, thousands of years ago. The overcoming of space and time are, in sum, the chief features of this second conception of communication.

Dialogue

The third conception, communication as dialogue, has roots in Plato. This view has some similarity to telepathy in its focus on the dyad and its fierce longing for ideal union, and indeed, Plato's distant influence can be found in medieval thought about angelic communication. But dialogue focuses on the dynamic process of interaction rather than telepathy's instant matching of thoughts. Plato's dialogic literary method suggests not just a way to present an unfolding philosophical argument, but something deeper: the progress of the soul toward truth, or more precisely, the coordination of two souls as they mutually progress toward truth. As Socrates argues in the *Phaedrus*, the best kind of rhetoric involves a knowledge of both the truth and the soul of the receiver, and an artful composition. This conclusion follows naturally from Socrates' belief that philosophical lovers may see in each other's beauty reminders of their heavenly origins and the truth they once knew. Ever since Plato, dialogue has served as one of the chief visions of communication: two participants, on an intimate and equal footing, who together pursue truth, love, and enlightenment. (Note that the "dia" in *dialogue* means *through* rather than *two*.) The fortunes of dialogue as a model of communication have waxed and waned, reaching two high points in the Renaissance Italian court and the French Enlightenment salon. The twentieth century was also such a high point. Business people, marriage partners, therapists, consultants, and political negotiators all extolled the virtues of dialogue. Such twentieth-century thinkers as Martin Buber and Hans-Georg Gadamer found in dialogue the recipe for an ethical human existence, as did Jürgen Habermas, though in a different key. Theologians, as well, found in dialogue or conversation an ennobling and undistorted model of religious discovery.

Dissemination

Our fourth conception, dissemination, is equally venerable and sharply opposed to dialogue. In the *Phaedrus*, Socrates repeatedly attacks forms of communication that are indifferent or open-ended to their audiences. Rhetoric, he says, can mistake the soul of the listener, and writing thoughts down is like a foolish farmer who scatters seeds abroad without regard for the soil in which they land. An apparent endorsement of just such agricultural folly is found in the New Testament parable of the sower, who casts seeds with apparent abandon anywhere—on the road and on stony, thorny, and good soil. Jesus concludes his narration of this parable with the gnomic imperative: let those who have ears to hear hear! The parable is thus recursive: the story of the sower is also the story of its telling. Those who hear the parable are left to wonder what kind of soil they are made of. Socrates seems to have preferred spreading his doctrine one-on-one to his intimate associates, while the Gospels typically portray Jesus as addressing great multitudes. His teaching was democratically open-ended in its offering and availability (even if the Gospels emphasize that both the multitudes and disciples had trouble understanding the fullness of his doctrine). In dissemination, we have a harbinger of what would come to be called broadcasting. Inside of Broadcasting House, the headquarters of the British Broadcasting Company since 1932, there is a statue of *The Sower*. The BBC, which has been the world leader in broadcasting for nearly a century, thus links its commitment to public service broadcasting directly to the New Testament idea of a free and generous offering available to everyone. Though advocates of dialogue may distrust a vision of communication that seems to lack interaction and intimacy, there is something powerful in broadcast forms of communication, whether they are found in radio and television, newspapers and books, or sermons and sculpture. Most of the material of human culture is not interactive. One Christian minister impressed with the powers of radio in its early years proclaimed that "God is always broadcasting," and diverse religious thinkers have found in mass communication a modern version of older religious ideas (such as the Christian Gospel or *euangelion*—literally *good news* in the original Greek). Religious preachers the world over find in satellites and cassette tapes divinely given vessels for their disseminations.

Typically, dissemination is understood as one sender and many receivers. There is, however, no good reason why there cannot be many disseminators and few recipients. Centralized message-senders such as broadcasters, advertisers, politicians, or evangelists are not the only disseminators. In cases such as strikes, protests, petitions, or elections many senders address a few; as in all dissemination, uncertainty of the reception remains open. In various liturgies, the members of the assembly are figured quite precisely as "communicants," i.e., senders of messages and not only recipients. In twentieth-century American communication research, mass communication (like broadcasting, a latter-day version of dissemination) was always viewed as central transmission and mass reception. Yet mass communication can also flow bottom-up: there can be mass disseminators as well as audiences. The concept of dissemination need not only favor people in power.

Ritual

The fifth and final conception of communication, ritual, dispenses with, or fully transforms, the notion of message. All four other conceptions see communication as the delivery of some kind of informational content in some sense, though there are important differences among their focus on other minds, conduits of contact, discovery of truth, or dispersion of seeds. Ritual is rich in meaning and poor in message. One typically learns nothing new at a circumcision, baptism, graduation, religious ceremony, or wedding. Indeed, the last thing one wants at a wedding is new information. A detailed answer to a greeting such as "how are you" would be a breach of decorum. And yet greetings do not lack meaning. Anyone who has been snubbed by a former friend or lover knows that not to be acknowledged feels like a kind of social death; one is excommunicated from the status of even being worthy to receive messages. Meaning is clearly more than the movement of messages. What Ezra Pound called literature—the news that stays news—could be said of ritual in general, religious and communicative. Communication can define our orientation to the universe, other people, and ourselves before it gives us any specific data. Here the religious sources are clear. The *logos* (word made flesh) that is central to the Gospel of John is not just a semantic meaning; it is a disclosure of the moral order of things. All religious traditions have ideas of communication that transcend the sharing of ideas. Though all religious institutions make use of all five conceptions of communication, and all five have religious roots, this last one shows most profoundly the inseparability of our ideas about religion and communication.

JOHN DURHAM PETERS

See also Organizational Communication; Political Communication; Profane Communication; Sacred Communication; Satellite Communication

Further Reading

Aquinas, S. T. (1952). *Summa Theologica*. Chicago: Encyclopedia Britannica.

Burke, P. (1993). *The art of conversation*. Ithaca, NY: Cornell University Press.

Carey, J. W. (1989). *Communication as culture: Essays on media and society*. Boston: Unwin Hyman.

Cooley, C. H. (1909). *Social organization: A study of the larger mind*. New York: Macmillan.

Innis, H. A. (1991). *The bias of communication*. Toronto, Canada: University of Toronto Press.

Percy, W. (1961). The symbolic structure of interpersonal process. *Psychiatry 24*, 39–52.

Peters, J. D. (1999). *Speaking into the air: A history of the idea of communication*. Chicago: University of Chicago Press.

Plato. (1995). *Phaedrus* (A. Nehamas & P. Woodruff, Trans.). Indianapolis, IN: Hackett Publishing.

Rothenbuhler, E. W. (1998). *Ritual communication: From everyday conversation to mediated ceremony.* Newbury Park, CA: Sage.

Scannell, P. (1996). *Radio, television, and modern life: A phenomenological approach.* Oxford, UK: Blackwell.

Simonson, P. D. (2003). Assembly, rhetoric, and widespread community: Mass communication in Paul of Tarsus. *Journal of Media and Religion 2,* 165–182.

Confession

Confession is a public or private affirmation of belief in ideas or doctrines considered to be essential to a particular faith system.

Meaning of the Word

To confess describes the making of a public statement of ratification or agreement. English *confess* derives from Latin *confiteri,* often also used to connote the idea of admitting or conceding a particular point of view. Early Greek sources employ the word *homologein,* the literal meaning of which is "to say the same thing," that is, to affirm one's agreement with a statement or proposition. Such an affirmation may apply to the context of law and the courts, to personal relationships, or to a central religious faith. In the Greek Bible, which includes the Old and New Testaments of Christianity, the word connotes the idea of agreeing with God about His holiness and about the sinfulness or absence of holiness in oneself. Thus one says about God and oneself the same thing that God says about Himself and the worshipper.

In the Hebrew Scriptures, several words are translated into English as *confess.* The most common, *lehodot,* is derived from a root that carries the base idea of praise. The implication is that appropriate praise of God necessarily implies acceptance of His holiness and goodness alongside one's own sinfulness. In postbiblical Judaism, the word *lehodot* acquired the sense of acknowledgement of guilt before God with such sincerity that God is moved to forgive the offending behavior, whether individual or corporate.

Other words used by biblical writers include *zakah,* "to remember," that is, to bring into present consciousness a deed of God from the historical memory of the Israelite community; *sapar,* "to tell, or retell;" and *lehagid,* "to make known" in public.

Islam extends the Jewish and Christian concepts of confession from the central idea of agreement with or praise of God by placing great emphasis upon the idea of bearing witness, of testifying to the basic truths of Islamic faith and praxis, often outside the faith community to a non-Islamic world. This idea is carried in the Qur'an by the *Shahadah* (Arabic root *shahadu*).

Personal or Private Confession

Personal or private confession centers around the idea of seeking forgiveness from both God and human beings who have been offended by actions deemed inappropriate (sin), that were committed by an individual religious believer. This link between confession and forgiveness (or atonement) is common to many religious traditions. In Judaism, personal confession is considered a private matter between an individual and God (Psalm 32:5). Within Catholicism, the practice of making personal confession to a priest is the result of a process lasting almost two centuries, beginning with required public admission of guilt, developing into the practice of "confession" between one Catholic and one priest in private; as the church observed that one individual making public notable details about his or her own sin could serve simultaneously to embarrass others who might have been involved, it recognized the need to limit public confessions.

Among Protestants, personal confession of sin in a public venue continued to find support among those who believed that only public declarations adequately fulfilled the New Testament prescription expressed by Paul (Romans 10:9) and Luke (12:8) and exemplified by leaders like Peter, Stephen, and Thomas. In this Protestant practice, the public avowal of belief and the private expression of regret about one's personal sins merge, but Protestantism also encouraged the confession of "faults" to other members of the believing community, to be accompanied by mutual prayer for one another (James 5:16).

In Islam, formal confession is limited to one formal creed only, the *Shahadah* (cited at the end of the previous section). Of the five major "Pillars of Islam," of which recitation of the *Shahadah* is the first, four reflect the Islamic concern with conduct or behavior in daily life rather than with any kind of confession. These include daily prayer, donation to charitable causes, fasting, and a pilgrimage to Mecca at least once in a lifetime. In addition to the *Shahadah,* the opening Surah (chapter) to the Qur'an, recited at least five times each day, functions for the Muslim much as the shema does for the Jew. In it are found ideas considered fundamen-

Selection from the Augsburg Confession (1530)

Article I: Of God

Our Churches, with common consent, do teach that the decree of the Council of Nicaea concerning the Unity of the Divine Essence and concerning the Three Persons, is true and to be believed without any doubting; that is to say, there is one Divine Essence which is called and which is God: eternal, without body, without parts, of infinite power, wisdom, and goodness, the Maker and Preserver of all things, visible and invisible; and yet there are three Persons, of the same essence and power, who also are coeternal, the Father the Son, and the Holy Ghost. And the term "person" they use as the Fathers have used it, to signify, not a part or quality in another, but that which subsists of itself.

They condemn all heresies which have sprung up against this article, as the Manichaeans, who assumed two principles, one Good and the other Evil—also the Valentinians, Arians, Eunomians, Mohammedans, and all such. They condemn also the Samosatenes, old and new, who, contending that there is but one Person, sophistically and impiously argue that the Word and the Holy Ghost are not distinct Persons, but that "Word" signifies a spoken word, and "Spirit" signifies motion created in things.

---

tal for the Muslim, including the mercy and compassion of Allah, the oneness of God, the duty of all Muslims to worship and serve God alone, and even an expression anticipating the great Day of Judgment, at which time the justice of Allah will become manifest and all people will receive their just reward or punishment. Notice should also be made of the statement recorded in the Qur'an 2:136:

> Say, We believe in Allah and that which is revealed unto us and that which was revealed unto Abraham, and Ishmael, and Isaac, and Jacob, and the tribes, and that which Moses and Jesus received, and that which the Prophets received from their Lord. We make no distinction between any of them, and unto Him we have surrendered.

Public or Communal Confession

Public confession is a religious exercise practiced by adherents of virtually all major faith traditions. Confession may be made via different means, and specific customs vary widely, but common themes include (a) the desire of the person making the public confession to identify with the basic themes of a particular religious group, (b) the desire to exclude those who cannot or will not make an appropriate utterance of confession, and (c) the need to reinforce central beliefs on a regular basis by including confession in the liturgy of public worship. The importance of public confession

to the three monotheistic faiths of Judaism, Christianity, and Islam may be seen in the wording of the summary statements demanded by each faith of its adherents.

The only confession in Judaism that enjoys virtual unanimity among all Jews is the shema, found in the biblical Book of Deuteronomy 6:4: "Listen [Heb: shema'], Israel. YHWH is our deity. YHWH is One." The shema is recited several times daily, both in private and in the synagogue, and pious Jews hope to be able to make its words their final utterance before death.

One of the most important developments within Judaism of the first Christian century was the addition of a carefully worded statement inserted into the primary prayer recited in the synagogues, the 'amidah, recited three times daily, as well as on Shabbat and holiday services. It contains eighteen benedictions recited by a congregation to express gratitude to God, to ask for wisdom, to pray for healing, and to anticipate the return of Jewish exiles to Jerusalem. In response to the efforts of Jewish Christians to use the synagogue as a platform from which to preach their doctrine of the divinity of Jesus, a special addition to the 'amidah was made. Known as the birkat ha-minim, "benediction concerning heretics," this statement invokes divine wrath on "slanderers" and asks God to "uproot, smash, cast down, and humble wanton sinners."

The birkat ha-minim originated during the Seleucid oppression of the second century BCE and was directed against those Jews who collaborated with the enemy. In the following century, the imprecation was directed against the Sadducees, who were quintessential opponents of rabbinic authority. Under Rabban Gamaliel II (first century CE) it was invoked for the first time against the Judeo-Christian and Gnostic sects and other heretics. To avoid any suspicion of heresy, the *hazzan* (prayer leader) had to be certain to recite this prayer in public worship. If he omitted it by error, he had to return and recite it. Furthermore, even a slight error in the recitation of the *birkat ha-minim* required a *hazzan* to correct his mistake. In the words of a prominent second century CE rabbinic authority, "if one passes before the ark and makes a mistake in any of the benedictions, he is not made to repeat it; but in the benediction concerning the sectarians he must be made to repeat it [even] against his will. The reason that he must repeat it is that, if he has in him any element of heresy, he will be cursing himself" (*Tanhuma de Rabbi Nathan*, cited in Elbogen 1993, 30).

It should be noted that errors were made often by a congregational leader reciting prayers during a service and they were accepted as inevitable and forgivable. Prayer was not stopped for such errors, nor attention drawn to them except in the case of the *birkat ha-minim*. For this one, the entire congregation paid close attention, to make certain that no word in the prayer was omitted or altered. Since its purpose was to make heretics uncomfortable, "a Jewish Christian could not recite this prayer if he did not want to curse himself and to make the congregation join in by saying 'amen'" (Elbogen 1993, 33). In other words, a Jewish Christian could neither serve as a prayer leader nor stand in silence in the congregation. He had to say "amen," or be revealed. The use of the *birkat ha-minim* is the background of the saying in John 9:22: "The Jews had already agreed that if any one should confess him [Jesus] to be the messiah, he should be put out of the synagogue."

As the citation from John indicates, Jewish Christians were stung by this use of the *birkat ha-minim*, feeling that they were being excommunicated. The Rabbis knew well how Paul and his followers had used the synagogue in missionary efforts and were determined to force Jewish Christians to reveal their identity before being allowed to speak publicly in a service of Jewish worship. Although they did not compose the *birkat ha-minim* to be used against Christians originally, they did revive its use in an effort to combat these Pauline methods.

Later Judaism attests thirteen principles of faith enunciated by the twelfth century scholar, Maimonides, each of which opens with the phrase, "I believe with complete faith." Intended to form an integral part of Shabbat worship, these thirteen principles range from belief in the oneness of God (monotheism) to belief in the coming of a messiah, and speak also about Mosaic literature, by which is meant the Hebrew Scriptures in general and the Pentateuch in particular. Because Judaism lacks a central authority, many Jews have resisted one or more of the thirteen principles believed by Maimonides to be basic to Jewish faith, and modern Reform prayer books omit the thirteen from their order of worship. Early Christians created specific statements of belief to be avowed in public as a symbol of one's conversion to and continued acceptance of the doctrines of the new faith. The most important of these was the second-century Apostles' Creed, which begins with an affirmation of one's acceptance of a trinitarian deity and continues to express other important beliefs held by Christians about the church itself—sin, salvation, and so on. The opening statement of this confession specifically excluded Jewish worshipers by placing Jesus and the Holy Spirit alongside God Himself as beings to be worshipped.

The Protestant Reformation of the sixteenth century witnessed a renewed interest in public confessions of faith that would distinguish their members from Catholic Christians. Among the most important of these were the Augsburg Confession in 1530 and the Westminster Confession of 1647. These public avowals of faith served both as models for conversion candidates and as a test of faithfulness among the membership. In particular, these Protestant confessions contained statements designed to separate Protestant beliefs from Catholic ones. These included carefully worded definitions of the role of the Church and the function and extent of canonical Scripture, as well as lines of demarcation defining the role of the clergy and the meaning of important sacraments used in Christian worship.

The first of the "Pillars of Islam," the short confession of belief, the *Shahadah*, is considered essential to the process by which one becomes and remains a Muslim: "I bear witness that there is no deity except Allah, and that Muhammad is His messenger."

Confession in Eastern Religions

The concepts of confession discussed with reference to Judaism, Christianity, and Islam are largely lacking in the two great eastern religions, Buddhism and Hinduism, neither of which adopts the view of monotheism that stands at the center of the Abrahamic faiths. In

Buddhism, emphasis falls on the need to find unity with all of creation and personal enlightenment, a task best accomplished by moderation and "calm detachment through which the wise person avoids the extremes of asceticism and self-indulgence" (Nigosian 1990, 300).

Hinduism, again absent a belief in monotheism, remains deeply involved in personal development through various stages of life, seeking to find ritual purification that makes one fit for the task of achieving mature development in each phase of life. The concept of confession or avowal of a prescribed set of beliefs, or even a private admittance of breaching one of those beliefs (sin), is foreign to the basis of Hindu religion and praxis.

Future Directions

It is certain that the specific expressions of faith discussed above will continue to be recited regularly in the worship of synagogues, churches and mosques. There is little disagreement among scholars about the viability of these statements, and their antiquity ensures their continuing prominence. As new or splinter groups are formed, one of the first decisions each will make will center on which classical expression best exemplifies the core beliefs of the group. Doubtless, the shema, the Apostles' Creed, the Westminster Confession, and the *Shahadah* will hold center place within most if not all such groups.

CHARLES DAVID ISBELL

See also Catholicism

Further Reading

Elbogen, I. (1993). *Jewish liturgy: A comprehensive history*. New York: Jewish Theological Seminary of America.

Esposito, J. L. (1999). *The Oxford history of Islam*. Oxford, UK: Oxford University Press.

Farah, C. E. (1994). *Islam* (5th ed.). New York: Barron Press.

Frend, W. H. C. (1984). *The rise of Christianity*. Philadelphia: Fortress Press.

Michel, A. (1967). Homologein. In *Theological dictionary of the New Testament* (Vol. V, pp. 199–220). Grand Rapids, MI: Eerdmans.

Nigosian, S. A. (1990). *World faiths*. New York: St. Martin's Press.

Schaff, P. (1984). *Creeds of Christendom*. Grand Rapids, MI: Baker Book House.

Scherman, N. (1984). *The complete art scroll Siddur*. New York: Mesorah Publications.

Wood, A. S. (1979). Creeds and confessions. In *International standard Bible encyclopedia* (Vol. I, pp. 805–812). Grand Rapids, MI: Eerdmans.

Confucianism

Kung Fu Tze, known to the West by his Latinized name, Confucius, was an exemplary teacher and sage of ancient China and its greatest communicator. The amazing vitality of his teachings and memory spread with China's ancient tributary relations to Singapore, Taiwan, Japan, Korea, and Vietnam. Today, the Confucian style of communication continues to influence East Asian communities around the world. Although the Confucian way of life is integrated variously into local societies and cultures in relation to different historical, economic, and geographical factors, it nevertheless provides an ideal model for family, state, and social structure. Confucius's temples can be found in East Asian communities everywhere. Confucius is undoubtedly one of the most prominent historical figures emerging out of China's long history.

Life of Confucius

Confucius was born at a time when China was threatened with disintegration, known in Chinese annals as the Spring and Autumn period (*Ch'un Ch'iu*), from 722 to 481 BCE. The golden age of the Zhou dynasty had fallen apart, and conflict and disruption had set in, threatening the rule of the emperor. Feudal princes, inspired by greed and the lust for power, were warring on each other, in contradiction to ancient codes of how to behave honorably. Corruption was rife, and massacres and bloodshed were rampant throughout the land. In the province of Lu, where Confucius was born in 551 BCE, the reigning duke was harassed by dissension, and lesser members of his house threatened to take over his royal power. It is likely that living in this time of great upheaval, Confucius understood the importance of order in both personal and political arenas where people communicate with one another.

Traditional accounts of Confucius's life relate that he was born of the illustrious Kung family, which could trace its roots back eighteen centuries, to its prehistoric founder Hwang-Ti. In the days of the grandfather of Confucius, political turmoil forced the family to leave their homes and settle in Lu, where the father of

Confucius, Kung Shu Liang-Hih was born. Confucius's father became famous as a military officer who exhibited strength and courage under fire. During the siege of Pihyang in 562 BCE, a group of his men were about to be trapped by a dropping gate that he caught and raised, enabling all of them to escape. Notwithstanding his many feats, he had nine daughters but no son to carry on his family name. At 70 years old, Shu Liang Hih approached the royal house of Yen and asked to marry one of his three daughters. Yen's two eldest daughters refused to marry such an old man, while the youngest, Chiangste, turned to him and said: "Merely designate your wish, father." Thus, Yen gave his youngest daughter to the warrior. She is remembered by Confucian families today as an example of filial piety. Feeling the pressure of responsibility to produce a son, Chiangste climbed the sacred Mount Ni and prayed for a son from heaven.

Legend has it that auspicious omens accompanied the birth of Chiangste's illustrious son, who was said to have been born in a cave in Mount Ni. Two dragons are believed to have appeared in the heavens, together with five sages, at the time of his birth. Music is said to have floated through the atmosphere when his mother went into labor. Upon the body of her son were forty-nine marks, signifying his unique destiny, and his head was shaped like Mount Ni. While there are many variations of the legend of the birth of Confucius, all report that he grew up in humble circumstances. Despite poverty, however, Confucius's mother persisted in her efforts to give her son the best possible education.

Confucius's father died when Confucius was only three years old, entrusting him to the care of his mother. It is said that his favorite childhood games were imitating ceremonial rites, which are fertile expressions of religious and cultural traditions. His passion for knowledge and public oration absorbed him, and at fifteen he became an assistant teacher. At seventeen, apparently, in need of material means, he sought employment to help to support his mother. He obtained a local position as a director of agricultural works, and it is said that the harvest was bountiful and the cattle thrived under his watch. At nineteen, he married the daughter of a noble Sung family and the couple had a son and two daughters. By the time his son was born, Confucius already had established his reputation, for the Prince of Lu sent him a symbolic gift of a carp. Confucius, aware of propriety, named his son Carp (Li). Thereafter, there is scant information in the historical record about his family.

Early Work of Confucius

Confucius's mother died when he was twenty-four years old, and in accordance with the profound significance attached to mourning for the dead, Confucius removed himself from public life for three years. He meditated and studied ancient ceremonial and political texts. Emerging from his reclusive retreat, he began his public speaking career. Throughout his life, Confucius humbly insisted that he was not an original thinker. Rather, he was a great synthesizer. He honed and developed his precepts from the literary and historical record left behind by ancient scholars. He believed that his scholarly pursuits were mandated by heaven. Heaven from the ancient Chinese perspective can be likened to a creative life-giving spirit that is immanent everywhere in nature and the human world. Like his predecessors, Confucius was a keen observer of nature and he believed in the sacredness of all natural life. Accordingly, the sage considered that his destiny was to lead men and women back to a love of their fellows. He thought that they could best serve heaven by serving each other. In a period when anarchy threatened to disrupt the nation, Confucius imparted to his students the ideals of justice and order that typified the ancient Shang and Yu kingdoms, which can be traced back in the archaeological record to the twenty-fourth century BCE.

Confucius thought it was important to put scholarly ideas into practice for the long-term benefit of society. Therefore, he traveled for most of his life, in search of a high political position that would enable him to use his great oratory skills for the service of humanity. He wanted to make life comfortable for everyone. Confucius yearned to implement the ancient philosophical principles, ethical doctrines, and political economy into the prevailing structures of government.

In 517 BCE, the political factions that threatened to disrupt the kingdom of Lu broke out into utter chaos and anarchy. Realizing the futility of remaining in his native province, Confucius traveled to the neighboring kingdom of Chou. He hoped that the local prince would offer him a government post so that he could communicate and implement his ideas more effectively in the public domain. However, the ruler only offered him a pension. Perhaps the prince thought that if Confucius were given real oratory power and authority, he would expose the already corrupt government. Refusing the pension, Confucius devoted the next fifteen years of his life to teaching and research. His ability to communicate abstract and cross-disciplinary ideas in a way that ordinary people can understand is remarkable. He is reputed to have studied philosophy with Loa Tze, music under Chang Hung and Su Hsiang, and politics under Tang Tau. Although it is not likely that Confucius was mentored by these heroic masters, it points to the reverence that Chinese people have for his thorough and well-rounded education.

Communication Style of Confucius

From the perspective of modern times, it is difficult to imagine that Confucius considered his first responsibility to be a great orator. However, during his lifetime, no one could even dream of becoming a civil servant or governmental official without also being an accomplished poet. This is because all formal communication between the emperor and his people took place through the form of flowery sayings and musical ballads. Ancient emperors listened to the heartbeat and pulse of the nation through the poetry and songs of its people. As stated in the *Book of Rites*, "Each five years, the Son of Heaven makes progress through the kingdom and the Grand Music Master is commanded to lay before him the poems of different states." These poems were carefully studied by royal scholars, for through them, in the absence of a press, the condition and well-being of each province was measured. Ancient Chinese rulers were well aware that the singing of poems provided a stress-releasing outlet for the people.

Poetry was also integral to the performance of religious and governmental ceremonies. No ceremonial ritual was complete without the recitation and singing of poetry. The cultivated man was knowledgeable in poetry. Confucius wrote in the *Analects*, "A man may be expected to act well in government service after he has mastered 300 lyrical poems." It is said that Confucius, eclectically, collected over 3,000 poems, out of which he selected and used only about 310. These poems covered diverse subjects from tributes to heaven or the emperor to love poems and poems about the beauty of nature.

Works of Confucius

The *Analects of Confucius* is one of the most reliable works on his life. It is a concise collection of Confucius's public speaking engagements, written by his disciples. It is said that Confucius wrote *Spring and Autumn* and edited the *Book of Poetry or Songs*, the *Book of Rites*, the *Book of Records*, and the *Book of Changes*. Later, during the Song dynasty (960–1279),

scholars brought together the *Analects*, the *Mencius*, the *Ta Hsueh* (Great Learning) written by Tseng Shen, a disciple of Confucius, and the *Chung Yang* (Doctrine of the Mean) written by Tzu Ssu, the grandson of Confucius. They named this collection the *Four Books*. The *Four Books* together with the *Five Classics* (collected, organized, and edited by Confucius) became the basis for education in China, from 1313 to 1912. They formed the basis for the competitive civil service exams that were mandatory for some 600 years. Even today, the effects of this examination system are visible in the national college-level entrance examinations of Taiwan, Japan, and Korea.

Teachings of Confucius

Master Confucius attracted a large following of students from different social, cultural, and economic circumstances. It is said that the number of his pupils reached 3,000. He refused no seekers his guidance, no matter how humble their origins. He was known to say to his students, "I was born with knowledge. I am the only one who has given himself to the study of antiquity and am diligent in seeking for the understanding of such studies." During his journeys he drew parables based on his personal experiences and observations of real social life that corresponded to the ideals of past scholars about familial and social life. His precepts have been followed for nearly three thousand years.

Confucius based his social teachings on those of the patriarchal Chinese family structure. He thought that the parent-child relationship was the foundation of the hierarchical nature of society. The fundamental loyalty of an individual was to his or her family. Confucius taught that younger generations should respect and obey their elders, women should be subservient to their men, and everyone should be obedient to the emperor, who was a parent figure. Today, Confucianism is still based on five relationships: ruler-subject, father-son, husband-wife, older brother–younger brother, and friend-friend. Except for the last, all of these relationships are based on differences in status and exemplify different power relationships in Confucian societies. However, Confucius also taught that those in superior positions were supposed to look out for the well-being and provision the needs of their subordinates. This ethical principle is one reason the modern nation states of Japan, Korea, Singapore, and Taiwan have taken a collectively oriented course to capitalist development, in sharp contrast to the competitive individualism and fragmented trajectory of Western Europe or the United States.

Confucius and his students traveled mostly on foot across China. They underwent many hardships, including starvation, humiliation, and persecution. Once, an assassin almost murdered Confucius. However, Confucius always showed himself to be an exemplary leader of impeccable moral character. He encouraged his disciples to strive to become superior human beings by living virtuous lives. This ideal was epitomized in the way Confucius communicated with others through his own words and actions.

At the age of sixty-eight, Confucius was invited back to Lu by the sovereign ruler, where he spent the rest of his life editing classical texts and continuing his teaching career. Despite his ardent desire to transmit his political theories into the structures of government, Confucius recognized that legitimate power and authority did not come from a high-sounding official title. When one of his students resented his not being in a public office, Confucius replied, "You remember the Book defines a good son as being ever-dutiful, and a friend of his brothers, thus, giving the example of good rule. This, too, is to rule. What need, then, of office?" In 479 BCE, Confucius died at the age of seventy-two and was buried in his hometown of Chufu.

Finally, Confucius stands as one of the world's greatest orators. He was devoted to teaching the public about ancient Chinese rituals and styles of communication that harkened back to a golden past. His influential ideas continue, today, to shape the way family life and societal life are constructed in East Asia, and beyond.

KATHLEEN NADEAU

See also Daoism

Further Reading

Cleary, T. (1998). *The essential Confucius: the heart of Confucius teachings in authentic I-Ching order.* Edison, NJ: Castle Books.

Confucius. (1979). *The analects.* Penguin Books.

Hawkins, B. (2004). *Asian religions.* New York: Pierson and Longman.

Kupperman, J. (2001). *Classic Asian philosophy, a guide to the essential texts.* Oxford, UK: Oxford University Texts.

Morgan, D. (2001). *The best guide to Eastern philosophy and religion.* New York: Renaissance Books.

Oldstone-Moore, J. (2002). *Confucianism, origins, beliefs, practices, holy texts, sacred places.* Oxford, UK: Oxford University Press.

Congregations

In the most general sense, the term *congregation* refers to a gathering of people. Persons congregate for a variety of events: weddings, baseball games, congressional sessions, soccer matches, festivals and holidays, and so on. While these general forms of assembly may reveal patterns of behavior similar to those often defined by scholars as religious (creed, cultus, community), they do not qualify as congregations in the particular sense of a body of believers or practitioners gathered in common communicative purpose. For example, some scholars of religion in the United States have described "the church of baseball" or have compared shopping malls to cathedrals. Indeed, both the stadium and the mall are ritual sites; however, the repetitive practices contained within are more often pseudo-religious, tied to larger patterns that transcend religious particularity (civil religion), even if they may have their roots in the particular. In contrast to the general and diffuse, religious congregations are localized spaces for gathering and communicating with reference to a divine or superhuman agent or entity, whether singular or plural.

Congregational Forms

Religious participants have been gathering themselves in different organizational forms across traditions as long as they have been practicing. The study of organizational arrangements, however, has historically been (at least in the West) a Jewish and Christian enterprise. The classification systems developed in nineteenth-century French and German sociology, along with accompanying theological advancements, provide the analytical schema upon which more recent congregational studies, both secular and theological, are constructed.

The French sociologist Emile Durkheim (1858–1917) argued that every social institution comes out of the womb of religion. Durkheim, along with Marcel Mauss (1872–1950) and others, tracked the evolution of religion alongside the evolution of society. Both religion and society evolved from the simplistic to the complex, or from the primitive to the modern. In each evolutionary step, however, solidarity was lost or threatened. For Durkheim, religion creates social cohesion and integrates individuals into society. As a principle site of integration, the congregation is a space where individuals are brought into moral community through their ritual participation. Max Weber (1864–1920), the German sociologist famous for *The Protestant Work Ethic and the Spirit of Capitalism,* also emphasized the importance of congregations as sites of moral formation. Weber proposed that ethics of neighborliness, often lost in the rise of modern societies, were recaptured and redistributed through the congregation. Thus, the congregation was a place of ethical maintenance and instruction.

Influence of Increased Diversity

Though they ranged across traditions in their scientific study of religion, both Durkheim and Weber focused on Jewish and Christian models of organized religious life. This narrow focus has continued in the study of religion in America. In the context of the United States, the term congregation has most often been used to describe a Jewish synagogue or a Christian church. Some scholars argue, however, that there is historical precedent for this specificity in the United States, where the Protestant congregational model has become the institutional norm, and religion in America post-1965 has demonstrated organizational convergence despite increased diversity.

For example, though previously present in recognizable numbers, Buddhism, Hinduism, and Islam have seen strong gains in the number of adherents in the United States after 1965—the year quotas were expanded for Asian immigrants. Some scholars, such as Diana Eck, have studied how new migrants are visibly transforming the American religious landscape. Almost every major American city now has a shrine or meditation center, a temple, or a mosque, not to mention the congregational forms of other religious traditions and movements present.

Despite the increase in pluralism and the demographic decline of Protestantism, a new wave of sociologists of religion in America, led by R. Stephen Warner, has observed a pattern of convergence (de facto congregationalism) in which new immigrant groups adopt and adapt organizational models forged in earlier Protestant experiences. In the United States, a Protestant congregational model of voluntary association replaced the parish system of Europe, where church membership was politically and regionally determined. The disestablishment of church and state led to a proliferation of voluntary religious associations. Congregations, particularly Protestant forms, have been the most successful of these associations.

"Americanist Controversy" in Roman Catholicism

The transition from European congregational forms to American forms caused some disruption in the Roman Catholic Church, culminating in the late nineteenth-century Americanist Controversy. Many leaders in the American hierarchy, such as Archbishop John Ireland and Cardinal James Gibbons, wanted to draw Catholics out of ethnic particularity and move them into a common culture that was both Catholic and American. Though somewhat approving at first, the Vatican retreated from this progressive movement, linking modern cultural developments (evolution and higher biblical criticism) with "Americanism." In 1899, the Vatican issued the *Testem Benevolentiae*, directly addressing the threat of Americanism. The Vatican strategy was to maintain orthodoxy through institutional control, opting for ethnic particularity over pan-ethnic American-Catholic movements. In short, the Vatican promoted a parish model in a congregationalist context arguably up until Vatican II (in 1965).

One concomitant outcome of the Vatican's unwillingness to address modernity was the rise of what Mary Ellen O'Donnell and others term "Cultural Catholics," persons who are Catholic by practical immersion over the course of their lives but are skeptical of Vatican authority and the institutional church. These Cultural Catholics test the limits of an observable congregation, as they continue to practice Catholicism outside the walls of the physical church.

Dominance of New England Puritanism

The descriptive currency of the term *congregation* then is strongest in relation to Protestant organizational forms in the United States. Though Catholicism presents another interpretive rubric for religion in America, the dominant narrative model, though not without its critics and revisionists, is still New England Puritanism. From the late sixteenth century on, Congregationalism, a Puritan organizational form, set the standard for later-arriving religious groups. Marcus Hansen, and later Timothy Smith, argued that immigrants adapt organizational models that suit their needs and succeed in America by adopting models that were successful for previous generations. Many scholars, Hansen and Smith included, consider Congregationalism, with its assertion that local congregations can govern themselves without interference from or reliance on an outside hierarchy, the most successful form of religious organization in America.

Even though religious options have increased in America over time, especially after 1965, religious congregations continue to move toward Protestant organizational models. For example, when forming new congregations, immigrant groups adopt organizational strategies of lay leadership and local authority, while acquiring nonprofit status. Paul Numrich has noted that in at least two immigrant Buddhist groups in Los Angeles and Chicago after 1965, new migrant Buddhist leadership oversaw the development of a parallel congregation for converts. In order to attract members, this second congregation was based on a more Americanized model. Though Numrich does not address this point directly, there is evidence that the parallel congregation of converts in turn influenced the migrant congregation, reinforcing Warner and Wittner's (1998) argument of structural convergence. Both congregations meet in the same space and overlap on multiple levels, illustrating the importance of organizational arrangements in the shaping of ritual life and congregational identity. As Joanna Waghorne (1999) put it in her study of a Hindu temple in the suburbs of Washington D.C., "in America all the gods live in the same house."

Congregational Identity

Media have played an important role in the shaping and maintenance of the congregation as a moral community. Congregations often share a body of sacred texts. Though the importance of texts differs with each tradition and movement, a canonical body of literature facilitates a recognizable vocabulary and common discourse. The congregation is a site of both maintenance and innovation of discourse. A textual record may preserve tradition and orthodoxy, as well as dissent; however, the textual account is continually interpreted through the ritual performances at the congregational level. Due to the public nature of texts, sociologists often reference social texts in addition to the printed word. Multiple meanings are inscribed in public performances and are shared in a variety of media. Thus, the identity of a congregation is never static; rather, it is constantly reenacted in ritual performances. Media, as vehicles of performance, are critical to the understanding of congregational identity.

The Eucharist as Medium

The Christian practice of Eucharist is a classic example of the use of media in the shaping of congregational and institutional identity. In his theoretical account of sacrifice, Durkheim argued that the congregation (as a body of believers) consumes ritual sacrifice. In the Eucharist, for example, congregants ingest the body and blood of Christ as sacrament. Historically, there has

been much debate among Christians over the proper meaning and practice of this ritual performance. The Roman Catholic Church and Eastern Orthodox Church split over this very issue, proving there is an iota of difference between same essence and like essence. Later, Protestants took issue with the power of the priest to sacralize the sacraments and the regulations of consumption dictated by the hierarchy to believers.

Changes in sacramental practice produced both intentional and unintentional changes in congregational identity. The Protestant Reformation produced schism (the division of religious institution into multiple organizations often referred to as sects), despite the desire of many early reformers such as Martin Luther to remain within the Church. This splintering produced an assortment of sacramental practices, transforming Catholic notions of sacrament and community into more individualistic Protestant forms. As Weber put it, the Protestant Reformation broke down the monastery walls, making priests of each individual.

Surveying the variety of sacramental practices among Christians in the United States, one can see the relative degrees in which the Protestant impulse of the priesthood of all believers is practiced—the more radical the impulse, the more individualistic the practice. For example, many Baptist congregations distribute the Eucharist individually, each believer receiving his or her cup and precut bread in a seated position. In contrast, most Methodist and Anglican congregants move to the front of the church and actively receive the body by means of bread broken in front of them and receive the blood of Christ from a common cup, usually by tincture—dipping the bread in the cup. It is crucial, though, how the sacrament is received, because the tincture method retains a degree of individualism that is subsumed in the Catholic sharing of the cup. Further, it matters whether the blood of Christ is wine or grape juice. More radical Protestants, such as Missionary and Landmark Baptists, stay as far away from transubstantiation (that is, the actual presence of Christ) as possible, opting instead for a symbolic interpretation. Thus, choosing grape juice over wine is both a moral and functional choice. All of these variations of media reflect theological interpretations of the Eucharist practice and different formations of congregational identity.

Significance of New Forms of Media

Innovations in ritual practices and the inclusion of new forms of media have consequences for congregational identity, intended or not. Media have long been a tool of evangelists in America, from Charles Finney and the "anxious bench," to Billy Graham and motion pictures, to Jerry Falwell and the *Old-Time Gospel Hour*. The adaptation of certain types of media by congregations facilitates greater access to a target audience while providing practitioners with ever-increasing options. Interestingly, even though Protestantism produces more options for religious believers, this religious plurality is susceptible to homogenization, in many ways paralleling other media markets, such as television and music.

For example, in terms of visual media, one of the biggest changes among mainline denominational worship in the last two decades has been the use of large-screen projectors and televisions in worship services. Placing the words of songs overhead in front of the congregation instead of the verses of hymns in the hands of each congregant produces a significant shift in congregational identity. Intended or not, this innovation dislocates denominational influence over a congregation, often replacing denominational hymnbooks with songs written and produced by other denominations or nondenominational publishing companies. This leads to greater similarity of ritual practices across denominations. Thus the choice and use of media has become as important as, or in some cases more important than, denominational affiliation in determining congregational identity.

CHAD E. SEALES

See also Audience; Sermons

Further Reading

Becker, P. (1999). *Congregations in conflict: Cultural models of local religious life*. Cambridge, UK: Cambridge University Press.

Butler, J. (1990). *Awash in a sea of faith: Christianizing the American people*. Cambridge, MA: Harvard University Press.

Durkheim, E. (1995). *Elementary forms of religious life*. New York: The Free Press.

Eck, D. (2001). *A new religious America*. San Francisco: Harper.

Numrich, P. (1996). *Old wisdom in the new world: Americanization in two immigrant Theravada Buddhist temples*. Knoxville: University of Tennessee Press.

Orsi, R. (Ed.). (1999). *Gods of the city: Religion and the American urban landscape*. Bloomington: Indiana University Press.

Tweed, T. (Ed.). (1997). *Retelling U.S. religious history*. Berkeley: University of California Press.

Vasquez, M., & Marquardt, M. (2003). *Globalizing the sacred*. New Brunswick, NJ: Rutgers University Press.

Waghorne, J. P. (1999). The Hindu Gods in a Split-Level World: The Sri Siva-Vishnu Temple in Suburban Washington, D. C. In R. Orsi, (Ed.), *Gods of the city: Religion and the American urban landscape*. Bloomington: Indiana University Press.

Warner, R., & Wittner, J. (1998). *Gatherings in diaspora*. Philadelphia: Temple University Press.

Weber, M. (1946). *From Max Weber: Essays in sociology*. New York: Oxford University Press.

Wuthnow, R. (1988). *The restructuring of American religion*. Princeton, NJ: Princeton University Press.

Cross, The

The cross of Jesus Christ is the central symbol of the Christian faith and raises some critical questions about the communication of religious conviction. While the fish was another early symbol of Christianity (*ichthus*—Jesus Christ, Son of God and Savior), the cross, like the Star of David and the menorah in Judaism and the crescent of Islam, became a major carrier of meaning within the Christian world. The oral proclamation of the Christian Gospel had as its center the atoning death of Jesus Christ, so the Apostle Paul declared that he "resolved to know nothing while I was with you except Jesus Christ and him crucified" (1 Corinthians 2:2). The two sacraments of baptism and the Lord's Supper have the cross of Christ at the core of their significance. The sign of the cross in the liturgy and the cruciform shape of many historic churches in Christendom underscore the cruciality (from crux, *crucis* in Latin, meaning the cross) of the sacrifice of Christ within the Christian faith.

The release of Mel Gibson's controversial movie *The Passion of the Christ* shows the potency of the themes set forth in the dying love of Jesus. The media became obsessed with the film and the divergent responses to it. All of the major news magazines had feature articles probing not only the phenomenon of interest in the film but also plumbing some of the reason and significance for the death of Christ in Christian theology. The film begins with Jesus crushing the head of the serpent in the Garden of Gethsemane, linking the Christ-event with the legion of Old Testament prophecies of the triumph of the seed of the woman over sin and death. In the Christian faith Jesus is not primarily a teacher of ethics, He is the divine Savior from sin through redemption achieved on the cross upon Mt. Calvary. The theme of the film is that all of humanity is responsible for the death of Jesus because we are all sinners and He bore that sin in His own body.

St. Augustine, the early theorist of Christian communication, speaks of how "things are learned by means of signs" (Augustine, *On Christian Doctrine*). In

The Crucifixion Depicted in the New Testament

Mark 10:45: For even the Son of Man did not come to be served, but to serve and to give his life as a ransom for many.

Romans 3:25: God presented him as a sacrifice of atonement, through faith in his blood.

Romans 5:10: For if when we were God's enemies, we were reconciled to him through the death of his Son, how much more, having been reconciled, shall we be saved through his life!

1 Corinthians 1:18: For the message of the cross is foolishness to those who are perishing, but to us who are being saved, it is the power of God.

1 Corinthians 2:2: For I resolved to know nothing while I was with you except Jesus Christ and him crucified.

Galatians 3:13: Christ redeemed us from the curse of the law by becoming a curse for us.

Ephesians 2:13: But now in Christ Jesus you who were once far away have been brought near through the blood of Christ.

anticipation of the modern discipline known as semiotics (having to do with words as signs), he believed that signs make an impression on the senses bringing something else to mind. Words are signs and the cross of Jesus is most especially a significant sign.

In his classic Gifford Lectures on religious symbolism, Edwyn Bevan argues that symbols are a reminder, a summons to remembrance as is the case with the cross of Christ. Human expressions are not adequate to the divine transcendent realities they describe, and hence the symbols of faith like the cross and the water of baptism and the bread and cup of communion are a gracious accommodation to our limited perceptive abilities. They are visual aids of the highest kind.

Some modern thinkers have seen the Resurrection of Christ as only a symbol or the wrath of God as exaggerated anthropomorphism. But there may well be a reality behind the symbol just as behind any religious metaphor. Some of the prophets in the Old Testament used symbolic action to convey truths about God's relationship to His people, as when Jeremiah broke a potter's earthen flask (Jeremiah 19:1–20:2) or Ezekiel carried the exile's baggage (Ezekiel 12:4). These symbolic acts had conceptual meaning, and this article will attempt to show that the cross as a venerable and powerful symbol has conceptual meaning.

Atonement for Sin

According to the Genesis account, God was the first to shed innocent blood in order that He might clothe the fallen couple, parents of the race (Genesis 3:21). The whole notion of a blood covenant was an ancient Semitic ritual and has had a worldwide sweep. One would give oneself to another by giving one's blood. Thus the principle obtained as held by the early Christians that "Without the shedding of blood, there is no forgiveness of sins" (Hebrews 9:22), based in Leviticus 17:10–14. The Israelitish slaves were liberated when the blood of the paschal lambs was shed and Christians have argued that, "Christ is our passover, slain for us" (1 Corinthians 5:7b). The slain lamb becomes a recurrent theme in Christian thinking about the cross. As John the Baptist cried: "Behold the lamb of God who takes away the sin of the world" (John 1:29). The whole sacrificial system in the Old Testament was understood as foreshadowing the vicarious suffering of the sinless Christ bearing the world's sins.

The Psalmist was believed to have seen the redemptive reality beyond any of his own personal anguish when he depicted one whose hands and feet were pierced and whose life was poured out like water (Psalm 22:12–18) and whose garments were divided with lots cast for their possession. Luther saw Isaiah 53 as the "golden passional" written as it were in the shadow of the cross. The suffering servant portrayed as the one "pierced for our transgressions, crushed for our iniquities" has from the earliest Christian perspective been the vicarious suffering of Jesus (Acts 8:32–35). Atonement for sin is the meaning of the cross. Christ took to Himself the penalty of death that in fact belonged to us sinners.

Jesus Himself spoke of His impending sacrifice for sins and in the earliest of the four Gospels as the "giving of his life as a ransom for many" (Mark 10:45). Jesus spoke of the eating of His body and blood (although variously understood in degrees of literality) as the very center of a Eucharistic meal for the faithful. The Lord's Supper sets forth the reality of being brought into the blood covenant. The promise of the covenanting cup was made good at the cross of Christ. Thus believers glory in the cross of Christ (Galatians 6:14).

Meaning of the Cross of Christ

The four Gospels portray the Crucifixion of Christ from four slightly different perspectives, each perspective shaping the selection of appropriate details. In recent years some scholars have seen the Gospels as stories of Christ's passion with introductions. Robert Gundry has seen Mark's Gospel as an evangelistic tract, essentially "an apologetic for the cross" (Gundry 1993). N. T. Wright has argued that the New Testament writers believed very deeply that these events really took place. If in fact Jesus died of influenza at age twenty-five, Christianity is gone.

In placing our interpretive grid over the Apostle Paul's teaching on the meaning of Christ's death, we sense different strands of meaning coming to the fore. Earlier Christians tended to emphasize a ransom theory. *Christus Victor* or the cross as triumph over sin, death, the world, and the devil sprang from Irenaeus. Abelard in the middle ages underscored an exemplarist view stressing Christ's death as the ultimate expression of the love of God (Romans 5:8). Governmentalists like Grotius expanded this notion to a larger canvas to demonstrate how God upholds His moral government throughout the universe by taking sin with the utmost seriousness. Anselm of Canterbury gave more weight to the transactional nature of the atonement in which a holy God's wrath was satisfied and the sacrifice of Christ's innocent life paid the price for the remission of the sins of the world. Although some more modern theories of the atonement like Vincent Taylor's "representative man" theory have been promulgated, the lines drawn by the historic positions pretty well stand today. Many Evangelicals today stress that even as there were five basic types of sacrifice in the Old Testament cultus (burnt offering, peace offering, meal offering, sin offering, and trespass offering), no one theory can adequately comprehend the profound nature of Christ's finished work on the cross.

The Australian Leon Morris insists that "Something happened at Calvary quite objective to man, and it is be-

A Celtic cross in a cemetery in Ireland.
Courtesy of Rebecca Mohr Schulz/istockphoto.com.

cause of this that we can have the completest assurance of our salvation" (1955, 275). The cross dominates the whole New Testament in this respect. John R. W. Stott, English Anglican, holds that the cross of Christ is "substitutionary from beginning to end" and that "The Biblical gospel of the atonement is God satisfying himself by substituting himself" (1986, 111f). Speaking of how the cross accomplishes the mutual satisfaction of mercy and justice, Stott confesses that "I could never myself believe in God, if it were not for the cross."

This would be supported by the Apostle Paul's contention that "Christ died for the ungodly" (Romans 5:6). Indeed our justification is made possible "by his grace through the redemption that came by Christ Jesus whom God presented as a sacrifice of atonement, through faith in His blood" (Romans 3:24–25). This imputation of our sins to Christ and the imputation of His righteousness to us is certainly set forth in Paul's words "God made Him who had no sin to be made sin for us, so that in Him we might become the righteousness of God (2 Corinthians 5:21).

The other New Testament writers, like the author of the Epistle to the Hebrews, likewise emphasize the perfect sacrifice of Christ for sins (Hebrews 9:26). Peter tells us that "Christ bore our sins in His body on the tree so that we might die to sins and live to righteousness" (1 Peter 2:24). The Apostle John stresses how Jesus is "The atoning sacrifice for our sins and not only for ours but also for the sins of the whole world" (1 John 2:2). The work of Christ for sinners then, in Christian theology, extends not only to deliverance from the very much deserved penalty of sin but also for the believer's deliverance from the power of sin (Romans 6). In the last book of the New Testament, the wounded Lamb is seen to be one with the conquering lion of the tribe of Judah (Revelation 5:6ff). Thus Christianity is suffused throughout with the centrality of the cross. In the substance of her theology and in the major symbol of her faith, the church of Jesus Christ is cruciform. The cross is to become a lifestyle for the followers of Jesus (Matthew 16:24). It is the enduring principle of the cross necessarily going before the crown, and life coming out of death (John 12:24). This cross was always in the mind of God as "the Lamb was slain from the creation of the world" (Revelation 13:8). Now actualized in time-space history it continues to show its potency.

The Cross in the Media

With the impetus and thrust of this Biblical and theological propulsion, we are not surprised to see that the death of Jesus has dominated artistic expression every bit as much as has the birth of Jesus. Michelangelo's *Jesus Carrying the Cross* is typical from the Middle Ages and the Renaissance as is Andrea Solario's glorious *Christ Carrying the Cross*. Holman Hunt of the Pre-Raphaelite Brotherhood in his *The Shadow of Death* shows Jesus in the carpenter shop and the shadow of the cross cast over Him even from before His birth. Rembrandt memorably painted the hill called Mt. Calvary and Him who died there as in the poignant *Descent from the Cross*, which can be viewed in the Hermitage in St. Petersburg, Russia.

Giovanni Battista Tiepolo's *The Crucifixion* is most extraordinary, as is Guido Reni's *Ecce Homo*. No painting is quite as theologically probing as the *Allegorical Trinity* by Frans Flori. The Jewish painter Marc Chagall returned again and again to the crucified Jesus draped in a Jewish prayer shawl. His *White Crucifixion* of 1938 reflects the agony of European Jewry. Theodore Prescott's *All My Sins* is searching, and it is significant that England's most noted painter in the twentieth century, Stanley Spencer, painted out his spiritual vision in his telling *The Crucifixion*. The cross continues to be an absorbing focus in Western thought and interest.

The world of music would not be the same without Bach's *St. Matthew's Passion* and his *St. John's Passion* or Handel's oratorio *The Messiah*, with its unforgettable arias from Golgotha. Stainer's *The Crucifixion* and DuBois' *The Seven Last Words of Christ* are typical of a more popular genre, the cantata. In our present postmodernist-tinged world, Gavin Bryars, the contemporary British composer, has written an aria in which a London derelict intones again and again, "Jesus' blood never failed me yet." And what would Christian hymnody be if stripped of Isaac Watt's "When I Survey the Wondrous Cross," or Charles Wesley's "And Can It Be That I Should Gain an Interest in My Savior's Blood," or Elvina Hall's "Jesus Paid it All"?

Christ-figures have abounded in great literature, like Herman Melville's *Billy Budd*, who dies being falsely accused. T. S. Eliot's Celia was consumed by the fixation: "I must atone." This theme surfaces much more satisfactorily in Ann Tyler's *Saint Maybe*, where Ian Bedloe lived his life in guilt over his brother's death and tried to atone for his guilt. He had joined the Church of the Second Chance that taught we must earn forgiveness when he met Rita, who pointed him to the cross of Christ where forgiveness is a free gift. In John Grisham's *Testament*, Nate is very confused but in the chapel "he studies the crucifixion." He experiences the forgiveness of sin and the wiping clean of the slate. He "saw the face of Christ in agony and pain, dying on the cross, dying for him" (Larsen 2004, 16).

Message of the Cross

From its earliest days, the church has been the venue of the oral communication of the word of the cross. The Apostle Paul reminds his readers "Before your very eyes Jesus Christ was clearly portrayed as crucified" (Galatians 3:1). This message of reconciliation has been at the heart of pulpit proclamation across the centuries of Christian expansion. Though varying in style and form, the huge literature on the preaching of the cross would include very close to the top the famous German preacher in the court of King Friedrich Wilhelm in Potsdam, F. W. Krummacher (1796–1869), and his volume *The Suffering Saviour*. Its sermons are divided into the outer court, the holy place, and the most holy place, setting forth different stages of Christ's suffering. The trilogy by the outstanding Dutch preacher, Klaas Schilder (1890–1952) is truly epochal as well.

Some of the finest preaching on the cross ever done in the English language can be found in two books by William M. Clow of Scotland (1853–1930). Both pastor and professor, Clow captured the Biblical and practical impact of Christ's death in *The Day of the Cross* and *The Cross in Christian Experience*. Of outstanding quality among American expositors of the meaning of the cross for our times have been the sermons of F. J. Huegel (1889–1971), missionary to Mexico and teacher at the Union Seminary in Mexico City, which have been collected in volumes such as *The Cross Through the Scriptures*. The oral proclamation of the cross continues to be an immense challenge.

Even Goethe confessed he was drawn to the cross:

I leaned on a little table beside me and I hid my tear-stained face in my hands, and who could ever express even in the dimmest way the experience that came to me then? A secret influence drew my soul to the cross where Christ once expired.

It was an inward leaning—I cannot give it any other name—an inward leaning like that which draws the heart to its beloved in its absence. As my soul drew near to Him who became mine and died upon the cross, in that moment I knew what faith meant and in that moment my spirit received a new uplifting. (from *Confessions of a Beautiful Soul* as quoted in Larsen 2004)

Thus it is clear that the cross of Christ is not only one of the most powerful religious symbols in human history but that its message and power continue to engage minds and hearts around the world, even into our postmodern times.

DAVID L. LARSEN

Further Reading

Augustine. (1952). *On Christian doctrine*. Chicago: Britannica Great Books.

Bevan, E. (1938). *Symbolism and belief*. Boston: Beacon Hill.

Clow, W. M. (1908). *The Cross in Christian experience*. London: Hodder and Stoughton.

Clow, W. M. (1909). *The day of the Cross*. London: Hodder and Stoughton.

Gundry, R. (1993). *Mark: A commentary on his apology for the Cross*. Grand Rapids, MI: Eerdmans.

Huegel, F. J. (1966). *The Cross through the centuries*. Grand Rapids, MI: Zondervan.

Krummacher, F. W. (1947). *The suffering savior*. Chicago: Moody Press.

Larsen, D. L. (2004). *The geography of Calvary: Sermons on the Cross of Christ*. Kearney, NE: Morris Publishing.

Morris, L. (1955). *The apostolic preaching of the Cross*. Grand Rapids, MI: Eerdmans.

Schilder, K. (1944). *Christ crucified*. Grand Rapids, MI: Eerdmans.

Schilder, K. (1944). *Christ in His suffering*. Grand Rapids, MI: Eerdmans.

Schilder, K. (1944). *Christ on trial*. Grand Rapids, MI: Eerdmans.

Stott, J. R. W. (1986). *The Cross of Christ*. Downers Grove, IL: Intervarsity Press.

Trumbull, H. C. (1893). *The blood covenant: A primitive rite and its bearing on scripture*. Philadelphia: John Wattles Publisher.

Van Bierma, D. (2004, April 12). Why did Jesus die? *Time*, *163*(15), 54ff.

Wright, N. T. (1994). *Jesus and the victory of God*. Minneapolis, MN: Augsburg and Fortress.

Culture Wars

"Culture wars" is a term used to describe struggles between various factions of a nation to determine the core principles on which societal norms are established. Though human beings have long been embedded in particular cultures and war has been a ubiquitous part of every civilization, the term "culture wars" is relatively new and best suited to describe specific aspects of late twentieth and early twenty-first century life, especially in the United States of America.

To best understand the concept, one must not only take into account historical trends, but also fundamental changes in religion and communication in the modern West. The historical roots of the culture wars can certainly be found in longstanding battles of conservatism and liberalism in Western Europe. In fact, the term *Kulturkampf* (culture struggle) was used in the 1870s to describe the battle between Otto von Bismarck's liberal government and his country's conservative forces—especially those with predilections for Roman Catholicism and the recent Vatican Council. Even so, culture struggle of the early German Empire is very different from the culture wars of modern America.

Historical and Religious Determinants

Postwar America had a radically different environment with very different characteristics than Europe had fifty years earlier. By midway through the twentieth century, the United States was enjoying the fruits of economic prosperity (the product of economic liberalism of the earlier century) but also beginning to feel the strains of its concomitant urbanization and cultural integration. Along with the growth of industry, government had burgeoned and spread into areas of interest Bismarck would have never imagined. Finally, the media of mass communication had developed and were providing entertainment and information to the average citizen on a daily basis.

One area where change from the late nineteenth to the late twentieth century is debatable is in the religious nature of the citizenry. Scholars have long studied and discussed the "secularization" of Western societies and at a certain level culture wars are manifestations of battles over that putative feature of modern life. However, some scholars see little empirical verification of the "secularization hypothesis," especially in the United States. And many feel the culture war phenomenon shows a strong *realignment* of religious identification and practice, not a lessening thereof.

Religious realignment is of particular interest given the long history of interreligious conflict in Western Europe and North America. Such conflict is easily visible in the history of Europe. It is evident in the tremendous abuse of Jews through the centuries. It is also evident in recurring Catholic-Protestant strife, most visibly in execrable historical events such as the Saint Bartholomew's Day Massacre of 1572. With all of this as a backdrop, Catholics, Jews, and Protestants found themselves cohabitating in the new world. That old suspicions and ill will lived on is not surprising. For much of U.S. history, all three major religious groups manifest occasional (if not frequent) animus toward one another.

Religious Realignment and Civil Religion

Traditional religious combatants found themselves in a very different milieu at the middle of the twentieth century. They were all material beneficiaries of a vibrant capitalist economy that was—to use a religious expression—no respecter of persons. In addition, they found themselves comingling more than at any point in history and interacting with a government that had grown significantly in size and had no formal ties to any religious denomination. Finally, people of different faiths increasingly found themselves sharing in a common, commercial, popular culture that was propagated with an underlying theme of religiosity, what some would call a "civil religion."

Looked at this way, civil religion and its interrelation to government and other broad cultural features is a defining element of the culture wars. As American society became more urbanized, homogenized, and mediated, struggles to define the civil religion of the nation became more heated. In this sense, Robert Wuthnow describes the culture wars as a "struggle for America's soul" (1989, xii). Much of that struggle relates to eco-

nomic power and government control over the lives of citizens. Moreover, argumentation over these issues often has a moral tone, even a religious dimension (in spite of claims of secularization). And, the battles that make up the culture wars are won or lost—or least they were *perceived* to be so—in the mass media.

Though traditional American religious antagonisms suggest warfare related to civil religion in America would create Protestant combatants, Roman Catholic combatants, and Jewish combatants, and that each of these groups would struggle against the other, this is far from the case. As has already been suggested, the twentieth century was a great period of religious realignment.

What one finds in studying cultural conflict in the late twentieth and early twenty-first century is that members of these religious groups are found on *both* sides of most cultural flare-ups. So instead of Roman Catholics battling Protestants and Protestants battling Jews, one finds Roman Catholics of one stripe battling Roman Catholics of another, Protestants who lean one direction battling Protestants who lean another, and Jews with certain predispositions battling Jews with other predispositions. In other words, one finds a coalition of Roman Catholics, Protestants, and Jews battling another coalition also composed of Roman Catholics, Protestants, and Jews. Though a contingent of secularists exists within each camp, these secularists abide with either group's religiosity as a means of achieving their goals.

Orthodox and Progressive Enclaves

Exactly what separates one side of the culture wars from the other is not easy to discern. James Davidson Hunter has suggested the two sides be called "orthodox" and "progressive" branches. Though there are some limitations to these terms, they are useful in explaining key features of the current situation. The orthodox wing of the culture wars sees religious tradition (for some, Scripture) as a primary and immutable source of moral authority. The progressive wing of the culture wars has respect for religious tradition, but sees it as one of many sources of moral authority and one with a high potential for error. Thus while one camp sees religion as a transcendent realm of revelation; the other sees it as a guide to be integrated within a broader worldview.

In this we see the actual term "progressive" is a useful label but does not indicate that one side adores progress and the other does not. Both sides are highly ambivalent about progress. In some instances they want a laissez faire government that celebrates change, in some they want a strict watchdog government that regulates change and defends the status quo. Even so, their reasons for acceptance or rejection are reflective of differences in perception of moral authority.

As an example, the orthodox group has largely been accepting of economic and technological change in American society and sees few moral reasons for government to mitigate change. On the whole, this portion of the American populace is neither averse to technology nor anticapitalist. Yet, they do feel some byproducts of modern technologically inclined capitalism are immoral and should be regulated.

Two examples of sites where the orthodox seek regulation are abortion and pornography. While abortifacients have been widely used for millennia, the 1900s introduced a wide range of technological options for abortion. One of the most hotly contested of these has been "dilation and extraction" (popularly called "partial birth abortion"), a prominent culture war battleground of the 1990s. The case of obscene communication is similar. Sexually explicit art and literature are not new to human civilization, but new technologies have allowed for wider dissemination thereof. As the orthodox interpret Scripture to support sexual chastity, here they would like less progress and more government intervention.

Though the political antagonists of the orthodox have been called progressives, they also show occasional ambivalence toward progress. Many of this set are highly suspicious of capitalism and technology. As examples, they fear the poor pay many of the costs of progress and that capitalists' use of modern communications media is often detrimental to what they perceive as native cultures or subcultures. The solution to these problems is presumed to lay with government intervention. For example, government redistribution of the wealth produced by capitalism is presumed to create greater equality. And government-sponsored media and arts programs can create a broader range of cultural awareness and promote diversity.

Government Arts Funding and the Zenith of the Culture Wars

All of the above suggests why some of the most divisive battles of the culture wars occurred in the late 1980s (continuing into the 1990s) and concerned government funding of the arts. Most notable were clashes over art exhibits by Andres Serrano and Robert Mapplethorpe. Both events received some funding—directly or indirectly—from the National Endowment for the Arts. Orthodox critics saw some elements in Serrano's oeuvre as sacrilegious and much of Mapple-

thorpe's as sexually perverse. Given this, they felt neither should receive government support. Progressives argued that Serrano's work was misinterpreted. It asked its audience to think critically about religion—something progressives have a natural proclivity for, as they constantly work to integrate new ideas into older traditions. In regards to Mapplethorpe, progressives claimed his work gave voice to an oppressed subculture. As progressive theology showed growing acceptance of homosexuality (the subject of much of his work), this posed no problems. Progressives perceived government sponsorship to be prescriptive since the dominant mass media excluded this minority voice.

The NEA controversies are representative of the culture wars in that they show how realigned elements of the citizenry had differing views on the role of government within culture. They also were representative because they show the power of the media in civic engagement. To understand this we should note that one of the most fascinating aspects of the NEA controversies of the late 1980s was that very few Americans ever directly experienced Serrano's *Piss Christ* or Mapplethorpe's *X Portfolio, Self Portrait*. But many were very aware of them. They read about them in their newspapers, saw them on the evening news, and heard them discussed on talk radio.

These people were the souls over which the culture wars are waged. During the NEA controversies, many who were not definitively tied to either the orthodox or progressive factions watched in amazement as both sides used the media to communicate. What most of the citizenry knew of the issues was the product of attributed quotations, soundbites, and news footage in which the committed explained their moral positions.

Future of Culture Wars

Much of the above indicates the development of deep structures that portend culture warfare to continue well into the future. In fact, what the 1980s and 1990s established might be called a "culture war industrial complex." When controversial issues develop, formal organizations that reflect the views of orthodox and progressive camps come forward to advance their positions. The newest narrow casting technologies (e-mail and the World Wide Web) allow these organizations to communicate very efficiently with their constituencies. The traditional media rely on the organizations and their formal spokespersons for contrasting views, allowing for balanced perspectives, but also allowing for cost-effective means of filling space (in media such as newspapers and magazines) or killing time (in media such as radio and television).

But if the culture wars are part of a battle for souls, there is a human element that must be considered. Quite possibly, the mass audience that the orthodox and progressive groups attempt to proselytize will grow tired of being wooed. Or, another significant shift in religious alignment could occur, drastically changing the nature of the groups doing the wooing.

Culture wars are the product of the current milieu of capitalist economics, powerful government bureaucracies, omnipresent media, and realigned religious groups with strong interests in defining the civil religion. A significant change in any one of these variables could make the culture wars relics of history.

RICK CLIFTON MOORE

See also Art; Censorship; Free Speech

Further Reading

Bolton, R. (Ed.). (1992). *Culture wars: Documents from the recent controversies in the arts*. New York: New Press, 1992.

Green, J. C., Guth, J. L., Smidt, C. E., & Kellstedt, L. A. (Eds.). (1996). *Religion and the culture wars: Dispatches from the front*. Lanham, MD: Rowman and Littlefield.

Hunter, J. D. (1991). *Culture wars: The struggle to define America*. New York: Basic Books.

Wuthnow, R. (1989). *The struggle for America's soul: Evangelicals, liberals, and secularism*. Grand Rapids, MI: Eerdmans.

D

Dance

Dance is a form of nonverbal communication that has long been associated with religion. Since it has the ability to transmit the ineffable and communicate a reality beyond words, it is historically and biologically a medium of spiritual expression. Examples of this use of dance abound in the history of Western, Eastern, African, and tribal religions.

Dance may be defined simply as intentionally patterned, rhythmic movement, often set to music. This broad definition then might include a range of activities, including ritual worship, but excluding utilitarian or pedestrian motives. Elements of dance include use of space and specific movements such as running, jumping, skipping, walking, hand gestures, bowing, and swaying. The key to determining if such movement is a dance might be the intended purpose, done with extraordinary movement (Hanna 1979, 17–28).

When such special movement conveys deep feelings and highly cherished values, the intention of the dance may be considered spiritual or religious. The setting for a dance might also determine its purpose. For example, ancient Greek temple dances expressed a certain theological belief about humans needing to perform this ritual action for the gods. However, historically dance also served as a bridge to express spiritual values in daily life. Throughout the world, community social dances following religious rituals served this purpose. Furthermore, sometimes dance has been performed for community viewing, with the intention of sharing an important religious ideal. Dances performed to tell stories of gods and goddesses in India would fall into this category.

How Dance Communicates the Sacred

Dance communicates what a culture considers sacred through metaphoric movement. Dance analysis of Rudolph Laban examines how to read such movement and begins to explain how dance conveys spiritual values. Laban theorized that there are universal movements of the body that express distinct emotions across cultures. His method considers the effort or amount of energy used in a dance, the space used, and the flow of movement.

The primary plane of motion is especially important in this method, as is rhythm. For instance, use of higher and vertical planes might indicate that one is reaching to the heavens. The strong vertical line and upward extended arm of the Sufi dancer is an example. A dance with strong horizontal, well-grounded movements like the Indian *Bharata Natyam* might indicate an appreciation of the earth.

Rhythms that are danced fast and furiously might communicate a metaphor of divine possession, while a stately slow dance might embody peace. Such movement might also be associated with psychological states and verbal metaphors (Espenak 1981, 35). For example, "lift up your heart" is a liturgical phrase with several meanings. It may indicate happiness, a call for help, or joy and is derived from bodily motion.

Linguists add to this idea, saying that religious and theological understandings are mainly metaphorical and embodied (Lakhoff and Johnson 1999, 566–567). Ritual scholars state this more directly, saying religion

is "danced out" as the body creates symbols of values (Driver 1981, 84). Religious scholars have long recognized this symbolic function of dance, even suggesting the activity is the basis for the idea of religion. In *The Elementary Forms of Religious Life*, Emile Durkheim claimed that dance was actually the impetus for the idea of religion, as it exhilarates participants:

> Commencing at nightfall, all sorts of processions, dances and songs had taken place; the general effervescence was constantly increasing.... The smoke, the blazing torches, the showers of sparks falling in all direction *and the masses dancing*.... So in the midst of these effervescent social environments and out of this effervescence itself the religious idea seems to be born. (Spencer 1985, 35)

In *Religion in Essence and Manifestation*, scholar Geradius Van der Leeuw seriously considered this point, equating dance with a feeling of power. Power being associated with the transcendent, dance then connects the spiritual world with lived reality:

> [Dance] is not merely an esthetic pursuit existing side by side with other more practical activities. It is the service of the god, and generates power.... In the dance life is ordered to some powerful rhythm

and reverts to its potent primeval motion, and thus it is possible to attain to all manner of things by "dancing."(1997, 374)

Philosopher Suzanne Langer also finds dance primary to the formation of religious awareness, creating a "mythic consciousness" (Spencer 1985, 35). Langer deals with stage performance, however, and her idea suggests that dance and ritual actions enact the truth of myth through metaphors of motion. In some traditions this is quite literal, as when medieval Christian dancers pantomimed scriptural stories (Taylor 1990).

Noted dance anthropologist Joann Kealiinohomoku reminds us, though, that dance involves much more than movement. She explains that it involves a configuration where "implicit as well as explicit aspects" and its "reasons for being" exist within "the entire conception of the dance within the larger culture." This means that besides looking at the movement of, for example, an Irish Ceili social dance, we might also consider why the dances were done after a church service. We might also consider the value of community in Irish Catholic culture. In other words, what people say and think, how they use movement to relay communication, and the larger, societal system of symbols are also factors to consider in understanding the language of dance (Kealiinohomoku 1974, 1–8; Hanna 1979, 237–238; Sautter 1986).

Dance in Religious Traditions

The values communicated by dance in religious traditions depend on the cultures in which they exist. In the West, the emphasis tended to be on dances stressing community and the importance of celebrating life. There are many examples of community group dances, sometimes led by specific individuals. In the Eastern religions, there are many more examples of dance done by performers for the benefit of the community. African and tribal traditions provide us with examples of healing associated with the activity. The following overview provides significant illustrations from around the world.

Judaism

Judaism has a rich history of dance in worship and community life. The purpose was primarily one of rejoicing, an important value of the religion. There are many examples of dance in the Bible, which were done outside of the temple (Gruber 1990). In the diaspora, Jews continued to dance for times of life passage, especially weddings and the Sabbath. One holiday, *Simchat Torah,* developed in the Middle Ages, was specifically for rejoicing in the Torah by dancing with a scroll. Two notable examples of Jewish dance are Mediterranean women's celebration ensembles and the practice of the mystic Hasidim of Eastern Europe. Called *Tanyaderas,* the women's ensembles led dance celebrations with drums and singing, especially for weddings. The Hasidim used dance as a means of creating joy, but also believed their effort invited in the holy presence of the *Shekinah* (Sautter 1986; Buxbaum 1994, 490).

Christianity

Christian scripture and early writings indicate that dance was an appreciated activity, building a sense of fellowship and heavenly pleasure. Some dances, like the labyrinth, symbolized belief in resurrection. One spiraled into death, then circled out into new life. Round dances were especially popular throughout the religion's history, and the church also developed a rich choreography of processions and liturgical motions. Carols, which are actually round dances with song, were especially popular among medieval Christians.

By the seventeenth century, most Protestants severely restricted dance activity. However, the Shakers were a notable exception. They found dance to be spiritually redemptive, spinning being an important part of their dance (Adams 1990; Taylor 1990).

Hinduism

Hinduism and its culture produced many forms of dance. As in most Asian religions, sacred reality mixes with daily life so religious art forms are found everywhere. There is even an entire scriptural text devoted to dance. The *Natyashastra* describes in detail the proper aesthetics for dance. Presumably, the descriptions were for temple dance, which is no longer done. However, it is clear that dances about the gods, devotional dance, and trance dance are still a part of the culture (Samson 1987, 9).

Dances done in the temple were done for the deity, by specially trained women. *Odissi* developed from a northern temple tradition in Orissa and is noted for its strong hip-sway. Tibetan Buddhist dance is similar in motion, though more improvisational and performed by men. *Bharata Natyam* developed out of southern Indian temple dance. Besides a deep, horizontal plié stance, the form is also well known for its facial expressions and hand gestures (*mudras*). As in many forms of Indian dance, the *mudras* are used for a storytelling portion, usually relating a myth about the gods. Such dances are also performed in elaborate outdoor public events that may last for days (Samson 1987; Gupta 2000).

Dance accompanying *kirtan* devotional singing is a means of expressing personal devotion to a deity in India. This *bhakti* yoga tradition encourages participants to fully engage in the practice, and some leaders even maintained wild movement was ideal. Chaitanya was a sixteenth-century *bhakti* master "credited with introducing devotional dance into *kirtan*." He found "full communion with the 'Beloved' deity possible through dance that included 'men' who sang and shouted at the top of their voices hour after hour, dancing and jumping about in ecstatic abandon." Chaitanya himself "would spring to his feet, ... with arms high above his head," and "begin to dance in the midst of the singers" (Puyang-Martin 1996, 190).

Trance dance is yet another form of religious expression in Hinduism. The festival for the goddess Durgha is known for participants becoming possessed by her. They will move wildly, in a trance-like state, when this occurs. Such dance is also performed throughout the year by individuals known to channel the goddess. Witnessing such possession is considered auspicious (Flood 1996, 220–221).

Vodoun Dance

Vodoun dance arises out of the West African Yoruban culture and expanded to the Caribbean. In this tradition's view, divine energy is living in all nature, and balancing the energy is important for maintaining the health of an individual or community. Dance is one means of doing so, with the basic stance reflecting this idea of balance. It is grounded through a strong bent-knee position, with the torso held slightly forward. Energy manifested by ancestor deities (*Loa*) possesses individuals in the vodoun dance ritual. Their energy is hot or cool and needs to be equalized (Pinn 1998, 11–53; Omofolabo 1998).

As performed in Haiti, the vodoun dance has a strong ritual form that provides a frame for possession. It includes an opening procession and a *mambo* priestess guide, who helps control the dance. Dancers will take on the movements of the *Loa* that enter them. Hot motions might include violent chest and arm movement and fast footwork, while cool motions might include gentle hip swaying. All are considered necessary for community balance, though some may be more appropriate at a particular time (Dunham 1983).

Other Traditions

Other traditions of note include shaman and Native American dances. Shamans might be described as healers who performed their work through a dance journey. Viewing the dance would be a means of changing reality or exorcising an evil spirit and thus bringing healing. This tradition was found especially in Korea, Siberia, and Africa. Some Native American dance might also fit under this category, though the tribes had many types of ritual and community dances. The Hopi, in particular, have a rich tradition of masked Kachina dancers, who are specially trained to perform throughout the year for the benefit of the community. Among the Plains Indians, there was a sun dance celebration and a Ghost Dance. The sun dance was a yearly ritual celebrating the solar cycle. The Ghost dance was performed by the community, mourning for the loss of their culture at the end of the nineteenth century (Wosian 1974, 18, 20; Kealiinohomoku 1987–1988; Marriot 1985).

The Future

There is a deep psychology to dance done for religious expression, as evidenced especially by tribal cultures. An understanding of this power of dance is still present today, with the popularity of global trance and dance "jam." As Durkheim and Van der Leeuw reminds us, the power of dance is in its ability to communicate spirituality. Within churches, there are liturgical dance performances, and services of progressive Jewish congregations often include simple line dances. As dance is symbolic movement that expresses what words cannot, it is likely such activity will continue in the future.

Cia Sautter

Further Reading

Adams, D., & Apostolos-Cappadona, D. (Eds.). (1990). *Dance as religious studies*. New York: Crossroad.

Backman, E. L. (1952). *Religious dances in the Christian church and in popular medicine* (E. Clauss, Trans.). London: Allen and Unwin.

Buxbaum, Yitzak (1994). *Jewish spiritual practices*. Northvale, New Jersey: Jason Aronson.

Devi, R. (1984). *Dance and music*. Santa Barbara, CA: International Lalita Kalas Foundation.

Driver, T. (1991). *The magic of ritual*. San Francisco: HarperSanFrancisco.

Dunham, K. (1983). *Dances of Haiti*. Los Angeles: Center for African-American Studies at UCLA.

Durkheim, E. (1965). *The elementary forms of religious life*. London: Collier Macmillan.

Espenak, L. (1981). *Dance therapy: Theory and application*. Springfield, IL: Charles C. Thomas.

Faruqi, L. I. (1976). Dance as an expression of Islamic culture. *Dancescope*, 43–51.

Flood, G. (1996). *An introduction to Hinduism*. Cambridge, U.K.: Cambridge University Press.

Grimes, Robert. (2000). *Deeply into the bone*. Berkeley: University of California Press.

Gruber, M. (1990). Ten dance-derived expressions in the Hebrew Bible. In D. Adams & D. Apostolos-Cappadona (Eds.), *Dance as religious studies*. New York: Crossroad.

Gupta, R. K. (2000). *A yoga of Indian classical dance*. Rochester, VT: Inner Traditions.

Hanna, J. L. (1979). *To dance is human: A theory of nonverbal communication*. Austin: University of Texas Press.

Kealiinohomoku, J. (1974). Dance culture as a microcosm of holistic culture. In T. Comstock (Ed.), *New dimensions in dance research: Anthropology and dance—The American Indian*. Tucson: University of Arizona Press.

Kealiinohomoku, J. (1987–1988). The Hopi Katsina Dance Event 'Doings.' In L. J. Bean (Ed.), *Seasons of the Kachina: Proceedings of the California State University Hayward Conference on the Western Pueblo*. Menlo Park, CA: Ballena Press.

Lakhoff, G., & Johnson, M. (1980). *Metaphors we live by*. Chicago: University of Chicago Press.

Lakhoff, G., & Johnson, M. (1999). *Philosophy in the flesh: The embodied mind and its challenge to Western thought*. New York: Basic Books.

Marriot, A. (1985). *The ten grandmothers: Epic of the Kiowa*. Norman: University of Oklahoma Press.

Omofolabo, S. A. (1998). *Yoruba dance: The semiotics of movement and body attitude in a Nigerian culture*. Lawrenceville, NJ: African World Press.

Pinn, A. (1998). *Varieties of African American religious experience*. Minneapolis, MN: Fortress Press.

Puyang-Martin, M. (1996.) *Kirtan: Devotional Music in the International Society of Krishna Consciousness in the United States* (Doctoral dissertation, University of California, Berkeley).

Samson, L. (1987). *Rhythm in joy: Classical Indian dance traditions*. Delhi, India: Lustre Press.

Sautter, C. (1986). *The dance of Jewish women as Torah* (Doctoral dissertation, University of Michigan, Ann Arbor).

Sautter, C. (2001). *Irish dance and spirituality*. Austin, TX: Sharing Press.

Spencer, P. (1985). *Society and the dance*. Cambridge, U.K.: Cambridge University Press.

Taylor, M. D. (1990). A history of symbolic movement in worship. In D. Adams & D. Apostolos-Cappadona (Eds.), *Dance as religious studies*. New York: Crossroad.

Van Der Leeuw, G. (1977). *Religions in essence and manifestation*. Tubingen, Germany: J. C. B. Mohr.

von Laban, R. (1975). *Laban's principles of dance and movement* (2nd ed.). Boston: Plays.

von Laban, R., & Redfern, H. B. (1965). *Introducing Laban's art of movement*. London. MacDonald & Evans.

Wosian, M. G. (1974). *Sacred dance: Encounter with the gods*. London: Thames and Hudson.

Daoism

Daoism is probably the least known and most poorly comprehended world religion, although it has been an essential element of Chinese civilization and other Eastern Asian cultures for more than two millennia. One reason for this is that knowledge of Daoism has been limited to a few philosophical texts. Another reason arises from the abstruse nature of the Daoist cannon. *Daode jing*, for example, is the second most translated work in the world, next to the Bible, yet it remains one of the most difficult and problematic texts of all Chinese literature. The various, and often times contradictory, interpretations of Daoist texts have led to incongruous answers to the question of what Daoism is. While the underlying unity of many other world religions is generally taken for granted, scholars of Daoism today are still searching for new conceptual ground to ease the discrepancies in views of the essence of Daoism.

Among the limited research done on Daoism, most centers on history, philosophy, and religion. Except for a few scattered insights, the field of communication remains uncharted territory for scholars of Daoism.

Definition and Central Belief

Because of the many distinctive forms of the Daoist tradition, a unified definition of Daoism has been difficult, if not impossible, to come by. The key concept in Daoism is Dao, meaning "way" or "path," which refers to "a nameless, formless, all-pervasive power that brings all things into being and reverts them back into non-being in an eternal cycle" (Oldstone-Moore 2003, 6). Dao is thus the source of the divine and the cosmic principle that permeates and transcends all things. The core philosophy of Daoism is *wu-wei*, meaning nonaction or noninterference, which suggests submission to or movement with, rather than against, natural process and change. Daoists assert that one's body is a microcosm parallel to the macrocosm of the universe. By following the forces of nature, one can be in harmony with them, thus cultivating Dao and achieving longevity and immortality.

The Legend of Laozi and *Daode jing*

Laozi (Old Master) and his teachings in *Daode jing* (*Classic of the Way and Virtue*) form the base of Daoism. The earliest available account of Laozi's biography appeared in *Shiji* (*Records of the Historian*) by Sima Qian (90 BCE). According to *Shiji*, Laozi (whose name is Li Er, also called Lao Dan), a contemporary of Confucius who taught Confucius funeral rituals, cultivated Dao and virtue. Upon witnessing the decline of the Zhou dynasty (1027–777 BCE), he departed the country. He committed his thoughts to writing, resulting in the two-volume, five-thousand-word *Daode jing*, dealing with

Dao and its virtue. His learning was devoted to self-effacement.

The figure of Laozi and the origin of the *Daode jing* remain a source of fascination, and the authorship and dating of the *Daode jing* continue to be debated. Nevertheless, Lao Dan was recognized as one of the greatest thinkers in Chinese history and the founder of the "Laoist" School, which was combined with Zhuangzi's philosophy in the fourth century BCE and became the basis of Daoism.

Early Daoist Movements

Based on distinctive intellectual histories and practices, Daoism has traditionally been categorized into two realms: philosophical Daoism and religious Daoism. Philosophical Daoism first emerged in the Warring States period of Chinese history (475–221 BCE). The fall of the Zhou dynasty created political chaos, and during that time sixteen states fought each other for dominance. In the vacuum of a central political ideology, the so-called hundred schools of thought materialized and competed for attention. The *Daode jing* emerged as a philosophy that could provide a remedy for a collapsing society through its ideal of *wu wi er zhi*—govern with minimum interference. During the following centuries Daoism gained substantial recognition; it was transformed when it merged with traditional yin-yan cosmology, notions of *chi* and *wu xin* (Five Phases), and certain Confucian administrative ideas. Along with Confucianism and Buddhism, this school of thought was firmly woven into the fabric of Chinese tradition and ontology.

Religious Daoism appeared during the late Han dynasty (206 BCE–220 CE). The turmoil at the end of the Han empire generated numerous mass movements, many of which espoused millenarian and messianic hopes. The spiritual terrain at that time also favored the development of religious characteristics in Daoism. Daoist magical practitioners were hired by imperial courts to experiment with medicines for immortality.

Two early Daoist movements preceded the formal organized religion. The first was the *Taiping* (Great Peace) Movement, also called Yellow Turbans, which rose in rebellion in 184 CE, but was eventually bloodily suppressed. Its leader Zhang Jue adhered to Daoist thought and possessed a talismanic text that might have been transmitted in *Taiping jing* (Scripture of Great Peace), a Daoist canonical text.

The second major movement was that of *Tianshi* (Celestial Masters), also known as the *Zhengyi* (Orthodox Unity) School, which emerged simultaneously with the Yellow Turbans. Founded by Zhang Ling, or Daoling, and later organized by his grandson Zhang Lu, this movement successfully managed an independent theocratic state for several decades and spread its doctrines and practices throughout the country. Zhang Ling is also said to have produced various texts to propagate his doctrine. One of them could have been the *Xiang'er*, a commentary on the *Daode jing*, which later became one of Daoism's sacred texts. Scholars argue that the movement's political compromises, rather than doctrinal factors, led later Daoists to identify more with the Celestial Masters movement than with the Great Peace movement.

Brief Historical Development

The Celestial Masters moved southward at the beginning of the fourth century when Han ethnicity lost control of the northern territory to a Hun regime. There the school encountered popular religious practices and divided into two distinctive denominations. *Shangquing* (Highest Clarity), popular among the elite, was founded through a series of revelations by spiritual beings. *Lingbao* (Numinous Treasure), on the other hand, was a communal form of Daoism that integrated *Shangquing*'s revelations, the Celestial Master's practices, and Buddhist ideas of universal salvation.

The popularity of Daoism reached another height during the Tang dynasty (618–907). The imperial family shared the same surname, Li, with Laozi, traced their lineage to him, and bestowed on him the state-protecting deity. The government established Laozi's birthday as a national holiday, mandated that citizens keep a copy of *Daode jing* at home, and added the text to the standard materials for civil services exams.

A war-torn China between Sung and Yuan (1279–1368) dynasties provided an environment for another religious boom. Many new Daoist schools emerged during this time and two remain active today. *Quanzhen* (Complete Perfection), established by Wang Zhe, became the most influential religious movement during the Mongol Yuan dynasty. *Quanzhen* amalgamated the "Three Teachings" (Buddhism, Daoism, and Confucianism) but nevertheless remained fundamentally Daoist because of its pursuit of immortality. Wang Zhe taught that to become immortal, one must be pure and tranquil by detaching oneself from earthly desires. He mandated celibacy and a vegetarian lifestyle; he also urged followers to withdraw from the secular world, to live as hermits or monastics, and to cultivate Dao through a liturgical framework and as a ritual specialty.

Zhengyi (Orthodox Unity) School, on the other hand, was a restoration of the Celestial Masters School. Unlike the *Quanzhen* School, *Zhengyi* believers cultivated themselves in secular communities. *Zhengyi* priests marry, live with their families, and perform rites in their communities. They pass on lineage to their descendants. The patriarchs are said to be the direct descendants of the founder of the Celestial Masters. The sixty-fourth Celestial Master, Zhang Yuanxian, resides in Taiwan today.

Neo-Confucianism was the moral guide for the feudal states during the Ming (1368–1644) and Qing (1644–1912) dynasties. Daoist ideas, however, were incorporated into Confucian thought, even though Confucianism tended to distance itself from popular religious practices, including Daoist rituals. After Mao Zedong took over China in 1949, Daoism, along with other religions, was deemed feudalistic, shamanistic, and superstitious, and after the Chinese civil war, many Daoists, including the sixty-third Celestial Master, Zhang Enfu, escaped to Taiwan, which preserved Daoist traditions while incorporating Buddhism and popular religions into its practices.

After Mao's rule, China grew more moderate, and religion experienced a renewal in both the academy and society, though it is still closely monitored by the state. The Chinese Daoist Association, established in Beijing in 1979, founded a journal to propagate Daoism. Different venues, such as universities, research institutes, and cultural organizations, also embarked on studies in Daoism. The recent tourist boom provides another motivation for the reconstruction and re-signification of Daoist temples and sacred mountains.

Daode jing and the Transmission of Daoism

The mythology of the immortal Laozi guiding the establishment of the Han dynasty put *Daode jing* in a prestigious position at the court. Early Han rule favored Laozi's nonaction philosophy in political policy. Laozi's five-thousand-word literature was bestowed as *jing* (classic or scripture) during Emperor Jing's rule, and he furthermore recommended regular recitation of *Daode jing* across the empire. On the local level, literati and local officials venerated and taught *Daode jing* to the common people. *Daode jing* was soon adopted by growing Daoist cults as a major sacred text, an emanation of the pure Dao instead of merely the work of a philosopher.

Laozi's divinity was established in the second century by the Celestial Maters. *Daode jing*, in this context, was the direct manifestation of the Dao and the key to the transmission of Daoist essences. According to a seventh-century encyclopedia, *Sandong zhunang* (Pearly Bag of the Three Caverns), a guardian of the western border, Yin Xi, pleaded with Laozi to write down his teaching before he left the country. God-Laozi tested Yin Xi in various trials, including reciting *Daode jing* ten thousand times over the period of three years. After Yin Xi completed his tests, as the legend goes, Laozi deemed him a worthy disciple, announced his immortality, and elevated him to the rank of "Highest Perfected." Laozi took him on a journey through the universe to the paradises and into the nine heavens. The two sages then went westward to India and Central Asia. This mythical journey was interpreted as a deed of *huahu*, or the conversion of the "barbarians" into Daoism. Laozi incarnated himself into the Buddha, who transmitted the Dao to suffering humanity and gave birth to Indian and other civilizations.

To Be a Disciple

Yin Xi's trials became an exemplary interaction between Daoist master and disciple. A new follower had to prove his inherent ability, determination, and loyalty. He had to declare his wishes, show what measures he had taken in realizing his goal, and pledge his allegiance to the Dao. As Daoism became an organized religion, rules directing members' behavior toward higher Daoist purity also became more clearly defined. The early Celestial Masters charted twenty-seven precepts for different levels of converts. The lower precepts are introductory guidelines for good citizenship in the community. The medium-level precepts encourage members to develop a positive attitude and help with the needs of the community and of others. The highest set, which includes keeping the divine law and not pursing worldly goods or revealing the group's esoteric teachings, enjoins service of the Dao and provides principles for immortality and happiness.

Recitation of *Daode jing* has been a crucial part of the Daoist lifestyle. The Celestial Masters used the text to glue followers together through daily recitations and for advancing behavioral guidelines; ultimately it created a sense of identity and community. While much of Western philosophical discourse, including religious texts, is informative, Chinese philosophical discourse in general, and Daoist texts in particular, are held to be transformative in their recitation. In other words, Daoist scriptures are a kind of speech act intended to alter the way of life of those who recite and hear them. Daoists believe in the power of the *Daode jing*; by reciting the sacred text constantly mortal beings can visualize, and even unite with, deity and eventually achieve immortality.

Daoist Rituals as a Form of Communication

Through rituals, Daoist priests stand as mediums between the supernatural world and the human world. Daoists believe that all harm comes from the spirits. The sick confess their wrongs to a Daoist priest who then reports the confession and negotiates with the other world to pardon sins, heal the illness, and permit longevity. The healed then accumulate good deeds by undertaking community service projects, such as repairing roads or helping the needy, to avoid future illness. The *Jiao* (communal offering) ceremony, dating from the fifth century, is a ritual for community welfare. During the *Jiao* ceremony, the priest's body is transformed to represent the cosmos. He visualizes energy traveling through his body to the cranium (where the highest emanations of Dao are located) and asks the gods for the replenishment of light, blessings, and life and growth for the community.

Talismans, music, chanting, and dancing are common forms of communication with the other world. Talismans, often used in conjunction with spells, function as a manifestation of cosmic energy, the representation of a deity, or an order issued by a Daoist god to keep demons and ghosts under control. Music can be used in rituals for comforting desolate souls, celebrating festivals, or sending memorials to the Daoist gods on special occasions. Daoist priests act as liaisons between people and gods. Through chanting *Daode jing* and other sacred texts (with or without instrumental music) and dancing before the gods, Daoist priests plead for joy, prosperity, health, and good fortune for the people.

Research Directions

The bulk of early work on Daoism either categorized the religion as superstition or imposed an Orientalist construct on it. Scholars in recent years have produced important insights through new critical analyses of the Daoist canon or fieldwork among living Daoists. The topic of Daoism, however, remains thinly explored and full of possibilities. Scholars in communication and media have not yet given Daoism much attention. Even though existing histories point to the communication of the religion as it expanded, the forms of Daoist communication themselves have yet to be identified. Many Daoist sacred texts have been widely interpreted for philosophical and religious meaning, but the question of how Daoist sages viewed communication is largely ignored. Some researchers allude to the role of Daoist priests in society, but none has specifically explained how Daoists communicate within and outside the religion. With the advancement of communication and media technologies, how does this traditional faith adapt itself to new ways of communication, how does technology alter the message, and how does the cyber community of Daoism, if it exists, redefine the Daoist community? An open and exciting area awaits exploration by communication and media researchers.

CHIUNG HWANG CHEN

See also Confucianism

Further Reading

Bokenkamp, S. R. (1997). *Early Daoist scriptures*. Berkeley: University of California Press.

Bradbury, S. (1992). The American conquest of philosophical Taoism. In C. N. Moore & L. Lower (Eds.), *Translation East and West: A cross-cultural approach* (pp. 29–41). Honolulu: University of Hawaii Press.

Creel, H. G. (1970). *What is Taoism? And other studies in Chinese cultural history*. Chicago: University of Chicago Press.

Graham, A. C. (1998). The Origins of the legend of Lao Tan. In L. Kohn & M. LaFargue (Eds.), *Lao-tzu and the Tao-te-ching* (pp. 23–38). Albany: State University of New York Press.

Hansen, C. (1992). *A Daoist theory of Chinese thought: A philosophical interpretation*. Oxford, UK: Oxford University Press.

Kohn, L. (1998a). The Lao-tzu myth. In L. Kohn & M. LaFargue (Eds.), *Lao-tzu and the Tao-te-ching* (pp. 41–61). Albany: State University of New York Press.

Kohn. L. (1998b). The Tao-te-ching in ritual. In L. Kohn & M. LaFargue (Eds.), *Lao-tzu and the Tao-te-ching* (pp. 143–161). Albany: State University of New York Press.

Kohn, L. (Ed.). (1993). *The Taoism experience: An anthology*. Albany: State University of New York Press.

Kohn, L. (Ed.). (2000). *Daoism handbook*. Koln, Germany: Brill Academic Publishing.

Kohn, L., & LaFargue, M. (1998). Editor's introduction. The Origins of the legend of Lao Tan. In L. Kohn & M. LaFargue (Eds.), *Lao-tzu and the Tao-te-ching* (pp. 1–19). Albany: State University of New York Press.

Kohn, L., & Roth, H. D. (Eds.). (2002). *Daoist identity: History, lineage, and ritual*. Honolulu: University of Hawaii Press.

Lai, C. T. (2003). Daoism in China today, 1980–2002. *The China Quarterly, 174*(June): 413–427.

Maspero, H. (1981). *Taoism and Chinese religion*. Translated by Frank Kierman. Amherst: University of Massachusetts Press.

Oldstone-Moore, J. (2003). *Taoism: Origins, beliefs, practices, holy texts, sacred places*. Oxford, UK: Oxford University Press.

Schipper, K. (1974). The written memorial in Taoist ceremonies. In A. P. Wolf (Ed.), *Religion and Ritual in Chinese Society* (pp. 309–324). Stanford, CA: Stanford University Press.

Schwartz, B. (1998). The thought of the Tao-te-ching. In L. Kohn & M. LaFargue (Eds.), *Lao-tzu and the Tao-te-ching* (pp. 189–210). Albany: State University of New York Press.

Zhang, D. (1998). The place of Daoism in the history of Chinese philosophy. *Contemporary Chinese Thought*, 29(3): 81–94.

Dead (Communication with)

Continuing communication between the living and the dead has served cross-culturally as a means to preserve bonds of affection across the space of death and as a method to allow the living to consult the dead about the conditions of the afterlife and how best to conduct life on earth. The dead, whether immediate ancestors or famous historical figures, are generally considered wiser than the living and are most often benevolent, giving advice or offering solace to the grieving. Whether contacted individually or brought back for a time-bound ritual in their honor, the dead's communication from beyond the grave assures the living of the continued presence of loved ones and the reciprocal care from living family and friends.

Communication consists of multiple possible forms ranging from speech acts like prayer and conversation, to the feeding of the dead, to types of commemoration. As a general rule, communication with the dead is understood to be a recuperation of the dead's actual presence rather than a trigger for memory, but many memorials are also created as a means of communicating an ongoing concern for the deceased. Communication may also be immediate, and particular dead people may be brought back to the realm of the living through the use of mediums, possession, or other forms of trance states. Large-scale rituals, such as the Day of the Dead in Latin America, often invite the dead back into the families' homes for a constrained period of time both to ensure the

dead's sense of perpetual affection and to ward off the possibility of an unwanted haunting by a neglected relative. Many societies have some belief that neglecting to communicate properly with the dead will produce meddlesome or even dangerous ghosts.

Mediums

Probably the most popular vehicle for communicating with the dead remains the human voice. Generally a person with some sort of official sanction—whether it is a priest, a healer, or a channeler—enters a trancelike state and serves as the intermediary for the spirit world. The figure of the medium often allows the spirits of the dead to speak through him or her, giving the living the opportunity to converse directly with those in the afterlife. While most often the petitioner is interested in contacting family and friends, it is also frequently the case that famous dead, such as statesmen, literary figures, and religious authorities, have been called upon to give advice to the living. The dead can be consulted for their knowledge of the afterlife, for particular problems like a plague of bad luck, or for their views on social or political platforms.

The gendered aspects of mediumship are a rich source of both scholarship and controversy, as women and sometimes children are often the primary resources for communication with the dead. While sometimes this allows the socially marginalized to occupy positions of semiclerical authority, it is also frequently the case that women are the loci for surprising or disruptive outbursts from the realm of the dead, sometimes coming in the form of possession. While the medical and psychological value of these mental states is hotly debated as performed, coached, or even faked, so too is the religious value of the communication for living women. Through the use of trance states, women may voice discontent and opposition to society without fear of repercussion, but only on the condition that it is not the woman speaking but rather the dead speaking through her. This paradoxical form of empowerment thus simultaneously gives voice to social discontent but potentially masks the author of the words.

Continued Care of the Dead

Communicating with the dead also serves as a way to keep families intact on both sides of the grave. Sacrifice and the burning or cooking of the sacred food has long been a traditional form of communication with both the gods and the dead in many cultures. Feeding

Cemetery with above-ground tombs near El Morro castle in Old San Juan, Puerto Rico. *Courtesy of Gary Hotson/ istockphoto.com.*

the dead at small shrines or domestic altars is common, and the smell or even smoke from the fire is thought to literally feed the ancestors. The dead are often invited back into the home for a ritual period of time each year, during which they are placated, fed, and assured of the family's continued care. Some religions, like vodoun, have elaborate rituals designed to retrieve the dead from a nebulous location and resituate them within the household economy. This relationship is one of reciprocity, with the family keeping the spirits of the dead content and the dead having the responsibility of being available for consultation and spiritual or magical aid.

Unwanted communication with the dead in the form of ghosts or demons is frequently attributed to a failure to care for the dead properly, such as improper burial or a lack of ongoing attention given to the dead. These hauntings may be personal forms of punishment or impersonal forces from anonymous dead who have been neglected and therefore seek attention from or revenge on strangers. Hostile possessions against the vehicle's will or poltergeist activity also account for a small percent of communication with the dead; oftentimes these messages from beyond require that the living right some ethical or criminal lapse in order for the dead to move on to the proper situation.

Research Directions

The continued existence of the dead and the continued need to communicate with them is a persistent religious motif across cultures and time. Forms of communication range from the immediate presence of the dead to a mediated attempt to ensure objectivity and the veracity of communication. Technology has often been mined for pursuing communication with the dead, with the telegraph, the telephone, and photography all having been conscripted into service. Devices such as the planchette and the Ouija board have been created specifically for this purpose, and more recently digital photography has been understood to capture images of spirits. While the techniques change over time and location, the content of the majority of communication with the dead has remained relatively constant—death is not a permanent impasse to communication but rather a bridgeable gulf allowing the living and the dead to remain connected in perpetuity.

CATHY GUTIERREZ

Further Reading

Ashforth, A. (2000). *Madumo, a man bewitched*. Chicago: University of Chicago Press.

Braude, A. (1989). *Radical spirits: Spiritualism and women's rights in nineteenth-century America.* Boston: Beacon Press.

Bremmer, J. N. (2002). *The rise and fall of the afterlife.* London: Routledge Press.

Carrasco, D. (1998). *Religions of Mesoamerica: Cosmovision and ceremonial centers.* Prospect Heights, IL: Waveland Press.

Chambert-Loir, H., & Reid, A. (2002). *The potent dead: Ancestors, saints, and heroes in contemporary Indonesia.* Honolulu: University of Hawaii Press.

Deren, M. (1983). *Divine horsemen: The living gods of Haiti.* Kingston, NY: McPherson & Company.

Keller, M. (2002). *The hammer and the flute: Women, power, and spirit possession.* Baltimore: The Johns Hopkins University Press.

McIlwain, C. (2003). *Death in black and white: Death, ritual, and family ecology.* Cresskill, NJ: Hampton Press.

Morris, I. (1992). *Death-ritual and social structure in classical antiquity.* Cambridge, UK: Cambridge University Press.

Spanos, N. P. (1996). *Multiple identities and false memories: A sociocognitive perspective.* Washington, DC: American Psychological Association.

Defamation

The media can be expedient means for religious groups to communicate their message in the public arena. However, the media are not always an ally to religious groups. Many instances can be cited where a member or usually members of a religious group have objected to the way in which the media have represented or portrayed their religion. The term *defamation* basically refers to slanderous communication, whether written or oral, that has a harmful impact on the reputation of an individual or a particular group. In this case we are focusing on defamation of a religion or religious group.

A religion can be defamed by a variety of different communications. These can be listed as follows:

1. Newspapers/magazines

2. Television and film

3. The Internet

4. Radio

5. Art and books

It can be noted that defamatory material can be communicated in oral, written, and electronic formats. It is probably not to overstate the case to suggest that at some point all religious groups (mainstream and alternative) have been affected by the issue of defamation and members within the group have voiced their objections either by communication to the wider public, by protests, or in some cases by pursuing their interests through legal channels.

History has revealed many examples of how certain groups have communicated defamatory material about other groups using the various forms of media. One of the more notable examples is the Nazi use of propaganda against the Jews. Such propaganda, as the Nazi campaign progressed, became communicated through more sophisticated means as mass media developed. A variety of forms of communication were used such as the radio, cinema, newspapers and publication. Indeed, even children's books were used as a means to promote the anti-Semitic caricature. With the resulting ghettoization and mass murder of the Jews, the enormity of widespread communication of defamatory material through forms of mass media can be clearly seen.

A more recent similarly tragic example can be found in the 1994 Rwanda genocide in which militant Hutus turned upon their Tutsi and more moderate Hutu neighbors. Again, mass media was used to spread defamatory information about the Tutsis. The newspaper and the radio in particular were used as weapons to spread hate propaganda and convince the Hutu tribe that the Tutsis were indeed the enemy and should be destroyed.

This section will address a number of issues that should be considered in any discussion of religion and defamation. These issues include the law, free speech, antidefamation groups, and the impact of the Internet, which is surely one of most significant areas that throw up complexities for any legal reasoning on the subject in the twenty-first century.

The United Nations Commission on Human Rights, combating defamation of religious groups (2003–2004), addresses the harmful impact of defamation against religion on the stability and harmony of society. The resolution emphasizes that a peaceful and tolerant society will only be properly realized when states, nongovernmental organizations, religious bodies, and the media address the issue of defamation. Overall, an important underlying concern that is highlighted in the resolution is the harmful impact of the events of September 11, 2001 seen in the negative stereotyping in the media of the Muslim community. The resolution particularly criticizes "the use of print, audio-visual and electronic media, including the Internet, and any other means to incite acts of violence, xenophobia or related intolerance and discrimination towards them of any other religion." The resolution recalls that all states have pledged themselves to promote respect for all their members without discrimination relating to religion or otherwise. The law against defamation differs from one country to the next and even within a country (such as the various states in Australia). It is a notoriously complex law that proves difficult to apply in many practical instances.

Defamation Law and Free Speech

The many complexities and nuances within any law against defamation would be too complex to delve into here. However, the following generic points can be highlighted.

There is within the law against defamation a distinction between libel and slander. This distinction generally refers to the mode of publication. Usually slander refers to oral communication and libel refers to written communication. The underlying basis for this distinction involves the permanency of form, that is, oral communication is more fleeting than the permanency of the written word. However, there are obvious complexities with radio and television broadcasts that have been stored in written format or have been archived permanently.

The main aim of the law against defamation remains relatively straightforward. It exists to protect an individual or group against misleading information that can harm their reputation.

The crucial question relating to the defamation law is the whole matter concerning freedom of speech. When does the right to criticize a particular belief system become defamation? Some religious members have been accused of being far too sensitive and thus blurring the distinction between constructive criticism and deliberate slander or libel. Any discussion or reform of the law against defamation in any country has to balance the protection afforded to religion and an individual's right to free speech.

There does seem to be a different emphasis on the law against defamation in different countries. Some legal commentators have purported that the law in the United States lends much more emphasis on freedom than countries such as Australia where free speech is not constitutionally protected as it is in the United States. In Britain the law against blasphemy (a distinct but in some senses a related law to that of defamation) has been successfully used in July 1977 by Mary Whitehouse against *Gay News*, a magazine that contained a poem depicting Jesus as an object of homosexual love. Issues surrounding free speech and defamation came under scrutiny again in the United Kingdom in the 1990s due to the impact of Salman Rushdie's book *The*

Satanic Verses on certain members of the Muslim community who wanted his novel banned for material contained within it that they believed slandered their faith and their prophet. Abdul Hussain Choudhury, a representative of the British Muslim Action Front, tried to pursue a ban on the novel using the blasphemy law. It was an unsuccessful attempt as the blasphemy law in the United Kingdom only applies to the established church. However, the mere attempt caused many to call for the extinction of the blasphemy law, which, they believed, was an antiquated law that contravened the intrinsic principle of free speech essential to democracy.

In order to protect themselves from attacks on their faith, members of both mainstream and alternative religions have formed their own antidefamation groups.

Antidefamation Groups

One of the most prominent antidefamation groups formed in the United States is the Anti-Defamation League of B'nai B'rith (ADL). The ADL was established in 1913 and was initially formed to protect Jewish people from anti-Semitic hatred. The ADL has expanded its concern to include other religious groups and races worldwide. The ADL has responded to numerous instances where it believes that a particular religion has been unfairly targeted and defamed. One example involved a newspaper in Melbourne that published an article with reference to a Jewish man who was charged with a criminal offense. The paper headlined the article "Jewish leader on $42 million charges." The ADL alleged that this was inappropriate language as it drew upon images of the negative stereotype of the Jew who is obsessed with money. They protested that the religion of the man charged was entirely irrelevant to the reporting of the incident and thus should not have been included. Further examples where the ADL have spoken out include right-wing Evangelical groups who have allegedly denied the Holocaust or promoted the conspiracy theory that Jews want to take control of the world. They have also criticized treatment and attacks, amongst other groups, against Islam, the Mormons, and various race groups such as African-Americans and Aborigines. In the latter instance the ADL was particularly critical of the way the Australian media handled and communicated the views of right-wing spokesperson Pauline Hanson, believing that the media devoted too much space publicizing her anti-Aboriginal view and her own ideology of "one nation."

There are other antidefamation groups whose views have been made widely available through the Internet—Hindu Antidefamation Coalition and the National

Alliance Against Christian Discrimination are just two examples. However, more often than not religious members express their concern not via a particular antidefamation league or group but rather via protests against material that they believe has defamed their faith.

Film is a medium that has caused much controversy over the decades. Christians all over the world have objected to films such as *The Last Temptation of Christ*, *The Devils*, *Monty Python's Life of Brian*, and *The Exorcist*. Some Muslims have spoken out against the negative way they believe their religion was portrayed in films such as *Not Without My Daughter*. In 2002 Hindus protested in India against a lesbian film that they allege causes disrepute to their culture and society and by association their religion.

Religions have also been accused of defaming each other. The ADL has specified right-wing Christian Evangelical groups who have defamed Judaism. The Palestinian crisis has provoked Muslims and Jews alike to publish heated defamatory material about each other's religion over the Internet. Indeed in Britain in 2002, the Home Secretary suggested that there should be a fresh attempt to outlaw acts of religious hatred that can be utilized by one religion to protect itself from another.

However, the ADL remains one of the biggest voices against defamation of religion and has itself come under a lot of criticism by proponents of free speech who criticize what they perceive as the ADL's "big brother" approach. The ADL has been accused of keeping "hate files" on individuals and groups it feels are a threat to religion and has also been condemned for its alleged links to Zionism. The ADL, in the twenty-first century, has committed itself to fighting defamation wherever it occurs, particularly on the Internet.

Defamation and the Internet

The Internet as a worldwide medium of communication presents difficulties when it comes to any legal discussion of defamation. The Internet is one of the fastest-growing global media and its impact is huge. Defamation over the Internet is increasingly a significant problem and legally it is hard to address. There are numerous reasons why this is so. Three of the major reasons are as follows:

1. Issues surrounding publication. If a member of a religious group believes that an individual or group has damaged his or her religion then it is an issue as to where the material was published. Is the point of publication where the material was downloaded or uploaded? Furthermore, the material could be sent from one country and accessed in another; and one country could have different nuances and emphases in their defamation law than the other.

2. People can publish defamatory material anonymously over the Internet (though it is true that there are various methods available to identify anonymous authors of defamatory material).

3. How far are ISPs (Internet Service Providers) liable? Are Internet intermediaries responsible for the material that they carry but did not create? In Germany in 1998 the Information and Communication Services Act was passed which gives responsibility to ISPs and the content of their client site if it is technically feasible for them to block the site.

As global communication gets easier and faster, defamation of religion becomes a cause for concern. The Internet has been widely used as a means for communicating criticism of religious groups and beliefs. In some cases it can be particularly hard to decide whether this criticism is harmful and misleading, and thus defamatory. Future debate about controls over the Internet has to take into account the issue of free speech as well as protection from harmful negative stereotyping and attacks upon religious groups. It is not unreasonable to suggest that governments need to take seriously the link between defamatory material and its influence and impact on those who wish to cause physical harm to members of a particular religious group.

Defamation of religion can be communicated over an array of different media: broadcasts over radio, television and film, as well as newspaper reporting and magazines. Even fictional novels and poetry can be a cause for protest from members of religious groups. Alternative religions are commonly protesting against the way they are being depicted in television and film; for example, Wiccans have formed their own antidefamatory group as they allege that they are one of the most discriminated-against religions in the United States. If a member of a particular religion desires to bring his or her case to court, then the onus is on the member to prove that the defamatory material in question is misleading or inaccurate and harmful to the person or the group. In most cases this has been a very difficult thing to do and the complexities arising from the law against defamation will be an area of continual debate and reform.

VICTORIA A. LA'PORTE

See also Free Speech

Further Reading

Anti-Defamation League of B'nai B'rith. (1997–1999). *ADL Briefing, 1*(1) & 3(2).

Akhtar, S. (1990). *Is freedom holy to liberals? Some remarks on the purpose of law in free speech.* London: Commission For Racial Equality.

Article 19. (1989). *The crime of blasphemy—Why it should be abolished.* London: Article 19.

United Nations Commission on Human Rights. (2004). *Racism, racial discrimination, xenophobia, and all forms of discrimination.* Geneva, Switzerland: United Nations.

Leo Cussen Institute. (1998). *Media law and defamation.* Melbourne, Australia: Leo Cussen Institute.

Leo Cussen Institute. (2001). *Defamation and the Internet.* Melbourne, Australia: Leo Cussen Institute.

Pipes, D. (1990). *The Rushdie affair.* New York: Carol.

Pullan, R. (1994). *Guilty secrets, free speech, and defamation in Australia.* Glebe, Australia: Pascal.

Drama

Theater is distinguished from other narrative arts, in that the story, if there is one, is presented using actors impersonating characters, as opposed to being recited or read. This element of mimetic representation is also the way *theater* is usually distinguished from *drama*. *Drama* generally refers to the written text that forms the principle basis for the live representation we call the theatrical text. Thus, a playscript, written or published, might be studied as drama, but it requires a performance to be considered theater.

Theater's Religious Origins

The most widely accepted theory regarding the origins of theater is that dramatic representation is directly related to religious ritual, although other theories have been proposed. Indeed, the first major theoretical discussion of theater, Aristotle's *Poetics* (c. 350 BCE), describes theater as evolving over time from dithyrambic choruses sung and danced in honor of the Greek god Dionysus, specifically at competitions that were part of the Festival of Dionysus in Athens, which began about 534 BCE. Tradition credits Thespis, winner of the first dithyrambic contest, with inventing the tragic form, by stepping out from the chorus and beginning a dialogue with it and with the choral leader. In Attic Greece, and later in Rome, plays were for the most part still limited to specific religious festivals, although the plays themselves became increasingly secular in content.

Of course, many other cultures outside Attic Greece have supported theatrical performances, and in Greek culture, mime flourished outside the state-supported religious festivals. It would therefore be reductive to suggest that all theatrical activities or performances derive from religious ritual. Nonetheless, most scholars would agree that at least some connection exists between ritual and theater. Quasi-theatrical elements in such pre-Athenian rituals as the so-called Egpytian Abydos Passion Play, and rituals from various ancient Sumerian, Babylonian, Hittite, and Canaanite cultures suggest a fairly widespread use of mimetic or theatrical elements in a variety of ancient religious settings. Of course, it is impossible at this far remove to reliably determine the degree to which such ritual texts were enacted, but it is at least possible that something resembling a mimetic performance may have been part of religious rites in many cultures across the globe.

In Asian theater, a connection between religious observances and theatrical performance can be seen. For example, the Sanskrit text *Natyasastra* (*The Science of Dramaturgy*, from ca. 200 BCE–200 CE), is both a sacred Hindu religious text and a very practical theatrical handbook, with detailed instructions regarding the dance, acting, costume, and makeup to be used in Sanskrit drama. The Hindu sage Bharata is credited with writing this remarkable work, having been taught it, according to legend, by Brahma himself. Jo Riley has demonstrated how the essentialist, pictographic aesthetic at the heart of Beijing Opera and other Chinese operatic forms reflects origins in Chinese exorcism and ancestor worship rituals, and such Japanese dramatic forms as Noh and Kabuki are both historically and aesthetically linked to Buddhism.

Theater as Separate from Ritual

Thus, theater may have evolved from ritual and may have many elements in common with ritual. At the same time, most theater theorists agree that a theater event is not quite the same thing as a religious ritual. Although both theater and ritual can involve an enacted performance, including mimesis, theater scholars usually distinguish between them by what we might call a presumption of efficacy. In other words, although both theater and ritual may involve representation, the ritual performer/celebrant is regarded by himself and by his audience/congregation as genuinely communing with some divine power, to the material and/or spiritual benefit of both. The theatrical performer, on

A dramatic scene showing a stone sculpture of an angel in front of a turbulent sky. *Courtesy of Firehorse/ istockphoto.com.*

the other hand, creates a representation on what is mutually agreed to be a more secular plane.

One way to distinguish between ritual and theater might be to look at a Catholic Mass, in which the celebrant is presumed to become Christ, just as the elements of the Eucharist host are transubstantiated into the body and blood of Christ. For devout congregants, mimesis becomes efficacious, a genuine communion with deity, but an actor in a play about a Mass may well use precisely the same language as one might find in a real Mass. Still, the audience at the play knows they are seeing a mere representation of the event. They agree to "suspend disbelief," or, in other words, they presume that what they are seeing is not efficacious. By the same token, we might compare a wedding ceremony in a play, as opposed to an actual wedding. Although the language and costumes used in both events might be identical, the audience at the play knows that what they are seeing is an elaborate fictional construct. The actors exchanging vows on stage are not actually committing themselves to each other, could quite possibly already be married to other people, and in fact are likely to exchange those same vows several times a week for many months in front of different audiences. In a real wedding, however, the participants agree to presume that a genuine change in status has taken place.

Thus, although at times, a ritual may involve the element of mimesis, a fairly clear line can be drawn between ritual and a theater event. In a ritual, the celebrant may be presumed by the congregation at some point to become Christ, or Osiris, or some other divine figure. A ritual may be, to that extent, mimetic, but in theater, both audience and performer agree to participate in the shared creation of an enacted illusion.

In addition to shared mimetic elements, theater and religion have often coexisted in what might best be described as a tense and uneasy alliance. In the Christian tradition, theatrical elements enhanced the medieval liturgy and eventually led to the creation of liturgical dramas. The Church festival of Corpus Christi often included mystery plays: large-scale community productions of works written in the vernacular but based on Christian scripture. Throughout Christian Europe, miracle plays celebrated the deeds of saints, and morality plays celebrated, in allegorical form, specific theological questions.

Despite the many historical links between religious observance and theatrical performance, theater has been consistently under attack from religious institutions, thinkers, and clergy. Jonas Barish (1981) has shown how, in the Christian tradition, opposition to theatrical performances has led to actors being denied the sacraments of the Church, denunciations of theatrical entertainments from pulpits, and a general attitude of suspicion toward actors and plays. Although censorship has generally been imposed on theaters and performers by civic authorities, it has often been in response to pressure from religious leaders.

The relationship between theater and religion has therefore been characterized by peculiar ambiguities and tensions, in which awkward and ineffective attempts to regulate or censor theatrical performances have alternated with moments in which theater is embraced as a valuable supplement to religious devotions. Thus, we see various ninth-century papal denunciations of 'mimi or histriones (actors), followed in the tenth century by Bishop Ethelwold of Winchester's *Regularis Concordia* (c. 965–975 CE), a compendium of liturgical playlets that included directions for their performance. The restrictive Catholicism of golden age Spain (c. 1550–1700) officially refused actors Christian marriage or burial, pressured civic authorities to censor plays, and intermittently succeeded in banning actresses from the Spanish stage. However, Spanish churchmen also hired actors to perform in religious pageants called the *autos sacramentales*, and most Spanish theaters served as fund-raising entities for such Catholic charities as the Cofredía de la Pasión y Sangre de Jesucristo. Japanese kabuki drama was first performed in 1603 by Okuni, a female dancer from the Izumo Grand Shrine, but the Shogunate found her dances too sensual and banned female kabuki performers in 1629. Safely in the hands of male performers, Kabuki would become the cultural touchstone it is today.

Return of Spirituality to Theater

With the rise of Romanticism in the Western world, the quest for supersensuous transcendence in nature and, ultimately, in art led to attempts to place spirituality at the center of the theatrical experience. Romantic spirituality found theatrical expression in new approaches to theatrical production, through a renewed study of and theatrical experimentation with the plays of Shakespeare, through a few actors whose forte was spiritual sensibility—Thomas Kean in England, Ludwig Devrient in Germany, François-Joseph Talma in France—and through the dramatic work of Romantic playwrights, particularly Friedrich Schiller and Victor Hugo. Romantic theater may not have been directly linked to institutional religion, but it represented an attempt to renew what was regarded as the foundational religious experience at the heart of the theatrical event.

Many of the various avant-garde artistic movements that flourished from the beginnings of modernism (c. 1870) through the end of World War I were self-conscious attempts to recover spiritual and religious values that artists felt had been lost with the onset of the Industrial Revolution. The director Aurélien-Marie Lugné-Poë founded the Théâtre de

l'Oeuvre in 1893 to place symbolist mysticism at the center of theatrical production. Influential designer and director Adolphe Appia's non-illusionistic approach was informed by his own interests in Asian religion and in his own fascination with eurhythmics, which promised a kind of kinesthetic/religious experience. German expressionism, which sought to bring external reality into harmony with humanity's spiritual nature, found a ready home in theatrical production, particularly through the works of such playwrights as Georg Kaiser, Eugene O'Neill, and Elmer Rice and such directors as Max Rheinhardt, Leopold Jessner, and Jürgen Fehling.

Following World War II, one branch of the theatrical avant-garde continued what remains the ongoing quest to return theater to what are regarded as its roots in religious ritual. The list of directors, theorists, and playwrights who have engaged in this effort is far too long for the scope of this article, but perhaps a few names will suffice. Richard Schechner has worked closely with anthropologist Victor Turner in efforts to recover the ritual nature of the theatrical event. Such theater companies as the Living Theatre and the Open Theatre have attempted to directly incorporate ritual elements in their productions. Polish director Jerzy Grotowski's experiments with Poor Theatre have centered performance strategy on a "holy actor" who embodies, and perhaps even atones for, the sins of the audience. Directors as disparate in their approach as Peter Hall, Peter Brook, and Robert Wilson and playwrights as widely ranging as Caryl Churchill, Wole Soyinka, and Suzan-Lori Parks have all enriched contemporary theatrical practice through their interest in ritual.

Relationship of Theater and Religion Today

Most contemporary theater remains secular entertainment, usually making at least a nod to moral issues, and frequently rooting dramatic conflict in some kind of ethical dilemma, but without any more substantial connection to mainstream religious practice. Some religious traditions incorporate theatricality in their devotions, and many churches sponsor pageants or short youth dramas as a supplement to worship. However, mainstream commercial theater, especially in the United States, and mainstream organized religion generally occupy different spheres of influence and responsibility and usually have little to do with each other. Aside from increasingly rare attempts by religious groups to censor theatrical productions, and aside from occasional efforts by commercial theater companies to mount plays designed to capitalize on religious holidays, the worlds of theater and religion are largely separate today. The historical link between religious ritual and theatrical representation, between spirituality and mimesis, must today be seen as somewhat marginalized, at least in the United States, found in avant-garde venues, in the world of theatrical experimentation and theory. However, in the heavily subsidized world of some European theaters, and in the best work of some Asian, South American, and African theater artists, we once again see the connection between religious ritual and mimetic representation.

ERIC SAMUELSON

Further Reading

Barish, J. A. (1981). *The antitheatrical prejudice.* Berkeley: University of California Press.

Riley, J. (1997). *Chinese theatre and the actor in performance* (Cambridge Studies in Modern Theatre). Cambridge, UK: Cambridge University Press.

Encyclicals

An encyclical is an official written communication in the form of a letter from the pope to the bishops of the Roman Catholic Church. The pope can use many different types of written communication to exercise the powers of his office, each with its own purpose, style, and authority. Examples of these include bulls, autograph letters, apostolic letters, decrees, rescripts, and briefs. There are significant differences between these forms of written communication. For example, when a pope wishes to explain or interpret the ordinary teachings of the Catholic Church, he might choose to write an encyclical, a general letter intended for the pastoral guidance of the whole church. But if he intends to issue a more formal definition of church doctrine, then he might choose a different form of communication, such as a bull, which he knows will be received with even greater solemnity.

The First Encyclicals

The word "encyclical" comes from a Greek word meaning "circular," which suggests a general letter circulated from church to church. In the first century, leaders wrote letters to mission churches throughout the Roman Empire, and many of these were copied and circulated from one Christian community to the next. This pattern can still be seen in the New Testament, which is partly a collection of letters. For example, the apostle Peter wrote a general letter to the churches of Asia Minor, which was copied, circulated among many Christian congregations, and eventually became part of the New Testament. In a similar way, modern popes also write letters of instruction and pastoral guidance to the Catholic faithful around the world. As in previous centuries, encyclicals are still written on paper and stamped with an official seal in ink. But computer technology and the Internet have also brought some changes. Today papal encyclicals can be read on many websites, including the official website of the Vatican.

During the early centuries of the Christian Church, bishops frequently wrote letters to individuals and to churches offering instruction, advice, correction, and censure on many topics. Most of this correspondence consists of letters that were directed to specific situations, individuals, or groups of Christian leaders, rather than of a general pastoral letter addressed to all the bishops of the church. Eusebius (c. 260–340 CE), a well-known bishop, quotes from a number of these letters. He writes that a group of bishops from Palestine "drew up a decree of the Church, in the form of letters addressed to Christians everywhere," and goes on to say that a similar conference of bishops at Rome also sent out a letter in the name of Victor, who was the bishop of Rome. These letters bear some resemblance to the modern practice of papal encyclicals, although today the forms of communication used by popes are more precisely defined. Today the use of the encyclical is limited to the pope in his pastoral leadership of the worldwide Catholic Church and is distinguished from the ordinary communications of bishops in their particular jurisdictions.

The form of these ancient letters followed the typical pattern of Roman correspondence, which began with the name of the writer and the name of the recipients, a pattern still evident in the letters of the New Testament. For many centuries popes identified themselves in this correspondence as "Bishop of the Catholic Church," but during the eighth century they began to write using their own papal names and to date their correspondence from the beginning of their pontificates. In the twelfth century, the official written communications of the popes began to be preserved in an ordered collection, and from this time forward the number of papal letters addressed to the wider Christian world grew.

The modern form and use of the encyclical is usually dated to the pontificate of Benedict XIV (1675–1758). Upon his accession to the papacy in 1740, Benedict issued a general pastoral letter that, in his words, would "revive the custom of the ancient Popes." The practice of addressing topics of faith and morals in a universal letter gradually became an important means of communication for popes to the present day.

Why Are Encyclicals Written?

Encyclicals are usually concerned with matters of doctrine and morals that are of contemporary relevance to the universal church. A pope might want to publish an encyclical for many reasons: to express his mind on unresolved theological issues, to address social or political problems, or to clarify the church's teaching on a matter and call the faithful to more diligent observance. A special class of encyclicals has been called "social encyclicals" because they primarily address issues of social justice, human rights, and world peace. Perhaps the most famous social encyclical is *Rerum Novarum*, issued by Pope Leo XIII (1810–1903) in 1891. Concerned about the problems of modern industrial capitalism, Leo chartered a new course for Catholic social thought. In this letter he affirmed the right to own private property, the right of workers to organize labor unions, and the responsibility of the state to protect workers. Political questions of the late nineteenth century thus became the occasion for the pope to guide Roman Catholics through the extremes of socialism and capitalism.

Encyclicals are meant to be pastoral. This means that they are intended to protect, guide, discipline, or instruct the leaders and members of the Catholic Church. This also means that they are practical rather than theoretical or speculative. Because encyclicals are pastoral letters, they are mainly written for members of the Roman Catholic Church. Since 1963, however, some encyclicals have sought to engage a wider audience by also being addressed to "all people of good will." Depending on the topic, encyclicals have ranged in length from a few paragraphs to long essays. The longest encyclical to date is *Splendor Veritatis*. Issued in 1993, this letter was a lengthy moral treatise that John Paul II (1920–2005) worked on for six years. But this is unusual. Most encyclicals have been much shorter.

Although encyclicals are issued in the name of the pope, they are usually not written by the popes themselves. More often, the pope relies on close advisors or groups of scholars to help him formulate his pastoral leadership in carefully constructed language. Once published, an encyclical is normally identified and referred to in discussion by its first two or three words. These titular words are usually in Latin, because the majority of encyclicals have been written in that language. However, the use of Latin is not officially required. In fact, one of the most famous modern encyclicals was written in German: called *Mit Brennender Sorge* (With Deep Anxiety), it offered a stinging rebuke of German fascism in 1937 prior to World War II. Although it was an important message for Catholics everywhere who faced the threats of radical nationalist and racist ideologies, this encyclical focused specifically on the threat of National Socialism to the freedom and independence of the German Catholic Church.

The Role of Encyclicals in Modern Times

Until the second half of the twentieth century, many encyclicals remained out of reach of most ordinary Catholics. But in the last fifty years, with advances in education and global communication, encyclicals have become more accessible to the common person. Of course, the clergy still bear a special responsibility to interpret and implement the pope's pastoral guidance. For instance, in 1956 Anne Fremantle commented that good English translations of some encyclicals were hard to come by. But today ordinary Catholics from around the world can easily read the pope's words for themselves. Some theorists have speculated that the use of modern digital media to reach the Catholic faithful directly will tend to increase the centralizing power of the papal office, because the pope can bypass bureaucratic intermediaries and speak directly to the church at large. Others, however, have suggested that the use of modern media may have a democratizing influence on papal power and authority. They reason that the distinctive authoritative character of papal declarations may be drowned out in an ocean of digital communications, or diminished by the endless array of competing critical views in digital space and time.

The frequent use of the encyclical in modern times has been controversial. For some critics, popes have made mistaken or poorly conceived declarations that have failed to express accurately the church's teaching on a particular subject. Others object that the use of encyclicals has become a political tool for suppressing legitimate dissent and disagreement among the church's theologians. This has given rise to a great deal of discussion on what kind of religious authority ought to be ascribed to encyclicals (as well as other authoritative communications of the pope). Should the teaching of a pope in an encyclical be regarded as final and in some special sense treated as infallible, that is, without error? Or is there room for some expressions of dissent and disagreement from teachings that do not claim for themselves infallibility?

Some Catholic theologians emphasize that papal teachings in an encyclical have less authority than statements that are explicitly identified as infallible and as extraordinary teachings of the church. This means that encyclicals should be given a proper religious respect, but that they are not necessarily infallible and do not require unconditional assent. In support of this view, Catholic theologians like Father Charles Curran have pointed out several examples of errors that have occurred in official papal teachings. For example, he cites as erroneous the teaching of Pope Pius IX (1792–1878) in *Quanta Cura*, which condemned modern ideas of freedom of conscience and worship as the right of every person. In addition, Curran has also advanced the argument that some areas of human knowledge are incapable of absolute certitude and, therefore, by definition, cannot exclude the possibility of error.

More traditional Catholic theologians disagree with Curran's viewpoint. They argue that because encyclicals contain the ordinary and received teaching of the church, they cannot be treated as different from other expressions of infallible teaching that do require assent and obedience. Advocates of this view often cite the statement of Pius XII (1876–1958) in *Humani Generis* in which he declared that if a pope purposely passes judgment on a debated subject, then that subject can no longer be considered an open question for debate.

Few modern encyclicals have generated more criticism and discussion than *Humanae Vitae*. Issued by Pope Paul VI (1897–1978) in 1968, this letter reaffirmed earlier teaching that forbade Catholics from using artificial methods of contraception. When some Catholic theologians openly questioned this teaching, the church hierarchy expressed fears that academic dissent would confuse church members and took steps to prevent contrary opinions from being taught in Catholic universities. Studies have shown that Catholics widely disregard the ban on birth control, prompting many Catholic theologians to call for a contemporary reformulation of the church's teaching on matters of contra-ception and human sexuality. Conservative bishops, however, have vigorously resisted changes to the received tradition, with the result that the Catholic Church remains divided on several of the teachings affirmed in *Humanae Vitae*.

The controversy over *Humanae Vitae* has led to an extensive ongoing discussion about the use and proper understanding of encyclicals and other authoritative pronouncements of the church hierarchy. These discussions suggest that there will continue to be changes in the way that the church hierarchy approaches complex social issues. But whatever changes may occur in the near future, the encyclical will continue to play an important role in a pope's pastoral guidance of the church.

DANIEL W. DRANEY

Further Reading

Encyclicals (2002). *The New Catholic encyclopedia* (Vol. X). Retrieved from www.vatican.ca, June 20, 2005.

Eusebius. (1965). *History of the church from Christ to Constantine* (G. A. Williamson, Trans.). New York: Penguin.

Fremantle, A. J. (1956). *The papal encyclicals in their historical context*. New York: Mentor Books.

Ihm, Claudia C. (1990). *The papal encyclicals: 1740 to 1981* (Vols. 1 –5). Ann Arbor, MI: Pierian Press.

May, W. W. (Ed.). (1987). *Vatican authority and American Catholic dissent: The Curran case and its consequences*. New York: Crossroad.

Schuck, M. J. (1991). *That they be one: the social teaching of papal encyclicals, 1740–1989*. Washington, DC: Georgetown University Press.

Enlightenment, The

The Enlightenment was a period in European and North Atlantic history, and a social movement that challenged humans to *Sapere aude!*, to "dare to know" by themselves, unaided by the tutelage of church, dogmatic religion, or intolerant traditions. While traditional histories of the Enlightenment put their emphasis on its European aspects and thinkers, the movement also spread through the United States, and what is today known as Latin America from the seventeenth through the eighteenth century. The Enlightenment would not have been possible without the commerce in commodities and ideas, and the general circulation of people among continents and nations that crossing the Atlantic made possible. Standard entries on the Enlightenment refer to it as an intellectual movement, and some even go so far as to name it a philosophical movement. Yet, this characterization of the Enlightenment misrepresents its material and social aspects. The Enlightenment was above all a radical transformation in the very nature of social interactions among citizens, consumers, rulers, societies, and cultures in general.

If Enlightenment refers to the power of the light of reason to vanquish and dissipate the shadows of superstition and ignorance, this light could not have lit the spaces of society without the explosion in the production and dissemination of books, learned societies, and newspapers. Religion or superstition, according to most readings, was replaced by reason during the Enlightenment. Those readings conceal, however, that this shift was only possible because of major developments in the means of religious communication. As a social movement, with a solid intellectual core, the Enlightenment continues to be contested, maligned, and praised. In this sense, Immanuel Kant's remark that he did not live in an enlightened age, but in an age of enlightenment, remains as true today as when he wrote it in December of 1784, when he penned his famous essay "Answer to the Question: 'What is Enlightenment?'"

New Interpretations

A major transformation took place in the study of history during the 1960s that spawned a spate of new interpretations of the Enlightenment. A shift away from great figures (popes, kings, philosophers), moments (revolutions, wars), and ideas (fideism, rationalisms, empiricisms) toward movements, institutions, *mentalités*, and the *longe duree*, the slow ebbing tide of historical processes, took place in historical research. This revolution in the production of historical research also affected the way historians studied and conceptualized the Enlightenment. The study of the Enlightenment must now also include reference to the different schools of its interpretation and analysis. At the very least three schools or currents of historiography of the Enlightenment can be discerned. The oldest and most prevalent school of interpretation is the one associated with the German philosopher Ernst Cassirer. In his 1932 text, *The Philosophy of the Enlightenment*, Cassirer presented an Enlightenment that was homogenous in terms of its debates and philosophical positions, which was dominant in Western Europe, and that above all reached its most elaborate expression in the work of Immanuel Kant. For Cassirer, the Enlightenment was principally about the philosophical championing of reason over superstition, custom, faith, and authority.

A second school is the one associated with Peter Gay, whose magisterial two-volume *The Enlightenment: An Interpretation* (1966–1969) opened up new research vistas. Each volume is entitled differently, and each gives an indication of Gay's line of interpretation. Volume one is entitled *The Rise of Modern Paganism*. Volume two is entitled *The Science of Freedom*. Like Cassirer, Gay conceived the Enlightenment as a unitary movement and period. In contrast, however, Gay included non-European figures such as Thomas Jefferson and Benjamin Franklin. Gay also offered a chronology of the Enlightenment that distinguished between the earlier, mostly French, and the latter, mostly German, Enlightenment thinkers. To the first period belong figures like François Marie Arouet Voltaire and Charles de Secondat Montesquieu, who were followed by a younger generation of philosophers, such as Denis Diderot, Jean le Rond d'Alembert, and Jean-Jacques Rousseau. To the late Enlightenment belong figures like Gotthold Ephraim Lessing and Immanuel Kant. In contrast to Cassirer, Gay infused his intellectual history of the Enlightenment with social history of the eighteenth century, paying attention to the social milieu of Paris in the eighteenth century. For Gay the Enlightenment was predominantly a struggle against religion, superstition, and the Church, and in tandem, a movement that sought political freedom through the elaboration of an art of living in freedom. By the end of the eighteenth century, Paris had become the cauldron of new means of social interaction, in general, and of religious communication in particular.

A third and more recent school of interpretation was initially championed by John Greville Agard Pocock and Quentin Skinner, in England, and Germán Arciniegas, in Colombia. This school has been advanced and popularized by Roy Porter, Daniel Roche, and Dorinda Outram. To this third school of interpretation also belong Robert Darnton and Ulrich Im Hof, although one is American and the other German. What unites all of these scholars, notwithstanding their different nationalities and fields of expertise, is their focus and point of departure. Invariably, all these scholars see the Enlightenment as a social movement that encompassed every imaginable aspect of society: trade routes, urbanization, newspapers, coffee houses, mail delivery, migrations and exiles of intellectuals and political leaders, and so on. They all depart from a study of everyday life, or quotidian existence, in the seventeenth and eighteenth centuries. Their studies, furthermore, begin with the insight that the transformation of European social existence in these centuries was a transcontinental and transatlantic phenomenon.

Selection from Kant's "An Answer to the Question: What is Enlightenment?"

In the extract below from an essay written in 1794, the philosopher Immanuel Kant seeks to define the concept of enlightenment.

Enlightenment is man's emergence from his self-imposed immaturity. Immaturity is the inability to use one's understanding without guidance from another. This immaturity is self-imposed when its cause lies not in lack of understanding, but in lack of resolve and courage to use it without guidance from another. *Sapere Aude*! [dare to know] "Have courage to use your own understanding!"—that is the motto of enlightenment.

Laziness and cowardice are the reasons why so great a proportion of men, long after nature has released them from alien guidance (*natura-liter maiorennes*), nonetheless gladly remain in lifelong immaturity, and why it is so easy for others to establish themselves as their guardians. It is so easy to be immature. If I have a book to serve as my understanding, a pastor to serve as my conscience, a physician to determine my diet for me, and so on, I need not exert myself at all. I need not think, if only I can pay: others will readily undertake the irksome work for me. The guardians who have so benevolently taken over the supervision of men have carefully seen to it that the far greatest part of them (including the entire fair sex) regard taking the step to maturity as very dangerous, not to mention difficult. Having first made their domestic livestock dumb, and having carefully made sure that these docile creatures will not take a single step without the go-cart to which they are harnessed, these guardians then show them the danger that threatens them, should they attempt to walk alone. Now this danger is not actually so great, for after falling a few times they would in the end certainly learn to walk; but an example of this kind makes men timid and usually frightens them out of all further attempts.

The economic, political, cultural, and social lives on the Continent, the British Islands, and the Americas were woven in a tight and intricate network of relations. For this reason, their works are more like social histories than intellectual histories. As social histories, their works provide thick material histories of culture, which elucidate the dependence of ideas on networks of communication.

Renaissance

As an intellectual and social movement, the Enlightenment is the summation of movements and the revolutionary social transformation that preceded it. Two of the most important precedents of the Enlightenment were the Renaissance and the Reformation. The Renaissance was also a movement and a period. As a movement, it signaled a revival of and return to the Greek and Roman roots of European culture. This return was made possible by the influx of learned scholars' ancient texts from Constantinople, when this capital of learning during the fifteenth century fell in 1453 to the expanding Ottoman Empire.

The fall of Byzantium to the Ottoman marked the end of the Middle Ages, and the inception of a period of cultural renewal. The cultural renewal, however, took place mostly in the Italian ports of the fifteenth and sixteenth century, in particular Venice, Genoa, and Naples. In these Italian cities, a wealthy merchant class had emerged that took under its patronage many of the scholars who would lead the rebirth of ancient culture. But, one of the things that the dispersion of the Byzantine scholars brought to Italy were the texts of Aristotle, Plato, Plotinus, and Roman scholars in the original Greek and Latin. The Renaissance was thus both a movement of return to the classical sources and an unprecedented rescue from oblivion of many scholars and texts that had been lost, forgotten, or that simply were never made available during the so-called "Dark Ages" between the fall of Rome in the fifth century through the fall of Constantinople. This revival was made possible by the very institutions of the church, such as its monasteries, where hundreds of scribes and monks patiently labored copying thousands of manuscripts. The image of a monk copying and reciting the words of ancient manuscript exists today as the most enduring

and material institutions of religious communication. In contrast to the medieval outlook, which emphasized above all the sinfulness of humans and thus imposed the imperative to have them lead by the authority and tutelage of the church, the Renaissance thinkers emphasized humanity's creativity, divine origins, perfectibility, and therefore, in the words of Pico della Mirandolla, the "dignity" of humanity. The Italian Renaissance was a compressed form of what was to take place in the Enlightenment, namely the synergistic convergence of a wealthy class, urban concentration, and the development of a culture of mass consumption of products that made available to great numbers of people the cultural inheritance of the world. And, although the Renaissance was not an antireligious movement, its contestation of the interpretation of the Holy Scriptures by the Church that emphasized the human fall can be said to have catalyzed a secularism that was to become full-blown with the Enlightenment. The turn to the sources of Christianity itself by the Renaissance thinkers, in its three sacred languages, Greek, Italian, and Hebrew, already inaugurated a questioning of the supreme authority of the church and its theologians.

Reformation

In contrast to the Renaissance, the Reformation was a confessedly anti-Church movement. It began as denunciation of the theological betrayal of the Christian doctrine and the corruption of Rome. Inaugurated by the German Martin Luther with his ninety- five theses against papal indulgences, which he affixed to the front of the All Saints Church at Wittenberg in 1517, the movement spread through Western Europe, the British Islands, and the northern area of France. The Reformation, however, rode on the back of the wave of learning inaugurated by the Renaissance. Desiderius Erasmus, for instance, a theologian and scholar, was a figure of both the Renaissance and the Reformation. Arguably, Martin Luther was also a figure of the Renaissance, if one considers his role as a translator of the Bible into German. Luther's relationship, as well as that of the Reformation in general, to the Renaissance and the humanism that it championed, is best illustrated by his twenty-eight-year collaborator, Phillip Melanchthon, who was trained as a humanist and who used his vast knowledge of the classical languages to promote a return to the sources of Christianity. Melanchthon used biblical and philological scholarship to refute papal primacy, although he advocated its acceptance for the sake of peace. A conciliator and pacifier, Melanchthon has subsequently been described by Reformers as a traitor, although he is buried next to Luther at Wittenberg. Like Dante Alighieri, author of the *Divine Comedy* and the important if neglected *De vulgari eloquentia*, Luther expressed one of the central aspects of the Reformation, namely the institutionalization of vernacular languages as national languages.

The contestation of the power of the Holy Roman Church in Rome took explicit expression in the proliferation of the vernaculars: Spanish, Italian, German, French, and English. The growth and formalization of these national languages displaced Latin as the lingua franca of the European cultural community. Interestingly, the fragmentation of the religious and cultural unity of the Christian Europe took place through the very institutions of the Church.

An illustrative parallel with the fall of the Roman Empire can be drawn. Just as the Christianization of the Roman Empire was made possible by the roads, highways, and postal system of the empire itself, the Reformation was made possible and diffused through the institutions of the Church itself. Monasteries, universities, theologians, and religious scholars, as well as church-financed and licensed printers were the main agents that spread the new methods of the production of books, precisely in the name of the Church and religious learning.

At the center of this diffusion, like an inexhaustible source of power and innovation, lay the book. The Reformation, in fact, was above all a revolution of the book, as French historians Lucien Febvre and Henri-Jean Martin argued in their classic work first published in 1958, *L'Apparition du Livre* (*The Coming of the Book*). The revolution of the book involved not only the development of new techniques of paper production, printing, binding, and distribution that essentially made the book into a mass commodity, but also the ways in which the book inaugurated and instigated national communities of scholarship, nonecclesiastical scholars, the promotion of national languages, and the emergence of a mass readership that was transnational and transcontinental in its tastes and readership. A movement that began with the central goal of granting everyone direct access to the Holy Word in the national language, ended up giving birth to both a mass readership and secular authorship that lay outside the control of any religious authority.

Public Sphere

The Enlightenment was made possible by the new social fabric and mental outlook that had been achieved, unwittingly, by both the Renaissance and the Reformation.

The preceding periods had championed a humanistic scholarship that celebrated humanity's incompleteness and futurity and a type of religious piety that revered the godly by way of the vernacular and local. In all, however, the three periods were about the consolidation of thick, expansive, and decentered networks of communication. What makes the Enlightenment sui generis and different from both the Reformation and the Renaissance, is that it was as much about the development of a mental outlook, a *mentalité*, as it was about the constitution of a new cultural sociability that found its proper home neither in the state, nor in the private sphere, nor even in what was called civil society, but in what German philosopher Jürgen Habermas called the "public sphere" (*Öffentlichkeit*). In this public sphere citizens encounter each other as equals and only the noncoercive power of reason prevailed; reasons were given and information exchanged. The republic of letters, belonging to neither empire nor nation, and to which all Enlightenment figures belonged, found its home in this space. Exposure to and participation in this public sphere promoted a new sociability that engendered a new form of social comportment, a new *habitus*, a way of behaving, that gave primacy to the public exchange of reason and the openness of a mutual give and take of arguments that celebrated the power of reason to resolve differences and conflicts. This public sphere is the name for a new social fabric woven by new sites and locales for the production and exchange of commodities, ideas, and news.

Academies were central in this new social fabric. Practically every monarchy during the eighteenth century set up an academy. These academies were established to promote scholarship, the diffusion of ideas, and the emergence of a local, national, and imperial scholarly community that would be the pride of the respective king or monarchy. These academies were a major vehicle for the promotion of talent, but also for upward social mobility. Members were appointed by the king or elected by the academy itself. Members were paid a stipend by the crown. Through its annual competitions, academies promoted innovative work while also engaging a wider public.

Salons performed a similar function, but outside the boundaries of the state. The salon was the academy for the rising bourgeoisie. It was organized, financed, and hosted with members of the nobility or upper classes. A wealthy matron of the letters and arts generally hosted these salons, and many of them were central to the diffusion of the Enlightenment. Enlightenment philosophers such as Bernard le Bouvier de Fontenelle, Charles de Secondat Montesquieu, Gabriel Bonnot de

Mably, and Claude Adrien Helvetius met at the salon of Madame de Tencin, while contributors to the *Encyclopédie*, Jean le Rond d'Alembert, Jean-François Marmontel, Ètienne Bonnot de Condillac, Michel Ètienne Turgot, and others met at the home of Mademoiselle de Lespinasse.

While salons were informal, reading societies tried to retain their spirit of open debate, although through a more formal structure. Reading societies had memberships, with paying dues, and came with privileges, such as access to libraries, lectures, or other literary events. Similarly organized but with more practical aims in mind, there also emerged utilitarian reading societies that promoted the production and dissemination of scientific work that could be directly applied in the fields of animal husbandry and agriculture. Most of these societies concerned themselves with improving the living conditions of farmers and modernizing the countryside.

The Freemasons also played an important part in this new social fabric. As a brotherhood and movement, it promoted social loyalty across class lines but also a type of ecumenical tolerance. These are the more prominent sites or nodes of the new social fabric that was the Enlightenment. Underneath them, alongside them, between them, however, there was the proliferation of other sites and milieux without which the Enlightenment could not have germinated and flourished. Enlightenment and eighteenth-century historian Robert Darnton drew up a "schematic model of the communication circuit" that illustrates the thickness and widespread character of the sites in which the Enlightenment thrived (1979). In this circuit, on one side, we encounter sites or milieux; on the other we encounter media. On the former, we encounter streets, markets, the court, cafés, taverns, public gardens, salons, private circles, printing shops, bookshops, libraries, and reading groups. On the latter, we encounter rumors, gossip, manuscript news, broadsides, posters, pamphlets, periodicals, and books. Careful attention to these ordinary, albeit indispensable, spaces of everyday social interaction discloses how the Enlightenment became established and how in turn the establishment became enlightened, to paraphrase historian Roy Porter. In tandem, what this type of thick social and material history of the Enlightenment discloses is that in its circuit of information, religion was essential but not determining.

Lasting Effects

According to Peter Gay, the Enlightenment was neither anti-Christian nor antireligious, although it was avowedly anticlerical. Enlightenment anticlericalism, however, flowed from the general antiauthoritarian character of its reverence for and deference to reason. The Enlightenment may have catalyzed the de-Christianization of Europe, but it hardly culminated in a thorough or even partial secularization of society. The very circuits of communication that facilitated the expansion of the Enlightenment were also the medium through which new forms of religiosity and piety were born and spread. What Martin Luther began in the sixteenth century was brought to fruition in the work of the American Enlightenment figures, which institutionalized freedom of conscience by writing it into the constitution of the new nation.

Religion, which etymologically means to bind and to be bound, was given a new life with the Enlightenment. The religion of the Enlightenment, its worship of reason, gave birth to an enlightened religion, a privatized and personalized religion that coexisted with the public use of reason. The Enlightenment's relationship illustrates what Hegel called the cunning of historical reason. Riding on the shoulders of the giants of the Renaissance and the Reformation, both movements and periods inaugurated and fomented by the church and the Christian religion, the Enlightenment, instead of consigning Christianity and religion to the dustbin of historical curiosities, gave both a new lease on life. Considering the level of superstition, heterodoxy, and polytheism that reigned during the Middle Ages, the Enlightenment could be said to have accomplished what the Church had failed to do: to spread the enlightenment and promise of the Holy Word. The Enlightenment, made possible by a new social fabric of unimpeded and relentless communication and exchange of reasons, gave birth to a new sociability in which religion was preserved so long as it did not seek to rule and silence the public sphere of unfettered reason.

EDUARDO MENDIETA

See also Middle Ages

Further Reading

Arciniegas, G. (1986). *America in Europe: A history of the new world in reverse.* San Diego, CA: Harcourt Brace Jovanovich.

Becker, C. (1932). *The heavenly city of the eighteenth-century philosophers.* New Haven, CT: Yale University Press.

Buchan, J. (2003). *Crowded with genius: The Scottish Enlightenment. Ediburgh's moment of the mind.* New York: Harper-Collins.

Cassirer, E. (1951). *The philosophy of the Enlightenment.* Princeton, NJ: Princeton University Press. (Original work published 1932)

Darnton, R. (1979). *The business of enlightenment: A publishing history of the encyclopédie 1775–1800.* Cambridge, MA: The Belknap Press of Harvard University Press.

Darnton, R. (1990). *The kiss of Lamourette: Reflections in cultural history.* New York and London: W. W. Norton & Company.

Darnton, R. (2003). *George Washington's false teeth: An unconventional guide to the eighteenth century.* New York and London: W. W. Norton & Company.

Darnton, R., & Roche, D. (Eds.). (1989). *Revolution in print: The press in France 1775–1800.* Berkeley: University of California Press.

Febvre, L., & Martin, H. J. (1976). *The coming of the book.* London and New York: Verso.

Habermas, J. (1989). *The structural transformation of the public sphere: An enquiry into a category of bourgeois society.* Cambridge, MA: The MIT Press.

Gay, P. (1966–1969). *The Enlightenment: An interpretation.* New York: Knopf.

Im Hof, U. (1982). *Das gesellige Jahrhundert. Gesellschaft und Gesellschaft im Zeitalter der Aufklärung.* Munich, Germany: C.H. Beck Verlag.

Im Hof, U. (1994). *The Enlightenment.* Oxford, UK: Blackwell.

May, H. F. (1976). *The Enlightenment in America.* New York: Oxford University Press.

Outram, D. (1995). *The Enlightenment.* Cambridge, UK: Cambridge University Press.

Porter, R. (2000). *The creation of the modern world: The untold story of the British Enlightenment.* New York and London: W. W. Norton & Company.

Rouche, D. (1998). *France in the Enlightenment.* Cambridge, MA: Harvard University Press.

Schmidt, J. (1996). *What is Enlightenment? Eighteenth-century answers and twentieth-century questions.* Berkeley: University of California Press.

Small, C. (1982). *The printed word: An instrument of popularity.* Aberdeen, UK: Aberdeen University Press.

Smith, A. (1979). *The newspaper: An international history.* London: Thames and Hudson.

Steinberg, S. H. (1996). *Five hundred years of printing.* London: The British Library and Oak Knoll Press.

Entertainment

People seek entertainment as a necessary distraction from the tensions of daily existence. But how can entertainment intersect with a commitment to religious contemplation?

Diversion at the Center of Entertainment

There has always been a tension between religious communication and entertainment because of the inherent nature of *diversion*, a key component of entertainment, which frequently centers on escape from the contemplation of serious issues. Religion calls for focused pondering and commitment to values with eternal consequences; entertainment calls for brief respites from intellectual and day-to-day cares. Although entertainment can be funny, sad, or merely diverting, it can also be as serious and as thought provoking as most religious communication.

In order for a culture to have time set aside to even consider entertainment as a normal part of existence, technology had to create opportunities for *free time*. Free time cannot exist in a culture that must work constantly in order to survive by providing the basic biological needs. As technological advances make the satisfaction of those basic needs easier, people find ways to "free up" unplanned time periods. All humans require rest, but sleep is not the only means to provide rest. Diversions through entertainment emerge in technologically advanced cultures to compensate for protracted periods of intense focus on survival issues; even God chose to rest on the seventh day after Creation.

But as God rested, did He *need* to be entertained? The tensions emerge again for strict religionists bent on forcing humans to live every aspect of their existence as though contemplation of the Divine was the only justifiable use of any free time. God may or may not require entertainment, but clearly in advanced cultures, His followers believe they do.

Modern mass media have never been able to escape confrontations with the variety of spokespersons for religious communication. Yet, in the midst of the culture wars, there have been examples of the extent to which modern mass media can communicate aspects of religious thought in new and refreshing ways.

Religious Messages in Motion Pictures

The late nineteenth century was not only a period of culture-changing media inventions, but a time in which the Roman Catholic and Christian Protestant commitment to media content was gaining adherents. Former stage magician and special-effects filmmaker George Méliès claimed a place in cinema history for his landmark *The Trip to the Moon* (1902), but few know that his earlier attempts at special effects resulted in the religious film, *Le Christ Marchant sur les Flots* (1899), in which he has an actor portraying Jesus Christ performing the miracle of walking on water.

Some insightful clerics recognized the potential values of portraying religious messages in this emerging art form. *The Religious Possibilities of the Motion Picture*, an essay written in 1911 by a Connecticut Congregational minister named Herbert A. Jump, called for the religious community to participate in the popular culture by attending these "movies." Many of these early religious motion pictures have been lost or destroyed, but famous mainstream films also offered religious references as a deliberate part of the narratives. D. W. Griffith's first four-reel feature-length film was *Judith of Bethulia* (1913–1914), a tale from Jewish history included in the biblical collection known as the Apocrypha. This was followed by his controversial epic *The Birth of a Nation* (1914), in which split-screen effects at the film's end reveal a heavenly city and hope for a better tomorrow in religious worship. Griffith chose to have two of his three stories in the failed epic *Intolerance* (1916) focus on religious issues: the life of Christ and His death and the persecution of the French Huguenots. As the movies became more daring in their portrayals of sensuality and relationships, the initial friendly coexistence with religious institutions began to disintegrate. Despite the conflicts, two noteworthy examples reveal the use by intention of religious messages: *The Jazz Singer* (1927), starring popular singer Al Jolson as an entertainer torn between his Orthodox Jewish family and traditions and his desire to be a popular singer; and Carl Theodor Dreyer's French film, *The Passion of Joan of Arc* (1928), which set the standard for religious biography or narrative in films to come later.

In 1930, Martin Quigley, a Catholic layman, and Daniel Lord, a Jesuit priest, crafted the Hollywood Production Code that became associated with moral restrictions and the Hays Office. Though never a directly censoring agency, the Hays Office became so influential that Hollywood films evolved into a codified representation of morality.

Hollywood producers chose to cast religious figures as stereotypical kindly agents, benevolent but largely supporting characters. An exception to this rule was the Academy Award-winning duo of Bing Crosby and Barry Fitzgerald as the sensitive and happy-go-lucky priests in *Going My Way* (1944). Also, Jimmy Stewart finds his way through a moral morass in the Christmas classic *It's a Wonderful Life* (1946) with help from Clarence, the angel striving to "get his wings."

Seeking a formula to place sexuality and biblical epic in the same context, director Cecil B. DeMille returned to remakes of his silent biblical epics and found new audiences in the 1950s for the special-effects-driven *The Ten Commandments* (1956). Three years later William Wyler made one of the most honored award-winning films in history, the biblical epic *Ben Hur* (1959).

Though the 1960s and 1970s generally ignored religious-based epics as too costly to gain a return on investment, a new approach to religious messages in film began to emerge in the 1980s as a natural connection to a character's personality or life choices. *Chariots of Fire* (1981) featured a lead persona who ran in the Olympics for Great Britain because of religious fervor and convictions. Controversies arise anew with cinematic interpretations of biblical events in such films as *The Last Temptation of Christ* (1988). But Hollywood should not be pigeonholed as antireligion, the proof being Robert Duvall's Academy Award-nominated Best Picture *The Apostle* (1997), which faithfully follows the tensions and joys of a Pentecostal Holiness preacher in the contemporary rural South. Hollywood now has a new breed of auteurs, directors and screenwriters interested in pursuing possible notions of spirituality in a wider context than organized religion. This can be seen in the films of M. Night Shyamalan, most notably *The Sixth Sense* (1999) and *Signs* (2002). Mel Gibson's independent film *The Passion of the Christ* (2004) has become the largest independent grossing film of all time. Irony comes full circle with the Gibson megahit because so many religious people who vowed to avoid R-rated films, known for sexuality, violence, and profanity, flocked to see a religious film so rated due to its historical recreations of Roman brutalities and perceived biblical accuracy.

Religious encounters with the film industry will always be potentially volatile. Yet, the commitment to truth in representation of credible stories and narratives draws screenwriters, directors, and producers back to religious messages.

Religious Messages in Radio, Television, and the Internet

Radio emerged in the early twentieth century as the entertainment medium of choice for many religious spokespersons. Prominent preachers would never claim that they were entertainers in the Hollywood sense; yet, many such as Sister Aimee Semple McPherson offered reporters the notion that had she not felt the call to the ministry she would have chosen a vocation on the stage or screen. McPherson created a new sermon format called "illustrated sermons" in which she would dress up in various costumes, sometimes descend by hidden wire from the balcony of her Angelus Temple in Los Angeles, or offer multiple-voiced characters for a sermon such as "The Cat and the Canary."

Beginning in radio and shifting to television in its infancy, faith-healing evangelist Oral Roberts had actual faith-healing services broadcast and televised to show the dramatic physical reactions to being "slain in the Spirit." Using a flair for emotional language and narrative, Billy Graham began a worldwide ministry in a tent service in Los Angeles in 1949, but eventually saw the need to have a weekly radio program entitled *The Hour of Decision* that would juxtapose actual revival-meeting sermons with studio conversational approaches to evangelism.

Virtually all of the radio evangelists made the transition to television, but perhaps none made the blurring of entertainment more noticeable than Catholic Bishop Fulton J. Sheen. Sheen, a gifted speaker who dressed in priestly religious splendor, maintained for several years in the 1950s a respectable television-ratings record when pitted against the very popular comedian Milton Berle. In the late 1960s and 1970s, Kathryn Kuhlman, a faith-healing evangelist, altered the entertaining quotient for religious messages by choosing a modified talk-show format with those who had been healed in her services. Blurring the entertainment notion even further was evangelist Pat Robertson, who created *The 700 Club*, a religious equivalent to a news debate and midnight talk-show hosting religious celebrities.

The allure of power, influence, and a focus on entertainment values led many evangelists down paths of disgrace and corruption in the 1980s. Jim and Tammy Faye Bakker and Jimmy Swaggart were merely a few of the noteworthy religious television personalities to have controversies and scandal destroy or seriously minimize their ministry impact. These people seemed to lose connection with their original religious calling and purpose by seeking the realm of entertainment exclusively.

Television dramatic series have recently experimented with religious personae in recurring roles. The most famous series to make religious messaging a normal part of its take on the world is, surprisingly, the long-running animated series, *The Simpsons*. Random sampling of its many episodes reveals that approximately 70 percent of episodes deal in some way with a religious message or a character or a passing reference to religion. *Touched by an Angel* found an audience that supported it through multiple seasons on the CBS television network. *The District*, a dramatic police series on television for three years, had recurring characters who blatantly claimed to have faith in Jesus Christ or were wrestling with faith issues. *Joan of Arcadia* has its teenage star meet various people who claim to be God, offering her spiritual advice and guidance. Television series do not shrink from dealing with religious messages or perspectives, even if the choice is to ridicule organized religion, as the animated series *South Park* frequently does. It is common today to find references to how characters in comedies and dramatic series confront issues of religious matters on a regular basis.

The technological advances of the Internet have opened up entertainment factors for religious message dissemination. Websites now provide sermon illustrations from popular cinema and television (e.g., Movieministry.com, Movieguide.org, or Ministryandmedia.com). Narratives with a religious bent are sent with regularity to households all over the world as downloadable e-mails. Burgeoning technology, even religious Internet gaming activities, provide entertainment opportunities within an acceptable range of morality and spirituality for many faith-oriented people.

Implications

In the very broadest sense, movies, radio, television, and the Internet are becoming more religious, or at least more open to offering religious outlets for perspectives. While the religious-epic genre (*The Passion of the Christ* being the noteworthy exception) seems to have waned, in actuality the religious genre has adapted, seeking a separate niche. Billy Graham's World Wide Pictures rents out theaters or carves out prime-time television hours for such films as *The Climb*. Mormon films (e.g., Ryan Little's *Saints and Soldiers*, Richard Dutcher's *God's Army*) have limited runs in select theaters and locations. Apocalyptic films such as *Left Behind* or *The Moment After* attract a few faithful supporters of the End-Times genre.

The motion picture, television, radio, and Internet industries do not seem to cater to religious groups, but they certainly have no problem providing entertainment products that religious people embrace as their own. As noted, these mediated communication forms do support the notion that God indeed has found outlets to reveal aspects of His nature through the diversions of entertainment. We cannot know for certain about God's *needs* (if any exist), but we freely admit that amusements make us ponder anew the extent to which God's nature, qual-

ities, and messages are represented in unexpected diversionary moments.

TODD V. LEWIS

See also Film; Music Video; Sports

Further Reading

Barsotti, C. M., & Johnston, R. K. (2004). *Finding God in the movies.* Grand Rapids, MI: Baker Books.

Billingsley, K. L. (1989). *The seductive image: A Christian critique of the world of film.* Westchester, IL: Crossway Books.

Corliss, R. (2004, August 16). The gospel according to Spider-Man. *Time Magazine,* 70–72.

Godawa, B. (2002). *Hollywood worldviews: Watching films with wisdom & discernment.* Downers Grove, IL: InterVarsity Press.

Hadden, J. K., & Swann, C. E. (1981). *Prime time preachers: The rising power of televangelism.* Reading, MA: Addison-Wesley Publishing Company.

Johnston, R. K. (2000). *Reel spirituality: Theology and film in dialogue.* Grand Rapids, MI: Baker Academic.

Lewis, T. (1988). Charisma and media evangelists: An explication and model of communication influence. *Southern Communication Journal, 54,* 93–111.

Lewis, T. (1998). Rhetorically exorcising the unseen demon: Charisma and consequences in *The Apostle.* Paper presented at National Communication Association, New York, NY.

Lewis, T. (2002). Religious rhetoric and the comic frame in *The Simpsons. Journal of Media and Religion, 1*(3), 153–165.

Lewis, T. (2003). *Loss of faith rhetoric in Signs: A Burkean analysis of rebirth.* Paper presented at National Communication Association, Miami, FL.

Lewis, T. (2004). Media logic and rhetorical issues of "Faith" in the television program, *The District.* Paper presented at National Communication Association Convention, Chicago, IL.

Lindvall, T. (2001). *The silents of God: Selected issues and documents in silent American film and religion: 1908–1925.* Lanham, MD: The Scarecrow Press, Inc.

Mast, G., & Kawin, B. F. (2003). *A short history of the movies* (8th ed.). New York: Longman.

May, J. R., & Bird, M. (Eds.). (1982). *Religion in film.* Knoxville: The University of Tennessee Press.

Newman. M. T. (Ed.). (1993). *A rhetorical analysis of popular American film.* Dubuque, IA: Kendall/Hunt Publishing Company.

Pinsky, M. I. (2001). *The gospel according to* The Simpsons. Louisville, KY: Westminster John Knox Press.

Pullam, S. J. (1999). *"Foul demons, come out!": The rhetoric of twentieth-century American faith healing.* Westport, CT: Praeger.

Romanowski, W. D. (2001). *Eyes wide open: Looking for God in popular culture.* Grand Rapids, MI: Brazos Press.

Schultze, Q. J. (1991). *Televangelism and American culture.* Grand Rapids, MI: Baker Book House.

Schultze, Q. J. (2003). *Christianity and the mass media in America: Toward a democratic accommodation (Rhetoric and Public Affairs Series).* Ann Arbor: Michigan State University Press.

Epistemology

The branch of philosophy encompassing the theory of how people know things is called *epistemology*. Epistemology comes from the Greek word *epistamai*, meaning "to know." Epistemology looks at how individuals acquire knowledge and also how they evaluate their beliefs. It is a normative discipline in that it seeks to create standards by which knowledge and beliefs can be considered legitimate, or illegitimate. A person practicing the discipline is called an *epistemologist*. Epistemology differs from *phenomenology*; that discipline seeks to understand how people experience reality. In religious circles the study of how people know God is very important. *Revelation* is the content of that godly knowledge.

Foundations: An Analysis of Knowledge

Epistemology starts with a very basic question: When does somebody know something to be true? The question has always dominated the thoughts of empiricists and rationalists. *Empiricism* believes that all knowledge comes from experience through the senses rather than being innate or inherent. Aristotle said that there is nothing in the mind that did not first come through the senses. Likewise, the English philosopher John Locke (1632–1702) thought that minds are blank slates that are written on by experience. *Rationalism* suggests that knowledge comes through reason and it tends to downplay experience as a source for knowledge. Both Plato (427–347 BCE) and René Descartes (1596–1650) believed that the mind is born with the natural ability to reason. Only through reason can one find absolute certainty.

Edmund Gettier (b. 1927) wrote a groundbreaking article called "Is Justified True Belief Knowledge?" A justified true belief is one that an individual is entitled to hold intellectually. Knowledge is the individual's awareness of beliefs, facts, or truths.

Justified true belief is explained in the following manner.

1. P is true;

2. S believes that P; and

3. S is justified in believing that P.

So, for example, you know that you have ten coins in your pocket, if and only if it is true that you have ten coins in your pocket, and you believe that you have ten coins in your pocket, and you are justified in believing so. Gettier proved that somebody could be justified in believing something, such as the existence of God, and yet still fail the test of true knowledge.

Directional Epistemology

Epistemologists can be divided into roughly two camps: internalists and externalists. An internalist is a knowledge theorist who believes that one knows things internally. That is, the criteria for justifying true belief primarily comes from within an individual. On the other hand, an epistemic externalist thinks that the criteria for knowing whether something is true comes externally to individuals. For example, Liz sees a flower and believes it to be yellow. Her belief that the flower is indeed yellow is justified solely by virtue of her own reasoning, her own point of view. Her belief comes internally. Contrastingly, Jill believes the flower to be yellow because a group of botanists has set criteria for yellow flowers. Her belief comes externally. However, there is overlapping in the second example. Jill's belief is internal also even though the primary locus of reason comes externally by way of the expert botanists. This also applies to religion. Some epistemologists believe that every individual can know God by way of internal intuition, while others believe that God makes himself known, externally, to the individual.

Skepticism

Another question dealt with by epistemologists is whether there are limits to one's knowledge or what one can know. For instance, can one know God, or is He beyond the scope of one's comprehensibility? Skeptics will sometimes argue that a certain set of beliefs should not be awarded any status. The set of beliefs is illegitimate. For example, some say that religious beliefs should not be recognized since they are highly subjective and unverifiable. Skepticism and skeptics are part of everyday life. Liz says the flower is yellow, but Jill corrects Liz and says, "No, you don't know what you're talking about, the flower is orange." Jill is skeptical of Liz.

Two philosophers associated with skepticism are René Descartes and David Hume (1711–1776). In his work *Meditations on First Philosophy*, Descartes argued that any belief that is subject to doubt should be counted as illegitimate. Unless one can arrive at a belief indubitably, then the belief and the method at which the belief is founded are subject to criticism. Beliefs that are indubitable are not so because of a subjective internal criterion of the believer. Rather, indubitable beliefs are so because there are no objective reasons to doubt them.

Hume takes Descartes a step further in questioning the methods by which people embrace beliefs without being able to rationalize them or test them using valid scientific means. However, this inability to apply scientific principles to beliefs did not stop Hume from questioning religious miracles and concluding that miracles contradicted nature. This conclusion led some philosophers to infer that Hume was logically inconsistent and in general, skeptical of all claims to knowledge. In the end he used rationalism to discredit the rational claims of others. Hume also rejected the notion of causation— that one cause affects another—because one cannot perceive the relationship of cause and effect. Hume's epistemology produced a reaction in philosophy called *common sense realism* that believes that the mind does not simply know representations of the world but has immediate access to the world. Thomas Reid (1710–1796) is considered to be the father of Scottish common sense realism.

Foundationalism and Coherentism

Rarely do people just know things. More likely one of a person's beliefs is based on one or more of their other beliefs. For instance, my belief that I will not be going to work tomorrow is based on my belief that it is snowing heavily. There is a connection between these two beliefs. This connection is called a *structure of knowledge*. Epistemologists like to discuss whether certain structures are more justifiable (or legitimate) than others. A reaction to this need for legitimacy is *foundationalism*, which counters that some beliefs do not need to be justified. Certain foundational beliefs stand alone and are independent of others.

Coherence theory is also concerned with structures of knowledge. This idea holds that justification of beliefs occurs in the cohesion of beliefs. Beliefs are related and are rarely independent of each other. Rather, beliefs exist in community with each other and therefore cohere. The relationship or structure of the beliefs gives them legitimacy.

Both foundationalism and coherentism are reactions to the *regress argument*. This argument demands that every belief must be based on evidence that justifies that belief. Seemingly, it would be impossible to ever justify a belief because one can always call into question its evidence. Foundationalism responds to this uncertainty by saying that some beliefs are basic and do not need evidence. Coherence theory responds by saying that there are no foundational beliefs, rather beliefs that can be justified without evidence as long as the beliefs converge at the agent (individual). In other words, a belief earns its credibility because of its interrelatedness to other beliefs.

A Priori and A Posteriori Knowledge

A priori knowledge is a belief that is known independent of experiences. This theory is very similar to foundationalism. *A posteriori knowledge* is a belief that is dependent upon experiences. For instance, everyone knows that 2 + 2 = 4. In addition, everyone knows that a female pig is called a sow. People do not need to experience these things to know that they are true. They know these truths a priori. The difference between a priori and a posteriori is fundamentally a question about how people get knowledge. People need not run tests, or conduct experiments, or have sophisticated data to prove that they know things. Somehow they acquired the belief, the knowledge. Along the way somebody taught them that 2 + 2 = 4 and that a female pig is a sow. However, simply knowing these things to be true need not justify belief in them.

Immanuel Kant (1724–1804) further distilled the two types of knowledge when he focused on the semantic domain of an a priori knowledge. He questioned how the relationship between meanings of words helps express beliefs. He said that an analytic proposition is one where the predicate concept is contained within the subject concept. For instance, consider the analytic phrase "All eagles are birds." Eagles are contained within the wider subject of birds. Kant also suggested that some propositions are synthetic because they add to each other. For instance, "Eagles have a wingspan of eighty inches" is a synthetic

Selection from William Paley's *Natural Theology; or, Evidences of the Existence and Attributes of the Deity*

Theologian William Paley (1743–1805) produced his classic text *Natural Theology; or, Evidences of the Existence and Attributes of the Deity* in 1802. The extract below is from Chapter XXIII, "Of the Personality of the Deity."

Contrivance, if established, appears to me to prove every thing which we wish to prove. Amongst other things, it proves the personality of the Deity, as distinguished from what is sometimes called nature, sometimes called a principle: which terms, in the mouths of those who use them philosophically, seem to be intended, to admit and to express an efficacy, but to exclude and to deny a personal agent. Now that which can contrive, which can design, must be a person. These capacities constitute personality, for they imply consciousness and thought. They require that which can perceive an end or purpose; as well as the power of providing means, and of directing them to their end (Note: *Priestley's Letters to a Philosophical Unbeliever*, p. 153, ed. 2.). They require a centre in which perceptions unite, and from which volitions flow; which is mind. The acts of a mind prove the existence of a mind: and in whatever a mind resides, is a person. The seat of intellect is a person. We have no authority to limit the properties of mind to any particular corporeal form, or to any particular circumscription of space. These properties subsist, in created nature, under a great variety of sensible forms. Also every animated being has its sensorium, that is, a certain portion of space, within which perception and volition are exerted. This sphere may be enlarged to an indefinite extent; may comprehend the universe; and, being so imagined, may serve to furnish us with as good a notion, as we are capable of forming, of the immensity of the Divine Nature, i. e. of a Being, infinite, as well in essence as in power; yet nevertheless a person.

No man hath seen God at any time. And this, I believe, makes the great difficulty. Now it is a difficulty which chiefly arises from our not duly estimating the state of our faculties. The Deity, it is true, is the object of none of our senses: but reflect what limited capacities animal senses are.

proposition because "eighty inches" adds to, or develops, the concept of "eagle." The analytic proposition is equated to a priori and synthetic proposition equated to a posteriori by some philosophers. However, we must bear in mind that the a priori/a posteriori distinction addresses the overarching concern of whether a proposition needs verification or if it can it stand on its own. Within that proposition we discover whether it is analytic or synthetic. When we think of this in terms of religion we are faced with the concern of whether true claims about God are known by our experience of God, or are they known apart from our experience of God.

Religion and Knowledge

Often proponents of religious beliefs have found themselves having to defend against attacks from atheistic and agnostic epistemologists. Can believers in God have justified true belief about God? Is belief in God reasonable or rational? Of course, skeptics will ask, Is there evidence that the belief is justifiable? A religious person might respond, like a foundationalist, that some beliefs do not, and cannot, be justified—they are basic and intrinsic to all human beings. This theory is typically called *general revelation*, or *natural theology*. The idea is that God has revealed Himself to all human beings; or in other words, God has enabled all human beings to know and understand him. Some theologians, namely Augustine (354–430) and Anselm (1033–1109), and most recently Karl Barth (1886–1968), understand that faith in God precedes understanding of God. They believe that the mind and rationality are fallible and not reliable. It is only when God breaks into a person's space and time and reveals Himself that the person can say that he or she knows God (*special revelation*). For example, in the Bible God shows Himself to Moses, and later God shows Himself to the people of Israel. This revelation results in actual, legitimate knowledge of God since their beliefs resulted in actions like the Exodus.

Thomas Aquinas (1225–1274) argued that both theology and philosophy could prove the existence of God. Theology begins with faith and revelation and works its way outward toward the created order. Philosophy begins with reason and seeks to understand creation, including God as the creator. Aquinas championed five ways that people have evidence for knowing God: change, contingency, motion, causation, and moral goodness. Aquinas believed that all rational beings would accept these evidences for the existence of God. John Hick argues that religious truths are verifiable, just not in this life. His argument became known as *eschatological verification*, which means that knowledge claims about God will be verified in the final days when God returns to earth.

In the latter part of the twentieth century, theologian Thomas F. Torrance rejected the claims of Isaac Newton (1642–1727) and others that people can abstract truth from nature and the universe. Newton divided time into two different realities: (1) real time and (2) absolute mathematical time. This division had the effect of approaching epistemology in a dualistic fashion. Similarly, the New Testament scholar Rudolph Bultmann (1884–1976) divided time and history into two different categories: (1) *historie* and (2) *geschichte*. *Historie* looks at time in terms of strict cause-and-effect relationships; *geschichte* approaches time in how it appears to one. Looking at time in either of these dualistic ways allows one to weed out beliefs that are not provable scientifically, and thus has the effect of reducing religious beliefs to mere myths.

Torrance rejected the notion of epistemological dualism and argued that there is only one real time. Like Albert Einstein (1879–1955) and other physicists, he understood time to be relative to observers. Most importantly, Torrance thought that it is illegitimate to force subjects of inquiry into one's frame of mind. Rather, for both science and theology one must allow oneself to be controlled, shaped, and matured by the subject one seeks to know. For religious epistemologists this means that they must subvert themselves to God if they truly want to understand God. There can be no forcing God into some kind of preconceived a priori understanding of God.

Epistemology and Post-Modernism

Postmodernism is simply the rejection of the presuppositions and ideals of modernism or of the Enlightenment. The terms *modernism* and *postmodernism* are very difficult to identify and define since they encompass slow cultural shifts over long periods of time that involve philosophy, science, art, music, architecture, and literature. However, the shift from modernism to postmodernism is generally thought to have occurred from the enlightenment to the present time.

Modernism holds that there are no limits to knowledge and that there are universal truths grounded in nature. Postmodernism is dubious about such universal claims to truth. Rather, postmodernism finds the validity of knowledge grounded in *subjectivism* (there is no objective truth) and *relativism* (truth is relative to the individual). Not only does postmodernism question the very nature of truth, it also is critical of the means by which one inquires truth. Michel Foucault (1926–1984) suggested that all claims to truth are conditioned by power and domination. These conditioners place epistemic methods in social contexts and constructs. Inquiry into beliefs does not happen in isolation from presuppositions and social, political, and economic situations.

ROBERT LEACH

Further Reading

Allen, D., & Springsted, E. O. (Eds.). (1992). *Primary readings in philosophy for understanding theology*. Louisville, KY: Westminster/John Knox Press.

Brown, C. (1968). *Philosophy and the Christian faith*. Downers Grove, IL: InterVarsity Press.

Crumley, J. S. (1999). *An introduction to epistemology*. Mountain View, CA: Mayfield Publishing Company.

Crumley, J. S. (1999). *Readings in epistemology*. Mountain View, CA: Mayfield Publishing Company.

Gettier, E. L. (1963). Is justified true belief knowledge? *Analysis, 23,* 121–123.

Lehrer, K. (2000). *Theory of knowledge*. Boulder, CO: Westview Press.

Shope, R. (1983). *An analysis of knowledge*. Princeton, NJ: Princeton University Press.

Torrance, T. F. (1969). *Theological science*. London: Oxford University Press.

Torrance, T. F. (1971). *God and rationality*. London: Oxford University Press.

Tsanoff, R. A. (1964). *The great philosophers* (2nd ed.). New York: Harper & Row Publishers.

Wolterstorff, N. (1976). *Reason within the bounds of religion*. Grand Rapids, MI: Eerdmans.

Evangelicalism

Evangelicals use any means possible to make a message of the gospel of Jesus Christ relevant for the culture of the time. Evangelicals create, consume, and are the subject of media as they strive to convert individuals to Christianity. History shows that Evangelical groups are adopters of new media forms and functions.

Who Are the Evangelicals?

Different parties use the word *Evangelical* to identify a variety of groups. This has been a problem for some Protestants who would want to call themselves Evangelical, were it not for the conservative overtones that the term carries. One useful definition is Protestants who believe that sharing the story of Jesus Christ is crucial in bringing about personal salvation for others. Many religious denominations would fall into this category, and many members of Protestant groups would define themselves as Evangelicals.

What Evangelicals Believe about the Media

Stepping back from the Reformation ideal of *sola scriptura* (deriving theological insights from scripture alone), Evangelical theologians worry about situating the biblical message in the context in which it is heard. There has been an effort of Evangelicals to change the course of American society through biblical messages. This is because for the Evangelical, religious belief pervades all aspects of life. The great commission "Go therefore and make disciples of all nations, baptizing them in the name of the Father, and of the Son and of The Holy Spirit, and teaching them to obey everything I have commanded you" (Matthew 28:19–20, NIV) compels Evangelicals to find innovative ways to share their beliefs. The first lead editorial in *Christianity Today* stated, "statesmen as well as theologians realize that the basic solution to the world crisis is theological" (*Christianity Today,* October 15, 1956, 20–23). In addition to faith in God, Evangelicals have shown a faith in technology. The work of the church, Evangelicals believe, is fundamentally about communication. Evangelicals have therefore used emerging technologies to promote their message. "From the founding of the Plymouth colonies to the present, the United States has been an incredible laboratory in which Evangelicals have been able to experiment with every imaginable form and medium of communication, from Bible and tract printing to tent revivals, gospel billboards, books, religious drama troupes, radio and television broadcasts, parade floats, motorcycle evangelism, periodicals, and even Rollen Steward, the rainbow-wigged sniper who holds up Scripture signs in front of the TV network cameras during sports events" (Schultze 1990).

While Evangelicals have a reputation for living in poorer and more isolated areas of society, in their desire to share their message, they have been innovative in their use of the media to appropriate the message for contemporary society. Large megachurches attract more than 10,000 people to weekend services and are founded on the principles of modern marketing. The styles and strategies of these churches are similar to techniques used by televangelists. In this way, church and parachurch groups have tried to create a "satellite" Christian experience that is dressed up like secular entertainment. Parachurch groups like Campus Crusade for Christ and Intervarsity Christian Fellowship use the media to spread their message. This skillful use of marketing techniques with media is critical for raising both ideological and financial support for these groups. As the financial and social standing of Evangelicals in North America has improved, their effectiveness in accessing and using communication technology has improved as well.

The majority of Evangelicals are optimistic about the promise of the media to change culture. A minority of Evangelicals see the media as a threat to a Christian worldview, producing tension in the views held by Evangelicals. Evangelicals believe that the media is powerful and can be used for good or evil purposes.

Parachurch organizations like the American Family Association and Focus on the Family produce materials criticizing the morality of mainstream media. Focus on the Family talks about political issues like gay rights but also talks about individuals raising children as good citizens. Focus on the Family provides both children's videos and ratings for parents on popular children's materials.

Overall, Evangelicals have embraced both the media and its technology. For example, overhead projectors and now PowerPoint presentations are found in many Evangelical worship services. Younger Evangelicals are seeking an experiential faith, and new media, enabled by computers, may help to facilitate this. Younger Evangelicals rely less on print media than older ones do.

Preaching as a Mass Medium

Evangelistic preaching is an intrachurch activity. In other words, the cause is bigger than the congregation. Preaching in the popular revivals of the eighteenth and nineteenth centuries was an early use of mass communication by Evangelicals. The crusade, or large-audience preaching opportunities, found in organizations such as the Billy Graham Crusade, Promise Keepers, and the Beth Moore seminars continue today as an effort to have one-to-many, live communication of the Evangelical message.

Print Media

Literature has been and continues to be an important component of Evangelical mission work. The ability to publish Bibles and tracts in vernacular languages is seen as important and is the impetus for Evangelical support for Bible publishing and translation organizations such as the American Bible Society and Wycliffe Bible Translators.

Dedicated Evangelical publishing started with small, private businesses. Large publishing houses like Word, Inc. and Thomas Nelson started with the efforts of individuals. As the private publishers grew more successful, the companies were bought out by larger media conglomerates or became independently publicly traded. Belonging to a publicly owned company means obligation to corporate stakeholders. Today, while contemporary religious publishers state that their purpose is Evangelical, these same publishers are owned by for-profit, public companies. The profit motive limits editorial freedom. It also draws criticism from the Evangelicals, who comprise the majority of the audience that these publishers reach. The books produced by Christian publishers tend to be inspiration or instruction for Christians. The works rarely reach out to doubters or nonbelievers. In the late 1990s and early twenty-first century, the *Left Behind* series transformed the idea of the second coming from straight evangelism to entertaining best sellers that did succeed in crossing to the popular market.

Christian magazines began largely as mainline denominational house organs, primarily reaching members of the sponsoring denominations. This began to change in the 1950s as the mainline magazines began to shrink in circulation and eventually died out entirely. Evangelical involvement in magazine publishing grew as the mainline publications dwindled. Billy Graham was involved in the launching of *Christianity Today* in 1956, as a part of the new Evangelicalism, which sought to both share the Evangelical message and to distance itself from fundamentalist concerns.

Over time, other magazines have attracted more of a lay audience, with *Christian Standard, Moody Monthly Magazine,* and *Sojourners* representing magazines by

Evangelicals for lay Evangelicals. Christian consumer publications such as *Christianity Today* and parachurch organizational magazines such as *Focus on the Family* have also grown. Magazines, like book publishing, have tended to move toward commercial models over time, creating the prophet-vs.-profit controversies found in other media. The Christian Booksellers Association and the Evangelical Press Association have been agencies of cooperation among different denominational publishing efforts.

The denominational press has continued in the publication of denominational newspapers. For example, the Southern Baptists continue to maintain a Baptist news service and national as well as state convention newspapers. Efforts to control the content of the publications by replacing editors have been an ongoing consequence of the intradenominational turmoil for Southern Baptists.

Electronic Media

The contemporary Christian music (CCM) industry is another example of Evangelical content being produced in a profit-oriented market. Although "Jesus Rock" has been around since the 1950s, it began to get a hearing later, in part because of the incorporation of praise music in Charismatic churches. As these churches moved toward a more postmodern, experiential style of worship, the praise song became an important part of an often extended portion of the worship service. Set to music similar to secular music the church attendee could hear on the radio, a market for recordings of this music grew. A major goal of CCM is to use music as a means to evangelize young people.

CCM as an industry has grown to the point that in 1985, gospel music, as it is categorized by the recording industry, was outselling jazz and classical music. In the 1980s, there was also a peak in the tension between the business and the mission of CCM as artists like Amy Grant and Michael W. Smith began releasing songs that were either hits on both the gospel and rock charts or made no mention of spirituality at all. Artists who "crossed over" the charts were criticized by some Evangelicals. Discomfort with the musical style of CCM has also been a problem. Setting the Christian message to a secular beat did not, by and large, attract nonbelievers, but rather attracted younger Evangelicals.

Evangelicals also present their message in film. The story of the coming apocalypse presented in both prophetic books and in Revelation in the Bible represents a dramatic story suitable to dramatic presentation.

As such, this story has been presented in films such as *The Omega Code* and quite profitably in the *Left Behind* series of books and movies. Although movies with Christian themes have been created for free-admission, church-based viewing in the past, the 1990s and beyond have seen new attempts to enter more mass-market movie production. The 2004 film *The Passion of the Christ*, directed by Roman Catholic Mel Gibson, was widely viewed by Evangelicals, who were encouraged to bring nonbelieving friends to viewings.

To the Christian, there is no difference between the secular and the sacred: every bush is a "burning bush" and all ground is "holy ground." Everything we do is to be offered up to God as our sacrifice of worship.

Bob Jones Sr. (1883–1968)

Billy Graham recognized the value of the media early in his ministry, using first radio and later television. Today, in Appalachia, relatively poor congregations donate money for airtime, believing that the broadcast is a form of Christian service. All Appalachian groups share a sense of mission—believing God calls individuals and gives them gifts to use in God's service. To fail to do this is to fail God. They are optimistic that their obedience provides rewards in both this life and the next. These broadcasts include music and preaching. There are stories shared about sinner friends who are converted as a result of the broadcast.

Christian radio has also become a force in some of the largest radio markets. Christian radio, which is almost exclusively Evangelical, grew such that most top markets had more than one station in the late 1980s. Although Christian stations do play some contemporary Christian music, many hours are spent broadcasting prerecorded programs syndicated by national ministries such as Focus on the Family, Atlanta pastor Charles Stanley's *In Touch*, and Texan Chuck Swindoll's *Insight for Living*. Christian radio attracts an audience mostly of existing Evangelicals.

Evangelistic television programs and networks, likewise, attract an audience of believers. The audience for religious broadcasting is predominantly older females. Media ministers address concerns of older adults like loneliness, failing health, and fear of impending death. Audience members also tend to have less education than nonviewers.

Most TV preachers would call themselves Evangelical Christians. Televangelism is a natural extension of Evangelicals' use of the mass media, starting with George Whitefield's open-air preaching. Changes in FCC regulations that no longer required networks to carry religious programming for free led to Evangelicals' initial purchases of inexpensive, Sunday morning airtime for their messages. As the televangelism phenomenon has grown, entire evangelistic networks such as the Trinity Broadcasting Network have developed.

Televangelism is one of the better-studied and more controversial modes of Evangelical communication. Televangelism differs from other religious programming in that it is audience supported. Fees for broadcasting can be in the millions of dollars. In order to draw these fees, televangelists need to attract not only viewers, but also donors. Many televangelists such as Jim Bakker and Pat Robertson were explicitly modeled on other entertainment media in format. Billy Graham, Rex Humbard, and Oral Roberts produce shows that fall into the category of religious spectacular, in which the focus is on the show more than the message. Miraculous events like faith healing often play a part. Modern televangelists also attract their audiences through a prosperity theology gospel. Seeking more faith will mean seeking greater earthly rewards. Donations to the televangelist's ministry will be a way of demonstrating the faith that can lead to the rewards.

Televangelism is also controversial for exercising influence to try to change America politically. In the mid-1970s, Evangelicals' involvement in politics brought them to the forefront of media attention. *Newsweek* named 1976 the "year of the Evangelical." The rise of the Christian right in the 1980s kept Evangelical Christians on front pages and in newscasts. The marriage of Evangelical media and politics has not been an easy one. Pat and Tim Robertson earned more than $200 million selling International Family Corporation (including the Family Channel) to Rupert Murdoch. When Robertson ran for office in 1986, he resigned his Southern Baptist ordination and tried to bill himself as a media executive, not a televangelist.

In addition to expressly religious shows, Evangelical-owned networks such as PAX and the Family Channel are broadcasting syndicated popular shows that appeal to the Evangelicals' moral sensibility. This family television blends Christian programming with selected secular programming. This remains a hard sell to the portion of the Evangelical audience that expects exclusively Christian programming.

Evangelical broadcasting makes up a large percentage of the number of hours broadcast across national boundaries but draws a small percentage of the audience. Religious groups transmitting into the Pacific Rim and South America, as early as 1931, made some of the earliest international radio broadcasts. Although efforts at international broadcasting continue, there are barriers to effectiveness for these broadcasts including technical restraints, cultural restraints, and political restraints. While in developed countries, the Internet is becoming a more important means of international communication, the radio will continue to be important in the developing world. Much of the area between the tropics, a focus for evangelistic mission work, will continue to use radio extensively.

News about Evangelicals

Reporters lack cultural understanding of Evangelicals, which influences coverage. For example, fundamentalist Evangelicals were covered in the Scopes "Monkey Trial" as parochial and backward in 1925, in a way that some feel indelibly hurt their image. Evangelicals withdrew from the media spotlight for a time. In the 1950s, the rise of televangelists such as Oral Roberts, Rex Humbard, and Billy Graham brought Evangelicals briefly back into media attention.

Religion has always been an important component of American culture. The press has been a part of this, from spreading religious ideas to determining through what is covered what is acceptable in the world of religion. This results in religious agenda setting by the media.

For example, reporters exposed to the politicking of the religious right emphasized the political power of Evangelicals in politics. This emphasis led to real power in the 1980s, when politicians actively sought support of Evangelical leaders like Jerry Falwell. As the actual, relatively small numbers of followers of televangelists like Falwell and Pat Robertson became known, media stories on their influence have faded.

In the 1980s, Christian groups attacked the entertainment industry, often through boycotts on advertisers on shows. The Moral Majority and the Rev. Donald Wildmon's Coalition for Better Television led the way in boycotts. Specific boycotts were effective in making some changes like the straightening of a gay character on *Soap*. Boycotts in general created more self-censorship among the networks—a trend that lasted into the mid-1990s. The American Family Association, founded by Wildmon, has crusaded against what they consider anti-Christian biases in the media including protesting *The Last Temptation of Christ* and organizing boycotts against companies that advertise on objectionable programs.

As subjects of news, Evangelicals are disappointed with the lack of coverage of their activities such as worship and service, misunderstanding the role of news to uncover the unusual. "Evangelicals as Evangelicals are not newsworthy to the secular media, nor have they been in the past seventy years, except as they misbehave, act politically, or stand against cultural change." Beginning in 1987, a series of scandals involving televangelists like Jim Bakker and Jimmy Swaggart brought coverage of Evangelicals to the forefront.

Emerging Media Technologies

In the 1990s and 2000s, Evangelicals continued their move into new media by establishing websites for individual churches and for parachurch ministries. One advantage for users is the ability to get information about a church without making the implied social commitment of a visit. Churches also report using e-mail to communicate within the congregation of members and regular attendees. Websites are used to attract visitors to come to the church, to promote the presence of the church in the community, and to support the basic activities of the church. While church websites are usually created by lay volunteers, some Evangelical denominations provide help to congregations in setting up websites.

Churches have used Internet-based communication such as e-mail and blogging, primarily as ways to keep up with members. As miniaturization and wireless communication continue to diffuse into the population, it is expected that Evangelicals will take advantage of new modes of communication.

The Future

As the information age has changed information into a commodity, religious communication will similarly become a commodity. As the rest of society becomes less book-oriented, so will religious communities, and new technologies will likely play an important part in future evangelizing. The challenges of balancing commercial viability and purity of the evangelistic message are likely to continue to raise questions. Also, within the realm of Evangelicalism, tensions between liberal and Fundamentalist stances remain. This has led to liberal- and conservative-focused publications and a division of the audience for Evangelical media. This division will continue to grow as long as the theological controversies remain.

AMANDA STURGILL

See also Protestantism, Conservative; Radio; Televangelism

Further Reading

Allan, J. D. (1989). *The Evangelicals: An illustrated history*. Grand Rapids, MI: Baker Book House.

Bachman, J. (1960). *The Church in the age of radio-television*. New York: Association Press.

Balmer, R. (2002). *Encyclopedia of Evangelism*. Louisville, KY: John Knox Press.

Board, S. (1990). Moving the world with magazines: A survey of Evangelical periodicals. In Q. J. Schultze, (Ed.), *American Evangelicals and the mass media* (pp. 119–142). Grand Rapids, MI: Academie Books.

Buddenbaum, J. M., & Mason, D. (2000). Introduction. In J. M. Buddenbaum & D. Mason (Eds.), *Readings on religion as news* (pp. 14–20). Ames: Iowa State University Press.

Caldwell, J. D. (1984). *Mass media Christianity*. Lanham, MD. University Press of America.

Calver, C., & Warner, R. (1996). *Together we stand: Evangelical convictions, unity and vision*. London: Hodder & Stoughton.

Dorgan, H. (1993). *The airwaves of Zion: Radio and religion in Appalachia*. Knoxville: University of Tennessee Press.

Ellens, J. H. (1974). *Models of religious broadcasting*. Grand Rapids, MI: Eerdmans.

Ellingsen, M. (1988). *The Evangelical movement: Growth, impact, controversy, dialog*. Minneapolis, MN: Augsburg.

Elvy, P. (1987). *Buying time: The foundations of the electronic church*. Great Wakering, UK: McCrimmons.

Ferré, J. P. (1990). Searching for the great commission: Evangelical book publishing since the 1970s. In Q. J. Schultze (Ed.), *American Evangelicals and the mass media* (pp. 99–117). Grand Rapids, MI: Academie Books.

Fortner, R. S. (1990). Saving the world? American Evangelicals and transnational broadcasting. In Q. J. Schultze (Ed.), *American Evangelicals and the mass media* (pp. 307–331). Grand Rapids, MI: Academie Books.

Grenz, S. J. (1993). *Revisioning Evangelical theology: A fresh agenda for the 21st century*. Downers Grove, IL: InterVarsity Press.

Hadden, J. K. (1987). Televangelism and politics. In R. J. Neuhaus & M. Cromartie (Eds.), *Piety and politics: Evangelicals and fundamentalists confront the world* (pp. 379–394). Washington, DC: Ethics and Public Policy Center.

Hart, D. G. (2002). *That old-time religion in modern America: Evangelical Protestantism in the twentieth century*. Chicago: Ivan R. Dee.

Hendershot, H. (2004). *Shaking the world for Jesus: Media and conservative Evangelical culture*. Chicago: University of Chicago Press.

Hoover, S. (1989). *Mass media religion: The social sources of the electronic church*. Newbury Park, CA: Sage.

Maus, M. (1990). Believers as behavers: News coverage of Evangelicals by the secular media. In Q. J. Schultze (Ed.), *American Evangelicals and the mass media* (pp. 253–273). Grand Rapids, MI: Academie Books.

Peck, J. (1993). *The gods of televangelism: The crisis of meaning and the appeal of religious television*. Cresskill, NJ: Hampton Press.

Schement, J. R., & Stephenson, H. C. (1996). Religion and the information society. In D. A. Stout & J. M. Buddenbaum (Eds.), *Religion and mass media: Audiences and adaptations* (pp. 261–289). Thousand Oaks, CA: Sage.

Schultze, Q. J. (1990). Keeping the faith: American Evangelicals and the media. In Q. J. Schultze (Ed.), *American Evangelicals and the mass media* (pp. 23–45). Grand Rapids, MI: Academie Books.

Schultze, Q. (1991). *Televangelism and American culture: The business of popular religion*. Grand Rapids, MI: Baker Books.

Schultze, Q. (1996). Evangelicals' uneasy alliance with the media. In D. A. Stout & J. M. Buddenbaum, (Eds.), *Religion and mass media: Audiences and adaptations* (pp. 61–73). Thousand Oaks, CA: Sage.

Stackhouse, J., Jr. (2002). *Evangelical landscapes: Facing critical issues of the day*. Grand Rapids, MI: Baker Academic.

Tidball, D. J. (1994). *Who are the Evangelicals?: Tracing the roots of today's movements*. London: Marshall Pickering.

Ward, M., Sr. (1994). *The story of Christian broadcasting: Air of salvation*. Grand Rapids, MI: Baker.

Webber, R. E. (2002). *The younger Evangelicals: Facing the challenges of the new world*. Grand Rapids, MI: Baker Books.

Feasts

The word *feast* conjures up an image of a table full of food and drink shared in celebration with family and friends. It has been thus since the earliest civilizations. When Isaac was weaned, his parents Abraham and Sarah gave a great feast (Genesis 21:8). When the adult Isaac made a treaty with Philistine king Abimelech and his aides, Isaac "then made them a feast and they ate and drank" (Genesis 26:30, NJB). Important feasts, the prophet Isaiah indicated, consisted of "rich food" and "well-strained wines" (Isaiah 25:6).

Feasting is a time-honored ritual that has manifested itself throughout all major religions and cultures. Most feasts have developed religious significance as an opportunity to honor God and renew bonds of family and community. As such, major religious holidays have come to be known as feasts. Regardless of how they are celebrated, feasts serve the purpose of nourishing the body, gathering people to strengthen communal bonds, giving thanks for blessings of abundant food, and acknowledging God's providence.

Despite the prevalence of food and drink, feasting can also emphasize sacrifice. To Christians, the Easter feast honors Jesus Christ's Resurrection. The Muslim feast of Id al-Fitr hearkens to the prophet Muhammad's instruction to be generous to guests and the poor. Jews abstain from leavened bread and other foods on Passover to commemorate the urgency with which their Israelite ancestors fled Egypt, and fast on the day before the first night of Passover.

Each of the major religions has its own feasts. All, in some way, involve food, community, worship, and remembrance.

Christian Feasts

Some feast days are common to most of Christianity. The best-known are Christmas and Easter, which commemorate the birth and death of Jesus. Christmas (from the Old English *Cristes maesse*, or "Christ's Mass") is observed on 25 December by Western churches and on 6 January in some Eastern churches, although Jesus' exact birthdate is unknown. In the United States and many European countries, churches and homes display a creche, with small statues depicting Mary, Joseph, and the baby Jesus in the stable where He was born. These are usually surrounded by figurines depicting shepherds, Magi, angels, and animals. Christians usually attend church services and prepare elaborate meals to commemorate the day. Christmas is preceded by Advent, a season of penance and preparation for Jesus' birth.

Christmas has acquired secular trappings, particularly in the past century, with Christmas carols, mistletoe, and the commercialized exchange of Christmas cards and presents. The day is personified by Santa Claus, who rides a reindeer-driven sleigh and slides down chimneys to give gifts to children. European nations have ascribed other names to Santa Claus. In England he is called Father Christmas, in France Pere Noel, and in Germany Kriss Kringle (from Christkindl, or "Christ child").

The feast of the Epiphany follows Christmas twelve days later. It commemorates the day when the Magi, three Arabian wise men, arrived at the Bethlehem stable to pay homage to the infant Jesus with gifts of gold, frankincense, and myrrh (Matthew 2:1–12).

Easter is a movable feast, meaning it can be celebrated on different days each year. Easter falls on the

A Jewish Kiddish cup with wine used to make a blessing before meals and ceremonial events.
Courtesy of Nancy Louie/istockphoto.com.

ples. As the apostle Luke recorded the event, "suddenly there came from heaven a sound as of a violent wind which filled the entire house in which they were sitting; and there appeared to them tongues as of fire; these separated and came to rest on the head of each of them." As a result, "They were all filled with the Holy Spirit" (Acts of the Apostles 2:2–3). Believers mark the day as the birth of the Christian church.

The Roman Catholic Church, as the oldest Christian Church, has more feasts than the Protestant denominations. One of the most prominent is All Saints' Day, which honors the saints of the church. This holy day is observed in the Western world on 1 November and by most Eastern churches on the first Sunday after Pentecost. Other feasts emphasized in Catholicism include the Immaculate Conception and the Assumption, which commemorate the conception of the Virgin Mary (mother of Jesus) and her physical ascent into heaven following her death. These are celebrated on 8 December and 15 August, respectively.

Jewish Feasts

In addition to Shavuot, the Jewish harvest feast that the Christians call Pentecost, major feasts in Judaism include Hanukkah, Passover, Rosh Hashanah, and Yom Kippur.

Hanukkah, the Hebrew word for "dedication," celebrates the victory of the Maccabees over the Syrian tyrant Antiochus IV and the subsequent reoccupation of Jerusalem. The Talmud, the Jewish holy book, reveals that only a one-day supply of holy oil remained in the temple when the Maccabees began removing Syrian idols so that it could be rededicated to God. However, the oil miraculously burned for eight days. Jews commemorate this by lighting Hanukkah candles, chanting blessings, and exchanging gifts. Hanukkah is a movable feast, celebrated in November or December.

Another eight-day observance is Passover, a movable feast in March or April that commemorates the flight of the Israelite slaves from Egypt. The term is derived from the tenth plague placed on Egypt for the Pharaoh's refusal to free the Israelites: the death of all firstborn Egyptian children. God told Jews to place blood from slaughtered one-year-old sheep or goats on their doorposts as a sign to God to spare their firstborn children. "When I see the blood I shall pass over you, and you will escape the destructive plague when I strike Egypt," God told Moses. "This day must be commemorated by you, and you must keep it as a feast in Yahweh's honor" (Exodus 12:13–14).

Rosh Hashanah marks the beginning of the Jewish year. It is a feast on which Jews examine their

first Sunday following the first full moon of spring, therefore placing it between 22 March and 25 April each year. Easter honors Jesus Christ's Resurrection. Tortured to death, Jesus returned from the dead on the third day and spent the next forty days on Earth, interacting with hundreds of his followers, Christians believe. Through Easter and the Resurrection, humanity has been offered the gift of salvation and redemption from sins.

Like Christmas, Easter has developed secular overtones. These usually include eggs (symbolizing imminent birth) and rabbits (symbolizing fertility).

Pentecost underscores the Jewish origins of Christianity. To the Israelites, this feast symbolized thanksgiving for the wheat harvest, and was celebrated fifty days after Passover. It was on Pentecost that the Holy Spirit descended on Jesus' twelve apostles and disci-

relationship with God and ask for blessings. Orthodox and Conservative Jews celebrate Rosh Hashanah for two days, while Reform Jews observe it for one. Rosh Hashanah feasts customarily include many sweet dishes made with honey, symbolizing the desire for a sweet and abundant year. Rosh Hashanah also serves as the beginning of the Ten Days of Penitence, during which Jews seek God's forgiveness and await His judgment.

The Ten Days of Penitence end on Yom Kippur, which means in Hebrew "the Day of Atonement." This is the holiest feast day in the Jewish calendar, during which Jews seek and grant forgiveness for sins and transgressions. On Yom Kippur, Jews emphasize sacrifice. They perform no work and abstain from food and sex, in obedience to scriptural rules in the book of Leviticus. "On the tenth day of the seventh month you will fast and refrain from work," God told Moses, "for this is the day on which the rite of expiation will be performed for you to purify you, to purify you before Yahweh from all your sins" (Leviticus 16:29–30).

Islamic Feasts

Islam's two major religious feasts are Id al-Fitr and Id al-Adha. Id al-Fitr marks the end of Ramadan, a month of fasting that honors God's revelations, through the archangel Gabriel, to the prophet Muhammad. These revelations comprise the Qur'an. Muslims more than twelve years old fast from sunrise to sunset during Ramadan. Since the Islamic calendar is lunar, the month of Ramadan can occur at any time during the Christian calendar. At its conclusion, Muslims celebrate Id al-Fitr by going to a mosque, decorating their houses, exchanging gifts, and consuming sweet foods and drinks. There are no dietary restrictions during this feast, and sheep, goat, or lamb is usually the featured meal.

Id al-Adha, known as "the Feast of Sacrifice," memorializes the day when Abraham was ready to sacrifice his son according to God's command. This feast is celebrated during the hajj, an obligatory pilgrimage to Mecca. Pilgrims sacrifice an animal, usually a lamb, at the sacrificial altar and derive their main meal from the meat of the sacrificed animal. This is usually accompanied by bread and a special type of rice called *biriyani*.

Buddhist Feasts

Wesak is a major festival in many Buddhist countries. Celebrated in May, it commemorates the birth, enlightenment, and death of the Buddha (meaning "Enlightened One"), Prince Siddhartha Gautama. This feast usually features entertainers, parades, and food, and emphasizes the virtue of charity. Many Buddhists visit monasteries on Wesak to decorate them or deliver flowers.

Specific countries have their own feasts. In Tibet, Losar denotes the Buddhist New Year. However, before they can celebrate Losar, Buddhists must complete unfinished business and dispel unpleasant thoughts. Thus, on the eve of Losar, during the festival of Gutor, people clean their houses, visit monasteries, and participate in religious ceremonies in an effort to banish evil spirits. Losar commences the following day, and consists of three days of feasting and dancing.

Thailand's chief Buddhist feast is Kathina, celebrated during October or November. It honors Buddhist monks who have kept the religion alive for two millennia. Thai Buddhists bring the monks gifts and the monks give their blessings, reminding the faithful that acts of kindness and generosity will be rewarded.

Hindu Feasts

Hinduism, a polytheistic religion about six millennia old, has many feasts that focus on one or more of its gods. Each features Hindus chanting prayers to the gods, and making and consuming sweets in honor of the gods. For example, the feast of Holi, which commemorates the triumph of good son Prahlaad over his demonic father Hiranyakashipu and aunt Holika, is celebrated with *chackli*, a type of pretzel. The feast of Ganesha Chaturthi, which entreats this elephant-headed god to aid believers in their difficulties, is accompanied by a sweet snack called *modhaka*. On Deepavali, the festival of lights celebrating victory of divinities over evil, Hindus make *badam burfi*, a diamond-shaped almond cake.

Kwanzaa

This is a purely secular seven-day feast for African-Americans. Created in 1966, it is a cultural celebration that begins 26 December each year. It is based on the year-end harvest festivals that take place throughout Africa. *Kwanza* means "first fruits" in Swahili, but the festival's creator, a professor of black studies, added an extra "a" to emphasize the African-American basis.

Secular Restrictions

In recent decades, secular society in some countries has outlawed public displays associated with religious feasts. In the United States, courts have ruled that it is illegal for a teacher to ask kindergarten students if they know whose birthday is celebrated on Christmas, and that schools and local governments may not display Nativity scenes. These rulings have been based on the U.S. Supreme Court's relatively recent reinterpretation of the First Amendment clause "Congress shall make no law respecting an establishment of religion, or prohibiting the free exercise thereof." Rather than the Founders' original intent that the new government would not create one national religion, the Supreme Court decided in 1947 that religious beliefs and practices must be kept out of the public arena.

Other nations have tried to suppress religious feasts. Troops under Fidel Castro violently disrupted a Havana religious procession celebrating the feast of Cuba's patron saint Virgen de la Caridad del Cobre, or Our Lady of Charity. Public displays of Christian or Jewish worship are illegal in Saudi Arabia, and Greece's constitution prohibits proselytizing and public exhibitions by churches other than the Greek Orthodox Church.

Despite this rising tide of intolerance, feasts in all major religions will continue to publicly communicate religious belief, honor sacrifices of forebears, and unify members.

RALPH FRASCA

Further Reading

Barton, D. (1992). *The myth of separation*. Aledo, TX: Wallbuilder.

Conner, K. J. (1980). *The feasts of Israel*. Portland, OR: City Bible Publishing.

Farah, C. E. (2003). *Islam*. Hauppauge, NY: Barron's Educational Series.

Fiszer, L., & Ferrary, J. (1995). *Jewish holiday feasts*. San Francisco: Chronicle.

Howard, K., & Rosenthal, M. (1997). *The feasts of the Lord: God's prophetic calendar from Calvary to the kingdom*. Nashville, TN: Nelson.

Kasdan, B. (1993). *God's appointed times: A practical guide for understanding and celebrating the biblical holidays*. Baltimore: Messianic Jewish Resources International.

Lewis, B. (1991). *The world of Islam: Faith, people, culture*. New York: Norton.

Niyogi, P. (2001). *Buddhist divinities*. New Delhi, India: Munshiram Manoharlal.

Parker-Rock, M. (2004). *Diwali: The Hindu festival of lights, feasts, and family*. Berkeley Heights, NJ: Enslow.

Sarkar, J. (1999). *Hindu feasts, fasts, and ceremonies*. New Delhi, India: Srishti.

Tylenda, J. N. (2003). *Saints and feasts of the liturgical year*. Washington, DC: Georgetown University Press.

Von Grunebaum, G. E. (1976). *Muhammedan festivals*. London: Curzon.

Film

The history of the religious film does not, or at least does not yet, accurately reflect the range and diversity of the world's religious practice and possibility. The beginnings of cinema, and the first many decades of its evolution, coincided with a continuing period of Western political and cultural preeminence. Accordingly in early film the Judeo-Christian, speaking very broadly, dominates to a disproportionate degree. It is true that since these beginnings a more diverse array of ideas has found expression. Still, since the scholarly record substantially depends on things to which our attention has been drawn, on the films and traditions to which we have access, then in the West, and in this Western account, an imbalance of attention and therefore of perception remains. Perspectives that would redress this imbalance have not always, or even very often, been broadly or sufficiently disseminated. In the cinema generally, and in this instance with regard to religious expression in film, many subjects that have been explored by filmmakers and by filmmaking communities await proper scholarly treatment.

Religion in Early Film

Starting in the late nineteenth century, the earliest projected films were predominantly actualities, precursors to the modern documentary or nonfiction film. There is a creation's morn sense of wonder to these films that set them apart as expressions of devotion, however much they may also have been commercial and ideological objects. As the century turned and the actuality gradually gave place to the narrative film, this religious feeling began to be more consciously and calculatedly evoked. The earliest film narratives did not have a coherent, comprehensible syntax. While cinematic grammar evolved, producers and audiences alike turned to familiar themes and stories, borrowing from them the clarity and sense that were not yet a consistent characteristic of the medium.

The life of Christ, and the Passion particularly, was a very common source of this sense. As film in the midst of the century's first decade began to signify more clearly and consistently, Christian stories, produced primarily but not exclusively in France and in the United States, continued to shore and brace. They lent a legitimacy that, for reasons both commercial and ideological, producers were anxious to attain. Together with adaptations of respectable theatrical and literary properties, religious films in several national settings were used to raise both the stature and profile of a medium that for many seemed suspect, an expression and dangerous incitement of lower impulse and lower classes alike.

Religious film (still almost exclusively Christian) continued to perform these linguistic and legitimizing duties as a fast-forming grammar was applied to longer and more elaborate story structures, as film production became increasingly rationalized and industrialized, and as the various motion-picture combines became more sophisticatedly and aggressively capitalized. Increasing cinematic sophistication, commercial calculation, and religious content are evident in a series of Italian spectacles produced between 1911 and 1914 and set in the classical and early Christian era. A kind of historical dialectic emerges between these productions, a conversation in which the pagan, declining and falling grandeur of Rome (*The Last Days of Pompeii* [1913], *Cabiria* [1914]) is set against and succeeded by Christ's more excellent, still cinematically grandiose way (*Quo Vadis* [1913]). The aesthetic and conceptual influence of these productions was strongly felt in the cinema of the United States, which, with the advent of World War I, perfected the mass production of film and assumed more or less permanent commercial dominance.

Productions like D. W. Griffith's *Judith of Bethulia* (1914) and *Intolerance* (1916) and Thomas Ince's *Civilization* (1916) reflected and in many ways extended the cinematic ambition and confidence of their Italian forebears. The religious undercurrent continued and expanded metaphorically into the present; both of the latter films use religious settings and sentiments to express antiwar feeling and argue an isolationist policy, going so far as to enact Christ's second coming to confirm their positions and conclude their narratives.

This august advocacy did not end up affecting American foreign policy (or helping the box office returns); after this, in commercial settings, religious precept would for the most part be expressed in more generalized, seemingly apolitical and unexceptionable ways. In a combination of conscious design and blind evolution, individual expression and plain industrial process, the American film industry gradually laid down a set of core, consensus values. These were to inform and underpin a cinema that was at least implicitly religious for decades to come. They were also to establish, whether in compliance or opposition, in the United States or internationally, parameters and possibilities for spiritual affirmation and inquiry that in many ways still prevail today.

Religious Films of the 1920s and 1930s

The American religious film in this period takes two main forms, though they are not exclusive of one another. Rooted in Victorian morality and early (1908–1913) Griffith, exemplified, for instance, in many of the films of Mary Pickford (i.e., *Daddy Long Legs* [1919], *Pollyanna* [1920], *Little Annie Rooney* [1925], *Sparrows* [1926]; see also Griffith's *Way Down East* [1920] and Henry King's *Tol'able David* [1921]), the Sunday school film was a commercially conservative, ideologically conformist entity that espoused the standard virtues or exposed the usual vices through contemporary tales that were occasionally cloying and often quite pretty and powerful. The biblical, or biblical era epic (i.e., *The Ten Commandments* [1923, also featuring its own modern Sunday school story], *Ben Hur* [1925], *King of Kings* [1927]) has the reputation of being an expensive, grandiose affair that appropriated the authority of its source and period to tell, and to sell, a rather easy, ecumenical view of Christian verity.

From a position of influence and popularity in their own period, these films have fallen into partial disfavor and even some critical dismissal. To be sure there are difficulties. The Sunday school film was prone to melodrama (i.e., a polarized view of good and bad or right and wrong) and facile solutions that betrayed a lack of social sensitivity or political sophistication. Its squeamishness about sin, or social crisis—not to mention its inclination to equate the two in an uncomfortably facile manner—was reflective of a Puritanism that could be, and often was, excessively proscriptive and censorious. (These contradictions can also be seen in the workings of Hollywood's self-regulating Hays Code [1927] and the impositions, also in the United States, of the Catholic Legion of Decency [from 1934].) For its part, the biblical film, especially as produced by Cecil B. DeMille, is often seen as being a hypocritical combination of conventional morality and open sensuality, where smug homilies vie uncomfortably with coy titillation.

Less obviously, Hollywood's conceit of a common set of moral and cultural values and of a homogeneous audience effaced real cultural and religious differences that deserved recognition, even celebration. This phenomenon extended beyond films with overtly religious subjects. Many of the movie industry's founding figures (Adolph Zukor, Samuel Goldfish/Goldwyn, Louis B. Mayer, Carl Laemmle, etc.) were Jewish immigrants from central or eastern Europe, men whose simultaneous success and failure was to suppress their particular backgrounds and convictions from their works and from the industry for which they were largely responsible. Here is another key point, a practically inherent limitation or, more fairly, delimitation of the commercial film. Its basic fiscal conservatism ensured that in the area of religion and elsewhere, diversity was only likely to appear as a strategy of product diversification and not as a true manifestation of searching and finding.

Clearly the seemingly untroubled surface of the Hollywood religious film of the 1920s masked potentially dark and ambiguous depths, depths that are more easily penetrated these many decades later. At the same time there are also real merits that the passage of time has obscured. For all of their shortcomings, Hollywood religious films before sound reveal more substance, more delicacy, and even more depth of feeling, than they are now given credit for. They set themselves a difficult task, often accomplished, of combining entertainment and instruction, commercial impulse and real sincerity. Their failures may be less due to calculated duplicity than to the difficulty of addressing the sacred in a medium that, in this instance, devoted itself unequivocally to profit, almost exclusively through escape. The combination of homily and sensuality, on the one hand hypocritical, is also a poignant reflection of the struggle and sometimes failing of any person, any community, and certainly any industry aspiring toward transcendence in a secular world and in a modern and materialistic age.

This period makes clear some of religious cinema's most basic paradoxes, challenges, and contributions. There is an assumption, based on a misreading of only part of the historical record, that religion, especially of a western variety, exerts a negatively conservative, censorious pressure on creative impulse and conscience and on film culture generally. This is only part of the picture. The caricaturing of factions—licentious Hollywood and censorious Heartland—had and continues to have some basis in truth, but the reality, broadly and fairly considered, is much more complex and much more interesting. Artists and industries and audiences have always engaged in a complex spiritual negotiation, a balancing of binary impulses that are essential not only to art but to the search for the sacred and for social survival: the individual and the communal, exploration and conservation, centrifugal and centripetal forces.

This dialectic is not restricted to a battle between the sanctimonious and the secular. The 1920s also saw the establishment of one of these binary alternatives within religious realms, one that affirmed at the same time that it continued to inquire and to constructively criticize. The art film favored spiritual exploration over the sometimes manipulations and pat declarations of the commercial cinema, and its individual, individualized search for truth did something to balance the pressures of consensus morality. Art films, here and afterwards, tended to thrive where film industries were less stable, hierarchical, or infrastructural. (Later, systems of subsidy, which is to say the partial protection from market forces, would provide them the same service.) This instability, or sometimes informality—where patronage, amateur values, and independent production held sway—often meant a greater possibility for innovation and individuation, for particular expressions of conviction and conscience. The art film's artisanal methodology and personal nature implicitly countered industrialization and mass production, something it paralleled in its view of religion. In these narratives transcendence was as often as not achieved through solitary struggles, often in opposition to institutional (congregational) imperatives.

The Danish writer/director Carl Theodor Dreyer exemplifies the independent and aesthetic possibilities of this approach. Most famously in his *The Passion of Joan of Arc* (1928), Dreyer sets forth the immemorial tensions between sectarian religion and individual spirituality, affirming that private conscience could, and repeatedly has, run afoul of the institutional church and of institutions generally. Far from being a mere negation, however, Dreyer's ringing ideological critique also attains great heights of reverence and conviction in the representation, through an artful and individual directorial style, as well as through the luminous performance of Renée Falconetti, of Joan's faith and martyrdom. Its condemnation of politics and priestcraft notwithstanding, the film accomplishes a remarkable and affecting transformation, a convincing portrayal of a world dominated, and not without benevolent affect, by religion.

The irony of the religious art film, evident in some discussions on Dreyer and many other masterly filmmakers, is that it leads as much to a kind of romantic reverence for the great artist as to any greater spiritual conviction and commitment. Here is another key to the consideration of religion generally and its relation to film. Religious desire is not only expressed denominationally, but in any search for transcendental signifiers, for first causes and last resorts. Systems and sects, philosophies and lifestyles, ideologies and individuals have all been consulted in this search, all suggesting their own answers to the great questions of origin and meaning, of purpose and destination, of the varieties of divinity and the possibility of human access thereto.

Thus it is that even Hollywood's hedonism, its materialism and its movie stars answered a yearning and inspired a kind of devotion (as well as directly giving rise to the Hays Code, the Legion of Decency, and the religious films discussed above). There is a faith expressed in the Soviet cinema of the 1920s and early 1930s, with its rejections of Christian and capitalist dogma and practice, its professions and proselytizing of Marxist-Leninist doctrine. There is conviction, as well as the coercion that so often accompanies it, in the Nazi era's film testimonies of Fuehrer and Fatherland. Religion informs and infuses Japanese cinema during the closing years of the Meiji era, echoing the prevailing state (*Kokka*) Shintoism and its enshrinement of the emperor and militaristic nationalism. In these demonstrable truths there is danger of religious and cultural caricature: The reality of these things in Soviet, German, and Japanese life cannot get near to the complexity of these things, nor of the range of belief and application that lies outside of them. What is clear is that an understanding of religious impulse and expression in film must be informed by ideological sensitivity and even a concomitant skepticism.

In this regard there is a less marked but nevertheless certain manifestation of religious impulse in film history, one that begins to come to the fore in the documentary film of the 1930s. In part defined and developed by the Scots theorist and producer John Grierson ("I look at the cinema as a pulpit, and use it as a propagandist"), the documentary film established a religiously and socially active, activist alternative to Hollywood homilies. The social aspect is self-evident and has remained in place into the present. As for religion, Grierson and many who followed found inspiration in the collective and communal doctrines not only of Marx, but of the New Testament. Although much documentary activity since Grierson has reflected a skepticism, even an agnostic or atheistic antipathy, toward institutions like the church, a very particular type of devotion has remained consistently in place. "Pure religion and undefiled before God and the Father is this, to visit the fatherless and widows in their affliction..." (James 1:27, KJV).

A similar activism informed a series of socially conscious American films of the period, with their implied and occasionally explicit critiques of the apparatuses of power, including the church (cf. the sanctimonious and ineffectual minister in *I Am a Fugitive from a Chain Gang* [1932]). There were also anomalous explorations like *The Green Pastures* (1936), a simultaneously condescending and deeply appreciative white fantasy about African-American religious experience and faith. For the most part, however, the commercial religious film in the United States continued to trace and update previously established patterns.

The 1930s and 1940s

The Depression informed a set of Sunday school sermons in films featuring Shirley Temple. As in the films of Mary Pickford, plucky innocence motivated adult improvement, and self-help led to a kind of divine intervention, this time in a more pointedly socioeconomic context. As Temple's career began to wane, the increasingly ambitious films of Walt Disney and his collaborators rose to commercial prominence and accomplished a significant merging. This is seen most clearly in *Pinocchio* (1940), describing as it does a kind of pilgrim's progress, culminating in its protagonist's sacrificial death and transfiguration. Here is a portentous development: The Sunday school story and the fairy tale film, with their similar sensibilities, audiences and didactic underpinnings, came together, and became somewhat interchangeable.

With the Depression's close and the eventual American entry into World War II, this hybridization extended to adult film fare. In both fantastic and erstwhile realistic settings, numerous films (*Here Comes Mr. Jordan* [1941], *Going My Way* and *A Guy Named Joe* [both 1944], and later *Angel on My Shoulder* [1946] and *The Bishop's Wife* [1947]) enact a standard situation and present a standard resolution. Man is born to trouble, but God, by means of a saintly or supernatural intermediary, intervenes and solves the problem. This is not so far from the sacred narratives basic to most religious traditions, all long established and substantially documented. The difference, and the difficulty, is that in these films religious verities meld with fantasy and move into the realm of wish fulfillment, even an indirect denial of religious assurances, not only of salvation, but of the nature of tribulation. There could be elegance (*Heaven Can Wait* [1943]), intensity (*It's a Wonderful Life* [1946]), and irony (*A Matter of Life and Death* [1946]) in the playing out of these semi- or pseudoreligious fantasies, but in the main, while aiming to comfort and console, they also enjoined passivity, even encouraging a kind of audience infantilization.

These developments reflect a quite understandable insecurity—a natural and deep-seated uncertainty. Other perspectives also reflected religion in this period and traced their own patterns of engagement and ambivalence. In occupied Denmark, Carl Dreyer's *Day of Wrath* (1943) linked the practices of a strict religious community with the methodologies and effects of totalitarian rule. Allied films about the war, which began with a God-on-our-side certainty, even pugnacity (*In Which We Serve* [1942], *Millions Like Us* [1943], *Mrs. Miniver* [1942], and Frank Capra and Anatole Litvak's documentary series *Why We Fight* [1942–1945]), gave way to the approach of victory to greater humility and ambiguity (*Fires Were Started* [1943], *This Happy Breed* [1944], and *They Were Expendable*, *A Walk in the Sun*, *Let There Be Light*, and *A Diary for Timothy* [all 1945]). In this, there is a move from colonial givens—the imposition of Western world views and institutions because of their clear superiority—to colonial questioning. Will our assumptions work in every setting? Are we really right after all?

This was an essential moment, especially in the diversification of religious expression in film. It is a truism that the experience of war forced the West to take closer and more careful account of the rest of the world. One result, relating to religion, was a more serious, sympathetic consideration of other traditions and other validities, as in John Ford's *The Fugitive* (1947) and Jean Renoir's *The River* (1951). Perhaps even more significantly, the West, in part through its cinema, began to doubt its own cultural and ideological preeminence. This is definitively expressed in Michael Powell and Emeric Pressburger's stunning adaptation of Rumer Godden's *Black Narcissus* (1947), where pale, proselytizing Western religion is no match for the color, sensuality, and ultimate impenetrability of utterly legitimate Eastern cosmologies.

Film Beyond Christianity

Bengali filmmaker Satyajit Ray's Apu trilogy (*Pather Panchali* [1955], *Aparajito* [1956], and *The World of Apu* [1959]) suggests some of the challenges and benefits of this process. Broadly speaking, it recounts the travails, from childhood to maturity, of the son of a Brahman priest. A masterful exploration of character and milieu, the films' religious elements are not pressed, but rather register as part of a very deep structure, fully constituted and lightly held. This is to say that its Hindu and Vedic complexities come naturally, are part of a more complex network of determinants and significations, and are bound to substantially elude the outsider.

A similar situation informs and complicates the reality and reading of Asian cinema, in which there is a widespread sensibility that derives, in form and content, from Buddhist thought, particularly as it evolved in and then radiated out from China. This can justly, if very generally, be found in a meditative, presentational style, reflecting and responding to the notion that life is made up of impermanence and suffering and that calm, kindly resignation is an appropriate response. Traces of this, explicitly and implicitly, consciously and subconsciously applied, are still found in a number of national settings in Asia. Each of these reflect the particular culture, as well as the perspectives of the individual or individuals expressing themselves therein. Here, for instance, is a root of the celebrated "sympathetic sadness" (*mono no amare*) in the films of Yasujiro Ozu.

Cinema of Charity

Another sort of spiritual expression in film offers itself here, providing a real path through inevitable cultural incomprehensions. The cinema of charity has the power to transcend sectarian and national boundaries. It is sometimes informed by but not necessarily dependent on doctrine or creed. More importantly, at least and especially for ecumenical conversations, it reflects a more general, accessible religious impulse, one central to practically all of the great religious traditions. Its narrative and stylistic characteristics are as diverse as the religions, cultures, and individuals that ply it. The cinema of charity is marked more than anything by its attitude toward cinematic subjects and spectators alike. This attitude is courteous, compassionate, generous, and sympathetic. These are films made with love.

The examples that come to mind tend to be individual filmmakers: Victor Sjostrom, Robert Flaherty, Jean Renoir, Alexander Dovzhenko, Frank Borzage, Ozu, Howard Hawks, Leo McCarey, Humphrey Jennings, Kenji Mizoguchi, Roberto Rossellini, Ray, Tom Daly, Jean Rouch, Ermanno Olmi, John Cassavetes, Stan Brakhage, Wim Wenders, Barbara Kopple, Charles Burnett, Agnes Varda, Abbas Kiorastami. In such lists—this one is just a sampling, and only deals with directors—lies a challenge, even a reproof to some believers. Leo McCarey's kindliness is undoubtedly a function and manifestation of his Catholicism, but in other artists the truth one feels is rooted in traditions to which one may not be able to subscribe. There may not even be a religious tradition. Jean Renoir's films, at least in terms of precept and practice, are decidedly secular, informed by nothing so much as his enormous generosity and his abiding humanist faith. The sectarian can make no points off of him and will doubtless disapprove of many of his central assumptions, yet he remains incontestably one of the most resonant, beneficent examples in world cinema of charitable filmmaking.

Here, perhaps, is the mystery of the religious film, if not of godliness. As with much sacred experience, the effects of all this diverse film work, as well as of our own cinematic and social attention and effort, are difficult to describe, and the causes of said effect difficult to grasp. The feelings, the result in generous inclination and charitable application, are nevertheless palpable. Charitable cinema, attending the entire history of the medium, has had and continues to have the power to smooth over cultural gaps and religious misunderstanding, to begin a binding of the heterogeneous in mutual appreciation and gratitude.

The 1950s

These enrichments and diversifications coincided with a period of existential uncertainty, attended as well by economic crisis, in the Hollywood industry of the 1950s. One of the responses was a return to Biblical subjects and grandeur. Although there were felicities, these films (i.e., *Samson and Delilah* [1949], *Quo Vadis* [1951], *The Robe* [1953], *The Ten Commandments* [1956], *Ben Hur* [1959]) generally lacked the subtlety and sincerity of the best of their 1920s predecessors. Part of this is due to their broad dramatic devices and their sometimes aggressive simplemindedness, all insufficiently balanced by the impression of actual belief. The usual sounding brass and tinkling coffers of the commercial cinema register as well, redolent perhaps of some greater spiritual desolation.

In addition, and perhaps more importantly, the fact that these spectacles utilized the techniques of escapist entertainment in the service of the spiritual led to very fundamental difficulties and distortions. Commercial films have always tended to simplify, to do much or most of the work for the audience. Passivity and even an unwillingness or inability to think or act have often been the result. Producers and consumers are mutually implicated in this process. Popular religious narratives simplify spiritual struggle, eliding difficult processes and manifesting internal advancements through external means (as in miraculous manifestations convincingly portrayed through special effects). This correlation of subject matter and style, of religion with (super) accessibility and (exaggerated) ease, was hinted at in the 1920s and came to full fruition in the 1950s. It embodied the basic contradiction of the commercial religious film: scripture from a number of traditions affirms that in the realm of spiritual manifestation and experience the Divine will not be found in the strong wind or the earthquake, nor in the fire, but in the still small voice. It will hold, with regard to our access to or control of such manifestation, that the wind bloweth where it listeth. Hollywood, and the commercial film in general, chose an easier, arguably less spiritually typical road.

As before, the European art cinema of the 1950s provides a salutary, challenging alternative to the facility of Hollywood religion. In films like Carl Dreyer's *Ordet* (1955) and Robert Bresson's *The Diary of a Country Priest* (1950), *A Man Escaped* (1956), and *Pickpocket* (1959), spectacle is countered by more subtle explorations of conscience and individual experience, by a more contemplative pace, and by a restrained, even ascetic style. The sparseness of these films, often bordering on severity, inscribes not only in the narrative but in its very cinematic articulation the rigor and reality of spiritual struggle. This is the opposite of easy cinematic salvation, and if its ways are strait and narrow, its rewards, for protagonists and sympathetic spectators alike, are proportionately great.

In addition to the magisterial effects of what Paul Schrader has called the transcendental style (cf. his study of the films of Bresson, Dreyer, and Yasujiro Ozu), agnostic and atheistic sensibilities also invigorate spiritual inquiry in the cinema of this period. These essential voices reflected prevailing intellectual and philosophical trends, providing a reminder that religion concerns not just the finding, but the seeking as well. Swedish director Ingmar Bergman's insistent, even obsessive, probing of the darkness (*The Seventh Seal* [1957], *Through a Glass Darkly* [1961], *Winter Light* [1962], *The Silence* [1963], *Cries and Whispers* [1973]) traces a doubting of Dostoievskian proportions, affecting precisely because of its insistence. As often as darkness prevails in Bergman's work, the continuation of the conversation becomes a de facto expression of faith, if not in certain answers, then in the continuing importance of the questions.

Bergman's cinema paradoxically validates spiritual process at the same time that it despairs of its efficacy. The spiritual substance and conviction in the films of the atheist Spanish director Luis Buñuel are even more paradoxical. The horrors of the Holocaust, among other things, had made of religious refusal a signal position of the period. Buñuel became an emblem and articulation of that refusal, though his films contain a less unequivocal message. He had indeed used blasphemy (*L'Age d'Or* [1930]) as part of a generally destabilizing, Dadaist critique of any number of institutions. Notwithstanding, a closer look at his later work reveals that surface sacrilege—as in the last supper sequence from *Viridiana* (1961)—might also be interpreted as a moralist's condemnation of hypocrisy, even his expression of righteous anger. Buñuel frequently targets the church, and his attacks are rooted in documented abuses of power (cf. *Las Hurdes / Land Without Bread* [1932]), but it is not simply religion he is after. A dialectic between honorable precept, the holy fools (the eponymous protagonists of *Viridiana* and *Nazarin* [1959]) who attempt to administer or carry it out, and the viciousness and unworthiness of those to whom they minister informs the films and gives them a bracing, healthy tension. Buñuel's negatory, frequently misanthropic cinema is not without regard or even reverence, as in his affecting defense of the principles believers so frequently fail to live up to.

The 1960s

By the mid-1960s years of ferment and unrest, added to a longstanding industrial instability, had left Hollywood out of touch with the leading edges of religious inquiry and ill-equipped to voice or defend its central values. The tepid institutional criticism of Richard Brooks' *Elmer Gantry* (1960), the hysterical wholesomeness of *The Sound of Music* (1965), to which audiences, frightened and polarized by the burgeoning counterculture, were drawn in droves, and the seeming elephantine irrelevance of *The Greatest Story Ever Told* (1965) seemed to confirm not only that commercial films were no longer able to address matters of religious concern, but that these matters had, in effect, ceased to matter.

In contrast to this failing old guard, a New Hollywood was emerging that rejected religion by assuming its inevitable affiliation with reactionary conservatism or bourgeois materialism (cf. the traitorous minister's daughter in *Bonnie and Clyde* [1967])—in other words, by fetishizing its worst manifestations and taking those parts to be the whole. Such criticism was far from being universal, but it did signal and inform an epochal change in direction. Absent the illusion of homogeneity or a clear mandate from the paying public, the American commercial film would from this point essentially withdraw from the active avowal of the religious values that for so long had constituted its nominal center.

Institutional, partly constructed consensus gave way to an ever more fragmented dialectic of spiritual searching and finding, affirmation and negation, along with everything in between. Other factors further obscure and enrich the discussion: the diversification of international filmmaking communities, especially in the developing world; the eventual democratization, through technology, of film production and distribution; ever increasing volumes of critical discourse. Out of all this the religious film emerges as a very mutable, protean object. The marking of historical pattern and theoretical possibility now becomes more difficult, obscured as it is by the advent of the present tense. From here, until the dust of contemporary practice settles into the scholarly record of coming decades, there are only strong impressions and speculations built on past practice.

Recent Developments

From the early 1960s through to his exile from the Soviet Union and death in the early 1980s, Andrei Tarkovsky's mystical cinema not only expressed its own elusive religious faith, but it also stood clearly as a counter to and refutation of state religion. Less clearly, but just as certainly, the humanism of the Czech New Wave in the mid-1960s constituted a similar response, as would affirmations of individual expression and worth in the Chinese cinema of the 1980s and 1990s. From 1968 (*The Night of the Living Dead*), the modern horror film emerges with intermittent effectiveness as a kind of negative image of conventional religious questioning, with its deep anxieties and pessimism attending and invigorating discussions of the usual issues.

Denominational cinema, productions made by and distributed to religious adherents by their chosen institutions, marked an important departure from and alternative to the impositions of film industries. It also identified an important point of rupture, as embattled believers found it more and more difficult to find themselves, their concerns, and their consolations in an increasingly boundary breaking and secular cinema. A whole range of pointed, ever more explicit investigations illuminate that gap.

Most pointedly in the individual works and collaborations of Paul Schrader and Martin Scorcese, transcendental impulse and aspiration would collide with an increasingly intransigent, often sordid naturalism. In films like *Mean Streets* (1973), *Taxi Driver* (1975), and *American Gigolo* and *Raging Bull* (both 1980), the result would be an operatic, even ecstatic treatment of sin and suffering intermingled. This cinema of mortification effectively rendered the aspiration and the emptiness of the age, and it was not without its powerful hints of salvation. John 9:25, the coda to *Raging Bull*, provides the intended rationale, and a great measure of justification for these films and their damaged protagonists. "Whether he be a sinner or no, I know not: one thing I know, that, whereas I was blind, now I see." This hard, clear vision also widened the gulf and inverted longstanding relationships between secular and sectarian constituencies. If in the 1920s, Sunday school cinema unduly caricatured the sin and the sinners that it sincerely tried to portray, then fifty and sixty years later a substantial and sin-ridden cinema could make little connection with many of the believing members of an alienated audience.

The controversy over Schrader and Scorcese's *The Last Temptation of Christ* (1987) exemplifies this alienation. It is a brave film, full of deep conviction, as well as significant lapses in decorum and taste. The hostility with which it was met may in part have reflected the high-handed philistinism of which the religious right is capable, but it also raised real and legitimate issues. This was not just conservatism, but conservation, not just intolerance, but an awareness of the potential dangers of its opposite. Faithful factions would have it that the over-inclination to take offense has to be factored against an opposite danger, which is the inability to be offended. The Western believer's call, occasionally answered by films like *Tender Mercies* (1983), *Places in the Heart* (1984), and Robert Duvall's historic *The Apostle* (1997), echoes a basic idea of the documentary film movement. Artistry and individual expression are essential and need to be subordinated to a sense of social responsibility and the pursuit of the public good.

Again, as always, there are international responses, resistances, and independent developments. Wim Wenders' *Wings of Desire* (1987) and *Faraway, So Close* (1993) reinvent Hollywood's intervening angel fantasy, using mythological suggestiveness and metaphor, irony, and a degree of humor to step back from the literalism and sometimes vulgarity of their least successful models. Set and beautifully shot in Berlin, the films also provide a preternatural preview of the fall of communism and of the geopolitical challenges and opportunities that would follow. There is mythological metaphor, some irony, and humor in this utilization of heavenly tropes. Still, for all their careful distancing, these are also graceful, informed parables about sorrow and salvation, testimonies to the power of cinema's loving look, and finally, especially in the conclusion of the second film, expressions of gratitude and belief. Here, amidst frequent divisive rhetoric, is encouraging evidence that popular artists and high modernists can meet and be edified on the rich, still common ground of religious film.

Nearby, Gabriel Axel's exquisite *Babette's Feast* (1987), featuring strategically cast and utilized actors from the ouevre of Carl Theodor Dreyer, provides a contemplation of and a lovely reconciliation between the abundant inclinations of Hollywood religion and the severities of the art film, as well as between the satisfactions of substantial secular pursuit and the more pressing needs of the spiritual life. Folk (*minkan*) Shintoism is essential to the delights and substance of recent animated films from Japan's Studio Ghibli (Hiyao Miyazaki's *My Neighbour Totoro* [1988], *Princess Mononoke* [1997], and *Spirited Away* [2001] and Isao Takahata's *The Racoon War* [1994]). Following ample

precedent, these films' value-specific manifestations—environmentalism, the refusal of good/bad polarities in its characters, a reverence for the domestic sphere—resonate outside that value system and have an inclusive, in-gathering effect, notwithstanding, or even because of their cultural and religious specificity.

Finally, and without doubt most important to a discussion of contemporary film and religion, the Iranian cinema of the 1990s and 2000s recapitulates many of the issues considered here, as well as providing new challenges and opportunities for productive discussion. Nowhere is the ease and danger of intrafaith incomprehension, nowhere is the necessity of generous effort and mutual appreciation more evident than in the interactions between Islam and the Judeo-Christian world. The tradition of Muhammad's forbidding the artistic representation of the human form has contributed to a paucity of artistic production generally, and film production particularly, in the Muslim world. However, notwithstanding this proscription some production has taken place. In the case of Iran, it has become some of the most bracing and challenging in world cinema.

Clichés must be considered and may have some bearing in the truth. Conservative, repressive forces in Iran are real, are substantially religious, and have ensured that free expression in the cinema has been substantially circumscribed. (It might also be justly argued that repressive forces in the United States [cf. a well-publicized refusal in 2002 to offer Abbas Kiorastami an entry visa to attend the New York Film Festival] have equally circumscribed the dissemination and celebration of this essential material.) A resulting inclination to find coded subversivities in Iranian film is appealing and will bear some fruit, but it may not be the most productive approach to the material, particularly with regard to the current conversation. As in Hollywood's heyday, as well as in numerous other politically restricting circumstances, limitation has sometimes served as a spur to creativity and to urgency. There are depths beneath the seemingly serene surfaces that bear investigation.

More importantly, it must also be granted that Iranian cinema is a diverse embodiment of a simple reality: Perhaps uniquely in film history, this national cinema unequivocally constitutes the collective expression of a community of faith. Its formal elements are challenging, even groundbreaking. If there is a great diversity—the homiletic cinema of Majid Majidi; the realist activism of Jafar Panahi; the diverse ministrations of the Makhmalbaf collective; the rigors, generosities, and comparative secularism of Abbas Kiorostami's intellectual art films—then it is partly a confirmation of the range of problem and possibility that religion, now too frequently caricatured as a uniformly constraining influence, can stimulate.

Through the course of its history film has consistently demonstrated its power to hold and to hog our attention. The lacunae in a summary like this, necessary in this setting and with this format, may actually resist its often unhealthy hypnotism. Films, filmmakers, even and especially when religion is at issue, should only serve as the beginning and as a part of a greater, more challenging exchange of precept and principle, one that expands one's outward comprehension and appreciation at the same time that it intensifies that which adheres and abides inside.

DEAN DUNCAN

Further Reading

Bazin, A. (1993). Cinema and theology. In J. McAuliffe (Ed.) *Plays, movies, and critics*. Durham, NC: Duke University Press.

Bliss, M. (1995). *The word made flesh: Catholicism and conflict in the films of Martin Scorsese*. Lanham, MD: Scarecrow Press.

Buñuel, Luis (1983). *My last sigh*. New York: Alfred A. Knopf.

Cowie, Peter (1982). *Ingmar Bergman: A critical biography*. New York: Scribner.

Dabashi, Hamid (2001). *Close up: Iranian cinema, past, present and future*. London; New York: Verso.

Fraser, P. (1998). *Images of the passion: The sacramental mode in film*. Westport, CT: Praeger.

Hardy, F. (Ed.). (1966). *Grierson on documentary*. New York: Praeger.

Hayne, D. (Ed.). (1959). *The autobiography of Cecil B. DeMille*. New York: Garland Publishing.

Lyden, J. (2003). *Film as religion: Myth, morals, rituals*. New York: New York University Press.

Medved, M. (1992). *Hollywood vs. America: Popular culture and the war on traditional values*. New York: Harper Collins.

Schrader, P. (1972). *Transcendental style in film: Ozu, Bresson, Dreyer*. Berkeley: University of California Press.

Skoller, D. (Ed.). (1973). *Dreyer in double reflection*. New York: Dutton.

Tarkovsky, A. (1987). *Sculpting in time: Reflections on the cinema*. New York: Alfred A. Knopf.

Free Speech

In Plato's *Republic*, Socrates asks Adeimantus whether he would "carelessly allow children to hear any casual tales which may be devised by casual persons, and to receive into their minds ideas for the most part [that are] the very opposite of those which we should wish them to have when they are grown up?" When Adeimantus responds in the negative, Plato concurs that censorship of "bad" stories is necessary to promote "good" ideas and to help children adopt those positive values and belief systems as they mature. This "paternalistic" rationale is consistent with some religious views maintaining that freedom of speech ought to be limited to protect believers from ideas or images that are perceived as spiritually threatening.

Ironically, although freedom of speech in Western society is rooted in a religious idea of God-given "natural rights" of individuals versus those of the state, Tony Rimmer (1996) demonstrated in his research that there is in fact an inverse relationship between levels of personal religiosity and tolerance of free speech in the United States. While there are diverse perspectives among various religious adherents, history suggests that many Christians and Muslims in particular are concerned with the potential harm of unfettered freedom of speech.

Free Speech as a God-given Right

From the perspective of politics and societal regulations, the simplest construct of free speech centers on the rights of individuals to express themselves without government censorship, punishment, or coercion. While there are varying theories about the value of free speech in society, the dominant free speech paradigm is motivated by Western ideals celebrating individual human rights. This emphasis on individualism can be traced to St. Thomas Aquinas' (1225–1274) belief that natural law (or God's law) overrides the laws of the state. In the seventeenth century, John Locke (1632–1704) and Baruch Spinoza (1630–1677) rooted religious liberty within the rights of individuals, placing in question the medieval doctrine of "natural subjection" (*plenitudi potestatis*: granting divine power to monarchs via the pope). Such emphasis on the individual was furthered by industrialization, urbanization, and democratization coupled with rationalism, science, and materialist-oriented ethics, resulting in greater religious and political toleration, and in laws and constitutions protecting speech and the press, and religious choice.

The outcome of this process is manifest in the First Amendment of the United States Constitution (ratified on 15 December 1791), which infers that religion and speech are "natural" individual rights that preclude government authority. It states, "Congress shall make no law respecting an establishment of religion, or prohibiting the free exercise thereof; or abridging *the* freedom of speech, or of the press...." [emphasis added]. Similar language is used in the United Nations' 1948 Universal Declaration of Human Rights, stating in Article 19 that "Everyone has the right to freedom of opinion and expression...." Drawing on the same ideology, the 1950 European Convention of Human Rights and Fundamental Freedoms (ECHRFF) declared, "Everyone has the right to freedom of thought, conscience, and religion" (Article 9 §1) and "everyone has the right to freedom of expression" (Article 10 §1). In all these instances, free speech rights are not given to individuals by governments, but are instead viewed as preexisting human rights (natural rights) that must be respected by political institutions.

Speech as Religious Practice

Protecting the speech rights of individuals advances religious diversity because the speech act is inextricably intertwined with religious practice and belief. Speech is manifest in printed form in the sacred texts of many faiths (see, e.g., Writings of Baha'u'llah, Wisdom of the Buddha, *Bhagavad Gita*, Qur'an, Talmud, Holy Bible, The Book of Mormon, the Vedas, etc.) and is a necessary element of religious practices involving proselytizing, preaching, and ritual. Examining religious belief as a socially constructed practice, sociologist Peter Berger emphasized the central role of speech (or discourse with others) in an individual's religious beliefs. According to Berger, a person's religious worldview "hangs on a thin thread of conversation" (Berger 1967, 17) with significant others (such as family members, friends, or spouses). These conversations are built and sustained over time through religious practices, rituals, and texts. Conversely, according to Berger's model, when empowered institutions quash religious speech, the viability of religious institutions is greatly threatened.

Religious Tolerance of Mass-mediated Speech

Religious institutions have historically struggled with speech as propagated through new communication technologies. Stout and Buddenbaum preface their compendium *Religion and Mass Media* (1996) by noting that Christian churches since the 1500s have demonstrated fear of the potentially harmful effects of mass-mediated speech (through the printed word, radio, television, the movies, and more recently, the Internet). In 1559, under the direction of Pope Paul IV, the Catholic Church issued the "Index of Forbidden Books" to discourage its members from reading some contro-

versial material. In the early 1800s, Protestant and Catholic clergy equated the newly popular novels with alcohol and tobacco. In 1973, Evangelical Methodist minister Donald Wildmon created the watchdog groups the National Federation of Decency (later the American Family Association) and the Coalition for Better Television (later renamed Christian Leaders for Responsible Television) in efforts to rid the popular media of sex, violence, and profanity. These and similar organizations influence media outlets by boycotting (or threatening boycotts) of products advertised during "objectionable" broadcast programming or by boycotting institutions that distribute or sell pornography or other "offensive" material.

I am a Canadian, a free Canadian, free to speak without fear, free to worship God in my own way, free to stand for what I think right, free to oppose what I believe wrong, free to choose those who shall govern my country. This heritage of freedom I pledge to uphold for myself and all mankind.

John Diefenbaker (former Prime Minister of Canada)

Sexuality and profanity are not only troublesome for Christian groups. Palmer and Gallab found that Islamic clerics have condemned much of Western media (and television in particular) as destructive and morally oppositional to the values of Islam. Furthermore, Yoel Cohen's analysis of Judaism and mass media highlighted conflict arising between various interpretations of the Talmud and media content emphasizing not only sexual content, but also gossip.

Government-enforced Speech Regulations (Obscenity Laws)

Laws in a number of countries recognizing freedom of speech and religion have, on occasion, been influenced by religious organizations and ideas. Blasphemy laws and regulations of sexually oriented speech are in large part driven by religious ideas.

One year following the ratification of the First Amendment of the U.S. Constitution, all fourteen of the then existing states made either blasphemy, profanity, or both, statutory crimes.

In the 1957 *Roth v. United States* (354 U.S. 479) decision, the U.S. Supreme Court rejected arguments that obscenity statutes offended the First Amendment by punishing incitation of "impure sexual thoughts" while offering no evidence that obscene material caused any overt antisocial conduct. Instead, the Court excluded obscenity from its definition of *speech*. Why the exception? The Court noted, "implicit in the history of the First Amendment is the rejection of obscenity as utterly without redeeming social importance." While there are several arguments offered by lawmakers in support of obscenity statutes, the traditional line of reasoning can be traced to Anthony Comstock who, in the 1870s, suggested that the purpose of sex was for procreation (rather than gratification) and that God laid down laws limiting sex to those who are legally married to each other. These laws, it was argued, could not change at the whim of society: "What was wrong yesterday is still wrong today and will be wrong tomorrow. Prohibitions against homosexuality, adultery, and promiscuity in the interests of preserving heterosexual fidelity, marriage, and the family reflect enduring, immutable values" (Linz and Malamuth 1993, 7). While the courts and lawmakers in the United States still struggle to determine what legally comprises obscenity, the religious and moral underpinnings allowing for the exception are still grounded in contemporary legal practice, as reflected by former U.S. Supreme Court nominee Robert H. Bork, who said that the free speech clause of the U.S. Constitution was intended to protect ideas, rather than to protect "self-gratification through pornography."

Government-enforced Speech Regulations (Blasphemy Laws)

Manny Paraschos's analysis of religious expression and the law in Europe cites legal conflicts in the union arising in countries that, while religiously homogeneous (dominated by one religion), are represented by lawmakers seeking to respect minority religious groups. One result of tensions between minority and dominant religious practices has engendered various statutes aimed at blasphemous speech. Paraschos notes two landmark cases—*Otto-Premiger-Instit v. Austria* (1993) and *Wingrove v. the United Kingdom* (1995)—that demonstrate the tension between blasphemy laws and the European Convention (ECHRFF).

In *Otto-Premiger-Instit*, a film trivializing the Christian creed while caricaturizing God the Father "as a senile, impotent idiot, Christ as a cretin and Mary the Mother of God as a wanton lady" was confiscated for violating the Blasphemy Act §188 of the Austrian Penal Code (1992). In a six-to-three decision, the regional court upheld the confiscation, noting the significant role played by religion in society and the need to allow discretion for authorities in different regions of Europe in such matters. The court concluded that con-

fiscation of the film acted to "ensure religious peace in that region" and to prevent some people from being "the object of attacks on their religious beliefs in an unwarranted and offensive manner" (*Otto-Premiger-Instit v. Austria* [1993], 5–17). The *Wingrove* decision centered on an 18-minute video titled *Visions of Ecstasy* that was denied approval for distribution and sale by the British Board of Film Classification because it was deemed blasphemous. The film offered erotic depictions of Jesus Christ with St. Teresa of Avila, a sixteenth-century nun. Citing the British statutory definition of blasphemy ("Every publication is said to be blasphemous which contains any contemptuous, reviling, scurrilous or ludicrous matter relating to God, Jesus Christ, or the Bible, or the formularies of the Church of England as by law established"), the court held that the board's action was within its legal rights to deny a license to the distributor. The court recognized that blasphemy laws are becoming obsolete in Europe but opined that because there is no uniform perception in the European Union regarding morals or religion, national laws regulating freedom of expression to "protect the rights of others" are consistent with the provisions of the ECHRFF. Despite upholding this law in defense of Christian churches, however, the British Divisional Court in 1991 refused to apply the same statute when British Muslim Groups challenged Salman Rushdie's *The Satanic Verses* on the grounds that the law, as written, did not apply to non-Christian faiths (*R. v. Bow Street Magistrate's Court* ex parte Choudhury [1979], 318).

Implications

There will always be occasions when religious ideals and other expressive acts conflict with one another. Because unfettered speech (both religious and secular in nature) is necessary in pluralist societies, balancing societal values and needs with those of religious institutions will continue to challenge political and religious organizations.

DAVID W. SCOTT

See also Boycotts; Culture Wars; Defamation; Tolerance

Further Reading

Ashcraft, R. (1996). Religion and Lockean natural rights. In I. Bloom, J. P. Martin, & W. L. Proudfoot (Eds.), *Religious diversity and human rights* (pp. 195–212). New York: Columbia University Press.

Berger, P. L. (1967). *The sacred canopy: Elements of a sociological theory of religion.* Garden City, NJ: Doubleday.

Bloom, I., Martin, J. P., & Proudfoot, W. (1996). *Religious diversity and human rights*. New York: Columbia University Press.

Claussen, D. (2002). *Sex, religion, media*. New York: Rowman & Littlefield.

Cohen, Y. (2001). Mass Media in the Jewish tradition. In D. A. Stout & J. M. Buddenbaum (Eds.), *Religion and popular culture: Studies on the interaction of worldviews* (p. 95–108*)*. Ames: Iowa State University Press.

Hart, H. L. A. (1994). *The concept of law*. Oxford: Clarendon Press.

Hill, M. (2002). *Religious liberty and human rights*. Cardiff: University of Wales Press.

Jelen, T. (1996). Catholicism, conscience, and censorship. In D. A. Stout & J. M. Buddenbaum (Eds.), *Religion and mass media: Audiences and adaptations*. Thousand Oaks, CA: Sage.

Johnson, L. T. (1996). Religious rights and Christian texts. In J. Witte & J. D. Van Der Vyver (Eds.), *Religious human rights in a global perspective* (pp. 65–95). The Hague: Martinus Nijhoff.

Linz, D., & Malamuth, N. (1993). *Pornography*. Thousand Oaks, CA: Sage.

Mendenhall, R. R. (2002). Responses to television from the new Christian right: The Donald Wildmon organizations' fight against sexual content. In D. S. Claussen (Ed.), *Sex, religion, media* (pp. 101–114). New York: Rowman & Littlefield.

Nimmer, M. B. (1984). *Nimmer on freedom of speech: A treatise on the theory of the First Amendment*. New York: Matthew Bender.

Palmer, A.W., & Gallab, A. A. (2001). Islam and Western Culture: Navigating Terra Incognita. In D. A. Stout & J. M. Buddenbaum (Eds.), *Religion and popular culture: Studies on the interaction of worldviews* (p. 109–123*)*. Ames: Iowa State University Press.

Paraschos, M. (2000). Religion, religious expression, and the law in the European union. In J. Theirstein & Y. R. Kamalipour (Eds.), *Religion, law, and freedom* (pp. 17–33). Westport, CT: Praeger.

Rimmer, T. (1996). Religion, mass media, and tolerance of civil liberties. In D. A. Stout & J. M. Buddenbaum (Eds.), *Religion and mass media: Audiences and adaptations* (pp. 105–122). Thousand Oaks, CA: Sage.

Stout, D. A., & Buddenbaum, J. M. (1996). *Religion and mass media: Audiences and adaptations*. Thousand Oaks, CA: Sage.

Stout, D. A., & Buddenbaum, J. M. (2001). *Religion and popular culture: Studies on the interaction of worldviews*. Ames: Iowa University Press.

Thierstein, J., & Kamalipour, Y. R. (2000). *Religion, law, and freedom: A global perspective*. London: Praeger.

Fundamentalism

In the study of religion, the term *Fundamentalism* generally refers to any religious ideology that militantly opposes the philosophical tenets of Western modernism by insisting on human access to an absolute divine authority. This general definition comes from an early twentieth century Protestant movement reacting to a perceived loss of connection with the divine in public discourse. The general definition is now used to refer to non-Christian religious ideologies that reject Western-style scientific inquiry and the secular values it suggests on the basis of a belief in human access to the divine. In media, Fundamentalists often use explicit citations of a text believed to be divinely authorized. Because the text is thought to be unquestionable, emotional and demonstrative assertions are often made without reasoned claims or appeals to broader standards of judgment. Because the pluralistic values of Western secularism appeal to standards of judgment beyond a single divine authority, they are often perceived as threatening by Fundamentalists. As a result, Fundamentalist media often seek to exclude or offer alternatives to mainstream secular media. This tendency in Fundamentalism has in many cases led to insular communities operating as radical activist subgroups in a more broadly inclusive society. As a result, Fundamentalist communities are often considered to foster intolerance for divergent beliefs, values, and perspectives. However, because they are often highly motivated subgroups, even minority Fundamentalist communities can exert significant political power.

The Rise of Christian Fundamentalism

The word *Fundamentalism* is historically associated with a series of twelve pamphlets called *The Fundamentals* published between 1910 and 1915 by the oil magnate and Protestant layman Lyman Stewart. The beliefs that developed from theologians and writers associated with this early form of Fundamentalism evolved from their shared belief in a strictly literal interpretation of the Bible. The complete authority and literal meaning believed to be contained in the divine texts of the Bible yielded the demonstrative and emotional norms Fundamentalist communication now exhibits.

Reacting to a perceived growth of secular influence both inside and outside Protestant institutions in the late nineteenth and early twentieth centuries, intellectual Christians became embroiled in heated debates. Particularly difficult was when Protestant leaders began to split on the proper Christian understanding of

Charles Darwin's (1809–1882) theory of evolution. For liberals, the Bible's description of Creation in the book of Genesis was figurative and hence not incompatible with Darwin's theory. For conservatives, Darwin's ideas replaced God's divine plan with random chance and human will. While liberal Protestant theologians like Walter Rauschenbusch (1861–1918) moved toward pluralism and social justice, conservatives like Lyman Stewart (1840–1923) focused on biblical literalism. For conservatives, an over-reliance on the authority of secular science was resulting in a worldwide decline in morals, rampant materialism, and growing militarism. In 1910, the year of the first issue of *The Fundamentals*, the conservative Presbyterian theologians at Princeton proclaimed the inerrancy of the biblical texts. By 1915, Protestant denominations in the United States were deeply divided into liberal and conservative camps.

In this environment, Lyman Stewart financed the publication and free distribution of *The Fundamentals*. One guiding editor of *The Fundamentals* was a minister named Reuben Torrey (1856–1928). Torrey's close friend was the most famous preacher at the time, Dwight D. Moody (1837–1899). Sometimes considered the progenitor of Christian Fundamentalism, Moody was a hugely successful Evangelical public speaker in the late 1800s.

Beginning in the early 1800s, the United States experienced a surge of interest in emotional expressions of religion. This tradition was associated with charismatic speakers like James McGready (1758–1817) and characterized by tent revivals or "camp meetings" that featured preaching, singing, and emotionally charged prayer. Bringing with him a more moderate style of preaching, Moody emerged into public view in the 1870s. Refusing to attach himself to any specific denomination, Moody did not alienate any segment of his audience. Instead, he offered a simple message that focused on personal morality, and he did so in a business suit and with a middle-class manner. As a result, he garnered a wide audience among many denominations of middle-class American Protestants. Because he also advocated a simple and literal approach to the Bible, a belief in biblical inerrancy, and a belief in an approaching apocalypse, Moody disseminated the underlying ideas that would come to unite themselves as Christian Fundamentalism in the decades after his death.

From 1914 through 1918, a series of huge conferences on "prophecy" attest to a growing interest in a literal understanding of the Bible. In 1917, the British government released a document that pledged support for a Jewish homeland in Palestine. Because the reestablishment of a Jewish homeland was overtly mentioned in the prophetic texts of the Bible, this document seemed to confirm a modern End Times narrative and fueled the growing apocalyptic or "premillennial" thinking. Emboldened by these sentiments, in 1918 the radically conservative minister William B. Riley (1861–1947) formed the World's Christian Fundamentals Association (WCFA). The WCFA focused on a political campaign to rid the denominational institutions of officials who were felt to be too liberal. Attempting to harness Moody's legacy, the WCFA advocated for an apocalyptically tinged struggle against the secular values in modern discourse. Making a doctrinal point, the editor of a Baptist paper first coined the term *Fundamentalist* to refer to those "ready to do battle royal for *The Fundamentals*" (Marsden 1980, 159).

While this battle was raging at a largely institutional level, the well-known Presbyterian politician William Jennings Bryan (1860–1925) launched his now famous campaign against the teaching of evolution in schools. Although Bryan may have been more concerned about a link between evolutionary theory and German nationalism than he was about a literal interpretation of the book of Genesis, he brought the theological issue of biblical authority into general public discourse. When John Scopes (1900–1970), a small town schoolteacher, was charged with breaking a new Tennessee state law against teaching evolution, Bryan prosecuted him. The popular secular writer and journalist H. L. Mencken (1880–1956) sensationalized the trial and it became a national spectacle. As a referendum on the values of its time, Scopes' defense attorney, Clarence Darrow (1857–1938), put Bryan on the stand and cornered him into denying a "literal" reading of Genesis. Bryan emerged looking inept and Darrow emerged looking rational and heroic. Bryan died on the Sunday following his catastrophic loss.

During the Scopes trial, journalists took hold of the term *Fundamentalist*. With Bryan's defeat and sudden death, the term became associated with a caricature of a hopelessly backward and rural brand of Christianity. Inside Protestant institutions, conservatives receded and disappeared. However, the term and its ideological opposition to modernist values persisted at a popular level outside of any denominational affiliations. Many middle-class Christian Protestants who considered themselves Fundamentalist were left feeling alienated from mainstream society.

After World War II (1939–1945), the Fundamentalist ideology began to slowly reemerge into public view. Seeking ways to reduce the possibility of another worldwide war, the United Nations was founded and international laws began to form out of a new conception of universal human rights. Concerned with the possibility of a single world government ultimately trumping the moral authority of biblical texts, conservative Christians again called for their literal interpretations of the Bible to guide public policy. Again finding cognates for their own times in ancient biblical prophecy, Christian Fundamentalists focused their attention on international politics and a perceived degradation of morality within the United States that pointed to an impending apocalypse.

By the 1970s, conservative Christian leaders like Jerry Falwell (b. 1933) and Pat Robertson (b. 1930) mastered a variety of media to locate and build support for their radically conservative and isolationist political agendas. In 1970, Hal Lindsey's (b. 1955) interpretation of biblical prophecy as foretelling cold war (1945–1991) politics sold 7.5 million copies and was the best selling nonfiction book of the decade. In the 1990s, the approaching end of the second millennium fueled a renewed interest in the End Times. In 1995, Tim LaHaye (b. 1926), another Protestant minister, began retelling the Fundamentalist prophetic narrative in the best selling *Left Behind* series of novels.

Today, expressions of Christian Fundamentalism can be found in a multitude popular press books, Christian music, cable television, movies, and on the Internet. Because of the emphasis on a literal interpretation of the Bible, Fundamentalist media often emphasize literal biblical quotations in support of political positions. Less political and more devotional or Evangelical media are often also often demonstrative. With a more emotional or sentimental tinge, this discourse tends to emphasize direct individual contact with the divine in prayer, personal experience narratives, and through stories of individual salvation. With this personal emphasis, Christian Fundamentalism can be thought of as a subgroup of Christian evangelicalism.

Because Christian Fundamentalism is nondenominational and has no single founding institution or text, it is difficult to differentiate from evangelicalism generally. Some Christians self-identify as Fundamentalists but may not be aware of the historical or ideological associations of the term. Others might reject the term but remain solid adherents to the ideological markers that are typically referred to as Fundamentalist.

After the collapse of the first wave of Fundamentalism in 1925, both mainstream Christians and Christian institutions largely rejected the term. Because of its negative portrayal during the Scopes trial and its subsequent rejection by Protestant institutions, the term has come to have a variety of often negative meanings. Thus, terming something Fundamentalist should be

done with great care. However, the basic ideas of Fundamentalism continue to evolve and develop at the popular level, and scholars have attempted to more rigorously define the term.

Ethnographic and experimental studies of Fundamentalism have yielded a descriptive definition based on manifestations of the religious ideology. Social scientists have defined Christian Fundamentalism as a "subgroup within evangelicalism that accepts biblical authority, salvation through Christ, and a commitment to spreading the faith" (Kellstedt and Smidt 1991, 260). Other researchers have more narrowly defined the term as "the conviction that the adherents have a special knowledge of and relationship to Deity, based either on a sacred and unquestionable text or on direct contact with and experience of God's message" (Perkin 2000, 79).

Sociologists have created a systematic catalogue of observable traits of existence of Fundamentalist discourse based on interviews with Christian believers. The following four traits can be seen as indicative of a discursive expression as participating in Christian Fundamentalism: (a) an "orientation toward biblical literalism," (b) "the experience of being reborn in faith," (c) "evangelicalism (or the obligation to convert others)," and (d) "an apocalypticism in its specifically end time form" (Strozier 1994, 5).

The discursive expression of these four traits can properly be termed Christian Fundamentalism. But even these relatively objective criteria do not wholly solve the problem of locating Fundamentalism in an example of human communication. Individuals often do not touch on all four of these definitive elements, even when all four ideas may be informing their expression. While locating some of these elements implies the others, this may not always be the case. Even when all four elements are present, different members of an audience may interpret the same communication very differently. Hence, naming someone or someone's communication as Fundamentalist should always be prefaced with a careful consideration of the term's meaning and an indication of its applicability to the case at hand.

Beyond the Christian Model

The complexity of defining Fundamentalism is nowhere more obvious than when it is used to refer to non-Christian religious ideologies or communication. Many researchers feel that when the term is used for a non-Christian ideological expression, the Christian history of the term prejudices our understanding of a wholly unrelated belief system.

While this probably is the case to some degree, the global surge in religious movements that seem to bear a basic similarity to Christian Fundamentalism make the term useful to help English speakers understand non-Western religious traditions in the new global communication environment. As a result, the general definition of Fundamentalism has come to refer a variety of non-Christian ideologies, and the need to understand non-Christian religious ideas around the globe is nowhere more evident than in what many have termed "Islamic Fundamentalism."

Islamic Fundamentalism refers to an ideology that emerged out of mainstream Islam as a reaction against Western-styled pluralist government and values. The Ottoman Empire (1301–1920) ruled the majority of the Islamic world until the end of World War I. During this period, the Ottoman Empire was officially Islamic but exhibited a remarkable degree of religious tolerance. After its defeat in World War I, the empire was divided and ruled largely as colonial holdings of European governments. Western ideas about government and values were imposed on the formerly Islamic communities. In 1948, Britain, The United States, and the United Nations cooperated in the founding of a new national homeland for the Jewish people. Many Muslims felt betrayed by the West. What is often termed Islamic Fundamentalism today took on its extremist tenor in opposition to European and American influence in the Middle East.

Wahhabism is the most well known form of Islam associated with Fundamentalism. Wahhabism is associated with the teachings of Muhammad Ibn 'Abd al-Wahhab (1703–1787). Wahhabi Islam emerged from a resistance to Ottoman rule by local political leaders in what is now Saudi Arabia. In Egypt, Sayyid Qutb (1906–1966) is credited with founding the Islamic Brotherhood movement as a militant reaction against Westernization and political tyranny. Although these and other contemporary militant Islamic movements bear some similarities to Christian Fundamentalism, many individuals feel that terming them Fundamentalist encourages a prejudice against and a misunderstanding of Islam.

Similar concerns arise when terming other religious ideologies, movements, or communications as Fundamentalist. Still, researchers have located Fundamentalism in the Zionist movement Gush Emunim or "Bloc of the Faithful." This political movement emerged was original a mixture of secular and sacred beliefs. Later, however, it became radicalized based on the growing popularity of an aggressively Zionist Rabbi, Zvi Yehuda Kook (1891–1982), son of the very influential Rabbi Abraham Yitzhak Kook (1865–1935). In response to the Iranian Revolution in 1979 that brought Fundamentalist-leaning religious leaders to power in that country, the Kookists emerged to argue for the expansion of Israel by settling lands currently occupied by Muslims.

The emerging Muslim governments in Iran and elsewhere were viewed by many Israelis as intent on the destruction of Israel. Kookists rejected the Israeli political system as an adequate means for addressing this threat. To pressure the Israeli government, the Kookists functioned as radical activists within Israel. Sometimes rushing their mobile homes onto hilltops in the dead of night, they would force the Israeli government to then forcibly remove them. With these sorts of aggressive tactics, Kookists advocated for a return to what believers felt was a more authentic form of Judaism than the government of Israel was exhibiting. This "authentic" Judaism included a belief that the Jewish people were chosen by God to occupy certain lands. As a result, the divine laws related to being God's chosen people trumped any adherence to international laws. This included the United Nations' ruling that forbade the expansion of Jewish settlements into areas already occupied by Palestinians. Although the Gush Emunim movement broke apart after the younger Kook's death in 1982, the aggressive tendencies in radical Zionism continue to be considered Fundamentalist by some researchers. In 1995, the Israeli Prime Minster Yitzhak Rabin (1922–1995) was assassinated by an Israeli law student who seems to have been influenced by radical Zionism in this tradition.

Even movements in non-Abrahamic religions are sometimes considered to exhibit the basic characteristics of Fundamentalism. In Hinduism, the nationalist movement Rashtriya Swayamsevak Sangh aggressively advocates for a Greater Hinduism that would destroy or absorb other political and religious traditions. In Sikhism, researchers have found examples of an extreme rejection of modernist thinking and the advocacy of a return to more "authentic" life-styles. Even in Buddhism, researchers have located nationalism attached to a religious revivalism in Thailand and Sri Lanka that some have termed Fundamentalist.

The Future of Fundamentalism

While debates still rage about what constitutes Fundamentalism in the world's complex and rich religions, the growing economic power of the Western intellectual tradition still spreads the same values that inspired Lyman Stewart's financing of *The Fundamentals* in 1910. As new technologies have made global communication and travel more readily available, it seems that the same sense of loss fosters a desire for a return to a closer connection with the divine. This desire has emerged as a militant ideology on the extreme fringes of all the world's major religious traditions. But these fringes cannot be ignored simply because they represent the minority of religious individuals. Instead, the intensity of the beliefs felt by many Fundamentalists renders their political activism potentially powerful whenever it emerges; even in communities or nations separated from these movements by vast geographic spaces.

After the attacks in the United States on September 11, 2001, the impact of Fundamentalist inspired violence can no longer be considered to be the problem of isolated nations. Instead, the technologies of global travel and communication have proven both to fuel confrontational religious beliefs and to offer avenues for very real confrontation. Global communication technologies brought Western values and culture to more traditional societies through television, movies, popular music, and the Internet. Access to representations of Western life has made some religious individuals feel threatened by the pluralist values of the Western democracies.

Meanwhile, these same technologies have made it possible for Fundamentalist activists to strike back at the very roots of the economic powers that fuel this Westernization. Through global travel, terrorist attacks can be carried out anywhere on the globe. Through global communication, extremist subgroups can seek to influence the political process of foreign nations when their acts of religious violence are portrayed in the global news media.

Global communication technologies have made it possible for individuals and groups to speak to each other with a speed and ease never before possible. In the coming decades, this exposure will surely continue to expand. In the global environment, the challenge presented by Fundamentalism remains the same even as it grows in scope. How will we as a global society find ways to manage our shared environment when our most fundamental beliefs are in conflict?

In the first decades of the twenty–first century, this conflict is unfolding at two levels. At the national level, each government is being forced to discover how to satisfy the concerns of a radicalized minority that feels its beliefs are divinely inspired even when those beliefs demand that the human rights of all citizens be limited. At the global level, international bodies of governance are struggling to develop equitable laws and systems of economic exchange that do not so deeply alienate re-

ligious conservatives that Fundamentalist activism devolves into global violence. Balancing the concerns of religion and secularism in this age of global information sharing will continue to present challenges for both individual nations and for international politics.

Robert Glenn Howard

See also Evangelicalism; Protestantism, Conservative

Further Reading

Abu-Amr, Z. (1994). *Islamic Fundamentalism in the West Bank and Gaza: Muslim brotherhood and Islamic jihad.* Bloomington: Indiana University Press.

Armstong, K. (2000). *The battle for God.* New York: Alfred A. Knopf.

Benjamin, D., & Simon, S. (2002). *The age of sacred terror.* New York: Random House.

Hadden, J. K., & Shupe, A. (1988). *Televangelism: Power and politics on God's frontier.* New York: Henry Holt.

Hadden, J. K., & Shupe, A. (1989). Is there such a thing as global Fundamentalism? In J. K. Hadden & A. Shupe (Eds.), *Secularization and Fundamentalism reconsidered* (pp. 109–122). New York: Paragon House.

Harris, H.A. (1998). *Fundamentalism and Evangelicals.* Oxford: Clarenton Press.

Howard, R. G. (1997). Apocalypse in your in-box: End-Times communication on the Internet. *Western Folklore, 56*(3/4), 295–315.

Howard, R. G. (2000). On-line ethnography of dispensationalist discourse: Revealed versus negotiated truth. In D. Cowan & J. K. (Eds.), *Hadden religion on the Internet* (pp. 225–246). New York: Elsevier Press.

Howard, R. G. (2005). The double bind of the Protestant Reformation: The birth of Fundamentalism and the necessity of pluralism. *Journal of Church and State, 47*(1), 101–118.

Kellstedt, L., & Smidt, C. (1991). Measuring Fundamentalism: An analysis of different operational strategies. *Journal for the Scientific Study of Religion, 30,* 259–278.

LaHaye, T., & Jenkins, J. B. (1995). *Left behind: A novel of the earth's last days.* Wheaton, IL: Tyndale House.

Larson, E. J. (1997). *Summer for the Gods: The Scopes trial and America's continuing debate over science and religion.* Cambridge, MA: Harvard University Press.

Lindsey, H., & Carlson, C.C. (1970). *The late great planet earth.* Toronto/New York: Bantam Books.

Marsden, G. (1980). *Fundamentalism and American culture.* New York: Oxford University Press.

Martin, W. (1996). *With God on our side: The rise of the religious right in America.* New York: Broadway Books.

Marty, M., & Appleby, R. S. (Eds.). (1991). *Fundamentalisms observed (The Fundamentalism Project), Vol. 1.* Chicago: University of Chicago Press.

Marty, M., & Appleby, R. S. (Eds.). (1993). *Fundamentalisms and society (The Fundamentalism Project), Vol. 2.* Chicago: University of Chicago Press.

Marty, M., & Appleby, R. S. (Eds.). (1993). *Fundamentalisms and the state (The Fundamentalism Project), Vol. 3.* Chicago: University of Chicago Press.

Marty, M., & Appleby, R. S. (Eds.). (1994). *Accounting for Fundamentalisms (The Fundamentalism Project), Vol. 4.* Chicago: University of Chicago Press.

Marty, M., & Appleby, R. S. (Eds.). (1995). *Fundamentalisms comprehended (The Fundamentalism Project), Vol. 5.* Chicago: University of Chicago Press.

Nielsen, N. S. (1993). *Fundamentalism, mythos, and world religions.* Albany: State University of New York Press.

O'Leary, S. D. (1994). *Arguing the Apocalypse: A theory of millennial rhetoric.* New York: Oxford University Press.

Perkin, H. (2000). American Fundamentalism and the selling of God. *Political Quarterly, 71*(1), 79–89.

Robertson, P. (1991). *The new world order.* Dallas, TX: Word Publications.

Strozier, C. B. (1994). *Apocalypse: On the psychology of Fundamentalism in America.* Boston, MA: Beacon Press.

Wojcik, D. (1997). *The end of the world as we know it: Faith, fatalism, and Apocalypse in America.* New York: New York University Press.

Woodberry, R. D., & Smith, C. S. (1998). Fundamentalism et. al: Conservative Protestants in America. *Annual Review of Sociology 24,* 25–56.

Hinduism

There is every indication that religion, including Hinduism, far from being rooted and static, is influenced by modern institutions such as those of media. We can draw at least four conclusions from this fact:

1. Since media enable novel modes of reception, religions can be practiced and espoused in ways that are different from their original forms.

2. The availability of new ways of mediating religion tends to be perceived and utilized by religious leaders and practitioners themselves, and thus new kinds of religious practice are tacitly legitimated.

3. In the process, not only are new religious identities created, but what it means to be religious itself changes.

4. These changes are signaled by the new visibility of communication itself, both as idea and as technical apparatus.

Features such as novelty, mutability, and technological dependency might seem to undercut the authority of a religion. In fact, the new visibility of media today should lead us to consider how our ideas about religion are reshaped when we consider the question of communication. This is true even of a religion many of whose practitioners consider changeless, like Hinduism.

Characteristics of Hinduism

The word *Hindu* was used by Persians to refer to those who lived east of the river Sindhu (now Indus). Over time, the sense of the word has shifted from a geographical to a religious one. In its current meaning, the term was first popularized by British writers around 1830, when the native population was categorized into Hindus and Muslims, disparate religious communities who were believed to require the force of British rule to coexist. Today the idea of the Hindu religion as a single entity has gained currency, especially in India. But until only quite recently, a single identity could be assumed for Hinduism only for specific purposes and in certain ways.

Hinduism is so internally diverse that no distinct creed or practice can be located that can classify the religion uniquely. Scholars tend to agree that this diversity itself constitutes its most distinctive feature, although it should be noted that this diversity is to some extent a product of how Hinduism is defined. But typically, no belief or practice is negated or rejected. On principle, doctrinal tolerance ranks high in comparison with other major religions. A Hindu may worship non-Hindu gods while remaining a Hindu. Deities and practices are usually distinguished in terms of adequacy and efficacy rather than in terms of good and bad or right and wrong. Disputes between monotheism and polytheism are not seen as crucial to the religion; religious beliefs are conceived as being ultimately harmonious with each other. Distinctions are made not on the basis of belief and principle (orthodoxy) so much as of custom and practice (orthopraxy).

No single central text and no single presiding authority or institution exists for all Hindus. As such, any attempt to provide a definition adequate to all Hindus has been deemed unsatisfactory by the major scholars of the religion. Few beliefs or practices can be identified that can precisely indicate who or what is Hindu. There is no Hindu in general; he or she is defined by caste and sect, language and region. Abstract and profound philosophical systems, generalized ethical principles, idol worship, animism, mysticism, and asceticism can exist in different combinations and can each lay claim to being Hindu. That is, what we see here is the operation of a range of religious practices and correspondingly a variety of communicational forms, whose apparent incompatibility is contradicted by their robust longevity.

Two Traditions

What this unusual congeries of religious practices indicates is the longstanding existence of multiple modes of power, operating within and across caste boundaries, resulting in a heterogeneous and fragmented picture. It indicates the accretion of new communication technologies upon older ones, writing over oral forms, print over writing and so on, with each new medium preserving or renewing older media contexts. The absence of a shared doctrine, text or clergy have combined with caste barriers, illiteracy, and linguistic pluralism to reproduce a unique communicational ecology.

This complex formation can be broadly categorized drawing on anthropological research. Hinduism, M.N. Srinivas argued, was divided into a Sanskritic, all-India tradition and a non-Sanskritic village-based tradition, as related but distinct elements. The former, sometimes called the great tradition, is based on recognition of the sacred texts, major deities like Siva and Vishnu, major pilgrimage centers, and the importance of the Brahman. The village tradition, sometimes called the little tradition, comprises diverse folk rituals and devotional practices, often only tenuously connected to the Sanskritic tradition. The terms indicate the centripetal powers of high-caste literati as opposed to the more centrifugal forces of local culture and religion.

Two phases of the recent development of Hinduism can be distinguished that are germane to this discussion. The first sought to transcend the village tradition from above, and the second saw what might be called a return of the repressed, albeit in a new context. We can illustrate these two phases in the figures of Swami Dayanand Saraswati and Mahatma Gandhi respectively.

In the nineteenth century, Hindu reform movements responded to Christian missionaries' criticism of native religious practices as superstitious and irrational. The prospect of conversion to Christianity, which promised exemption from caste discrimination, also spurred internal efforts at Hindu reform. The Arya

Samaj, founded in 1875 and still active today, was the most influential of these reform movements. The authority claimed by this movement was textual and located in the Vedas, although the latter were a revealed and closely guarded text, heard and memorized by Brahmans, rather than available to be read by all. If the Vedas had been a locus of Brahmanical caste power, however, the Arya Samaj's founder, Dayanand Saraswati, presented caste divisions as functional rather than intrinsic, seeking in a sense to modernize casteism without challenging the institution of caste. Thus, for example, Vedic authority was claimed to be scientific, as opposed to the barbarism of the little tradition.

Dayanand's declaration that Hinduism was modern before the West, and that its current appearance was a decline from its ancient glory, became the model of later arguments for Hinduism, and as well for nationalists of all stripes. Although the popular spread of Hindu reform was limited, it helped create a cultural platform for educated Indians and was important in stimulating anticolonial nationalism. But nationalism remained an elite tendency dominated by British-educated lawyers until the proper medium for communication with the masses could be located. Here we can describe the second phase in Hinduism's recent development.

Politics and Religion

Nationalist politics was conceived around utopian conceptions of an egalitarian community yet to be formed. Not only education and print-based communication limited its reach, but the language of politics, drawing as it did on a European blend of liberalism, was as yet alien to the majority.

Beginning in the late nineteenth century, however, appeals to a Hindu/Indian audience developed through newly public rituals, such as the Ganesh festival, and new Hindu symbols and slogans were devised such as Bharat Mata, Mother India, a deity meant to represent the South Asian subcontinent; and Vande Mataram, Hail Mother, conceived by the Bengali writer Bankim Chandra. These forms of identification were not simply spiritual in their inspiration. For most of its duration, British rulers forbade political activity on the part of their colonial subjects. Religion, however, was deemed a private matter, where for the most part the British observed a policy of noninterference. Therefore the repressed political energies of Indian subjects could most safely seek expression precisely in the realm of religion. Not all the uses of religion were new. In some cases old themes were revitalized, such as Ram Rajya, the rule of

A Hindu temple in the suburbs of Houston, Texas. *Courtesy Mark Jessup/ istockphoto.com.*

Ram, representing the golden age when Lord Ram, an incarnation of Vishnu, was king. Mahatma Gandhi presented the goal of independent India as the restoring of Ram Rajya, drawing on Hindu imagery in order to present the struggle of anticolonial nationalists in popular terms. In Gandhi's view, Hindu religion was a basis for political identity although not in an exclusive way; his daily prayer meetings, for instance, drew on scriptures from all the major religions. Gandhi was steadfast in his attempts to bring Hindus and Muslims together and was eventually assassinated for being "pro-Muslim." In a context where religion and culture were completely intertwined, and few secular symbols existed for popular identification, Gandhi's choice was a revealing one.

Gandhi was the first leader in the independence movement to find a nationwide audience, breaking out of the urban-educated circles previous nationalist leaders had largely been confined to. The language of political interest and economic needs had failed to connect with a largely rural constituency; appropriate symbolism had to be found for the purpose. Not only was

163

Gandhi's solution religious in its inspiration, it was distinct in sparking connections across the cultural gulf that separated educated and uneducated, urban and rural in India.

If the Arya Samaj had sought to get rid of much of the little tradition, and failed, Gandhi sought to bridge the two traditions instead, and succeeded. It would be a mistake to see this as simply affirming the indomitable character of popular religion, however. Gandhi had grasped the conditions for successful communication with the Indian masses. Politics could not be separated from questions of religion and of self transformation. If politics really mattered, it would affect the whole of your life and not be regarded as a set of opinions that could be changed like a suit of clothes. Nor did Gandhi merely advocate political independence. He sought to embody the ideas he propounded, from matters of dress, food, and intimate life to ahimsa, or nonviolence. It is no accident then that he established a bond with the poorest of the land.

The mediation of religion in new communicational contexts alters its character in ways that may be consciously utilized by religious leaders. These communicational contexts are never purely technological, but are also social and historical in character. Popular tradition was transmitted through oral and print media, but it came to fruition amidst a countrywide struggle and through a quasi-religious figure.

What had earlier been a localized and varied tradition was now anointed as a medium of national awakening. Moreover, with the achievement of independence, claims of national greatness vis-à-vis the West seemed to be validated. Thereafter, Hindu identity and Indian nationalism could more easily be yoked together with claims of civilizational superiority, while similar appeals for secular or composite identities had to perform far greater critical labor, and with less success. Gandhi's use of popular religion was crucial for national politics, but his philosophy became an increasingly marginal phenomenon, "Gandhism," marooned on the memory of a charismatic leader.

Hinduism Today

Meanwhile Hindu religion, by virtue of having tacitly been nationalized, came to appear modern in its appeal without undergoing significant reforms; it is noteworthy for instance that caste discrimination remains alongside laws that prohibit it. Political Hinduism has become an attitude and an identity, bearing little rela-

tion to preexisting tradition as such. It invokes an ancient history, and a demographic majority that in fact remains to materialize electorally, although it can be a potent and terrifying weapon at times. More and more, Hinduism is available for piecemeal appropriation and public display, and intricately differentiated rituals become homogenized as equally Hindu in character. Ironically, the attempt to consolidate Hinduism as a nationwide political identity has resulted precisely in the opposite outcome. From the early 1990s onwards in Northern India, there has occurred a spectacular growth of lower-caste parties, which guarantees that Hindu nationalism will have to rely, for the foreseeable future, on coalitional politics and fail to achieve the dominance it has imagined for itself. The story of Hinduism is, in this sense, one where the influence and visibility of communication and politics has increased precisely as Hinduism has begun to be mediated through more channels and sought to be unified at the same time.

ARVIND RAJAGOPAL

Further Reading

Doniger, W. (2003). Hinduism. *Encyclopaedia Britannica.* Retrieved June 25, 2003, from http://www.britannica.com:80/eb/article?eu=108344.

Fuller, C. J. (1992). *The Camphor Flame: Popular Hinduism and society in India.* Princeton, NJ: Princeton University Press.

Hawley, J. S. (1991). Naming Hinduism. *Wilson Quarterly, 15*(3), 20–34.

Jones, K. W. (1976). *Arya Dharma: Hindu consciousness in nineteenth-century Punjab.* Berkeley and Los Angeles: University of California Press

Rajagopal, A. (2001). *Politics after television: Hindu nationalism and the reshaping of the public in India.* Cambridge, UK: Cambridge University Press.

Sontheimer, G. D. (1991). Bhakti in the Khandoba Cult. In D. Eck & F. Mallison (Eds.), *Devotion Divine: Bhakti Traditions from the Regions of India: Studies in Honor of Charlotte Vaudeville.* Groningen/Paris: Egbert Forsten/Ecole Francaise d'Extreme Orient.

Sontheimer, G. D. (1991). Hinduism: The five components and their interaction (pp. 197–212). In Sontheimer and Hermann Kulke (Eds.), *Hinduism Reconsidered.* South Asian Studies 24. New Delhi: Manohar.

Srinivas, M. N. (1952). *Religion and society among the Coorgs of south India.* Bombay: Asia Publishing House.

Van der Veer, P. (2001). *Imperial encounters: Religion and modernity in India and Britain.* Princeton, NJ: Princeton University Press.

Humor and Laughter

It is first necessary to define and clarify the differences between *humor* and *laughter*—terms that are commonly misunderstood and mistakenly used as if they were interchangeable. Laughter is an event in the physical world, a respiratory and muscular response that is typically both visible and audible. Laughter is emitted both voluntarily and involuntarily and is most similar physiologically to crying. Although laughter is frequently defined as a response to or an indication of amusement, research indicates that most laughter in social settings is produced not in response to attempts at humor, but as a conversational lubricant and group mood modulator (Provine 2000). Other causes of laughter in the absence of amusement include tickling, breathing nitrous oxide, psychosis, intoxication, tension, relief, fear, surprise, disgust, exhilaration, exhaustion, and the intent to cheer or deride.

Humor is a construct created to explain why certain types of stimuli elicit laughter even though several recognized categories of humor, such as irony and sarcasm, typically do not elicit laughter. Humor is notoriously elusive of precise definition; dictionaries take a circular approach by using near synonyms such as amusing or funny. Humor scholars define humor as a stimulus containing an incongruity followed by its surprising resolution or sometimes as the incongruity alone.

Humor and Values

Sense of humor, defined as the pattern of things a person finds amusing and, more importantly, fails to find amusing, stands as a reasonable proxy for values and worldview. Of special interest in the study of humor in religious groups is discovering what if anything the members collectively fail or refuse to find amusing under any circumstances. Most religions identify certain things as being sacred and, therefore, inappropriate and unacceptable topics for humor. These include deities, personages living or dead believed to possess divine authority or power, physical objects such as relics, activities such as ordinances and prayer, and doctrinal teachings. A group member who uses humor that makes light of, ridicules, or points out faults, weaknesses or contradictions in things deemed sacred is viewed suspiciously by the devout. In extreme cases, use of such humor may be viewed as blasphemy or sacrilege or as evidence of apostasy. There is no surer way for an outsider to antagonize a group of believers than to deliberately make light of those things the group holds sacred.

Because of the widespread misconceptions concerning the relationship between laughter and humor, involuntary laughter resulting from a nonhumorous cause, such as nervousness or embarrassment, and occurring during a solemn religious activity is often misinterpreted as a sign that the laughing person finds something about the activity funny and is, therefore, displaying irreverence.

Nevertheless, there are several circumstances in which even devout group members will tolerate humor about the sacred. One is when the representation of the sacred in the humorous context is stylized to the point that there is a disconnect between the stylized representation and the physical or mental representation of the same sacred object in its religious context. For example, in a comic strip Gary Larsen, creator of *The Far Side*, depicts God outscoring a mortal competitor on the *Jeopardy* game show. For many readers, this cartoon representation of deity is completely unassociated with the deity that they worship.

A more grudging and guilt-producing indulgence in humor occurs when the humorous item is simultaneously offensive to a person's religious sensibilities and so funny as to be irresistible. This results in the paradoxical image of a person with tears of laughter streaming down his or her face saying, "That's not funny, you know!"

Humor and Group Identity

Religious groups are also cultural groups with their own history and folklore, music, art, drama, and literature, which frequently include forms of humor that are cherished and celebrated. Many groups also have a distinctive cuisine and dietary restrictions, dress and grooming practices, and unique names, vocabulary and phraseology; humor that turns on insider knowledge of any of these components of culture reinforces the identity of the group and distinguishes insiders from outsiders. Insider humor, when presented by an outsider to an insider, is often less than well received.

Groups that take pride in their uniqueness and separateness as "a peculiar people" tend to have especially well-developed and treasured collections of insider humor. This is particularly true of groups that have been marginalized, oppressed, or otherwise persecuted because of their religion and whose members have utilized humor as a coping strategy to comfort and encourage each other. One description of this phenomenon is *Laughter in Hell: The Use of Humor During the Holocaust* (1991) by Steve Lipman.

Noah's Second Ark

In the year 2004, the Lord came unto Noah, who was now living in the United States, and said, "Once again, the planet has become wicked and over-populated and I see the end of all flesh before me. Build another Ark and save two of every living thing along with a few good humans."

He gave Noah the blueprints, saying, "You have six months to build the Ark before I will start the ceaseless rain for 40 days and 40 nights."

Six months later, the Lord looked down and saw Noah weeping in his yard, but no ark.

"Noah," He roared, "I'm about to start the rain! Where is the Ark?"

"Forgive me, Lord," begged Noah. "But things have changed. I needed a building permit. I've been arguing with the inspector about the need for a sprinkler system. My neighbors claim that I've violated the neighborhood zoning laws by building the Ark in my yard and exceeding the height limitations.

We had to go to the Development Appeal Board for a decision. Then the Department of Transportation demanded a bond be posted for the future costs of moving power lines and other overhead obstructions, to clear the passage for the Ark's move to the sea. I argued that the sea would be coming to us, but they would hear nothing of it.

Getting the wood was another problem. There's a ban on cutting local trees in order to save the spotted owl. I tried to convince the environmentalists that I needed the wood to save the owls. But no go!

When I started gathering the animals, I got sued by an animal rights group. They insisted that I was confining wild animals against their will. As well, they argued the accommodation was too restrictive and it was cruel and inhumane to put so many animals in a confined space. Then the EPA ruled that I couldn't build the Ark until they'd conducted an environmental impact study on your proposed flood.

I'm still trying to resolve a complaint with the Human Rights Commission on how many minorities I'm supposed to hire for my building crew. Also, the trades unions say I can't use my sons. They insist I have to hire only Union workers with Ark-building experience.

To make matters worse, the IRS seized all my assets, claiming I'm trying to leave the country illegally with endangered species.

So, forgive me, Lord, but it would take at least ten years for me to finish this Ark."

Suddenly, the skies cleared, the sun began to shine, and a rainbow stretched across the sky. Noah looked up in wonder and asked, "You mean, you're not going to destroy the world?"

"No," said the Lord. "The government beat me to it."

Mass-mediated portrayals of religious groups often contain faux-insider humor based merely on stereotypes of these distinctive cultural features. Sometimes a scriptwriter will exploit a well-known distinctive cultural feature merely as a convenience to service plot without any obvious intention to actually portray the group. This is seen in films such as *Paint Your Wagon* and *Chicago,* which contain brief references to the well-known historical association of the Mormons with polygamy.

Conversely, believing writers will often incorporate humor into an otherwise serious presentation as a way to communicate the group's perspective and message to outsiders in an appealing and nonpedantic fashion and to gain support and sympathy.

Humor and Within-group Dynamics

Humor that elicits derisive laughter is a "social corrective" that can be used to enforce conformity to group mores and to teach people the boundaries of their roles. The classic discussion of this topic is *Laughter: An Essay on the Meaning of the Comic* (1911) by Henri Bergson. Humor can be used to define and either strengthen or weaken a group's hierarchy. In situations where there is a rigid hierarchy and large power distances, a leader who uses self-deprecating humor judiciously increases loyalty and lessens resentment in the lower ranks. Additionally, leaders who skillfully employ humor that activates a group's sense of identity can, at times when their authority is threatened, increase compliance and support for themselves. Conversely, fear of popular humor that exposes hypocrisy and other personal weaknesses of the leader is an effective deterrent to abuses of power. These effects of humor on group structure have been observed in nearly all groups, from families to nations; the operation of the principles involved should not be notably different in religious groups.

Psychologically, either creating humor about or pointing out the existing humorous incongruities in a situation or relationship can reduce stress and anxiety and act as a socially acceptable outlet for frustrations and aggressive feelings. Sometimes the only way for people to openly complain or criticize without bringing their own faith into question is by using the disclaimer "I was just kidding." Humor also provides a type of forum for acknowledging ambiguities and stating opinions about sensitive controversies.

Studying Humor as Religious Communication

Humor scholars in fields such as history, anthropology, and sociology collect and analyze examples of the humor of specific groups, including religious groups, as a unique window into the group's culture and as reliable indicators of the group's current status, internal dynamics, relationships with the outside world, and the development of these over time. Because informal humor is created to serve an immediate social or psy-

chological need and not for the record that it inadvertently creates, examples of popular humor provide candid snapshots that are rarely found in intentional histories.

The Future of Humor

It is likely that the use of humor in religious media communication will increase in the future and that a lively sense of humor and the ability to use humor strategically will be increasingly valued in religious leaders. These developments are predicted as a natural part of a larger cultural movement which celebrates and promotes the use of humor and laughter as beneficial to physical and mental health and to interpersonal relations. One consequence is that high-level leaders are no longer always represented as staid. A nonreligious example: U.S. presidents starting with Ronald Reagan are shown smiling with teeth visible in their official portrait. This cultural movement began in the 1970s and coincides with the development of humor scholarship, which will continue to investigate humor in religious communication.

DIANA MAHONY

Further Reading

Bergson, H. (1911). *Laughter: An essay on the meaning of the comic* (C. Brereton & F. Rothwell, Trans.). London: Macmillan.

Lipman, S. (1991). *Laughter in hell: The use of humor during the Holocaust*. Northvale, NJ: Jason Aronson, Inc.

Provine, R. (2000). *Laughter: A scientific investigation*. New York: Viking.

Idolatry

Simply defined, idolatry is the worship of any created object as a god or the assignment of magical or supernatural powers to any image. The object can be an animal or a plant or a nonliving natural feature like a mountain, hill, or river. However, idols are more often associated with carved figures or figural representations and symbols that have become objects of worship or to which certain supernatural qualities have been attached. The root meaning of "idol" is image, whether visual or carved; and in the modern era some images are described as works of art.

The concept of idolatry includes the description of images and their transmission as cultural products across time and cultures. As forms of religious communication, images convey history, ideas, and emotions; they reinforce customs and values; and they evoke the experience of the transcendence.

Monotheistic religions commonly make a distinction between true and false religion; they consider idolatry to be either the worship of false gods or the association of created (and therefore false) beings or objects with a monotheistic God. Idolaters are assumed to be acting in ignorance or incapable of reason because they devote their attention to created objects rather than to the God who created them. Monotheists have traditionally considered religions that practice devotion to images inferior.

Idolatry takes many forms—the worship of nature (for example, the sun, moon, and stars); the worship of heroes and ancestors (for example, emperor worship in the Greco-Roman world before the fourth century); and fetishism (for example, believing that natural objects like trees, stones, and hills have supernatural or magical powers). Even nationalism as excessive devotion to one's nation can be regarded as idolatry.

Objects invested with sacredness played a significant role in the lives of non-Western peoples, and the first encounter of Europeans, mostly explorers and missionaries, with these people inspired curiosity and perplexity, and early reports described a devotion to these objects as idolatry. This perspective was taken up by anthropologists in the nineteenth and early twentieth centuries and they tried to locate the most rudimentary form of religion in the worship of objects. Terms such as "totemism," "animism," and "fetishism" were used to describe the worship of images and the assigning of souls or supernaturalism to objects or animals or their symbolic representations.

A better understanding of the cultures and religions of these people has led to a rejection of anthropological evaluations of the religions of non-Western peoples. Labeling nonmonotheistic religions, non-Western images, and cult objects as idolatry is now understood to be a subjective manner of classifying and condemning non-Christian religions. It represents, on one hand, the clash over cultures, and on the other, the promotion of the belief that monotheistic religions are superior to polytheistic ones. And in fact, nineteenth-century anthropological evaluations did not regard the nonliterate religions as true religion but rather as a misconception of religion.

However, since every religion makes use of images and symbols, the condemnation of one image and the approval of another cannot be based on any coherent religious standard. And the labeling of an image as idolatrous has nothing to do with the quality of the artistic fabrication, since both crude and refined images have been destroyed by iconoclasts. The fear of images arose from the belief that they had an intrinsic power that could dominate the minds of worshippers. Consequently, idolatry was often used simply to describe anything that was not officially endorsed as part of orthodoxy.

Idolatry and Monotheistic Religions

References to idolatry are common in the scriptures of monotheistic religions such as Judaism, Christianity, and Islam. These three religions commonly demand the total worship of a Supreme Being and prohibit the adoration or worship of any created object.

Idolatry is strongly condemned in Islam. The Qur'an and hadith forbid any art representation of Allah, and the association of any creature with Allah is considered *shirk*, a grievous sin. Nevertheless, in some periods of Islamic history, one can find images in manuscripts, architecture, tapestries, and other devotional items. Islamic orthodoxy is made even stronger by claims that pre-Islamic Arabs were idol worshippers who persecuted the Prophet Muhammad. Upon conquering Mecca in 629, Muhammad destroyed all the idols in and around Mecca and encouraged his followers to follow suit, arguing that the destruction meant the elimination of falsehood and the revelation of truth. These precedents, with the doctrine of *tawhid*, belief in one Allah, have formed the basis of the Islamic rejection of idols and idolatry. However, the Kaa'ba, a pre-Islamic monument that was associated with idolatry, was nonetheless left intact and simply invested with a new meaning (that it was connected with the revelations of Allah to Muhammad). Consequently, orthodox Islam after the seventh century could be seen as a replacement of polytheism and idolatry with a monotheistic belief in Allah.

The condemnation of idolatry by Christianity is partly rooted in the Judaist belief in the oneness of God. Yet the biblical history of Israel is replete with instances of Israelites engaging in idolatrous practices similar to their neighboring nations. Hence, the total rejection of idolatry and the upholding of monotheism was likely a gradual process that took some time. For example, in the book of Exodus (32:1–35), not long after the promulgation of the Ten Commandments, there was a conflict surrounding the golden calf made by Aaron for the people to use as an object of worship. To Moses, this was a violation of the part of the Ten Commandments that legislated against the worship of images and the association of Yahweh with such images

(20:3–7). The prophets constantly condemned idolatry as rebellion against Yahweh and hence deemed it a national sin, and the conquests and exile of the Israelites were partly explained as divine punishment for the sin of idolatry. On the domestic level, punishment as grievous as death was prescribed in Exodus 22:20 and Deuteronomy 13:1–10 for those found guilty of idolatry.

In the New Testament, the apostle Paul, a first century Christian leader, constantly warned Christians against a belief in and an association with idols, which was common in many cities in Asia Minor at that period. As Christianity became a popular religion after the fourth century, iconoclasm emerged as a response to idolatry; it reached its height during the Protestant Reformation in the sixteenth century. John Calvin, Ulrich Zwingli, and Andreas Karlstadt, along with other reformers, rejected religious images and promoted their removal from churches and their destruction. They argued that the use of images in worship was not sanctioned in the Scriptures. This iconoclastic tradition was followed by Western missionaries in their encounters with the religions of non-Western peoples from the sixteenth century to the early twentieth century.

Idolatry and Iconoclasm

Throughout human history, there have been periods when religious leaders have displayed iconoclastic tendencies and have urged their followers to adopt the same attitude. Iconoclasm, the practice of destroying images because of their association with religion or worship, is often the official or semiofficial response to idolatry, providing a subtle justification for persecution and religious violence. The destruction of anything labeled idolatry has often been justified on the grounds that it maintains religious purity by removing images not sanctioned by the religion. Because idols were associated with superstitions and regarded as the product of ignorance, some religious leaders preached that their destruction would be a liberation. As David Morgan argued in his review article on the subject of iconoclasm, iconoclasm may not always be the destruction of images but rather a strategy of replacement, simply because none of the monotheistic world religions has ever operated without images (2003, 171).

Iconoclasm reached its zenith in the encounter of Christianity with other cultures and religions. Christian missionaries in many lands attached religious significance to images and encouraged new converts to Christianity to either abandon these images or destroy them. In the twenty-first century, radical Evangelical Christian groups in many parts of the world have

Deuteronomy 13: 1–10 (KJV)

If there arise among you a prophet, or a dreamer of dreams, and giveth thee a sign or a wonder,

And the sign or the wonder come to pass, whereof he spake unto thee, saying, Let us go after other gods, which thou hast not known, and let us serve them;

Thou shalt not hearken unto the words of that prophet, or that dreamer of dreams: for the LORD your God proveth you, to know whether ye love the LORD your God with all your heart and with all your soul.

Ye shall walk after the LORD your God, and fear him, and keep his commandments, and obey his voice, and ye shall serve him, and cleave unto him.

And that prophet, or that dreamer of dreams, shall be put to death; because he hath spoken to turn you away from the LORD your God, which brought you out of the land of Egypt, and redeemed you out of the house of bondage, to thrust thee out of the way which the LORD thy God commanded thee to walk in. So shalt thou put the evil away from the midst of thee.

If thy brother, the son of thy mother, or thy son, or thy daughter, or the wife of thy bosom, or thy friend, which is as thine own soul, entice thee secretly, saying, Let us go and serve other gods, which thou hast not known, thou, nor thy fathers;

Namely, of the gods of the people which are round about you, nigh unto thee, or far off from thee, from the one end of the earth even unto the other end of the earth;

Thou shalt not consent unto him, nor hearken unto him; neither shall thine eye pity him, neither shalt thou spare, neither shalt thou conceal him:

But thou shalt surely kill him; thine hand shall be first upon him to put him to death, and afterwards the hand of all the people.

And thou shalt stone him with stones, that he die; because he hath sought to thrust thee away from the LORD thy God, which brought thee out of the land of Egypt, from the house of bondage.

---

continued this iconoclastic tradition as a conversion strategy. For example, in 2003 the Warriors of David, a dissident Baptist group based in southern Chile, burned a statue of the Roman Catholic Virgin of Carmen, claiming that the statue was an idol and that therefore the festival associated with it was a pagan event.

But it is difficult to find a single criterion that can be used to judge an image as idolatrous because there are so many varieties of images and so many varieties of devotion. For example, while Protestant reformers discarded and destroyed images during the Reformation and Catholics viewed such destructions as abominable, both claimed to practice the true Christian religion. Indeed, the polemics against images are associated with the history of Christian inner rejuvenation, the promotion of a sectarian faith, and the sustenance of evangelical revival.

Although there is a better appreciation of religious and nonreligious art in the modern world, iconoclasm has continued between fringe and radical religious groups. A widely reported iconoclastic violence was the destruction of the two 125-foot-high statues of Buddha in Baniyan, Afghanistan, in early March 2001 through the orders of Mullah Muhammad Omar, the leader of the Taliban, who described the statues as idols insulting to Islam. Despite pleas from international quarters, many of which regarded the statues, which have been standing for about 1,500 years, as archaeological monuments of significant cultural history, the Taliban used mortars and canons to destroy them.

It is doubtful whether iconoclasm ever succeeded in eliminating any nonliterate religion or any genre of art altogether; rather, it has succeeded only in limiting the power of images, by depriving them of their economic advantage and privatizing the worship associated with them. Overall, iconoclasm is a complex social phenomenon. It can be described as vandalism, as an aspect of social conflict, as a process of refinement of art (when the objects destroyed are accorded less significance), as the promotion of rationality, or as the strengthening of religious bigotry.

Idolatry and Art

By the late nineteenth century, iconology and the study of iconography had promoted a keen understanding of the expression of religious thought and worship in images. Consequently, there was a new interpretation and a better appreciation of "idols" as works of art. Colonial authorities, explorers, traders, and missionaries benefited from this new understanding and images were no longer destroyed; some were preserved locally while some were taken to the West and housed in art museums where they were deprived of their religious association or displayed as trophies of Christian conversion. Images that were once condemned as idols assumed new meaning as works of art. However, iconoclastic violence still erupted from time to time and this violence has continued into the twenty-first century.

Idols are a form of communication that promotes creativity from one generation to the other. They carry forward a significant part of the culture of many non-Western people and reflect their spirituality. Though not all images are connected with religion, the ones associated with idolatry suggest how religion supplied the content and the characteristics of traditional art in non-Western cultures. These powerful creations of non-literate people reflect their worldview and their conception of the supernatural.

Certain images have been viewed as idolatry because in the non-Western world, art and religion are interwoven. But art not only depicts a particular culture, it also provides a manifestation of the sacred, and some images are closely associated with the spiritual source of power. The polemical construction of "idolatry" is embedded in social and ethnic contacts between the West and the East, between the "civilized" world and the "primitive world," and between organized monotheistic religions and unorganized polytheistic religions.

MATTHEWS A. OJO

See also Islam

Further Reading

Apostolos-Cappadona, D. (Ed.). (1984). *Art, creativity and the sacred: An anthology in religion and art.* New York: Crossroad.

Besançon, A. (2000). *The forbidden image: An intellectual history of iconoclasm* (J. M. Todd, Trans.). Chicago: University of Chicago Press.

Child, A. B., & Child, I. L. (1993). *Religion and magic in the life of traditional peoples.* Englewood Cliffs, NJ: Prentice Hall.

Dupré, W. (1975). *Religion in primitive cultures: A study in ethnophilosophy.* The Hague & Paris: Mouton.

Gamboni, D. (1997). *The destruction of art: Iconoclasm and vandalism since the French Revolution.* New Haven CT: Yale University Press.

Hackett, R. I. J. (1996). *Art and religion in Africa. (Religion and the arts).* London & New York: Cassell.

Hawting, G. R. (1999). *The idea of idolatry and the emergence of Islam: From polemic to history.* Cambridge, UK: Cambridge University Press.

Laeuchli, S. (1980). *Religion and art in conflict: Introduction to a cross-disciplinary task.* Philadelphia: Fortress.

Mills, K. (1997). *Idolatry and its enemies: Colonial Andean religion and extirpation.* Princeton, NJ: Princeton University Press.

Moore, A. C. (1977). *Iconography of Religion: An Introduction.* London: SCM Press.

Moore, A. C. (1995). *Arts in the religions of the Pacific: Symbols of life.* London: Pinter.

Morgan, D. (2003). The vicissitudes of seeing: Iconoclasm and idolatry. *Religion, 33,* 170 –180.

Information

Religion cannot be understood without attention to information. Religious information includes symbol, ritual, prayer, sermon, blessing, and all verbal and nonverbal expression in a spiritual context. The distinction between sacred and profane information is recognized in most religious cultures. Sacred information sustains belief and forms the core of religious doctrine, while profane messages inform parishioners about the larger society or secular realm. In the current media age, the lines between sacred and secular have blurred; individuals experience religion within and without religious institutions. In this article, religious information is examined in terms of (1) *evolution*, or how the nature of religious information has changed through time; (2) *levels*, which suggests that information has several functions at different levels of religious experience; and (3) *accommodation*, which is the process of accepting religious groups in society based on information available.

Evolution

The nature of religious information has evolved through time and is best understood within distinct historical periods.

Orality

Orality characterizes religious communication of the preliterate era. Before writing became widespread, the voice was the essential transmitter of messages. Ruben (1992) gives two compelling examples of ancient belief in the connection between information and reality. In the Middle East, utterances like *abrakadabra* were assumed to cure a fever. Similarly, the Old Testament phrase "Let there be light and there was light" reflects the belief that the creation of the world began with the spoken word.

Ancient Greek religion embraced a rich oral tradition of religious stories, rhetoric, and festivals. The gods were honored through poetry and state-sponsored drama about ethics and aesthetics. Orality also defined Europe in the Middle Ages; parishioners engaged mostly in word-of-mouth communication and the church was a central forum for information exchange. St. Thomas Aquinas encouraged theatrical techniques to enhance learning of sacred information. Cathedrals with their altars and statuary reinforced the religious voice of the priest, serving as reminders of the sacred.

Literacy

Literacy led to early libraries and scriptoriums in the eleventh and twelfth centuries. For example, Catholic monks hand-copied holy scripture and restricted its access. Possession of sacred texts increased the power of the priests, who served as information gatekeepers. It wasn't until the era of printing that religious information became accessible to common citizens. Greater access to the Bible was sought by Martin Luther, who favored access to sacred texts. Printing, then, standardized and reproduced holy writings, enabling their diffusion to distant lands and decentralizing the power of the church. No longer were religious messages bounded by time or space. The spread of all ancient world religions from Buddhism to Islam has been greatly aided by the portability of printed materials.

Effects of Radio and Television

In the electronic era, radio and television became important media vehicles. In the early twentieth century, traditional church meetings were broadcast to large audiences via radio, making it possible to hear sermons without being physically present in houses of worship. In 1930 a Christian radio station in Ecuador broadcast religious messages to most of the Western hemisphere (Bendroth 1996). By the 1950s, Billy Graham and Oral Roberts were reaching millions through the medium of television. "Televangelism" combined the traditional church meeting with television entertainment formats. Recent programs like *The 700 Club* depict prayer,

preaching, and sacred music in a talk-show approach that includes live interviews and video news reports. Entertainment programs like *Touched by an Angel* and *Joan of Arcadia* convey religious information within the genre of television drama. This synthesis of religious and secular forms has raised new questions about whether entertainment media like television can adequately preserve the sacred character of religious information.

The Internet

The present postindustrial era of the information society creates opportunities and challenges for churches (Schement and Stephenson 1996). The Internet offers new information sources such as religious websites, blogs, and cyberchurches. This technology creates new ways of accessing information and forming relationships across denominations. One out of every six teenagers says he or she plans to use the Internet as a substitute for institutional church (Barna 1998). These developments signal an emerging trend of personal autonomy in religious worship. Information that was once obtained directly from clergy in face-to-face meetings can now be accessed from online sources. While the Internet offers greater access to religious information, the degree to which it maintains religious community is not yet known. Studies indicate, however, that specialized relationships built around topical religious information characterize the Internet more than general primary relationships (Wellman and Gulia 1999).

Levels

Denominational structures are systems, and information has different functions at various levels. The primary levels are intrapersonal, group, and societal. At the intrapersonal level, information is exchanged between God and the individual through prayer, chanting, or meditation. Other forms are more demonstrative, such as animal and human sacrifice, a common practice in ancient Polynesian, Roman, and Christian religions. Among Charismatic Christians, intrapersonal information is conveyed by speaking in tongues, and inspiration can also be received through dreams. Contemplation of sacred texts such as the Koran, the Bible, and the Hindu Vedas is also a form of intrapersonal communication.

Information is also exchanged in groups. Within temples, mosques, and churches people interact and build religious community. Not only are these buildings for personal worship, but they are environments for informal communication that builds cohesion and group identity. Informal exchange of information helps adherents relate religious teachings to everyday life. In Chinese religion, Buddhist and Taoist temples function as community centers and places for family gatherings. While Islamic mosques are primarily for prayer obligations, groups also discuss health issues, child rearing, and service opportunities. Similarly, modern synagogues serve as social and recreational environments in addition to places for liturgical services.

Groups create important information networks for the flow of religious information. Such networks vary greatly across denominations. Catholics, for example, participate in a structure where information flows from the pope down several levels to clergy and then to parishioners. Judaism, on the other hand, is organized around autonomous synagogues centered in local communities; intracongregational communication is less formalized. The point is that each religion has a different system, with its own networks of information flow.

Recent questions have been raised about the Internet and whether it will strengthen or weaken religious communities. Thus far, studies indicate that online communication does not necessarily replace face-to-face communication but usually augments and supplements these relationships (Campbell 2004). Research also indicates that online communication creates new opportunities for volunteerism but that long-term intimate relationships may take more time on the Internet compared with face-to-face relationships (Wellman and Gulia 1999).

Accommodation

At the societal level, information is key to a religion's acceptance and survival. Whether a group is accommodated by society is directly related to information available to citizens. Throughout history, misinformation has resulted in hardship for many denominations and sects. When the Black Plague killed one-third of Europe's population in the fourteenth century, rumors spread that Jews had poisoned the wells. Although these rumors were completely unfounded, numerous Jewish communities were burned to the ground. A more recent misconception is that Mormons are polygamists, despite the fact that the practice was officially discontinued over a hundred years ago. Organizations such as the Anti-Defamation League and American Hindus Against Defamation work to correct such falsehoods in the media.

In this regard, news coverage of religion is also an important matter. According to Buddenbaum (1998),

journalists are often ill prepared to cover stories about religion, and as a result, a number of stereotypes result. For example, conservative Christians are frequently portrayed as antiscience, and news stories often make an erroneous connection between Islam and terrorism. However, the assumption that coverage of religion is inherently biased has been challenged by Silk (1995), who argues that the values in news stories about religion turn out to be the same as those embraced in the larger society (e.g., honesty, tolerance, inclusion). Nevertheless, efforts are being made to improve journalists' coverage of religion. The Religion Newswriters Association, for example, offers educational programs in comparative religion, and some television stations employ religion-news specialists for their newscasts.

The Future

The evolving nature of information demands new definitions of "information" and "information environments." In this mediated era, individuals will undoubtedly experience new points of contact with religious messages. These will come in both traditional and nontraditional forms. This situation requires new forms of literacy and critical skills in order to manage information as well as to assess its relevance and quality.

Daniel Stout

See also Information Society; Knowledge; Libraries

Further Reading

Barna Research Group. (1998). *The cyberchurch is coming: National survey of teenagers shows expectation of substituting Internet for corner church.* Oxnard, CA: Barna Research Group.

Bendroth, M. (1996). Fundamentalism and the media: 1930–1990. In D. A. Stout & J. M. Buddenbaum (Eds.), *Religion and mass media: Audiences and adaptations* (pp. 74–84). Thousand Oaks, CA: Sage.

Buddenbaum, J. M. (1998). *Reporting news about religion: An introduction for journalists.* Ames: Iowa State University Press.

Campbell, H. (2004). Challenges created by online religious networks. *Journal of Media and Religion 3*(2), 81–99.

Ruben, B. (1992). *Communication and human behavior.* Englewood Cliffs, NJ: Prentice Hall.

Schement, J. & Stephenson, H. (1996). Religion and the information society. In D. A. Stout & J. M. Buddenbaum (Eds.), *Religion and mass media: Audiences and adaptations* (pp. 261–289). Thousand Oaks, CA: Sage.

Silk, M. (1995). *Unsecular media: Making news of religion in America.* Champaign: University of Illinois Press.

Wellman, B. & Gulia, M. (1999). Virtual communities as communities: Net surfers don't ride alone. In M. Smith & P. Kollock (Eds.), *Communities in cyberspace*. London: Routledge.

Information Society

In the contemporary period of late capitalism known as the information society, citizens rely on communication technology and are increasingly engaged in information work. Similar concepts are Daniel Bell's *postindustrial society* and Manuel Castell's *informational society*, which is used interchangeably with popular terms such as *information revolution* and *information age*. It is a period when information technology is tied to industrial production and the dissemination of information in various fields. Schement and Stephenson (1996, 263–265) identify specific "tendencies and tensions" of the information society for religious groups. Dominant tendencies include information as commodity, a robust information economy, increased interconnectedness between citizens, pervasive information technology, and the creation of media environments in the home and workplace. Conversely, there are a number of tensions or liabilities associated with the information society such as information inequity, privacy, decreasing access to political discourse, lower levels of literacy, and reliance on image over substance.

The information society is characterized by *integrated communication*; that is, points of contact with religious institutions have increased—individuals receive information from books, magazines, signage, television, the Internet, and even direct-mail brochures. Church websites provide access to religious texts from anywhere in the world. Personal information is stored in databases by some groups for missionary purposes; others use credit-card systems for tithes and offerings in order to track donation histories of parishioners.

Commercial Influences

Commercial influence is strong in the information society. Religious retailing and religious marketing are common practices among many denominations. Annual sales of religious books, music, gifts, and jewelry are now over $3 billion (Haley, White, and Cunningham, 2001), and many department stores have separate sections for religious products. Contemporary Christian music (CCM) is one of the fastest growing music genres (Perry and Wolfe, 2001). The brand

WWJD (What Would Jesus Do?) is a popular jewelry and clothing line designed to promote religious values. The mixing of religion and commercialism has ignited criticism in some circles. According to Haley, White, and Cunningham (2001), consumers are divided about whether marketing is an appropriate means of religious worship.

Reproduction of Religious Symbols

Another characteristic of the information society is the prolific reproduction of religious symbols. Some images like the crucifix (the Christian cross) are now so ubiquitous that few connect them with specific institutions. Known as *symbol flattening*, this phenomenon involves the distribution of symbols beyond the borders of the physical or immediate congregation (Hoover, 2001). This occurred when promoters of the film *The Passion of the Christ* created products such as a Passion Nail Necklace, Passion Pocket Coin, and Passion Pocket Card and marketed them globally. Other examples include media depictions of the popular singer Madonna wearing a crucifix and portrayals of Krishna in the television program, *Xena, Warrior Princess*.

Effects of the Internet

Perhaps the most salient question is whether religious community will be significantly altered in the information society. Will the Internet create greater information access and quality interaction between church members, or will it weaken primary relationships that presently exist in traditional congregations? The reality is probably something in between. Studies indicate that online interactions do not necessarily replace face-to-face relationships but can extend them in new and unique ways (Campbell, 2004).

Wellman and Gulia (1999) conclude that information exchanged on the Web is specialized, and a greater willingness exists to communicate with strangers. The Web is also global, combining both local and global relationships. Related to the community question is the emergence of "cultural religion," or religious practice focused on media of popular culture such as television, film, and popular music (Albanese, 1996). For example, Sylvan (2002) found that Deadheads (followers of the rock band, the Grateful Dead) displayed several elements of what it means to be religious, including psychological, sociocultural, ritual, and spiritual elements. However, the extent to which cultural religion replaces or complements institutional religion remains unclear.

Hand holding PDA with bible text. Verses are from Matthew 6, The Sermon on the Mount. *Courtesy of Linda and Colin McKie/ istockphoto.com.*

Use of the Media

To deal with changing events in the information society, many churches offer educational programs in religious media literacy. These initiatives, whether through websites, classes, or printed materials, instruct church members in using media in optimal ways that are consistent with religious goals. For example, Davis et al. (2001) uses narrative and theological analysis in suggesting ways of "reading" television through the lens of religious values. And Hess (2001) argues that particular TV programs and movies can be used in religious instruction.

Stout (2002), however, observes that tendencies of religious audiences often create impediments to media literacy such as (1) an overreliance on second-hand or secondary sources in assessing the worth of media such as television and film, (2) the simplification of texts to the exclusion of the aesthetic dimension, and (3) the tendency to extend institutional rules intended for specific genres to a broader range of media. Religious media literacy as a practice is still unfolding, and additional research is needed to understand how it is developing across denominations.

DANIEL STOUT

See also Internet and Cyber Environments; Satellite Communication; Technology

Further Reading

Albanese, C. L. (1996). Religion and American popular culture: An introductory reader. *Journal of the American Academy of Religion, 59*(4), 733–742.

Campbell, H. (2004). Challenges created by online religious networks. *Journal of Media and Religion, 3*(2), 81–99.

Davis, W. T., Blythe, T., Dreibelbis, G., Scalese, M., Winans-Winslea, E., & Ashburn, D. L. (2001). *Watching what we watch: Prime-time television through the lens of faith.* Louisville, KY: Geneva Press.

Haley, E., White, C., & Cunningham, A. (2001). Branding religion: Christian consumers' understandings of Christian products. In D. A. Stout & J. M. Buddenbaum (Eds.), *Religion and popular culture: Studies on the interaction of worldviews* (pp. 269–288). Ames: Iowa State University Press.

Hess, M. (2001). Media literacy as a support for the development of a responsible imagination in religious community. In D. A. Stout & J. M. Buddenbaum (Eds.), *Religion and popular culture: Studies on the interaction of worldviews* (pp. 289–311). Ames: Iowa State University Press.

Hoover, S. M. (2001). Religion, media and the cultural center of gravity. In D. A. Stout & J. M. Buddenbaum (Eds.), *Religion and popular culture: Studies on the interaction of worldviews* (pp. 49–60). Ames: Iowa State University Press.

Perry, S. D., & Wolfe, A. S. (2001). Branding religion: Christian consumers' understandings of Christian products.

In D. A. Stout & J. M. Buddenbaum (Eds.), *Religion and popular culture: Studies on the interaction of worldviews* (pp. 251–268). Ames: Iowa State University Press.

Schement, J., & Stephenson, H. (1996). Religion and the information society. In D. A. Stout & J. M. Buddenbaum (Eds.), *Religion and mass media: Audiences and adaptations* (pp. 261–289). Thousand Oaks, CA: Sage.

Stout, D. A. (2002). Religious media literacy: Toward a research agenda. *Journal of media and religion, 1*(1), 49–60.

Sylvan, R. (2002). *Traces of the spirit: The religious dimensions of popular music.* New York: New York University Press.

Wellman, B., & Gulia, M. (1999). Virtual communities as communities: Net surfers don't ride alone. In M. Smith & P. Kollock (Eds.), *Communities in cyberspace.* London: Routledge.

Internet and Cyber Environments

The *Internet* is a term used to describe the vast array of wires and computer connections people access when they log on to a computer and navigate though websites or access their e-mail. While the word *Internet* is what most people use to identify the World Wide Web (WWW), it represents much more than one application. It has been defined as the network of all networks, providing the infrastructure that allows computers around the world to communicate with one another. The Internet hosts technology that allows users to interact in chat rooms, conduct database searches, and send instant messages to their friends.

Cyberspace is another word often synonymous with the Internet. It denotes a "virtual" world where technology and fantasy meet beyond the user's computer screen. William Gibson, in his science fiction novel *Neuromancer* (1984), used the term *cyberspace* to describe the digital realm the story's hero enters when he connects a computer directly into his brain. As a "virtual-reality grid space," cyberspace becomes a somewhat mystical realm where people do not simply use technology; they become part of the computer network.

Cyberspace and the Internet have been described as a new frontier. This is a space that allows people to engage with each other and with information in new ways, as the Internet is seen to facilitate a transition between the real and the virtual. The idea of moving between spaces can be found in the prefix "cyber," rooted in the Greek word for steersman or pilot, someone who guides others from one point to another. Cyber environments are computer-created spaces representing a

realm made of digital images, icons and texts. The movement between the "real" or offline and the online environment is facilitated by Internet technology. Thus the Internet becomes a tool that shapes both the space and the journey.

The Internet is used in many ways: as an information source, a discourse tool, a sphere for identity construction, and a communication forum. Yet amongst its numerous uses it is also increasingly being used as a religious space, providing people connection with spiritual information, activities, and like-minded believers. For over two decades the Internet has been a space where spiritual rituals are conducted and traditional religious beliefs discussed.

Emergence of Religion Online

Religious use of the Internet can be traced back to the early 1980s when religious computer enthusiasts began to explore ways the Internet could be used to communicate about issues of faith. The first religious-orientated online group was the Usenet "net.religion" discussion list, a forum dedicated to dialogue on religion, ethics, and the "moral implications of human actions" (Ciolek 2004). It steadily grew until the mid-1980s when it split into the hierarchies of "alt.philosophy," "alt.religion," "soc.culture," "soc.religion," and "talk.religion" during a reconfiguration of Usenet. Throughout the 1980s, other religious computer hobbyists and programmers formed various online groups dedicated to their specific religions, such as the first Christian e-mail newsletter "United Methodist Information," and the "net.religion .jewish" Usenet group.

A key event for religion and the Internet occurred in 1986 when a memorial service was conducted online in remembrance of the U.S. space shuttle *Challenger*, which exploded soon after takeoff. Organized on the Unison network discussion board, it involved a liturgy of Christian prayers, scripture, and meditation followed by a "coffee hour" designed to allow individuals to post reactions to the tragedy. This online service "demonstrated the power of the computer medium to unite a community in a time of crisis beyond the limits of geography or denomination" (Lochhead 1997, 52). While religion had always been about communication, the Internet was recognized as potentially offering unique and vibrant opportunities for traditional religious expression.

Throughout the 1990s, more religious groups and mailing lists emerged online such as Ecunet, an ecumenical Christian e-mail listserve (www.ecunet.org),

Beliefnet Statement of Principles

Beliefnet hopes to help people meet their own religious, spiritual and moral needs by providing information, inspiration, community, stimulation and products.

Beliefnet will be respectful of the wide range of religions and spiritual approaches.

Beliefnet will not exclusively promote one particular religion or belief system.

Source: Beliefnet Statement of Principles. Retrieved November 9, 2005, from http://beliefnet.com/about/index.asp

H-Judaic (www.h-net.org/~judaic/), and BuddhaNet (www.buddhanet.net). Another notable first was the establishment of The First Church of Cyberspace (www.godweb.org) in 1992, a "virtual" Christian congregation created by American Presbyterians to be the first nondenominational online church. By the publication of *Time* magazine's special issue on religion online in 1996, dozens of religious websites and online resources could be found: from the first monastic website, Monastery of Christ in the Desert (www.christdesert.org) to the first Islamic e-periodical, *Renaissance: A Monthly Islamic Journal* (www.renaissance.com.pk) and the establishment of the Virtual Memorial Garden tribute to people and pets (catless.ncl.ac.uk/vmg/). The article "Finding God on the Web" (Chama 1996) proved significant, demonstrating the mass media's recognition that the Internet was being used and cultivated as a spiritual space.

Numerous expressions of religion online have continued to emerge, including cybertemples, online rituals, religious online communities and e-vangelism. The Internet provides religious practitioners new opportunities to explore religious beliefs and experiences through a growing number of websites, chat rooms, and e-mail discussion groups dedicated to a variety of faith-related issues. Some online religious seekers chose to cultivate traditional religions in a new context. Connection-hub websites such as Crosswalk (www.crosswalk.com) provide Christians with access to online bible study tools and various interactive devotional or fellowship groups. Others experiment with new forms of religion, altering and adapting ancient beliefs to this digital environment. Ancient religions, such as Wicca, and new religions unique to the Internet such as technopaganism (neo-paganism adapted and celebrated in a technological context) have found homes online. Experiments in interreligious net-

working can also be found such as Beliefnet, (www.Beliefnet.org), a "multi-faith e-community," which offers thoughts for the day from the Dalai Lama, inspirational screensavers, and access to sacred text from different faith traditions. Religion online gives spiritual seekers the opportunity to explore diverse forms of religion easily.

Cyberchurches and Cybertemples

Cyberchurches and cybertemples are unique forms of religious Internet use. These are online environments where electronically linked groups aim to reproduce in some aspects of conventional church or temple life. While they are often in the form of websites, they differ from the thousands of "real world" churches or temples represented online though webpages. These entities exist solely on the Internet and have no equivalent structure offline. Hundreds of these online worship spaces exist. Cyberchurches and cybertemples provide online resources for religious devotion such as providing e-mails of daily religious reading or hosting archives of recordings of real audio/video sermons. Others offer bulletin board services (BBSs) that allow people to post spiritual questions or prayer requests. Cybertemples, or cyber-cathedrals, are often websites designed, using the language and images of a traditional building, to provide visitors a framework in which to navigate. They can include such features as "chapels" for prayer and reflection, a "nave" where people can meet and interact, and a "scriptorium" housing online religious texts and other resources. They have been referred to as churches without walls; examples include the often-cited First Church of Cyberspace or newer experiments that have received much media attention, such as the Church of Fools (www.shipoffools.com/church). The Church of Fools was the UK's first web-based 3D church, allowing an online congregation to attend weekly services in a multiuser environment. The site enabled participation through computer avatars that can join in hymn singing and communicate synchronously with others logged on. Within its first twenty-four hours online, the church had 41,000 visitors and raised much discussion in the international press about the implication of online church for organized religion. While the weekly gatherings have ceased, the church still offers online parishioners the opportunity to drop in and visit the sanctuary or crypt and interact with others.

Online Rituals

The Internet can also be used as a sacramental space, being set apart as a space for spiritual ritual. Many religious traditions have been proactive in cultivating the Internet as a sacred sphere. One of the first demonstrations of this was in 1996 when Tibetan monks based in New York performed a special ceremony and ritual to bless cyberspace for use in Buddhist religious practices. The monastery's website describes this, stating:

> In using the Internet we noticed the Net breeds both positive and negative behaviors, reflecting the very human nature of we who use it. In this sense it became apparent that the space known as cyberspace was very appropriate for a tantric spiritual blessing—to help purify how it is used and the "results" it yields. (The Blessings of Cyberspace, www.namgyal.org/blessing.html)

During the thirty-minute ceremony monks chanted while "envisioning space as cyberspace, the networked realms of computers."

Other religious groups have also sanctified the Internet as a religious cyber environment. Brenda Brasher in her survey of online religion offers numerous examples of online rituals such as a cyberseder, an online celebration of Passover that helps Jewish people reengage with their faith in the privacy of their own homes. Brasher argues that by invigorating the concepts of sacred time, presence, and spiritual experience, religion online allows people to see the religious cultural heritage of many faiths and thus can contribute to interfaith understanding. Common rituals include cyberpilgrimages, whether they be to virtual shrines of a Catholic saint such as Mary (hometown.aol.com/theBVMPage/) or the Japanese Culture Club's Shinto virtual shrine (www.asahi-jc.com/shrine.htm). Other cyberpilgrimages involve online visits to traditional pilgrimage spots; Virtual Jerusalem (www.virtualjerusalem.com) enables Jews to explore cultural and religious information on Judaism or even "email a Prayer" to be placed in the cracks of the Western Wall in Jerusalem.

By using IRC software (internet relay chat, which allows multiple users to log on to the same "channel" simultaneously and hold typed group conversations) or chat rooms, religious Internet users can also participate in online prayer meetings. In many cases users meet in another online forum but then choose to gather weekly at a specific time for moderated prayers. A study of prayer meetings in a multiuser virtual-reality environment found that although online prayer meetings are not the same as conventional prayer services, they reproduce some essential features of conventional church life "albeit in novel ways" (Schroeder, Heather, and Lee 1998). These examples illustrate the diverse ways religious leaders and practitioners around the world have attempted to duplicate traditional expressions of religious practice online.

Online Religious Communities

Online religious communities are groups that facilitate interactions with believers who are separated by geography, but share some sort of spiritual connection or conviction. Some online communities are created intentionally by a church or denomination. These can be formed through a website and may employ RealAudio/Video technologies, attempting to create electronic congregations similar to attempts made by televangelists to construct television congregations of faithful viewers.

Other communities are formed at a grassroots level by individuals rather than institutions. These often emerge as people find others online while searching to become part of a group conversation on a specified topic. Online religious communities congregate around an issue of faith, from a general topic, such as mysticism or spiritual disciplines, to a specific focus on a belief like the gift of prophecy or a religious affiliation such as Anglican or Baptist. While many websites refer to themselves as online communities, most provide interaction with hypertext and images only. Online religious communities are interactive groups, facilitating two-way interaction through various computer technologies such as e-mail or IRC.

No matter what technology is used, online religious communities revolve around common themes: experience, interaction, and connection. Members select the community they wish to join based on the type of experience they are looking for. The strength of the connection is based on the affinity an individual feels for the group or topic. Several in-depth studies have been conducted on the character and consequences of the online religious community on a member's ideas of religiosity, considering different traditions from Christianity to Paganism (Campbell 2005; Linderman and Lövheim 2003). These studies investigate how members' participation in text-based online environments influenced their definition of religious identity, individually, and communally. In each case, research found that the Internet provides a way to reexamine traditional understandings of religious participation by facilitating engagement between people of shared beliefs or religious experiences who would have normally been separated due to geography or time. For some of these members, online community life was perceived as more vibrant than that which they experience in their face-to-face religious community. For others the Internet provided a tool to test and solidify the personal religious narratives related to their faith and practices. Community online remains a popular religious use of the Internet.

Online Witnessing (E-vangelism)

Besides challenging ideas of what it means to gather as a church or religious community, the Internet is changing the ways people communicate ideas of faith. A movement in witnessing online, often referred to as "e-vangelism," has emerged on the Internet. Various books and online resources have been created to provide guidance in this activity. Online witnessing focuses on presenting a purposeful religious presence in cyberspace through a variety of means, through websites, in chat rooms and on e-mail lists. While in some cases, this is being promoted in a top-down manner, with religious organizations encouraging these activities and providing resources, in many instances it is individual Internet-savvy religious practitioners undertaking these tasks.

One of the first organizations to describe the Internet as a potential "mission field" was Gospel Communication Network (Gospelcom, www.gospelcom.net). Launched in 1995, its goal was to "provoke people to think deeply about the nature of God" by "saturating Cyberspace with the greatest news of all." Gospelcom provides webpage space, set-up services, and technological support for Christian ministries such as the Billy Graham Center (www.gospelcom.net/bgc/) and the International Bible Society (www.gospelcom.net/ibs/). Other Christian e-vangelism resource pages have surfaced providing instructions and training for those

looking for strategies for witnessing. Brigada's Online Web Evangelism Guide (www.brigada.org/today/articles/web-evangelism.htm) offers suggestions on creating web environments directed towards non-Christians to "introduce them to Christ." Other websites are designed as interactive tracts, such as Who is Jesus? (www.ccci.org/whoisjesus?) presenting an apologetics argument about the person of Jesus Christ.

Andrew Carega's book *E-vangelism: Sharing the Gospel in Cyberspace* (1999) addresses issues raised by doing "surf evangelism in online conferences" or through visiting web sites. He advocates online missionaries be fluent in the language of technology as well as being aware and sensitive to this new culture of the Internet before venturing into cyberspace. Yet e-vangelism is not just an Evangelical or Protestant phenomenon. E-vangelism has been given sanctioning and support by the Catholic Church in an official Vatican online document (Pontifical Council for Social Communications 2002) and in a book by Catholic educators presenting a theology of ministry for the Internet (Zukowski and Babin 2002). Using the Internet as a tool for proselytizing is also found amongst other religious communities. One interesting example is how some sectors of Ultra-Orthodox Judaism have developed websites as tools to reach out to secular Jews, examples being Chabad.org (www.chabad.org/) or Shofar News (www.shofar.net/site/index.asp). Many creative uses of the Internet for missionary activities continue to surface online.

Studying Networked Religion

In the mid-1990s, religion online began to catch the attention of many researchers and religious practitioners, yielding diverse reactions and methodologies. Religious Computer-mediated Communication (CMC) researchers attempted to describe and investigate the Internet as a new realm to engage the religious. Research investigating the Internet as a spiritual space has taken many different directions. These include looking at the general phenomenon of cyber-religion (Brasher 2001), commenting on religious ethics and virtual reality (Houston 1998), considering how Internet technology reconnects people with spiritual beliefs (Cobb 1998; Wertheim 1999), exploring adaptations of traditional religious practices online (Bunt 2000; Zaleski 1997) and identifying new religious expressions (Davis 1998). A range of religious critiques of the Internet have been produced from strong critiques (Brooke 1997) and enthusiastic advocacy (Dixon 1997) to reflective approaches of addressing both the benefits and weaknesses of Internet technology (Schultze 2002).

In the twenty-first century, religious CMC research is beginning to be considered as a serious field of inquiry. Some early explorations specifically focused on categorizing, defining and interpreting the phenomenon of religion online. Hadden and Cowan's *Religion on the Internet-Research Prospects and Promise* (2000) offered the first critical survey of religion online, addressing different theoretical approaches to studying the phenomena of religion, including work on new religious movements, traditional religious organizations, and cults. This included Helland's work (2000) and a popular distinction that has been employed by many researchers: religion-online (importing traditional forms of religion online) and online-religion (adapting religion to create new forms of networked spiritual interactions).

The Barna Research Group and the Pew Internet and American Life Project have also produced significant reports on trends related to online religious users. Barna's *Cyberchurch Report* (2001) asserted an estimated 100 million Americans at that time used the Internet for religious or spiritual experiences, with common activities including listening to archived religious teaching, reading online "devotionals," and buying religious products online. Similarly Pew surveys showed in 2000 that 21 percent of Internet users had already looked for religious or spiritual information online (Larsen 2000); this rose to over 30 percent in Pew's 2004 study (Hoover, Clark, and Rainie 2004). Pew's 2001 *Cyberfaith* report also observed the most popular activities of "religion surfers" online were solitary ones used to supplement offline religious involvement (Larsen 2001).

Increasingly studies of religion online are asking questions that concern not just the phenomenon of religion online, but how practices within a specific online community context may point to larger cultural shifts in our information-based society. Religious CMC studies are tackling issues such as religious authority online, the process of identity construction, the redefining of traditional roles, and community networking. Discussions of online ethics taking place in religious context also seek to address larger issues of social trust, authenticity, and moral obligation online (Wolf 2003). More in-depth, systematic studies of religious use of the Internet continue to emerge, raising the profile of religious CMC studies, offering innovative methodologies and critical reflection on online culture as a whole (Dawson and Cowan 2004). These add to larger discussions about how the Internet is becoming embedded in our everyday lives and changing the ways people see others and interact in the world.

Challenges of Online Religion

For some the thought of practicing religion online can be theologically problematic. Practicing religion in a "disembodied" medium challenges many people's image of what it means to be part of a church or religious community. However, the fact remains that the Internet is increasingly being used as a space to seek out traditional religion or create new forms of community and practice. Those who fear a mass exodus from the pews by those practicing religions through a screen should realize that while Internet and online churches are useful for some things, such as encouraging social interaction and building relationships, they lack other qualities people value, such as face-to-face interaction and embodied worship experiences such as communion. This is supported by research on Internet use such as Katz and Rice's *Social Consequences of the Internet* in which they state that the Internet "does not supplant other communication forms, but rather supplements them" (2002, 329) in many types of social organizations, including religious groups. They also found Internet use appears to encourage and stimulate overall social interaction in these context.

Religion online is different from being involved in an offline faith community, yet it does not need to be seen as disconnected from a person's daily spiritual practice. Practicing religion online—whether in a cyberchurch, online prayer meeting, or seeking spiritual information online—simply represents one arena for individuals to express their overall religious life, albeit in a novel format.

HEIDI CAMPBELL

Further Reading

Barna Research Group. (2001). *More Americans are seeking Net-based faith experiences*. Retrieved June 2, 2004, from http://www.barna.org/cgibin/PagePressRelease.asp?PressReleaseID=90&Reference=D

Brasher, B. (2001). *Give me that online religion*. San Francisco: Jossey-Bass.

Brooke, T. (1997). *Virtual gods*. Eugene, OR: Harvest House.

Bunt, G. (2000). *Virtually Islamic: Computer-mediated communication and cyber Islamic environments*. Lampeter, UK: University of Wales Press.

Campbell, H. (2003). A review of religious computer-mediated communication research. In S. Marriage & J. Mitchell (Eds.), *Mediating religion: Conversations in media, culture and religion* (pp. 213–228). Edinburgh, UK: T & T Clark/Continuum.

Campbell, H. (2005). *Exploring religious community online: We are one in the network*. New York: Peter Lang Publishing.

Carega, A. (1999). *E-vangelism: Sharing the Gospel in cyberspace*. Lafayette: Vital Issues Press.

Cobb, J. (1998). *Cybergrace: The search for God in the digital world*. New York: Crown Publishers.

Ciolek, T. M. (2004). Online religion: The Internet and religion. In H. Bidgoli (Ed.), *The Internet Encyclopedia* (Vol. 2, pp. 798–811). New York: John Wiley & Sons, Inc.

Chama, J. R. C. (1996, December 16). Finding God on the Web. *Time, 149*(1), 52–59.

Dawson, L, & Cowan, D. (Eds.). (2004). *Religion online: Finding faith on the Internet*. New York: Routledge.

Davis, E. (1998). *Techngnosis*. New York: Random House.

Dixon, P. (1997). *Cyberchurch, Christianity and the Internet*. Eastborne, UK: Kingsway Publications.

Gibson, W. (1984). *Neuromancer*. New York: Ace Book.

Hadden, J. K., & Cowan, D. E. (2000). *Religion on the Internet: Research prospects and promises*. New York: JAI Press.

Helland, C. (2000). Online-religion/religion-online and virtual communitas. In J. K. Hadden & D. E. Cowan (Eds.), *Religion on the Internet: Research prospects and promises* (pp. 205–223). New York: JAI Press.

Hoover, S., Clark, L. S., & Rainie, L. (2004). Faith Online: 64 percent of wired Americans have used the Internet for spiritual or religious information. *Pew Internet and American Life Project*. Retrieved June 2, 2004, from http://www.pewinternet.org/reports/toc.asp?Report=119

Houston, G. (1998). *Virtual morality*. Leicester, UK: Apollos.

Larsen, E. (2000). Wired churches, wired temples: Taking congregations and missions into cyberspace. *Pew Internet and American Life Project*. Retrieved June 2, 2004, from http://www.pewinternet.org/reports/toc.asp?Report=28

Larsen, E. (2001). CyberFaith: How Americans pursue religion online. *Pew Internet and American Life Project*. Retrieved June 2, 2004, from http://www.pewinternet.org/reports/toc.asp?Report=53

Linderman, A., & Lövheim, M. (2003). Internet and religion: The making of meaning, identity and community through computer mediated communication. In S. Marriage & J. Mitchell (Eds.), *Mediating religion: Conversations in media, culture and religion* (pp. 229–240). Edinburgh, UK: T & T Clark/Continuum.

Lochhead, D. (1997). *Shifting realities: Information technology and the church*. Geneva, Switzerland: WCC Publications.

Nightmare, M. M. (2001). *Witchcraft and the Web: Weaving Pagan traditions online*. Toronto, Canada: ECW Press.

Pontifical Council for Social Communications. (2002). *The church and the Internet*. Retrieved June 2, 2004, from http://www.vatican.va/roman_curia/pontifical_councils/pccs/documents/rc_pc_pccs_doc_20020228_church-internet_en.html

Schroeder, R., Heather, N., & Lee, R. M. (1998). The sacred and the virtual: Religion in multi-user virtual reality. *Journal of Computer Mediated Communication, 4*. Retrieved June 2, 2004, from http://www.ascusc.org/jcmc/vol4/issue2/schroeder.html#LANGUAGE

Schultze, Q. (2002). *Habits of the high-tech heart*. Grand Rapids, MI: Baker Academic.

Wertheim, M. (1999). *The pearly gates of cyberspace*. London: Virago.

Wolf, M. (Ed.). (2003). *Virtual morality: Morals, ethics and new media*. London: Peter Lang Publishing.

Zaleski, J. (1997). *The soul of cyberspace: How technology is changing our spiritual lives*. San Francisco: HarperSanFranciso.

Zukowski, A., & Babin, P. (2002). *The gospel in cyberspace: Nurturing faith in the Internet age*. Chicago: Loyola Press.

Interpretive Community

The concept of interpretive community has been one of the most important in audience studies since the mid-1980s. It has been particularly useful in addressing the enduring question of how people interpret (or decode) media content. While most theories grant that audience members will always "read" media messages differently, the interpretive community approach locates the source of these differences at the social, not individual, level. That is, social collectives generate the interpretive codes and strategies people use when they encounter media in their lives. The community may already be in existence, such as ethnic groups or youth subcultures. In such cases, the media are one of many resources in the construction of collective identity. But some interpretive communities also form around a specific media text, genre, or technology. The emergence of such media-based interpretive communities may span or crisscross sociodemographic categories such as gender, age, class, race, and ethnicity.

In either case, empirical study of an interpretive community will reveal the members' rules and standards for engaging with media texts as well as how media use relates to aspects of the community's ideology, morality, or cultural values. As this article will discuss, the concept is a potent metaphor for characterizing the religious audience.

Origin of the Concept

The notion of the interpretive community originated in the humanities, and specifically in questions of what literacy is and how it functions. Although the nineteenth-century philosopher Charles Peirce is credited with the idea that knowledge is always interpreted in public communities of inquiry, it was Stanley Fish (1938–) who coined the term *interpretive community* and argued that the meanings of any text derive from the authority of a critical community. A proponent of the 1970s reader-response movement in literary studies, Fish rejected the idea that there is an objective hierarchy of value in the literary canon. In his 1980 book *Is There a Text in This Class*, Fish claimed that texts are neither good nor bad in themselves, nor do they represent meanings in any direct sense. Instead it is the reader who activates the meanings of a text and gives it value by deploying the appropriate strategies of interpretation; in effect, the reader "writes" the text by bringing to bear his or her knowledge of genre, style, literary tradition, and so on.

Readers, however, do not operate as free agents. Reading strategies, wrote Fish, are "community property, and insofar as they at once enable and limit the operations of his [or her] consciousness, [the reader] is too" (1980, 14). In other words, one cannot be a reader at all unless one has been socialized into a community of readers.

As influential as it was in prompting literature scholars to rethink their assumptions, Stanley Fish's version of the interpretive community was not yet ready to be used to study mass media. For one thing, Fish only discussed readers who were highly practiced in making critical judgments. Popular media, on the other hand, exist in the warp and weave of everyday life. The readings produced by audience members tend to be informal, improvisational, and tied to pragmatic concerns. Secondly, the critical community that Fish presupposed is an idealized entity. But to understand the worlds of real users of media, one needs to closely examine where they live, their lifestyles and beliefs, what they cherish and what they avoid or disavow—and, of course, what media they actually consume, how they evaluate the content, how they perform the act of media use, and how their usage and interpretations articulate with the rest of their lived experience.

Interpretive Community and Media Studies

The work that brought the concept of interpretive community to the attention of media scholars, and had a major impact in spreading its usage, was Janice Radway's 1984 volume *Reading the Romance*. In focusing on a popular genre—romance novels—Radway analyzed readers in their social context and thus achieved what Klaus Bruhn Jensen termed a "bridge between cultural and social scientific approaches to the media audience" (Jensen 1987, 29). Radway set her inquiry among a group of women who patronized a bookstore in the town of "Smithton," and employed several methods—questionnaire, interviews, group discussions—to elicit their understandings of the genre. Among the areas she explored in *Reading the Romance* were the women's motives for reading romance fiction; how they classified examples (both "good" and "bad") of the genre; how they described the typical (and atypical) plots, stories, and characters of the novels; the way they negotiated reading in their homes; and how the fantasies of gender relations they constructed from the novels related to the realities of their own lives. Throughout the book, Radway interweaves her analysis of the Smithton women's interpretations through several conceptual frameworks, among them: feminist critiques of patriarchal culture; narrative and reader-response theory; and institutional analysis of romance publishing and its marketing practices. *Reading the Romance* was a masterful study in how complex evaluations and styles of usage can characterize even the most lowbrow genre.

After the publication of Radway's work, the interpretive community concept was noticed, discussed, and adopted by many communication researchers. Notions of the "active audience" dominated the field of mass communication in the early and mid-1980s, particularly in the uses and gratifications and cognitive-process approaches, and the interpretive community was clearly aligned with an active audience view. However, uses and gratifications and cognitive research typically ignore the cultural agency of audience groups. The concept of interpretive communities had much more in common with other emerging areas of study—cultural studies, social semiotics, and reception analysis—which are concerned with the production of meaning in audience discourses.

From the mid-1980s through the 1990s, the interpretive community became a popular concept among researchers using ethnography and other qualitative methods to study audiences. The audience formations studied under the rubric have been quite varied. The most common type, following from Radway's work, is the genre audience. Popular genres like romance fiction enable troubling or contentious subjects to be treated within well-understood conventions of narrative and character type. Studies of the interpretive communities for televised news and sports, soap operas and talk shows, and self-help and science fiction books, among others, demonstrated that fans pursue distinctive ways of making sense of, and gaining pleasure from, these genres. In some studies, varying—or even conflictive—readings among regular consumers of a genre have been found. This variation seems to be evidence of two related phenomena: (a) A single genre can support multiple communities; and (b) interpretive communities are flexible enough to allow, or encourage, creative voices to be heard. In fact, studies of fans of such genres as soap operas (Harrington & Bielby, 1995) and science fiction (Jenkins, 1992) disclose how the audiences revise and remake the very texts that brought them together in the first place.

Other audience formations beyond the genre audience have been investigated. People whose only relationship to each other is a media text and the shared resonance it has in their lives may, under certain circumstances, be studied as an interpretive community. For example, Aden, Rahoi, and Beck's (1995) study of visitors to the site of the film *Field of Dreams* supports "the notion of individuals finding a secure, metaphorical place as a result of their interpretations" (374). An interpretive community can also flourish around a technology, as suggested in Seibert-Davis's study of vinyl record aficionados. Similarly, a significant portion of cyberspace studies focus on communities that are based entirely on technological mediations (Smith & Kollock, 1999). However, the interpretive strategies that virtual community members use, and the topics that attract their interest, do not often differ radically from those of their face-to-face counterparts. Finally, it should also be noted that the concept of interpretive community has been used productively in studies of mass communicators. Zelizer's (1993) study of journalists' discourse about critical events of reportage such as McCarthyism and Watergate is an outstanding example.

The Religious Audience and Interpretive Community

Recently, the concept of interpretive community has been invoked by scholars who study the media in religious contexts. Religious communities, of course, devote much of their communicative activity to fostering a particular way of understanding personal identity,

spiritual experience, and the world at large. Many churches are also highly sensitive to the power of the media; some even view secular media as competitors in the winning of hearts and minds. As such, one might expect the religious community to be a factor of some importance in the private media uses of members. Research has in fact found that people tend to interpret religious media content, such as televangelist programs, in a variety of modes: for example, as resources for personal growth, as extensions of the institutional church, and as elaborations of their own faith histories. To date, however, few studies of religious genre communities have been conducted. This may change as the marketplace for religious culture expands, because, as Thomas Lindlof (2002) observes, "there is no shortage of fans and devoted audiences for popular religious texts, ranging from the *Veggie Tales* video series…to the burgeoning Christian pop music scene" (67).

Because religion is a "transportable" community—that is a communal identity that can be enacted in a variety of sociotemporal circumstances—members of faith communities must often decide how they will orient to a widespread, largely secular media environment. There may be thematic connections, for example, between how people "read" their scriptural texts, the ways in which they "read" secular media material, and the ways they "read" other symbolic phenomena in their surroundings. A study in this vein is Daniel Stout's (2004) exploration of Mormons' perceptions of the media-saturated scene of Las Vegas and the interpretive coping strategies they have devised for living there. Recent studies have also examined the tensions felt by people of faith between their church teachings and secular media genres, and how the religious opponents of controversial media content argue their positions with reference to their own and others' communities. In studies like these, the codes of one or more conflicting worldviews can be inferred from the discourses of individual actors.

Research Directions

This section discusses directions for future study of the interpretive community. It remains unclear, for example, how fan groups and subcultures differ in kind from an interpretive community. There is also a need to know what difference it makes to define an interpretive community as a "discursive formation" (Schroder 1994, 339), compared to a preexisting group of people who happen to use media in distinctive ways (e.g., white male viewers of NASCAR events). Additionally, the concept has probably not been utilized to its fullest. For example, it is not difficult to see how interpretive communities play a role in such theories as the diffusion of innovations or in social-perceptual processes like parasocial interaction—both of which are vital in understanding facets of the religious audience.

The field of consumer research has contributed the idea of the *brand community*, which is "a specialized, non-geographically bound community, based on a structured set of social relationships among admirers of a brand" (Muniz & O'Guinn 2001, 412). Such consumers honor and perform the rituals and symbolic acts that go with usage of such brands as Macintosh computers, BMW automobiles, and Nokia cell phones. Although it is possible to take the analogy too far, one's choice of a religious commitment is not unlike a brand loyalty—particularly in light of the growing numbers of people who "shop" for a spiritual home. The role that mediated communication plays in brand decisions, and the shift in media choices and interpretations that may occur once a commitment takes hold, are issues for future study.

Finally, the media environment continues to trend toward mobile, digital technologies, and people's notions of interpretive community will probably change with it. Although the audience seems to be "fragmenting," this breakup is true only from the perspective of media companies trying to hang onto their market shares. From the perspective of people living in this new world, the technologies they use form an interconnected—and seamless—series of platforms that enable them to access different information sources as well as multiple versions of the same content (Livingstone, 2004). New technologies are also enabling people to produce their own media texts. From compiling songs on CDs to designing websites to sending their own video over the Internet, people are less willing than ever to confine themselves to a traditional audience role. These and other creative practices are spreading into existing interpretive communities—including religious settings—and should merit the attention of communication scholars in the future.

Thomas R. Lindlof

Further Reading

Aden, R. C., Rahoi, R. L., & Beck, C. S. (1995). "Dreams are born on places like this": The process of interpretive community formation at the *Field of Dreams* site. *Communication Quarterly, 43*(4), 368–380.

Anderson, B. (1991). *Imagined communities: Reflections on the origin and spread of nationalism*. London: Verso.

Fish, S. (1980). *Is there a text in this class? The authority of interpretive communities*. Cambridge, MA: Harvard University Press.

Harrington, C. L., & Bielby, D. D. (1995). *Soap fans: Pursuing pleasure and making meaning in everyday life*. Philadelphia: Temple University Press.

Jenkins, H. (1992). *Textual poachers: Television fans and participatory culture*. New York: Routledge.

Jensen, K. B. (1987). Qualitative audience research: Toward an integrative approach to reception. *Critical Studies in Mass Communication, 4*, 21–36.

Jensen, K. B. (1995). *The social semiotics of mass communication*. Thousand Oaks, CA: Sage.

Lindlof, T. R. (2002). Interpretive community: An approach to media and religion. *Journal of Media and Religion, 1*(1), 61–74.

Livingstone, S. (2004). The challenge of changing audiences: Or, what is the audience researcher to do in the age of the Internet. *European Journal of Communication, 19*(1), 75–86.

Muniz, Jr., A. M., & O'Guinn, T. C. (2001). Brand community. *Journal of Consumer Research, 27*, 412–432.

Radway, J. (1984). *Reading the romance: Women, patriarchy, and popular literature*. Chapel Hill: University of North Carolina Press.

Schroder, K. C. (1994). Audience semiotics, interpretive communities and the "ethnographic turn" in media research. *Media, Culture & Society, 16*, 337–347.

Seibert-Davis, J. (2003). *"Vinylphilia": Consumption and use of the "obsolete" vinyl record among the vinylphiles*. Unpublished doctoral dissertation, University of Kentucky, Lexington.

Smith, M. A., & Kollock, P. (Eds.) (1999). *Communities in cyberspace*. London: Routledge.

Stout, D. A. (2004). Secularization and the religious audience: A study of Mormons and Las Vegas media. *Mass Communication & Society, 7*(1), 61–75.

Zelizer, B. (1993). Journalists as interpretive communities. *Critical Studies in Mass Communication, 10*, 219–237.

Islam

Islam has become a subject of increasing importance in media studies because of controversies concerning media portrayals of the religion and its adherents (Muslims) and debates over the role of democracy and democratic media within Islam itself. There are approximately 1.3 billion Muslims concentrated primarily in thirty nations in the Middle East, North and West Africa, and Asia, where they are an overall majority. Fifty-seven nations are affiliated with the Organization of the Islamic Conference (OIC), an international coordinating agency that represents Islam globally in economic, social, and political affairs. Only fifteen percent of the world's Muslims are Arabs, yet the faith is regarded as centered in the Middle East. Muslims regard the seventh-century figure Muhammad as a prophet and the Qur'an as direct revelation by God to Muhammad through the archangel Gabriel.

Muslims regard themselves, together with Jews and Christians, as "people of the book," or followers of monotheistic religions who also received divine revelation, or books, from God and share beliefs in some prophets, such as Moses. This designation is a notable media-defined identity that is unique to Islam. Islam outlines five religious duties or "pillars" of faith for adherents. They are (1) the profession of faith (*shahadah*), (2) five daily prayers (*salat*), (3) fasting during the month of Ramadan (*sawm*), (4) giving to the poor (*zakat*), and (5) religious pilgrimage (hajj) once in each person's lifetime to the holy shrine of Mecca in Saudi Arabia. Muslim dress varies across nations and traditions. Some Muslim women wear veils and coverings (such as the *hijab,* burka, and *nikab*), and some men wear headgear (such as the turban and *kalansua*). Muslims worship in buildings called mosques (or *masjids*).

Islamic Traditions

The Sunni and Shia are among Islam's distinct traditions. The differences between these two main groups are more political than doctrinal or spiritual. Sunni and Shiite beliefs arose from historical disputes over the ancestral authority of the Prophet Muhammad. Customs and practices of Sunnis and Shia are diverse and varied, and relations are sometimes marked by co-operation; other times by strife and conflict. Both groups share common beliefs in the obligation of the sacred pilgrimage to Mecca and other holy sites in Saudi Arabia. Sufi Islam crosses both groups and represents the diverse mystical expression of Islam. Sufi mysticism has historically been less observed than the dominant religious beliefs and practices of Sunnis and Shia because of its solitary individual search for religious truth. Other Islamic movements, such as Wahhabism, are gaining increasing strength in some regions. Wahhabism is the dominant form of Sunnism in Egypt. It holds that some groups, like the Sufis and Shia, follow novel, non-Islamic religious practices. The oldest and most distinct Islamic movements in North America are the Nation of Islam religious community (sometimes known as "Black Muslims") and the Moorish Science Temple, which draws from an Asiatic racial identity. There are between five to eight million Muslims in the United States, 30 to 40 percent of whom are African-American, while the rest come from Arab, South Asian, African, European, and other American origins.

While Islam possesses liberal and conservative trends, Fundamentalist beliefs are often highlighted in Western media. A concept popularized in discourse about Fundamentalist Islam is Jihad, defined by devout Muslims as "religious struggle," but understood narrowly by most Western observers as "holy war." Islamic leaders debate the acceptability of Western popular values and modernity, including the concept of a democratic "public sphere" as an arena for common discourse and the proper role of the media. Traditional Islamic interpretations of the sayings (*sunnah*) and actions (hadith) of the prophet Muhammad or canonical laws (shari'ah) have had little to say directly about the function of mass communication beyond embracing the Qur'an as the central medium of communication. Muslim scholars in communication science point, however, to the neglected importance of desert caravans as a communication pattern in the historic past, creating enduring patterns of social relations and cultural exchange in the arid Middle East, and the unprecedented scope of the annual *hajj,* gathering as many as four million people from diverse cultural origins focused on a single, peaceful religious goal. From these unique social origins have arisen distinct understandings of communication and society.

Responses to Negative Stereotyping

In the Western media, negative stereotypes of Islamic people and cultures have been a mainstay for movie producers. Thomas Edison made a short film, *Fatima Dances,* in 1897 for his early moving-image Kinetoscope in which "Arab women" with enticing clothes dance to seduce a male audience. Many subsequent media portrayals of Arabs and Muslims have been gross caricatures of wealthy oil barons or crazed terrorists. Even seemingly innocent cartoon images of Aladdin and Sinbad raised antipathy in Muslim and Arab critics. Similarly, news coverage in the West in the twentieth and early twenty-first centuries often characterized Islam as a violent and fanatical religion that represses women and is generally antagonistic toward Western liberal democratic ideals.

In the 1970s, entangled in the political and economic alliances of geopolitics, the news flowing along East-West media channels about Middle East conflicts, especially between Israelis and Palestinians, further enflamed tempers and passions about Muslims. These conflicts included the Suez crisis in 1955, the Arab-Israeli wars of 1967 and 1973, the oil crisis of 1973–1974,

The Mohammed Ali Mosque in Cairo, Egypt. *Courtesy istockphoto.com.*

and the Iranian revolution of 1978–1979. By the late 1970s, complaints about the distorted and stereotyped images of non-Western nations took shape in the New World Information and Communication Order (NWICO), inspired by a 1978 paper submitted to UNESCO by Tunisian Minister of Information Mustapha Masmoudi. His proposal to equalize the flow of information included prohibitions on all media activities likely to misrepresent or show in an unfavorable light the activities of developing countries, the regulation of the gathering and transmission of news across national borders, and the creation of an international agency to regulate activities of foreign journalists.

In a similar tone, Edward Said (1978) argued that Western values were dominating the Arab and Islamic worlds by a curious twist of geopolitical consumerism. He maintained Arabs exchanged their oil in the open world marketplace for a foreign and antagonistic Western culture. Faced with economic and cultural colonization, Muslims were presented with two radical alternatives: either sever relations with Western nations, or promote aggressive internationalization of Islamic values and institutions. Some writers see deep religious and cultural conflict arising from these tensions in a clash of civilizations (Huntington 1996); others argue that Islam has a long history of tolerance and respect for other religious traditions. These conflicting views are frequently the focus of contemporary debates about the evolving place of Muslims in a modern pluralistic world.

In the early 1990s, with complaints about Western reporting of the Gulf War in 1991 and the banning of Salman Rushdie's controversial book *The Satanic Verses* by Shiite leaders in Iran, the deep rift between Western modernity and traditional Islam became more concrete. The Council of Europe demanded improvements in the West's negative images of the Islamic world, and the Euromed Non-governmental Platform (Forum Civil Euromed) warned that economic and political ties between the European Union and the Mediterranean region would improve only if stereotypes ceased and media performance on all sides improved.

Islamic-Western relations worsened in late 2005 and 2006 when most of the Islamic world voiced its strong objection to cartoon depictions of the Prophet Muhammad in European newspapers and magazines, originating in the newspaper *Jyllands-Posten* in Denmark. Many Muslims view such cartoons as sacrilegious and insulting because of their widely held belief that caricatures of the prophet are banned to prevent idolatry. An OIC-coordinated response to the cartoons was a unified response to protest over the cartoons, but resulted in violence in many Islamic nations. Defenders of the cartoons argued that such depictions, even if distasteful, are a free-speech issue and must be tolerated. The controversial cartoons became another flash point in the escalating debate over the compatibility of democratic liberalism in traditional Islam, and respect for traditional beliefs in Western democracy.

Analysis of Media Stereotypes

Media analysis has focused on intercultural dimensions of media stereotypes of Arabs and Muslims in news outlets, literature, and film. Such stereotypes are distortions that create what one writer described as deep feelings of frustration and dismay as Arabs and Muslims "continue to experience prejudice, intimidation, discrimination, misunderstanding, and even hatred" (Haddad 1991, 3). Using a strategy of protest and resistance, political action groups in North America and Western Europe have raised awareness of ethnic and religious objections to unfair media portrayals. These groups include the Council on American-Islamic Relations (CAIR), American-Arab Anti-Discrimination Committee, and Arab Media Watch.

Much of the strategy of media response by Muslims has been predicated on theories of stereotyping. Most theories of stereotyping can be divided between those focusing on individual cognitive processes and those interested in sociocultural causes. Individual theories of stereotyping are based on particular motives and personality traits, while sociocultural approaches draw upon conflict theories and social learning models to explain the process of stereotyping.

In the closing years of the twentieth century, contemporary approaches to Islamic media analysis have sought alternatives to stereotyping by suggesting that cultural dialogue draw on different assumptions about the social foundations of communication. Kai Hafez outlined several specific steps to improve Western media performance regarding the Islamic world, and likewise, Islamic views of Western modernism. These steps include encouragement of critical domestic media environments; formulation of a code of journalistic conduct to include respect for other cultures and traditions; diversification of journalistic sources; improved crisis coverage by news media aimed at de-escalation of tensions; creation of channels of cultural dialogue; and creation of a Mediterranean observatory for comparative media monitoring and studies.

Islamic Democratic Media

Several nations with Islamic traditions have had notable success in cultivating democratic media. Among those nations are Lebanon, Egypt, Jordan, and Morocco. These nations have been at least modestly successful in encouraging democratic dialogue through their national media, creating policies to allow space for privately-owned print media, although most governments still maintain a firm hold on public broadcasting. Free-press advocates are wary, however, about the dangers faced by journalists who confront opposition from religious fundamentalists, such as the Wahhabis.

Considerable interest has also been focused on the emerging television industry in the Middle East, particularly the news coverage of the war and its aftermath in Iraq from Qatar-based studios of broadcaster al-Jazeera. Al-Jazeera has been on the forefront of a shifting perspective in Middle Eastern broadcasting, challenging the dominant global view of Western media.

The American terrorist attacks of September 11, 2001 were pivotal in terms of Islamic and Arabic images in the Western media. While media coverage after September 11 was initially drawn from old stereotypes and caricatures of Arabs and Muslims, subsequent coverage of the religious identities and motives of the actors has opened a window onto some of the complex social and political dimensions of Islam and Middle Eastern societies and their changing relationships with Western Europe and North America.

ALLEN W. PALMER AND ABDULLAHI A. GALLAB

See also Jihad; Mosques

Further Reading

Ahmed, A. S. (1988). *Discovering Islam: Making sense of Muslim history and society*. New York: Routledge.

Barber, B. R. (1995). *Jihad vs. McWorld: Terrorism's challenge to democracy*. New York: Ballentine.

Eickelman, D. F. & Anderson, J. W. (2003). *New Media in the Muslim World: The Emerging Public Sphere*. Bloomington: Indiana University Press.

Gareeb, E. (1983). *Split vision: The portrayal of Arabs in the American media*. Washington, DC: American Arab Affairs Council.

Haddad, Y. (1991). *The Muslims of America*. New York: Oxford University Press.

Hafez, K. (1999). *The West and Islam in the mass media: Fragmented images in a globalizing world*. Cresskill, NJ: Hampton Press Inc.

Huntington, S. P. (1996). *The clash of civilizations and the remaking of world order*. New York: Simon & Schuster.

Hussain, M. (1986). Islamization of communication theory. *Media Asia*, 13(1), 32–36.

Kamalipour, Y. R. (1995). *The U.S. media and the Middle East: Image and perception*. Westport, CT: Greenwood Press.

Leonard, K. I. (2003). *Muslims in the United States: The state of research*. New York: Russell Sage Foundation.

Palmer, A., & Gallab, A. (2001a). *Beyond antipathy: a dialogic approach to conflict between Arab and Western cultures.* Paper presented at Arab Stereotypes Conference. Retrieved June 22, 2005, from http://www.lau.edu.lb/centers-institutes/bima/papers.html

Palmer, A., & Gallab, A. (2001b). Islam and Western culture: Navigating terra incognito. In D. A. Stout & J. M. Buddenbaum (Eds.), *Religion and popular culture: Studies on the interaction of world views*. Ames: Iowa State University Press.

Qumsiyey, M. B. (1998, January). 100 Years of Anti-Arab and Anti-Muslim Stereotyping. *The Prism*. Retrieved June 22, 2005, from http://www.ibiblio.org/prism/jan98/anti_arab.html

Said, E. (1978). *Orientalism*. New York: Vintage Books.

Said, E. (1981). *Covering Islam. How the media and the experts determine how we see the rest of the world*. New York: Pantheon.

Schlesinger, P. (1993). Islam, postmodernity, and the media: An interview with Akbar S. Ahmed. *Media, Culture and Society, 15*(1), 29–42.

Shaheen, J. (1984). *The TV Arab*. Bowling Green, OH: Bowling Green State University Popular Press.

Shaheen, J. (2001). *Reel bad Arabs: How Hollywood vilifies a people*. Brooklyn, NY: Olive Branch Press.

Terry, J. (1985). *Mistaken identity: Arab stereotypes in popular writings*. Washington, DC: American Arab Affairs Council.

Israel, Media in

The centrality of religion in the Jewish State has made religion a characteristic of the Israeli mass media. The tensions between religion and state in Israel are subject of regular coverage and discussion in the mainstream general media. There is also a separatist religious media providing the informational requirements of the ultra-Orthodox Haredim (Hebrew for "pious ones") and the modern Orthodox *dati leumi* ("national religious") populations, the two dominant religious streams in Israel. A changing media structure including the place of religion in public broadcasting and Internet, and changes within the two religious Haredi and *dati leumi* communities, has made mass media a subagent of contemporary religious identity and a channel of comunication between religious and secular communities in Israel.

The General Press

The media are the main channel through which the secular and most of the traditional, though not specifically religious adult population (accounting for 70 percent of the Israeli Jewish population) receive information about religion. Coverage of religion in the general media may be divided between reporting religion-related news stories and the reporting of fewer stories on religion per se not concerning the daily news.

Religion coverage on the news pages mostly focuses upon aspects of state–religion relations including the religious political parties (which generally hold a fifth of the one hundred twenty seats in the Knesset and participate in the coalition-style government), government funding for yeshivot (educational institutions of higher religious leaning), army exceptions for yeshiva students, the status of the small but growing non-Orthodox religious streams (Reform and Conservative which do not enjoy official recognition by the government) and the question of the official status of religious conversions carried out by them, and Sabbath and kashrut observance in public institutions. Other national newspapers, radio, and television each have a religious-affairs correspondent covering the beat in most cases on a full-time basis. Internal religious matters such as synagogual life, liturgy, rabbis, religious educational institutions (with the exception of government funding), and religious youth groups receiver scant attention. Unusual *pesukim* (religious decisions) are sometimes covered in the popular media, including *Yedioth Aharonot* and *Maariv*, if only as reflecting the eccentrity of religion. One exception is the religious holidays which are usually covered through photographic illustration and television reports on the eve of the holiday, including the high prices of Passover (*Pesach*) food, children's fancy dress for the Purim holiday, or the contrasting manners in which the religious and secular Israelis spend the vacations during the week-long Passover and Tabernacles (Sukkot) holidays.

The Haredi population, which makes up 450,000 of Israel's five million Jewish population, is the most covered religious stream due both to to their political clout and their anti-modern lifestyle. The modern Orthodox (180,000) are today less focused on narrow questions concerning state–religion relations and more in the forefront of Jewish settlements in the West Bank (or the biblical territories of Judea, Samaria) captured in 1967. The Reform and Conservative receive far less coverage except when they appeal to the courts or the government against the Orthodox monopoly. There is almost no religion-related coverage, neither of the Israeli

Muslim population, despite that they make up a sixth of the population, nor of the Christian communities, despite the presence of key Christian churches in Jerusalem, Nazereth and the Palestinian-controlled Bethlehem (Cohen 2005).

Purely religious content in the press is mostly confined to a column in the Friday weekend edition on the weekly Bible reading in each of the three national newspapers, the quality *Haaretz*, *Yediot Aharonot* and *Maariv*. Current trends in religious behaviour are occasionally the subject of features in the newspapers.

The Haredi Press

Structure

The religious media may be divided between the Haredi media and the modern Orthodox media. The Haredi press has been party- or institution-affiliated press. There are two daily newspapers. *Hamodia* (The Announcer), founded in 1949, is the organ of Agudat Israel political party, representing the Ashknazi Haredi Hasidic community, most closely identified with the Gerar Hasidic court. *Yetad Neeman* (Torah Opinion Daily) is the organ of the Degel Torah party which represents the Ashkenazi Haredi non-Hasidic or Lithuanian community. It was founded in 1985 by followers of Rabbi Eliezer Shach, head of the elite Ponovezh Yeshiva in Bnei Beraq, after the latter was thrown out of the Council of Torah Sages, an umbrella group of Ashkenazi Haredi rabbis. The paper's readers count also Haredim from the Sephardi or non-Ashkenazi background. Each have an estimated circulation of 30,000 copies. With the exception of radio, these have been the only mass media seen by this population. The newspapers act as important agents of political recruitment; 67 percent of Haredim surveyed read *Hamodia* or 30 percent *Yetad Neeman* (Israel Advertisers' Association, 1995).

The Sephardi Shas political party founded its own daily newspaper, *Yom LeYom*, (From Day to Day) in 1993 but it became a weekly shortly afterwards. Its estimated circulation is 3,000. By contrast to *Hamodia* and *Yetad Neeman*, which are primarily media covering the news, *Yom LeYom* allots more space to covering the activities of the party and its spiritual mentor Rabbi Ovadiah Yosef. Other institutional publications include *Hamahaneh Haharedi*, the weekly of the Belze Hasidic court; *Kfar Habad*, organ of the Habad (Lubavitcher) hassidim, *Haedah* of the Council of Torah Sages; and *Hahomah* of the Neturei Kartya, part of the Satmar Hassidic court. These are less news but more political commentaries with the exception of *Kfar Habad* which

reports Habad's worldwide outreach programme and contains articles memorializing past rebbes who led the movement.

Since the 1980s, the monopoly enjoyed by the party papers has been successfully challenged by a commercially-orientated Haredi weekly media which has blossomed. These are attempts by journalists from a Haredi background to deploy the techniques such as modern graphics, fetching headlines, covering a broader range of subjects than those in the party "establishment" Haredi media. The first papers, today obsolete, were *Erev Shabbat* and *Yom Shishi*. The main weeklies are *Mishpacha* (Family), and *BeKehila* (In the Community), both of which were established in 1997. Vain attempts by the Haredi rabbis to stop the phenomenon of the commercial media may be attributed to a desire within sections of Haredi society to be better informed and in particular to be less estranged from the modern Israeli state. When the state was founded Haredi religious leaders denounced the state as before its time—as requiring the coming of the Messiah before a sovereign Jewish state could be established. Agudas Israel party declined to participate in the country's coalition style of government. Haredim declined to serve in the army.

Content

Haredi press is heavily influenced by Jewish principles. Its mandate reflects less what reality is and more what it should be. Drawing upon the biblical edict that "the Israeli camp shall be holy" (Leviticus 19), Haredi editors seek to ensure that the newspaper that enters the Haredi home does not "impure" the family atmosphere. Each newspaper has a rabbinical censor whose job is daily before edition time to check the next day's edition. Above him is a board of rabbis who determine editorial policy.

There is no editorial content about entertainment, sport, singers, or women, or sexual abuse. AIDs, for example, is referred to as "a contagious disease." To get around the limitations when important information needs to be published, *Hamodia* and *Yetad Neeman* carry a column "From Day to Day" and "On the Agenda," which through attacking a subject as un-Jewish—for example an Israeli success in an international sporting event—are thereby informing their readers that it occurred. The party media also see the censor's role in inclusionary terms. For example, the way a newspaper describes a religious leader as gaon (most learned) or simply "rabbi," is an allusion to that individual's standing in the eyes of the paper and its sponsors.

Moreover, the censor sees the role of the Jew as possessing a responsibility to build the model society. The

Haredi media report the secular world from a perspective of superiority, hostility and self-correction. There are Jews—Haredi—and there are Israelis—secular Jews. Drawing upon Jewish social responsibility as an ideal, Israelis or Jewish heretics need to be rescued. Secular Jewish education is coined progressive education in a derogatory sense, decried as a factor in rising crime patterns. The Left are associated with the universities and academics. The modern religious are criticized as misled religious Jews. Non-Jewish religions are not referred to. Most criticism is reserved for Zionism. The Israeli Army is not called by its formal name, the Israel Defence Forces, since the true defender of Israel is God. The Supreme Court is criticized for not basing its decision on Jewish religious law (halakhah); court decisions are therefore not described as rulings, instead "the court decided" is written. The secular media is pictured as being permissive, anti-establishment, and athiestic.

Haredi press have few reporters, relying mostly upon the news agencies. Most of the material produced in-house comprises analyses, op-eds and interpretations of news developments, according to the Haredi viewpoint. One major scoop, for example, was that of Israel Katzover, a reporter then for *Shearim,* who in 1977 reported that an official ceremony for Israel's first F-15 airplanes from the United States had run into the Sabbath. The story triggered a government coalition crisis that eventually brought down the Rabin government. The commercial Haredi media, while respecting the code of not publishing immoral matter that would upset Haredi Jewish sensitivities, have introduced a new level of press freedom in an otherwise highly hierarchical society. It reports and discusses behind the scenes wheeling and dealing of the Council of Torah Sages, the politics inside the Haredi political parties, and instances of corruption in Haredi institutions. It has also opened a Pandora's box of issues previously denied in Haredi circles such as the problem of Haredi drop-outs from the yeshivot, discrimination in the Ashkenazi Haredi school system against Sephardi children, and Down-syndrome children.

A major qualitative difference in religion reporting between the religious press and the general press is that the latter cover a far broader range of religious themes. These include inspiring portraits of religious sages, Jewish history, discussion of contemporary questions of Jewish religious law (halakhah), suitable material at times of holidays, sections of special interest for women, and book reviews of religious publications. Some of this is contained in a separate supplement with the Friday Sabbath eve edition of the newspaper. The separate supplement also enables these religious readers who prefer not to read "secular" subjects on the Sabbath holy day to read only the holy, or *kadosh,* supplements.

The Modern Orthodox Press

The National Religious Party publishes a daily *Hatzofe* (The Spectator) (9,000 circ. daily, 14,000 Sabbath and holy day eve). Unlike the Haredi papers, its impact is less, given that the modern Orthodox read the general press. A nationalist press has evolved in recent years, which is read by many modern Orthodox, reflecting the ties between the NRP and settlement in Judea, Samaria and Gaza. The weekly *BaSheva* (In the Week), established in 2002, is financed through advertising. The quality weekly *Mekor Rishon* (First Source), established in 1997, is less narrowly or religiously identified.

Religious Broadcasting

Broadcasting is broken down between religious content in the general broadcasting, and broadcasting stations geared for religious populations. Religious broadcasting has been heavily influenced by the public broadcasting model that exists in Israel. Israel Radio and Israel Television has since 1965 and 1968 existed as a public broadcasting authority. Prior to this, they were part of the Prime Minister's office. A religion department exists each in Israel Radio and Israel Television. Under the Broadcasting Law, the function of the religion department of the Israel Broadcasting Authority is to "strengthen ties with the Jewish heritage and its values and deepen knowledge about it." Programming covers topical Jewish developments in Israel and in Jewish communities abroad, cantorial music and chassidic music, discussions about the Bible weekly reading, and relevant programming at times of the holy days. Under a coalition government agreement in 1950 the modern Orthodox National Religious Party (NRP) was given the religion department in Israel Radio, and after Israel Radio became a public authority the department's staffing was closely identified with members of the NRP. Program content has an Orthodox accent, particularly modern Orthodox, with little program involvement of the non-Orthodox Conservative and Reform movements, in part reflecting their small size in Israel. Minority Muslim religious tastes are covered in their own Arabic-language public radio and televsion channels in Israel.

The objections of the Haredi community to the general media extend to Israel radio—both because its content is also regarded as unsuitable for the Haredi home and because it is part of the state Zionist structure.

Some listen to the news channel of Israel radio. Others used a pirate nationalist-modern religious station, Arutz 7, which broadcast from 1988 until it was closed in 2003. In 1996, the Israel Government, recognizing the need to provide the religious communities with their own station, approved the establishment of Radio Kol Chai (The Voice of Life).Though geared to both the Haredi and modern Orthodox communities, Haredim managed to take control of the station and such features as women announcers and women singers, which are anathema to Haredi ears, were dropped. There are a large number of pirate radio stations, mostly religious, and many of which are affiliated with supporters of the Shas religious party. Radio Emet (The Radio of Truth), Radio 2000, Radio 10 mostly broadcasting inspirational content comprise religious lessons (*shiurim*), and religious songs. The Shas Party unsuccessfully lobbied in the 1990s to legalize the stations.

The modern Orthodox listen to public radio and many also watch public television. Yet Arutz 7, identified with the settler movement, was until its forced closure a popular station also providing news. Dissatisfaction among some in the modern Orthodox with television programming led to the creation in 2003 of an independent television channel (Techelet) geared toward the traditional Israeli public with creative programming about Jewish history and history, but it failed economically to sustain itself.

Advertising and Public Relations

Haredi rabbis have long used the wall poster (*pashkevil*) pinned in religious neighborhoods to attack or excommunicate those individuals or companies which they regard as behaving inappropriately. Today, Orthodox rabbis in Israel make certain use of mass media as supplementaries to such traditional channels of communication as the synagogue pulpit. These include appearances on religious radio and in religious newspapers. A new phenomenon in synagogues are professionally produced synagogue weekly bulletins containing essays by rabbis, mostly on the weekly Bible reading, and questions on Jewish law, which are distributed on the Sabbath at the synagogue. Some of these are sponsored by political bodies with rabbis slanting their writings to fit a particular political message concerning the Arab-Israeli conflict. Former chief rabbis Mordechai Eliahu and Ovadiah Yosef give weekly lectures via the satellite to their followers in Israel and abroad. Rabbis are little sought after by the general media, reflecting partly that the dogmatic rabbinical personality is un-

suitable for the type of one-on-one dialogue which characterizes reporter-source relations.

In advertising, Orthodox, as well as feminist groups, have campaigned against sexually explicit advertising, and some Haredi bodies have imposed boycotts on the products of companies which use provocative advertising.

A more recent trend is that as economic standards have improved within the Haredi community, companies have earmarked the population, and target the potential audience within the Haredi press, using motifs suitable for that audience. A number of commercial advertising companies have developed focusing on this sector.

Audience Patterns

Religious communities are not as exposed to the mainstream media as the general Israeli Jewish population. 28 percent of religious people (Haredi and modern Orthodox) defining themselves as religious do not see a daily newspaper in contrast to 17 percent of secular Israelis (Israel Advertisers' Association, 1997). This is particularly true of the Haredi community. 32 percent of Haredim do not read any newspaper, and only 14 percent see general, non-religious newspapers. 46 percent of Haredim do not listen to radio—30 percent of which said they do not do so for religious reasons. 24 percent of Haredim are estimated to listen to Kol Chai's newly created news department. Beforehand, many listened to Arutz 7, which was surprising given the station's ultra Zionist agenda. Only 14 percent listen to Israeli radio, and 6 percent to the Galei Zahal military radio station. The low figures for radio are surprising given the rapidly changing security situation in the country. The inspirational pirate radio stations have a regular following: 20 percent and 19 percent of Haredim listen to Kol Neshama (The Voice of the Soul) and Radio 10 (Israel Advertisers' Association, 1995). Television is banned in Haredi communities because its content is regarded as morally inappropriate; while entertainment per se is not invalidated the Haredi perspective is nevertheless critical of it being seen as more than a relief from such higher values as religious study.

There is considerable variance among the Israeli Jewish public in religion. Only 2 percent and 3 percent of secular Israelis listened frequently to *shiurim*, and programes on religion and tradition, in contrast to 21 percent and 17 percent of traditional Israelis, 44 percent and 37 percent of modern Orthodox Jews, and 55 percent and 51 percent of Haredi Jews (Rokeach, 1997).

The Media and Secular-religious Relations

The mass media influence mutual religious and secular perceptions of each other, having implications for the uneasy relationship between the two communities. In attacking the lifestyles of secular Israelis, the Haredi media delegitimize this population in the eyes of the Haredim. Conversely, the preoccupation of religion coverage in the general media with the religious political parties, and with the wheeling and dealing over state-religion matters, notably funding for Haredi in institutions, distorts the perception of Haredim in the eyes of the secular population. As a stereotyping agent, the media impact could be seen, for example, in the difference in which the rabbi is perceived: whereas he is glorified within the religious media, the rabbi is villified in the general media. Television and newspaper photo images of the Haredim construct an image of them as backward and generally fail to penetrate their inner world. So does the demographic trend among the Orthodox population toward large families. The 1995 assassination of Prime Minister Itzhak Rabin by a nationalist from the modern Orthodox community exacerbated secular-religious tensions yet further. In 2004, 61 percent of Haredim said in 2004 that the general media were antagonistic, and a further 19 percent said this was true in the case of some of the media (*Mishpacha*, 28 September 2004). Asked to rate their confidence in the media on a score of 1 to 5, Haredim replied 2.32, and the modern Orthodox 2.65 in contrast to 2.98 given by traditional and 3.07 of secular respondents (Herzog Institute, 2003).

While aspects of state–religion tensions and the political clout of the religious political parties are subject of discussion frequently, and in the electronic media in particular, enabling different sides to give vent to their feelings, discussion inevitably focuses on the conflictual aspects. As a result of media diversification, both in licensed radio and television, and in pirate radio, public discussion has become more populist, with each audience listening and viewing its "own" station. The modern Orthodox community has sought to improve its media image by encouraging its members to enter the journalistic profession, and more journalists identified with the community are today employed in the general media. Media studies have been introduced into the state religious educational curriculum. The Maale School of Arts, in Jerusalem, has sought to provide training in filmmaking within the confines of religious law. Yet, whatever sensitivity and knowledge this trend causes, it reduces only incrementally the fundamental state-religion tensions.

Jewish Internet

The Internet has created a revolution in accessibility to information about Judaism and Jewish-related matters. There were an estimated 8,500 Jewish websites in 2005. The sponsors of Internet sites may be broken into grassroots groups and individuals; organizational; news; and commercial. Religious content in grassroots group and individual category includes the Bible, commentaries, the Talmud and Jewish law codes. Sites enable the surfer to partcipate in the daily study of a page of the Talmud (the *daf Yomei*) and hear inspirational talks about the weekly Torah reading (*divrei Torah*). This category includes a number of Jewish outreach programs; among early leaders in identifying the potential of the Internet were Habad and Aish Torah (a yeshiva for returnees to Jewish observance). Organizations include the Conservative, Orthodox and Reform movements, synagogues, and community organizations, with listings of synagogues, kosher restaurants, places of Jewish interest, and other services. News includes the website versions of Jewish and Israeli newspapers.

The commercial category, which was relatively late in developing on the Web, today sells most current Jewish books and Judaica.

The "virtual synagogue" has not evolved since these are not regarded as fulfilling Jewish Law criteria for communal prayer (the *minyan*). The "virtual rabbi" replies to questions of Jewish law (*sheiltot*) and offers counseling. A large number of questions deal with marriage, relationships and sexuality.

The virtual rabbi offers anonymity where questions put to the local community rabbi have not. Participation in forum and chat questions on religious belief, as well as participation in religious lessons (*shiurim*) conducted on the Web, contribute to creating virtual communities. The Internet's impact upon Jewish identity is in making religious information much more accessible to those seeking it. Two of the most popular subjects on the Web are Jewish geneology and Jewish dating. The formal ban by Haredi sages upon the use of the Internet necessarily limits the question of its impact to those not adhering to the prohibition. The Internet also has the potentrial of reaching Jewish communities in closed countries.

Jewish Diaspora Media

Mass media has played a role within communities in Jewish diaspora for 350 years. There are 8,300,000 Jews living in the diaspora, 5,700,000 of which are in the

United States. The media provide local Jewish news, national Jewish community news, and news from Israel and overseas Jewish communities. In addition to providing news, articles, essays and reviews on Jewish identity, culture and religion are included. In addition to its informational function, the media fulfills an important role in maintaining Jewish identity and solidarity with Jews elsewhere.

The first newspaper, *The Gazeta de Amsterdam,* was founded in Amsterdam in 1675. The first Jewish newspaper in the modern sense of providing news was the *Allgemeine Zeitung des Judenthums,* launched in Leipzig in 1837 and surviving until 1922. The London *Jewish Chronicle,* founded in 1841, survives to this day. Jewish newspapers grew in the eighteenth century parallel to the growth of the Jewish Emancipation movement (*Haskalah*) mainly in Germany; by the end of the nineteenth century there were over one hundred Jewish newspapers and journals in Europe, published in German, Hebrew, English, Yiddish, French and Ladino. By the 1930s there were also Yiddish dailies in key East European capitals, which folded after the rise of Nazism. A number of underground papers were published during World War II in areas under Nazi control including the Warsaw ghetto.

The arrival of masses of Jewish immigrants to the United States at the end of the nineteenth century and the first half of the twentieth century created a daily and weekly Yiddish press. In addition to news, it provided information about immigrants' rights and the new homeland. Today there are fifty weekly newspapers and a large number of biweekly and monthly publications in the United States.

There are fifteen weekly Jewish newspapers in Europe, seven in Canada, three in Latin America, and two elsewhere in the world. In addition, there are many which appear fortnightly or monthly in different centers of Jewish population. The ex-Soviet republics have seen a rebirth of Jewish press with about forty publications.

A major source of information for the Jewish press worldwide is the Jewish Telegraphic Agency. Established by Jacob Landau in The Hague, and based since 1922 in New York, it has a far-flung network of correspondents, mostly part-time, in North America and around the world. It is partly funded by The Council of Jewish Federations. Economic difficulties facing the Jewish press has produced a trend of local Jewish federations buying out the Jewish press, which it sees as a channel to the Jewish community. Yet, this trend has in effect limited the newspaper's freedom of reporting about the Jewish establishment.

News from Israel is an important ingredient of the coverage in the Jewish media today. Although the Israel-Arab conflict is covered already by the daily general media, the Jewish media is less critical and covers a broader gamut of issues such as internal Israeli politics, the economy, religion, and society. Introspective of criticizing the Jewish State, the Jewish media generates diaspora sympathy for Israel.

There are Jewish radio stations in many countries, in most cases broadcasting a few hours weekly. The most developed Jewish radio stations are those in France, Argentina, and New York which broadcast throughout the week. Attempts to create Jewish television have not generally succeeded owing to its high cost; in a few countries, state television allots time to Jewish religion. The Internet has become an important means for following Jewish news, with many Jewish news organizations producing online editions.

The Arab Media

Religion is a topic of interest in the Arab media in Israel and in the media in the Palestinian territories. Inside Israel, the Arab media—comprising weekly magazines, including *Kol al-Arab* and *A-Sinara*, and a regional radio station for the country's Arab population, Radio Shames—cover religion among its content. But only a journal of the Islamic movement is sponsored by a religious organisation or comprises mostly religious content. 24 percent of Israel Arabs are very interested in religion news, and 45 percent are somewhat interested (I'lam, 2005). Religion content comprises two types. Religious broadcasting includes Friday prayers and prayers during the Ramadan month, and lectures by Muslim clerics. Religion-related news has included coverage of the status of the al-Aqsa mosque (the third most holy shrine in Islam) situated on the Temple Mount in Jerusalem where some Jewish groups aspire to rebuild the Jewish Temple, and a dispute in Nazareth over the construction of a mosque on the site of the Church of the Basilica. The Arab-language broadcasts of Israel Television and Israel Radio cover religion to a lesser degree. Coverage of Christianity, and such related events as the Christmas Mass in Bethlehem, is less than coverage of Islam, given that Christian Arabs comprise only 15 percent of the Israeli Arab population. A similar pattern of coverage of religion is found in the media of the Palestinian-controlled territories. Some of the Palestinian daily newspapers publish a weekly sermon on Fridays discussing current topics from an Islamic perspective. Palestine Television, which is controlled by the Palestinian Authority, covers

Islam, including broadcasting the weekly Friday service from a Gaza mosque, phone-in programs about Islam, and during the month of Ramadan expanded coverage including dramatic portrayals of personalities and key events in the history of Islam.

YOEL COHEN

Further Reading

Baumel, S. D., (2002). Communication and change: Newspapers, periodicals, and acculturation among Israeli Haredim. *Jewish History* 16.

Cohen, Y., (2005). Religion News in Israel. *Journal of Media & Religion*, 4 (3).

Cohen, Y., (2001). Mass Media in the Jewish Tradition. In D. A. Stout & J. M. Buddenbaum (Eds). *Religion and popular culture: Studies on the interaction of worldviews*, Ames: Iowa State University Press.

Heilman, S. C. (1990). Religious Jewry in the secular press: Aftermath of the 1988 elections. In C. Liebman (Ed.) *Religious and secular: Conflict and accommodation between Jews in Israel*. Tel Aviv: Avi Chai Foundation.

Herzog Institute of Communications, Society, Politics. (2003). *Public confidence in the media*. Tel Aviv. Tel Aviv University.

Israel Advertisers' Association (1995). *Survey of Exposure to mass media: Haredim*. Tel Aviv: IAA.

Jemaal, A. (2005). *I'lam, Survey of media exposure of Israeli Arabs*. Nazareth: Media Center for Arab Palestinians.

Israel Advertisers' Association (1997). *Survey of exposure to mass media*. Tel Aviv: IAA.

Levi. A., (1990). The Haredi press and secular society. In C. Liebman (Ed.): *Religious and secular: Conflict and accommodation between Jews in Israel*. Tel Aviv: Avi Chai Foundation.

Micolson, M. (1990). The Haredi press in Israel. *Kesher, 8.*

Rokeach, E., (1997). *Israeli governmental inquiry into strengthening Jewish values through radio*. Unpublished manuscript.

Sasson-Levi, O. (1998). *Secular Israelis as reflected in the Haredi press*. Ramat Gan: Am Hofshi.

Jihad

The Arabic word *jihad* literally means "to strive" or "to make an effort." It is derived from the verb *jahada*, which means "to exert." The word has been interpreted differently at different times and there is no consensus among scholars on its exact meaning. As a concept, it has been used to mean both a private struggle to attain perfect faith and a public struggle to establish a just Islamic society. Historically it has been identified with the idea of a "holy war," a war that all Muslims are bound to carry out against all non-Muslims and apostate Muslims.

Historical Development

During the early phase of Muhammad's ministry, *jihad* meant that Islam was to be spread by peaceful means. It was only after Muhammad moved to Medina and established an Islamic state that fighting in self-defense was permitted by the Qur'an. At this point, *qital* (fighting or war) began to be referred to as one form of jihad. A distinction was now made between jihad as a peaceful endeavor and jihad as a form of war. However, warfare was still regarded as a secondary form of jihad.

The Qur'anic Revelation

The hadith (traditions) quote Muhammad saying on his return from battle: "We return from the little jihad to the greater jihad." His words have been interpreted to mean that the more difficult and crucial effort to conquer the forces of evil in oneself and in one's own society, in all the details of daily life, was the greater endeavor.

Yusuf Ibish, an Islamic scholar and political scientist, highlights the distinction between greater and lesser jihad. He sees the greater jihad as the internal fight of individuals to overcome their animal tendencies and the lesser jihad as fighting on behalf of the community, in its defense. According to Karen Armstrong, there are several Arabic words denoting armed combat, such as *harb* (war), *sira's* (combat), *Ma'araka* (battle), and *qutal* (killing), that the Qur'an could have used if war had been the Muslims' principal way of engaging in this effort. However, *jihad*, a vaguer, richer word with a wide range of connotations, was chosen instead. Thus, the duty for Muslims is to commit themselves to a struggle on all fronts—moral, spiritual, and in the material world. The peaceful concept of jihad flourished later, in the teachings of the Sufi divines.

The Medieval Phase

The spread of Islam through conquest and the expansion of the territory ruled by the Arabs necessitated a further elaboration of the idea of jihad. Islamic jurisprudence between the eighth and the eleventh century defined jihad as a divinely ordained struggle to establish Muslim rule over non-Muslims and thus pave the way for the spread of Islam. Thus, it was argued that the world was divided into two spheres—*Dar-al-Islam* (land of Islam), where Islamic law prevailed, and *Dar-al-harb* (land of war or unbelievers), where the absence of Islamic law led to immorality and chaos. It was the duty of the Islamic state to absorb *Dar-al-harb* into *Dar-al-Islam*—by peaceful means if possible, by war if necessary.

According to the jurists, it is ordained by God that every individual Muslim, except the handicapped and the blind, must learn to fight. Those who devoted themselves to the study of the Qur'an were exempt from participating in battle but not from learning to fight. The Qur'an restricted Muslims themselves to the cause or path of God in three major areas: to defend Muslims from attacks; to liberate people from an oppressive power; and to call people to Islam and convey its message to all people using courtesy and consideration. Significantly, Muslims are reminded to follow the path of justice: "That person is not of us who inviteth others to aid him in oppression; and he is not of us who fighteth for his tribe in injustice; and he is not of us who dieth in assisting his tribe in tyranny" (Suhrawardy 1997, 77).

Complex rules for jihad also evolved. Jurists differed on whether the two realms could coexist. It was felt that peace could be maintained for a period of ten years if it was in the interest of the Islamic state. A jihad could be declared and led only by an imam. Those enemies who chose not to accept Islam or fight were given *dhimmi* (protected) status on payment of *jaziya* (tax). This applied initially to Christians and Jews only, but was later extended to all communities. The rules of engagement and protection were stricter against Muslim rebels, but the idea was to reintegrate them quickly into the Muslim fold, without unnecessary antagonism.

The version of jihad as warfare became more pronounced as Muslim armies and Christians from Europe clashed for the control of West Asia, which was claimed by both as their right. It is from this time that jihad came to be understood as a holy war.

Modern Interpretations

The word *jihad* came to be understood in different ways in modern times. The first view, which can be called "apologist," emphasizes the spiritual aspect of jihad and denies the legitimacy of any holy war. The second view, a modernist theory, reiterates this view with a significant difference—jihad, as warfare, is compared to the Western concept of a just war—that is, war is permissible if the aim is to defend Muslim lives and society. A third view, which can be called "revivalist," rejects both these notions and stresses the idea that war is justified in order to establish a society on Islamic principles. It is this third view that is finding wide acceptance among Islamic societies, and the one that serves as the inspiration for militant Muslim organizations.

Political Islam

The concept of jihad today has to be understood in the context of political Islam. Political Islam draws heavily on a traditional Islamic lexicon, but in the process it transforms conventional religious notions into contemporary political tools. There was a sudden proliferation of Islamist groups in the 1970s that called for establishing an Islamic state and launching jihad. Three important theoreticians of the Islamist movement were Mawdudi in Pakistan, Qutb in Egypt, and Khomeini in Iran. The decisive battlefield for the Islamists proved to be Afghanistan, where a successful jihad was financed by Middle Eastern monarchies and the United States.

The economic success of the oil-rich states has not trickled down to the majority of the people. The poverty belts around the big cities have proved to be a natural breeding ground for a militant, antielitist, anti-Western view of Islam. Widespread disenchantment with corrupt regimes, economic failure, and dictatorship gave a further impetus to militant Islam.

The establishment of the radical Islamic Taliban in Afghanistan, the presence of U.S. forces in Saudi Arabia following the Gulf War, and the Palestinian uprising against the Israeli occupation of the Gaza Strip and the West Bank gave a boost to groups such as Hamas, al-Qaeda, and Islamic Jihad. Small, well-trained groups engage in attacks against U.S. interests worldwide and stage suicide bombings against Israelis, secular Arabic governments, and all those seen to be assisting the West (who are considered un-Islamic). The attacks by al-Qaeda in the United States led to the ouster of the Taliban and the elimination of the Saddam Hussein regime in Iraq. Opponents of the United States–backed regime in Iraq continue to attack U.S. troops and their allies and supporters. Militant Islamic groups have also been responsible for attacks in Indonesia, Russia, Spain, and India.

Jihad Communications

Although they denounce the West, jihad groups use modern means of communications for propaganda and for planning their activities and maintaining communication links with each other.

Information Transfer and Operations

The Internet is a favorite tool of jihad groups. The Laskar Jihad in Indonesia makes extensive use of the Internet to coordinate its operations. The al-Qaeda training manual gives detailed instructions to its members regarding the various modes and tactics of intragroup communication, and cautions them to take extensive security measures. Communication within the group includes the use of cell phones and satellite phones, although these phones can also threaten group security. The movements of Osama bin Laden, the head of al-Qaeda, were tracked by U.S. satellites by homing in on his satellite phone signals. It is believed that groups such as al-Qaeda have not only used the link between the global banking system and the Internet to transfer funds from one location to another, but that they have also played the stock markets in some countries in order to raise funds for their activities.

Propaganda

The fact that the means of information are easily available to virtually anyone has revolutionized the use of propaganda by jihad groups. The Palestinian organization Hamas, for instance, has several websites maintained by the Palestinian Information Centre, Qassam Brigades, and the London-based Return Center. Many of these websites are using American sermons in mosques, which can be recorded and passed on in the form of audio cassettes, compact discs, and videos. Most of Osama bin Laden's threats to the West have been made available in this manner. They can be exchanged, sold, or shown on satellite television stations, or through conventional means such as the newspaper, pamphlets, and faxes.

Al-Jazeera: A Case Study

Politically independent television network al-Jazeera claims that it is the only one in the Middle East. The Qatar-based network was initially funded by the emir of Qatar and aims to become financially independent through advertisements. Run by former BBC staff, it is the most watched network in the Middle East, since it is widely believed among Arabs that government-run stations are biased. The network became prominent in the post–September 11 period when al-Qaeda used it to broadcast bin Laden's messages. It has also broadcast tapes of kidnappings and executions by militant groups. It was the only network to show the bombings of Afghanistan from within the country. The website, in English and Arabic, has been forced to change its host server numerous times.

The fact that al-Jazeera is willing to air much of what it receives from militant groups combined with its unwillingness to censor its coverage of the war in Iraq has given it enormous credibility with Arab viewers and made it the choice of militant groups for propaganda purposes. Their policies have also led to charges from the U.S. government and some U.S. media that the network is supporting terrorism.

Outlook

The concept of jihad has always depended on the historical, social, and political context in which the word was used. In the late twentieth and early twenty-first centuries, Islamic radicals and their support groups have brought a new, narrowly focused connotation to the word. They see jihad solely as a violent struggle against non-Muslims and those supporting them; they believe that the original, moderate understanding of the term is possible only in a pure Islamic society.

RINA KASHYAP

See also Islam

Further Reading

Akbar, M. J. (2002). *The shade of swords*. New Delhi, India: Roli Books.

Cooley, J. K. (1999). *Unholy wars: Afghanistan, America, and international terrorism*. London: Pluto Press.

Esposito, J. L. (1988). *The straight path*. New York: Oxford University Press.

Gunaratne, R, (2002). *Inside al Qaeda*. New Delhi, India: Roli Books.

Hamidullah, M. (1961). *Muslim conduct of state*. Lahore, Pakistan: Shaykh Muhammad Ashraf.

Hasmi, S. H. (1998). *Encyclopaedia of politics and religion*. Washington, DC: Congressional Quarterly.

Heikal, M. (1992). *Illusions of triumph. An Arab view of the Gulf War*. London: Fontana.

Hitti, P. K. (1970). *History of the Arabs*. New York: St. Martins Press.

Inayatullah, S., & Boxwell, G. (2003). *Islam, postmodernism and other future: A Ziauddin Sardar reader*. London: Pluto Press.

Jurgensmeyer, M. (2000). *Terror in the mind of God: The global rise of religious violence*. Berkley: University of California Press.

Kelsay, J., & Johnson, J. T. (Eds.). (1990). *Just war and jihad: Historical and theoretical perspectives on war and peace in Western and Islamic tradition*. New York: Greenwood Press.

Kepel, G. (2002). *Jihad: The trail of political Islam*. London: I. B. Tauris.

Khaddduri, M. (1955). *War and peace in the law of Islam*. Baltimore: John Hopkins University Press.

Morteza, A. M. (1985). *Jihad: The holy war of Islam and its legitimacy in the Qur'an*. Tehran, Iran: The Islamic Propagation Organization.

Noorani, A. G. (2002). *Islam and jihad*. New Delhi, India: LeftWord Books.

199

Peters, R. (1979). *Islam and colonialism: The doctrine of jihad in modern history*. The Hague, The Netherlands: Mouton.

Surawardy, A. (1997). *The Sayings of Muhammad*. New Delhi, India: Goodword Books.

Turner, B. (2003). *Islam-critical concepts in sociology* (Vol.1). London: Routledge.

Wallerstein, I. (1999). Islam, the West, and the world. *Journal of Islamic Studies, 10*(2), 109–25.

Zubaida, S. (2002). Trajectories of political islam: Egypt, Iran and Turkey. *The Political Quaterly*, 60–78.

Journalism

Religion is a subject for news coverage, but the nature of news about religion varies among media. Within any particular medium, it also varies over time in response to changes in the religious climate. Nevertheless, there are two basic journalistic approaches that have remained relatively constant: religious journalism and religion journalism. Religious journalism is the reporting of news, including news about religion, from a particular religious perspective. Religion journalism is the reporting of news about religion from the perspective of a relatively neutral, objective, and detached observer.

Early American Journalism

Three hundred years ago, religious journalism was the norm. Printer/publishers usually saw their newspapers as performing both civic and religious functions. For example, on 25 September 1690 a short item in the first issue of the first American newspaper, *Public Occurrences Both Foreign and Domestic*, gave as the paper's purpose, "First, That Memorable Occurrents of Divine Providence may not be neglected or forgotten, as they too often are. Secondly, That people everywhere may better understand the Circumstances of Publique Affairs, both abroad and at home" (Harris 1690). Similarly, on 20 March 1727 the first issue of the *New-England Weekly Journal* (1727–1741) told readers the paper would publish "Remarkable Judgments, or Singular Mercies, more private or public, Preservations & Deliverances by Sea or Land: together with some other Pieces of History of our own, &c. that may be profitable & entertaining both to the Christian and Historian" (Kneeland 1727).

Although those papers and most others were primarily business ventures, a few were started solely for religious purposes. The best known of these is the *New-England Courant* (1721–1726). In August 1721 as a smallpox epidemic raged in Boston, wealthy Anglicans started the paper, with James Franklin (1697–1735) as printer/editor, because they thought having their own newspaper would help them gain ecclesiastical and political control over the colony. From the debut issue of 21 August through late September, they filled the paper with letters and essays attacking the prominent Puritan clergyman, Cotton Mather (1663–1728), for his support of smallpox inoculations, which they likened to "playing God." Newspapers such as the *Boston News-Letter* (1704–1776) and the *Boston Gazette* (1719–1741) published letters and essays in which the Reverend Mather and his supporters defended inoculation as a gift from God.

In addition to the letters and essays supporting an issue or cause, colonial newspapers also carried short news items portraying good news as signs of God's favor and bad news as evidence of God's wrath, along with the occasional crime story constructed as a cautionary tale warning of the consequences of straying from the faith.

Although newspapers published very little news that was truly local, news from elsewhere sometimes had local impact. During the First Great Awakening, for example, letters from people who had heard the Reverend George Whitefield (1714–1770) preach in other colonies piqued the curiosity of readers in towns where he was scheduled to appear. Each new appearance generated more media attention. But as was the custom, editors who accepted Whitefield's message published favorable letters and commentaries; those who disagreed with him criticized his theology.

That pattern prevailed until well into the nineteenth century. Newspapers carried some news of events, but much of the space in each paper was given to letters or essays commenting on issues of the day. For many of those issues, arguments pro and con were rooted in religion. But because each paper was understood to be presenting the viewpoint of its editor/publisher, very few papers provided anything approaching balanced coverage.

Religion Journalism

But by the 1840s that pattern was beginning to break down. Industrialization led to an increasingly urban, immigrant, and diverse population that had little interest in the kind of letters and essays favored by the newspapers of that era and that, in any case, could not afford to pay in advance for a year's subscription. Thus, the penny press was born. Instead of catering to an educated elite, the penny press provided news and entertainment to a working-class audience for the price of just a penny an issue.

The Birth of Religion Journalism

Benjamin Franklin (1706–1790) could be considered the founder of religion journalism because of the openness to publishing diverse viewpoints he expressed in his "Apology for Printers," published on 10 June 1731 in his *Pennsylvania Gazette*, and his editorial practices as editor/publisher of the *Gazette* from 1729 to 1750. However, that honor is usually given to James Gordon Bennett (1795–1872), who began publishing his penny paper, the *New York Herald*, in 1835.

The irreverent tone Bennett used in commentaries and satires made his paper a "must read" by both his fans and his detractors. However, a bigger factor in the success of his paper came from the emphasis Bennett placed on news of things that his readers really cared about and that had an impact on them. During the Second Great Awakening, one of those things was religion.

The Second Great Awakening was a time of great religious fervor. New religions sprang up. Protestant missionary activity, revivals, and camp meetings flourished. Anti-immigrant and anti-Catholic sentiment increased. Bennett covered it all, but in a way that represented a radical break from tradition. As a Scot and a Catholic in a predominantly Protestant America, Bennett reported from the perspective of an interested but uninvolved observer. Instead of writing to promote or defend a particular religious understanding, he wrote to show what religious people were doing and what impact it might have on others. From that perspective, he covered all religions. No religion was singled out for praise; none received exclusively critical coverage.

His favorable coverage of individual examples of charitable and moral behavior and the neutral to favorable attention to church histories, worship services, and revival meetings as well as to the annual meetings each May and June of the Bible, tract, and missionary societies eventually became the model for stories on church pages. His thorough but critical coverage of church finances, clergy sexual improprieties, meddling by Catholic and Protestant clergy in congregational and political affairs, and anti-Catholic and anti-Mormon attacks by Protestants paved the way for modern hard-news coverage of religion.

While Bennett's approach to religion apparently delighted his audience, it had little immediate effect at other newspapers. As debates over slavery and states'

rights led inexorably to the Civil War, newspapers on both sides of the issues and in both North and South routinely published prayers, the full texts of sermons, and other commentaries in which their authors used the Bible to argue for the rightness of their cause. But when the Civil War ended, so, too, did the highly polemical and divisive religious journalism it had spawned. The number and frequency of articles using religion to support or oppose a cause decreased. Neutral to favorable stories about religious people and events increased.

The Religion Page

In response to public demand for news during the Civil War some papers began to flout "blue laws" that made it illegal for most businesses to operate on Sunday. They also increased the number of pages of news they published each week. As papers got bigger, they also began to group stories together by subject.

Since about 1900, at least four-fifths of all daily papers have had a "church page," usually on Saturday. These pages became the repository for brief stories about local religious people and events as well as for brief announcements of the topics for the Sunday sermons in prominent local churches. From the 1920s until well into the 1950s some larger papers such as the *New York Times* published a second church page on Monday devoted to synopses of those sermons.

Whether because of the religious beliefs of their owner/editors or deference to the sensibilities of the religious majority in a community, many stories were about large, well-established Protestant churches. Papers also published some news from large, local Catholic churches, but the generally smaller conservative Protestant churches and those serving ethnic or racial minorities rarely got coverage. Except in urban areas with large Jewish populations, stories about non-Christian religion were even rarer. Both on and off the church page, newspapers promoted Protestant churches and their activities and causes, in the process making celebrities of prominent evangelists such as Dwight Moody (1837–1899) and Billy Sunday (1862–1935).

With religion defined as a local beat and with space on the "church page" allocated among congregations primarily on the basis of church size and prominence, most papers paid little attention to national or international news about religion or to religious issues or controversies. When they did, reporters working other beats usually wrote the stories.

Although some stories about the 1925 Scopes trial tried to explain conservative Protestants' concerns about evolution, many treated them as a threat to progress and their beliefs as a joke. During prohibition and the 1928 presidential election campaign of the Catholic, Al Smith (1873–1944), stories often portrayed Catholicism as a threat to American culture and to democracy itself. Quakers and Jehovah's Witnesses got similar treatment during World War I and World War II.

Efforts to Improve Religion Journalism

Surveys conducted for the American Newspaper Publishers Association indicate that as recently as the 1960s most readers were very happy with the short people- and event-oriented stories published on the typical church page. However, many smaller denominations were unhappy because church pages of the era typically ignored them.

In 1912 the Seventh-day Adventist Church created its own publicity bureau to counter criticism of the Church for its opposition to Sunday blue laws, which prohibited most businesses from operating on Sunday. In 1929 Protestant churches banded together to create the Religious Public Relations Council in an effort to improve church public relations practices, and garner more, and more favorable, news coverage for member churches. In hopes of countering anti-Semitism at home and abroad, the National Conference of Christians and Jews started the nondenominational Religious News Service in 1934.

More efforts to improve religion news occurred after World War II, as the euphoria of victory quickly gave way to a cold war against "godless communism." In 1949 the Religion Newswriters Association, a professional organization for journalists who cover the religion beat for secular media, held its inaugural meeting in conjunction with the opening of Syracuse University's nonsectarian program in religious journalism, as religion reporting was called at that time.

After about twenty-five years Syracuse discontinued the program, but by the 1980s schools around the country had begun to offer occasional courses in religion reporting. In 1994 both Temple University and the Medill School of Journalism at Northwestern University started offering a master's degree in religion reporting.

And in 1994 Newhouse Publications bought Religious News Service and changed its name to Religion News Service to better reflect the kind of stories the service has always provided. At about the same time, Religion Newswriters Association established a permanent office and hired Debra L. Mason as its first executive secretary. Since then, RNA membership has grown to over four hundred members and affiliates, most of whom are actively engaged in religion reporting.

Where early efforts to improve religion reporting came from the churches, developments during the 1980s and 1990s were news-driven. With the election of the born-again Christian Jimmy Carter (b. 1924) as president, the resurgence of religious Fundamentalism in Iran, the birth of modern televangelism, and the increasing political influence of the Christian right, religion became a "hot" topic.

Contemporary Newspaper Coverage of Religion

In response to growing awareness of religion's impact on individuals and society and of people's interest in religion, papers increased the space set aside for religion from an average of just over a page in 1980 to between two and three pages a decade later. They also hired more and more experienced reporters to fill that space. In 1980 only two papers, the *New York Times* and the *Los Angeles Times,* had two reporters assigned to the religion beat; by 2000 that number had more than quadrupled.

By the mid-1980s newspapers had retired the old title of "church page," with its distinctly Christian connotation, in favor of names such as "religion and values" or "faith and ethics," which both better reflect the reality of American pluralism and also the broadened definition of religion news. In place of short, routine stories of people and events, the newly expanded religion sections began to showcase long, complex depth features examining the interplay between religion, science and medicine, economics, law, and politics from a variety of religious and ethical perspectives. In the process, the number of stories about mainline Protestants decreased. The number about conservative Protestants increased, as did coverage of churches serving racial and ethnic minorities and new and alternative religious movements. Stories explaining the theology and practices of organized religions alternated with stories about personal quests and forms of spirituality unattached to any particular religion. Feature stories about Ramadan, the summer solstice, and Hanukkah became as common as ones about Christmas and Easter.

Although religion remained a local beat at most newspapers, very few papers continued to confine religion news to the religion section. Since at least the 1980s most papers have expected their religion reporters to produce at least some hard news and news features that can compete successfully for space in other sections of the paper as well as on the front page. Nevertheless, religion reporters continued to produce only a relatively small fraction of all the stories about religion. Journalists working other beats still report most breaking news stories and most national and international news with a religious dimension.

Magazine News Coverage of Religion

Even before newspapers began taking religion news seriously, it was a staple in many magazines. The popular *McClure's Magazine* (1893–1929), for example, routinely published articles about religious history, the Holy Land, prominent clergy, and religious revival and reform movements as well as short stories and investigative reports on other topics.

From its beginning in 1923, *Time* magazine devoted a regular section to religion and often featured religious subjects on its cover. Other weekly news magazines followed suit. At first, the religion sections appeared weekly, but stories in them were very short. More recently, the sections have appeared less regularly, but the stories are longer and have greater depth. Magazine issues with cover stories exploring Christian theology, biblical archaeology, or the faith of average Americans are consistent best sellers, but for the most part, the news magazines emphasize conflict and controversy. Although *Time* and *Newsweek* have always employed talented religion reporters, most stories are team efforts. They also are heavily edited to conform to the magazines' editorial position and style.

Other magazines do not have religion sections or religion writers, but they often carry religion news. Some of the best religion reporting can be found in quality publications such as *Atlantic Monthly, Harper's,* and the *New Yorker.* All regularly carry articles with significant information about the role of religion in the Middle East, the religious dimension of domestic and international terrorism, and the influence of political leaders' religious beliefs on the policies they advocate.

Broadcast News Coverage of Religion

In contrast to magazines, radio has never devoted much attention to religion news. With the advent of television, radio lost much of its news audience. As a result, few stations engage in active newsgathering or subscribe to special religion feeds from the wire services. Since at least the 1960s, the trend at most stations has been to provide just headline news; religion becomes a part of that news only when there is a major event, such as a papal visit to the United States, or when a prominent religious person is accused of wrongdoing. The major exception to that pattern is National Public Radio, which is one of the few networks that both engages in active

news gathering and has a reporter assigned specifically to the religion beat.

Unlike newspapers, which operate on a beat system, television reporters are usually generalists. With the exception of a few years in the 1990s when Peggy Wehmeyer covered religion for ABC, no network ever employed a reporter specifically to cover religion news. Although a few local stations such as WFLA in Tampa–St. Petersburg have made arrangements to share a religion reporter with the local newspaper, only a handful have ever employed their own religion reporter. Only about a dozen broadcast journalists have ever been members of Religion Newswriters Association.

Nevertheless, since at least the 1970s about 5 percent of all stories on network television newscasts might be classified as religion news. With the exception of holiday features, chosen as much for their visual appeal as for their news value, and an occasional depth story produced for a special segment, most religion stories are shorter than thirty seconds. Most of those simply mention religion in a story that is really about some other subject. Of those mentions, almost all come in coverage of international news from traditional religious trouble spots such as the Middle East or in stories about political activities of the Christian right.

At the local level, attention to religion news is generally even more rudimentary. Religious holidays and holy days get perfunctory coverage. Churches may serve as a backdrop for newsworthy funerals or weddings. People involved in accidents or disasters or who have been victorious in a sporting event are shown thanking God for their good fortune more frequently than was true even as recently as the 1980s. But, for the most part, religion makes news only when it intrudes in a way that makes it impossible to ignore: crimes committed by or against a religious person or institution, a religious challenge to the law or to public policy, or a major event such as a papal visit.

Religious Journalism

Religious journalism has never completely disappeared from the mass media. Traces linger in opinion columns and letters to the editor, but since the middle of the nineteenth century, religious journalism has, for the most part, been the province of specialized religious media.

Print Media

The first religious magazine, *Christian History,* appeared in Boston in 1743. Like it, most of the early periodicals were short-lived, nondenominational "miscellanies" intended to promote religion and the diffusion of useful knowledge. In 1789 the Methodist Episcopal Church started *The Arminian* to spread church teachings. After the revolution, religion news and commentary were so popular that in the first half of the nineteenth century religious newspapers such as the *Boston Recorder* (1816–1867) competed successfully with secular papers, which also provided extensive coverage of revivals and other religious events, full texts of sermons, and other kinds of religious commentary.

By 1825 there were almost two hundred Christian publications. Foremost among these were the publications of the Bible and tract societies that sprang up during the Second Great Awakening. These publications, which were inspired by and helped fuel the American sense of "manifest destiny," featured narrative accounts from Protestant missionaries and appeals for support from Protestant missionaries. That sense of destiny also inspired many of the earliest denominational publications such as the *Spirit of Mission*, which was started by the Episcopal Church in 1836 and later became *Forth,* and then in 1960 *The Episcopalian.*

As those name changes suggest, for almost a century Protestant religious publications inspired and entertained their readers with tales of missionary activity on the American frontier and overseas. But by the 1930s, missionary magazines were losing their appeal. Denominational publications like *The Episcopalian,* with its mixture of feature articles, designed to educate and inspire church members, and news of church programs and activities, became the norm.

In contrast to Protestant periodicals, early Catholic ones such as Boston's *Irish and Catholic Sentinel* (1834–1835) were started to defend the faith against Protestantism, provide news from the old country, and interpret American culture for immigrants. Like the *Sentinel* most nineteenth-century Catholic publications operated independent of church control. But because they delighted in reporting controversy, in 1899 Pope Leo XIII issued a pastoral letter that led to an era of institutional control that lasted until Vatican II. Since the 1960s, however, the Catholic press has become an increasingly diverse mixture of official church newspapers and magazines, ones published by Catholic religious orders and organizations, and ones that are truly independent.

Because most Americans are at least nominally Christian, most religious publications are Christian. However, by 2000 there were at least one thousand publications representing every religious orientation from atheism to Zen. Like the early Catholic papers, many Jewish, Muslim, Buddhist, and Hindu publications carry features, news, and commentary designed to defend the faith or interpret American culture and provide news from the homeland for an immigrant audience.

Although denominational magazines and other publications published by or for people of a particular religion often have larger circulations, independent Christian magazines such as *Christian Century* (moderate, mainline Protestant; 1884–), *Christianity Today* (conservative, Evangelical Protestant; 1956–), *Sojourners* (socially oriented, Evangelical Protestant; 1971–), *America* (Catholic, Jesuit; 1909–), and *Commonweal* (Catholic, lay-edited; 1924–) tend to be the most influential because they circulate widely among clergy, lay leaders, academics, and policy makers. Since its inception in 1986, *World* has become increasingly influential on political matters by promoting itself to conservative Protestant church members as a Christian alternative to the secular newsweeklies. James Dobson's *Focus on the Family* (1982–) is equally important for its conservative Protestant perspective on lifestyle and family issues.

Among magazines publishing from other religious perspectives, the Buddhist *Tricycle* (1990–), Jewish *The Reconstructionist* (1935–), and secular humanist *Free Inquiry* (1980–) are most similar to the general circulation Christian publications, though none matches them in influence.

Broadcasting

When broadcast licensing began in the early 1920s, just a few frequencies were made available for use by religious organizations. However, since the demise of the fairness doctrine in 1988 and the attendant changes in broadcast regulation, which opened up radio to narrowcasting, the number of Christian radio stations has more than quadrupled. While most of the 1,965 Christian stations on the air in 2004 employed a Christian music format, Christian stations have become an important outlet for news and commentary from a conservative Christian perspective.

Ever since the Moody Bible Institute acquired a license in 1925 to operate radio station WBMI, its *Christian Perspectives on the News* has been a highly respected source for news from a conservative Protestant perspective. However, since the 1980s it has lost ground to M. G. "Pat" Robertson's CBN Radio Network, and, more recently, to the increasingly popular syndicated news and commentary produced by Focus on the Family and featuring James Dobson.

With the change in broadcast policy in the mid-1980s, television has also become more hospitable to religious journalism. Since then, Robertson's *700 Club* has become the primary outlet for news and commentary from a conservative Protestant perspective. However, Jack Van Impe's *Today in Bible Prophecy,* with its more apocalyptic interpretation of world events, also has a large and loyal audience. Some public-access cable channels carry news and commentary from other religious perspectives, but none has the reach or the influence of the conservative Protestant programming.

Culture, Controversy, and Competition

Early-twentieth-century efforts to improve religion reporting gave newspapers greater access to information from the churches themselves. That, in turn, allowed papers to broaden coverage somewhat so that it included news from denomination headquarters as well as from local churches. The more recent efforts, with their twin focus on improving journalists' understanding of and sensitivity to all religions and on improving active newsgathering techniques, broadened coverage even further. By the end of the century, religion journalism's emphasis on depth features and hard news about many different religions made it equal in quality, at least by the standards of the profession, to news coverage on other specialty beats. Nevertheless, problems remained.

The mass media have always considered religion an expendable beat. When interest is high and economic times are good, as they were in the 1990s, they hire religion reporters and give them the time and space to do good work; at other times they cut back as some media have done since about 2000. But even in good times, almost all broadcast news and most national and international newspaper stories that have or should have a religion dimension are produced by reporters from other beats who have no special knowledge of or interest in religion. As a result, stories are sometimes missed or mangled in ways that fuel public criticism.

While most journalists approve of the broader definition of religion and the depth-feature and hard-news emphasis, the public has been more divided. Surveys conducted by Stewart M. Hoover during the 1980s indicate that the public considers religion news more important than sports news. Readership is about equal. But in terms of satisfaction, sports news moves to the top of a list of nine kinds of specialty news while religion news falls to the bottom. Here, the problem is that one group likes the broad definition and the more substantive reporting, but notices the instances of shoddy coverage and wants better. But another and more vocal group sees coverage of religions and forms of religi-

osity that are outside the mainstream and hard news stories, especially when they touch on scandal, as evidence of anti-Christian bias in spite of surveys showing that most religion reporters are religious and most of those are Christian.

Although research indicates people are highly unlikely to choose or abandon a faith because of something they have seen or heard from the mass media, there is evidence that some people create their own religious worldview by incorporating things they have learned from the media into whatever belief system they already have. However, research also indicates that, by consistently using certain frames or *topoi* that are themselves derived from a Judeo-Christian culture, religion journalism supports conventional notions of religiosity; emphasis on activities and issues important to conservative Christians and reliance on them as spokespersons may even suggest that conservative Protestantism is synonymous with true Christianity.

Nevertheless, concerns about mass media effects translate into a substantial market for religious media, which have been readily available in America at least since Harvard set up its printing press shortly after the university founding in 1636. Like religion news in the secular press, religious media flourish during times of heightened religious fervor. If the Second Great Awakening was "the age of religious journalism," as scholars have often dubbed it, the late 1900s and early 2000s can appropriately be called "the second great age of religious journalism."

Although the number and popularity of Muslim and Buddhist publications grew rapidly during the period, once again it is the Evangelical Protestant media that really define this second period of religious journalism. However, judging their quality is more difficult. Technically, many of them are as good or better than secular media. But because these are religious media, their quality must also be judged by religious standards—by whether or not they present a particular religious understanding properly and in doing so achieve their intended purpose. Here, research evidence is again mixed. While studies show that people do learn from the media they attend to, they also show that people tend to choose media that support their basic beliefs. Therefore, there is little evidence that religious media alone convert anyone to a faith. There is, however, evidence that these media reaffirm and strengthen the beliefs their fans already have as a result of socialization through home and church, and then mobilize them to action in ways that can have real impacts.

The continued coexistence of religious journalism and religion journalism as complementary and sometimes competitive media systems can be construed as both effect and cause of what sociologist James Davison Hunter has dubbed a culture war. More benignly, it can also be taken as a testimony to the robustness of the freedom of religion and press Americans enjoy as a result of the First Amendment to the Constitution of the United States.

JUDITH M. BUDDENBAUM

See also Media; Media Activism; Media Literacy; Newspapers

Further Reading

Abelman, R., & Hoover, S. M. (Eds.). (1990). *Religious television: Controversies and conclusions*. Norwood, NJ: Ablex.

Buddenbaum, J. M. (1986). Analysis of religion news coverage in three newspapers. *Journalism Quarterly, 63*(3), 600–606.

Buddenbaum, J. M. (1987). Judge…what their acts will justify: The religion journalism of James Gordon Bennett. *Journalism History, 14*(3–4), 54–67.

Buddenbaum, J. M. (1990). Network news coverage of religion. In J. P. Ferre (Ed.), *Channels of belief: Religion and American commercial television* (pp. 57–78). Ames: Iowa State University Press.

Buddenbaum, J. M. (1990). Of Christian freedom fighters and Marxist terrorists: The image of SWAPO and the Namibian independence movement in the religious and secular press. In Y. Alexander & R. Picard (Eds.), *In the camera's eye: News coverage of terrorist events* (pp. 131–150). Washington, DC: Brassey's.

Buddenbaum, J. M. (1998). *Reporting religion news: An introduction for journalists*. Ames: Iowa State University Press.

Buddenbaum, J. M. (2003). Religion. In F. Cropp, C. M. Frisby, & D. Mills (Eds.), *Cross-cultural journalism* (pp. 159–184). Ames: Iowa State Press.

Buddenbaum, J. M., & Mason, D. L. (Eds.). (1999). *Readings on religion as news*. Ames: Iowa State University Press.

Dart, J., & Allen, J. (2000). *Bridging the gap: Religion and the news media*. Nashville, TN: Freedom Forum First Amendment Center of Vanderbilt University.

Fackler, M., & Lippy, C. H. (Eds.). (1995). *Popular religious magazines of the United States*. Westport, CT: Greenwood.

Hafez, K. (2000). *Islam and the West in the mass media: Fragmented images in a globalizing world*. Cresskill, NJ: Hampton.

Hoover, S. M. (1988). *Mass media religion: The social sources of the electronic church*. Newbury Park, CA: Sage.

Hoover, S. M. (1998). *Religion in the news: Faith and journalism in American public discourse*. Thousand Oaks, CA: Sage.

Hubbard, B. J. (Ed.). (1990). *Reporting religion: Facts and faith*. Sonoma, CA: Polebridge.

Hunter, J. D. (1991). *Culture wars: The struggle to define America*. New York: Basic.

Marty, M. E. (1963). *The religious press in America*. New York: Holt, Rinehart, & Winston.

Nord, D. P. (2004). *Faith in reading: Religious publishing and the birth of mass media, 1790–1860*. New York: Oxford University Press.

Olasky, M. (1988). *Prodigal press: The anti-Christian bias of the American news media*. Wheaton, IL: Crossway.

Said, E. W. (1997). *Covering Islam: How the media and the experts determine how we see the rest of the world* (2nd ed.). London: Vintage.

Schultze, Q. J. (Ed.). (1990). *American Evangelicals and the mass media*. Grand Rapids, MI: Academie.

Silk, M. (1995). *Unsecular media: Making news of religion in America*. Urbana: University of Illinois Press.

Silk, M. (Ed.). (2000). *Religion on the international news agenda*. Hartford, CT: Leonard E. Greenberg Center for the Study of Religion in Public Life of Trinity College.

Sloan, W. D. (1991). The New England Courant: Voice of Anglicanism. *American Journalism, 8*(2–3), 108–141.

Sloan, W. D. (Ed.). (2000). *Media and religion in American history*. Northport, AL: Vision.

Underwood, D. (2002). *From Yahweh to Yahoo: The religious roots of the secular press*. Urbana: University of Illinois Press.

Judaism (Communication & Mass Media)

Judaism's perspective on communication and mass media may be divided between motifs in the Old Testament comprising communications, and principles of Jewish religious law concerning behavior of mass media.

The Jewish religion does not preach social asceticism or a social isolation but encourages social participation and, therefore, communication between men. In order to regulate social communication a number or principles may be extrapolated in Jewish sources. Given that the Five Books of Moses, or Torah, the prophets, and later Jewish law works like the Mishnah and Talmud, and such codifers as Maimonides predated the mass media age, it is necessary, in determining Judaism's view of mass media to locate points of contacts between Judaism and social communication.

The Torah and Communication

Modern ideas of communication proliferate in the Bible. These include the question of complete and honest reporting. The sin of the misreporting by ten out of the twelve spies about the Promised Land was not only that they added their own ideological views to their factual report but also, according to the Bible commentator Abravnel, that instead of reporting back directly to Moses they went public with their report to all the Israelites, generating public pressure against Moses. Calls to public opinion were part and parcel of public life in ancient Israel. Korach, in charging that Moses exploited his position, defamed Moses about a woman who had nothing and was forced to give up her sheep to the priest (*Yalkut Shimeoni* commentary on Numbers, Chapter 16). The deliverances of the Jews from Egypt and in the Purim saga at the city of Shushan, Persia were examples of messages by God to international public opinion. Another media-related concept found in the Bible is slander—the most famous case being when Miriam spoke badly of Moses for "the Cushan woman he married," for which she was smitten with leprosy (Numbers 12:1).

Divine Communication

Communication has played an important role in the development of Judaism. Communication by God is of a number of types: first, informational, such as details of statements and biblical events; it is noteworthy is that almost every command to Moses is accompanied by the word "to say," i.e., to pass on, or communicate, to others. Second, emotional, such as the binding of Isaac, the Crossing of the Red Sea, the capture of the Promised Land; in chronicling such dramatic events, the Bible is not very different from the news media. Third, values or commandments (mitzvot), such as the six hundred thirteen positive and negative commands providing a code of spiritual and social behavior. For example, the verse "Hear O' Israel, the Lord is Our God, the Lord is One" (Deuteronomy 6:4) commands belief in His omnipotence. As an ethical religion, Judaism regulates man's relationship with God and with his fellow man. While not rejecting the "good life," the Jewish weltanschauung is that man should use his free choice to raise his stature to emulate the characteristics of the infinite God.

God is an activist god both for the Jewish people as a whole and in the life of individual Jews. Given both a desire for knowledge about God and the infiniteness of God, the acts and messages of God are the only knowledge about him and his attributes. The prophets have fulfilled a primary role as messengers of God (Haggai 1:13) and as witnesses of God's power and mercy. Yet the prophet was more than a messenger; he was a par-

ticipant standing in the presence of God (Jeremiah 15:19). His communication was not neutral but comprised ethical monotheism or a religion of morality, raising the spiritual standards and moral fiber. Since the end of Jewish prophecy in the fourth century BCE, the hidden divine meaning of events cannot be extrapolated, and prophecy was replaced by faith (*emunah*) and thrice-daily prayer as the staple ingredient of the relationship between the Jewish people and God.

Halakhah and Mass Media

The main spheres of social communication where Jewish religious law (*halakhah*) has legalized are firstly, the individual's right to privacy and his social reputation, and secondly, drawing on the biblical precept that "the camp shall be holy" (Deuteronomy 23:15), that sexual modesty should characterize media content. A third sphere concerns the functioning and exposure to the media on the Sabbath and holy days. This suggests that the overlap between mass media behavior and Judaism appears conflictual. To be sure, where there is a confluence of interests between Judaism and mass media—such as the provision of information about events and societies which contributes to understanding and the building of peaceful relationships—this is not generally identified as a specifically religious goal.

The Right to Know and the Right to Privacy

The major innovation of Jewish theology in mass media behavior—which later influenced also Islam—concerns the divulging of previously unknown information. Leviticus 19:16, in warning against not being "a talebearer among your people, or standing idly by the blood of your neighbour," imposes substantial limits on the passage of information. The rabbis have divided types of information into a number of categories. Most severe is divulging secret information to the wider public which is intended or has the effect of damaging somebody's reputation (*loshon hara*). When Miriam spoke ill of Moses for "the Cushan woman he married," she was smitten with leprosy. Also forbidden, but with lesser severity, is the disclosure of even positive information about somebody if it will indirectly lead others to voice negative opinion about that individual (*rehilut*) (Israel Meir Ha-Kohen, 1873).

In contrast to modern society, characterized by the right to privacy as subservient to the right to know, in Judaism the right to know is subservient to the right to privacy. Invasion of privacy is regarded as sinful;

information and photos obtained from inside a neighbor's private territory is private, its publication being tantamount to an invasion of privacy, and gossip (Talmud Tractate Babba Bathra 60a). These restrictions in Judaism profoundly affect the work of the professional journalist in disclosing previously unpublished information. The journalist draws much of his information from sources who disclose selectively, often in order to weaken a political opponent. However, once the information is known to three people it is no longer forbidden, and it is permitted to be heard. As the Talmud Tractate Erachin (16a) notes, once the information is known to three people, it is the same as announcing it to the world." Information therefore takes on a relative value. The journalist and his informant have carried out a most heinous act in making the information public, but that same information may be heard by other people.

While modern society permits everything to be published apart from that which personally damages somebody's reputation—including a large middle category of information which is not of vital importance to know—Judaism does not acknowledge an automatic right to this middle category of information. Scholars have differed regarding the middle category of information. Maimonides, for example, distinguished between information about "distant" events, such as one associated with the elite, and about individuals "nearer" to the discloser of the information of which it is forbidden. While also not favoring this, Maimonides says that this category is not forbidden by Jewish law. More recently, the stringent approach represented by Israel Meir Ha-Kohen (1838–1933), known as the Chofez Hayim, of Vilna, contrasts with Abraham Kook (1865–1935), the chief rabbi of Palestine during the British mandate period, who recognized that the press had an integral part to play in modern nation-building, and favored that media behavior should be more attuned to Jewish values.

In Judaism the only rights to know are: first, the right to know Jewish knowledge, i.e., the Torah and national laws; and secondly, information which if kept secret would cause damage to somebody. In the latter, the Bible acknowledges the fourth estate role, or societal watchdog, fulfilled by the media (Korngott, 1993). The Torah says that it is not only permitted to publish information which if kept unpublished would damage society but obligatory. That the same verse (Leviticus 19:16) which prohibits the disclosure of secret information continues "...do not stand idly by the blood of your neighbor," and suggests that if somebody, including a journalist, hears of information, such as cor-

ruption committed by a government minister or an official, he has an obligation to take steps to rectify the situation. The Bible is possibly unique in its time period in not only praising its heroes but also criticizing them. There is a long tradition of freedom of expression by the prophets speaking out against wrongdoings of the leadership and the people, and against the exploitation of the poor. Public accountability was reflected, for example, in the running of the Temple treasury, with the priest responsible for having his priestly garments checked for any secret pockets in order that even undesirable elements would not suspect that if he was rich the wealth came from Temple funds, or that if he was poor it wasn't because he sinned and took Temple wealth (Talmud Tractate Shekalim Chapter 3: Mishna 2).

If the matter can be dealt with by other means than press disclosure this is preferred. If not, media disclosure is necessary. Thus, Judaism distinguishes between the large flow of otherwise interesting information disclosed by the media which does not come under this category, disclosure of which it prohibits, and the much smaller category of information of social value (Chwat, 1995). Moreover, much depends on the motives of the journalist in disclosing the information. Did the journalist do it for the watchdog function or his own professional need to publish exclusive information? To avoid committing *loshon hora*, the Chofez Hayim conditions that such information be published only if, in addition to the information being entirely accurate, that in disclosing it the reporter has the public good as his goal, and that there is no other way to achieve the social goal other than by going public. Information that reveals that a public official is not capable of functioning if given to him privately, might persuade him to stand down.

A related question which has occupied some rabbis today concerns the disclosure of information of corruption or sexual improprieties committed by rabbis. Such disclosures defame the religion and even God (*hilul hashem*), are regarded with considerable gravity. Instead of emulating a rabbi-like figurehead as somebody behaving in God's way, people will emulate the wrong deed. Moreover, there may be no way to correct inappropriate behavior by a specific individual other than by going public with the wrong deed. Over the centuries rabbis have generally favored covering up rather than disclosure even if it may be in the social interest for people to know. By contrast, modern society is characterised by such matters being brought to public attention rather than being ignored. Even the Bible

The flag of the State of Israel. *Courtesy of Holger Franke/ istockphoto.com.*

was not averse to publishing details of the sins of the righteous as means toward moral teaching. One of a number of examples is Moses's sin in smiting the Rock instead of speaking to the Rock to bring forth water, which would have otherwise publicized a miracle—a means toward moral teaching. Another concerns the public dimension to the punishment given to idol-worshippers: "the idol-worshipper shall be put to death—the hand of the judges being first and after them all of Israel, and all Israel shall hear and see, and there shall not be evil any longer" (Deuteronomy 17:7). Moreover, there is a Jewish principle of collective responsibility, according to which a Jew is responsible for warning his fellow Jew about his wrongdoing, and that failing to do so makes the former himself punishable by heavenly decree.

Sexual Modesty

Although the Jewish tradition is critical of sexual exposure in the news media, notably in film and in photographs, this is less obvious than it appears. Physical pleasure from sexual relations within marriage is regarded in a positive light in Judaism. Biblical discussion of modesty as an ethical value concerns mostly the manner in which a person behaves in his social relations. Yet, the Israelite camp in the wilderness in "which God walked shall be holy . . . that God should

not see anything unseemly and turn Himself away from you" [Deuteronomy 23:15] is an allusion to nudity being looked on negatively. A concern of Jewish teaching is that as a result of his exposure to images alluding to sex, a man could be sexually aroused to masturbation or "improper emission of seed" (onanism) [Genesis 38:9]. Different branches of Judaism interpret the requirement of sexual modesty differently. Orthodox Judaism forbids a man to look on a female immodestly attired; in the ultra-Orthodox community it includes the uncovered hair of a married woman. Similarly, they forbid a man to listen to a woman singer lest he be sexually aroused; the modern Orthodox community permit this if the song is prerecorded and the listener does not know how the singer looks. The same prohibition on men does not apply on women. These restrictions raise profound artistic questions of how love can be portrayed and expressed in a manner which is religiously acceptable. Conservative and Reform Judaism takes a more liberal attitude, but the latter, in defending women's rights, takes a stand on the sexploitation of women in the media.

The Haredi Community. Of all the religious streams, the Haredi (Hebrew for fearful ones) community or ultra-Orthodox Jews have felt most threatened by changing mass media. Reflecting its philosophy of withdrawal from modernity, seeking to maintain religious values in a cultural ghetto framework, their rabbis have over the years issued religious decrees (*pesuk din*) against media as a threat to Torah family values. From the appearance of newspapers in the nineteenth century, through to the appearance of radio and television, and latterly video, computers and the Internet, haredi rabbis have enacted such decrees against media. The modern orthodox (*dati leumi*) rabbis have not issued legal rulings regarding media exposure, which reflects their broader philosophy of seeking to create a synthesis between Judaism and modernity. Yet some of their rabbis, particularly those identified with the Hardal (*haredi leumi*) substream encourage controlling exposure particularly of children to the general media.

When Israel Television was established in 1968, haredi rabbis banned their followers from watching television because its content was considered inappropriate. The ban on television was the most successful of the bans against media with the overwhelming number of Haredim respecting it. The earlier ban on radio—drawing on the prohibition against hearing gossip (*loshon hara*)—while enjoying some respect, is much less respected than the TV ban because radio is more of an informational than entertainment tool. The ongoing political-defence problems of the country make it more difficult for people to adhere to the ban.

When videos cameras were produced—with many haredi families using them to record family celebrations—no rabbinical ban was introduced initially because their usage could be controlled. However, after it was discovered that television programs could be seen if videos were plugged into computers, haredi rabbis in 1993 banned videos.

In 1998 haredi rabbis imposed a ban on computers. Initially, it covered the computer in its entirety but the recognition that computers are an integral part of modern business life led to a revision, and they distinguished between allowing computers in business but not at home. Not all haredi rabbis agreed to the ban, notably haredi rabbis from a Sephardi (or non-Ashkenazi) background. There is a recognition that the computer is a useful tool for religious study. For example, the Bar-Ilan University CD-rom Responsa Project is a database of the most comprehensive collection of traditional texts from the Bible, biblical commentaries, Mishnah, the Babylonian and Jerusalem Talmuds, and later Jewish codes, covering 3,300 years of Jewish written scholarship. The development of the Internet resulted in a special *bet din* (religious law court) of haredi rabbis to issue a ban on its use. It was regarded by them as a far worse

moral threat than television: whereas television was supervised, the Internet enabled access to pornographic sites. Haredi rabbis have been faced with the realisation that the ban on computers and Internet has not been entirely accepted—an estimated 40 percent of haredi houses in Israel have personal computers at home. Parallel to the rabbinical bans upon computers have been a number of attempts by haredi entrepreneurs of computer filtering programs.

In 2002 haredi rabbis forbade talmudical college students from using mobile phones, seeing them as a threatening the appropriate atmosphere for the tamudical college study hall. But as the mobile phone's capabilities widened, notably providing Internet access, haredi rabbis saw the mobile phone as a threat to the entire community and established a rabbinical committee for communication affairs which began negotiating with mobile phone companies to provide only land telephone lines. The variegated bans by haredi rabbis against new media forms have caused the wider meaning of modesty in Judaism, as concerning personal behavior such as regarding wealth and self-assessment, to be somewhat lost in the overwhelming concern about sexual modesty.

Accuracy, Advertising, and Copyright Ownership

Knowledge and information also possess Jewish ethical dimensions in terms of copyright ownership and accuracy. Information reported in the media has to be complete, accurate and objective, the penumbra of deceit and bias, in order to avoid the audience being deceived. The requirement for accuracy is problematic when a news organization, under tight deadlines, faces news sources which do not wish to give their account of events. *Halakhah* rules that compensation be given if somebody's reputation was damaged as a result of inaccurate reporting.

The problem of deception has taken on special importance in advertising and public relations. Whereas Judaism allows products to be promoted attractively to draw custom, it disallows giving false information resulting in a person deciding to, say, buy a product which he would not otherwise do (*geneivat daat*), if he had complete information.

Judaism recognizes a prohibition of stealing knowledge. Material, such as a book or song, which is the exclusive property of one person may not be copied without their permission. Where news coverage concerns events are publicly known no claim to copyright ownership may be made. But investigative journalism in which one news organization is the exclusive source of the information may claim exclusivity. "News borrowing" of information in the latter category is, therefore, only permitted where such permission has been obtained. Rabbis have condemned as stealing the copying for commercial purposes of entire computer programs. However, if only a small section of a program is copied for ad hoc use there is greater leniency. Printed Bible-related material is regarded by rabbis as not being the exclusive property of one party, and, therefore, no copyright stipulation exists for Bible-related materials. Some rabbis exclude serrmons and other material authored by a specific rabbi which they say should not be published without the author's permission.

Media Exposure on the Sabbath

The prohibition of work on the Sabbath Day, as enjoined by the fourth of the Ten Commandments (Exodus 20:8), has implications for the Jew's exposure to the media on the Sabbath and holy days. The prohibition of work—or "acts of creativity" as defined by Jewish law—includes activating electricity on the Sabbath and holy days, with the result that television and radio cannot be switched on (Auerbach, 1996), or the Internet accessed. Reform Judaism, however, does not rule against using electronic media. Since the Sabbath Day is not only characterized by restrictions on work but also as a spiritual experience of prayer, study and rest on the holy day, haredi rabbis have questioned whether such mundane activities as newspaper exposure take away from the Sabbath atmosphere. Furthermore, even though a radio or television set could theoretically either be left on from before the Sabbath, or be turned on automatically by a time-clock (the device by which many Jews have heating and lighting on the Sabbath), it would distract from the Sabbath experience, unless the program is of a religious nature. (In Israel the electronic media functions on the Sabbath and holy days, with the single exception of the Yom Kippur fast day, but newspapers are not published.) In one instance during the 1991 Gulf War, when Israel's civilian population was targeted by Iraqi missiles, rabbis allowed for the radio to be left on in order for the people to follow the instructions of the emergency forces. Certain types of information in newspapers, such as advertisements or economic and other articles directly related to an individual Jew's work, are regarded as inappropriate reading lest he come to make even a mental decision regarding work.

A Jew may not benefit on the Sabbath from work carried out specifically for him, such as having a newspaper delivered to his house or from news gathered on the Sabbath. The subject of Sabbath observance in the modern technological age is one that occupies rabbis today. Amongst media-related questions are whether a religious Jew may give an interview to a broadcast journalist on the weekday in the knowledge that it will be broadcast on the Sabbath; and whether a Jew living in Israel may listen or see a rebroadcasting of a program first broadcast by Jews on the Sabbath.

Cyberspace Prayer

Judaism does not recognize the idea of a "virtual synagogue" existing in cyberspace. Orthodox rabbis (*haredi* and *dati leumi*) do not allow for participation in religious services except for those physically present. To fulfil a person's obligation to hear the prayer reader, or cantor, that person has to be able to hear the cantor's voice directly, not a voice filtered by, say, a microphone. For a person who does not wish to fulfill his obligation but merely wants to say "amen" it is not necessary to hear the voice directly; in the giant synagogue in Alexandria, Egypt, one who did not hear the blessing knew when to answer "amen" when an officiant waved a flag. Conservative Judaism allows for participation in a religious service from a distance as long as there is an audio connection, preferably two-way; participation by written communication, such as e-mail and chat room, does not suffice. Moreover, like the orthodox, the Conservative rabbinate insist on the basic requirement for a Jewish religious service of a quorum, or ten men (*minyan*), physically gathered together (Reisner, 2001).

Writing the Divine Name

An extension of the Jewish law prohibition to pronounce the Holy Name, the Tetragrammaton, Jewish law regards as sacrilegious the destruction of texts with other names of God. To overcome the problem, texts such as prayer books are by tradition buried in a cemetary. In the past orthodox rabbis debated whether or not newspapers should print sermons and other religious material. The preferred means of the religious media is to use God's name in an abbreviated form (for example, G-d). Some rabbis limit the prohibition to the printing of full Scriptural verses and not to other types of references to God. With the introduction of computers and Internet, rabbis have addressed the question of the name of God appearing on screen, and have ruled that the prohibition on erasing God's name occurs in print, not when in electronic form, which is not regarded as writing since this involves firing electrons on a luminous substance painted on the inside of the screen which lights up in the form of letters. The leniency does not extend to material saved to disk.

YOEL COHEN

See also Israel, Media in

Further Reading

Ariel, A. (2001). *Damaging somebody's reputation in the public sphere*. Tzohar (5–6).

Auerbach, S.Z. (1996). Radio broadcasts on the Sabbath. Alon Shevut, *Tehumim* (16).

Barkai Y., Priman M. (2003) Media events in the Bible. *Mayim Medaliah*, (15).

Chwat, A.I., (1995). Newspapers & news—an obligation or a prohibition. Elkana, *T'Lalei Orot*.

Israel Meir Ha-Kohen, (1873). *Chofez Hayim,* Vilna. For an English edition: Z. Pliskin. (1975). *Guard your tongue: A practical guide to the laws of* loshon hara *based on the Chofez Hayim*. Jerusalem: Aish HaTorah.

Korngott, E. M. H. (1993). *The Light of Ezekiel: Contemporary issues in Jewish law*. Petach Tiqva, pages 329–366.

Reisner, A.I. (2001). *Wired to the* Kadosh Barukh Hu *[God]: Minyan via Internet*. Committee on Jewish Law and Standards. The Rabbinical Assembly of America.

Knowledge

The study of knowledge raises multiple issues and questions about the framework we use to make sense of the world. This includes discussions about worldviews, paradigms, and how a person's presuppositions determine what will be accepted as knowledge. Discussions about knowledge often compare and contrast various frameworks for knowing, including the theistic, modernist, and postmodernist structures and how these perspectives dramatically change what someone accepts as knowledge. Knowledge that comes from the intersection of religious conviction, communication, and media touches on the very core of how we know as humans. This concept will be examined from a religious perspective and then from a communication and media perspective.

Religious Assumptions

The religious emphasis on knowledge has two divisions (particularly in the Western Orthodox Christian perspective) that include the key Greek words used to talk about knowledge and systematic theology's basis for understanding knowledge.

Key Greek Words

Gnosko and *epignosko* are the two words translated as "knowledge." *Gnosko* is understood to be a "seeking to know," an inquiry, or an investigation. *Epignosis*, on the other hand, denotes exact or full knowledge, discernment, or recognition—the latter being a greater participation by the knower in that which is known, thus showing greater influence over the person or object known. Other words related to knowledge are belief (*doxa*), to understand (*epistamai*), and to perceive (*oida*). These words depict various degrees of knowing and can be further investigated for insight. Essentially, though, the key Greek words depict knowledge both as complete and as an ongoing process. This does not mean that knowledge is depicted as subjective and relative; rather, it is objective and static in the mind of God but unfolding and limited for humanity. This is explained more clearly from the discipline of systematic theology.

Systematic Theology's Explanation

Western Christianity's systematic theology divides knowledge into two categories: that which comes from general revelation and that which comes by special revelation. The emphasis on Western theology here is significant because Eastern religions generally do not recognize special (or particular) revelation as a distinct theological category or as a separate knowledge that is revealed to a distinct people chosen by God.

Western Christianity has come to appreciate Augustine's comment that "all truth is God's truth," but its theologians also understand that humans know imperfectly because we are limited by our incarnated existence. This is the idea of general knowledge; it is seen as imperfect and incomplete because humans are flawed and rebellious against God. The theological idea of common grace presumes that God reveals knowledge to all of humanity in and through ordinary means and objects of life. The apostle Paul refers to this in Romans 1, when he talks about how God has revealed knowledge of Himself to all of humanity. This results in knowledge about the existence of God, God's creation, and human creative activities such as those found in the arts and the sciences. General knowledge helps humanity to understand the seasons, how they change and the fact that rain falls on the godly and the ungodly alike. These things are what we usually recognize and accept as knowledge and hold in common with believers and unbelievers alike.

Special revelation, on the other hand, is that particular knowledge about salvation or other aspects of God's plan for His people that are revealed through direct speech from God (for example, Moses and the burning bush), the words of the prophets (those who speak God's words), the teaching and preaching of the apostles, and, most significantly, through the incarnation of the God-man, Jesus. The Gospel of John talks about Jesus as the *logos*, the special revelation of God to humanity. Special revelation does not necessarily give a believer greater insight into mathematics, science, or the arts than that known by the nonbeliever, but it does give particular knowledge about God's plan of salvation and a person's eternal destiny. Jesus, as the special revelation of God, shows us that knowledge is not just a collection of data and facts but that it is relational and embodied in a God-man, Jesus.

The intersection with communication and media becomes significant because general knowledge is available from God to all who are alive by means of the knowledge of God that is "inborn" and available to all (Romans 1:18–ff). Special revelation, on the other hand, is revealed through two particular means: the embodied person of Jesus Christ and the secondary means of humans using symbols in order to communicate the special revelation with other humans. It is this secondary means of conveying God's special revelation that employs communication (symbolic interaction) and the media.

Communication and Media

Communication scholars generally tap into the philosophical arguments from the discipline of epistemology to talk about the basis for knowledge. Cherwitz and Hikins (1986) define knowledge as "justified true belief" and distinguish between belief (mere *doxa*), true belief, and justified true belief. Neither "belief" nor "true belief" is qualified to count as knowledge, they contend. Knowledge stands apart from these other two because it is not only believed, it is not only true, but it is justified by some means of evidence to others. These

two scholars argue for the need for a fair and just approach to argumentation to help us "come to know." Their perspective on knowledge is classified as "rhetorical perspectivism" and is classified as a realist perspective rather than a relativist or intersubjectivist approach to knowledge. Within the study of communication there are three main positions about knowledge. Knowledge is realist (based on a knowable world that stands apart from the knower) or it is subjective (based only on how the knower generates meaning) or it is intersubjective (how groups of people agree on a meaning for the phenomenon they encounter).

Esther Meek (2003), influenced by the philosopher Michael Polanyi and the theologian John Frame, argues for a definition of knowing as "the responsible human struggle to rely on clues, to focus on a coherent pattern and to submit to its reality." She also contends that the information only attains the status of knowledge through the help of authoritative guides in our lives who help us recognize and understand the "coherent patterns." All of these scholars, among many others, recognize the place that other humans have in shaping what we accept as knowledge.

The role of the media becomes significant in all of these interactions because the media presents data through sounds and images that we can choose to interpret as true and accurate or that we reject as inaccurate. The various media that exist dominate our ability to know what is taking place in the world and place an emphasis on the visual means of knowing. Most any information conveyed will more likely be conveyed through some form of media communication rather than face-to-face interaction. This places the media in a powerful position to determine what we know and how we come to know.

Intersection Between Religion, Communication, and Media

The intersection between religion, communication, and media is intriguing because a post-Christian culture tends to disregard those who believe in special revelation and accept those who emphasize that which is deemed public knowledge. Thus, what is accepted as knowledge becomes dependent upon those who are able to convince a viewing and listening audience that what they have to say is true. This can become a vicious cycle because if the audience will only pay attention to that media which reinforces its own presuppositions, then those who offer a differing opinion about knowledge may be silenced. On the other hand, if various voices are heard through the media, then audience presuppositions may be challenged and definitions of "public knowledge" are more likely to be changed.

MARK A. GRING

See also Information; Libraries

Further Reading

Berkhof, L. (1996). *Systematic theology*. Grand Rapids, MI: William B. Eerdmans Publishing Co.

Calvin, J. (1999). *Calvin: Institutes of the Christian religion* (Vols. I & II; J. T. McNeill, Ed.; F. L. Battles, Trans.). Louisville, KY: Westminster John Knox Press. (Original work published 1585.)

Cherwitz, R., & Hikins, J. W. (1986). *Communication and knowledge: An investigation into rhetorical epistemology*. Columbia: University of South Carolina Press.

Clark, G. H. (1986). *Religion, reason and revelation*. Jefferson, MD: The Trinity Foundation.

Frame, J. M. (1987). *The doctrine of the knowledge of God*. Phillipsburg, NJ: Presbyterian and Reformed Publishing Company.

Kittle, G. (Ed.). (1964). *Theological dictionary of the New Testament* (Vol. 1; G. W. Bromiley, Trans.). Grand Rapids, MI: William B. Eerdmans Publishing Co.

Kuhn, T. S. (1962). *The structure of scientific revolutions*. Chicago: University of Chicago Press.

Kuyper, A. (1931). *Lectures on Calvinism*. Grand Rapids, MI: William B. Eerdmans Publishing Co.

Meek, E. L. (2003). *Longing to know: The philosophy of knowledge for ordinary people*. Grand Rapids, MI: Brazos Press.

Van Til, C. (1969). *A Christian theory of knowledge*. Phillipsburg, PA: Presbyterian and Reformed Publishing Co.

Vine, W. E. (n.d.). *Vine's expository dictionary of New Testament words*. McLean, VA: MacDonald Publishing Company.

Libraries

The purpose of all religious rites and ceremonies is that of communication, whether oral or written. From the beginning of time, men and women have had thoughts and feelings of worship through the divine illumination of both sight and knowledge. And these were shared among men and women and became words, which in turn became the languages of communication often conveying religious or spiritual messages. Humans sought to preserve these spoken words, so they invented symbols and began to inscribe them onto many kinds of media: tortoise shells, birch bark, tablets of stone, metal, papyrus scrolls, animal skins, and paper. Writings on paper and papyrus then became books and scrolls, which were copied and kept in priestly and princely libraries. Libraries began with the externals of spirituality called religion. As religions and civilizations evolved and became more literate, these private libraries then evolved into temple, public and university libraries, enabling further religious and intellectual progress of humankind's mind and soul.

Libraries then attained the laudable distinction of being many things, at many times, to all people: congregations of disparate media, services for communicating knowledge, and sanctuaries of learning. "Libraries…exist to bring humankind closer to the experience of both humanity and divinity" (Tucker 2000, 3). Even the study of religious texts could be worship, for Einstein said that the pursuit of truth and beauty is a sphere of activity in which we are permitted to remain children all our lives. This "holy reading" is the key and harks back to the Garden of Eden when Yahweh appointed Adam and Eve to name and classify the animals of the earth. Literacy of any kind imparts a portion of divine authority to every person, whose Bible, Qur'an, Book of Mormon, hymnal, psaltery, the *Bhagavad Gita*, missal, books of hours, prayer book, the Tripitaka, and other sacred writings mirror the important tasks of Adam and Eve. Martin Luther went so far as to say that the Levites of ancient Israel not only were given stewardship over the ark of the covenant, but over the early records that later made up Hebrew Scriptures.

If one of the chief uses of religion is to attack the ageless problems of humanity, libraries are important media as well as a means of communication. The story of libraries at their best is one of diversity, freedom, tolerance, and egalitarianism: they are counter-institutions to the Tower of Babel by bringing together nations, cultures, languages, and religions, as well as a non-censoring environment for learning. Whether public and private, ecclesiastical or monastic, academic or princely, libraries lead to education, awareness, understanding, and a respect and reverence (worship) for all things on earth and in heaven. While helping combine the life of the mind with the life of the spirit, libraries provide information, knowledge, and wisdom that can improve our judgment in many avenues of life. We "don't know what we don't know," but libraries have always helped to cross that threshold, sometimes merely through chance discovery (serendipity) and timeliness (synchronicity), often called "divine inspiration" in many religions. A major emphasis of the Reformation leaders, especially of Luther and Melanchthon, was on the utility of books and libraries for the new faith.

History of Religious Libraries

In the linear march of history, modern man believes that the twenty-first century has to be the pinnacle of a

L

217

gradual progression of religious enlightenment. However, there were periods in ancient times when religious groups began to create their own libraries: the library at Shuruppak and Eresh in Mesopotamia in 2500 BCE, the temple libraries in Egypt (1256 BCE), which contained religious and astronomical texts, as well as a tradition that eventually resulted in the Chenoboskian (Nag Hammadi) library of codices. The Hittite Empire was very literary as well, possessing both archives *and* a library of mythological and religious texts, while Ashurbanipal boasted the first systematically collected library in the ancient Near East (Nineveh, 639 BCE). Qumran had its library of Dead Sea scrolls. In Nepal manuscripts existed on Tantrism, philosophy, Sanskrit grammar, astrology, rituals, religion, medicine, and Vedic literature. Religious libraries in India, China, Tibet, and Nepal may even have pre-dated Near Eastern libraries, although libraries in Africa appeared much later because of the predominance of an oral tradition. (Alex Haley in *Roots* characterized African oral *griots* as living, walking archives of oral genealogical and religious history, and wrote that "When a griot dies, it is as if a library has burned to the ground.") During the Medieval period when Western civilization was in a "dark age," the Arab-Islamic civilization of the Abbasids flourished in their capital of Baghdad, where sixty-three libraries housing large collections of books and manuscripts were open to Islamic scholars and the public alike. In 1037 the Sofia Cathedral in Kiev contained a library, and libraries and translation centers sprang up in Toledo, Segovia, and Cordoba, where Jewish, Muslim, Slavic, Greek, and Christian scholars worked respectfully side by side, ensuring a veritable "apostolic succession" of Western culture (twelfth and thirteenth centuries). Such is the diverse history of libraries, which eventually gave rise to famous religious collections such as the Vatican Library, the Bodleian Library, and the Abbey of Kells in Ireland.

Religious Libraries Today

The philosophy of libraries in the twenty-first century insists that libraries are to be places of pluralism, tolerance, diversity, and ecumenism. They never exist for themselves but to serve the interests of the patron, satisfying both intellectual and spiritual curiosity. Much more than collections of books, they fulfill the following in a quiet, humble, and worshipful manner:

- redeemers and restorers from society's ills, especially ignorance, intolerance, indifference and illiteracy;

- providers of checks and balances in a less political manner than government or ecclesiastical institution;

- facilitators, along with laboratories, to help speculations become truths and better understandings of basic realities;

- reconcilers of truth and reason; and

- creators of "unlimited Paradise." (Jorge Luis Borges)

The great Swedish scientist and mystic Immanuel Swedenborg even claimed from personal revelations that great libraries exist in the world of spirit (heaven), following John the Revelator's prophecy about the books being opened on Judgment Day (Revelation 20:12).

There are more than 1,347 denominational libraries in the United States alone, a vast majority of them being housed in monasteries, convents, and theological seminaries. In addition, Christian Science reading rooms are a familiar sight in many communities. Denominational libraries and information centers thrive in many nations throughout the world, fulfilling an obligation by their religious traditions to propagate the faith and educate the faithful. Islamic libraries are among the most profuse, particularly in the Middle East, Indonesia and North Africa. In recent years Hindu libraries have been discovered in Visakhapatnam, Nepa Nagar, and Uran, India, and there are currently nine Jain libraries in Delhi. Yayasan Belia Buddhist Malaysia (also known as the Young Buddhist Foundation of Malaysia) sponsors Buddhist libraries and study centers throughout Malaysia. Sri Guru Singh Sabha in Southall, England, the leading Sikh institution in Europe, sponsors reference and lending libraries throughout the island. Finally, religious libraries are the heart and substance of universities throughout the world. It is worth noting that *Princeton Review* reported that the number one American academic library in 2004 was at a private religious university (Brigham Young University), which was founded by The Church of Jesus Christ of Latter-day Saints.

How do religious libraries affect religious practice? That depends partly upon the individual practice and worship enjoined by the thousands of different belief systems, and very often their proliferation encourages converts, although it would be more impossible to determine how much more the general use of libraries has resulted in conversions than the reading of specific books. In our more diverse and pluralistic age, libraries exist not solely for scholarly work or for the faithful to help deepen their faith through reading and contemplation of holy texts and commentaries: they just as frequently serve truth seekers from outside a given tradition, whether that be a casual Saturday reader in a public library who washes his hands before

Mission Statement of the American Theological Library Association

The mission of the American Theological Library Association is to foster the study of theology and religion by enhancing the development of theological and religious libraries and librarianship. In pursuit of this mission, the Association undertakes:

To foster the professional growth of its members, and to enhance their ability to serve their constituencies as administrators and librarians;

To advance the profession of theological librarianship, and to assist theological librarians in defining and interpreting the proper role and function of libraries in theological education;

To promote quality library and information services in support of teaching, learning, and research in theology, religion, and related disciplines and to create such tools and aids (including publications) as may be helpful in accomplishing this; (and)

To stimulate purposeful collaboration among librarians of theological libraries and religious studies collections; and to develop programmatic solutions to information-related problems common to those librarians and collections.

Source: American Theological Library Association. Retrieved December 14, 2005,
from http://www.atla.com/about.html#mission_and_ends

---

reading Luther's works, or a Baptist student at Baylor University browsing in the stacks and finding a fascinating book on the Baha'i religion. Most of this open and tolerant atmosphere has been fostered by the keepers of the books—librarians. In society today most librarians are the unsung heroes of organized knowledge and wisdom, providing access to and preservation of a given religious heritage. They have been given appellations and attributes that often evoke a sacred and religious vocation and would almost be fitting enough for royalty or even deities: missionary of the mind, apostle of culture, minister of knowledge, purveyor of light, steward of thought, lighthouse of truth. And whether a librarian fulfills his natural role or not, the Internet provides anyone, whether in a library or not, with religious texts, online praying, worship, and absolution of sins. Official websites are now commonplace for all religious traditions, supplementing the printed word in libraries and making the propagation of the faith virtually worldwide.

Future of Religious Libraries

Even as libraries embrace the information commons and the collaborative learning center as major forces for change, so are libraries and their professional organizations reaching out beyond their walls in many ways. For example, some religious libraries that are members of the American Theological Library Association (ATLA) are involved in the building up of African libraries, and their librarians attend ATLA conferences where selected denominations are chosen to offer worship services before each day's meetings, and where an interdenominational choir participates in those services. These activities support the best in library philosophy and its interdisciplinary nature, while denominational-specific professional organizations like the Association of Jewish Libraries bring together librarians in any field who happen to be Jewish.

Libraries today seem to reflect an idealism about unfettered knowledge and learning that has long been the dream of monastic and university librarians throughout the centuries. On the one hand there is increasing recognition that there is both systematic *and* revealed theology. On the other, there is the desire to work with the oral traditions of Native American and African cultures, along with their religious traditions. Without libraries man probably would have destroyed himself by now, for civilization and its many attributes cannot be truly great without great libraries. The most striking feature of the library of the twenty-first century will not be its physical form, but the intellectual ferment that takes place within both it and the people who gave it life. Its librarians will be humble and teachable seekers after eternal realities, knowing that ultimately all men are products of so-called "alien" ideas that have come by both study and by faith. Finally—and more idealistically—Joseph Knecht, in Hermann Hesse's *Glass Bead Game*, hopes that he can one day arrange and "sum up all the knowledge of time, symmetrically and synoptically, around a central idea." Then, he believes, man could "come near to perfection, pure being, and the fullness of reality." Such should be the mission statement of all libraries that seek to make learning and scholarship both a sacred activity and a form of worship.

GARY P. GILLUM

See also Information

Further Reading

ALA World Encyclopedia of Library and Information Services. (1986). Chicago: American Library Association.

Casson, L. (2001). *Libraries in the ancient world.* New Haven, CT: Yale University Press.

Maxwell, N. A. (1995). The disciple-scholar. In H. B. Eyring (Ed.), *On becoming a disciple-scholar.* Salt Lake City, UT: Bookcraft.

Polkinghorne, J. (2004). *Science and the trinity: The Christian encounter with reality.* New Haven, CT: Yale University Press.

Rubenstein, R. E. (2003). *Aristotle's children: How Christians, Muslims, and Jews rediscovered ancient wisdom and illuminated the dark ages.* Orlando, FL: Harcourt.

Schrodt, P. (1996). Theological librarianship and theological education. *Proceedings of the American Theological Library Association* (pp. 133–149). Chicago: ATLA.

Shera, J. H. (1971). *"The compleat librarian" and other essays.* Cleveland, OH: Case Western Reserve University.

Tucker, J. M. (2000). Logos, biblos, & bibliotheke: Christian influences in library development. *Proceedings of the 66th International Federation of Library Associations and Institutions Council and General Conference, Jerusalem.* Retrieved December 30, 2004, from www.ifla.org/IV/ifla66/papers/013-145e.htm

Wright, H. C. (1977). *The oral antecedents of Greek librarianship.* Provo, UT: Brigham Young University.

Literature, Religious

Religious literature frequently consists of stories published in books designed for the global marketplace. Between 1990 and 2005, religious book publishing for the mass market became highly profitable; religious-fiction profits rose 35 percent, and translations, adaptations, and interpretations crossed geographical and denominational boundaries, adding to the mixed genre of fiction and spiritual advice.

For example, a new book by a Buddhist Vietnamese monk, Thich Nhat Hanh, anticipated sales of 75,000; one by New Age writer Marianne Williamson 250,000; a book relating Disneyworld and Gospel messages by the journalist Mark Pinsky 25,000. The Dalai Lama is listed as the "author" of more than 240 book titles, all of which experience robust sales, as do books by popes, former president Jimmy Carter, and the Reverend Billy Graham. Books popularly called "religious" cater to a broad social and economic spectrum of religious and economic tastes, reaching global markets through consolidated media corporations that include publishers specializing in religion as well as standard trade publishers.

More Than Money

Mass-marketing expertise is applied to religious books as well as to Christian rock on DVDs and related media. Popularity is not a sign of higher literary worth but indicates the trend in popular taste and the marketing savvy of publishers. The market for popular literature with religious themes aimed at eighteen- to thirty-year-olds is more than $2 billion a year, according to the Christian Booksellers Association. Landmark events such as the publication of *The Da Vinci Code* typically spawn a number of counterarguments, spin-off products, and often extensive news coverage.

One series of novels has outsold all other top-thirty Christian marketplace bestsellers: Timothy LaHaye's *Left Behind* series, a storyline about the Book of Revelation and prophecies about the end of the world, sustained through twelve books and more than twenty-five children's books, resulting in a near-cult following of readers. A related category, Christian romance novels published by Harlequin, routinely sells seventy-five thousand copies in six months.

Types of Religious Literature

The intention of religious storytellers is often evangelistic; readers are potential converts. However, the better-crafted stories are written more subtly, intended to engage the reader's imagination rather than the rigors of believing in narrow doctrine or strict denominational dogma. This way of writing about religion is not new: many of the classics in literary history reflect the struggles of believers with the realities of life.

Diverse storylines of historical and romantic fiction and formulaic devices can be found in the Publishers Weekly list of the top ten Christian novels published within the past decade. For example, Tracy Groot's *Stones of My Accusers* (2004) tells the story of a man named Orion, Pontius Pilate's liaison to the Jews, whose moral lessons set a high standard for compassion. Ryan Gordon's *Eyes at the Window* (2003) is a mystery set in an Amish pioneer settlement. Another example seems drawn from the daily newspapers: Randy Singer's *Dying Declaration* (2004) is about accusations of murder brought against Fundamentalist parents when their prayers alone fail to heal their son. In Suzanne Wolf's *Unveiling* (2004), an art restorer travels to Italy to work on a medieval panel of the Crucifixion, and as she strips away the layers of old paint, she discovers new levels of her spirituality. Ruth Axtell Morren's *Wild Rose* (2004) creates a historical romance in an 1873 seacoast town in a spin on Pygmalion, where a sea captain befriends an orphan, educates her, and falls in love. Rene Gutteridge's *Splitting Storm* (2004) is about an FBI agent trying to find his brother's murderer: his avocation is tornado chasing, where he find the mystery of God in storms. All these storylines are typical in that they contain a moral problem that reaches a crisis, as well as a triumphant denouement because the individual lives according to religious principles.

All religious literature involves the interpretation of lived experience, or autobiography, and the exercise of the imagination, which can be a visualization of the images of holiness or the narration of experience, how religion seems to appear to the narrator or author.

Characteristics of the Genre

Out of the enormous body of world literary classics representing pluralistic religious traditions, examples from the modern and postmodern era can demonstrate how media, religion, communication, and literature come together to shape a genre distinguishable by a bridging or boundary-spanning relationship between the author and reader, where the audience is not merely the receiver of the message but an interpreter of the story.

The element of direct address, the communication between the author and the reader as an I-you relationship, remains an important element of religious literature today, with one major exception. Spiritual journalism strives for objectivity about real events, reported on by a participant-observer to a mass-media marketplace.

In religious literature, reader and author have separate identities from church, mosque, synagogue, temple: they are engaged in a conversation based on entering an imaginative world. While belief provides the context or frame within which the author created

the story, the reader may resist the idea of such beliefs. The purpose of religious literary art is to unify author and reader and to transcend the psychological, orthodox, and material culture.

Traditionally, the purpose of classic religious art is to observe the existence of a higher power; the definitive characteristic of religious literature after 1850 is the search for the value of the individual within the context of community, linked by an understanding of a natural religion, tolerant of pluralistic beliefs, embedded in a transcendentalist philosophy.

Common Interfaith Themes

The word "natural" describes religion that springs without dogma or doctrine from the interactive experience of human beings with other people, with nature, and in communities. In this experience of pluralistic religion, there are commonalities in the values and principles of many faiths. *Listening* is very important: it is the stillness valued in Buddhism and in all contemplative practices that employ meditation, sitting, silence, and quiet as part of their rituals. *Solitude* is valued in many religions as an avenue toward greater self-knowledge, with the aim of achieving peace. Though the self is valued as the source of psychological reality in the material world, many religions place the value of the "no-self" or "selfless being," whose priorities are focused on community, above the individual's own profit or self-centeredness. *Balance* as a virtue is similarly to be found in many Eastern and Western faiths: it is a reconciliation of opposites, positives and negatives, silence and song, listening and speaking, interior and exterior attention. *Transformation*, or change, and *forgiveness* lead to rebirth and triumph over the negative powers. All these themes occur frequently in religious literature.

Settings for religious stories in all traditions have similarities: they are either domestic—a study of interiors, stories about class and society—or natural, a study of exteriors; the human within the framework of the unknown. There is often the use of parables, riddles, or koan-style questions threaded throughout the larger narrative structures. Thinking about dichotomies is a helpful way to dissect plots but is not intended as an exact critical science. Rather, looking for opposition and tension within a religious plot is a good way to segregate or categorize types of stories, including those concerning war, travel, romance, mystery, discovery, and the tradition of the bildungsroman, the journey of the person through episodes of life events that lead to growth, change, and ultimately maturity (or salvation).

Five subcategories of narrative story frames define the genre of religious literature: historical and romance fiction (as discussed above), autobiography, fictional and spiritual geography, travelogues, and spiritual journalism.

Autobiography

The best-selling spiritual autobiography of the twentieth century was Thomas Merton's *The Seven Storey Mountain* (1948). Merton was born in Britain, was orphaned as an adolescent, and led a dissolute life as a teenager, after which he enrolled in Columbia University, converted to Catholicism, and joined a Trappist monastery. Historically, St. Augustine's *Confessions* is the model for such literature. The sinful episodes of youth are a necessary scaffold for the moral memoir and for later maturity, when guilty hindsight provides the writer with a clearer vision and deeper levels of conviction in a mature spiritual identity.

Fictional and Spiritual Geography

Geographical religious fiction concerns the identity of a person but within the context of a cultural place that is nearly alive, with its own mysterious, powerful nature to shape the subject. Susan Monk Kidd's *The Secret Life of Bees* (2002) may be thought of as a work of religious literature because it is the story of a lonely, misunderstood adolescent who runs away from home to adopt a new family and community among eccentric people she claims as her spiritual kin. She needs to replace a white mother who rejected her and find new religious icons, which she does in a black wooden Madonna. Kidd's storyline is a conventional "coming of age" narrative told with humor.

Anne Patchett's *Patron Saint of Liars* (1992) is about a rebellious young adult who abandons her identity as a young wife, leaves her husband of three years when she finds out she is a pregnant, and returns to her roots to live in a home for unwed mothers run by nuns in rural Kentucky, a place known among the locals for its "magical" waters, which once healed her as a child. She goes home to escape herself and to experience rebirth while she herself gives birth.

Wendell Berry's *Jayber Crow* (2000) is an example of recent religious literature: an impoverished young man from Appalachia promises to study for the ministry because he is poor and is offered a scholarship. Yet his honest speech about his failure to believe in God gets him expelled from the school. So begins his life of wandering: he settles in a new town as the barber, where he listens to the confessions and confidences of his customers as would their pastor or confessor. He escapes one disaster after another, including a flood of biblical proportions, to enter the mystery of love with a woman whose feelings for him are as deep and unspoken as his, yet mutually understood, a metaphor for the love of God.

Kathleen Norris's *Dakota: A Spiritual Geography* (2001) is about growing in the spirit even though she is limited by her life in a dying Midwestern town, where she has moved with her husband from Manhattan into a house she inherited from her grandmother. Norris's pastiche of geographical comment, autobiography, and journal seeks holiness in the ordinary, as did Henry David Thoreau on Walden Pond. Norris is not in Concord, Massachusetts, however, but in Lemmon, South Dakota.

She is a Protestant lay minister, a wife and poet who decides to enter the Benedictine order as an oblate, a novice practitioner of the ancient contemplative wisdom of the Desert Fathers, including silence, solitude (easily found in her location), and contemplation, which she finds among the monks in a nearby monastery. This type of religious realism describes the bond between human spiritual growth and knowing a place intimately, a kind of marriage between the woman and the geography that surrounds her, which parallels the relationship she has with her husband.

Comparing Norris's with Kidd's world, or with the novels of many authors who wrote stories about being "on the road" (e.g., Jack Kerouac), shows the value of "stability," a commitment to one community and one place for one lifetime that defines religious boundaries.

The point of religion is not to learn what it means to love God but to learn what it means to be human, one of God's creatures. Some writers are solitary and write about lonely people without a great many friends; because of this solitude, their imagination animates natural places such as a river, a mountain, or a forest much as others might express their love for people. Though many writers use this style, two award winners are Annie Dillard (*Pilgrim at Tinker Creek*, 1974), and Gretel Ehrlich (*The Solace of Open Spaces*, 1986, and *The Future of Ice: A Journey into Cold*, 2004).

Travelogues

Patricia Hampl's *Virgin Time* (1993) is a good example of a religious travelogue with a humorous understanding of religious anachronism—the performance of rituals and habits that have outlasted their original purpose—and how paradox and contradiction are central to the

Selection from *The Confessions of Saint Augustine*

Woe is me! An dare I say that Thou heldest Thy peace, O my God, while I wandered further from Thee? Didst Thou then indeed hold Thy peace to me? And whose but Thine were these words which by my mother, Thy faithful one, Thou sangest in my ears? Nothing whereof sank into my heart, so as to do it. For she wished, and I remember in private with great anxiety warned me, "not to commit fornication; but especially never defile another man's wife." These seemed to me womanish advances, which I should blush to obey. But they were Thine, and I knew it not: and I though Thou wert silent and that it was she who spake; by whom Thou were not silent unto me; and her wast despised by me, her son, the son of Thy handmaid. Thy servant. But I knew it not; and ran headlong with such blindness, that among my equals I was ashamed of less of a less shamelessness, when I heard them boast of their flagitiousness, yea, and the more boasting, the more they were degraded; and I took pleasure, not only in the pleasure of the deed, but in the praise.

Source: St. Augustine. (1975). *The Confessions of Saint Augustine*. (p. 23). New York: Pocket Books. (Original work written 397 CE)

comic side of religion. She travels in order to move forward emotionally and spiritually and to understand her own past. She meets a cast of characters, as did the troubadour poet Geoffrey Chaucer centuries earlier, as she travels on pilgrimage from one miraculous shrine to another, in Assisi, at Lourdes, and with new-age groups in northern California. The title signifies her moment of transcendence and revelation: "virgin time" is the point between daybreak and sunrise, the beginning of things all over again, of starting anew. Rodger Kamenetz's *Jew in the Lotus* (1994) (see also *Stalking Elijah*, 1998) recounts the story of a Brooklyn Jew who, along with a group of Orthodox rabbis, travels to Asia to meet the Dalai Lama and encounter Buddhism.

Spiritual Journalism

Azar Nafisi's *Reading Lolita in Tehran* (2003), which spent more than six months on the *New York Times* best-seller list, is about Islamic responses to Western values in Iran in 1995. Reporting on her work as a literature professor in Iran, Nafisi argues that one's public identity is inseparable from the private acts of the imagination that transcend ideology. Her central question is, "How does the soul survive" under the constant threat of death. Nafisi's journalism is an unsentimental memoir: she captures conversations about Western culture as her students meet in her living room to discuss Western literary classics by Nabokov, James, Austen, Fitzgerald. Nabokov's *Lolita* (1958) resonates in postrevolution Iran,

when the age a woman could be married was lowered from eighteen to nine.

Nafisi reports that for women in an Islamic state the story of Lolita is not the rape of a twelve-year-old by a dirty old man but how one's individual soul can be swallowed up by the identity crisis of another individual or, for that matter, in the civil strife of a nation-state. "How would it be different if people read in a newspaper a story about an individual, a female, married to a man decades her senior who robbed her of her virginity and identity?" Nafisi asks (this is a similar storyline to the 2004 Cannes award winner *Osama*). In a country where the government's chief film censor was blind, the newspaper is popularly accepted as ideological only.

Reading Lolita in Tehran is useful to examine because it illustrates the difference between fiction and journalism within a communication context. The line is blurred in state-controlled journalism between nonfiction and truth. The purpose of a book is to tell the story that cannot be told: nonfiction is not "real" life as in journalism, and the power of a novel or nonfiction book is not to report but to stir controversy.

The exercise of the human imagination, to envision alternatives to ideology as a value, is to set the architecture of the human heart within the framework of religion, the public expression of soul. Religion may describe the architecture of the state, and so play a civic role, but the public expression of religion is limited by the space in which it is exercised. To imagine is to envision an alternate reality to the existing culture that is printed and broadcast in the news.

Nobel Prize winner V. S. Naipaul's *Beyond Belief: Islamic Excursions Among the Converted Peoples* (1999) reports on the lives of ordinary people, many of them journalists, in four non-Arab Muslim countries—Indonesia, Iran, Pakistan, and Malaysia—over five months in 1995. The stories recount life in countries where "everyone is a convert," since Islam was originally an Arab religion. "Conversion" means identity change for these individuals—and not only in their worldview: a non-Arabic individual's holy places and sacred language are all Arabic. In societies where the entire non-Arab population is converted, the social order is disturbed.

Naipaul's premise is that the conversion experience is complex, unfinished, a process of crossing over from old beliefs about cults, tribes, rulers, to revealed universals, Christianity and Islam. Naipaul notes that fiction can be used by writers to render the "news about a changing society, to describe mental states," but his narration is like journalism without the reporter. The "purity" is in how an individual lives—how they once were and what they became after their conversion to Islam.

Framing the Storyline

Of those storylines that define the genre of religious literature outlined here, books of historical and romance fiction represent a very popular media product that serious writers disparage as too close to magazine writing. The oldest types of religious literature are parables and the spiritual autobiography, where the purpose has always been the conversion of the reader. Newer forms of religious literature are those that combine autobiography within a fictional framework celebrating the importance of cultural place, or spiritual geography. Similarly, the recent development of the spiritual travelogue, though as classic a literary form as Chaucer's tales, aspires to document the subjective life in as objective a manner as possible.

It is the subcategory of spiritual journalism that is cutting edge—a style of communication based on mass media rather than on classical models. Seeking objectivity, immersed in the news events and cultural values of the day, the writer tries to understand how religious belief shapes not only literature but the writer's and reader's reality, so that rather than being purely fictional or autobiographical, a travel story, or a historical romance, spiritual journalism puts the writer and reader on a level playing field. Both are seekers, and the act of

writing, for the author, and the act of reading, for the audience, is part of a larger spiritual conversation.

CLAIRE BADARACCO

Further Reading

Albanese, C. (Ed.). (2001). *American spiritualities: A reader.* Bloomington: Indiana University Press.

Badaracco, C. (Ed.). (2005). *Quoting God: How media shape ideas about religion.* Waco, TX: Baylor University Press.

Buchman, C., & Spiegel, C. (Eds.). (1994). *Out of the garden: Women writers on the Bible.* New York: Fawcett.

Dean, W. (2002). *The American spiritual culture and the invention of jazz, football and the movies.* New York: Continuum.

Mort, J. (2002). *Christian fiction: A guide to the genre.* Westport, CT: Libraries Unlimited.

Nord, D. P. (2004). *Faith in reading: Religious publishing and the birth of mass media in America.* New York: Oxford University Press.

Literature, Secular

Secular literature may signify a cultural site of communication about religions and religious life, an ideological term that marks off one realm of culture against other (religious) realms or a frame of reference for interpreting literary works. The term implies its partner term, *religious literature*, and this pair suggests two realms of literature that can be clearly distinguished and investigated, each on its own terms. However, the meaning and use of this term and the identity of a literature that can be clearly identified as *secular* and its relation to religious literature and religious life reveals a complex set of issues that resists straightforward historical analysis. While literary works that stand in some way independent of religious life can be identified in many historical periods (in Western cultures), this term is perhaps better considered in the context of modern Western culture as a product of the past five centuries—the Renaissance, the Enlightenment, and Romanticism. In this long and complex era, we can see the development of forms of creative expression (e.g., the modern novel) and cultural-political structures that operate independently of religious authorities. Nevertheless, the terms *secular* and *literature* and their relation to religious life need to be explored before we can turn our attention fruitfully to consideration of anything that might be considered *secular literature*.

Any attempt to delineate the relations between religious and other realms of culture or religious and other modes of interpretation of cultural products needs to be carefully situated in particular historical-cultural contexts. The term *literature* will have a different range of meanings in East Asian or South Asian cultures (and there, it will also differ over time), in relation to its scope and meaning in Western or other cultures. Likewise, any attempt to delineate a realm of culture as *religious* (sacred) or *secular* will take on different contours in these cultures. Here, examples are drawn from twentieth- and twenty-first-century English-language literature. Rather than taking these examples as definitive for this topic, these examples should be used for further reflection, analysis, and comparison with other historical eras and cultures.

Use of *Secular* as an Identifying Term

The distinction between the secular and the religious or sacred has recently become problematic in the study of religions. Thus, in order to understand and make useful the term *secular literature*, we need to consider the problems and possible uses of secular and religious. Secular, along with some of its extensions (secularism, secularization), suggests a realm of culture, an ideological perspective on culture, and a cultural process, all offered as distinct from and perhaps in opposition to a religious realm, perspective, or process. As a theoretical construct for understanding religious phenomena, these terms are now used less and in more limited ways, in comparison to the ways they were used through most of the twentieth century. While some interest is expressed in abandoning such terms, their ongoing use suggests that such a wish is not likely to be realized. We do better to use, and observe the use of, these terms as carefully as possible.

The significant way in which these terms have gone into eclipse as theoretical constructs is in their attempt to identify a clear and decisive process of modernizing social change, in which cultures transition from being shaped by religious institutions and ideologies to the development of institutions and ideologies that operate independently of and in opposition to the religious. This relation was understood to be one of opposition and eventual replacement. As cultures modernized, they would become secular, and so religious life would be privatized, marginalized, or eliminated. Whether such processes were interpreted as progress or decline depended on the attitude of the interpreter toward the value of religious life.

In any case, this idea of secularization as replacement for or the means to eliminate religion seems, at this stage, not to have materialized. While secular realms of culture have developed in modern societies, the persistence and resurgence of religiosity in these same societies in the late twentieth century shows that the relation between religious and secular realms of culture must be reconsidered. What has developed instead are vigorous religious and secular realms of cultural life that exist symbiotically, even when their representatives are antagonistic to the other realm of culture. Thus, modernity seems to have brought to Western cultures multiple, interactive realms of culture, some of which are primarily religious, some of which are primarily secular, but which do not exist in complete independence of each other. In this broad context, then, terms such as *secular* are used more often by representatives of religious communities who are seeking to make clear the identities of their own communities by contrast with other parts of a culture that are deemed to be insufficiently or inappropriately religious.

Man is the religious animal. He is the only religious animal. He is the only animal that has the True Religion—several of them. He is the only animal that loves his neighbor as himself and cuts his throat, if his theology isn't straight. He has made a graveyard of the globe in trying his honest best to smooth his brother's path to happiness and heaven.

Mark Twain (1835–1910)

The term *secular* (and *religious* or *sacred*) may be used to refer not only to a cultural location but also to a context or frame of reference for interpreting cultural products. Thus, as we identify a realm of culture as primarily religious or secular, we may also interpret or represent cultural phenomena from any realm of culture in secular or religious terms.

Use of *Literature* as an Identifying Term

While the term can take a variety of modifiers, such as secular or religious, the term *literature* needs to be considered alone in relation to some understandings of religious phenomena. While this term is perhaps less problematic than *secular*, at least in the context of its relation to religious phenomena, some consideration of possible complexities is in order. If literature is taken here to designate those linguistic products (such as novels, short stories, drama, poetry) that result from the exercise of human imagination and creativity, then some religious texts will be, even though they may appear in the form of poetry or dramatic narrative, not literature at all, at least under some religious interpretations. If, for instance, one takes the scriptures of the Christian traditions as the words of God (rather than the works of humans) that are merely transcribed, preserved, and transmitted by humans, then such texts might not be called literature. Granted, this perspective is not widespread; nevertheless, it is worth noting. Another, perhaps more common, perspective on texts that are considered sacred—i.e., Scripture, by a particular religious community or tradition—is that such works do engage human creativity and imagination as humans strive to represent religious experience to each other.

One other complication of the term *literature* needs to be noted, even though it does not specifically relate to religious concerns; that is, literature has been often taken (perhaps less so now) to designate an aesthetic and cultural standard, an elite or high-culture category of imaginative products, in contrast with other imaginative products that are identified as "popular." This distinction has proven to be indefensible and is not endorsed here.

Secular Literature

Given these many qualifications and complexities, one might be concerned that we have qualified the concept of secular literature out of existence. However, the term has use, both as a loose identifier of a particular realm of cultural products and locations of production and as a broad term of reference, interpretation, or reception of such products. We may proceed most fruitfully by identifying a continuum of possibilities within which we can identify some useful points of reference.

Religious Context vs. Fully Secular

At one end of the spectrum are those products that exist primarily (but, again, not exclusively) in a religious context. The clearest examples are those texts identified as sacred Scriptures, produced and received primarily in the context of religious communities, and that are interpreted by those communities in terms that clearly mark off the Scriptures from other linguistic products that are the result of human agency. Such texts could nevertheless be interpreted by others in secular terms and could, for nonmembers of those religious communities, be considered another category of secular literature. At the other end of the spectrum, in principle at least, would be a fully secular literature that in no way considers anything religious at all and

that, because of its lack of interest in considering anything religious, would be unlikely ever to be subject to religious interpretation, either favorable or critical.

Independent Engagement

Between these hypothetical poles of fully religious or fully secular literature are those imaginative linguistic works produced outside the direct auspices of religious communities but that deal with religious life or experience in some way. Such works are unlikely to be received as Scripture or sacred (except in an extended or metaphorical sense), yet they reflect a serious engagement with religions. It is at this point that we may be most clearly able to identify a useful meaning of secular literature in relation to religious life: Secular literature is a site of independent engagement with religious life and a location of communication about religious life. With this in mind, we should not be surprised to see novelists, poets, essayists, and others deeply and seriously engaged with the implications of religious life. While the forms of engagement are many, we can identify three modes that can help guide our reflections.

First, secular literature may treat religious life in a way that, if not apologetic, is at least consistent with or corroborates the experiences of particular religious communities or experiences. The *Left Behind* series (LaHaye & Jenkins 1996–2004) is an important contemporary example of such literature. Because of the mass-market popularity of these books with conservative American Christians, and because of their lack of critical acceptance outside those circles, such writing remains too much ignored in discussions of relations of literature and religious life. Some might argue that the *Left Behind* books are not properly secular, because these books are written by explicitly religious persons on explicitly religious themes. However, if we recall that this literature is produced, promoted, and to a great degree consumed in an environment independent of church authority, we can consider it as an item of secular literature that is deeply engaged with religion, in ways that are more complex than one might initially suspect. In such work, we can see not only the advancement of a particular religious perspective but also the critique of alternative religious lives and, of course, a critique of secular culture.

Use of Secular Literature to Critique Religiosity

A similar example, though one that many might hesitate to include in the same discussion with *Left Behind*, is the work of Flannery O'Connor (1925–1964). In

O'Connor's short fiction (e.g., *Revelation*, 1971) and novels (e.g., *Wise Blood*, 1952), we see a deeply religious writer whose stated aims were to write from her Roman Catholic tradition and to critique both the conventional Christianities she experienced in the American South and the secularized culture she saw developing in mid-twentieth-century America that in her view threatened traditional and authentic expressions of religiosity.

This complex strategy of critique and advancement of religiosity and alternatives to it can be seen as well in a second category of secular literature whose primary aim is to critique religious life in a way that aims to be critical or subversive. In the modern West, this critical use of secular literature is most directly a product of the Enlightenment conception of religion as an impediment to social progress. In the twentieth century, some of Mark Twain's (1835–1910) works, such as *Letters from the Earth* and The Mysterious Stranger still provide good examples. Salman Rushdie's *The Satanic Verses* (1988) provides a clear use of religious materials for critical purposes. Even here, however, the critique of religion may focus more on a conception of conventional religiosity that fails to live up to its own ideals.

Power of Religious Symbols in Literature

While these two modes of engagement are most obvious, what may be most interesting is a mode between these, one that is neither clearly aligned with nor critical of religious life but that recognizes the cultural and psychological power of religious symbol and narrative and thus takes these materials as at least part of its subject matter, in order to dramatize some aspect of the human condition that invariably includes religious life. Examples abound but can include works by such authors as Graham Greene (*The End of the Affair* 1951), Yann Martel (*Life of Pi* 2003), and J. R. R. Tolkien (*The Lord of the Rings* trilogy 1954–1955), each of whom explores religious life, in terms that recognize the presence and power of religion in individual and cultural life.

MARK W. GRAHAM

Further Reading

Brooks, C. (1995). *Community, religion, and literature*. Columbia: University of Missouri Press.

Carey, P. (1997). *Wagering on transcendence: The search for meaning in literature*. Lanham, MD: Sheed and Ward.

Comstock, W. R. (1981). Religion, literature, and religious studies: A sketch of their modal connections. *Notre Dame English Journal, 14*(1), 1–28.

Detweiler, R. (1983). *Art/literature/religion: Life on the borders*. Chico, CA: Scholars Press.

Detweiler, R. (1996). *Uncivil rites: American fiction, religion, and the public sphere*. Urbana: University of Illinois Press.

Gordon, D. J. (2002). *Literary atheism*. New York: Peter Lang.

Hesla, D. H. (1978). Religion and literature: The second stage. *Journal of the American Academy of Religion, 46*(2), 181–192.

Jasper, D. (1987). *The New Testament and the literary imagination*. Atlantic Highlands, NJ: Humanities Press International.

Jasper, D. (1989). *The study of literature and religion*. Philadelphia: Fortress Press.

Jasper, D. (1992). The study of literature and theology: Five years on. *Journal of Literature and Theology, 6*(1), 1–10.

Jasper, D., & Ledbetter, M. (1994). *In good company: Essays in honor of Robert Detweiler*. Atlanta, GA: Scholars Press.

Kazin, A. (1997). *God and the American writer*. New York: Alfred A. Knopf.

May, J. R. (1989). The art of steering: Theological literary criticism after three decades. *Religion and Literature, 21*(1), 1–7.

McDonald, J. J. (1984). Religion and literature. *Religion and Literature, 16*(1), 61–71.

Salyer, G., & Detweiler, R. (1995). *Literature and theology at century's end*. Atlanta, GA: Scholars Press.

Ziolkowski, E. J. (1998). History of religions and the study of religion and literature: Grounds for alliance. *Literature and Theology, 12*(1), 305–325.

Magazines

Magazines have been published by religious organizations and denominations for centuries as tools for outreach and for reinforcing faith in those who worship a deity or adhere to a particular set of beliefs. The religious paperbound magazine has, like secular magazines, gravitated toward a strong presence on the World Wide Web as well.

International Religious Magazines

Communications scholar Doug Underwood makes the case for British Quaker George Fox being one of the earliest religious journalists in England. He published pamphlets in the mid-1600s defending Quakerism against the censorship and condemnation of the English government and rival clerics. This was the same period in which poet John Milton wrote his famous tract *Areopagitica* (1644), calling for freedom of expression. Frances E. Mineka has written that "perhaps the earliest forerunner of the numerous influential miscellanies of the eighteenth and nineteenth centuries" was the monthly *Post-Angel,* published in 1701–1702 by John Dunton (Mineka 1972, 27). Religious magazines were the dominant type of religious periodical in eighteenth century England, printing poetry, moral essays, general news, obituaries, biographies, and sermons.

Contemporary religious magazines based in London include *Church Times,* a Church of England publication; *Jewish Quarterly,* and *Q News,* a Muslim periodical. One of the oldest Christian news magazines in France is *Dimanche en Paroisse,* established in 1885. Germany has many religious magazines, including a large number of Catholic publications. These include *Katholische Sonntags Zeitung fur das Bistum Augsburg,* published for the Augsburg Diocese, which has a circulation of some 42,000.

Early Religious Magazines in America

The first magazines to appear in America were secular, general-interest periodicals founded by Andrew Bradford and Benjamin Franklin in 1741, the former beating the latter by three days. Bradford's periodical, *The American Magazine, or a Monthly View of the Political State of the British Colonies,* lasted for only three issues. Franklin's *The General Magazine, and Historical Chronicle, for All the British Plantations in America,* fared little better, folding after six issues.

The first purely religious magazine in the British colonies was *The Christian History, Containing Accounts of the Revival and Propagation of Religion in Great-Britain and America,* which lasted from 1743 to 1745. The magazine was born during the Great Awakening of revivalism that swept through New England, challenging the established conservative church. *The Christian History* was editorially guided by and supportive of influential and popular Evangelical preachers such as the Anglican George Whitefield and Presbyterian Gilbert Tennent. The magazine was written and published by the Reverend Thomas Prince of South Church in Boston, with minor assistance by his son, Thomas Prince, Jr. Detailed accounts of revivals in Massachusetts, New Jersey, and Pennsylvania were commonplace in *The Christian History.* Such details eventually became monotonous for readers, and the magazine folded in February of 1745 as the flame of the Great Awakening was fading as well.

According to magazine historian Algernon Tassin, the second religious magazine in America appeared in Germantown, Pennsylvania, twenty years later in the 1760s and was printed in German. Some twenty years after that, Methodist Episcopal Bishops Thomas Coke and Francis Asbury edited *The Arminian Magazine* in Philadelphia from 1789 to 1790. Printing sermons was its forte, especially those of denominational founder John Wesley, whose writings were scarce in the newly established United States. Coke and Asbury hoped to create a sense of unity among the blossoming and numerous Methodist societies scattered about the young nation. Limited content and a decentralized readership no doubt contributed to the magazine's rapid demise. Conversely, the influential *Christian Advocate* was begun by the Methodist Church in 1826 and continued well into the twentieth century, merging with the Methodist publication *Today* (1956) in 1974 to form *United Methodists Today*.

Pious content also permeated other religious magazines in the late eighteenth and early nineteenth centuries. The earnest offerings included biographical portraits of the clergy, religious poetry, and tales of conversions. Charles Lippy has written, "Indeed, magazine journalism in general during this period did not seek so much to entertain or to advance knowledge in a specialized field as to provide a means for moral improvement" (Lippy 1986, xi).

Minority Publications

Minority religious magazines existed in the early nineteenth century, but one denominational publication stood out from the rest, having been the only antebellum black periodical to survive into the twentieth century. "The *Christian Recorder* was less a propaganda organ than a church news magazine and discussion forum for its founder, the African Methodist Church," according to media historian John Tebbel (1969). Beginning in 1818, the magazine struggled with illiteracy among its potential audience, the majority of whom lived in slave states. The magazine picked up steam by 1841 as a quarterly, supported by the church's New York Conference and a literate black population in the North. By 1852, the magazine was considered dangerous by Southern slaveholders and banned in slave states. After the Civil War, Christianity among blacks flourished and so did other prominent minority magazines. Two of these were the *A.M.E. Zion Review,* a quarterly published by the African Methodist Episcopal Church, and the *Star of Zion,* published by the North Carolina Zion Methodists.

Although Protestants dominated, religious minorities had their magazines as well. The prolific Unitarians published, among others, the *Christian Examiner* (1824) for almost fifty years. Roman Catholicism was represented by the *U.S. Catholic Miscellany,* published in Charleston, South Carolina, from 1822 to 1832. A handful of Jewish journals began in the mid-1800s, including the *American Israelite* (1854).

Other Antebellum Magazines

The *Biblical Repertory* was founded in 1825 as a voice for the antirevival movement, and was one of the first periodicals written for a professional readership, namely the Presbyterian clergy.

The abolitionist movement was firmly entrenched in American society by the mid-nineteenth century. The majority of the religious publications of this period came from Baptists, Methodists, Presbyterians, and Congregationalists. Along with the numerous newspapers and tracts editorializing against slavery, religious magazines published a number of reform-minded articles. The Congregationalist-focused *Independent* (1848), for example, printed the text of Harriet Beecher Stowe's novel *Uncle Tom's Cabin.*

Religious Magazines After the Civil War

Religious magazines in the United States grew rapidly after the Civil War ended in 1865. In his famous historical study of American magazines, Frank Luther Mott put the number of religious periodicals at 350 that year, doubling by 1885 to more than 650 titles. Sunday school periodicals accounted for more than half of the titles published in 1885. Religious reviews sold as many as 10,000 per issue, while circulation for some weeklies reached 100,000. Most of the content was dull, delving deep into theological issues and controversies, and the weeklies often battled in their pages with one another. Because of Protestant fear of Catholic growth and power, many denominational publications condemned Catholicism, spurring growth in that Church's own press. By this same year, 1885, Tebbel notes that Catholics had 74 publications to lead the field, one more than the Methodists. Baptists published many magazines in the late nineteenth century, but they tended to have short lives. The Presbyterian and Unitarian Church presses tended to be split between North and South, liberal and conservative.

Nondenominational journals included *The Christian Herald,* an offshoot of a London magazine, and the

Salvation Army's *War Cry*, which began in 1882 and is still being published.

Religious periodicals were so diverse by the end of the nineteenth century that Mott divided them into as many as thirteen types, such as:

- Periodicals that commented on national and international affairs and literary developments from a religious perspective

- Denominational journals with a liberal slant

- Denominational periodicals aimed at laymen

- Quarterly or monthly theological reviews sponsored by denominations

Innovations by the Religious Press

Magazines early on proved to be an effective tool for teaching and distributing religious information to a wide audience, and the medium was adopted early on by Protestant Christians for conversion and evangelical purposes. Christian Evangelical denominations have traditionally been on the cutting edge of printing technology and have often led the way in innovations in printing and distribution. American Evangelicals, for example, ushered in the concept of religious mass media through the establishment of dozens of Bible and tract societies between 1805 and 1815, according to scholar David Paul Nord. From these various groups emerged two dominant national organizations, the American Bible Society, founded in 1816, and the American Tract Society, begun in 1825. These two societies were responsible for the widespread use of power printing (the use of steam and other methods for faster press operation), stereotyping (making metal plates so movable type could be reused quickly), and cheaper papermaking. These innovations produced astounding results. The American Tract Society, for example, went from printing 700,000 tracts in 1825 to more than six million just four years later.

Modern Religious Magazines

According to Lippy, the academic study of religion has expanded beyond seminaries, where religious training took place prior to the twentieth century, to nonreligious and state colleges and universities. This shift toward establishing religion departments at secular institutions changed the way religion is viewed and studied. Additionally, the study of religion has become increasingly specialized, leading to a number of religious periodicals of various stripes. Titles include *Biblical Archaeology Review* (1975), the *Journal of Church & State* (1959), the *Catholic Biblical Quarterly* (1939), the *Jewish Quarterly Review* (1889), and *Dialogue: A Journal of Mormon Thought* (1966).

Less scholarly popular periodicals offer commentary on current events and modern society for an educated and religiously literate audience. These include the *Christian Century* (1884), a liberal to moderate magazine, and the more conservative *Christianity Today*, begun in 1956 by the Billy Graham Evangelical Association. *Christianity Today* has a circulation of 155,000 and publishes other titles such as *Christian History* and *Books and Culture*. *World* magazine, edited by religious journalist and professor Marvin Olasky, has the look and style of a hard news magazine such as *Time* or *Newsweek* but covers national and international events with a Fundamentalist Christian worldview. *Bodhi* magazine (1997) is a periodical published for Buddhists. *Commonweal* (1924) focuses on a conservative Catholic viewpoint, and *Commentary* (1945) reflects conservative Judaism. *Hadassah Magazine* (2000), a monthly for contemporary American Jewish readers, has a circulation of 309,000.

Religious Press Associations

There are two national religious press associations with which many periodicals identify themselves. The Associated Church Press (ACP) was founded in 1919 by a group that later became the National Council of Churches. The Evangelical Press Association (EPA) was begun by Biblical literalists as an alternative to the more liberal ACP. According to scholar Ken Waters, the EPA started out with 103 member publications in 1949. By 1998, the EPA "quadrupled in membership, far outpacing its older sister, the ACP" (Waters 2001, 309).

Special Categories

Religious magazines continue to proliferate, and there are specialty titles in both print and online form. Many of these cater to special tastes, even pious religious humor. One such magazine is *The Door*, which bills itself as "Pretty Much the World's Only Religious Satire Magazine." *The Door* is published by a Christian outreach community in Dallas, Texas, called the Trinity Foundation. Spiritual renewal and social justice were behind the founding of the Evangelical *Sojourners* magazine, based in Washington, D.C., which began life in 1971 as the *Post-American*. *Killing the Buddha*, according to its website, "is a religion magazine for people made anxious by churches, people embarrassed to be caught in the 'spirituality' section of a bookstore, people both hostile and drawn to talk of God. It is for people who somehow want to be religious, who want to know what it means to know the divine, but for good reasons are not and do not."

The Future of Religious Magazines

Since 1980—with events such as the election of conservative President Ronald Reagan, the flourishing of the Moral Majority, the rightward shift at many Protestant seminaries, and the prominence of religious conservatives in politics—news media in the United States have paid more attention to religion. With the emphasis on religion in both the American presidential races in 2000 and 2004, many news organizations paid more attention to religion. Secular publications such as *Newsweek, Time,* and *U.S. News & World Report* produce religion stories on Easter and at Christmas, and cover cultural topics throughout the year such as religious movies and books, as well as trends such as megachurches and new spiritual movements.

More specialty religious magazine titles can be found on the newsstand, including *CCM* and *Relevance,* both aimed at the youth audience that buys contemporary Christian music. As new generations seek new ways to express their religiosity, magazines of this nature will continue to grow, perhaps existing primarily on the Internet. Religious publishers have always been innovators, and will embrace whatever new technology exists in the future in order to spread their gospel.

ANTHONY HATCHER

Further Reading

Blanchard, M. A. (Ed.). (1998). *History of the mass media in the United States.* Chicago: Fitzroy Dearborn Publishers.
Emery, M., & Emery, E. (1988). *The press and America: An interpretive history of the mass media* (6th ed.). Englewood Cliffs, NJ: Prentice Hall.
Fackler, P., & Lippy, C. (Eds.). (1995). *Popular religious magazines of the United States.* Westport, CT: Greenwood Press.
Lippy, C. (Ed.). (1986). *Religious periodicals of the United States: Academic and scholarly journals.* Westport, CT: Greenwood Press.
Mineka, F. E. (1972). *The dissidence of dissent: The monthly repository, 1806-1838.* New York: Octagon Books.
Mott, F. L. (1930). *A history of American magazines, 1741–1850.* Cambridge, MA: Harvard University Press.
Mott, F. L. (1971). *American journalism, a history: 1690–1960* (3rd ed.). New York: MacMillan.
Nord, D. P. (1984). The evangelical origins of mass media in America, 1815–1835. *Journalism Monographs, 88.*
Richardson, L. N. (1931). *A history of early American magazines, 1741–1789.* New York: Thomas Nelson and Sons.
Schultze, Q. J. (1990). *American Evangelicals and the mass media.* Grand Rapids, MI: Academie/Zondervan.
Tassin, A. (1916). *The magazine in America.* New York: Dodd, Mead, and Company.
Tebbel, J. (1969). *The American magazine: A compact history.* New York: Hawthorn Books.
Underwood, D. (2002). *From Yahweh to Yahoo!: The religious roots of the secular press.* Urbana: University of Illinois Press.
Waters, K. (2001). Vibrant, but invisible: A study of contemporary religious periodicals. *Journalism & Mass Communication Quarterly, 78*(2), 307–320.
Willings Press Guide Vol. I. (2003). Chesham, Bucks, UK: Waymaker Ltd.

Mantra

The ritual verbal formulas known as mantras are a distinctive feature of a number of South Asian religious traditions, including both Hinduism and Buddhism, and have been carried by those traditions in their spread across Asia and, in more recent times, to Europe and North America. Although mantras are distinctive to South Asian traditions, they bear a number of characteristics in common with similar formulas in other cultures. In particular, they share with many such formulas their highly repetitive character; the use of numerous poetic devices including alliteration and palindromes or quasi-palindromes; and their magical function. As such, mantras have often been identified with various genres of ritual language including spells, charms, incantations, and prayers. Actually, mantras are a bit of all of these. In some cases they are used primarily for worship of the gods, or to show reverence. In other cases they are intended to achieve a purely practical objective, such as destroying one's enemies.

The use of mantras in South Asian traditions goes all the way back to primeval antiquity. The original referent of the term mantra were the formulas of the Vedic hymns composed approximately 1500–1200 BCE. As Frits Staal has pointed out, parts of many Vedic mantras consist of strings of nonsense syllables, or vocables without any apparent semantic content. This pattern accelerated in the later texts known as Tantras that began to appear from about 600 CE. Tantric seed (*b¥ja*) mantras such as *hr¥m, kl¥m, Êr¥m,* and the ubiquitous *om,* which actually goes back to late Vedic times, are not words in the ordinary sense, although they have a deeply encoded symbolic value.

In Vedic times, when the primary mode of ritual was sacrifice, the mantras often constituted the central or operative portion of the ritual. This continued to be the case in Tantra, where mantras were employed both with and without accompanying physical operations. Tantra for this reason was often referred to as "the science of mantras" (mantraÊÇstra). According to a popular Tantric folk etymology, "Mantra is that which saves as a result of thinking" (mananÇttrÇ yate iti mantrah). The word *mantra* derives from a combination of the verbal root *man*- (thinking, contemplation) and the agentive suffix -*tra*, thus meaning something like "an instrument for thinking with."

Imitating the Cosmogony

In the late Vedic period, various ritual texts prescribed that the chanting of any mantra should be preceded and/or followed by the pronunciation of *om*, the so-called proclaimer (*pra ava*), the most sacred syllable in Hinduism. Although the form and style of mantras changed in the Puranas and Tantras, the requirement of adding *om* generally continued. In Tantric texts numerous rituals were developed with the purpose of making mantras effective (*siddha*). These rituals often involved adding *om* or other seed mantras at the beginning and end of a mantra in forward and reverse order, respectively, a practice known as enveloping (*sa pu a*). The significance of this practice lay in very ancient Hindu cosmological ideas. The process of creation was conceived as a cycle of evolution and involution, or expansion and contraction. By adding *om* and other vocables at the beginning and end of the mantra in such a way as to produce a roughly palindromic or chiastic shape, Tantric ritualists produced a verbal imitation of the cosmic cycle. This was supposed to make mantras more creative and effective, especially for magical purposes. Tantric mantras in this way also imitated various other creative processes, including the cycle of breath, the path of speech, and the cycle of sexual reproduction, all of which were associated in the mythology with the cosmogonic cycle.

Buddhist Mantras

Buddhist mantras, as Agehenanda Bharati has shown, exhibit many of the same patterns as Hindu mantras, while following their own distinctive tradition. The use of mantras accelerated in Mahayana Buddhism (c. 100 CE onward) and especially in Tantric Buddhism or Vajrayana (c. 600 CE onward). Perhaps the most famous mantra in Tibetan Tantric Buddhism is *om mani padme h¥m* which translates literally as "*om*, the jewel in the lotus, *h¥m*," and encodes the symbolic meaning of nondualism and the union of male and female. The use of esoteric or encrypted language in the Buddhist Tantras is not confined to mantras, and extends to the so called twilight or intentional language (*sandh(y)ÇbhÇsa*), in which sexual terms are given metaphorical significance or, conversely, apparently nonsexual terms have an encoded sexual reference. Buddhists carried their mantras with them as far as Japan, where in the tradition known as Shingon or esoteric Buddhism, the use of Sanskrit mantras was a staple of ritual practice.

Mantras Compared with Other Spells

As previously noted, the repetitiveness of mantras is similar to that of spells and prayers in many other cultures. Such formulas may be divided into two broad categories, according to their origin in folk or civilization traditions. Folk charms in many cultures, such as Bengali folk mantras (*laukik mantra*) used by snake bite healers (*ojha*), use repetition and nonsensical magic words. Sanskrit Tantric mantras, like the spells of the Greek Magical Papyri, are distinguished from folk charms by their frequently elaborate nature and the manner in which they encode a complex cosmology. In both types of spells, however, it is clear that poetic imitation contributes to their binding or magical power.

The Future of Mantras

An important question is the fate of mantras and similar formulas in modernity, when magical practices have been largely discarded as "superstitious." The use of mantras continues to be common in modern South Asia for household and temple worship (*p¥jÇ*) and, in villages, for practical purposes such as healing. However, reflecting the influence of Western rationalism and Protestant missionaries, early Hindu reformers such as Rammohun Roy (1772?–1833) and Dayananda Sarasvati (1824–1883) argued for a restriction of the use of mantras, especially those associated with image worship. Among the modern westernized South Asian elite, mantras have largely lost their traditional devotional and especially magical function. A recent exception is the adoption of personal mantras for private meditation, a fashion that parallels some Western New Age movements, but with a distinctively Hindu flavor.

ROBERT A. YELLE

233

Further Reading

Abe, R. (1999). *The weaving of mantra: Kukai and the construction of esoteric Buddhist discourse*. New York: Columbia University Press.

Alper, H. (Ed.). (1989). *Mantra*. Albany: State University of New York Press.

Avalon, A. [Woodroffe, J.] (1998). *The garland of letters: Studies in the mantra sastra*. Madras, India: Ganesh.

Beyer, S. (1973). *The cult of Tara: Magic and ritual in Tibet*. Berkeley: University of California Press.

Bharati, A. (1993). *Tantric traditions* (rev. ed.). Delhi, India: Hindustan Publishing.

Gonda, J. (1975). The Indian mantra. In J. Gonda, *Selected Studies IV* (pp. 248–301). Leiden, Netherlands: E. J. Brill.

Padoux, A. (1990). *Vac: The concept of the word in selected Hindu Tantras* (J. Gontier, Trans.). Albany: State University of New York Press.

Patton, L. (2004). *Bringing the gods to mind: Mantra and poetry in early Indian sacrifice*. Berkeley: University of California Press.

Staal, F. (1996). *Ritual and mantras: Rules without meaning*. Delhi, India: Motilal Banarsidass.

Wayman, A. (1984). The significance of mantras, from the Veda down to Buddhist Tantric practice. In G. Elder (Ed.), *Buddhist Insight* (pp. 413–430). Delhi, India: Motilal Banarsidass.

Yelle, R. A. (2003). *Explaining mantras: Ritual, rhetoric, and the dream of a natural language in Hindu Tantra*. London and New York: Routledge.

Material Culture

In the intersection of religion, media, and communication, the term *material culture* implies a strong relationship between religious artifacts and human behavior in a spiritual, communicative, and cultural context. The term causes researchers to analyze the multiple interactions that take place between religious objects, the creator and/or consumer of the religious items, and the culture. The analysis could include, among other things, the manufacture, use, consumption, and implications of religious toys, books, theme parks, jewelry, clothing, entertainment venues, and architecture.

Further, material culture studies in this context analyze how consumers perceive themselves and others from a religious and cultural perspective through the means of commodities (objects for sale) and seek to find the technological, social, and ideological meaning in the common religious artifacts that surround individuals as part of their everyday existence. That which is considered to be sacred could include places and tangible things such as icons, clothing, furnishings, shrines, artifacts, and possessions that are associated with the sacred. Also, intangible things such as dances, songs, names, and rituals could be included in this sphere. In addition, persons and other beings could represent the sacred.

Multiple Definitions

There are varying definitions of material culture, with various disciplines defining the concept in different ways. By its nature, material culture spans scholarly disciplines, with studies ranging from art, folklore studies, history of technology, and cultural and social history. Material culture encompasses the ideas about substances outside of the mind arising from human behavior as well as the beliefs about human behavior needed to produce these objects. These could include religious foundational beliefs or practices that lead to certain types of economic systems, or alternatively, they could focus on religious artifacts that reflect economic prosperity or poverty. As an economic term, *material culture* involves ideas concerning manufacture or usage and articulated theories about the production, use, and character of material objects.

The idea underpinning material culture, in a religious context, is that artifacts that are made by individuals reflect the religious convictions and ideas of those individuals, and thus, also reflect the religious, mental, and spiritual configurations found in the society as a whole. The religious artifacts and cultural panoramas that artisans create reflect the widely accepted, systemic, and taken-for-granted concepts of usefulness and value that have developed over generations. These objects and practices represent the religious group's idealistic vision of tradition and orderliness. The religious artifacts help individuals to gain reassurance in the midst of the changeability and uncertainty of the physical world. They also serve as mechanisms for societal interaction. Humans infuse these objects with meaning and symbolism, and as a result, these objects bring enjoyment to their possessors.

The term *material culture* also encompasses the idea of man conquering his physical environment deliberately in conjunction with designs shaped by religious beliefs, expectations, and ideals. An example of this would be when the early American settlers conquered the wilderness and designed colonies that were shaped by their religious beliefs or values.

Historical Debates

These multiple manifestations of material culture can be traced through historical periods, as scholars scrutinize the historical development of the relationship between goods and identity and analyze how systems of inequality have been replicated and challenged through material cultural practices and ideas. Scholars have debated whether economic structure affects culture and religion or whether religion affects economic structure. Karl Marx believed that economic structure affected culture and religion. In that context, it was felt that religion was the opiate of the masses and part of a tripartite rule of power. In this view, religion was seen as a problematic variable with regard to the economic system. However, Max Weber saw certain religious beliefs as foundational building blocks of an efficient and highly productive economic system. Religion, under this theoretical foundation, was viewed as a positive factor with regard to the shaping of an economic system and societal structure. However, scholars have observed that there is a paradox inherent in this view of the Protestant ethic. This religious ethic encourages hard work, thrift, and earning money as a sign of God's blessing but discourages the enjoyment of the money thus earned.

Premodern to Postmodern Material Culture

Other scholars view the relationship between religion and material culture through a different lens, arguing that societies can progress from a time of intense religious focus to a materialistic focus as a society shifts from a premodern to a postmodern state. During the pre-Enlightenment premodern period, humankind was deeply religious or superstitious, with communities that revolved around religious beliefs and communal living conditions. Religious artifacts of premodernity included the medieval renditions of the Madonna and Christ child, Gregorian chants, cave petroglyphs, and Roman and Greek statues and temples built to the gods.

The modern phase began during the Enlightenment, as humankind searched for meaning in scientific discoveries, rationality, and a quest for an ultimate truth.

The postmodern phase began after World War II and signaled the beginning of splintered subsocieties and an emphasis on individualized spirituality. During this phase, there was an increased acceptance of the notion of multiple truths and diverse religious expressions and practices, which included pop culture religious rites. The religious artifacts of postmodernity might include New Age candles, individualistic religious jewelry, religious websites, televised church meetings, and Bibles targeted toward teenagers containing quizzes or teen pop-cultural references.

Some scholars have observed that as a society becomes more economically secure and materialistic, traditional religious fervor tends to fade and church attendance declines. Ronald Inglehart (*Modernization and Postmodernization,* 1997) observed this phenomenon in forty three European countries as they progressed through historical and economic stages. Curiously, researchers have observed that the United States has not followed that trend to the same extent as European countries. However, other scholars feel that the level of spirituality in Europe is still high but is manifested in different ways and through different rituals and artifacts. Still other researchers observe a resurgence of religion in formerly Communist countries, such as China and Russia, and feel that religion is still a vibrant force throughout the world.

Commodification and Spirituality

In current society, the intertwining of material culture and religion is a growing trend that involves the commodification of that which is spiritual and sacred. Commodification involves the process of turning something into an economic good—something that can be bought, sold, exchanged, or exploited. Different scholars and laypeople see this through different lenses, with some decrying the increasing materialism that they see to be the antithesis of religion. Other scholars argue, when viewing the meaning making of individuals, that the commodification of religion simply involves individuals who are seeking to acquire and incorporate objects into their lives that will help them reach their idealized selves. It is felt that believers infuse meaning into the commodified religious objects that bring them to greater spiritual heights. One example of this phenomenon would be the "What Would Jesus Do?" (WWJD) rings, T-shirts, and other objects that some Christians defend as objects that help them lead better lives and aid in sharing the message. However, some other Christians decry what they perceive as the overly dominant display of Christianity as part of the products and state that religion should be manifested solely by individual actions and thoughts.

Another example of the incorporation of religious objects as part of living a better life can be found in the "Choose The Right" (CTR) rings of The Church of Jesus Christ of Latter Day Saints, which help children to remember to make correct choices as they live their lives. The children infuse meaning into those rings as an outward manifestation of an inward commitment or, alternatively, as a manifestation of an idealized self. Both the WWJD products and the CTR rings represent to the consumers commodified spiritual objects that help them make correct decisions, aid in building a sense of community, and represent an outward manifestation of a follower who wants to make correct decisions.

Religious Artifacts in the Marketplace

This aspect of material culture has been viewed as a potent economic force. *Marketing News* reported in 2005 that the value of the Christian retail industry grew from $2.6 billion in 1991 to $3.75 billion in 2002. The market share of the Christian music genre grew from 4.5 percent in 1997 to 6.3 percent in 1998. Also, according to most recent statistics available in 2005, the religious card industry had grown to such an extent that it had captured 26 percent of the market share in card and specialty stores.

Church construction is also big business, with Christians financing the $20 billion-per-year industry, which gives an indication of the financial resources Christians have. In like manner, Christian consumers have also embraced Christian magazines, clothing, vacations, tapes, home schooling supplies, crafts, books, and other products.

Other faiths also have religious objects that are for sale to help in maintaining religious standards. Websites have proliferated that aid Muslim women in dressing in a manner consistent with their faith. These Internet stores offer products that attempt to integrate Muslim standards of modesty with current professional and popular fashions.

Thus, when scrutinized against the rubric of commodification and with respect to the material culture, religious organizations can be viewed as both fighting the materialism that is seen as detrimental to religious values and embracing material culture as a manifestation of that which helps its members grow more spiritual.

Culture Wars

One of the current material cultural debates revolves around the perceived beneficial or detrimental effects of pop culture. One argument isolates television as a harmful factor with regard to religion and society. Some researchers mourn the loss of social capital and the human and societal interconnections that were lost as television came into widespread use. Some religious organizations decry the array of immorality and pop cultural references found on TV, with the thought that these influences could harm spirituality. The battlegrounds of the religious culture wars have included Hollywood, movies, clothing, music, TV shows, and

Disneyland. However, other ministers and religious organizations have embraced television and pop culture as an aid in spreading the faith. Religious gatherings in Disneyland and televised church meetings are examples of this intermixing of religion and media.

Material Culture and Materialism

In the realm of marketing research, some scholars have analyzed the evolution from meaning making through the artifacts of material culture (which is considered to be a positive effect), into meaning making through materialism (which is considered to be negative). These scholars observe that sacred holidays, such as Christmas, evolved from that which is sacred and holy to an event that celebrates the acquisition of items out of a sense of materialism and greed. Materialism is defined by these scholars as a consumption-based orientation to happiness seeking. In spite of those who see wealth as a reward for righteous virtues such as hard work, industry, and thrift, this research stream has observed that Buddhism, Hinduism, Islam, Judaism, and Christianity all condemn concentrating on building excessive material wealth. They write that religion has become secularized and the secular has become sacred in contemporary Western society

Material Culture and Religious Holidays

One of the religious holidays identified as a major element in the studies of material culture and materialism is Christmas. This holiday displays multidimensional sacred and secular meanings, including religion (formal sacredness), interpersonal relationships (communalism), secular materialism, cynicism, commercialism, gift giving, sensuality, and hedonism (the festival of excess). Consumer behavior researchers observe that the Christmas observance challenges us to create, during a relatively brief holiday, a reality that is fundamentally different from that which most of us construct during the rest of the year. Critics within marketing scholarship feel that Santa Claus is a symbol of American attempts to bring commercialism and materialism around the world.

In like manner, Halloween grew from prehistoric Celtic festivals that celebrated the day of the dead or day of the harvest. Gallic celebrants wore disguises, banquet tables were prepared for visiting ghosts, and harvest beggars asked for food. Now, some marketing scholars feel that Halloween has multiple meanings. It elicits a sense of community, a struggle between light and darkness, a sacred pilgrimage, an exercise in the mastery of fear, and materialism. When analyzing the materialistic aspect of the celebration, some marketing critics feel that this celebration has also been transformed from a festival of meaning into a materialistic ritual that socializes children into the characteristics of acquisitiveness, possessiveness, and gluttony.

Interpreting Material Culture

Material culture can be interpreted in multiple ways. The term can have either positive or negative connotations with respect to the religious and cultural aspects of a society. At its very foundation, the term asks the viewers of the culture to look at religious artifacts and seek to ascertain the meanings that individuals draw from them as a reflection of the greater societal traditions and beliefs.

ANNE V. GOLDEN

See also Bells; Clock; Cross, The; Museums; Relics; Religious Marketplace; Signage

Further Reading

Belk, R. W. (1987). A child's Christmas in America: Santa Claus as deity, consumption as religion. *Journal of American Culture, 10*(1), 87–100.

Belk, R. W. (1990). Halloween: an evolving American consumption ritual. *Advances in Consumer Research, 17,* 508–517.

Belk, R. W., Dholakia, N., & Venkatesh, A. (Eds.). (1996). *Consumption and marketing: macro dimensions.* Cincinnati, OH: South-Western College Publishing.

Belk, R. W., Wallendorf, M., & Sherry, J. F. (1989). The sacred and the profane in consumer behavior: Theodicy on the Odyssey. *Journal of Consumer Research, 16,* 1–38.

Fielding, M. (2005, February 1). The halo effect: Christian consumers are a bloc that matters to all marketers. *Marketing News, 39,* 18–20.

Hirschman, E. C., & LaBarbera, P. A. (1989). The meaning of Christmas. In E. C. Hirschman (Ed.), *Interpretive consumer research* (pp. 136–147). Provo, UT: Association for Consumer Research.

Inglehart, R. (1997). *Modernization and postmodernization: cultural, economic, and political change in 43 societies.* Princeton, NJ: Princeton University Press.

Lyon, D. (2000). *Jesus in Disneyland: religion in postmodern times.* Cambridge, MA: Polity Press.

Putnam, R. D. (2001). Tuning in, tuning out: the strange disappearance of social capital in America. In R. Niemi & H. Weisberg (Eds.), *Controversies in voting behavior.* Washington, DC: CQ Press.

Santino, J. (Ed.). (1994). *Halloween and other festivals of death and life.* Knoxville: The University of Tennessee Press.

Schlereth, T. (Ed.). (1985). *Material culture: a research guide.* Lawrence: University Press of Kansas.

Stout, D. A., & Buddenbaum, J. M. (Eds.). (1996). *Religion and mass media: Audience and adaptations.* Thousand Oaks, CA: Sage Publications.

Stout, D. A., & Buddenbaum, J. M. (Eds.). (2001). *Religion and popular culture: studies on the interaction of worldviews.* Ames: Iowa State University Press.

Media

Religions and religious cultures have always been defined in part by the media through which they are remembered, ritualized, expressed, and passed on. We assume that the earliest of these media used the basic human senses of sight, touch, hearing, and smell in combinations of ritual, story, art, music, and movement. The way we think about the media of religious cultures today, however, is influenced by historical developments in the economic, political, and technological spheres. In the history of the West—in particular—what once were thought to be the *natural* media of religion have taken their place among more *modern* media of communication, with far-reaching consequences.

Link to Religion and Empire

The Canadian economist Harold Innis is generally credited with the development of a theory of communication linking it to the prospects of religion and empire. According to Innis, the history of empire is partly explainable through the dominant media typical of their times. Those media that overcame *time* (such as stone carvings) favored the interests of religion, according to Innis, and those that overcame *space* (such as the lightweight and easily transportable papyrus scroll) favored the development of empire. Innis's larger project of developing a grand theory of media, politics, and religion remains intriguing, influencing such important twentieth-century thinkers as Marshall McLuhan and Jacques Ellul.

Today, there is good reason to think of all media as overcoming *both* time and space. Looking back from such a modern perspective, there are examples even in the early history of Christianity. The letters of Paul, for example, were significant both for their transcending of time (they endure) and of space (they depended on the complex infrastructure of the Roman road and postal system). Further, the Epistles are not the only example of interactions between religious history and media history in the West. The signal event is probably the development of moveable-type printing in Europe in the fifteenth century (though the technology first emerged in Asia centuries before). Gutenberg's innovation had far-reaching implications for Christianity, making it in fundamental ways a religion of "the book."

In addition to the production and distribution of Bibles, the Reformation led to the spread of the literacy needed to consume them. The historian Elizabeth Eisenstein has pointed out that almost more important (and more significant to the subsequent interactions between media and religion) was an impact that Gutenberg probably did not anticipate: the development of the social and market role we know of today as "the publisher."

Development of Publishing

The power to publish was a new social role, one that was potentially independent of state or clerical authority and thus influential on subsequent developments, including what we now think of as the sphere of public discourse. The independence of publishers and their publications led to direct conflict with the church and state, and the potential of conflict came to define the nature of Anglo-American press traditions and press theory, establishing the notion that the press should naturally be in a state of tension with these other authorities.

As with state authorities, religious authorities developed their own means of publishing, using the new medium of print for a variety of purposes. Besides Bibles, formal and informal religious organizations also produced tracts, posters, pamphlets, newspapers, magazines, "church school" materials, and books. In the case of the United States, religious publishing was among the earliest forms of printing in the colonies and new nation, forming the foundation for the secular printing and publishing industries that followed.

Development of Other Media

What we think of today as "the media," however, developed during the nineteenth century in Europe and North America as the result of the development of the first truly *mass* medium, the mass-market newspaper. This was made possible by the industrialization and mechanization of printing, one of the waves of innovation that contributed to the industrial revolution. This revolution in printing brought about massive changes in the speed and volume in which communication artifacts could be produced, further eliding Innis's distinction between the time and space capacities of the media. Because of the production speed and volume of

the modern mass media, both time and space became fluid, and the ability of individual messages to reach large, heterogeneous, and relatively anonymous audiences became the essential feature.

The rapidity of change in the media themselves also became a feature of the communication realm from the nineteenth century onward, with the revolution in printing coinciding with the first telecommunications (meaning "rapid communication") medium—the telegraph—followed soon after by an ever-quickening pace of invention. Motion pictures, radio, the phonograph, television, satellites, the Internet, the World Wide Web—each of these brought great promise and new challenges to the worlds of secular and religious communication. Besides the technologies involved and their abilities to transcend limitations in reach, time, and space, the mass-media era also brought about a revolutionary change in the way the media were financed. Prior to the mass press, media were largely directly supported by various political or sectarian interests or depended for their income on sales to readers or audiences. The mass press for the first time made it possible to support media through "third-party" or advertiser financing. This led to increasing independence, particularly in the journalistic media but also set the stage for one of the characteristics that came to define the media of the late twentieth century: commodification.

Growth of Religious Broadcasting

As the broadcasting era dawned, religion played an important role. The first radio stations on the air in the United States included religious broadcasts, and the public-service broadcasters who came to control the medium in Europe and elsewhere commonly included religion as one of their areas of service. In fact, what came to be known as the "public-service" model of religious broadcasting dominated most airtime for the first half of the twentieth century. This model stressed programming that served the great common religious values of a given culture, avoiding sectarian controversy. This so-called "broad-truths" approach to religion was in fact rooted in an essential characteristic of the mass media: that large, heterogeneous, and anonymous audiences necessarily demanded a kind of religion that was consensual and general in nature.

Particularized religion, however, found its place in the medium of broadcasting as well, even from the earliest days. The "radio preacher" that became a common social stereotype was a fixture of late-night and small-market radio from the 1920s onward in the United States. These Evangelical ministries were rooted in a sense that this new medium was an exceptional tool for the propagation of the Gospel, and with the development of international shortwave broadcasting, a number of such ministries began to develop worldwide outreach.

Religious Themes in Film

Film was also a medium where religion appeared from the earliest days. A number of major Hollywood films on biblical themes, including *Samson and Delilah* (1949), *David and Bathsheba* (1951), *The Robe* (1953), *The Bible* (1956), and *The Ten Commandments* (1923 and 1956) had important impacts on the world of religion and subsequent development of religious media in two ways. First, they helped create a film audience out of a previously skeptical religiously motivated middle America, thus domesticating film going, something that had previously been derogated in those contexts. Second, these helped create for that audience a taste for mediated religious imagery and a sense that mediated religion was thinkable and doable.

Sectarian Film

Commercial film continues to be an important medium for religious exploration, in both its theatrical and its sectarian forms. This latter area—sectarian film—has also been a prodigious producer of religious media. Evangelical organizations began producing films as early as the 1940s, and by the 1950s, films were regular fare in church basements throughout the United States, in Europe, and in mission fields elsewhere. The commercial success of film as an industry led to the development of ever-larger audiences, and today film remains among the most influential and "high culture" of the visual media. Struggles over access to film and over its content also continue, with a major event in 2004 the release of *The Passion of the Christ*, one of the most successful religiously themed films of all time.

Integration of Media into Religion

The media of radio, film, and publishing came to be integrated into the fabric of religion, particularly in the industrialized West, in a number of ways. Not only did they help establish the terms of religious understanding and the symbols of religious discourse for large audiences, they also increasingly came to form the outlines of the religious public sphere over the course of the twentieth century. The evangelist Billy Graham was one of the most prominent figures in this, playing an important role in the development of a new, more acceptable form of conservative Protestantism, moving beyond the Fundamentalism of the early century to the Evangelism of mid-century. For this purpose, it was important that Graham was soon able to establish himself both as a public figure and as a media figure.

Graham's rise also signaled the transition from the print and audio era to the visual era of religious media. Not only did Graham's ministry become a major producer and distributor of films, Graham himself became an important independent religious voice in American television. The Catholic bishop Fulton Sheen preceded Graham as a regular on American network television, but Graham's series of televised revivals beginning in the 1950s stretched into the twenty-first century, and he remained the dominant figure in American and British Evangelism and an important figure in Protestantism overall.

Television and Religion

Television has been a revolutionary medium for religion. As the medium that more than any other coalesced mass domestic and international audiences, it provided the foundation for cultural and social symbolization and discourse to finally move out of the realms of traditional authorities (clerical and state) into a freer space beyond, where commodified, voluble, and influential symbols and messages came to determine the nature of public culture, religious and otherwise.

Television's early days, like radio's, were defined by the "public-service" model. Up to the video revolution of the 1970s, the costs of terrestrial television broadcasting were prohibitive for any but the largest commercial and public organizations. In Britain and the United States, that meant that distinct versions of a public approach to religion held sway. In Britain, with an established church, the prerogatives and perspectives of the Church of England were at the center of output on the public-service BBC, though with careful provision for other voices and perspectives also to appear. In the United States, the "broad-truths" approach carried the day, though in practice the three dominant religions of mid-century America—Judaism, Catholicism, and Protestantism—were given preferential access to airtime.

In both the United States and Britain (and indeed in most public-service television systems) religion was largely relegated to what came to be known as the "religion ghetto" of Sunday mornings and late nights, its traditional times in the private sphere's domestic week, but also times where it posed little competition to programming favored by larger audiences.

Billy Graham on Evangelism and Media

Ironically, just at the time I find my own strength waning, God has provided new ways to extend our ministry through technology. As I have said elsewhere in these pages, until this century the extent of an evangelist's outreach was determined by the limits of his voice and the distribution of his writings. Now modern technologies have leapfrogged these barriers. Within the last few years, it has literally become possible to proclaim the Gospel to the entire world.

I am sure we would have staggered if we could see what will be possible a hundred, fifty, even ten years from now. If Jesus were here today, I have no doubt He would make use of every means possible to declare His message.

Source: Graham, B. (1997). *Just as I am: The Autobiography of Billy Graham* (p. 722). New York: HarperCollins Publishers.

All of this began to change in the 1970s with the twin innovations of satellite broadcasting and small-format videotape. The video and satellite revolutions made it possible for a wide range of producers to enter the television market. Small-format video greatly reduced the costs of television production and ultimately its distribution as well. As the costs of video-production equipment, the videotapes themselves, and VCRs fell through the 1970s and 1980s, new commercial, non-commercial, sectarian, and secular producers entered the television business, and television began to flood the globe in unprecedented ways.

Impact of Satellite Broadcasting

Perhaps more important to the prospects of religious television, however, was the development of satellite broadcasting. A series of regulatory and market changes in the 1970s made the widespread distribution of television no longer the monopoly of large networks or state broadcasting institutions. Anyone with the capital to do so could set up a network, and the increase in cable television in North America and the emergence of satellite "piracy" elsewhere meant that those networks could be connected with larger and larger numbers of receiving households and larger and larger audiences.

These largely technological changes had profound and lasting impacts on the nature of religious television. Evangelical broadcasters who had long been active in radio, in film production and distribution, and to an extent in television that was often relegated to the least desirable times and outlets were ready to take advantage of satellite and cable television. Being prodi-

gious fund raisers and armed with a theology that saw these developments as opportunities for expanded outreach, a number of ministries emerged as national and international broadcasters, seemingly overnight. Among these were Pat Robertson, who went on to a position of political prominence and whose *700 Club* remained as a significant ministry well into the twenty-first century; Jim and Tammy Bakker and their *PTL Club*; and Paul and Jan Crouch's Trinity Broadcasting Network, which continues as the only true religious television network to survive the market restructuring and shakeout that this industry has experienced. Literally hundreds of religious television broadcasters remain in the marketplace today, using a variety of production and distribution means. They range in size and influence from Trinity, which has produced theatrically released films, down to producers of one hour a week. They also range across the conservative theological spectrum, from the Catholic Eternal World Television Network, to the Pentecostal Benny Hinn.

Decline of the Public-Service Model

Self-defined and self-evident "religious television" is only part of the phenomenon, however. The decline of the public-service model in secular broadcasting came as a result of competition from commercial broadcasting, where a range of commodified cultural expressions are the heart of content. As a central site of cultural and social expression and meaning making, it stands to reason that what we once might have called simply "secular" television would also carry a significant amount of religious content.

In fact by the 1990s, commercial broadcasting had overcome whatever reluctance might have endured from the public-service era (where religious content was carefully segregated in schedules) and began scheduling programs that regularly dealt with religion and spirituality. In the U.S. context, the groundbreaking example was the very successful *Touched by an Angel*, which premiered on the CBS network in 1994 and ran through nine full seasons as a ratings success. CBS is also home to *Joan of Arcadia*, which premiered in 2003 and has achieved strong ratings. These were only the most prominent examples as a wide range of programs regularly deal with religion and spirituality in a variety of ways. Research with television audiences has revealed that an even wider range of programs are found to be religiously or spiritually significant by viewers, from *The Simpsons* to *The X-Files* and even *Walker, Texas Ranger*.

It thus appears that in the television era religious media have come full circle, with the everyday practices of religious or spiritual meaning making defining the extents and limits of religiously or spiritually significant communication. To see things this way necessitates a shift in perspective, however, away from an orientation focused on the various technologies of the media and their history, toward an orientation that focuses on audiences' practices of reception of these media. Such a view is consistent with trends on contemporary cultural analysis, which focuses on the reception rather than the production of culture. Such a view necessarily leads to a consideration of religious media in combination and interaction with one another. With increasing concentration and cross-ownership in the media industries, audiences' growing multimedia practice has coincided with an economic and cultural multimediation as well.

In the world of religious media and media about religion, this multimediation is not new. Many independent ministries have produced books, audio and videocassettes, magazines, journals, pamphlets, CD-ROMs, and DVDs in addition to television and film. Increasingly, such media are cross-promoted, with published materials marketed through radio and television and vice versa.

Media Enterprises

Much of religious media has been rooted in the conservative wings of Christianity and Protestantism. But other religions have their media, too. The so-called new age, or seeker-oriented faiths have spawned prodigious media enterprises, though they have been less present in television and radio than the more traditional religious groups. Scholars have begun to look across these mediated practices in the context of a wider concern with the material culture of religion. Studies in this area have looked at everything from greeting cards to funeral practices, to gifting, to calendar art, to vernacular art, to the wide range of ways that religion can be commodified, expressed, experienced and celebrated. Different media are also differentially relevant to various demographic categories, religious and otherwise. For example, a large and influential publishing industry supports a range of religious organizations, sensibilities, and groups, with magazines such as *Christianity Today* and its various other publishing enterprises playing a central role on the conservative end of the Protestant spectrum, *Sojourners* magazine and its activities positioned at the other end of that range, and an array of Catholic and Jewish enterprises also significant players.

Different demographic categories also consume popular media in unique ways, ways that are often religiously or spiritually significant as well. Youth culture has been a particular area of interest in this regard, being particularly active in appropriating a range of media to its own quests for spiritual or religious meaning.

Among the media most identified with generational cultures are those technologies most significant in the late twentieth and early twenty-first centuries: the digital media of the Internet, personal communication devices, and the World Wide Web. These media emerged with substantial promise in the spheres of religion and spirituality. A wide range of websites, meetings, list servs, and other online practices have self-conscious and less-obvious religious themes and implications. While the Internet and World Wide Web show great potential to be a new frontier in the evolution of religion, there is reason to suspect that a good deal of what goes on there is rather more mundane. At the same time, emerging digital media such as instant messaging may portend even more change in the articulation and realization of religion. Change has always been the rule in the evolution of media, and the media's interaction with religion will continue to be rooted in both technological and cultural change.

STEWART M. HOOVER

See also Journalism; Media Activism; Media Literacy; Newspapers

Further Reading

Boudoin, T. (2000). *Virtual faith: The irreverent spiritual quest of Generation X.* San Francisco: Jossey-Bass.
Brasher, B. (2001). *Give me that online religion.* San Francisco: Jossey-Bass.

Carpenter, J. (1985, April). *Tuning in the Gospel: Fundamentalist radio broadcasting and the revival of mass Evangelism, 1930–45.* Paper delivered to the Mid-American Studies Association, University of Illinois, Urbana.

Clark, L. S. (2003). *From angels to aliens: Teenagers, the supernatural, and the media.* New York: Oxford.

Crowley, D., & Heyer, P. (2003). *Communication in history.* Boston: Allyn and Bacon.

Eisenstein, E. (1980). *The printing press as an agent of change.* New York: Cambridge University Press.

Habermans, J. (1991). *The structural transformation of the public sphere.* Cambridge, MA: MIT Press.

Hadden, J., & Cowan, D. (Eds.). (2000). *Religion on the Internet.* New York: JAI Press.

Hendershot, H. (2004). *Shaking the world for Jesus: Media and conservative Evangelical culture.* Chicago: University of Chicago Press.

Hoover, S. M. (2002). The culturalist turn in scholarship on media and religion. *Journal of Media and Religion, 1*(1), 25–36.

Hoover, S. M. (in press). Islands in the Global Stream: Television, Religion, and Geographic Integration. *Studies in World Christianity.*

Hoover, S. M., Clark, L. S., Alters, D. F., Champ, J. G., & Hood, L. (2004). *Media, home and family.* New York: Routledge.

Hoover, S. M., Clark, L. S., & Rainie, L. (2004). *Faith online.* A technical report of the Pew Internet and American Life Project. Retrieved June 13, 2005, from http://www.pewinternet.org/pdfs/PIP_Faith_Online_2004.pdf

Hoover, S. M., & Wagner, D. K. (1997). History and policy in American broadcast treatment of religion. *Media, Culture and Society, 19*(1), 7–27.

Innis, H. A. (1972). *Empire and communications.* Toronto, Canada: University of Toronto Press.

Mahan, J., & Forbes, B. (Eds.). (2000). *Religion and popular culture in America.* Berkeley: University of California Press.

Marsden, G. (1982). Preachers of paradox. In M. Douglas & S. Tipton (Eds.), *Religion and America* (p. 155). Boston: Beacon Press.

McDannell, C. (1998). *Material Christianity.* New Haven, CT: Yale University Press.

Morgan, D. (1999). *Visual piety.* Berkeley: University of California Press.

Morgan, D., & Promey, S. (Eds.). (2001). *The visual culture of American religions.* Berkeley: University of California Press.

Nord, D. P. (2004). *Faith in reading: Religious publishing and the birth of mass media in America, 1790–1860.* New York: Oxford University Press.

Pinsky, M. (2001). *The Gospel according to the Simpsons: The spiritual life of the world's most animated family.* Louisville, KY: Westminster John Knox Press.

Roof, W. C. (1998). *Spiritual marketplace.* Cambridge, MA: Harvard University Press.

Schultze, Q. The mythos of the electronic church. *Critical Studies in Mass Communication, 4*(3), 245–261.

Wright, C. (1986). *Mass communication: A sociological perspective.* New York: McGraw-Hill.

Media Activism

To some scholars, juxtaposing the two terms "media" and "activism" sounds like a species of nonsense. The nonsense is not from any lack of clarity about the terms themselves. The term "media" readily refers to all the technologies of discourse that engulf public and private life today. John McHale identifies media used in activism as "publications, mailings, mass media, the Internet, interpersonal contact, meetings, phone calls, demonstrations (including speeches, testimony, banners, disruptive tactics, and slogans at demonstrations), and other media." The term "activism" is also a well-known phenomenon of principled expression advocating social change. Put these two familiar terms together and what emerges are "messages sent through the media that promote shifts in the social and political construction of legitimate limits of social, political, or economic conditions" (McHale 2004, 3). But meaningful media activism, says Todd Gitlin, is precisely what does not easily happen. Thanks to "the media's political skew toward the hypervaluation of private life and the devaluation of public life," the concerns of civic life are "largely reduced to a sideshow" (Gitlin 2002, 164). Criticism of and by the media aiming to improve democracy must swim against a gigantic tide towards passivism and privatism encouraged by the media themselves.

Still, as scholars of social-movements communication know, media activism does occur both globally and regionally, addressing such issues as environmentalism, health care, capital punishment, unilateral military action, and, most pertinently for this essay, the role of religion in public life. Despite the arguments of Richard Rorty and others that religion is best when it is most private, citizens in contemporary democracies are often quick to take up media arms against a sea of religious troubles, especially misrepresentations of religious groups, crude depictions of sexuality, and human-rights abuses. Religion, media, and democratic politics make for an exceedingly complicated triad, but not one likely to dissolve anytime soon.

Examples of Religious Media Activism

Gitlin has identified eight ways people tend to engage with the media: the fan, ironist, content critic, paranoid, exhibitionist, jammer, secessionist, and abolitionist. Although he uses these "styles of navigation" (2002, 118) to describe mostly secular engagement with the media, his terms are also useful for framing representative examples of religious media activism.

The *fan*, or the avid consumer of available mass-mediated fare, offers probably the largest and most varied activist demographic across the globe. Consumer choice is an important kind of activism, an implicit message that the pop-cultural industry should keep churning out material. In the United States, such media consumption appears to be relatively unaffected by religious convictions. There is, admittedly, a sizeable market for religious media fare—television shows like *Touched by an Angel*, movies like *The Passion of the Christ*, and music offered by the contemporary Christian music industry. Even so, being an Evangelical, mainline Protestant, or Roman Catholic does not appear to significantly influence what media consumers do with their remote controls. Unlike the trusting enthusiasm of the fan, the *ironist* both distrusts and depends on the mass media. Perhaps the people depicted in the title of a book chapter by William D. Romanowski, "Christians Who Drink Beer," are fans and ironists by turn.

For every contingent of amenable consumers, however, there is a vocal *content critic*. Great Britain's Malcolm Muggeridge and France's Jacques Ellul were two of the twentieth century's most notable Jeremiahs, indicting the mass media for their falls from grace. Other examples include "politically courageous reporting from the church-based press" in Kenya (Fackler 1990, 323), biblically informed cultural analysis from the Virginia-based *Mars Hill Audio Journal*, and small but determined pockets of Reformed Christians in Central and Eastern Europe (in organizations such as SEN) who attempt to nourish media literacy in religious citizens of young democracies.

Such prophetic attempts to speak from religious perspectives about the mass media contrast sharply with the habits Gitlin ascribes to the *paranoids*, those who believe that powerful media will have a pathogenic effect on their consumers. In 1996, for example, the Southern Baptist Convention (SBC) issued a resolution against The Walt Disney Company, encouraging a boycott by the faithful of the institution for its engagement with homosexual concerns. What was remarkable was that of the five things listed as failings of The Walt Disney Company, four of them were mass-mediated. The clear implication was that the real danger of The Walt Disney Company lay not in its specific institutional practices and policies regarding homosexual employees, so much as in its powerful mass-mediated messages. The SBC's solution to this problem was not to counsel communities to cultivate discerning criticism, but rather for individuals to practice activism by stopping The Walt Disney Company's access to their pocketbooks.

On the other hand, the *exhibitionist* is supremely confident of the ultimate religious serviceability of the mass media. The televangelist Jimmy Swaggart's "People of Love" centers, Jerry Falwell's Moral Majority, and Pat Robertson's *700 Club* mustered so much support by the American electorate that scholars like Jeremy Rifkin and Jeffrey K. Hadden conclude that Evangelical activism is a most potent (if not *the* most potent) political force in the United States. Unlike the glittering earnestness of the television preachers, the *jammer* has a quirky, savvy activism that positions a message (often a defacement of a corporate message) in an unexpected public place. The catchy black and white "God speaks" billboards are a religious example of jamming by means of preachments such as "That 'Love Thy Neighbor' thing—I meant it," and "Don't make me come down there." All the statements are signed, by proxy, "God."

The habits of the *secessionist* appear in the policies of conservative religious liberal arts colleges, especially those in the American Bible Belt, which forbid students to have televisions in their dorm rooms or to go to movie theaters after class. Extreme examples of the *abolitionist* draw on religious fervor to practice acts of terror, counting on the quick eye of national television to communicate a religio-political message. The September 11 terrorists are the most infamous example of media activists with purported religious motivations. To link these examples of abolition and secessionism in a single paragraph is not to argue for an essential connection between Christian and Islamic Fundamentalism, because as the next section of this essay will show, the activist habits of conservative religionists in America have had a quite markedly different impact on the mass media than has the activism of religious conservatives from other faith traditions in other countries.

Nature and Impact of Religious Media Activism

The careful reader will note two common traits of the examples of religiously informed activism just offered. First, most of the examples featured American media activism. As the largest exporter of public culture, the United States quite naturally offers some of the richest examples of religionists' efforts to influence others by means of the mass media. Second, Gitlin's categories are uniformly negative in formation, suggesting the unlikelihood of substantive activism. His bleak portrayals of resistance to the media tsunami suggest that, apart from acts of violence, religionists really have very little capability to effect change by means of the media. But American religionists have managed to engage with the media in order to address the question of how much influence persons of faith have had on and by the media industry.

Quentin Schultze insists, "The interaction of the mass media and Christianity taking place in the United States is not mirrored anywhere else in the world—even in other democracies with Christian tribes" (2003, 351). There are good historical reasons for the exceptional nature and impact of American religious media activism. As James Carey has argued, the American experiment finds significant roots in a kind of religious media activism. Because the Pilgrims saw the transmission of ideas from one point to another as a worthy redemptive project, they understood their journey across the Atlantic in piously communicative terms: the *Mayflower* was a kind of mass medium for missiological enterprise. Later, the founders of the American republic saw the mass transport of ideas, by means of good roads, as a means of making a large liberal democracy possible. Although James Madison's argument in the *Federalist Papers* about roads as communication technology was not avowedly religious in nature, later American technologies of communication were understood in religious terms. In the 1840s Samuel F. B. Morse described the telegraph with a pious rhetorical question, "What hath God wrought?" Radio and television would subsequently be understood as means of conveying Christian truth in what the subtitle of Paul Freed's *Let the Earth Hear* called "the thrilling story of how radio goes over barriers to bring the gospel of Christ to unreached millions." Mass communication and religious activism have never been fully separated in the American imagination.

This linkage between religiosity and the mass media, as Schultze has argued, has influenced not just believers, but broad swaths of the American populace. He explains that there are marked tendencies, even among secularists, to understand the media as means of "conversion" (to American notions of multicultural harmony) and "communion" (in broad myths of prosperity such as the American Dream) and "praise" (in the preoccupation with celebrity) (2003, 9). Americans understand media activism in essentially religious terms.

Not that religious activism in the media has been entirely optimistic. Religious activism in the United States has what James Carey calls a dystopian side, resulting in negative takes on the media, even among those who do not subscribe to a particular religion. Schultze identifies, for example, faith-inspired dialects of "discernment" and "exile" (2003, 9). In other words, religionists in America have tended both to judge the media and to distance themselves from it. When not condemning the excesses of the media, Americans sometimes feel alienated by it. As an occasion for prophetic or pilgrim activism, the mass media have a recognizably religious register.

But the impact of religious activism on the media is reciprocal. The cost paid by American religionists for retooling public life by means of the media is that religion has been influenced by its own tools. Marshall McLuhan famously said that the medium is the message, an aphorism that communication scholar Em Griffin summarized as "We shape our tools, and they in turn shape us" (2003, 343). The emergence of religious celebrity groupies, the manipulativeness of televangelists, the flattening of the supernatural—all these are, according to Clifford Christians, unlooked-for ways that religion has, in the course of activism, been shaped by its own implements. Still, as Schultze argues, the mass media has an interdependent relationship with religion. "A healthy tension between the media and Christianity is ultimately a good thing for democracy in America, as long as both sides are civil even when they disagree" (2003, 6).

Study of Global Religious Media

This essay has emphasized the exceptional nature and consequences of religious media activism in America. In many ways, this emphasis is only natural, because the conversations between religion and the mass media in the United States have been so complex and so surprising that it is hard to think of exact parallels in other parts of the world. But if Gitlin is right to say that "Hollywood is the global cultural capital" and that increasingly everybody lives "under the sign of Mickey Mouse & Co." (2002, 176–177), then the study of global religious media activism may reasonably begin by an analysis of American media advocacies. But more research should be done elsewhere. In Argentina, for example, the 2004 closing of the controversial art show of León Ferrari found Jews and Catholics applauding and leftist literati protesting the negotiation of religion, politics, and media in a struggling democracy. Across the planet, Rosalind I. J. Hackett has pointed out that

Nigeria's secular democracy, whose "media scene...is arguably one of the most lively and developed on the African continent" (2003, 48), has witnessed depictions of Christians and Muslims that have both deepened and diminished distrust between these religious groups. But "media issues, notably in connection with religion, are under-researched when it comes to Nigeria or indeed Africa as a whole" (2003, 61). Will the increase of revivalist forms of religion in struggling democracies manipulate the mass media to the ends of philistinism and violence? Communication scholarship needs to investigate how earnest religionists everywhere can practice energetic advocacy via the mass media to the benefit of piety and polity alike.

CRAIG E. MATTSON

Further Reading

Abercrombie, N., & Longhurst, B. (1998). *Audiences*. Thousand Oaks, CA: Sage.

Campbell, R. (2003). *Media and culture: An introduction to mass communication* (4th updated ed.). New York: St. Martin's Press.

Carey, J. W. (1989). Communication as culture: Essays on media and society. In D. Thorburn (Ed.), *Media and popular culture*. New York: Routledge.

Christians, C. (1990). Redemptive media as the evangelical's cultural task. In Q. J. Schultze (Ed.), *American evangelicals and the mass media*. Grand Rapids, MI: Academie.

Fackler, M. (1990). A short story of evangelical scholarship in communications studies. In Q. J. Schultze (Ed.), *American evangelicals and the mass media*. Grand Rapids, MI: Academie.

Fackler, P. M., & Lippy, C. H. (Eds.). (1995). Popular religious magazines of the United States. In *Historical guides to the world's periodicals and newspapers*. Westport, CT: Greenwood.

Freed, P. E. (1980). *Let the earth hear: The thrilling story of how radio goes over barriers to bring the gospel of Christ to unreached millions*. Nashville, TN: Nelson.

Gitlin, T. (2002). *Media unlimited: How the torrent of images and sounds overwhelms our lives*. New York: Henry Holt.

Griffin, E. (2003). *A first look at communication theory* (5th ed.). Boston: McGraw-Hill Higher Education.

Hackett, R. I. J. (2003). Managing or manipulating religious conflict in the Nigeria media. In J. Mitchell & S. Marriage (Eds.), *Mediating religion: Conversations in media, religion and culture*. London: T&T Clark.

Herrick, J. A. (2003). *The making of the new spirituality: The eclipse of the western religious tradition*. Downer's Grove, IL: Intervarsity.

La DAIA replicó a Ferrari y Negó que la Iglesia Católica fuera antisemita. *La Nacion Line*. Retrieved December 22, 2004, from http://www.lanacion.com.ar/cultura/nota.asp?nota_id=663812&origen=amigoenvio

May, J. R., (Ed.). (1997). *New image of religious film*. Kansas City, MO: Sheed & Ward.

McHale, J. P. (2004). Communication for change: Strategies of social and political advocates. In R. E. Denton, Jr. (Ed.), *Communication, media, and politics*. Lanham, MD: Rowman.

Peters, J. D. (1999). *Speaking into the air*. Chicago: University of Chicago.

Pieper, J. (1988). *Abuse of language, abuse of power* (L. Krauth, Trans.). San Francisco: Ignatius.

Pierce, D. L. (2003). *Rhetorical criticism and theory in practice*. Boston: McGraw-Hill.

Postman, N. (1985). *Amusing ourselves to death: Public discourse in the age of show business*. New York: Penguin.

Romanowski, W. D. (2001). *Eyes wide open: Looking for God in popular culture*. Grand Rapids, MI: Brazos.

Rorty, R. (1999). *Philosophy and social hope*. New York: Penguin.

Rouillon, J. (2004). Abrazo simbólico en el Centro Recoleta. *La Nacion Line*. Retrieved December 18, 2004, from http://www.lanacion.com.ar/cultura/nota.asp?nota_id=664187&origen=amigoenvio

Schrader, P. (1972). *Transcendental style in film: Ozu, Bresson, Dreyer*. New York: Da Capo.

Schultze, Q. J. (2003). Christianity and the mass media in America: Toward a democratic accommodation. In M. J. Medhurst (Ed.), *Rhetoric and public affairs series*. East Lansing, MI: Michigan State University Press.

Squier, S. M. (2003). *Communities of the air: Radio century, radio culture*. Durham, NC: Duke University Press.

The Southern Baptist Convention's "Disney" Resolution. Retrieved June 12, 1996, from http://www.religioustolerance.org/new1_966.htm

Media Literacy

Promotion of general literacy has been intimately linked to religious communities for centuries, and media literacy, in particular, has had dramatic interactions with religious communities.

History

Although the printing press made texts widely accessible and was thus "important to mass literacy" in Europe, "of equal importance was an Augustinian monk,

Martin Luther (1483–1546), whose claim that each person ought to be able to the read the Word of God for herself or himself brought a text with an immediate and huge market to the new technology" (Tyner 1998, 20). In the United States, literacy was heavily promoted, particularly in the late 1800s and early 1900s, by religious communities. The rush to teach people how to read served "similar purposes of religious propagation, maintenance of political order, and the formation of a national character" (Graff and Arnove 1995, 275). Christian Evangelical efforts to promote literacy as a means to spread the Gospel led to the formation of the Sunday School Union and its libraries which helped "to prepare for the development of the public school"; indeed, "statistics in an 1859 *Manual of Public Libraries* document that 30,000 of the 50,000 libraries in the nation were Sunday school collections" (Boys 1989, 31).

In each of these examples, religious communities used promotion of literacy to pursue specific religious goals. The underside of that history, however, is the suppression and loss of indigenous languages and the promotion of "alphabetic literacy," or literacy based on written texts at the expense of oral and other modes of language. Scholars argue that literacy is "one of many discourses in a multicultural, multilingual society" (Tyner 1998, 28), and that communication through language involves far more than simple utterance of words.

Freire and Literacy

It is this understanding of literacy as a form of discourse that permeates Brazilian adult literacy expert Paulo Freire's (1921–1997) essential work on literacy. Freire understood literacy education as a process by which those most oppressed by societal structures could gain their own voices learning to read and write through the "conscientization" of their situations.

As Freire's ideas began to permeate beyond Brazil's borders, the discussion of media literacy began to emerge with more energy and force. Two definitional threads resulted from this discussion—literacy as a tool for promulgating already produced meaning, and literacy as a form of discourse that can illuminate structures of power. Educators following both of these threads, already conscious of the pervasive presence and influence of nonprint-based materials, particularly television, in the meaning making of their students, mined the field of communications for conceptual frameworks that would help them incorporate emerging media technologies into literacy.

Instrumental Media Literacy

In the U.S. context, where communication studies focused primarily on questions of media effects and other instrumental notions, the combination of communication studies with either of these understandings of literacy led to a definition of media literacy that stressed strongly its ability to "inoculate" students against damaging effects. The melding of conceptual frames drawn from communication studies with the definition of literacy as a tool for promulgating already produced meaning led to a definition of media literacy. From the "tool end" of the media literacy spectrum came a desire to teach people how to use new media to broadcast already defined religious messages that would serve to displace "negative secular" messages. The goal was to use media to effect a new form of evangelism that would spread the Gospel more broadly. Not much thought was given as to whether or not the use of this new tool fundamentally altered the message being promulgated through it (Horsfield 1984).

From the "power of discourse" end of the literacy spectrum came a media literacy focused on deconstructing dominant messages, thus "conscientizing" students so that they could critically participate in rebuilding a new society. The goal here, particularly within religious communities, was to engage mass media critically and thus negate their destructive effects. An excellent example of this approach can be seen in the early years of the Center on Media and Values. Media-literacy advocates in the religious realm worked hard to create critical engagement with popular culture, but refused to acknowledge the ways in which that critical engagement forced a new approach to religious community as well. Deconstructing dominant meaning is only part of the media-education process described by Freire, which begins and ends in creative construction of active subjects. Religious persons have a life as religious subjects just as much as they do as media subjects. Religious media-literacy advocates were missing the second part of the process described by Freire, the crucial claiming of voice and construction of active religious subjectivities. "If literacy can be halved into two universes, reading and writing, the literature...follows a one-way mass media paradigm that is increasingly anachronistic in comparison to the two-way, interactive potential of technology. In the mass media equation, students are primarily receivers of information selected by others" (Tyner 1998, 85).

In each instance of religious communities practicing media literacy, media engagement was focused on "reading" not on "writing." In the tool mode of spreading a positive message, or in the discourse mode of deconstructing a negative message, media engagement in religious communities was essentially focused on ways to get beyond mass-mediated popular culture, rather than seeing it as an original and crucial matrix in which to do theological reflection and live faithfully. Such a limited view was directly linked to the communication theories educators were drawing upon.

Expressive Media Literacy

With the advent of global systems of telecommunication—particularly the World Wide Web—religious communities, media scholars, and literacy advocates finally began to learn more directly from each other. The shift to a global system opened up new lines of collaboration, both within and outside of communities of faith, between scholars and activists, between producers and receivers. This shift has made it possible for communication theories that are based on cultural reception rather than on instrumental effects to make their way into the U.S. context, at the same time as communities throughout the world grow ever more cognizant of the need to support indigenous cultural expression in the face of the dominance of United States-originated programming.

For more than four decades, there has been an explosion of literacy work in multiple contexts across the globe. "Research and practice about media education has been ongoing since the 1960s....Notably it is embedded in the curriculum in most industrialized countries—except the United States. It is mandated in the curriculum in Canada, England, Australia, and New Zealand, and offered in a host of non-English-speaking countries, including Austria, Brazil, France, Germany, Mexico, and Spain" (Tyner 1998, 92–93). Media education is only one of the rubrics being advanced. Computer literacy, network literacy, technology literacy, information literacy, visual literacy, and finally, multiliteracies have all been proposed as crucial elements of capacity for citizens of the twenty-first century. Literacy education "emphasizes how negotiating the multiple linguistic and cultural differences in our society is central to the pragmatics of [our] working, civic, and private lives" (New London Group 1996, 60).

Media literacy no longer accepts the simple reading tasks of earlier forms, but requires that students be able to write in particular media as well. It also builds on a more nuanced and culturally receptive understanding of the process of communication. Rather than envisioning communication as a one-way process of "sender-message-receiver," scholars and activists are increasingly describing an active engagement on the part of audiences with the "texts" that they consume, using words such as "resist," "negotiate," "contest," and "rewrite" to highlight the process. Alongside this more active analysis of how media function is a more complex and active description of how teaching and learning take place.

Teaching and Learning Paradigms Shift

Many U.S. media-literacy activists missed the more radical aspects of Freirean literacy theory when they were working on communication theory, not only because communication theory in the U.S. context tended to be so instrumental but also because educational theory owed so much at the time to notions of "schooling," or what Freire called a "banking" understanding of teaching, in which teachers make deposits of knowledge in heretofore "empty" students' heads (Freire 1985, 59). He contrasted that description of education with a problem-posing approach in which students gained literacy through engaging their own contexts and coming to voice—and thus reading and writing—words as a means of liberation. The words they began learning to read and write grew out of the words they were struggling to find to name their reality in situations in which they were oppressed, in which their reality was quite literally "written out."

This transformational understanding of education paired well with cultural-studies theories emerging in Europe, and grew into what media education experts Len Masterman and Francois Mariet call an "experiential, democratic pedagogy." They summarize the principles of media education in the European context thus:

1. The central and unifying concept of media education is that of representation.

2. A central purpose of media education is to "denaturalize" the media.

3. Media education is primarily investigative; it does not seek to impose specific cultural values.

4. Media education is organized around key concepts, which are analytical tools rather than an alternative content.

5. Media education is a lifelong process.

6. Media education aims to foster not simply critical understanding, but critical autonomy.

7. The effectiveness of media education may be evaluated by two principal criteria: (a) the ability of students to apply what they know (their critical ideas and principles) to new situations; and (b) the amount of commitment, interest, and motivation displayed by students.

8. Media education is topical and opportunistic. (Tyner 1998, 117; Masterman and Mariet 1994, 53–57)

Tyner suggests that these principles are shared by media educators all over the world, noting in particular media-studies expert Roberto Aparici's work in Spain and his analysis of media education in other parts of the world (Tyner 1998, 118).

It is crucial to note this shift in underlying paradigm in relation to a consideration of media literacy's interaction with religion. From an instrumental, and thus "protectionist" or "inoculative" approach to media, media literacy or media education has moved to a fundamentally transformative approach in which media become one of a number of avenues in which students become capable of "writing their lives." In some sense *media* has grown closer to what might have been an original meaning of the term, a plural for *medium*, or that in which something can be grown and nurtured.

Where historically religious communities were at the forefront of pushing print-based literacy, now more and more of them are struggling to figure out where they stand in relation to media literacy. Both communication theory and media-literacy practice have moved away from instrumental notions and toward more culturally receptive positions. This shift has pushed some religious communities into a renewed examination of their role in relation to culture. In some parts of the Christian context, for instance, theologian H. Richard Niebuhr's categories still carry power. Churches may define themselves as inhabiting a "Christ vs. Culture" position, or a "Christ transforming culture" position (Niebuhr 1951, vii–viii). Niebuhr's categories, however, are increasingly being reconsidered and challenged in light of the diverse local cultures that flourish amidst an increasingly global culture (Lee 2000). Indeed, religious appropriations of the concept of culture are increasingly fluid and diverse, drawing upon postmodern debates within anthropology and notions of social constructivism within pedagogy.

This challenge to received notions is particularly strong within religious communities that are struggling to come to terms with the diverse meaning-making practices of their younger generations. Where before

mass media were pipelines through which Evangelical messages could be piped, thus helping their congregants avoid "secular popular" contexts, or similarly, where mass-mediated popular contexts were engaged primarily as a means to deconstruct negative messages, now communities of faith are slowly and often painfully coming to realize that mass-mediated popular culture has become the primary database from which younger generations are drawing to make sense of their religious experiences.

These people—and they are not all young—are increasingly not only "reading" their experiences as holding transcendent significance but also are "writing" their experiences in popular culture genres, even in some cases using digital tools to incorporate popular culture references into their religious meaning making. One striking consequence of this shift has been a move away from formal religious institutions as arbiters of meaning and credibility, of religious authority (Hess, Horsfield, and Medrano 2004).

The challenge of media literacy now becomes a very fruitful and compelling one for religious educators: How can they foster identity within and loyalty to a specific community of faith while at the same time respecting the pluralism of the world context and the integrity of spiritual practices that reside within popular culture frameworks as much as within traditional church practices? The answers to this question are just beginning to emerge, and are at least as varied as the contexts in which they arise. Some scholars look to popular culture contexts as rich ground for religious meaning making. Theologian Thomas Beaudoin, for instance, points to texts as varied as Broadway musicals like *Rent*, MTV videos done by Madonna, and science fiction scenarios (2000). Others have gone searching in the various religious traditions to reclaim meaning-making practices that are rich in image and experiential sensorium, reclaiming daily practices of faith such as hospitality, testimony, household economics, and so on as a basis for renewing commitment to traditional communities of faith (Bass 1997). Still others are experimenting with worship spaces, believing that ritual is at the heart of understanding faith, and finding ways to incorporate digital media into liturgy and other forms of prayer (Sample 1998; Anderson and Foley 1997).

Indeed, some scholars suggest that media literacy holds the promise of enculturating religion in the twenty-first century, if religious communities can find ways to engage media literacy that respect its transformational character, and that focus on "writing" in media as much as they do on "reading" it. The paradigm shift that has emerged within communication studies—from an instrumental to an expressive approach—has emerged within religious education as well. Religious communities are now trying to determine if religious "truth" is something that can be objectively known and thus deposited through linear practice directly into passive minds and hearts, or, in contrast, if "truth" is something that is intimately relational, growing out of contextual engagement and revealed in an ongoing fashion through its participants' practice. These are the questions that religious communities continue to struggle with as they engage media literacy.

MARY HESS

Further Reading

Anderson, H. & Foley, E. (1997). *Mighty stories, dangerous rituals: Weaving together the human and the divine.* San Francisco: Jossey-Bass.

Aparici, R. (Ed.). (1996). *La revolución de los medios audiovisuales: Educación y nuevas tecnologías* (2d ed.). Madrid, Spain: Ediciones de la Torre.

Aparici, R. & García-Matilla, A. (1989). *Lectura de imágenes.* Madrid, Spain: Ediciones de la Torre.

Bass, D. (1997). *Practicing our faith.* San Francisco: Jossey-Bass.

Bazalgette, C. (Ed.). (1993). *Proceedings of the 1992 UNESCO conference on media education.* London: British Film Institute, CLEMI, and UNESCO.

Beaudoin, T. (2000). *Virtual faith: The irreverent spiritual quest of Generation X.* San Francisco: Jossey-Bass.

Bevans, S. (1992). *Models of contextual theology.* Maryknoll, NY: Orbis Books.

Boys, M. (1989). *Educating in faith: Maps and visions.* San Francisco: Harper & Row.

Buckingham, D. (1994). *Children talking television: The making of television literacy.* Basingstoke, UK: Falmer Press.

Buckingham, D. & Sefton-Green, J. (1996). *Cultural studies goes to school: Reading and teaching popular media.* Basingstoke, UK: Taylor & Francis.

Center for Media Literacy. Retrieved June 28, 2005 from www.medialit.org.

Delpit, L. (1995). *Other people's children: Cultural conflict in the classroom.* New York: The New Press.

Fairclough, N. (1989). *Discourse and social change.* Cambridge, UK: Polity Press.

Freire, P. (1985). *Pedagogy of the oppressed.* New York: Continuum Press.

Gee, J. P. (1996). *Social linguistics and literacies: Ideology in discourses.* Bristol, PA: Taylor & Francis.

Giroux, H. (1988). *Schooling and the struggle for public life.* Minneapolis: University of Minnesota Press.

Graff, H. J. & Arnove, R. F. (1995). National literacy campaigns in historical and comparative perspective. In H. J. Graff (Ed.), *The labyrinths of literacy: Reflections on literacy past and present* (pp. 270–298). Pittsburgh, PA: University of Pittsburgh Press.

Hart, A. (Ed). (1998). *Teaching the media: International perspectives.* Mahwah, NJ: Lawrence Earlbaum Associates.

Hess, M. (1999). From trucks carrying messages to ritualized identities: Implications for religious educators of the postmodern paradigm shift in media studies. *Religious Education, 94*(3), 273–288.

Hess, M. (1998). Media literacy in religious education: Engaging popular culture to enhance religious experience (Doctoral dissertation, Boston College, 1998). *Dissertation Abstracts International.*

Hess, M., Horsfield, P., & Medrano, A. (2004). *Belief in media: Cultural perspectives on Christianity and media.* Burlington, VT: Ashgate Publishing.

Horsfield, P. (1984). *Religious television: The American experience.* New York: Longman.

Jesuit Communication Project 1804–1877. Retrieved June 28, 2005 from http://interact.uoregon.edu/MediaLit/JCP/

Kress, G. (1985). *Linguistic processes in sociocultural practice.* Oxford, UK: Oxford University Press.

Lee, B. (2000, November). A post-colonial feminist analysis of the dynamics of Christianity and culture in the Korean Christian religious education context. *Proceedings of the Association of Professors and Researchers in Religious Education*, 311–324.

Macdonnel, D. (1986). *Theories of discourse: An introduction.* Oxford, UK: Basil Blackwell.

McLaren, P. L. (1989). *Life in schools: An introduction to critical pedagogy in the foundations of education.* New York: Longman.

Masterman, L. & Mariet, F. (1994). *Media education in the 1990s Europe: A teachers' guide.* Croton, NY: Manhattan Publishing.

Media Literacy Online Project. Retrieved June 28, 2005 from http://interact.uoregon.edu/MediaLit/HomePage

Niebuhr, H. R. (1951). *Christ and culture.* New York: Harper & Row Publishers.

New London Group. (1996). A pedagogy of multiliteracies: Designing social futures. *Harvard Educational Review, 66*(1), 60–92.

Sample, T. (1998). *The spectacle of worship in a wired world: Electronic culture and the gathered people of God.* Nashville, TN: Abingdon Press.

Schreiter, R. (1997). *The new catholicity: Theology between the global and the local.* Maryknoll, NY: Orbis Books.

Shweder, R. (1991). *Thinking through cultures: Expeditions in cultural psychology*. Cambridge, MA: Harvard University Press.

Tanner, K. (1997). *Theories of culture: A new agenda for theology*. Minneapolis, MN: Fortress Press.

Tyner, K. (1998). *Literacy in a digital world: Teaching and learning in the age of information*. Mahwah, NJ: Lawrence Earlbaum Associates.

Van Gelder, C. (Ed.). (1996). *The church between gospel and culture: The emerging mission in North America*. Grand Rapids, MI: William Eerdmans Publishing.

Meditation

The Search for Ultimate Reality

Meditation is much misunderstood. Many who do not understand it fully use it mechanistically to create an effect. In an attempt to "increase our inner awareness" and to "find ourselves," some superficial and nonspiritual meditation techniques produce an experience that is exciting and exhilarating, but divorced from its religious anchorage, and often has little lasting effect. This form of meditational exercise is often a form of escapism. Meditation is most effective when it is based on the quest for an understanding of the ultimate reality, for it is then that the soul is truly liberated. For this, the mind must be stilled. As a form of communication, it works most effectively at an intrapersonal level when the mind is placid and calm. This is because meditation is communication by the human soul with the human soul at a spiritual level.

For effective spiritual communication to occur, meditation must overcome the natural tendency of the mind to diffuseness, by learning to apply it to a single point to the exclusion of all else. This allows for the birth of true understanding. This is also the bedrock of all mind control. This method of mind management is used by those who wish to make a spiritual intrapersonal communication. Otherwise, meditation cannot free the mind from its general zeal to be the master of all matter. This, however, is inimical to spiritual communicative meditation. For that to happen, the art of concentration must be learned. The control of thought must be mastered. Eastern meditative techniques and philosophy taught this with a view to liberating the soul. This is because we are the result of what we have thought. What we are is founded upon our thoughts. It is made by our thoughts. Patanjali explains that "The mind is trained so that the ordinary modifications of its action are not present, but only those which occur upon the conscious taking up of an object for contemplation, is changed into the likeness of that which is pondered upon, and enters into full comprehension of the being thereof" (Judge 1889).

Self-realization and the Ultimate Reality

To overcome the natural tendency of the human mind to diffuseness, meditation is used to prevent new evil from entering one's mind, to remove all evil that is there, to develop such good as is in one's mind, and to acquire still more unceasingly. To achieve this requires "right effort." This involves the right use of one's energies, directing them to secure the maximum results with the minimum expenditure of force. This involves the whole field of modern psychology, in the elimination of every "complex" and mental inhibition that results in friction and consequent loss of power. In this way, the connection with the spiritual part of one's being is made.

Meditation is, therefore, part of a much longer process of self-realization. Meditation cannot work if the mind cannot be controlled. It is necessary, therefore, to first acquire a degree of moral and physical control. Then, as Eastern philosophy teaches, one can approach *Bhavna*, the control and evolution of the mind. Every Eastern school of practical philosophy has emphasized this since the dawn of history. This is because, just as a high standard of ethics is a prerequisite for the grasp of pure philosophy to prevent a power thereby gained from being abused, so mind control in its widest sense is vital to tread the path to enlightenment.

The conditions required for spiritual communication to occur are such that the thought process must first be stilled. This is because one is trying to communicate with one's soul and through the soul with the ultimate reality. To achieve this, one must sit in *samadhi*. This is a state of mind in which the waves of confusion aroused by thought are stilled. It is far more than trance or mere psychic ecstasy; it is awareness of the still center of the turning world. In this way, mind development is carried to heights beyond our normal understanding. *Samadhi*, however, is far short of *prajna* (wisdom), which together with its twin sister *karuna* (compassion), is known by the faculty of *buddhi*, the intuition or direct cognition by which the evolving consciousness recognizes and knows its oneness with the All of which it is part. When *samadhi* merges with *prajna/karuna*, the individual has earned the title "free," free from the fetters of *avidhya* (ignorance) and

A young woman meditating in a forest setting. *Courtesy of J. Morse/ istockphoto.com.*

free from the snares of the self, and being free he knows that he is free and finds himself upon the threshold of Nirvana.

The "Monist" Conception of the Ultimate Reality

This is how meditation works best: as a form of communication between the self and the ultimate reality. This ultimate reality may or may not be God. The ultimate reality is how the individual conceives him. Religion is based on the human conviction that beyond the physical world there is a transcendent or absolute reality. Eastern and Western religions have different conceptions of the ultimate reality. Both conceive of a reality that is greater than the physical universe, but they have radically different conceptions that lead to radically different accounts of the relationship of the individual to the ultimate reality. That in turn leads to differences over such questions as evil, suffering, salvation and liberation and even matters such as time and space.

In Western tradition (comprising the Judeo-Christian and Muslim orthodoxies) the transcendent reality is given in the name of God, who is a personal, omnipotent, omniscient being. God here is the creator and is conceived of as being wholly other than His creation. He is described variously as being both wrathful and avenging and kind and beneficient. Above all he has a will and a purpose for human beings. The cosmos is an arena for the interaction between God and inhumanity. In the Eastern traditions of Buddhism, Daoism, Hinduism (particularly the *Adviata Vedanta* school) as well as newer eastern religions like Sikhism, there is no concept of God as a person. The ultimate reality is rather a process, a truth, or a state of being. It is a concept that is posited as one of "absolute reality," suggesting that there is a single reality in the cosmos. Everything else is either a relative or contingent reality or is illusory or nonxistent. It is the Absolute that is transcendent and immanent. It cannot be described as an aspect of the phenomenal world. This is because it is devoid of all empirical determinations. This absolute reality is called *Brahma* in Hinduism, *Dao* in Daoism, *Paramartha* in Mahayana Buddhism, and *Akal Murat* or *Akal Purakh* in Sikhism.

In the context of these differences, Eastern religions can be described as "monist" depicting only one fundamental reality in the world, whereas Western religions can be described as "dualist" or "theistic," being composed of the two different realities of God and humanity. These two radically different conceptions of the ultimate reality lead to radically different perceptions of life and how it should be lived. In the dualist traditions suffering is the result of sin. Sin results from the breaking of God's will. This in turn is caused by the disobedience of human will. In the monist traditions suffering is due to human ignorance (*avidhya*) or delusion. The physical world is an illusion (*maya*) and human beings suffer because they become overly obsessed with worldly gain. In the dualist tradition, salvation from the commission of sin caused by a failure to follow the law of God can only be remedied by turning towards God and his written laws. In the monist traditions, because the source of all evil and suffering is human ignorance and the failure to perceive the real state of affairs, the path to salvation lies in the acquisition of knowledge and wisdom. This is above all intuitive and experimental knowledge gained through meditation, breathing exercises, contemplation, and discipline of body and mind. In Hinduism, the wisdom gained by seeing through illusion (*maya*) is called *jnana*; in Buddhism it is called *prajna*. In either event, whether one's conception of the ultimate reality is as a monist or as a dualist, meditation allows one, through the control of thought, to communicate with that ultimate reality.

Monist and dualist religions both refer to a paradise or heaven after death, just as they both describe a hell or place of suffering. However, the treatment of these two states is markedly different in the two religious systems. In Western tradition, they describe a place where the soul finally finds its resting abode, which may be either a place of eternal pain or of happiness. In Eastern traditions the cycle of life is continuous through birth and rebirth, with heaven and hell both being temporary sojourns before one returns back to earth in a reincarnated form. There is no final end. The soul continues, surviving in one reincarnated form and then another. Salvation for the soul comes through liberation from the process of reincarnation. In Hinduism, this is referred to as *moksha* (in Sikhism it is referred to as *mukti*). The goal of the wise is to achieve this state in life through deep meditation and self-control. When this happens, it is called *jivanmukti*, and such a person is said to have attained *sat-chit-ananda*, namely, a state of existence-consciousness-bliss in this life. For Buddhists, the liberation of the soul through meditation leads to *nirvana*, namely, a state of being "blown out," whereby all craving, desire, and attachment to the world is extinguished.

The Liberated Soul and the Ultimate Reality

It is in the liberation of the soul that meditation is most effective. This is because it is a form of thought-communication, through control of the thinking process, leading to an intrapersonal communication with the senses. Meditation works by stopping the normal flow of thought. The individual opens up to concepts and ideas that would not otherwise have emerged in the human consciousness. In its most perfected form meditation can bring about an altered state of consciousness. However, as a communicative form, different religions employ meditation differently. Hinduism has developed the art of meditation to its highest levels. In Hinduism, there are a range of practices, from controlling bodily functions such as breathing (*pranayama*), to concentrating on visual images (*mandalas*), to repetitive chanting of a word or a phrase (*mantras*), to a repetitive bodily movement (*mudra*). In Thervada Buddhism, the method employed is to focus on some object or concept (as the Buddha did himself). Zen Buddhists contemplate a koan. This is a question or a problem put to a student, forcing him to view reality in a new way, thus leading to the enlightenment of his soul. It involves a creative technique of propelling a disciple into a new vision and thus into a new life though the use of words. Zen Buddhist technique involves also becoming aware of one's thought, sensations, and breathing, while ensuring at all times that one is not distracted by it. The Sufi tradition of Islam involves repetitive chanting. In one Sufi order, it even involves a whirling dance. All such techniques are designed to create a state of altered consciousness. Christian meditation involves long prayer vigils, contemplation of the Cross, or repetition of simple prayers. The Baha'i people meditate daily but do not require a technique to be followed.

Ultimate Reality as a Cognitive Knowledge of Spiritual Truths

Meditation is also closely associated with mysticism. This is because people who believe that the central religious experience can best be re-created through achieving altered states of consciousness are often described as "mystics." These states of consciousness can be reached in two ways. The first is the path of increased psychological arousal, achieved, for example, by rhythmical chanting or dancing. This culminates in mystical chanting, which in Sufism is known as *wajid* or *hal*. The second way is the path of decreased mental activity, leading to a deep state of meditation, which in yoga is called *samadhi*. Both these paths lead to a trance state. In this state of being in a trance, the believer can see reality and lead himself to the liberation of his soul. In mysticism, one common technique used to achieve this altered state of consciousness is the ritual repetitive chanting of a name or a short formula. This practice is found across the religious world. In Eastern Orthodox Christianity, it is called *hesychasm*, in Sufism it is *dhikr*, in Hinduism it is *japa* (the reciting of mantras), and in Sikhism it is *Jaap* (the reciting of the name of God).

Both Eastern and Western religious traditions include this type of religious experience. However, it is mostly associated with the monist religions of the East. In the theistic traditions of the West it is viewed as being somewhat heretical. For example, it is central to the Sufi orders of the Islamic faith. It is not central to Islam itself. This is because mysticism is closely associated with gnosticism, which, on the journey of mysticism, requires a spiritual master to act as a teacher in order to bring about the trance-like state of mind that leads to cognitive knowledge of spiritual truths. For this reason, the Judeo-Christian world follows mysticism only as a peripheral practice engaged in by a minority. Outside it, and the closer one gets to the Eastern traditions, mysticism flourishes, so that the tenets of Hinduism and Buddhism are greatly dependent on it. Those who enter the states of trance or ecstasy report the experience of a monist state where the dualist division between oneself and other breaks down, leading to an intense sense of unity with the Ultimate Reality. The subject-object differentiation is dissolved and the self and the world become one and the same. In this feeling, time slows down to the point that one even has the sense of it standing still. Yet, the realization of the Ultimate Reality cannot be communicated because the phenomenon is based on a state-bound knowledge and meaning. People who achieve this experience a heightened sense of sensory perception. Those who have experienced this altered state of consciousness claim not to need external evidence for their reality because of the intense "feeling of reality" that has no connection with any objective judgment of reality. Such is meditation.

Satvinder Singh Juss

See also Mantra

Further Reading

Bishop, D. H. (Ed.). (1975). *Indian Thought: An Introduction*. New York: John Wiley & Sons.

Hiriyanna, M. (1975). *Outlines of Indian Philosophy* (10th ed.). London: George Allen & Unwin, Ltd.

Humphreys, C. (1962). *Buddhism* (3rd ed.). London: The English Universities Press, Ltd.

Momen, M. (1999). *The Phenomenon of Religion*. Oxford: Oneworld Publications.

Judge, W. Q. (1889). *The Yoga Aphorisms of Patanjali*. Retrieved January 25, 2006 from http://www.theosociety.org/pasadena/patanjal/patan-hp.htm

Medium Effects Theory

The principle question with regard to *medium effects theory* concerns whether the medium in which messages appear produces significant and specific influences on the transactions of meaning taking place between sources and receivers. The topic is of particular importance to religious communicators as they make decisions about whether and how to adapt their messages to and in largely secularized mass media environments. The numerous contested perspectives concerning this topic may be summarized by examining three representative positions on the matter. Orientations adopted from Marshall McLuhan, Neil Postman, and Nicolas Negroponte offer insight.

Medium Defined

First, a brief word about the term *medium*. As Postman, and others, argue, the term *medium* relates more strongly to *media uses* than to *media technologies*. In other words, the term *medium* more accurately refers to the ways that audience members use mediated communication resources than to the types of transmitters and reception devices used. For example, television is often called a medium. When speaking of television as a medium, one means more than network and cable broadcasts transmitted using a particular technology and viewed via a screen. The medium of television concerns not only those technological factors, but also the variety of ways that audience members experience television. To wit, many audience members rely on television as a primary source of information about the world, use television content as the subject of social conversations with friends and relatives, meet and socialize during live televised events, and interpose television watching during meals, travel, and other social rituals. Although a given medium does not express itself in identical ways across demographic audience segments (not everyone uses a given medium in the same way), the uses to which mediums are put tend to coalesce within specific "demographics" (sets of people sharing certain characteristics tend to put a medium to similar usages).

Marshall McLuhan and Mediums: Medium is the Message

Marshall McLuhan was an early popularizer of questions about *medium effects*. McLuhan coined the now-famous aphorism "the medium is the message," by which he meant that the real meaning of a given mediated message was not to be found in the content (be it linguistic or nonverbal) of the transmission. Rather, McLuhan argued that the really important effects from mediated communication transactions were to be found in the medium itself. McLuhan proposed that the technological infrastructure enabling the delivery of the material played a key role. From this perspective, the background (what the technology could do and what, thereby, became expected from it) was more important than the foreground (the content of the message). Additionally, McLuhan argued that given mediums enhance or mute human senses. For example, printed writing virtually requires (and thereby privileges) sight, while modern electric technologies stress touch and sound (electricity vibrates our nervous systems as it works to transmit messages). For McLuhan then, the principle message is the change in sense ratios encouraged by the ubiquitous use of a given medium.

McLuhan adapted a theological idea from Teilhard de Chardin that further illustrates the importance of perspectives about mediums for religious communicators. McLuhan's concept of the *global village* is an adaptation of de Chardin's articulation of the noosphere, a universal environment featuring a global consciousness encouraged via broadly distributed communication connections. To McLuhan, people in the global village share a lot of information about each other. However, where de Chardin envisioned this factor as evidence of the "mystical body of Christ," McLuhan notes that sharing information about others, in itself, does not guarantee peace. In fact, McLuhan pointed out that, historically, villages have sometimes been very bloody places. Yet the medium effects from global interactivity would produce changes in users' nervous systems. McLuhan's insights seem to foretell some of the outcomes of digital communication and the World Wide Web as many contemporary authors now note the "edgy" quality of communications in an increasingly connected world.

Neil Postman and Mediums: Medium Modifies the Message

Neil Postman modifies McLuhan's take on the concept by noting that, perhaps, the principle medium effect is that mediums transform the content that appears within them. Postman is more concerned about the nature or function of message content than is McLuhan and extends McLuhan's proposal that particular mediums have preferences for specific types of content.

For example (and this is Postman's archetypal instance), according to Postman, the medium of television is ruled by commercialism to such an extent that the medium trivializes (virtually) all of its content. On television, according to Postman, entertainment value is the alpha and omega, and any attempt at "serious" television is both mistaken and misleading. Since television must present ubiquitous advertising, content is "sliced and diced" in ever-decreasing segments; content only appears to fill up the black spaces between the ads. This means that no matter how serious the content of a given segment might be, it is preceded and followed by a sales pitch for something unrelated (and usually sensational) such that even truly serious content is trivialized. Further, entertainment value is so important for holding an audience on television that otherwise serious content, such as education, news, or religion, must be presented in increasingly entertaining formats; otherwise programs draw neither audience nor support.

Postman illustrates the specific application of his perspective for religious communicators when he argues that television, as a medium, cannot be used (effectively) as a religious space. Postman laments televangelism for its over-reliance on showmanship and spectacle and for its strong connection to advertising, as abundant amounts of time during broadcasts are spent pleading for money. Most tellingly, with regard to his theories of medium effects, Postman notes that not all content may be effectively translated across mediums. He argues that televisions can not be consecrated as sacred spaces and that sacred spaces are crucial to worship ceremonies. Postman notes the many secular uses to which television, as a medium, is put as well as the "non-sacred" places in which they appear in homes (bedrooms, bathrooms, kitchens). As a result of these and other factors, Postman proposes that the medium of television transforms the messages carried therein so strongly as to compromise the use of television for serious content, including that of a religious nature.

McLuhan's insights were developed, primarily, in the post–World War II years of the 1950s and 1960s, during which modern advertising and commercial (broadcast) television came to the fore. McLuhan wrote about the effects of electricity, and his examples included film, radio, television, print advertising, as well as the newly developing computer industries. His untimely death, in 1980, prevented him from fully integrating his ideas into the new media environment that he seemed to prophesy with some profundity.

Prior to his death in 2003, Neil Postman eschewed the use of many modern technologies (to the degree that was possible). He wrote his books using pen and paper (later to be typed by others) and he sought out low-tech transportation alternatives when possible (trying, for example, to avoid electric functions on the cars he purchased); Postman did not use e-mail, spent little time seeking information on the World Wide Web, and he firmly believed that television's best (and virtually only justifiable) use was for watching live sporting events. Though he claimed to not be a "techno-phobe" (one with irrational fears about using technologies), he was proud to be a Luddite (one who is cautious of the social changes brought about by technology, especially when those changes are allowed to take place without careful and self-conscious consideration of their costs and benefits).

Neither McLuhan nor Postman write about medium effects with a view to the possibility that computational digitization may have changed the very nature of the questions they were asking (let alone the answers to those questions).

Nicholas Negroponte and Mediums: Medium Embodies the Message

Nicholas Negroponte offers a contrasting perspective to those of McLuhan and Postman. Negroponte believes that computational digitization supercedes and obviates the duality presented by either of the formulations "the medium is the message" or "the medium shapes the message." Negroponte argues that in digital communication, the medium constitutes the message; in computational communication, the digital code, programming algorithms, networks, and the like embody both the medium and the message. For Negroponte, medium and message are one. This perspective carries thought-provoking implications for those who are interested in religious communication.

From Negroponte's perspective, one could speak of information as a medium that transcends all (previous) mediums. One then begins to consider relationships among biological, chemical, and computational information as they reflect universal organizing principles. Such parallels carry ontological implications as questions of genesis and propagation come into view. To what degree is life as we know it based on "information" with computational implications? To what extent will life become increasingly technologized through the use of digital communication?

Authors considering questions of medium effects theory often discuss the material in terms of *media determinism, technological determinism,* and/or *medium theory*. Although not interchangeable, these terms describe material with overlapping scope, so readers looking for information about medium effects theory may want to search these additional terms as well.

Communication interactions are complex events for which reductionistic explanations are often overly simplistic and under-informative. More than likely, polarized claims that mediums constitute either the most or least important part in the communication interaction equation are overstated. The views of McLuhan (the medium *is* the message), Postman (the medium *shapes* the message), and Negroponte (the medium and the message are *constituted* by the same aspects) provide insight into the various perspectives about medium effects theory.

EDWARD LEE LAMOUREUX

Further Reading:

Ebersole, S. (1995). *Media Determinism in Cyberspace*. Retrieved February 2, 2006 from http://www.regent.edu/acad/schcom/rojc/mdic/md.html

McLuhan, E. & Zingrone, F. (Eds.). (1995). *Essential McLuhan*. New York: BasicBooks.

Negroponte, N. (1995). *Being Digital*. New York: Vintage Books.

Postman, N. (1985). *Amusing ourselves to death: Public discourse in the age of show business*. New York: Penguin Books.

Middle Ages

Religious communication played an essential role during the Middle Ages in Europe (476–1450). During the years following the collapse of the Roman Empire, the religious practices of European peoples passed from a welter of pagan and nature cults to one dominated by Christianity—after 1054 Roman Catholic Christianity reigned in Western Europe and Eastern Orthodox Christianity in Eastern Europe. Various means of religious communication both spearheaded and then solidified this transformation. Oral, symbolic, and written communications were the dominant forms of religious communication. Oral forms included the Mass—which actually combined the oral and symbolic forms, sermons and homilies, hymns and songs, recited creeds.

Extract from Peter Abelard, *Sic et Non (Yes and No)*, 1120 CE

We must also take special care that we are not deceived by corruptions of the text or by false attributions when sayings of the Fathers are quoted that seem to differ from the truth or to be contrary to it; for many apocryphal writings are set down under names of saints to enhance their authority, and even the texts of divine Scripture are corrupted by the errors of scribes. That most faithful writer and true interpreter, Jerome, accordingly warned us, "Beware of apocryphal writings...." Again, on the title of Psalm 77 which is "An Instruction of Asaph," he commented, "It is written according to Matthew that when the Lord had spoken in parables and they did not understand, he said, 'These things are done that it might be fulfilled which was written by the prophet Isaias, I will open my mouth in parables.' The Gospels still have it so. Yet it is not Isaias who says this but Asaph." Again, let us explain simply why in Matthew and John it is written that the Lord was crucified at the third hour but in Mark at the sixth hour. There was a scribal error, and in Mark too the sixth hour was mentioned, but many read the Greek *epismo* as *gamma.* So too there was a scribal error where "Isaias" was set down for "Asaph." We know that many churches were gathered together from among ignorant gentiles. When they read in the Gospel, "That it might be fulfilled which was written by the prophet Asaph," the one who first wrote down the Gospel began to say, "Who is this prophet Asaph?" for he was not known among the people. And what did he do? In seeking to amend an error he made an error. We would say the same of another text in Matthew. "He took," it says, "the thirty pieces of silver, the price of him that was prized, as was written by the prophet Jeremias." But we do not find this in Jeremias at all. Rather it is in Zacharias. You see then that here, as before, there was an error. If in the Gospels themselves some things are corrupted by the ignorance of scribes, we should not be surprised that the same thing has sometimes happened in the writings of later Fathers who are of much less authority....

Source: Tierney, B. (Ed.). (1972). *Great Issues in Western Civilization, Vol. 1* (p. 412). New York: Random House.

Symbolic forms included the rituals associated with holidays and church architecture and ornamentation. Written expression included the Bible, Papal decrees and decisions of Church councils, patristic writings, scholarly writings by churchmen, and feast-day calendars. These modes of communication served to moor both peasant and powerful Europeans in a harbor of a Christian worldview.

Oral

On worship days, congregations of the faithful and their clerical leaders participated in a formal worship service or Mass. It consisted of a range of oral communication along a standard order of worship, or Ordinary. Its major features included the Introit, or formal entrance by the priest, an offertory, in which an offering was collected to support the church, the canon and consecration, in which the elements of communion were set apart, the Eucharist, and a final prayer and dismissal. The Ordinary included a range of oral and symbolic communication including responsive recitations taken from the Bible, typically from the Psalms, in which the priest would recite a line and then the congregation would recite the following line. Typically, the priest and the choir, or the priest, choir, and congregation, would sing responsively an antiphon or anthem. The clerical, choral, and congregational singing used biblical texts for source material—often literally the Scriptures in song—and had as its end the reinforcing of core Christian concepts, especially Christ's atonement for human sin. The priest would then read a longer passage of Scripture. And the congregation would recite the Apostles' or the Nicene Creed, which, like hymns, outlined essential religious beliefs. The Nicene Creed was especially important from a doctrinal sense. Reflecting a decision by a church council during the fourth century, it emphasized Christ's being of the same substance as God the Father and was an important rhetorical tool to combat early church heresies that were spread among many of the Germanic barbarians that Jesus was only similar, not the same, materially as God the Father. In this way, creedal recitation could serve to promote at least the appearance of doctrinal conformity.

The vital worship exercise in the Mass was the Eucharist, or Holy Communion, in which both the priest and the congregation repeated ritual words and consumed ceremonial foods. The words of the priest were vested with transformative power. "*Hoc est corpus meum* [This is my body]…*Hic est sanguinis meus* [This is my blood]," said the priest as he held the unleavened bread and the wine that represented the flesh and blood of Jesus Christ. These utterances were understood to transform the bread and wine into the actual flesh and blood of Jesus, a process defined by the Church as transubstantiation. The human words of the priest spoken under divine direction accomplished a supernatural end.

The homily or sermon was often part of the Mass, and missionaries often used the sermon form to convert the Germanic tribes to Christianity in the early Middle Ages (476–800). An exercise in persuasive rhetoric, the sermon served two essential functions: comfort and correction. The faithful might be reminded of a state of future rewards, while the unregenerate and unfaithful would be told of eternal torment that awaited them upon their deaths. The priest's words were doubly vested with God's authority. First, he began his homily with references to scripture or to authoritative patristic writings about scripture. His rhetorical touchstone was thus divinely sanctioned. Second, drawing his office through the Pope, he was considered to be speaking with divine power. When the sermon was part of the Mass, it was pronounced in Latin, but missionaries especially would use appropriate vernacular languages when their goal was to convert the unchurched.

The priestly homily and the words of the Eucharist composed one unique sound of oral communication. Another distinct sound was the chant-style singing in the church, which from about 600 until about 1300 was the approved form of worshipful singing. Perhaps to distinguish church music from the lusty songs of German barbarians and the clever bawdiness of troubadours, the church adopted a monadic style of singing in which everyone sang the same note (although usually with older males singing an octave lower than women and young males). This singing, known as the Gregorian chant, provided an auditory clue that one was moving into a sacred place.

In addition to the oral ritual of worship, religious communication sometimes took the form of a public speech. In November 1095 at Clermont, Pope Urban II proclaimed the need for a crusade to liberate Palestine from the Seljuk Turks. Standing on a raised platform before an assemblage too large to fit inside a cathedral, he abandoned the form of the Mass for an oration rich in righteous rhetoric, calling upon all those gathered to redeem the land where Jesus walked from the hands of men he considered infidels. Urban repeated the speech in various forms over the next nine months, usually in the vernacular of the audience. The gist of his speech was preserved not only by papal scribes but spread by word of mouth and in epistles written by members of the audience.

Symbolic

The evolving sacramental system was the core symbolic communication of institutional Christianity. Through various rituals—codified at seven during the thirteenth century, the Church dispensed divine grace on the faithful. The sacrament of baptism, in which the earthly parents of a child gave him over to Christ, served both as a rite of initiation and, in Church teaching, removed the stain of original sin by which all people since Adam were rendered estranged from God. Other important sacraments included confirmation, in which a young person was acknowledged to possess all the rights and obligation of the faithful; penance, in which sinners confessed their misdeeds and were assigned some deed—the giving of alms or making a pilgrimage—to atone for the misdeed; the Eucharist; matrimony, by which the church extended control over marital sexual relations, procreation, domestic politics, and property; and extreme unction, in which a priest heard the last confessions of the dying and absolved them from hell. Through this sacramental system, the church effectively communicated its position as the earthly mediator between humanity and God. Those who sought to become priests or nuns took the sacrament of Holy Orders, effectively separating themselves from worldly concerns and focusing solely on the concerns of Christianity and its institutional church.

Other rituals and feasts served to link the seasons of nature with Christian theology. Traditional pagan rites had historically followed the solstice and represented the victorious sun over the increasing darkness. The Church linked this primordial rite with the birth of Jesus, which most likely had occurred in April. Hence the Feast of the Nativity and the Christ Mass represented the turning back of the night of sin by the birth of the Christian savior. Other important ritual days included Easter, in which the Christian resurrection was superimposed over Germanic fertility rituals. As part of this rebirth, the faithful bathed, and men shaved their beards and cut their hair, acknowledged their sins, and received the Eucharist, in effect having a renaissance of the body and soul.

Easter Mass culminated Holy Week, which was the time for dramatic reenactments of Christ's Crucifixion.

These Passion plays were public events designed to convey in visual form the suffering and death of Jesus, which according to Christian theology, had atoned for the sins of all humanity.

The co-option and transmogrifying of pagan rituals represented a necessary and powerful manipulation of folk tradition and culture, communicating to ordinary people Christian truths. But this negotiation over ritual and practice represented compromise between the institution of the Church and peasant practice. The emergence of the cult of Mary, the mother of Jesus, as a pillar of theology and ritual began most likely with common people linking pagan and classical images of earth mothers with the Virgin Mary. The rituals associated with Mary seem to have represented the need to temper divine justices with maternal mercy. And feasts commemorating the major events in Mary's life—the Annunciation, for example—became part of the symbolic ritual days that throughout the calendar year provided a pleasant reminder of the core teachings of Christianity.

Just as feast and holy days represented an attempt to imprint Church teachings on the peoples of Europe, other important symbolic communication had political ends. Because of the collapse of central secular authority that accompanied the fall of the Roman Empire, the Church attempted to constitute itself as the political epicenter, especially from the eleventh century onward. Hence, through ritual and symbol, the Church repeatedly asserted its claim to political as well as moral supremacy in Europe.

In the same way that the human soul was believed superior to the body, the Church held that it was superior to earthly kingdoms, and its officials, especially the pope, answered to no secular ruler. Hence, in the eleventh century, the pope ordered secular rulers to abstain from bestowing symbols of secular authority on church officials who worked for these rulers. The Church feared that both the churchmen and common people would assume that the churchmen answered to whoever bestowed the symbols of office. This practice, called lay investiture, was never completely halted, but the Church was adamant that its officials answered only to their religious superiors and to no secular rulers.

Like rituals, the material structures of medieval Christianity served as important symbols of religious belief and power. Especially after 1000, large cathedrals and their adornment served to communicate truth and belief. The basic floor plan—a long rectangle cut by a transept—was essentially a Latin cross, which represented the Crucifixion. It was nearly always oriented toward Jerusalem. Large windows of stained glass let in light, illuminating the physical space of the aisles and altar in the way the teachings of the Church were to illuminate the soul. The stained glass often portrayed saints or the apostles and behind the large altar was a depiction, sometimes a mural, of the Crucifixion. The edges of the aisles were adorned with statuary, often featuring the Virgin Mary. The aesthetics and architecture of these cathedrals served as a material testament to the message of the Church and was a measure of its power to convey it.

Of course, architecture and adornment were not rigidly uniform across Europe any more than Europeans were completely uniform in their religious beliefs. Christians in the Byzantine Empire differed from their counterparts in Western Europe on important matters such as the source of the Holy Spirit, the Third Person of the Trinity, the authority of the pope over churches within their borders, and the use of statuary, so basic to Christianity in Western Europe but contrary to preferences in the East. The result of these disputes was a division between Roman Catholic Christians and Eastern Orthodox Christians in 1054. Here the problem was less about the effectiveness of communication but rather a dispute over whose words, rituals, and structures best reflected and received the evolving traditions of Christianity.

Written

The Bible served as the foundation for Christian doctrine and, in the years before printing, was valued not just for its authority but also for its scarcity. The authoritative text was compiled and translated from earlier Greek and Hebrew sources by Jerome in the late fourth century. Known as the Vulgate, because it was written in the common or vulgar Latin of the day, it is considered the major literary achievement of the fourth century and remains the basis for the Catholic Bible today.

Copies of the Vulgate were painstakingly produced by hand, richly and ornately bound in leather with pages lavishly decorated. Because of the labor and cost involved in producing Bibles, not every parish had one. The famous Irish Book of Kells is a product of this tradition. It consists of just the four Gospels, laboriously recopied by Irish monks and decorated with illuminated letters and symbols, likely inspired not by Western Christianity, but rather from motifs common to Islam and the Byzantine Empire.

The necessities of making copies had important consequences. It required copyists to agree on a set form and shape of lettering, first the minuscule set of the ninth through the eleventh centuries and the Gothic lettering that typified medieval writing until the advent of the printing press. Written matter of any kind was rare and expensive; it cost a parish priest a year's salary to purchase a full text of the Bible and it took a competent scribe a full year to make a copy.

Nevertheless, the written word played important roles for religious communication. Churchmen studied available religious books in their seminaries and many priests and most monasteries had libraries. In addition to the Bible, hand-copied patristic writings—writings of the early Church fathers—and religious commentaries were staple items in these meager libraries. Many of these writings had their genesis in the later years of the Roman Empire when Christianity was becoming the official religion of the Empire (fourth century) and when there were opinions on a host of issues, especially on the nature of Jesus (human or divine) and the relation between the state and the church.

These patristic writings provided the definitions and explanations of Christianity as defined by the institutional Church. The writings of Augustine (354–430), Bishop of Hippo in North Africa, were the most influential and important. In his treatise *On Free Will*, Augustine developed and explained the doctrine of Original Sin, in which all human beings share the tendency of Adam to commit sin and only God can alter that human nature. His autobiographical *Confessions* related how he moved from debauchery through divine grace to salvation. In *The City of God*, he postulated humanity as struggling between citizenship in the city of the Earth and citizenship in the city of God. Relying on Augustine's authority, the Church took the position as the earthly representative of the heavenly city and thus justified its claim to supremacy over secular powers.

Religious questions and disputes did not end with Augustine, and throughout the Middle Ages churchmen recruited the written word to aid their cause. The Church had a vital interest in protecting the issue that divided Plato and Aristotle: is an idea more real than a thing. The Church held that ideas were more real than things; such a position enhanced the claims of Church power and, intellectually, lessened the damage done by lustful priests to its status. Hence, Anselm's (1033–1100) *Monologue* argues that universals are more real than particulars.

Thinking people also struggled with the contradictions between faith and reason. Abelard (1079–1142) in *Yes and No* suggests that a vital faith must meet the tests of reason. His *On the Divine Unity and Trinity* suggested that the trinity reflected different modalities of a unitary God, hardly an orthodox postulate in the Middle Ages but quite a rational one.

Thomas Aquinas (1225–1274) likewise used the written word to solve the conundrum between reason and faith. Prolific, Aquinas published over 10,000 double-columned pages in his brief life. His twenty-one volume *Summa Theologica* seeks to defend Catholic dogma by showing that it is indeed rational. And he asserted that human sin made reason a fallible guide. In his own mind, Aquinas had affirmed his faith in a reasoned way but in 1277 Pope John XXI found two hundred nineteen of Aquinas' assertions to be heretical.

In addition to facilitating scholarly disputation about theology, writing promoted important Church functions. Not only could papal decrees or bulls (from *bulla*, the signet ring employed by medieval popes) be copied and broadcast, but important administrative tasks could be compelled by letters or receipts recorded in registers or roll books. In 1075, Pope Gregory VII wrote a formal letter of complaint to German King Henry IV in which he demanded that the king cease the practice of lay investiture or face excommunication.

Over time, however, the rules and regulations of the Church, especially the canon law, which defines how and why the Church operates and specifies appropriate Christian behaviors, had become discordant, seemingly contradictory, and nowhere compiled. Gratian, an Italian monk, compiled and published a *Reconciliation of the Discordant Canon Law* (*Concordia discorandtium canonum*) in 1148. Although it was never made the official volume of canon law, it was nonetheless the indispensable digest on canon law for the late Middle Ages and was widely circulated.

Written religious communication served a range of purposes and appears in a variety of places. Thomas Bede's (673–735) *Ecclesiastical History of the English Nation* is nominally a history of the Anglo–Saxon conquest of England but from his faith-based view is essentially a providential history of God's handiwork in the process. And it was Bede who popularized dating events from before or after the birth of Jesus. Similarly, the surviving versions of *Beowulf* contain additions, likely made by a churchman, to make the piece appear Christian enough to be preserved. It is not unlike the love letters of some medieval people who use the language of theology and the Bible as metaphors for more earthly passions.

Significance

In oral, symbolic, or written form, religious communication in the Middle Ages helped to form and then supported common personal assumptions about religion and served as a bulwark for the evolving and expansive institutional Church. Its forms and rituals provided meaning, explanation, and structure in the precarious millennium following Rome's collapse. The discourse of religion helped move pagan barbarians toward the world of the Christian Europe of the Renaissance and Reformation, becoming a major part of European culture in the process.

EDWARD R. CROWTHER

Further Reading

Bergeron, K. (1996). *Decadent enchantments: The revival of Gregorian Chant at Solesmes*. Berkeley: University of California Press.

Brown, P., & Lamont, R. (1986). *Augustine of Hippo: A biography*. New York: Dorset.

Caciola, N. (2003). *Discerning spirits: Divine and demonic possession in the Middle Ages*. Ithaca, NY: Cornell University Press.

Cantor, N. (1993). *The civilization of the Middle Ages*. New York: HarperCollins.

Collins, R. (1991). *Early medieval Europe, 300–1000*. New York: St. Martins.

Cook, W. R., & Herzman, R. B. (2004). *The medieval world view: An introduction* (2nd ed.). Oxford, UK: Oxford University Press.

Durant, W. (1950). *The age of faith: A history of medieval civilization (Christian, Islamic, and Judaic) from Constantine to Dante, A.D. 325–1300*. New York: Simon and Schuster.

Fossier, R, (Ed.). (1986). *The Cambridge illustrated history of the Middle Ages* (3 vols.). Cambridge, UK: Cambridge University Press.

Jungman, J. A. (1961). *The mass of the Roman rite: Its origins and development*. New York: Benziger Bros.

Kuttner, S. G. (1960). *Harmony from dissonance: An interpretation of medieval canon law*. Latrobe, PA: Archabbey Press.

Latourette, K S. (1938). *The thousand years of uncertainty: A. D. 500–A.D 1500*. New York: Harper and Brothers.

Marenbon, J. (1987). *Later medieval philosophy (1150–1350)* (2nd ed.). London: Routledge.

Marenbon, J. (1988). *Early medieval philosophy (480–1150): An introduction* (2nd ed.). London: Routledge.

McKittrick, R. (1983). *The Frankish church under the Carolingians*. New York: Longman.

Oakley, F. (1979). *The western church in the Later Middle Ages*. Ithaca, NY: Cornell University Press.

O'Brien, J. M. (1968). *Medieval church*. Totowa, NJ: Littlefield, Adams, & Co.

Quasten, J. (1983). *Music and worship in pagan and Christian antiquity*. Portland: Oregon Catholic Press.

Tellenbach, G. (1959). *Church, state and Christian society at the time of the investiture contest*. Oxford, UK: Basil Blackwell.

Wilson, C. (1990). *The gothic cathedral: The architecture of the great church, 1130–1530*. New York: Thames and Hudson.

Wolfson, H. A. (1970). *The philosophy of the church fathers* (3rd ed.). Cambridge, MA: Harvard University Press.

Miracles

Miracles are extraordinary events that witnesses attribute to supernatural causes. These events or actions are so extraordinary that they appear not to have a rational or scientific explanation; therefore witnesses claim them as evidence of the divine acting in nature or through an individual. While miracles can constitute any sort of transformation of natural phenomena, they often include physical healing or the exorcism of spirits.

In many instances, miracles are considered to be the sign of communication between the spiritual world and the material world. Sometimes adherents see a miracle as a signal from the spiritual world that tells them what they should do. Often, miracles are interpreted by someone who is thought to have communication with the supernatural realm. In fact, miracles are sometimes performed to convince witnesses that the practitioner has this type of communication with the spiritual world.

History of Development

Miracles have always been a part of religious traditions. In early indigenous religions, magicians, shamans, or prophets performed miracles. These miracles included healing, vision quests, divination, and sometimes the transformation of physical matter. The ability to perform miracles was an indication to members of the community that an individual had communication with the spiritual world. The most important function of the shaman in indigenous traditions, whether Australian Dieri, American Cherokee, or West African Yoruban, or others, was to interpret information between the spiritual and human realms. This was often done by interpreting dreams or various techniques of divination: reading bone or stick patterns, charting the stars, or reading other natural signs. Members of the community believed the shaman's information to be credible because of his ability to perform miracles.

In Egyptian religion, the goddess Isis reportedly gave the gift of healing to many humans, but she is also said to have healed anyone seeking refuge in her temples. Isis and Osiris, husband and wife, were considered to be symbolic of the renewing energy evident

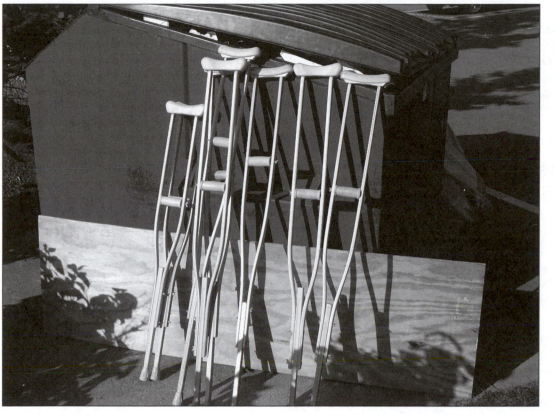

Crutches found abandoned after a revival in Columbus, Ohio. *Courtesy of Michael Devnay/ istockphoto.com*

in nature. Isis was the giver of life and the great protector of humanity. Her priests and priestesses, therefore, were thought to have the powers of healing. A healing by one of these individuals was evidence of the care that Isis had for humanity. This is, then, another example of communication of a deity through the use of miracles.

In India, Hindu yogis and Buddhist monks have been credited with miraculous powers. In both of these instances, however, while the ability to perform miracles is considered to be evidence that the person has advanced to a high level in their spiritual quest, the use of these gifts is a detriment to the individual. In the case of Hindu yogis, while they might have the power to change matter or to heal others, the use of these gifts binds them to this world and they cannot attain *moksha*, or release, in this lifetime. In the case of Buddhist monks, while they might be able to gain deeper insight, know the thoughts of others, have a developed sense of hearing, or be in two places at once, the use of these gifts is discouraged, as they are a distraction from achieving Nirvana. In these cases, the communication is not necessarily between the spiritual world and the human world. Rather, it is a sign to witnesses that advancement in their spiritual lives is possible. It is, there-

fore, more accurately a communication between believers.

In ancient Israel, the prophets, as spokesmen for God, often had the power to perform miracles. These were considered to be signs from God, first to communicate his wishes and second to show that the prophet spoke for him. The most notable of these was Moses, who performed miracles in order to demand the release of the Israelites from Egypt, and performed some miracles during their exodus. These were miracles that included the transformation of matter: changing his staff into a serpent, changing water to blood, causing locusts to rain from the sky, and so forth. Each of these was considered to be a sign of wrath from God in retribution for the Egyptian pharaoh's refusal to release the Israelites. In this case, the deity is communicating his wishes through the prophet's performance of a miracle.

In early Christianity, part of the ministry of Jesus was his performance of miracles. While he was capable of transforming matter, such as the changing of water into wine or calming the seas, he is most notable for his healing miracles and exorcisms. For Jesus, it would seem that two conditions were necessary for working miracles: prayer and belief. The healing miracles often happened as a result of prayer on his part or on the part of the afflicted, while he often told the person who was healed that their faith had made them well. Thus, after communicating their wishes to the divine, the sick person was made well—the divine answered the request with a miracle. In addition, of course, witnesses believed that the power of Jesus to heal was a sign that he was from God.

Miracles were not as much a part of early Islam, since Muhammad rejected requests for the performances of miracles, but they are a part of Sufi and devotional Islam. The only miracle that Muhammad is reported to have performed was the reception of the Qur'an. When his disciples asked him to perform miracles, he refused, saying that these were signs of God and he was but a simple man. Later, in Sufi practice, however, the veneration of saints, or *wali*, developed. These individuals had been mystics, possessed by God, during their lifetime. This closeness with God, this union, reportedly left its mark on the *wali*. After their possession, they were said to be able to perform miracles such as walking on water, flying through the air, resurrecting the dead, and being in more than one place at a time. Because of this closeness with God, devotees believe that saints, once they leave this world, are able to mediate between the spiritual and material realms. Thus, the devotee communicates with the saint through prayers and offerings, and the saint communicates with God on behalf of the supplicant.

Miracles in the Modern World

Many of the world's traditions continue to believe that miracles are the way that the spiritual world communicates with the human world. The shamans of indigenous traditions still mediate between the spirit world and the human world. Hindu yogis and Buddhist monks are still credited with the ability to change matter in unexplainable ways. In the rabbinic tradition of Judaism, rabbis are sometimes thought to have special gifts from God. Rabbinic literature often describes miraculous feats performed by rabbis; much of the third chapter of the Tractate *Taanit*, or the "Chapter of the Saints," describes such rabbinic miracles.

In Christianity, there are different types of miracles that are currently accepted. Healing, particularly in the case of chronic or terminal diseases, is often considered to be miraculous and is usually attributed to the power of prayer. In Catholic devotional practice, Mary is thought to perform miracles. There have been several apparitions of Mary, a few of which are sanctioned by the church. In the apparitions, she often asks the witness to build a shrine on that location and leaves be-

hind miraculous properties such as the healing waters at Lourdes, France. In addition, Mary is considered to be a mediator between the human world and the spirit world according to those devoted to her. This is due to her role as co-redemptrix; she participates in the redemption of humanity due to her miraculous conception of the savior Jesus. This is an example of a witness or several witnesses being necessary in order for a miracle to have the desired affect. Because the miracles are attributed to Mary, as a mediator between the worlds, human witnesses are necessary for the miracles to be considered thus. The communication in this case is between the supernatural realm and the human realm.

In Judaism, Christianity, and Islam, witnesses to miracles believe that the miracles are natural manifestations of God. They believe that the miracles are signs or communications between the supernatural world and the material, or human, world. If an individual performs the miracle, then that individual is believed to have God working through them.

In contrast, in other traditions such as Hinduism, Buddhism, or Christian Science or other New Thought traditions, miracles are evidence that the material world is but an illusion. For instance, for Christian Science, the material body is an illusion; what is real is the spiritual body. Therefore, all sickness or mental disease is attributed to the mistaken belief that this physical body is real and ignorance of the divine nature within individuals. Healing can occur when the individual realizes the illusory nature of physical and mental sickness. Christian Science founder Mary Baker Eddy believed that this was the message that Jesus was trying to send with his ministry of healing; she believed that the Christian Church misunderstood His message. Therefore, for these traditions, miracles are not so much a communication between the divine and material realms as an understanding of the actual nature of reality. If miracles are a communication at all, they might be evidence of the illusory nature of the world that one individual could show another.

Implications of Miracles and the Media

In the contemporary world, media are utilized to show miracles to more people, so that more people might witness evidence of the supernatural world. Both television and the Internet have been widely utilized for this purpose. Many Evangelical Christian traditions have utilized television to broadcast the performance of miraculous healing. Generally, an afflicted person in the live audience will come to the stage for the preacher to heal in the name of Jesus. This was a practice used by the disciples of Jesus after his ascension. Those who have tuned into the broadcast can witness the transformation of the afflicted person. For instance, a person who was limping as he or she climbed the stairs might descend the stairs after the healing, miraculously walking in a regular fashion. Sometimes the healing is not as evident on the screen; a person may have asked that Jesus heal their stomach troubles or some other internal illness. One of the critical elements of miracles is the presence of witnesses. Television broadcasts are therefore a modern convention of reaching many more witnesses than were previously available.

In addition to television media, the Internet has also added more witnesses to miracles that are performed. Religious groups post "eye-witness" accounts of miracles or offer to pray with the individual for miraculous healing. The Elk Transmission Meditation Group has a website entitled "The Miracles Page." This page organizes articles written in various magazines and newspapers about miracles. The articles are organized by the type of miracle witnessed, for instance, "crosses of light," "healing waters," "signs of the Mother," "Buddhist miracles," and the like. The Real Presence Association has a website that reports various Eucharistic miracles throughout history. These miracles, according to Catholic devotional practices, show that the person of Jesus is present in the Eucharistic elements. Miracles include the host transforming to human flesh or being preserved through fire. When possible, web pages show the miracle, such as "Our Lady of Clearwater," an image of Mary that appeared on an office building in Clearwater, Florida. The Internet has been a valuable tool for religious groups wishing to spread the word about miracles.

Looking Ahead

Miracles clearly continue to be of vital interest to many people. Articles in popular publications such as *Time* magazine carry stories told by witnesses to miracles. News organizations such as CNN and the BBC often carry stories about unexplained supernatural phenomena as well. These news organizations generally document the story of a witness to a miraculous event. Religious people regard miracles as communication from the divine, as evidence that the supernatural exists.

DAWN L. HUTCHINSON

Further Reading

Cavadini, J. C. (Ed.). (1999). *Miracles in Jewish and Christian antiquity: Imagining truth.* Notre Dame, IN: University of Notre Dame Press.

Eliade, M. (Ed.). (1987). *Encyclopedia of religion.* New York: MacMillan.

Mullin, R. B. (1996). *Miracles and the modern religious imagination.* New Haven, CT: Yale University Press.

Mormonism

Mormonism is the informal title by which The Church of Jesus Christ of Latter-day Saints (or the LDS Church) is popularly known (referred to hereinafter as the Church).

The Church was officially organized by the prophet Joseph Smith (1805–1844) on 6 April 1830 in Fayette, New York, with six official (baptized) members, and began immediately to grow exponentially. By 1845 there were an estimated fifteen thousand Mormons living in Nauvoo, Illinois (by then the headquarters of the Church), with numerous others in other locations. This growth was facilitated by use of the printing press to publish the *Book of Mormon*, and other Mormon literature, including missionary tracts and hymnals that communicated unique Mormon theology.

Joseph Smith was murdered by an anti-Mormon mob in 1844 in Carthage, Illinois. Brigham Young, the new Church leader, subsequently led Mormon pioneers in an exodus forced by persecution, across the plains to the unsettled West.

The Church has been headquartered in Salt Lake City, Utah, since 1847. By 2004, it had an estimated 12 million members, with more than half of its membership outside of the United States. Again, this growth has been facilitated by the Church's use of print and broadcast media, as well as structured internal communication networks. Mediated and non-mediated communications have facilitated extensive missionary activity. Constant internal communications directed to members have allowed this centrally organized religion to maintain consistent doctrine and practices throughout its worldwide church organization. This article examines the Church's use of and attitudes toward the media and discusses modes of communication within and outside of the religion.

Embracing and Resisting the Media

In July 2004, the Church celebrated the seventy-fifth anniversary of the Mormon Tabernacle Choir's first radio broadcast of "Music and the Spoken Word." The Choir began its weekly broadcasts on 15 July 1929 (when the radio industry was still very new) and is the longest continuous radio broadcast in the history of United States network radio.

The early adoption of radio is an example of the Church's historical and contemporary enthusiasm for and readiness to embrace all media to achieve its communication purposes. Church presidents and other leaders consistently have taught that communications media are tools to assist in spreading the gospel message throughout the world. For example, Church President Gordon B. Hinckley said, "The Lord has inspired skilled men and women in developing new technologies which we can use to our great advantage in moving forward this sacred work" (Rasmussen 2000, 278). The Church also views the media as appropriate "tools for family enjoyment and edification" (Stout, Scott, and Martin 1996, 85).

On the other hand, the Church also strongly encourages resistance to the media. Leaders regularly warn Church members of the dangers, evils, and negative effects of the media, and instruct them about proper media use. In the official Church magazine, the *Ensign* (September 2004), Hinckley wrote about "the flood of pornographic filth, the inordinate emphasis on sex and violence" in the world, and of "a weakening rot seeping into the very fiber of society." Much of this he attributes to the media. He counsels Church members to discipline themselves in terms of media use, to be careful about the media their children use, and to speak out publicly in support of suitable programming.

Hinckley (b. 1910) has been a consistent presence in Church media planning and direction since he started working for the Church in 1935. He is widely regarded as the father of and the reason for the Church's successful use of communications in the twentieth century. He exemplifies the Church's embrace of and responsiveness to the media. He held a press conference when he was first appointed to be President of the Church in March 1995 (the first Church President to do so). He has spoken at the National Press Club, appeared on *Larry King Live*, been interviewed by Mike Wallace on *60 Minutes*, and received the Presidential Medal of Freedom from President George W. Bush in June 2004.

Primary Religious Texts

The primary religious texts of the Church are known as the four standard works: *The Holy Bible*, the *Book of Mormon: Another Testament of Jesus Christ*, the *Doctrine and Covenants of The Church of Jesus Christ Of Latter-day Saints* and the *Pearl of Great Price*. The Church publishes the authorized King James version of the Bible with explanatory notes and cross-references to the other standard works. The *Book of Mormon* is a sacred record of peoples in ancient America that was engraved upon sheets of metal and later translated by the prophet Joseph Smith. The Church has published, translated into more than ninety languages, and distributed worldwide more than 100 million copies of the *Book of Mormon*. The *Doctrine and Covenants* contains revelations given to Joseph Smith, the prophet, with some additions by his successors in the presidency of the Church. The *Pearl of Great Price*, produced by Joseph Smith, is a selection of materials touching many significant aspects of the faith and doctrine of the Church.

Church Media Ownership

Print

The Church owns one of America's longest existing daily metropolitan newspapers, *The Deseret Morning News* (previously known as *The Deseret News*). It was started in 1850 on a press that the pioneers transported across the plains in wagons.

The Church publishes numerous magazines including the *Ensign* (for adults), the *New Era* (for youth twelve to eighteen), the *Friend* (for children), the *Liahona* (an international magazine available in forty-seven languages), and the *Church News* (an English-only weekly publication of current Church events). The Church also prints scriptures, hymnals, lesson manuals for all age groups, and leadership manuals for all of the auxiliary organizations and activities within the consistent organizational structure of Mormon congregations throughout the world. The Church also owns a publishing company, Deseret Book, which publishes LDS inspirational literature and fiction, and also functions as a full-service bookstore with forty-one retail outlets.

Broadcast

Many authors have observed that the Mormon Church is a formidable broadcast institution because of its wide media holdings of extensive radio and television networks and outlets. Despite its commitment to spread the Gospel throughout the world, the Church has not viewed its media holdings as conduits for direct proselytizing. The bulk of Church-produced media content over the years has been in the form of public service programming.

Satellite

Church-owned Brigham Young University, which manages a PBS television station, also launched in January

2000 a direct-broadcast satellite network called BYU Television (BYUTV) that by 2004 was able to reach more than 26 million homes across the United States, and was beginning to be carried by international cable and satellite companies. BYUTV focuses on uplifting and family-appropriate programming produced by the Church, BYU, and LDS-owned Bonneville International Corporation.

Internet

The Church launched its official website, www.lds.org, in 1996, and in 1999 a filtered DSL service known as the Millennial Star Network (www.MSTAR.net) with the objective of providing both value-laden content and Internet access. Also launched in 1999 is a genealogy website, www.familysearch.org, that contains the records of the world's largest family history library and includes multiple tools for doing family history and genealogy.

Communicating with Members and Nonmembers

The ability to transmit the Church's semiannual General Conference has been especially important to communication with its members. General Conference is the forum in which Church leadership makes general announcements about church activity, progress, and organizational matters, and expounds on theological and spiritual issues. It has been broadcast on radio since 1924, on television since 1949, and is now available by cable, satellite, and Internet.

The Church also produces an extensive array of religious videos and movies to be used in Sunday schools, seminaries, institutes, Church visitors centers, missions, and families.

In nonmedia communications, specific instructions about how local congregations should be managed, as well as other administrative issues or advice to members, are sent by letter from the First Presidency of the Church to area and local leaders, who then read the instructions over the pulpit at regularly scheduled Sunday worship services. These directives range widely in terms of the topics they address, from financial to administrative to social matters. The Church specifically requires that politics not be discussed during Church meetings. Church advice to members about voting and other political matters is extremely rare and limited to issues that the Church considers to be moral matters (such as gambling and same-sex marriage).

The Church communicates with nonmembers primarily through its extensive missionary program. In 2003 there were more than fifty-six thousand full-time Mormon missionaries of many nationalities serving in countries all over the world. The Church also has an extensive public affairs operation, with headquarters in Salt Lake City, Utah, and satellite offices around the globe. Many nonmembers are aware of the Church because of press coverage of the Mormon Tabernacle Choir, Brigham Young University sports teams, and the growing number of LDS temples being built around the United States and the world. Temple Square in Salt Lake City is a major tourist attraction, with nearly 5 million visitors annually.

Noninstitutional Mormon Media

There are many Mormon-related media products that are produced not by the institutional Church, but by Mormons who wish to communicate about their religion, express and discuss their culture or theology, and make connections with other members. These products include books, art, music, websites, and a new genre of cinema that explores Mormon cultural themes.

Verbal Communication

This is a lay church with a strong central structure. Mormons are engaged in verbal communication and presentation from early childhood. In church meetings, men, women, and children present lessons, talks or sermons, offer prayers, and participate in congregational singing. Each local congregation (ward) has a choir. Members are organized in their wards to visit every ward member or family each month with in-home visits. They share a short theological message, inquire as to the physical and spiritual needs of the members they visit, and report verbally through the ward organization to the ward leader (the Bishop) about any needs that need to be met. Members in local areas also engage in extensive social activities by age groups, by gender groups, and as a whole. Families are encouraged to meet weekly on Monday nights (known as Family Night) for religious lessons, prayers, songs, games, and activities. Missionary work also is conducted in face-to-face conversations with individuals and families.

Spiritual Communication

Mormon theology and culture strongly emphasize education, self-reliance, rational thought, and mental and physical engagement in mortal life. Mormons also are strong believers in spiritual communication and extra-rational guidance from deity (inspiration and revelation) about temporal, spiritual, and emotional affairs ("As the Dew From Heaven Distilling," 2005). They believe that God still communicates with mankind, just as He did during Biblical times. The President of the Church is considered to be a latter-day prophet who receives direction and guidance from God about matters relating to theology, the proper conduct of believers, and the affairs of the Church. Individual members of the Church are encouraged to pray for personal guidance and inspiration relating to all aspects of their lives. Nonmembers who are investigating the Church are encouraged to read the *Book of Mormon* and other Church literature, and to ask God through prayer for a confirmation from the Holy Ghost as to the divinity of Jesus Christ, and as to whether the *Book of Mormon* and Church theology are true.

The Future

Inasmuch as the Church has wholeheartedly embraced the media for its communication purposes for more than 150 years, it is to be expected that it will continue to do so in the future. It can be expected to build upon its past successes in media use especially for proselytizing, member instruction, and public relations. At the same time, however, the Church can be expected to continue to warn its members of the harmful effects of certain media content—especially of Internet pornography.

As the twenty-first century begins, noninstitutional member-produced Mormon cultural media is beginning to burgeon. It can be expected that this trend will increase dramatically, both in the United States and internationally, as Church membership continues to grow worldwide.

There is a strong body of literature that has studied Mormons and the media, particularly the ways in which Mormons have been discussed or represented in the media. This literature will continue to grow as scholars address fresh questions such as Mormon media use and gratification, and media effects upon Mormons.

Finally, with the eventual passing of President Hinckley, the future is uncertain as to how the relationship between the institutional Church and the media might change with succeeding Church presidencies.

SHERRY PACK BAKER

Further Reading

"As the dew from heaven distilling: Revelation is the means our Heavenly Father uses to communicate divine truth to us." (2005). *Ensign*, *35*(2), 10-15.
Ashton, W. J. (1950). *Voice in the West: Biography of a pioneer newspaper*. New York: Duell, Sloan & Pearce.
Baker, S. & Stout, D. (2003). Mormons and the media, 1898–2003: A selected, annotated, and indexed bibliography (with suggestions for future research). *BYU Studies, 42* (3 & 4), 125–189.
Dew, S. L. (1996). *Go forward with faith: The biography of Gordon B. Hinckley*. Salt Lake City, UT: Deseret Book Company.
"Diamond Jubilee for America's Choir," *LDS Church News*, published by the *Deseret Morning News*, July 24, 2004, pp. 6, 8–9.
Garr, A. K., Cannon, D. Q., Cowan, R. O. (Eds.). (2000). *Encyclopedia of Latter-day Saint history*. Salt Lake City: Deseret Book Company.
Hinckley, G. B. (2004). In opposition to evil. *Ensign, 34*(9), 3–6.
Ludlow, D. H. (Ed.). (1992). *Encyclopedia of Mormonism*. New York: Macmillan Publishing Company.
Rasmussen, R. C. (2000). Computers and the internet in the church. In *Out of obscurity: The Church in the twentieth century*. Salt Lake City, UT: Deseret Book.
Sidney B. Sperry Symposium. (2000). *Out of obscurity: The Church in the twentieth century*. Salt Lake City, UT: Deseret Book Company.
Stout, D., Scott, D. W. & Martin, D. G. (1996). Mormons, mass media, and the interpretive audience. In D. Stout & J Buddenbaum (Eds.), *Religion and mass media: Audiences and adaptations*. Thousand Oaks, CA: Sage.

Mosques

"Mosque" in English (*masjid* in Arabic) has roots that predate Islam and even means more than just a building type in Islam itself. The word *masjid* is found in Aramaic as early as the Jewish Elephantine Papri (fifth century BCE), and it also appeared in Nabathean inscriptions with the meaning "place of worship." *Masjid* in Islam is formed from the verb *sajada*, "to prostrate oneself," but it is now used exclusively to refer to an Islamic place of worship.

Mosques as Sanctuaries

During the lifetime of the Prophet Muhammad, there were two sanctuaries of highest esteem to the Prophet, as mentioned in the Qur'an: the Mecca sanctuary (al-Masjid al-Harâm, Sûra 11:144, 149, 5:2, 8:34, 17:1 etc.) and al-Masjid al-Aqsâ (Sûra 17:1). The latter means the Jerusalem sanctuary, though scholars argue that the reference is more likely referring to a place of prayer in heaven rather than on earth.

The Meccan sanctuary has always been the principal mosque known as Bayt Allah (the house of Allah), even before the time of the Prophet. It was the sanctity and the uniqueness of the Ka'ba—the name given to the cube-shaped temple in the center court of the Great Mosque of Mecca—that led the Prophet to reclaim and sanctify it for the use of the Muslims in the worship of one God in 630 CE. According to tradition, before the Hijra (622 CE) Muhammad himself performed *salât* (obligatory prayer) in secret in the narrow alleys of Mecca with his male followers and sometimes beside the Ka'ba or in his own house in Mecca. Yet we must remember that the Prophet taught that a sanctuary for worship was not a fundamental necessity, since the entire surface of the Earth is mosque.

Mosques as Places of Worship

By the time the Prophet Muhammad settled with his followers in Medina, the idea of a corporate place of worship became necessary for easy access to hear the message of the Prophet and to receive instructions on both political and economic strategies for sustenance and the spread of Islam. The original type of mosque set up by Muhammad was decisive in setting the pattern for future mosques. Islamic tradition champions the decisive impact of a single building on the evolution of the mosque, which developed from the house of the Prophet in Medina. It is agreed by scholars generally that apart from borrowed ideas from conquered territories, which later gave the impetus to what is now known as Islamic architecture, the house of the Prophet in Medina became the prototype that later rulers followed to structure their mosques; this has been described by Umbarto Scerrato (1972) as "a modest structure, a square plot of land some 165 feet on each side, surrounded by an outer wall of unbaked bricks and only about 10 feet high." Mud huts housed the Prophet's wives and followers who had come with him from Mecca.

Leone Caetani (1915) observes that the earliest *masjid* had nothing of the character of a sacred edifice. It was enlarged while the Prophet was still living, in 628 and then in 644 by the Caliph 'Umar and once again in 649–650 by 'Uthman. Caetani notes further that it was only gradually that Muhammad's house became public in nature and eventually sacred.

The great change took place after 'Alî moved the seat of government outside Arabia, and Medina fell to the rank of a provincial town and a place of memories. When the bustle and worldliness of the capital of a great empire gave way to the monotonous calm of provincial life, people no longer came to Medina in quest of position, wealth, or honors but only out of obsequiousness to the memories of the great past. And it was in this period, in part through the grafting of religious ideas of non-Arab peoples, that there developed the concept of the holiness of the house of Muhammad and the transformation from a private abode to a sacred and public temple took place.

Prayer in the Mosque

The mosque has been defined as a place of prostration and a community center, but it also has four levels of prayers that are established or attached to it. There are obligatory prayers performed in the mosque, and certain types of mosques accommodate certain types of prayers. There are prayers for the individual, the congregation, the total population of a town or city, and the entire Muslim world, as George Michell (1978) has rightly observed. For three of these there are distinct liturgical structures.

Mosques as Structures for Prayer Levels

The first structure is the *masjid*, a mosque used for daily prayer by individuals or small groups of believers but not for the Friday worship. It therefore has a *mihrâb* (prayer niche) but no *minbar* (pulpit). The prayer rug also corresponds to this level. The second is the *jâmi'*, the congregational or Friday mosque (*masjidal-jâmi'/jumu'a*), used for the main weekly service. It is normally much longer than a *masjid* for the daily obligatory prayers and is provided with a *minbar*.

The third is the *'îd* prayer ground. This is usually an open space, with the *mihrâb* representing the *qibla* locating the direction of prayers and used during major Islamic festivals.

The fourth level is the annual ritual of the pilgrimage, which is a congregation of all the Muslims of the world in Mecca. Within these liturgical types of mosques, a range of architectural variation is possible.

Characteristic Symbols

In the development of the mosque, the building has acquired some characteristic symbols that identify it with the requirements of the faith: on the outside, a fountain for ablutions is provided so that Muslims can pray in ritual cleanliness. A minaret serves to call the believers to prayer, while inside a small empty niche (*mihrâb*) on the center of the *qibla* wall indicates

Ertogrul Gazy, a modern mosque that Turkey paid to have built in Ashgabad. It is said to be modeled after the famous Blue Mosque in Instanbul. *Courtesy of Jacques Croizer / istockphoto.com.*

the direction of prayer. In communal Friday mosques a pulpit (*minbar*) is placed to the right of the *mihrâb* for the prayer leader (*khatib*) to deliver the sermon (*khutba*). Other optional elements and features are an enclosed area for the ruler (*maqsûra*), the respondent's platform (*dikka*), and a cantor's lectern (*kursî*), from which the Qur'an is often read. It is noteworthy that most of these elements had already been established within the first century of Islam.

Earliest Mosques

Within the first century mosques had been built in various centers. In Syria a church was taken and turned into a mosque. Churches at that time were normally built with the sanctuary facing east. In order to turn them into mosques, K. A. C. Creswell (1968) notes, it was only necessary to close the western entrances, pierce new entrances in the north wall, and pray across the aisles toward the south, the direction of Mecca. Thus, when al-Kanîsat al-Ûzmâ (the Great Church) in Hama was converted into a mosque in 15 AH (636–637 CE), the west front became the west end of the sanctuary.

In Jerusalem, the remains of the biblical hall of Herod were used as a mosque. In Persia, at Persepolis and Qazwîn, the *apandanas* or hypostyle audience halls of the Persian kings, with their roofs resting on columns with double bull-headed capitals, seem to have been taken. In Iraq, the situation was different because the Arabs founded new towns, so preexisting buildings could not be employed.

It is quite interesting that the great Umayyad Friday mosques, with the exception of those in Damascus and Jerusalem, started in a primitive manner. The same situation definitely occurred in other conquered territories where Muslims had to build new structures. However, the development of the various Islamic mosque structures has been a great contribution to architecture in general and religious building technology in particular.

Internal Features of the Early Mosques

The internal features of the mosque developed as Islam grew. The first primitive mosque did not have distinctive features of any architectural value. However, as the early Muslim communities continued to grow, these features became necessary. The first to change was the mosque itself, which developed from a demarcated space—partly roofed and partly open to the sky to provide accommodation for the congregation at prayer—to a magnificent edifice of historical importance.

The principal factors affecting the size of the mosque are the numbers of worshippers to be accommodated and the nature of the prevailing climate region by region. The prayer hall is usually rectangular or square in plan.

Internal features include the *mihrâb* (small niche indicating direction of prayer), *minbar* (pulpit), *kursî* (lectern), *maqsûra* (enclosed area for the ruler), carpet and other floor covering, lighting, and incense burner. Each one of these features came into existence during the period of the evolution of the mosque structures.

External Features of the Early Mosques

The external features of the mosque, which also developed over time and have similar values to the internal features, are the minaret, the dome, the ablution foun-

tain (water supply), the entrance to the mosque, the portal, and the courtyard (*sahn*).

One of the outstanding external features of the mosque is the minaret. The word "minaret" entered English in the seventeenth century from the Turkish *minaret*. Its immediate source may be the French *minaret*, with a silent "t." It may also have derived from the Spanish *minarets*, the Portuguese *minaretto*, or the Italian *minaretto*. These ultimately come from the Arabic *manâr* or *manâra* (light house or turret), two words that today universally designate mosque towers.

The minaret was motivated, as suggested by Michell (1978), by the need for a height from which to broadcast the call to worship by the *mu'adhadhin*. The higher one gets, the greater the area over which the sound can be distributed. Creswell (1965), however, shows that the minaret developed out of the corner towers, or of the temenos of the Church of St. John the Baptist at Damascus when the entire area was taken over to build the Umayyad mosque. The minaret continued to be part of the mosque structure from the time of the Umayyads, as a consensus of the religious community to provide a high place for the *mu'adhadhins*.

During the lifetime of Muhammad, the call to prayer was given from the roof of his house in Medina, and it was not until the fourteenth and fifteenth centuries that the building of minarets became universal.

A single minaret was generally provided, although under the Ottoman and Mughal empires, twin minarets (signifying royal patronage) were frequently built. The Sultan mosque in Istanbul has four, while the Ahmet mosque has six, a figure exceeded only in Mecca, where there are seven minarets in the Ka'ba mosque.

Functions of Mosques in Early Islam

The mosque has developed as the Islamic building par excellence and as such the key to Islamic architecture. The various types of mosques can be considered under three broad headings: the mosque as a religious center, the mosque as a social center, and the sectarian mosque.

Mosques as Centers for Divine Worship

As noted previously, there are four categories of religious mosques. The first level is the *masjid*, a smaller mosque that accommodates individuals and groups for the five obligatory daily prayers. The structure of such a mosque ranges from a space wide enough to allow an individual to prostrate himself before Almighty God to the simplest architecture of a structure covered to protect worshippers from sunshine and rain. Development of this simple structure means that Muslims and Muslim communities need never be without a mosque.

The *masjid al-jâmi'*, even from the early days of Islam, has been a more ambitious kind of building, in keeping with its grander function. The religious obligation imposed on every adult male and female free Muslim to meet for communal worship every Friday for public service or *salât* created the need for a much larger building than a *masjid*. The word *jâmi'* is derived from the Arabic root meaning "to assemble." In early Islam, a *jâmi'* was required to be erected in a city.

The *'îd* prayer ground is the mosque used during the Muslim festivals because of the nature of the ceremonies. It is always a *musallâ*, an open-air mosque, with only two structures: the *mihrâb* to show the direction of prayer and a *minbar* for the leader to deliver the festival sermon. The *'îd* prayer ground is used for the two great festival prayers and also for intercessory prayers in the time of drought, famine, and the like.

The Ka'ba or pilgrimage mosque is the central shrine in Islam and represents the concept and the center of *al-tawhîd*. The al-Masjid al-Harâm in Mecca became the pilgrimage center for Muslims after the cleansing done by the Prophet Muhammed in 630 CE. Other centers include the Medina mosque—the mosque of the Prophet—and *al-Masjid al-Aqsâ* in Jerusalem, in their sequence of importance.

Salâhaddîn was the one who introduced the monastic mosque in Egypt, founding the country's first *khanaqa* in a private house, the dar Sa'id as-Suada in 1173–1174.

The monastic mosques are used as retreat centers—that is, places for quiet contemplation and prayer—and are residential mosques with all their concomitant facilities. Monastic life goes back to the Sunna of the Prophet Muhammed, whose habit it was to go into retreat, or *i'tikâf*, for ten-day periods. Through various religious practices, the members of Sufî orders became absorbed into God. They lived a life of holiness in word, in conversation, and by example. The monastic mosques are sometimes used as centers for learning and for initiation into their mystical order and also provide shelter for wandering scholars.

Mosques as Social Centers

Mosques as a social center were instituted for education and charity; e.g., distribution of *zakat*, dispensation of justice, and political mobilization. Other types of social-center mosques are the tomb mosque and the collegiate mosque.

The tomb mosque is a place of worship that includes the founder's tomb, such as the mosque of al-Juyûshî, perched on the cliff edge of Mount Muqat'am overlooking Cairo. Dating from 1085, it is a *masjid* pure and simple, according to Michell (1978), but with the added distinction of being the first mosque to have a tomb as an integral part.

The collegiate mosque serves as a social centre, taking care of the intellectual development of the adherents of Islam. In Islam elementary as well as higher education is based on religious sciences and related philological disciplines. Students are arranged in cells around a master on a *kursî*, next to a pillar. It is the residential factor that relates the collegiate to the monastic mosque.

Sectarian Mosques

Those mosques built in response to certain needs of particular groups of people are known as sectarian mosques. Among these were mosques reserved for certain tribes, which flourished especially in Arabia during the first century of Islam and were a potent force for disunity, and mosques for separate quarters in a town or, as a logical extension of this, for certain crafts or occupations. Sometimes mosques reflected theological differences—not only the obvious Sunni and Shia differences but also the relatively minor distinctions between the various *madhhabs* (law schools).

Some of these mosques function as *jâmî*, the Friday congregational mosque, while others are used as *masjids*, smaller mosques, and also as a meeting place for the people in the community. The tribal mosque was a sign that the independence of the tribe was still retained under Islam. In fact, it is noteworthy that sectarian mosques are never shared with other tribes.

There were many such tribal mosques during the lifetime of the Prophet in Mecca and in Medina. Evidences of these types of mosques are found all over the Muslim world. During the wars, Pedersen (1991) points out, these tribal mosques were the natural rallying points for the various tribes; for example, the mosque was a *majlis*, where councils were held.

Mosques in Western Cultures

Since the terrorist attacks of September 11, 2001, Muslim communities outside Islamic countries have sometimes met with resistance to the construction of mosques in Western countries, especially in the United States. However, as Muslims emigrate to Western nations in increasing numbers, mosques will no doubt become more frequently seen in North American and European cities.

Fola T. Lateju

See also Islam

Further Reading

Caetani, L. (1915). *'Uthman and the recension of the Koran.* N.p.

Creswell, K. A. C. (1989). *A short account of early Muslim architecture.* Aldershot, UK: Scholar Press.

Hillenbrand, R. (1994). *Islamic architecture: Form, function, and meaning.* New York: Columbia University Press,.

Michell, G. (Ed.). (1978). *Architecture of the Islamic world: Its history and social meaning,* New York: Thames and Hudson.

Pedersen, J. (1991). Masdjid. In Bosworth, C. E., et. al. (Eds.), *Encyclopaedia of Islam.* Leiden, Netherlands: E. J. Brill.

Rivoira, J. T. (1975). *Moslem architecture: Its origin and development.* New York: Backer Art Books.

Scerrato, U. (1972). *Monuments of civilization: Islam.* London: Cassell & Company.

Museums

The idea of a museum is not a stable concept. Formal definitions are regularly debated, and often they differ from culture to culture. Generally speaking, a museum displays four characteristics: a legally organized permanent institution established for the purpose of giving educational value to communities; the collection, preservation, research, interpretation, and presentation of objects and other evidences of people and their environments; the continuing accessibility of these collections and presentations of objects and evidences by the public; and designated and delimited space or spaces in which the institution exists and the activities occur.

The above conditions can be applied to a variety of disciplines including anthropology, archaeology, art history, natural history, politics, religion, the sciences, and technology. The descriptive titles of these institutions are not limited to the term "museums." Depending upon their context and collections, they also can be termed aquaria, arboreta, art galleries, botanical gardens, historic sites, monuments, nature centers, visitor centers, vivaria, and zoological gardens. They can be either governmentally or privately sponsored, and they can be centered in a single space or spread across a number of independent spaces. The great diversity of institutions comprehended under the "museum" des-

ignation and the ongoing reevaluation of what a museum is reflect the complex history and multitude of purposes embodied within them.

The importance of museums to religion and communication lies in two domains: On the one hand, the designation of sites for the protection and signification of objects and discourses in order to enlighten a curious visitor is a practice that has occurred in religious situations for many centuries and has informed museums in their work; on the other hand, the kind of epistemological procedure that the museum demands of its visitor is one that is often referred to in terms that connote a religious experience. These two conditions underscore the parallel and mutually informing paths that religious institutions and museums have followed.

Early History

The ancient Greek word *mouseion* signified the home or seat of the muses—the nine daughters of Mnemosyne and Zeus. Each daughter was considered the goddess of a domain of learning, providing inspiration for the creation of history, astronomy, tragedy, comedy, dance, music, and poetry in three realms: epic, love and lyric. While none of these domains had within their central methodology the observation of objects removed from their natural surroundings for the purpose of analysis, the context in which learning took place was one of reflection and speculation aloof from the mundane activities of life. In classical Greece, the studies of philosophy, ethics, and religion were intermingled. However, by the time the Museum of Alexandria in Hellenistic Greece was established, that orientation had changed to an emphasis on the study of facts.

By the second century BCE Greek temples were receiving, either by gift or commission, sculptures, paintings, and similar objects as votive offerings to deities, and thus they became the first repositories of works of art in Greece. For the worshipper, however, these objects functioned not as independent aesthetic forms with content drawn from life but as reverenced vehicles for the transportation of one's mind to the realm of deity.

Precursors to the Modern Museum

By the seventeenth century, three quite distinct precursors to the modern museum and its mission were apparent. These forms emerged as responses to discrete social demands, each one primarily unrelated to the material nature and value of the objects that it was organized to preserve. Indeed, it is these nonmaterial

A display of old sitting Buddhas located in the Intrarawiharn (or Intharavihan) Temple/Wat complex, Bangkok, Thailand. *Courtesy of Didier Faucher/ istockphoto.com.*

aspects of each one's purpose that is more significant to the development of the modern museum and that remain responsive to contemporary social demands.

Cabinets of Curiosities

With roots in classical times, and influenced by increasing opportunities for educated and wealthy people to travel and observe the world beyond their domestic locale, cabinets of curiosities, or *Wunderkammer*, emerged as complex but idiosyncratic methods of ordering and understanding one's place in the world. Specimens and objects including, among other things, shells and geological specimens, preserved specimens of flora and fauna, coins and small machines, and paintings and sculptures were collected and assembled in a room of cabinets within one's home, especially prepared for effective visual display. While the earliest forms of these cabinets did not present the collections in a systematic way, by the seventeenth century relatively complex encyclopedic taxonomies had evolved.

The Princely Gallery

The term "gallery" accurately connotes a long, often grand corridor through which one would pass in a processional movement. Landowners, mostly wealthy kings, princes, dukes, and other noblemen, maintained preeminence among their peers and adversaries on the one hand, and their subjects on the other, by a constant and conspicuous display of power and knowledge. Perhaps the most visible architectural evidence of power was the gallery of art works accumulated as booty from conquests and commissioned and purchased from personal wealth. These objects were carefully organized in such a way that one's procession along the gallery would declare a number of intimidating messages: that the owner's strength was sufficient to defeat opposing armies and peers; that the owner's knowledge was superior by virtue of his easy relationship with the content and figures presented in the works; that the owner's genealogy (actual or cultural) was directly aligned with the great cultures and figures of the world; and that the owner's wealth was vast, demonstrated by the volume of works hung floor to ceiling in the gallery. Only invited visitors entered the gallery, which made them feel privileged, and they were expected to demonstrate gratitude and reverence to the owner.

The Temple or Cathedral

Temple or cathedral collections fall generally into two domains. Relics—pieces of wood, metal, fabric, bone, and other materials, promoted as real or transubstantiated fragments of original religious instruments, clothing, or even people—were displayed in elaborately decorated reliquaries, the design of which was intended to increase the significance of the relic and at the same time keep it removed from direct contact with the worshipper. While viewing and reflecting upon the object, the worshipper imaginatively magnified the object's history and significance, thereby simultaneously feeling a more privileged relationship with the deity.

The second domain includes paintings, sculptures, and other similar objects, as well as the architecture of the building, including the treatment of light. These forms were carefully arranged in a schema in order to provide an educational and inspirational narrative that taught both the posture that was to be adopted by the worshipper toward the priests and toward the deity, as well as the essential tenets that the worshipper was expected to know. This schema began at the building's exterior prospect and progressed across the threshold and throughout one's procession through the building and the religious ceremony. It involved the communication of certain prescribed meanings conveyed by the imagery and form of objects and by the space and organization of the building. In this environment, the objects in the temple's collections and the building's architecture functioned as utilitarian forms in the service of the religion, bringing about particular awareness and behavior in the worshipper.

The Modern Museum

While still evolving in response to social and cultural forces, the formation of the modern museum was largely complete by the mid-nineteenth century. Places set aside for the collection, preservation, research, and display of material and other evidences of humanity and its environment had been established to promote scholarship and to edify the public. On the surface, the modern museum is a secular environment—one in which knowledge is acquired and justified by the evidences in material and documentary form placed before the viewer. However, the cultural conditioning of the viewer—the codification that had created the appropriate behavior and, more particularly, the appropriate psychological and intellectual posture in relation to the evidences being observed—was a direct consequence of the cabinet of curiosities, the princely gallery, and the temple.

The "Gaze"

In 1914 the visual artist Marcel Duchamp (1887–1968), by placing a relatively common utilitarian object (a bottle rack) as if it were a sculpture in a museum, demonstrated that museums cause viewers automatically to adopt a particular kind of gaze that intends to obtain from the object significance and value beyond that which would have been obtained if the object were viewed in its common context. That gaze, sometimes referred to in religious terms as "beholding," has embodied within it a sense of reverence for the object, a willingness to accept its role as emblematic signifier, a subjection to the authority that has identified the object as being worthy of display, and a positive hope that knowledge and value will be obtained from one's interrogation of the object. In the process of beholding, one imaginatively magnifies the importance and discourse of the object. This effect is produced more by the context of the object's presentation—the museum—than by the inherent qualities of the object, although the two factors are interdependent.

Moral Discernment

In the nineteenth century, following the establishment of nation-states and the resulting formation of the concept of "the public," society leaders were faced with the challenge of managing large bodies of citizens using methods that respected the citizens' new social autonomy. Cultural reformers utilized public institutions that taught and exemplified the kinds of attitudes and behaviors that ensured a self-regulated, moral, and productive life. Central to the ideology was the idea that a citizen exposed to humankind's highest expressions of thought, creativity, beauty, and craft would be able to recognize the difference between these forms and the more mundane expressions of life. A citizen able to recognize the difference would automatically prefer the higher forms, thereby becoming more discerning, self-governing, and righteous.

Indeed, the nineteenth-century use of the word "aesthetic" denoted the causal relationship between the appreciation of beautiful and virtuous forms and the improvement of one's inner grace and moral bearing. Museums were frequently identified by cultural reformers as one of the most influential instruments in the execution of this strategy. The following declaration by Sir Henry Cole, the British cultural reformer, provides an example of a widely held confidence in the museum's capacity to perform the difficult and sensitive task of elevating society:

> If you wish to vanquish Drunkenness and the Devil, make God's day of rest elevating and refining to the working man; don't leave him to find his recreation in bed first, and in the public house afterwards;…Open all museums of Science and Art after the hours of Divine service; let the working man get his refreshment there in company with his wife and children, rather than leave him to booze away from them in the Public house and Gin Palace. The Museum will certainly lead him to wisdom and gentleness, and to Heaven, whilst the latter will lead him to brutality and perdition. (Bennett 1995)

Cultural Authority

The sequence of objects and ideas to which the citizen was exposed in the museum taught another kind of doctrine, one intended to generate strong respect for the state and the ruling establishment. Collections were placed in large neoclassical buildings, with the works purposely arranged to be viewed in logical procession, echoing the princely galleries of the past. They were designed to signify to the citizen that the building and the nation-state it represented were seamlessly aligned with the great cultures of the past and therefore possessed the same cultural authority and excellence. The objects were typically arranged in a strategic sequence that began with works from the classical cultures and ended with the best works from the nation (or region) in which the museum was located. The works displayed were selected according to a cultural measure of objects most likely to inspire reverence, loyalty, and moral rectitude.

Current Conditions

In the political context of the twenty-first century, museums do not place moral discernment at the forefront of their mission statements; however, the idea of personal and social improvement and enlightenment is regularly embodied in mission-statement rhetoric and in practice. And while considerable emphasis is placed upon the significance of the particular object and evidence, most major modern museums organize the public display of their collections according to historical and cultural orders laid out in the nineteenth century.

While the traces of the cabinet of curiosities, the princely gallery, and the temple are now combined in varying degrees in each kind of museum, the influence of these traditions remains clearly discernable in museum architecture, displays, and educational programming. In an interesting turnaround, religious organizations have adopted many of the techniques used by secular museums (such as visitors' centers, educational brochures, and guided tours) to teach tenets to their members, to proselytize, and to educate the surrounding community.

Campbell B. Gray

See also Material Culture; Relics

Further Reading

Aagaard-Mogensen, L. (Ed.). (1988). *The idea of the museum: Philosophical, artistic and political questions.* New York: The Edwin Mellen Press.

Bazin, G. (1967). *The museum age.* New York: Universe Books Inc.

Bennett, T. (1995). *The birth of the museum: History, theory, politics.* London: Routledge.

Carbonell, B. M. (Ed.). (2004). *Museum studies: An anthology of contexts.* Malden, MA: Blackwell Publishing.

Duncan, C. (1995). *Civilizing rituals: Inside public art museums.* London: Routledge.

Hein, H. (2000). *The museum in transition: A philosophical perspective.* Washington, DC: Smithsonian.

Karp, I., Kreamer, C. M., & Lavine, S. D. (Eds.). (1992). *Museums and communities: The politics of public culture.* Washington, DC: Smithsonian.

Karp, I., & Lavine, S. D. (Eds.). (1991). *Exhibiting cultures: The poetics and politics of museum display.* Washington, DC: Smithsonian.

Lorente, J. P. (1998). *Cathedrals of urban modernity: The first museums of contemporary art, 1800–1930.* Aldershot, UK: Ashgate Publishing Company.

Preziosi, D., & Farrago, C. (Eds.). (2004). *Grasping the world: The idea of the museum.* Aldershot, UK: Ashgate Publishing Company.

Prior, N. (2002). *Museums and modernity: Art galleries and making of modern culture.* Oxford, UK: Berg.

Sherman, D. J., & Rogoff, I. (Eds.). (1994). *Museum culture: Histories, discourses, spectacles*. Minneapolis: University of Minnesota Press.

Wittlin, A. S. (1949). *The museum: Its history and its tasks in education*. London: Routledge and Kegan Paul Limited.

Music

From the beginning religion has communicated through music. Sacred music serves monotheistic, polytheistic, and totemic religions; it served the early high civilizations of China, India, and the near East as well as the New Guinea tribes almost completely secluded from the modern world. In Western culture, most musicians depicted in early Mesopotamian and Egyptian art participate in sacred rites. In the Bible, music is the third profession to be listed (after animal husbandry and agriculture; Genesis 4:2 and 21), and song accompanies the creation of the earth (Job 38:7). Music has always resonated with the magical, the sacred, and the mysterious essence of things.

Music as a Medium of Cosmic Truth

The earliest known music theorist is Pythagoras, a Greek religious leader active in the waning sixth century BCE. Pythagorean religious philosophy holds that relations among numbers govern or even create the world and that music manifests this order. The harmonious motions of the heavenly bodies create actual music—the Music of the Spheres—which humans, hampered by too coarse a nature, cannot hear.

Pythagoras investigated musical intervals (the distance between two pitches). He found that simple ratios generate consonant (pleasing or concordant) intervals and that progressively complex ratios generate progressively more dissonant (grating or discordant) ones. The most consonant interval is the octave. Pluck a string and listen. Then put a bridge at the midpoint of the string so that only half the original length vibrates and pluck again: Now the note is an octave higher. Hence, a ratio of two-to-one (whole string to half string) creates an octave. Pythagoras saw this correlation of simple ratios to consonant intervals as a key to understanding cosmic order.

Christianity assimilated much Greek thought. Since Medieval times, musicians refer to the Greek consonances as perfect intervals and the discords as imperfect. The perfect intervals are closer to God's nature

than the mundane imperfect intervals. In metaphorical harmony with this intervalic theology, Medieval pieces begin and end on perfect intervals, which also stand at the strongest rhythmic positions. Imperfect intervals arise from and sound fleetingly between the perfect. Similarly, the late Middle Ages called triple rhythms perfect by analogy to the Holy Trinity, in contrast to the imperfect duple rhythms associated with human bipedal motion (walking, marching, dancing).

The imperative to end music with a perfect interval was so strong that it survived long after musical style had arguably made the practice obsolete. The elemental sonority of Western music for more than five centuries now has been the triad (such as C-E-G). Yet for a couple of centuries after triads became standard, the last sonority in a piece was still customarily reduced to perfect intervals (such as C-G). Even today, with no theological rationale and despite a poor fit with musical style, our vocabulary bears the imprint of these now long-abandoned ideas: For half a millennium, musicians have had to learn that one of the perfect consonances—the fourth—functions as a dissonance.

Pythagorean ideas were accepted for over two thousand years, from the sixth century BCE until the scientific revolution in seventeenth-century Europe. Even after Galileo had started publishing works that would overthrow the old cosmology, Johannes Kepler, in his magnum opus, *Harmonice mundi* (1618), derived musical scales from planetary motions and wrote out the music sounded by the planets.

When Newtonian mechanics silenced the Music of the Spheres, the ratios of intervals remained crucial for the scientifically oriented Enlightenment music theorists, especially Jean Philippe Rameau, who synthesized modern music theory. Indeed, the correspondence of consonance to the harmonic series still inspires theorists to ask how far music manifests some universal principle of nature.

On a more explicitly spiritual track, Romantics in the later eighteenth century saw music as the highest of arts, the ideal medium to convey the spiritual, intuitive truth they strove to apprehend. The most extravagant philosophical exponent of the Romantic view is Arthur Schopenhauer, who claimed that music is the pure manifestation of the will that creates the world in *Die Welt als Wille und Vorstellung* (1844).

The Romantic idea that music communicates truth too deep for words leads us to accept a composer as a genius or seer, a notion that has turned concert halls into temples of art. Composers, starting most notoriously with Beethoven, see themselves as vessels to convey

Rejoice, the Lord is King!

Rejoice, the Lord is King! Your Lord and King adore;
Mortals give thanks and sing, and triumph evermore;
Lift up your heart, lift up your voice;
Rejoice, again I say, rejoice!

Jesus, the Savior, reigns, the God of truth and love;
When He had purged our stains He took His seat above;
Lift up your heart, lift up your voice;
Rejoice, again I say, rejoice!

His kingdom cannot fail, He rules o'er earth and heaven,
The keys of death and hell are to our Jesus given;
Lift up your heart, lift up your voice;
Rejoice, again I say, rejoice!

He sits at God's right hand till all His foes submit,
And bow to His command, and fall beneath His feet:
Lift up your heart, lift up your voice;
Rejoice, again I say, rejoice!

sublime truths. This has spurred composers to make extravagant claims, culminating with Aleksandr Skryabin's plans for *Misteriya*, a week-long, multimedia event to be performed by thousands of participants in the Himalayan foothills. The performance of *Misteriya* would bring about the end of the world and transform Earth and its inhabitants to a higher spiritual plane.

Music as a Medium of Ethics

Accounts of music's significance are usually more modest than those listed above, but all acknowledge its powerful spiritual impact. The Greeks concluded that music not only affects our moods and behavior but molds our character and changes our nature—an idea called the Doctrine of Ethos. The effect on the soul depends on the type of music. Different instruments, modes, and rhythms suit different contexts: The aulos (an oboe ancestor) is played in worship of Dionysus, while the kithara (a large lyre) honors Apollo; music that builds bravado and aggressiveness benefits soldiers but harms politicians. These effects are cumulative, so a youth who listens to too much decadent

music ends with a flawed character. Plato recommended banning a long list of scales and rhythms as morally damaging. Variations on this Greek theme have pervaded talk about music's role in society ever since: The Soviet Union controlled music in order to curb revolutionary tendencies and buttress political enthusiasm, and American religious leaders often attack new music as degrading or evil.

That music influences us is beyond question, and it is not difficult, especially within a culture, to agree that lullabies sooth and marches energize, that if we play a melody in major and then in minor, the major version will seem more buoyant to a Westernized listener. However, history rules out a simplistic view of ethos. To name one difficulty, adults usually judge youth culture to be decadent, yet that culture is routinely absorbed into the next generation's mainstream. Around 1800, waltzes were condemned as lascivious, but by mid-century, they had become a fixture among polite dances. Similarly, the jazz that once so disgusted the proper has now migrated from the dance hall to the concert hall and from raunchy bars to the smoke-free environs of public radio.

Those who rail against the evils of music assume—with Plato—that musical materials can be inherently or essentially evil. Some such see the process of assimilation as evidence of a long-term decline in cultural values that is leading the world to its doom. Others consider musical style to be morally neutral, so accidental factors—words, visual information, and social context—determine the ethical quality of a work. In this view, one redeems music by replacing objectionable content with uplifting alternatives as the Christian music industry does in offering sanitized versions of most current popular styles.

A related practice occurs when a congregation requires a new repertory of music. The rise of the Protestant churches in the sixteenth century created a need for chorale melodies, which was often satisfied with *contrafacta*, melodies for which the original text has been replaced by a new one. The originals were often secular. Indeed, the most moving crucifixion hymn of all, the *Passion Chorale*, was originally a lively song in which a boy whines about his girl (*Mein G'müth ist mir verwirret*, by Hans Leo Hassler).

Music Media

While some ancient cultures developed systems of musical notation, these had fallen out of use by late antiquity, so in the early Middle Ages music was transmitted orally. Medieval notation was first invented for Catholic liturgical music, apparently in response to a political need.

Charlemagne and his family aspired to revive the Roman Empire. In pursuit of this goal they set about to unify their domains with a common currency, law code, educational system, liturgy, and music. The Franks searched for the most authoritative liturgical practice as their model. The music for the Roman liturgy they chose soon came to be called Gregorian chant for Pope Gregory the Great (r. 590–604 CE), who they believed had written down the large corpus of Roman liturgical chant by dictation from the Holy Spirit. Iconography represents Gregory writing down the music that a dove sings into his ear. This legend admirably suited the imperial mandate to unify church music.

However, Frankish rulers found their attempts to unify chant repeatedly frustrated. Complaints about corrupted chant abound in eighth- and ninth-century records, even after multiple attempts to fix the repertory. Music notation helped solve this problem. At first, in the ninth century, notation functioned as an *aide-mémoire* for musicians who had already learned the chants. By the thirteenth century, notation placed individual pitches on a staff, as it does today. Rhythmic notation was developed to synchronize the voices of sacred polyphony. By the seventeenth century, notation had acquired most of its modern features. Although notation is still incomplete in many ways, trained musicians can now learn new pieces without help from a teacher. The first printed music appeared in the late sixteenth century, and the music publishing industry hit its stride in the nineteenth, when large numbers of the middle class became affluent enough to study music.

In the twentieth century, sound recording radically transformed the transmission of music. Once music is recorded, listeners no longer need the intermediaries of teachers, notation, publishers, performers, and concert halls.

Congregational Song

Catholic liturgical music had been sung by clergy, and most chant would be difficult for a congregation to learn and perform. Martin Luther wanted the entire congregation to experience the ethical and educational power of making music and spurred the development of an important new repertory. The Lutheran congregational hymn—or chorale—is a short, simple melody with straightforward rhythms and syllabic text-setting in strophic form that sets a poetic rhymed text. Chorales are easily learned, easily remembered, and easily sung by a congregation. They change the experience of church services by giving a group of worshipers the means to approach God, unanimously immersed in musical communion.

Inevitably, the qualities that make an effective chorale exclude other possibilities. Like much spiritually ecstatic music, chant has the effect of a single voice inventing music as inspired by the Holy Spirit. Such melodies can be unpredictable, unpatterned, and difficult to reproduce in myriad ways. The musician's fervent concentration on a single word or idea often yields melismas: chains of sometimes dozens of notes sung on just one syllable. Such music is beyond a normal congregation's capacity. Still, a congregation wants to exult, and we find modest, clearly patterned, simple melismas in some hymns (in the Easter Hymn, with the text "Christ the Lord is Risen Today," on the word *alleluia* or in "Angels We Have Heard on High" or "Ding, Dong, Merrily on High" on the first syllable of *gloria in excelsis deo*).

Music and Symbolism

The Catholic response to the Protestant movement, the Counter-Reformation, was institutionalized by the

Full Gospel Choruses

Pentecostals sang these choruses, many of which were carried over from previous holiness traditions. The choruses below are categorized into the following themes: Jesus, Eschatological, Revival, Healing, and Prayer.

Jesus

Oh, how I love Jesus. Oh, how I love Jesus. Oh, how I love Jesus,
Because He first loved me.
I'll never forsake Him. I'll never forsake Him. I'll never forsake Him,
Because He first loved me.

Eschatological

Sing the wondrous song of Jesus, Sing His mercies and His grace,
In that mansions, bright and blessed, He'll prepare a place for me.
When we all get to Heaven, What a glory that will be,
When we all see Jesus, We will shout and claim the victory.

Revival

Oh, Holy Ghost, Revival comes from Thee,
Send a revival, start the work in me.
Thy Word declares, Thou wilt supply our need,
For blessings now, O Lord, We humbly plead.

Healing

I am the Lord that healeth thee,
All of your sickness bring to me,
Come with your pain, and you will see,
That I am the Lord that healeth thee.

Compiled by Stan and Ruth Burgess

Council of Trent in the mid 1500s. The council considered abolishing polyphony in church services because it obscures the words being sung. According to legend, a performance of Palestrina's polyphonic *Pope Marcellus Mass* showed the council that textual clarity depends on a composer's skill, not a style of music. While this legend has long been discredited, its earlier acceptance resulted in Palestrina's style being held in near canonical status for centuries. When, in subsequent eras of music, composers such as Handel, Mozart, or Verdi wrote church music in Baroque, Classical, or Romantic styles, conservatives condemned them in comparison to Palestrina's style. In the nineteenth century, the Cecilian Movement (after St. Cecelia) fought newer trends in an effort to keep Palestrina's style from degenerating. The style became a symbol for such things as orthodoxy, the faith of the fathers, and the purity of an earlier age.

Indeed, a style of music often communicates some extra-musical idea. The *sicilienne*, a Baroque pastoral dance, is found in many Christmas works to represent the scene in which angels tell shepherds in the fields of Christ's birth (the best-known are Bach's *Christmas Oratorio*, Handel's *Messiah*, and Corelli's *Christmas Concerto*). The "French Overture," invented to accompany the entrance of the Sun King, Louis XIV, is used in Handel's *Messiah* to invoke the Son of God and King of Heaven. Beethoven used a military-band style in the

Missa Solemnis to evoke warfare before setting the words *dona nobis pacem* ([Lord] grant us peace).

Music symbolism often depends on text. Most Renaissance composers wrote at least one Mass in which they quote the melody of *L'homme armé* ("The Armed Man," a secular call-to-arms tune), arguably as an admonition to put on the whole armor of God (Ephesians 6:11). Starting with Berlioz's *Symphonie fantastique*, at least a score of concert works quote the opening phrase of *dies irae* (Day of Wrath) from the Roman Catholic Requiem (funeral) Mass. The melody migrated to popular culture and sounds in dozens of film scores, TV shows, and popular music tracks, where it might symbolize supernatural evil (*The Shining*), destruction (*Demolition Man*), death (*The Seventh Seal*), or judgment day (*It's a Wonderful Life*).

Recent Developments

The two most sweeping changes in recent religious music have roots in the 1960s. Contemporary Christian music (CCM) is a billion-dollar industry fed especially by Evangelicals. CCM's roots are in the counterculture trends of the 1950s and 1960s, which were often spiritual, if irreligious. The values of the 1960s found Christian expression in Jesus-Movement music. In the 1970s and 1980s CCM became an increasingly large business but was hampered by a reputation of low-budget amateurism compared to the rising standards of secular commercial music. As the audience grew, so did financial resources, and the 1990s saw a professionalization of Christian pop that has redressed this imbalance. At the turn of the millennium, CCM had become a billion-dollar business that outsold classical, jazz, and new-age combined and, incidentally, could not exist without inexpensive mass-distribution of recorded sound.

Today, modern worship music is written for church services and is primarily distributed by print. Most of it is characterized by toned-down popular style characteristics. CCM, by contrast, is entertainment distributed as recorded sound that competes directly with popular styles. Indeed, CCM is an umbrella term that encompasses styles from adult contemporary and country, to punk, rap, metal, and beyond.

In CCM the rare ethnic face is usually found in a group of whites. Astonishingly, even the most popular Christian rap, hip-hop, and R&B artists are white. The only commercial category not dominated by white musicians is black gospel, which some commentators put in a separate category from CCM. Clearly, the segregation found in churches also divides the music industry.

While the rise of CCM has changed the sacred music landscape of America, the other change has a much larger global impact because it affected Roman Catholics, at one billion plus, the earth's largest denomination. The Vatican II council in the 1960s changed worship music virtually overnight. The switch from Latin to vernacular liturgy rendered an entire repertory obsolete. The new music that replaced it aspired to be contemporary and relevant and to increase the active participation of the congregation. As a result, this highly conservative church heard guitar-accompanied, popular-music styles in the liturgy sooner than most ostensibly more liberal main-line Protestants. In recent decades Catholics have worked to preserve the cultural identity of worshipers. In a Mass one can now hear the influence of Flamenco music, African rhythms, Native-American rituals, or even thousand-year-old Japanese court music. Within cultures, a plethora of musical styles address distinct constituencies. The Catholic church has now officially discarded the ideal of worldwide unity in favor of fostering music that more directly communicates to the lay soul.

For further study and current bibliographies, the best place to start on every topic except CCM is the *New Grove Dictionary of Music and Musicians*, second edition (2000), the most exhaustive music encyclopedia in any language. For CCM, start with Mark Allan Powell, *The Encyclopedia of Contemporary Christian Music* (2001), but the serious student will soon move on to a search of recent issues from the most relevant scholarly journals.

BRYCE RYTTING

See also Chanting; Music Video; Silence

Further Reading

McKinnon, J. W., Stevens, J., & le Huray, P. (1987). *Music in early Christian literature*. Cambridge, England: Cambridge University Press.

Powell, M. A. (2001). *The Encyclopedia of contemporary Christian music*. Peabody, MA: Hendrickson Publishers.

Stanley, S. (Ed.). (2000). *New grove dictionary of music and musicians*, 2nd edition. Oxford, England: Oxford University Press.

Thomas, M. J. (1999). *Apollo's lyre: Greek music and music theory in antiquity and the Middle Ages*. Lincoln, NE: University of Nebraska Press.

Wilson-Dickson, A. (2003). *The story of Christian music: From Gregorian chant to black gospel*. Minneapolis, MN: Augsburg Fortress.

Music Video

Since the advent of film with sound, the combination of music and moving pictures has been a popular form of entertainment. The term "music video" is, however, most often reserved for the kind of medium, combining music and television images that has become common within popular music, particularly since the launch of MTV in 1981. A music video in a strict sense is a short film clip released as a supplement to a music track, ordinarily a single that functions as soundtrack for the video. Music videos are an essential part of the marketing of records and artists within contemporary popular music. Such promotional music videos are also produced within various forms of religious music, such as that in Islam, Reformed Judaism and, most notably, contemporary Christian music or Christian rock.

Contemporary Christian Music Videos as Alternative to Secular Music

Contemporary Christian music (commonly abbreviated CCM), as well as Christian music videos, can be defined in several ways. According to one definition of the genre, the Christian character of CCM and Christian music videos depends on the message of the songs, a message that is also conveyed by the visual images in the video. A second, more sociological definition states that CCM as a whole, as well as the music videos, are Christian in the sense that they are produced, distributed, and consumed within an institutional Christian framework.

CCM functions as a Christian alternative to "secular" or mainstream popular music and as such attempts to provide a Christian audience with Christian artists and products as similar to the mainstream market as possible without compromising what is perceived as the Christian character of the products. This is also true of the videos. A closer look at music videos within CCM and a comparison with mainstream videos (e.g., those on MTV) show that there are many similarities, in the fast camera movements and editing that are characteristic of music videos, in the structure of the videos, and in the often trendy looks of the artists themselves.

Structure of Videos

Typical of the music video structure is the blend of images of the artist performing, live in concert or in a situation reenacting a live performance in various milieus, with images conveying a narrative that may or may not be connected to the lyrics of the song.

Many music videos consist entirely of images of the artist performing; such videos are common within CCM. These videos are easier to produce than a video resembling a short film and are therefore better suited for a narrow genre with smaller resources than those available to the major mainstream stars. But the videos showing live performances with an audience are also perfectly suited to accommodate "praise" or "worship" music, a growing niche within CCM, as exemplified in several videos by the group Third Day.

An important part of the visuals of any music video is the artist or group performing. The appearance of attractive young people in the video is arguably a major contributor to the success of the whole medium. This same observation can be made of the videos in CCM; in comparison with mainstream videos, however, there is a noticeable difference in one aspect of the artists' appearance: their clothing. The minimal attire on both men and women often featured in mainstream videos is rare in the videos in CCM. The appearance of the artists in CCM videos can therefore be seen as a visual representation of a lifestyle perceived as compatible with Christianity.

Other Visual Aspects

There are also other, more explicit visual aspects to Christian music videos that can be interpreted as representations of Christianity and as visual expressions of a Christian message. Many videos feature objects closely related to Christian tradition, such as churches or bibles; or persons in the video use poses and gestures recognizable as parts of Christian worship; e.g., holding their hands together as if praying. Christian symbols and imagery are also evident in many videos, both quite explicit imagery, such as crosses or bread and wine, and more ambivalent symbols, such as lights shining from the top of the frame or water; e.g., in scenes reminiscent of baptism. An example of a video heavily featuring objects, gestures, and symbols representing Christianity is the video to one of the major CCM hits of the 1990s, "Jesus Freak" by dc Talk.

Visual Narrative

In some CCM videos, the visual narrative is a central part of the Christian character of the videos. There are a few types of narrative that are common. Many videos contain a conversion narrative; e.g., "Reborn" with Rebecca St. James. Other examples are narratives of liberation from problems such as a stressful job or an inhospitable environment, a theme covered in different ways (e.g., in "Consume Me" with dc Talk or "One of These Days" with the group FFH); and conflicts and their resolution; for example, in "Irene" with Toby Mac.

An important message often conveyed in CCM videos is the call to charity toward those less fortunate, as comes out very clearly in "When Love Takes You In" with Steven Curtis Chapman or "You Raise Me Up" with Selah, which strongly features news footage of starving African children.

The Use of Music Videos

A central function of a music video is to serve as an advertisement for records and other commercially distributed products related to the artist, as well as promoting the image of the artist. Within CCM, the logic of advertisement often becomes conflated with the evangelistic purpose of the music, because the aim of selling more records is well suited to the desire to spread the message conveyed on these records.

The advertisement function influences both the form and the content of the videos. In order to be interesting enough to invite several viewings and allow the advertising message to be consumed repeatedly, the videos often are quite complex. A music video must contain elements that are thought provoking and open to interpretation. The music videos in CCM must be especially open to interpretation, as they must function on the one hand as a contemporary music video and on the other as a medium for a Christian message.

Limited Market of CCM Videos

As CCM is a relatively small—albeit growing—genre of popular music, access to distribution on mainstream music channels is very limited. Apart from distribution on Christian cable television and on the Internet, CCM videos are distributed in commercially available collections on VHS and DVD; for example, the hit collections jointly released annually from 1996 onward by the major CCM distribution companies under the brand name "WoW." In addition to the distribution on channels specific to the genre, a small number of CCM artists cross over into the mainstream and are shown on MTV. Examples of major CCM crossover artists from the 1980s and onward are the hard-rock groups Stryper and P.O.D., as well as the female artists Amy Grant and Stacie Orrico.

The vast majority of consumers of CCM are, however, young people already engaged in the Christian church. The main use of CCM videos is therefore not as a tool for evangelization but rather as accepted entertainment for Christian youth. Beyond this, the videos serve as models for the musical activities in local parishes and youth groups and may also feature in actual worship and concerts where videos with the performing group are displayed on big screens adjacent to the stage.

The use of the video format is not entirely restricted to contemporary popular music. One example of a wider use is the attempt to promote new hymnals in the national Lutheran churches of Finland and Sweden at the end of the 1980s, when both these churches arranged nationwide contests in the production of "hymn videos."

Religious Themes in Videos Outside CCM

Commercial popular music and the medium of the music video is to a great extent a Western phenomenon, and the evangelistic theology of Christianity emphasizes the use of modern means for spreading the gospel. But the use of music videos within a religious framework is not restricted to a Christian context; there are artists who in their music and their videos refer, for example, to Islam, African-American religions, or Satanism.

Islam

There are American hip-hop artists who belong to the Nation of Islam and Senegalese *mbalax* artists who are followers of the local Muslim Sufi leaders; many of these artists sing of their faith and release videos of their songs. An example of a hip-hop song with evident Islamic influence in the text as well as in the video is "Allah U Akbar" by Brand Nubian.

African-American Religion

A well-known example of religious influence in popular music is the connection between Jamaican reggae and Rastafarianism. The visual aspects of reggae clearly feature symbols of Rastafarianism, such as the dreadlock hairstyle and the colors of the Ethiopian flag, red, yellow and green. This is, for example, evident in several videos by the legendary Jamaican Reggae artist Bob Marley. Reggae is not the only example of African-American religious influence in popular music, as is evident, for example, from the conspicuous appearance of Cuban Santeria rituals as well as a depiction of the trickster god Elegua in the video

"Mambo Yo Yo" by the Los Angeles–based artist Ricardo Lemvo.

Satanism

Another popular music genre where the references to the views and beliefs of a particular religious tradition are quite central is the hard-rock genre black metal. The use of references to Satanism within black metal is not limited to song lyrics but is part of the iconography in the genre; this is also present in music videos with black metal groups. In addition to religious imagery, these videos typically feature a violent, somber aesthetic reminiscent of gothic film, as evidenced in the video "Progenies of the Great Apocalypse," by one of the more successful groups in the genre, Dimmu Borgir from Norway. It must also be noted that in the context of metal music it is notoriously difficult to determine the difference between religious conviction or belonging on the one hand and image and irony on the other.

Other Uses

Going outside the stricter definition of music video as a short film clip accompanying one song, there are other examples of religious themes in media combining music and moving pictures. There are videos used as tools for meditation that draw on various religious traditions, notably traditions common within the "New Age" spectrum. These videos typically use calm instrumental music and images of natural scenery. In the musical numbers in Indian films, references to Hindu religion and use of forms of traditional devotional music are not uncommon. And commercially available live video recordings of the performance of religious music are abundant.

It must also be pointed out that the use of religious reference in music videos is not limited to videos produced within a religious context. The references to Satanism central to black metal, for example, are also present in various forms in other metal genres. An artist within the commercial main stream of popular music who has been prolific in her use of religious imagery in her videos is Madonna. Her video "Like a Prayer" is a clear example of this, and both academic scholars and religious commentators have found important religious as well as political messages in it. The interpretations of a video such as "Like a Prayer" serve as an important reminder that the reception and interpretation of a video play a great role in deciding whether a work such as a music video is "religious" in some sense and what function such a work may have in a religious context.

The Future

The academic research on the relations between popular music and religious traditions or institutions is still quite limited. Considering the importance of the medium of the music video in contemporary popular music, including contemporary Christian music, it must be stated that the research in this area is particularly scarce.

Further research is needed on the production, reception, and content of videos that draw on different religious traditions or are produced within the institutional contexts of different religions; and on the use of religious elements such as symbols and iconography in mainstream music videos and the interpretations of these elements in different viewer categories. There is an increase in scholarly awareness of the relevance of the visual aspects in religious practice, including Protestant Christianity, as well as a growing body of research on religious aspects in feature films, but so far these research interests have only to a very limited extent inspired studies of the religious aspects of music videos.

ANDREAS HÄGER

Further Reading

Booth, G. (2000). Religion, gossip, narrative conventions and the construction of meaning in Hindi film songs. *Popular Music*, 19(2), 126–144.

Frith, S., Goodwin, A., & Grossberg, L. (Eds.). (1993). *Sound and vision: The music video reader*. London: Routledge.

Gow, J. (1998). Saving souls and selling CDs: The mainstreaming of Christian music videos. *Journal of Popular Film and Television*, 25(4), 183–188.

Häger, A. (1996). Like a prophet: On Christian interpretations of a Madonna video. In T. Ahlbäck (Ed.), *Dance, music, art and religion* (pp. 151–174). Åbo, Finland: The Donner Institute for Research in Religious and Cultural History.

Häger, A. (forthcoming). Visual representations of Christianity in Christian music videos. *Temenos*.

Howard, J. R. & Streck, J. M. (1999). *Apostles of rock: The splintered world of Contemporary Christian Music*. Lexington: The University Press of Kentucky.

Hulsether, M. (2000). Like a sermon: Popular religion in Madonna videos. In B. D. Forbes & J. H. Mahan (Eds.), *Religion and popular culture in America* (pp. 71–100). Berkeley: University of California Press.

Reid, J. E. & Dominick, J. R. (1994). A comparative analysis of Christian and mainstream rock music videos. *Popular Music and Society, 18*(2), 87–97.

Romanowski, W. D. (2000). Evangelicals and popular music: The contemporary Christian music industry. In B. D. Forbes & J. H. Mahan (Eds.), *Religion and popular culture in America* (pp. 105–124). Berkeley: University of California Press.

WoW Hits 2005. (2005). The year's top Christian artists and music video hits. EMI. [DVD]

Myths

Myths are powerful stories through which cultures express their deepest values and concerns. If there are modern myths, or if ancient myths live on in contemporary society, we will find them expressed in the stories told through the mass media.

Myths are popularly understood to be stories about ancient gods and heroes, which may be interesting but which no longer have power and meaning in the modern scientific world. Yet throughout the twentieth century scholars renewed their interest in myth and considered what myth might tell us about people today.

Function of Myths

Mircea Eliade (1907–1986) argues that powerful myths continue to shape our thinking in the contemporary world. These myths interpret the origin of things, express shared values, and give shape and meaning to our experience. In order to understand these claims, and recognize the myths embedded in modern media, it is helpful to know something about myth in the ancient world and to contrast myths with folktales.

Though they take the form of stories, ancient myths are more than folk or fairy tales. To the societies where they emerged, they were precious cultural possessions that carried deeply shared truths.

Folktales entertain and often illustrate a moral lesson, as we see in Aesop's fables, where the lesson is included at the end of the tale, but they are not assumed to be about actual events. One can read *Little Red Riding Hood* as a cautionary tale for little girls, but it is not presented as an account of an actual wolf and girl whose actions set in place unchangeable relationships between wolves and girls.

In contrast to folktales, myths are assumed to express actual events of such significance that they shaped the nature of reality. Eliade describes myths as tales set in a time prior to ordinary time, or in a world above the world of everyday life. Thus myths explain both the origin of things and their meaning. To outsiders they may appear as fanciful as fairy tales, but to the culture that produced them they are windows to a "time of origins" (Eliade 1959, 71).

Joseph Campbell (1904–1987) argues that a myth serves four critical human needs by providing (1) a sense of awe about the universe, (2) a description of the world aligned with the scientific understandings of the day, (3) ritual support for the social order, and (4) direction for the individual in facing the psychological traumas of life. It is easy to look back and see the way the myths of Greeks, Romans, the Norse, or Native American peoples serve these purposes. It is harder to think about one's own cultural material in this way.

For instance, Jews and Christians are often resistant to the suggestion that the Bible contains material that can be seen as myth. The familiar story of the Garden of Eden (Genesis 2:4b–3:24) is one example of a biblical account that can be read as myth. This myth of origin tells of the creation of humanity by an all-powerful Creator who must be treated with awe. It supports the social order by making hierarchy between the sexes and the traumas of work and childbirth a part of an explanation of how the relationship between God and humanity emerged.

Myth as Literature

Ancient cultures understood their myths to be true. But later cultures treated that claim as naive. Disconnected from belief, myth becomes purely literary, as happened to classic Greek and Roman myth in modern Europe. Myths came to be regarded only as archaic stories that might provide literary allusions, but were not to be taken literally. Thus over time describing something as a "myth" came to mean that it was untrue, reversing the original meaning of the word.

While popular discourse largely dismissed myth as archaic and untrue, myth remained a rich source of powerful images and narratives from which artists drew in every era. The versions of ancient myths that we know are later literary reworkings of myths that had long existed in oral culture. Subsequent authors and visual artists turned to myth as a source of engaging human concerns, themes, characters and images. Northrop Frye (1912–1991) wrote that "Myth is and has always been an integral element of literature, the interest of poets in myth and mythology having been remarkable and constant since Homer's time" (Frye 1963, 21). Sometimes, as in Keats's "Ode on a Grecian Urn," there are direct references to ancient myth. At other times, as in cartoons where Wile E. Coyote appears as an update of the trickster coyote of Native American mythology, the references are veiled.

Myth and Psychology

The idea of myth captured the imagination of early psychological theorists. In the work of Sigmund Freud (1856–1939) myth came to be seen as the expression of deep human or social truths. In exploring the incestuous wishes that he believed were at the heart of human development, Freud turned to the Greek myth in which Oedipus kills his father Laius and marries his mother Jocasta to give form to his idea of the Oedipus complex.

Freud's disciple Carl Jung (1875–1961) broke with Freud about 1913 and developed his own system of psychological thought. He argued with Freud's assertion that the roots of psychological complexes were to be found in the traumatic experiences of childhood. Jung turned from external experience and argued that there were deep internal structures, a collective unconscious, that shaped our development and understanding of the world. Jung argued that there were enduring symbols in the unconscious that are part of our human legacy and which shape the way we experience and think about the world around us. Figures such as the shadow, the hero, the trickster, the earth mother, and other powerful reoccurring images appeared in the dreams, myths, and stories of people from many different cultures.

Archetypal Approaches

By the middle of the twentieth century, these rich literary and psychological approaches to myth produced renewed interest in traditional mythologies. Scholars like Eliade and Campbell looked for the common themes, concerns, and structures in myth in many different cultures. Campbell argued that myths and religion follow common or universal archetypes, much as Jung had argued that such archetypes shaped the internal world of dreams and the collective unconscious.

Frye broke with the literary criticism of his day, which focused on literature's effect on the modern reader, to develop a criticism that understood literary expression in light of the origins of literary themes and form. He sought to enrich our reading of the text by letting us see its connection to earlier and lasting literary and mythic forms and concerns.

Earlier thinkers had dismissed myth as the product of ancient or "primitive" cultures and suggested that it had no place in a rational scientific world. Thinkers like Freud, Jung, Campbell, Eliade, and Frye provided ways to consider how myth lives on in the unconscious life of modern people, and in contemporary storytelling forms like the novel, film, and television. They suggest that myth continues to shape the way that people think about their experience in the world.

Myth and Popular Media

The idea that myths and archetypes lived on in contemporary media provided new ways for scholars to think about popular culture. Popular culture had been dismissed as merely generic or formulaic entertainment. Now it appeared that these formulas were worth serious attention. John Cawelti suggested that at the root of such formulas as the adventure, mystery, and romance were powerful myths or moral fantasies. He argued that the romance formula expressed a moral fantasy in which love is all-sufficient and triumphant. Understanding the formulas gave access both to their aesthetic satisfactions and to the masked cultural myths behind a TV show, film, or novel.

Mythographers like Campbell and Eliade think of myths as cultural possessions that become part of a shared world of meaning. Thus producers of media can draw on or express myths from their culture without being aware of that process. They may be bemused by the suggestion that their work is more than entertainment. As we see in Frye's discussion in *Fables of Identity* of writers ranging from Milton (1963, 119 ff) and Blake (1963, 138 ff) to Dickenson (1963, 193ff) and Joyce (1963, 256 ff), many writers are quite conscious of their borrowing. Filmmaker George Lucas has discussed his awareness of writers like Campbell and Jung and the way their influence shaped the *Star Wars* films.

Some argue that while the creations of popular media may be "like" myths, they are not really myths. We do not, after all, "believe" that popular culture is true in the way that ancient Greeks apparently believed the accounts of Zeus, Hera, and Hermes. They suggest that the stories of popular media are more like folktales, moral lessons in the midst of fanciful tales that no one takes seriously. This argument helps us to see that it is more accurate to say that the myth lies behind these particular media expressions. The modern tale is like a mask that both hides and reveals the myth.

As one example, consider the way science fiction provides an explanation of our place in the universe in stories suitable for a modern culture. The *Star Trek* series was popular on television in the late 1960s and gave birth to subsequent movies, follow-up TV series,

The Creation Myth of the Tukano People

An indigenous people in Brazil and Columbia, the Tukano Indians have a creation story that revolves around a battle between the sun and moon.

In the beginning there were the Sun and the Moon. They were twin brothers. At first they lived alone, but then the Sun had a daughter, and he lived with her as if she were his wife. The Moon brother did not have a wife and became jealous. He tried to make love to the wife of the Sun, but the Sun heard about it. There was a dance up in the sky, in the house of the Sun, and when the Moon brother came to dance, the Sun took from him, as a punishment, the large feather crown he wore that was like the crown of the Sun. He left the Moon brother with a small feather crown and with a pair of copper earrings. From that time on the Sun and the Moon have been separate, and they are always far apart in the sky as a result of the punishment that the Moon brother received for his wrong-doing.

The Sun created the Universe and for this reason he is called Sun Father (pagë abé). He is the father of all the Desana. The Sun created the Universe with the power of his yellow light and gave it life and stability. From his dwelling place, bathed in yellow reflections, the Sun made the earth, with its forests and rivers, with its animals and plants. The Sun planned his creation very well, and it was perfect.

Source: Reichel-Dolmatoff, G. (1971). *Amazonian cosmos: The sexual and religious symbolism of the Tukano Indians* (p. 24). Chicago: University of Chicago Press.

and a fan culture supported by clubs and conventions that continues up to the writing of this encyclopedia. Like Genesis, *Star Trek* puts humans at the center of a vast and interesting universe. While no God or gods are explicit, *Star Trek* expresses a powerful myth of progress, a belief that things will evolve for good in the future. At the same time *Star Trek* confirms a largely paternal and military social order with its ranks and obligations. When Michael Jindra quotes *Star Trek* fans as saying, "It's about faith in the future," it sounds very much like *Star Trek* serves the same function as ancient myths or religion.

A Myth of Origin

Another example of how contemporary media function as myth can be found in the Western. From dime novels written at the closing of the frontier such as Edward Wheeler's *Calamity Jane the Heroine of Whoop-up* (1878) through television series of the 1950s like *Roy Rogers* to 2004's HBO series *Deadwood*, the Western has been an enduring tale about the origins of America. The Western justifies violence and suggests that the nation was forged in the clash between wilderness and civilization. Western heroes embody individualism and yet sacrifice their lives for an emerging civilization.

If there is an active myth behind these tales, it ought to inform Americans' understanding of their place in the world and meet Campbell's four human needs. The Western does provide a sense of awe about the universe, expressing how small the human being is in the vastness of the frontier while simultaneously expressing the importance of bringing eastern civilization to the West. The stories fit with the scientific understandings of its day, replacing magic or gods as shapers of the world with heroes of strength and character. The stories provide ritual support for the social order by defining gender roles and suggesting that the western expansion and the extermination of native peoples is an inevitable expression of fate or divine will. Finally, the Western provides direction for the individual in facing the psychological traumas of life, by valorizing individualism and suffering on behalf of the community. That these stories continue to find an audience suggests that a powerful myth of origin lies behind the Western through which some Americans continue to interpret their place in the world.

Implications

Myth is a narrative process through which people explain the origin of things, align themselves with deity or the fates, give meaning to cultural structures and attitudes, and interpret their place in the world. Evident in ancient cultures, we find it at work in modern media as well. Understanding the myths that lie behind popular tales helps us to understand the power of modern media to shape and interpret the world.

JEFFREY H. MAHAN

Further Reading

Campbell, J. (1959). *The masks of God: Vol. 4. Creative mythology*. New York: Viking.

Campbell, J. (1972). *Hero with a thousand faces*. Princeton, NJ: Princeton University Press.

Cawelti, J. G. (1976). *Adventure, mystery, and romance*. Chicago: University of Chicago Press.

Eliade, M. (1959). *The sacred and the profane: The nature of religion*. New York: Harcourt Brace Jovanovich.

Freud, S. (1966). *The complete lectures on psychoanalysis*. New York: W. W. Norton. (Original work published 1920)

Frye, N. (1963). *Fables of identity: Studies in poetic mythology*. New York: Harcourt Brace Jovanovich.

Head, J. G., & MacLea, L. (1976). *Myth and meaning*. Evanston, IL: McDougal, Littell.

Jewett, R., & Lawrence, J. S. (1977). *The American monomyth*. Garden City, NY: Anchor/Doubleday.

Jindra, M. (2000). It's about faith in our future: *Star Trek* fandom as cultural religion. In B. D. Forbes & J. H. Mahan (Eds.), *Religion and Popular Culture in America*. Berkeley: University of California Press.

Jung, C. (1964). *Man and his symbols*. Garden City, NY: Doubleday.

Turner, V. (1982). *From ritual to theatre: The human seriousness of play*. New York: PAJ Publications.

Native American Religion

If eyes are mirrors into the soul, then religion reflects a culture. Native American cultures and their religions inform the lives and identities of their peoples. When viewed over the changing currents of history, the religions of Native Americans reflect deep spiritual sensibilities, political change, and cultural adaptations.

Identity

Native Americans, also known as First American peoples, probably inhabited parts of the Americas as early as 9,000 BCE. Scientific and anthropological evidence suggests that these early humans crossed from Asia to the far northern tip of the Americas via an Ice Age land bridge. This area, today known as the Bering Strait, provided a portal for these migrating peoples to settle eventually along the coasts and the interior, moving both south and east. Following nomadic patterns, these first Americans traveled in order to follow the fish and game they hunted for survival.

By around 5,000 BCE, however, some of these peoples learned how to cultivate their lands and grow life-sustaining crops in one area. This, coupled with their ability to domesticate some of the animals around them, meant that Native Americans were able to create alternatives to nomadic life. For those able to settle in one place, their ensuing societies grew more complicated, and communities more structured. Some groups, like the Incas, Mayans, and Aztecs, developed powerful empires. Regardless of how elaborate or straightforward their societies, Native Americans followed the rhythm of habit, custom, and ritual. These factors help define commonalities among Native American religions.

In 1492, Christopher Columbus landed his ships in the Americas, mistaking them for India. Thereafter, he dubbed the indigenous people he met "Indians," and the designation unwittingly gave rise to the practice of early European explorers to group all the peoples they encountered as monolithic Indians. Subsequently, the religious practices of Native Americans—when recognized at all—were viewed as barbaric, crude, or nonexistent.

The Americas once hosted as many as five hundred tribes, or nations, at the time of first contact between Europeans and Native Americans. Indigenous religious expression was as diverse as their languages. One approach to classifying Native American religions is by type of ritual. These could include such practices as the Corn Dance, the Sun Dance, and the Blessingway. Another way to examine, collectively, the religions of Native American nations is to look at their religious narratives and their common themes, such as accounts of creation and the afterlife. These, in turn, can be contrasted with Christianity, reflecting a major dichotomy between the two worldviews. Finally, a more recent construct offered by Vine Deloria Jr. (2003) argues that American Indian religions can best be understood in terms of their linkages to space and place.

Rituals

Examining Native American religions through key rituals can give partial insight into their seminal beliefs. In the Corn Dance of the Zuni people, for instance, corn (or maize) is personified as Corn Maidens. These deities influence patterns of plenty or famine, depending upon their presence among the people. The Corn Dance is a ritual that honors and respects their importance, so that they will always remain close to the Zuni.

The Sun Dance is traditionally celebrated by the Plains Indian nations, such as the Arapaho, and is a sacred ceremony of renewal. Taking place in late spring or early summer, the Sun Dance involves four intense days of ritual sweats and retelling of narratives detailing the formation of some stars, land formations, and the sun.

Such ceremonies emphasize beneficial outcomes for the whole nation or tribe. For example, the Lakota Sun Dance is performed so that "the people might live." And for the Navajo the Blessingway refers to an assortment of myths and rituals that chart the cycles of the Creation and the emergence of First Peoples to Earth. These rituals, intended to ensure a good life, mark such key ceremonies as birth, marriage, and house blessings.

Narratives

Storytelling and oral tradition are bedrocks of Native American religions. Despite the specific variances, these sacred stories and histories reflect two basic sensibilities about time. One is a chronological sense of time, marking periods in segmented order. Another is a transcendental view of time, where past, present, and future can merge and interact with each other. This mythic view of time recognizes, for instance, the presence of spirit beings alongside humans and interactions where humans, animals, and plants can communicate with each other.

Invariably, Native American religions are recognized for their abilities to see a "oneness" in everything, expressing connections between a Creator, humans, animals, plants, and inanimate objects. This emanates from mutually shared beliefs that the Creator made everything, whether animate or not, with a similar spirit. Thus, Native American religious rituals tend to reinforce mutual respect and unity among all things, seen and unseen.

Christianity

Christian missionaries arrived in the Americas virtually with the early explorers. Conceived as an important adjunct of colonization, missionary workers accompanied explorers and adventurers with the expressed goal of evangelizing "heathens" to the Christian faith. In fact, the activities of the church—first represented by Roman Catholics and then later, Protestants—formed a key aspect of political and military strategy known as pacification.

For example, the priest Bartolome de Las Casas (1484–1566) earned a reputation of being sympathetic to Indians because he openly criticized atrocities against them by his Spanish countrymen in the Caribbean, Mexico, and Latin America. However, his solution proved to be, in the long term, extremely destructive to native cultures. Emulated by subsequent missionary efforts in the Americas and Africa, La Casas's "reduction strategy" evangelized indigenous peoples by relocating them in tightly controlled "missions," where they would be stripped of their native customs and enjoined to adopt European language, values, and customs.

Later, beginning in 1828, Congregationalist missionaries, along with others from Methodist, Moravian, and Baptist faiths, protested government plans to relocate Cherokees from Georgia. Arguing in favor of Cherokee sovereignty, some missionaries like Samuel Worcester and Elizus Butler received jail sentences for their support. Still, even this rally behind Cherokee interests fed into missionary notions of how much "progress" Cherokees had made as members of the so-called "Five Civilized Tribes."

As missionaries settled around Indian settlements, they approached their goals of religious conversion with dogged zeal. Missions, "praying towns," and similar communities separate from mainstream Indian life became the focal points for conversion activities. Contrasted against native beliefs, Christianity presented some challenges. First, the Christian message, and its messengers, accompanied soldiers and military dominance. Therefore, when Christian beliefs were presented as an antidote to suffering, such a premise seemed incompatible with actual experience. Philosophically, the Christian God and the Great Spirit were compatible beliefs. Yet, the tenets of Christian faith, rested upon a messiah figure from another culture and locale foreign to native eschatology. The Christian sacred stories were codified in a book and written in a foreign language. Native faiths relied upon oral traditions. Finally, Christian conversion required that Indians reject, wholesale, centuries of their own tribal histories, customs, and ritual in order to be accepted into an uncertain and unseen faith.

Over time, Christian conversions, representing various sects, have made significant inroads into native cultures. As a result, traditional Indian beliefs and Christianity have accommodated each other in various ways. The erosion of Indian cultural beliefs and customs in the face of Christian conversions has inspired a modern-day revival of traditional rituals, languages, and ceremonies. In other instances, Native Americans

A Native American totem pole found at Tillicum Village on Blake Island in the Pacific Northwest.
Courtesy of Jeffrey Logan/ istockphoto.com

have learned to incorporate both belief systems into their lives. For example, in some Pueblo cultures, Catholicism and traditional ceremonies coexist. Finally, many Native Americans have become Christians and have developed leadership in various Christian faith expressions. Today, Christianity represents a vibrant and significant aspect of Native American religious expression.

Native American Church

A more contemporary adaptation of native traditions to Christianity blossomed with the formation of the Native American church or Peyote Church. Scientists have documented the use of the peyote cactus as a sacrament to a pre-Columbian era. When peyote is used in religious rituals, believers are said to experience a mystical revelation from the Creator. The peyote rituals, when acknowledged as honoring a Christian God as the Creator, blend traditional beliefs with Christianity.

Peyote rituals had been practiced for centuries among many tribal nations; however, opposition to these practices and to Indian traditions in general, motivated proponents to formally organize their church. On 10 October 1918, the Native American

Church incorporated in Oklahoma, with the stated intent of promoting Christian beliefs and morality using the peyote sacrament. The rituals of the Native American Church usually fall into one of two practices: the Half Moon Way or the Cross Fire Way. Although the design of the altar and the pattern of the rituals practiced differ between the two, Native American Church adherents share some essential commonalities. Church doctrine promotes the avoidance of alcohol and advocates strong adherence to hard work and monogamy. Church services include prayer meetings, as well as those services that accompany weddings, funerals, healing rituals, and thanksgiving ceremonies. Officiants from Native American church services include roadmen, or ministers, who are accompanied by firemen, drummers, and other participants.

Religious Freedom

Even after the legal establishment of the Native American Church, the struggle for religious tolerance of Indian beliefs and rituals continued. In 1921, the Office of Indian Affairs banned native ceremonies and traditional rites. The 1934 Indian Reorganization Act ended restrictions against the practice of native religions. However, resistance and public disapproval reenergized after World War II, when the U.S. government adopted termination and relocation policies against Native Americans. These practices, which removed some sacred lands from Indian control, were aimed at integrating Native Americans into American society by removing them from reservations and placing them in urban areas.

After arrests of Native Americans in the early 1970s, Congress held hearings in 1978 on American Indian religious freedom. That same year, the American Indian Religious Freedom Act (AIRFA) passed, promising the protection and preservation of American Indian religious freedoms. However, since its passage, AIRFA has been criticized for being vague and for lack of enforcement.

Later, in 1993, Congress passed the Religious Freedom Restoration Act (RFRA), which was supported by a wide-ranging alliance of religious groups. Included within this act were provisions to protect native religious practices in prisons. This worked for only a short time. In June 1977, the U.S. Supreme Court struck down RFRA as unconstitutional, and native religious practices—such as participation in sweat lodges; possession of sage, cedar, and tobacco herbs; and wearing long hair—were quickly banned.

Lasting Impact

Native American religious beliefs are not monolithic, so they cannot be understood simplistically. Perhaps the best framework for knowing the essence of these beliefs, however, is to recall Vine Deloria Jr.'s (2003) framework of the importance of space and place. All of the concepts associated with Native American religions, such as a reverence for nature and the multiplicity of rituals tied to seasonal changes, find their anchoring in specific spaces and meaningful places. Likewise, it is easier to comprehend how severely the forced migration and family dislocations have affected traditional native beliefs in their reliance upon kinship ties, sacred landmarks, and dance rituals.

Today, Native American religious practices thrive in their unique expressions. They have also influenced Christian faith expressions, as seen in the Native American Church. In the Americas, Native American religions offer philosophical ideals that have influenced societal beliefs in natural healing, ecology and preservation, and religious freedom.

META G. CARSTARPHEN

Further Reading

Deloria, V. Jr. (2003). *God is red: A native view of religion.* Golden, CO: Fulcrum Publishers.

Hampton, C. (2004). Missions and missionaries. *Encyclopedia of North American Indians, 1–2.* Retrieved December 21, 2004, from http://college.hmco.com/history/readerscomp/naind/html/na_022700_missionsandm.htm.

Hirschfelder, A. B. (2000). *Encyclopedia of Native American religions: An introduction.* New York: Facts on File.

Kidwell, C. S., Noley, H., & Tinker, G. E. (2001). *A Native American theology.* Maryknoll, NY: Orbis Books.

Martin, J. W. (1999). *Native American religion.* New York: Oxford University Press.

Native american spirituality. (n.d.). Retrieved December 14, 2004, from http://religiousmovements.lib.virginia.edu/nrms/naspirit.html, 1-10.

Tinker, G. E. (2004). Native American Church. *Encyclopedia of North American Indians, 1–4.* Retrieved December 21, 2004, from http://college.hmco.com/history/readerscomp/naind/html/na_025000_natamch.htm

Tinker, G. E. (2004). Religion. *Encyclopedia of North American Indians, 1–3.* Retrieved December 21, 2004, from http://college.hmco.com/history/readerscomp/naind/html/na_032600_religion.htm

Vernon, I. S. (2004). Religious rights. *Encyclopedia of North American Indians, 1–3.* Retrieved December 21, 2004, from http://college.hmco.com/history/readerscomp/naind/html/na_032700_religiousrig.htm

Newspapers

Diversity in faith and practice has characterized religion in the United States since the nation's colonial period when dissenters of all stripes left their European homelands seeking freedom of worship. That same multitude of voices echoes well into the twenty-first century—especially in the pages of the nation's daily newspapers.

Early Years

The cacophony is in keeping with the country's religious history. Even before it became a nation, America featured divergent religious voices, ranging from the Puritans who established the Massachusetts Bay Colony to the Anglicans who dominated in some Southern colonies. Most Americans who were religious were Christians and the vast majority of those were Protestant, a reality that shaped both the nation's politics and its newspapers.

The Puritans viewed America as a place set apart, destined by God to be a "city on the hill." Early on, they focused on education and literacy, setting up Harvard University, newspapers and printing presses. Through their publications, they tried to spread their ideas. So did other Christian groups, using the religious literature of sermons and tracts, and books and newspapers to spread their messages. For many years, newspapers were expected to represent the viewpoint of their founders. In the press's early years in the United States, rare was the publication that tried to present all sides of an issue. As Buddenbaum and Mason note in their foundational book on religion news, "From the establishment of the first newspaper in 1690 through the era of the Party Press, the prevailing view was that people should have the courage of their own convictions" (Buddenbaum and Mason 2000, 2).

Nineteenth Century

Historians continue to argue over the intent of the religious language used in America's founding documents such as the Declaration of Independence. But the prevalent mind-set early in the republic's history was grounded in Evangelical Protestantism. Because mainstream America possessed a certain religious character, the press covered religion as a matter of course in the nineteenth century, often as it covered other events of the day. Newspapers of the era did not require a religion writer or a religion section or page, something that became commonplace a century later.

Back then, however, the nation's business, politics, and public life in general were dominated by a white male mainstream that usually belonged to established, socially-acceptable Christian groups including the Congregationalist, Presbyterian, and Episcopal churches. Indeed, writes church historian Martin E. Marty, "Many newspapers covered Sunday sermons of the prominent. What the Episcopal bishop did, or the Presbyterian Stated Clerk said, or the Congregationalist theologian thought, had cultural import" (Hubbard 1990, ix).

Certainly other Protestant Christian groups were at work in the nineteenth century society, particularly among African-Americans and poorer whites. In addition, there were growing numbers of Jewish and Catholic Americans. But those populations—and usually their activities—rarely made headlines. If they were covered at all, such groups usually were covered by their own publications. Some of those were religious in character while others were of a more ethnic or political nature. Often they played a central role in the lives of new immigrants. For example, the Yiddish press performed a major educational function among an estimated 3 million Jewish immigrants to the United States at the beginning of the twentieth century.

Twentieth Century

In the secular press, a growing clash between biblically based worldviews and modern secularized ideas combined with the exploits of a few colorful religious figures moved religion onto the front pages of the nation's dailies early in the twentieth century. Among the most famous of those stories was the Scopes Trial pitting William Jennings Bryan against Clarence Darrow, and the biblical book of Genesis against Darwinism. After World War II, religion again began to attract coverage as the ranks of the nation's synagogues and churches swelled. For a while, it seemed that most firmly established American religious groups—Protestant denominations and the largest Catholic dioceses—enjoyed frequent press coverage. But over time, serious distrust was manifest as outright hostility wedged itself between the press and the religious community. Even though the First Amendment protects the freedom of expression of both, believers and reporters seemed increasingly uncomfortable with each other. Though studies indicate there is more discomfort with and ignorance about religion than bias in the nation's newsrooms, more citizens began to see the press as challenging rather than supporting religious institutions.

The religion "beat" as it is known today at secular newspapers slowly evolved as a reporting specialty in the aftermath of a series of events. Those events shaped both American and international religious life and influenced how the press covered religious events. Among the catalysts in the beat's development in the second half of the twentieth century were the ecumenical movement, the civil rights movement, Roman Catholic reforms of the early 1960s, global religious strife and the advent of an educated, vocal, and highly conservative religious wing in American politics.

One can trace the roots of heightened modern newspaper coverage of religion to several points in American cultural history including the 1976 election of a Georgia peanut farmer, Jimmy Carter, as the country's president. Carter declared himself a "born-again" Christian, using terminology familiar to many in the South but largely unknown among the Washington press corps. In politics and specific religious beliefs, Carter parted company with many of his fellow Southern Baptists. But he shared a cultural history with them, a history in which a heretofore uneducated and largely poor slice of the American electorate rose to greater economic and cultural dominance.

Just as the printing press drove the spread of new ideas across Europe during the Enlightenment, technology helped drive the spread of newspaper coverage of religion almost two centuries later. Carter's elevation to the White House took place at about the same time as a cross section of conservative voices began to make themselves heard on the airwaves with the growing prominence of television ministries such as those of Jerry Falwell in Lynchburg, Virginia, and Pat Robertson in Virginia Beach, Virginia.

With the election of conservative Republican Ronald Reagan as president in 1980, clergy such as Falwell and his "moral majority" became a force with which to reckon. Their names and their ministries made headlines in newspapers small and large. The televangelism scandals of the 1980s seemed to attract more, rather than less press attention to those ministries. Over the next two decades, Fundamentalists' and Evangelicals' social and moral agenda—including opposition to abortion and gay marriage and support for homeschooling and heterosexual marriage—largely paralleled that of the GOP. When George W. Bush won reelection in 2004, Evangelical voters embraced the president as one of their own.

Political times had changed, and newspaper coverage changed with it. Though the stories were written as often by political reporters as by religion writers, newspapers struggled once again to understand and report on the deep religious sensibility in American life. In the wake of Bush's reelection, newspapers explored how the Democratic Party seemingly had failed to articulate voters' moral concerns, and they examined whether voters elected Bush because of his strong moral positions or because of national security concerns.

Long before Bush's election, in the 1990s, the perceived great divide between the average American's values and the values promoted in media appeared to widen, becoming known as the "culture wars." In a memorable speech, Vice President Dan Quayle in 1992 told a convention of Southern Baptists that he wore the media's scorn as "a badge of honor."

Cost concerns and competition with broadcast and online media pressed newspapers to reconfigure their coverage in the final years of the twentieth century. Some added more religion coverage, beginning special weekend day sections devoted to religion and called by such titles as Religion & Ethics and Faith & Values. Other media continued to "mainstream" religion stories with articles on the nation's faith groups and ethical issues vying for front-page coverage along with stories on domestic politics and international affairs.

As fairness and objectivity had developed into central standards for American journalists, religion coverage in newspapers had broadened and deepened. However, too often when budgets got tight, religion writers were cut or veteran writers were replaced with less expensive and younger reporters. A quick examination of U.S. newspaper coverage from the 1990s forward suggests it might be divided into five broad categories: sectarian, biblical, faith in public life, privatized faith, and new religious groups. The stories carried by larger papers include denominational coverage of annual meetings, judicatory legislative sessions and the ruminations of large religious boards and agencies; stories about the Bible ranging from detailed analysis of the newest biblical criticism to the Scripture-reading habits of the average American; faith and public life stories exploring how faith shapes voting patterns, political alliances, business practices and personal behavior; personal belief and practice articles uncovering everything from home altars to patterns of prayer and meditation; and stories about alternative spiritual beliefs and new religions.

Into the Twenty-First Century

Surveys continue to show that the United States is probably the most religious of the world's developed nations. Nine out of ten Americans profess belief in God and as many as half are estimated to be affiliated with a religious group. But this high level of religiosity is taking place in a nation facing great challenges at home and abroad.

In response, religion writers themselves have worked to increase the knowledge and professionalism of reporters working the beat.

Knowing that good reporting on religion is a key component of a responsible press in a free society, the Religion Newswriters Association (founded in 1949) has expanded and retooled its outreach. Made up of 260 journalists covering religion in the secular news media, the organization provides education and resources for religion writers, including newcomers and longtime reporters. In addition, it works to raise awareness of the importance of religion coverage in the secular media.

Even into the twenty-first century, religion reporters, newspaper editors, and religion scholars were debating the best sort of reporter to cover religion. Central questions in that ongoing discussion included: Is a religion specialist the best person, perhaps, the only truly fit reporter, to cover all stories with a significant religion angle? That would mean exporting a religion writer from the local newsroom to the frontlines of the world's religious battles: from the discord in the Middle East to the misery of ethnic infighting with religious roots in Russia. Or, the discussion goes, is it better that a journalistic generalist cover stories with a religion angle, leaving more traditional stories such as denominational meetings, papal trips, and the opening of new houses of worship to a religion specialist?

The long-standing relationship between media and religion in the United States long has been an adversarial pairing. The press is often skeptical of religious people and communities. The religious community and its leaders, in turn, usually mistrust the press. But in an increasingly global world, an understanding of religion's role in public and private matters is essential to informed news coverage. Moreover, despite declining readership, newspapers continue to offer the most indepth daily coverage of overseas and domestic matters, suggesting good reporting will continue to require a strong grasp of religion's role in public and private life.

CECILE S. HOLMES

See also Journalism; Media

Further Reading

Buddenbaum, J., & Mason, D. (2000). *Readings on religion as news*. Ames: Iowa State University Press.
Hubbard, B. J. (1990). *Reporting religion, facts & faith*. Santa Rosa, CA: Polebridge Press.

Novels

The novel's status as a form of religious communication depends heavily on the way in which religion is defined. The novel has not historically served the needs of orthodoxy, theology, doctrine, dogma, or other official types of religious discourse. In fact, novels and their various antecedent forms in the romance, satire, and novella, for example, are not only distinct from orthodox forms of religious discourse, but often stand against them. Over the course of the novel's development since the mid-1700s, the bulk of published works in this genre have been escapist forms of entertainment. As such, they were often considered to be frivolous at best and depraved at worst. Clearly, novels have accomplished more artistically and socially than entertaining and satisfying the prurient interest of their readers. Many of the earliest novels had their foundation in the moral instruction of youth, primarily that of young women. Samuel Richardson's novels *Pamela* and *Clarissa* grew out of this tradition, laying a foundation for the didacticism of some novels; however, almost immediately, the novel opened itself up to themes beyond maintaining one's virtue and sexual purity, notably with Henry Fielding's *Tom Jones*, the story of a young man's sexual exploits and adventures.

Rise of the Novel

Women were the primary readers of novels during the first hundred and fifty years of the genre's development. The overt sexism of the eighteenth and nineteenth centuries helped foster a climate in which the novel was thus seen as a lesser literary form, ancillary to the epic poem, philosophy, and scientific writing. Despite the existence of masterpieces from the early development of the novel (works written by both men and women alike), the bulk of published novels could be categorized, then as now, as mass-market works directed toward an audience looking not so much for art as for entertainment. Nevertheless, many of the foundational works enjoyed great market success in addition to laudatory critical reception.

It is generally agreed that the first novel in any language is Lady Murasaki Shikibu's eleventh-century Japanese court romance, *The Tale of Genji*. Miguel de Cervantes's Spanish masterpiece, *Don Quixote*, with its publication in 1605, marks an important evolutionary step from the epic tradition toward the novel proper. From the time of *Don Quixote*'s publication, many long prose works in English were published: Aphra Behn's *Oroonoko* (1688), Daniel Defoe's *Robinson Crusoe* (1722),

Defoe's *Moll Flanders* (1722), and Jonathan's Swift's *Gulliver's Travels* (1726). While part of the development of a prose fiction form that would ultimately become the novel, these works, particularly *Robinson Crusoe*, are generally not considered to be properly novels because they were constructed as fictionalized autobiographies with elaborate narratorial constructions fabricated to create distinctions between the authors and the narrators of the works. An illusion of truth was maintained by author and publisher alike, which helped ease these works into the marketplace. The above works dealt with moral and ethical issues, but they were not religious as such, which is to say, they were not the product of any particular doctrine, dogma, or denomination. In fact, novels and romances were, and to some extent still are, rejected by orthodoxies.

Samuel Richardson's epistolary novel, *Pamela* (1740) is perhaps most widely considered to be the first novel in English, followed by *Clarissa* (1747–1748) and then by Henry Fielding's *Tom Jones* (1749). These works mark a structural break from the fictionalized autobiographies of the works mentioned above and begin to assert the presence of a new, protean form: the novel. In fact, contemporary critics cite the novel's lack of clearly defined characteristics as its primary defining feature. There are, of course, numerous long standing battles over the inception of the novel in English, and the criteria for a given work either being or not being a novel is often contradictory.

Definition of the Novel

Quite simply, a novel is a work of prose fiction, distinguished from the tale, short story, and novella by its length. Any definition beyond that is difficult to sustain. For many, any definition beyond that is useless. Almost as soon as the rise of the novel in English began, the form began to feed off itself. Fielding's *Joseph Andrews* (1742), for example, reengages Richardson's *Pamela*, parodying its themes and borrowing its characters (Joseph Andrews is Pamela's brother). The "proto-novels" of Swift and Defoe are certainly long works of prose fiction, yet are often not considered to be "proper" novels because of their lack of a coherent unity of the plot; they are episodic and picaresque like *Don Quixote*. A quick look at many novels shows that for almost any proscriptive feature ascribed to the novel, there is a violation or subversion of the rule. This subversion of form is matched by a subversion of anything resembling "official content." The novel is rarely a good vehicle for propaganda, religious or otherwise. Nevertheless, the invented or imagined nature of the novel's content is challenged, for example, by the roman à clef, which takes real events and characters and presents them in a thinly-veiled fiction that is only nominally "imagined." A contemporary example of this is the novel *Primary Colors* (1996), which portrays the pursuit of the American presidency by a couple very much like America's forty-second president and his wife, Bill and Hillary Clinton. The roman à clef, then, challenges the novel's fictionality. Length is another variable feature. The works of Samuel Richardson, George Eliot, and Charles Dickens were often quite long, presented in multiple volumes or serialized in newspapers of the day. Current novels might be two to two hundred and fifty pages. Add to this the complication of the "short novel" and the indeterminacy of definitions of the novella, and length becomes a complicating feature rather than a defining point.

The Novel and Social Realism

While the novel is a literary form so varied that any defining feature is faced with instant exceptions, scholars have attempted to assert that any of a number of features (length, structural unity, focus on character) are what distinguish it from other analogous forms. Perhaps the most profound and problematic of these asserted features is made by Ian Watt in his seminal study of the development of the novel in English, *The Rise of the Novel*. Watt argues that the primary difference between the novel (as it developed in eighteenth-century England) and fictional prose from earlier periods such as the classical era and Renaissance is the novel's reliance upon what is commonly known as realism. Watt defines *realism* as a quality in art that stands in opposition to idealism; he also argues that realistic fiction is distinct from the romances (*romans*) published on the European continent during the eighteenth century and earlier. Romances often dealt with the elite, while the first novels dealt with "all the varieties of human experience." More important, however, Watt argues that the novel's realism is not the result of its subject matter, but is the result of how that subject matter is presented. Religious fiction, on the other hand, tends to depict the world in idealistic terms, showing how things ought to be rather than how they are.

This kind of realism was clearly part of the novel's foundation and is a feature found in a high percentage of novels published during the last three centuries; however, during the course of the twentieth in particular, realism has been less and less of a concern of writers, particularly with the introduction and

Selection from Sinclair Lewis' *Elmer Gantry*

Sharon was one of the first evangelists to depend for all her profit not on a share of the contributions nor on a weekly offering but on one night devoted entirely to a voluntary "thank offering" for her and her crew alone. It sounded unselfish and it brought in more; every devotee saved up for the occasion; and it proved easier to get one fifty dollar donation than a dozen of a dollar each. But to work up this lone offering to suitably thankful proportions, a great deal of loving and efficient preparation was needed—reminders given by the chief pastors, bankers, and other holy persons of the town, the distribution of envelopes over which devotees were supposed to brood for the whole six weeks of the meetings, and innumerable newspaper paragraphs about the self-sacrifice and heavy expenses of the evangelists.

Source: Lewis, S. (1927). *Elmer Gantry*. New York: Harcourt, Brace and Company, Inc.

development of the stream-of-consciousness and surreal novel, mastered by Virginia Woolf and William S. Burroughs, respectively. In any case, both the development of a realistic aesthetic and the movement away from it over the last hundred years show in aesthetic terms how the novel has tried to be distinct from devotional or religious writing while still maintaining a social function. As mentioned, most devotional writing treats subjects as the given religious system believes they ought to be. The realistic novel, on the other hand, deals with things as they occur in the world. So, by the time Austen and Dickens began publishing, the novel's main function was as a tool for social critique. Perhaps the most profound social change engendered by a recent novel came from Upton Sinclair's *The Jungle* (1906). Its portrayal of the Chicago meatpacking industry in the late 1800s/early twentieth century caused a public outrage and prompted President Theodore Roosevelt to initiate legislation that would constitute the first pure food and drug laws in the United States. The work of socially conscious novelists such as John Steinbeck, Arundhati Roy, and others has continued in this vein.

The departure of novels from strict social realism also distinguishes them from devotional writing and other forms of orthodox religious communication. As novels moved away from realism, they headed into the human psyche and into language itself. Like the work of abstract expressionist painters, the nonrepresentational novels of writers such as James Joyce, Gertrude Stein, Joseph Heller, and Jean Cocteau were more about the surfaces of language than its interpretability. Such works were not interested in uncovering the truth. In fact, such works arose at the time that truth—religious, philosophical, or otherwise—was being called seriously into question.

Rise of Secularism

Long before the development of the novel, Western culture had been turned from its religious foundations. The development of science, empirical philosophy, and political theory through the work of Francis Bacon (1561–1626), René Descartes (1596–1650), John Locke (1632–1704), David Hume (1711–1776), and others marks a clear path toward secularism that blends into the rise of the novel as well as the development of the middle class in England. This secularizing process was not an event but a gradual exchange of one value system for another. The novel began to occupy a space in both the cultural and literal marketplaces in major cities such as London. In addition to poetry and philosophy, devotional reading such as spiritual autobiography, theology, sermons, moral instruction manuals, and the like formed the central core of libraries, curricula, and private reading practices. The reading of romances and other fantastic works was considered anathema to intellectual growth. Novels were initially denounced but quickly rose to prominence in the marketplace, creating an immediate sensation and forming, within a span of twenty to thirty years, a powerful new arm of the English economy. Writers and booksellers formed a new elite class within the burgeoning middle class, which brought along an upward mobility past eras did not enjoy. Again, this was not an overnight change for the establishment of a middle class or the diminishment of religious discourse. Clive T. Probyn points out that it took more than a hundred years for the publication of novels to "outstrip the publication of religious books" (1987, 5).

Novels Featuring Religion

Though novels have rarely functioned as forms of religious communication, they have often had religion as their theme or subject; however, unlike proto-novels such as John Bunyan's religious allegory, *Pilgrim's Progress* (1678), novels have taken a critical view of religion, often satirizing religion, exploring hypocrisies, and addressing personal struggles of faith. Because fiction is rooted in the exploration of conflict and tension, novels taking religion as their theme most often address religion, theology, or belief in conflict. Voltaire's *Candide* (1759) is a prime example of a novel that satirizes religion, more particularly piousness. The central character, Candide, having fallen on hard times, is denied food by a preacher who had just finished a sermon on the blessings of charity. James Joyce's *The Portrait of the Artist as a Young Man* (1915), is a bildungsroman about a Stephen Dedalus, whose struggle with Catholicism is represented by wild swings between holiness and hedonism. Chaim Potok's *My Name Is Asher Lev* (1972) presents Asher Lev, a Hasidic Jew struggling between the traditional world of his faith and his life as a world-renowned painter.

Struggles and crises of faith constitute the lion's share of the novel's religious themes, with perhaps one great exception. The eschatological *Left Behind* novels (1996–2004) of Tim LaHaye and Jerry B. Jenkins are a publishing anomaly. There are twelve novels in this series, with sales figures outstripping the best of best-selling novelists. Even though these novels are overtly religious, they are not based on orthodox Christian theology, but instead feature a hybridization of biblical principles and the rapture theology of John Nelson Darby called *premillennial dispensationalism*. Despite their wide readership among devout Christian readers, the *Left Behind* novels are just as far from orthodox theology as any irreligious or unreligious novel written in the last three hundred years. The curious success of these books is surely the exception to the rule.

Salman Rushdie's *Satanic Verses* constitutes another interesting take on the religious novel, perhaps more apropos of the novel's struggles with faithfulness. Rushdie is not a practicing Muslim, though he was born one. His novel satirizes aspects of Islamic code, parodies the Ayatollah Khoemeni, Muhammad,

Muhammad's wives, and even the Qur'an itself. The now-infamous fatwa was issued against Rushdie in 1989, which called for his death along with the publishers of the book. After the fatwa was issued, Rushdie went into hiding, the Japanese translator of the book was killed, and the Italian translator was seriously wounded. The fatwa remained in effect (subsidized financially by the Iranian government) for nine years. While the case of Rushdie's *Satanic Verses* might appear extreme, it is more representative of the position most novels have with respect to religious systems.

TODD ROBERT PETERSEN

See also Bookstores; Literature, Religious; Literature, Secular

Further Reading

McKeon, M. (1987). *The origins of the English novel: 1600-1740*. Baltimore: Johns Hopkins University Press.
Probyn, C. T. (1987). *English fiction of the eighteenth century: 1700-1789*. London and New York: Longman.
Watt, I. (1957). *The rise of the novel*. Berkeley and Los Angeles: University of California Press.

Numinous

The "numinous" is a term used by Rudolf Otto to describe the holy. It is also used by Otto as a term that helps communicate religious experience cross-culturally. In addition, it is a term that describes the experience of a human encounter with the holy. The human experience of the numinous may thus be understood as an experience of nonrational communication between the holy and the human.

Examining Otto's Numinous

Though the term itself appeared prior to Otto, it is Otto who gives the numinous a precise and technical meaning for the study of religions. Otto's category of the numinous appears most notably in his book *Das Heilige* (1917), translated into English as *The Idea of the Holy* (1923). For Otto, the holy is marked by an "overplus of meaning" (Otto 1950, 5), meaning that the holy exceeds human comprehension. From this perspective, humans' ability to perceive the numinous comes not through analysis but through experience.

Otto distinguishes the term "numinous" from the term "holy" because he does not wish to simply equate the holy with goodness. The holy is something beyond our category of the good; the holy contains the good but is not exhausted by the good. The term "numinous" thus distinguishes Otto's understanding of the holy from more general uses of the term. The numinous is, in Otto's terms, "*mysterium tremendum et fascinans.*" The numinous is thus wholly other (*mysterium*), capable of evoking both awe and fear in human beings (*tremendum*). At the same time, however, the numinous attracts and fascinates us (*fascinans*). Though the numinous is wholly other and terrifying, it affects human experience because of human fascination, human desire. That is, humans are drawn toward the holy or the numinous even as it inspires fear and awe in them.

For Otto, human experience of the numinous is an *individual* experience that is beyond rational explanation and description. Yet this experience of the numinous is not purely subjective, in Otto's view. Rather, "The numinous is . . . felt as objective and outside the self" (Otto 1950, 11). Otto's primary concern here is to stress the presence of the holy as something really real. For Otto, the holy exists as something outside of human experience, though it can only be approached through human experience. Otto's ability to make such a claim stems from his unique reading of and elaboration on the work of Immanuel Kant, which is examined in more detail below.

Otto and Religious Experience

Otto's emphasis on the individual's religious experience leads him away from theories of religion that stress the textual and rational over the nonverbal and nonrational. By emphasizing an individual's experience of the divine, Otto attempts to break free from earlier understandings of religion that view religious texts and documented theological reflection as indicators of more sophisticated, or even more valid, religious experiences. Otto's desire to break free from purely "rational" understandings of religion is demonstrated in the very first chapter of *The Idea of the Holy*, entitled "The Rational and the Non-Rational." In this chapter, Otto notes that conceptions and descriptions of God always include analogy to what humans perceive as their best or most noble attributes. Yet, he argues that these analogies are limited. That is, God or the holy so greatly exceeds humans' ability to describe and characterize it within reason that they must admit that the holy is beyond our reason. Thus the holy is understood by Otto to be nonrational because he understands rationality as a human trait.

On this subject Otto writes that:

So far are these "rational" attributes from exhausting the idea of deity, that they in fact imply a non-rational or supra-rational Subject of which they are predicates. They are "essential" (and not merely "accidental") attributes of that subject, but they are also, it is important to notice, synthetic essential attributes. That is to say, we have to predicate them of a subject which they qualify, but which in its deeper essence is not, nor indeed can be, comprehended in them; which rather requires comprehension of quite a different kind. (Otto 1950, 2)

In plainer terms, Otto understands the holy as both rational and non- or suprarational. That is, rational attributes can be understood as coming from the holy, yet the holy cannot be contained by them. The holy therefore must be understood both through analysis and through direct nonrational experience, that "comprehension of a different kind." By stressing the importance of individual experience, Otto understands religious experience as being accessible to all who are drawn to the numinous.

Otto's understanding of the human experience of the numinous can be understood as a vital form of communication between the human and the divine. This communication between the human and the divine is, as noted above, marked by the nonrational. This type of communication is beyond language, beyond humans' rational comprehension. As it is experienced, it immediately evokes emotion and feeling, rather than thought and reflection (though thought and reflection may certainly arise later as a result of this experience). For example, Otto notes the prophet Ezekiel's religious experiences take the form of dreams and parables. These dreams and parables are not understood as wholly rational forms of communication. That is not to say that these communications are mistaken or flawed. Rather, Otto understands the divine as being capable of communicating differently than the human. These exchanges are more immediate and potentially more affective than rational, verbal communication.

Communication between the human individual and the divine is thus, for Otto, an experience in which "creature-feeling" plays a larger role than philosophical reflection. "Creature-feeling" is a term used by Otto to describe "the emotion of a creature, submerged and overwhelmed by its own nothingness in contrast to that which is supreme above all creatures" (Otto 1950, 10). Creature-feeling is thus a descriptor for Otto of the human encounter with the divine, an encounter that leaves the human being full of awe and without words capable of describing the experience.

Rudolf Otto in Context

Rudolf Otto's thinking was significantly influenced by the work of Immanuel Kant and Friedrich Schleiermacher. Though the influence of both of these thinkers appears throughout *The Idea of the Holy*, some specific examples of their influence will help the reader better understand the basic philosophical and theological context out of which Otto's thought arises. Examining these influences more closely will likewise demonstrate the uniqueness of Otto's theories of religion.

Otto explicitly gives credit to Schleiermacher for identifying the element in religious experience called the "feeling of dependence." Yet as important as this discovery is, Otto notes, Schleiermacher's term may lead to a misunderstanding of what religious experience really is. The feeling of dependence one feels during a religious experience, Otto argues, is both a feeling of dependence and something much greater than a feeling of simple dependence. It is for this reason that Otto coins the term "creature-consciousness" or "creature-feeling." As noted above, this creature-feeling is the emotion the creature has when faced with the numinous. This is a feeling not only of dependence and inferiority, but also of amazement and wonder at the utter superiority of the holy. Creature-feeling thus supplants Schleiermacher's "feeling of dependence" by stressing not only feelings of dependence, but also feelings of awe present in human encounters with the divine.

Kant's categories of the true, the good, and the beautiful, developed in his *Critiques*, are supplemented by Otto's "fourth category" of the holy. For Kant, the categories are understood explicitly as being a priori or necessary conditions for human knowledge. Otto, however, seems to find Kant's categories lacking, as they rely heavily on an understanding of the rational within consciousness. Otto therefore takes Kant's understanding of the categories as absolutely necessary and applies this idea to his nonrational or supra-rational category of the holy. Thus, as noted above, Otto understands the nonrational holy as being both objective and outside of human consciousness. This "fourth category" lies closest to Kant's category of the aesthetic, though Otto would argue that the holy is not fully contained within the aesthetic.

In addition to these major philosophical influences, Otto's work also seems to have been influenced by the early psychological theories of his day. In particular, William James's *Varieties of Religious Experience* is referenced several times in *The Idea of the Holy*. In these references, Otto presses James to take account of the nonrational consciousness at play in religious experience. Thus Otto's understanding of religious experience is marked by an emphasis on the nonrational element once more, perhaps pointing to the nonrational within human consciousness itself, but certainly pointing to the human ability to perceive the non-rational holy.

Critiques of Otto

Rudolf Otto's influence on the study of religions has been significant. Otto is a foundational figure for the comparative study of religion. Otto's *Das Heilige* influenced such thinkers as Martin Buber, Joachim Wach, and Mircea Eliade, among others. The works of these thinkers have, in turn, greatly influenced (and continue to influence) contemporary theories of religion.

Though foundational for the field of comparative religion, Otto's work has been the subject of numerous critiques. First, Otto's work is understood as not purely phenomenological or philosophical; it is instead theological. Otto seeks not only to describe religious experience, he seeks also to identify characteristics of the divine, a desire that his own work seems at times to contradict. In addition, Otto's tendency to *evaluate* religious experiences, rather than simply observe religious experiences, has similarly let to criticism. That is, scholars might wonder why Otto is qualified to evaluate what does or does not constitute a viable experience of the numinous.

Further, Otto's understanding of the divine as fascinating, as capable of evoking fear and awe, and as wholly other may well describe Otto's understanding of the Christian God, however, this may not adequately describe religious experiences across cultures. Though Otto's theories are written as though they are descriptive of all religious experience, they are decidedly Christian in tone. Thus these theories and formulations may not satisfactorily describe the varied religious phenomena encountered and religious experiences faced by all of the world's religious peoples.

Yet despite these criticisms, Otto was, for his time, relatively sensitive to the problems encountered when attempting to describe wide-ranging religious experiences. As a pioneer in the comparative study of religions, Otto strove to create categories that could be used to describe widely divergent religions by focusing on human experiences of encounters with the divine. Though Otto's work is now generally understood as somewhat limited in scope and flawed in presentation, it continues to stand as a foundation in the comparative study of religions, even as it is criticized. As such, it continues to influence and challenge contemporary and future scholars of religion.

Implications

Otto's numinous can be understood as an attempt to describe the holy or the divine cross-culturally. That is, Otto desires to develop a way of speaking about religions without marginalizing or simplifying unique human experiences. Yet, as has been noted above, Otto's numinous is criticized for being too Christian a term, too Western an understanding of religion, and too theological in tenor. Otto's theories of religion may be regarded as limited; however, these theories and the criticisms of them give us an idea of the difficulties faced when attempting to examine religions comparatively. The desire to communicate religious experiences across cultures presents scholars with the problem of identifying language and terminology adequate to the complex phenomena of religion. When communicating religion, the scholar, journalist, or conversationalist must be sensitive to the particularities of religions, while at the same time not being simply struck dumb by the daunting task of communicating such a complicated and vital element of human experience.

CHRISTA SHUSKO

Further Reading

Almond, P. C. (1984). *Rudolf Otto: An introduction to his philosophical theology*. Chapel Hill: University of North Carolina Press.

Capps, D. (1997). *Men, religion, and melancholia: James, Otto, Jung, and Erikson*. New Haven, CT: Yale University Press.

Capps, W. H. (1995). *Religious studies: The making of a discipline* (pp. 1–52). Minneapolis, MN: Fortress Press.

Eliade, M. (1996). *Patterns in comparative religion* (R. Sneed, Trans.). Lincoln: University of Nebraska Press. (Original work published 1958)

Gooch, T. A. (2000). *The numinous and modernity: An interpretation of Rudolf Otto's philosophy of religion*. Berlin, Germany: Walter de Guyter.

James, W. (1985). *The varieties of religious experience*. Cambridge, MA: Harvard University Press. (Original work published 1903)

Kant, I. (1990). *The critique of judgment* (W. S. Pluhar, Trans.). Indianapolis, IN: Hackett Publishing Company. (Original work published in German 1790)

Kant, I. (1993). *The critique of practical reason* (L. W. Beck, Trans.). Upper Saddle River, NJ: Prentice-Hall. (Original work published in German 1788)

Kant, I. (1999). *The critique of pure reason*. Cambridge, UK: Cambridge University Press. (Original work published in German 1781)

Kunin, S. D. (2003). Rudolf Otto: The idea of the holy. *Religion: The modern theories* (pp. 62–68). Baltimore: Johns Hopkins University Press.

Otto, R. (1950). *The idea of the holy* (J. W. Harvey Trans.). London: Oxford University Press. (Original work published in German 1917; first English translation published 1923)

Raphael, M. (1997). *Rudolf Otto and the concept of holiness*. Oxford, UK: Clarendon Press.

Schleiermacher, F. *On religion: Speeches to its cultured despisers* (R. Crouter, Ed.). Cambridge, UK: Cambridge University Press. (Original work published in German 1799)

Wach, J. (1951). Rudolf Otto and the idea of the holy. *Types of religious experience, Christian and Non-Christian* (pp. 209–227). Chicago: University of Chicago Press.

O

Orality

The term *orality* (communication by speech without writing) has consistently been conceived and defined in opposition to *literacy* (communication mediated by symbolic notation). This "great divide" was initially associated with two types of society: oral (primitive, illiterate) and literate (advanced, civilized). Over the past thirty years, significant developments in the study of orality and orally derived thought and expression have contributed to an understanding of oral modes of communication as information technologies for preserving and transmitting history, religion, and other cultural knowledge. Evidence from fieldwork in living oral societies has amassed, and researchers from ancient, medieval, and contemporary traditions now question the assumption of a fundamental division between oral and written communication. Orality is now conceived as a spectrum, extending from ongoing oral traditions, to oral traditions that persist alongside and in interaction with written traditions, to highly literate compositions that still manifest trace evidence of oral derivation, through to new forms of orality mediated by electronic media (radio, cellular telephone, television).

Dimensions of Orality

The study of orality encompasses primary orality (civilizations with no exposure to writing), oral tradition (communication preserved in human memory and transmitted through time by word of mouth) involving verbal art (epic, poetry) or narrative (either in elevated or everyday language), oral literature (works composed without writing and then recorded), oral history (accounts of events that took place during the speaker's lifetime), and secondary orality (aural and/or visual communication via electronic media).

Orality and Religious Communication

Stories and histories as vital to religion as the Old Testament scriptures, the ancient Greek *Illiad* and *Odyssey*, and much of early European and Asian literature have roots in orality and were passed down through generations by oral traditions before they came to be documented in writing. Research on the ecology of orality shows the pervasiveness of oral and orally derived modes of communication throughout the world. More than a hundred national literatures presently involved in the study of orality include Albanian, Arabic, Bulgarian, Chinese, English, French, German, Greek, Japanese, Russian, Serbo-Croation, Spanish, Turkish, as well as numerous North American Aboriginal traditions, the languages of the Bible, African language families, and the rural folkpreaching of the southern United States.

Fields of Inquiry

Orality is a key concept in religion, classics, archaeology, and history; a focus of inquiry in literary studies, linguistics, education, and music; a major subject of investigation in anthropology, ethnography, folklore, and performance studies; and the basis of research in the study of media ecology, cultural studies, and information and communication technology.

History of the Field

The study of orality began with the pioneering research of American classical scholar, Milman Parry (1902–1935). Before Parry, scholars assumed that Homer's *Illiad* and *Odyssey* were either literate compositions created by a single author or the composite result of a long-term process of editing. In 1928 Parry published two theses that proposed a novel answer to the centuries old "Homeric Question" of *who* Homer was and *what* exactly his *Iliad* and *Odyssey* represented. Parry pointed to the complex patterns of organization in the verse and argued that one person could not have created this elaborate construction. The language rules governing this style would have required a long development time and could only be the cumulative product of an entire tradition to which generations of poets and rhapsodes (sewers of songs) contributed over centuries (Parry 1971). He arrived at this conclusion by demonstrating that frequently repeated phrases in the verse— epithets such as "divine Odysseus" or "wine-dark sea"—were threaded together into an intricate tapestry. He called these stock expressions *formulas,* which he defined as a "group of words regularly employed under the same metrical conditions to express a given essential idea" (Parry 1971, 272). Each formula was made of expressions that fit into a section of verse and was tied together with those that came before and after to create six measures in a line (hexameter).

What was the purpose of this complex system? Parry argued that formulaic techniques were mnemonic aids created by poets living in a wholly *oral* society in the ages before the advent of the phonetic alphabet. He theorized that the epics were too long to memorize line by line without writing. Instead, the poets improvised in performance by selecting expressions from a huge storehouse of formulas—a poetic diction—and stitching them "into the mould of the verse after a fixed pattern" (Parry 1971, 268). The storehouse of formulas, together with the principles for fabricating them into a composition, constituted a completely unified technology for verse making.

Parry's hypotheses concerning the oral traditional nature of the epics challenged the central orthodoxies of Homeric studies. His second major contribution was to carry out field expeditions to the former Yugoslavia with his assistant, Albert Bates Lord (1912–1991), to test theories of orality developed from the ancient manuscript tradition by comparison with the Serbo-Croatian oral epics of the unlettered *guslari.* These studies of a living tradition, completed by Lord following Parry's early death, demonstrated that techniques similar to Homer's (though not as elaborate), were developed in the oral poetry of other societies.

In 1949 Lord defended a thesis entitled *The Singer of Tales* at Harvard University. His comparative study, first published in 1960, applied the information from the analysis of the Yugoslav material to poems in ancient and Byzantine Greek as well as Old English. Lord extended the definition of the formulaic style still further in this work to encompass stock elements he called "themes" and "subthemes," defined as "groups of *ideas* regularly used in telling a tale in the formulaic style" (Lord 1964, 68). Words and phrases vary in different parts of a composition, while themes and subthemes repeat an identical order of actions, events, and objects. Every journey, for instance, reiterates the same sequence of loading, embarking, disembarking, and unloading ships.

In 1958 Homeric scholar Cedric M. Whitman (1916–1979) built on the Parry–Lord research concerning formulaic phrases and themes by showing that the entire plot of Homer's epics has a completely unified "geometric structure of the most amazing virtuosity" woven from interlocking formulaic structures at various orders of magnitude. The plot of the *Illiad* is "spun out" by expanding, compressing, or altering an initial formula to create an ordered series of topics (places), themes, and episodes. After the middle of the composition, the previously mentioned order reiterates in reverse, so that the concluding passage returns full circle to the initial formula. Mnemonic ring patterning helped the poet keep track of the episodes in the story because they were organized into an A-B-C-B̃-Ã series with a symmetry of topics and themes on either side of the midpoint (Whitman 1958). Each place encapsulates additional levels of information. A, for instance, is subdivided further via the sequential and symmetrical pattern so that information is condensed in a hierarchical arrangement that moves from general to specific.

Serious research on orality and oral literature began with the publication of the findings of Lord and Whitman. Nearly half a century later, thousands of published studies testify to the significance of the research on orality and oral tradition for understanding religious and cultural phenomena. The study of oral communication has become one of the most important critical perspectives on Homer and a major theoretical nexus in the study and comparison of numerous other ancient, medieval, and contemporary literatures (Foley 1985).

Orality, Religion, and Communication Technology

The findings of Parry, Lord, and Whitman provided the impetus for an approach to culture and communication developed by scholars associated with the Toronto School of Communication: Harold Innis, Eric Havelock, Marshall McLuhan, Walter J. Ong, and Northrop Frye, who extended orality and literacy studies to a range of religious and cultural phenomena. This approach has been both controversial and deeply influential.

Harold Innis (1894–1952) refined the Parry–Lord comparative method of confirming hypotheses concerning ancient communication technologies by analogy with technologies used in other cultures. His *Bias of Communication* traced the historical development of technologies that predominated in subsequent civilizations, showing how communication technology both reflects and helps shape the organization of society. Innis cautioned that the communication technology that predominates in a culture produces a mental "bias" that makes it difficult for users to comprehend communication embedded in alternative modes of communication.

Eric Havelock (1903–1988) built on the implications of oral poetry as the central vehicle of communication in Greek culture. His landmark, *Preface to Plato,* suggested that Homer's epics were instruments for transmitting education, a "container" for all cultural information, a "massive repository of useful knowledge, a sort of encyclopedia of ethics, politics, history, and technology," and an "indoctrination which today would be comprised in a shelf of text books and works of reference" (1963, 27, 43). He argued that oral and literate media are associated with different kinds of human mentality and the transition to literacy had far-reaching psychological, social, and cultural effects. The banishment of Homer and the poets by Plato's Socrates marked the rejection of mnemonic modes of communication in favor of the language, categories of thought, and forms of social organization designed to store knowledge in writing. According to Havelock, Homer represents the culmination of the memory technology, and Plato is the pivotal figure in the transition from orality to literacy. Havelock's theory concerning the causal effects of literacy has been extensively critiqued.

Marshall McLuhan (1911–1980) drew on the research of Parry and Lord and built on the findings of Innis and Havelock to urge a theory of three fundamental revolutions in communication technology. He noted in the prologue to his *The Gutenberg Galaxy* that the work was "complementary to *The Singer of Tales* by Albert Lord," in that "the enterprise which Milman Parry undertook with reference to the contrasted *forms* of oral and written poetry is here extended to the *forms* of thought and the organization of experience in society and politics." McLuhan argued that the "Literate Revolution" that ensued in the wake of the phonetic alphabet culminated in new forms of human mentality and radically different forms of social organization. He proposed that the shift from orality to literacy was a model for understanding the effects of subsequent transformations in communication technology. The "Gutenberg Revolution" following the invention of printing with movable type in the fifteenth century accelerated the pace of change. The "Electronic Revolution" that commenced with the telegraph in 1844, followed by radio, telephone, films, television, and computers, is creating a new era of secondary orality that will one day link all societies in a "global village." McLuhan asserted that the "medium is the message," indicating that meanings inhere in the medium of communication, so that the form of a technology transmits messages over and above the explicit meanings in the content.

Walter Jackson Ong (1912–2003), who completed his master's thesis under the direction of McLuhan, furthered Havelock's research on the Greek tradition and contributed groundbreaking research on the history of mnemonics. He developed a comprehensive account of the evolution of human consciousness that has had a formative influence on cultural studies, media ecology, American Catholicism, Renaissance intellectual history, and the history of print culture. His "relationist" thesis is that major developments in culture and consciousness relate to the "evolution of the word from primary orality to its present state" (Ong 1977, 9–10). One of his lasting accomplishments was to demonstrate that "residues" of traditional mnemonic techniques can be found in texts composed hundreds of years after the technology of writing had theoretically prevailed over the old oral tradition.

Northrop Frye (1912–1991) developed a synoptic view of the evolution of literature from poetry to prose. He drew from Havelock and Ong, especially in his late works, *The Great Code* and *Words of Power* (Frye 1982, xix, 8) which dealt with repeating patterns in the Bible. Frye saw the Bible as a "halfway stage" between oral tradition and a "fully developed writing tradition." "Words of power" are formulas that became codified into "typology," an archetypal "mode of thought," or a "form of rhetoric" that provides a framework for the arrangement of words in scripture so that "all facts and all ideas are linked together" in "a single, complex structure of repeated images" (1982, 80, 204). Repeating patterns in the Bible form a "cultural framework" for comparing myths and literature from different ancient traditions.

Research by John Miles Foley, a student of Lord and Ong, detailed how traditional patterns were a kind of language in themselves. Formulaic phrases, themes, and plot patterns were "ancient technologies of representation" that bore meanings beyond the literal sense of the words in a composition (Foley 1999, 3). Patterns at different orders of context functioned as a "code" that referred "institutionally toward a traditional network of associations" that people steeped in a culture tune into but that go unrecognized by those unfamiliar with this background context (1999, 31). Traditional formulas formed an index to meanings stated in the content. Individual details were "slotted" into different places in the framework that served as a familiar context to informed audiences. *The content changed with the performance, but the overall form of the ideas remained constant.* In this style the audience is responsible for figuring out what the work means. If listeners or readers do not have the background, training, or experience, then the communication is not received.

Controversies

Controversies in religion focus on how different forms of media transmit ineffable meanings in sacred texts. In classics, archaeology, and history, questions surround the origin of the alphabet, the translation of traditions into texts, the diffusion of writing, and the spread of literacy throughout the ancient world. Discussions in education concern the changing role of media and technology in the context of learning and teaching. In anthropology, ethnography, and folklore studies, the dialogue revolves around the documentation of oral histories, living oral traditions, and folktales (via tape recorder, film, video, or in writing). In the study of contemporary culture and technology, arguments converge on the psychological, sociological, and political effects of new information and communications technologies and the extent to which technology acts as a causal force in determining cultural forms.

The Future of the Religion–Orality Interface

Studies of oral modes of communication may be applied to a range of problems that serve as the focus of

discussion in a number of disciplines today. The findings concerning the patterns of communication in Homer have been subjected to standards of verification and proof similar to those in the sciences; these methods may be extended to the study of other traditions as well. Acknowledging that works of literature have roots in orality will provide new answers concerning the interaction between religion and media. Recognizing the bias of communication will help us devise appropriate methods for observing and recording oral histories, living oral traditions, and for interpreting folktales. Comparing data concerning the advent of the technology of the computer, the Internet, and other current innovations in information technology with the historical evidence for the adoption of the alphabet and the spread of writing and literacy opens new avenues for understanding the role of technology in different cultures.

Studies in orality are an essential background for understanding and interpreting religious phenomena. It is not possible to fully understand orally derived literature or living oral societies without some recognition of the meanings encoded in traditional forms of communication. Acknowledging the importance of findings concerning orality will provide solutions to issues, both ancient and contemporary, that are the focus of current debate and suggest new opportunities for further research.

TWYLA GIBSON

See also Mantra; Music; Sermons

Further Reading

Foley, J. M. (1985). *Oral-formulaic theory and research: an introduction and annotated bibliography.* New York: Garland Publishing.

Foley, J. M. (1990). *Traditional oral epic: The* Odyssey, Beowulf, *and the Servo-Croatian return song.* Berkeley and Los Angeles: University of California Press.

Foley, J. M. (1991). *Immanent art: from structure to meaning in traditional oral epic.* Bloomington: Indiana University Press.

Foley, J. M. (1999). *Homer's traditional art.* University Park: The Pennsylvania State University Press.

Frye, N. (1963). *The educated imagination.* Toronto: CBC Publications.

Frye, N. (1982). *The great code: The Bible and literature.* Toronto: Academic Press Canada.

Frye, N. (1990). *Words with power: being a second study of the Bible and literature.* Markham, Canada: Viking.

Goody, J. (1987). *The interface between the written and the oral.* Cambridge, UK: Cambridge University Press.

Havelock, E. A. (1963). *Preface to Plato.* Cambridge, MA: The Belknap Press of Harvard University Press.

Havelock, E. A. (1982). *The literate revolution in Greece and its cultural consequences.* Princeton, NJ: Princeton University Press.

Havelock, E. A. (1986). *The muse learns to write.* New Haven, CT: Yale University Press.

Innis, H. (1951). *The bias of communication.* Toronto: University of Toronto Press.

Lord, A. B. (1964). *The singer of tales.* Cambridge, MA: Harvard University Press.

Ong, W. J. (1977). *Interfaces of the word: Studies in the evolution of consciousness and culture.* Ithaca, NY: Cornell University Press.

Ong, W. J. (1981). *The presence of the word: Some prolegomena for cultural and religious history.* Minneapolis: University of Minnesota Press. (Original work published 1967)

Ong, W. J. (1991). *Orality & literacy: The technologizing of the word.* New York: Routledge. (Original work published 1982)

Parry, M. (1971). In A. Parry (Ed. & Trans.) *The making of Homeric verse: The collected papers of Milman Parry.* Oxford, UK: Clarendon Press.

Thomas, R. (1992). *Literacy and orality in ancient Greece.* Cambridge, UK: Cambridge University Press.

Vansina, J. (1985). *Oral tradition as history.* Madison: University of Wisconsin Press.

Whitman, Cedric Hubbel. (1963). *Homer and the heroic tradition.* Cambridge, MA: Harvard University Press.

Organizational Communication

The study of organizational communication emerged in the academy as rhetorical studies sought greater relevancy in a society that was becoming increasingly linked through business communication. As scholars examined the function of the American business corporation, they looked for explanations that would lead toward greater organizational efficiencies (Barnard 1938). Initially focused on medium, organizational communication quickly evolved into a highly theoretical practice that included the creation and adaptation of metaphors to understand a new and changing organizational environment (Morgan 1997) and the process of human sense making within the corporation (Weick 1995). Organizational communication incorporated theories of learning, knowledge (Argyris & Schon 1978), and social-network construction (Barabasi 2002).

While at a glance the first layer of organizational communication theory is clearly associated with busi-ness, deep rhetorical connections (Tompkins, Tompkins, & Cheney 1989) tie the field to religion. The identity, hierarchy, and orthodoxy ideas of rhetorical and social critic Kenneth Burke (1936) were appropriated by rhetorical scholars studying organizations to make knowledge claims. Through Burke's conception of identity, hierarchy, and orthodoxy, the tie of religion to organizational communication becomes evident.

Identity

The creation of identity is a central subprocess in organizing. Creating through communication the image and role of a superior, subordinate, pastor, parishioner, professor, or any other organizational title is a symbolic, sense-making function and a prerequisite to behavior. According to organizational behavior expert Karl Weick, "Identities are constructed out of the process of interaction. To shift among interactions is to shift among definitions of self" (1995, 21). Weick notes that a positive self-concept allows one to deal with the discrepancies of perception inherent in the organizing process.

The creation of self-identity through interaction was used by organizational-communications expert George Cheney to understand professionalism and culture at Gore and Associates, and by public administration expert Herbert Kaufman to understand the culture in the U.S. Forest Service. The intellectual genealogy follows back to Burke who originally conceived of identity construction in the context of religion. Burke argued that identity construction is the first function of any symbol system. Human beings, he reasoned, need to construct an identity for themselves that distinguishes them as individuals and establishes them within a hierarchy. The simple hierarchy in a religious context is always about whether or not someone is orthodox.

In simple terms, identity construction distinguishes who is in the church, who is outside the church, and who within the church is closer to God. The interaction and communication that is part of distinguishing identity creates the meaning behind hierarchical position in the church. For example, the identities of priest or cardinal and layman or parishioner are constructed through negotiation and interaction. Note that the construct of identity is not just individual but also organizational. The hierarchical titles found in this example follow those found within corporations, like vice president and president, or employee and subordinate. Each of these terms represents an individual and corporate identity within a hierarchy.

Hierarchy

To Burke, human symbol systems are inherently hierarchical. Creating symbolic order through hierarchy allows humans to determine who is closer to God. Similarly, corporations have a hierarchy-building process in place. H. L. Goodall Jr., an expert in organizational communications, describes how the parking lot near a corporation (or university) is a symbolic representation of the organizational hierarchy. The president, with his or her reserved spot, parks closest to the building. Managers (or faculty) do not have individual spaces, but do have preferred parking locations. Employees (or students) park even farther away.

The idea of creating a hierarchy to define who is more and who is less important is not just materially represented in organizations. Individual identities are also constructed in hierarchy to determine who is closer to the truth. A person holding a doctorate in philosophy is seen as having more authority than a person with a master's degree, while one with a master's degree trumps a bachelor's, and a bachelor's degree trumps a nongraduated student. If a student disagrees with a professor who has a doctorate, and if independent verification is not available, a default belief based on hierarchical identity is that the highly educated person is more likely to be right. According to Burke, people are captives of their own symbolic hierarchies.

The notion of formal authority, or position power, is found throughout management literature (Morgan, 1989). It could be argued that position power is the symbolic recreation of religious authority within a corporate setting. The manager, like the priest, is "closer to God" by virtue of his or her position in the hierarchy, demonstrating the idea that the higher one is in the organization, the more likely he or she is to be identified as the one who knows best and is most virtuous.

Orthodoxy

Burke argues that orthodoxy drives the symbolic creation of the hierarchy. Alan Wilkins, an organizational behavior expert, suggests that orthodoxy within the corporation is transmitted and understood through stories. Management and organizational-studies expert David Boje describes organizational stories as the method through which experiences are communicated and by which organizational members make sense of

their environment and others with whom they work. Much like the parables found in Christian scripture, organizational stories serve to tell individuals what is really valued within the organization. They establish orthodoxy by saying who is a hero and who is a villain. The stories tell who is "closer to God."

Community

Corporate and individual identity, hierarchy, and orthodoxy lead to social-clustering or community-building. Outside the connection to Burke ideas, organizational communication has drawn on religion to understand how communities emerge. In the conceptualization of how community comes into being, it is argued that communities are not as much places of common belief as they are places of common communicative processes. These processes can be either dialectic or dialogic in nature.

Dialectic communities promote forms of argumentation to establish orthodoxy. Weick refers to arguing as a belief-driven form of sense making. Michael Cohen, James March, and Johan Olsen suggest that organizations are forums and socially constructed processes for truing through argumentation. Thus communication within an organization is inherently polarizing and results in controversy. Both Burke and later Eric Eisenberg noted that the organizational or community-building process is one of argument followed by transcendence. Transcendence, according to Burke, is a human but "god-like" characteristic.

Dialogue has emerged for communication scholars as an alternative way to understand and organize communities. Though dialogic processes run deep in many cultures, in some cases going back thousands of years, most dialogic processes are rooted in religious practice. For example, Parker Palmer, an education activist, notes how dialogue was used in Quaker traditions not only to worship but also to make decisions in a clearness committee. A clearness committee is a group of wise people who gather at the invitation of an individual. They are charged with asking questions to help the individual become clear about a key life question the individual faces, such as marriage or career change. The assumption of the Quaker clearness committee is that the truth is within the individual, and that caring questions can help surface that truth to a level of individual understanding. This process is remarkably similar to the future search, or conference method, of organizational strategic planning that assumes that with the right people interacting in the room a clear future for the company can be developed.

Without a doubt, most practitioners and scholars of management and organization have little knowledge of the religious roots of their practices and theory. Throughout a history of organizations predominated by small, craft-oriented, family-owned businesses, the only large organizations were either military/government or religious in nature (McGregor, 1985), and in many cases the two were not distinguishable. It is not surprising that much of the knowledge of how organizations work came from an understanding of military, government (Morgan, 1997), and religion. It is also not surprising that communication and rhetoric drew on these religiously based constructs to make sense of the corporation as it rose to social prominence in the nineteenth century. Certainly the symbolic construction of identity within a religious or organizational hierarchy helps us understand the orthodoxy of our values that often dialectally or dialogically contract with other identities within the same hierarchy.

SCOTT C. HAMMOND AND DAN W. PETERSON

Further Reading

Argyris, C. & Schon, D. A. (1978). *Organizational learning: A theory of action perspective*. Reading, MA: Addison & Wesley.

Barabasi, A. L. (2002). *Linked: The new science of networks*. Cambridge, MA: Perseus.

Barnard, C. I. (1938). *The functions of the executive*. Cambridge, MA: Harvard University Press.

Boje, D. (1991). The story-telling organization: A study of story performance in an office-supply firm. *Administrative Science Quarterly, 36*, 106–126.

Burke, K. (1936). *Attitudes toward history*. Berkeley: University of California Press.

Burke, K. (1969). *A rhetoric of motives*. Berkeley: University of California Press.

Cheney, G. (1991). *Rhetoric in an organizational society: Managing multiple identities*. Columbia: University of South Carolina.

Cohen, Z. M. D., March, J. G., & Olsen, J. P. (1972). A garbage can model of organizational choice. *Administrative Science Quarterly, 17*, 1–25.

Eisenberg, E. (1990). Jamming: Transcendence through organizing. *Communication Research, 17*, 139–164.

Goodall, H. L. (1989). *Casing a promised land: The autobiography of an organizational detective as cultural ethnographer*. Carbondale: University of Southern Illinois Press.

Kauffman, H. (1967). *The forest ranger*. Baltimore: Johns Hopkins University Press.

McGregor, D. (1985). *The human side of enterprise* (2nd ed.). Boston: McGraw-Hill.

Morgan, G. (1997). *Images of the organization*. Newbury Park, CA: Sage.

Palmer, P. (1998). *The courage to teach: Exploring the inner life of a teacher*. San Francisco: Jossey-Bass.

Tompkins, E. V. B, Tompkins, P. K., & Cheney, G. (1989). Organizations as arguments: Discovering, expressing, and analyzing the premise for decisions. *Journal of Management Systems, 1*, 35–48.

Weick, K. E. (1995). *Sensemaking in organizations*. Newbury Park, CA: Sage.

Wilkins, A. L. (1984). The creation of company cultures: The role of stories in human resource systems. *Human Resource Management, 23*, 41–60.

Orthodoxy

The word "orthodoxy" derives from the Greek term for "correct doctrine" (*orthodoxia*). The term first made its appearance in the fifth century as early Christian writers began to contrast the "tradition of the fathers" with the varieties of "heretical deviance" (false opinion or heterodoxy) that were increasingly being classified by Episcopal theologians as the canon of major historical heresies.

Early History

Orthodoxy, in early Christian theology, is thus the opposite of heresy and is seen to be the unique possession of the church (an idea that ranges back to the late Catholic epistles of the New Testament—1 John 2: 18–19; 1 John 4:1–6; 2 John 10; 2 Peter 2:1–2; 1 Timothy 6:3; 2 Timothy 1:13) and was developed intensively by the second- and third-century teachers Irenaeus and Origen), while heresies are the invention of sectarians. This contrasts significantly with the meaning of orthodoxy in pre-Christian Greek philosophical thought, where it was a school term that referred to a correct conception and where heterodoxy simply meant a variant opinion from the norm (not necessarily a right or a wrong position—just one that differed from the opinion of the majority, especially in philosophical matters that were open to various interpretations).

The early Christian "firming up" of the sense of orthodoxy in sharp distinction from heresy was probably a legacy of the church's vision of itself as the heir of Israel, inheriting the Scriptures and a new sense of being the "covenant people." For Christians the heart of the Torah, or covenant experience, shifted from the observance of the prescripts of the law to the celebration of

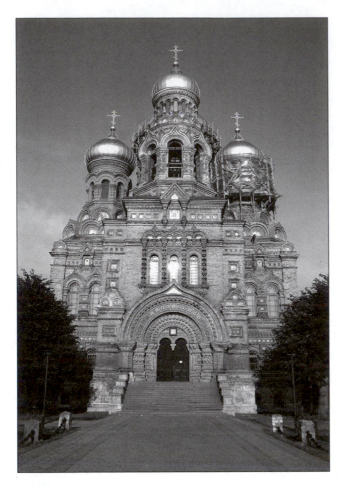

Orthodox church in Karosta, Liepaja, Latvia.
Courtesy of Gunta Klavina/istockphoto.com.

the person and witness of Jesus and the maintenance of the "apostolic tradition." For this reason in the patristic understanding of revealed tradition, heterodoxy (that is, the departure from orthodoxy) was always seen as a culpable lapse into error. The last letters of the New Testament (the epistles of John, Jude, and Peter especially) even see the rise of heresy as a deliberate strategy of Satan, designed at hurting the community of the New Israel, in the same way that apostasy and false cult had damaged Israel's integrity in the records of the Torah and prophets.

Changes in Meaning

By extension from all this, in recent times the word orthodox has come to mean the "classical" exposition of the position of various church and religious groups: hence "Orthodox Catholic doctrine" or "Orthodox Lutheranism." In this analogous sense the word has been applied to the more rigorous obser-

vance of Judaism (Orthodox Judaism as distinct, for example, from Conservative or Reform Judaism).

After the ninth century the word "Orthodoxy" (usually designated with a capital letter) came to be used as a more common designation of the "church" (alongside the four "marks" or "notes" of the church as listed in the Creed, namely that the church is One, Holy, Catholic, and Apostolic). When the church as a whole is referred to as "Orthodox," it meant that it was in possession of a certain "charism of truth," an instinct—or something like it—for knowing what was or was not important and integral to the appropriation of the Gospel experience in each different generation. This was akin to the doctrine of the infallibility of the church (based on Jesus's promise to Peter that "the gates of Hell would never prevail" against it; Matthew 16:18). Roman Catholicism in the late modern period greatly developed this notion of the infallibility of the church along the discrete lines of papal infallibility (especially as formulated in that official doctrine at the Vatican Council in 1870), but the other churches retained a sense that this was rather a charism of truth that belonged to the church as a whole.

Eastern Churches

From the seventeenth century onward "Orthodoxy" was a term that was increasingly used to connote the Eastern churches (the Orthodox Church) as distinct from the Western Catholic Church (Roman Catholic, as it was designated after the Reformation era). The Eastern Christian world increasingly wanted to distinguish itself from the Western churches, which (by implication) it felt had departed from the clarity and integrity of early Christian teaching. Accordingly, it designated itself as the true locus of Orthodox Christianity, and thus, in nuce, as the Orthodox Church in toto. Classical Orthodox theology, to this day, recognizes only itself as the true and unique Church of Christ, maintaining that by manifold and various heretical deviances all other Christian groups have declined from church into denominations.

Even when it used this shorthand title of "Orthodox," however, the Eastern churches still invoked the other and ancient "descriptors" or marks of the Church, so the Eastern Orthodox formally designated themselves as the Holy Catholic Apostolic Orthodox Church of the East. It is in this sense that the word "Orthodoxy" is often used to connote whole families of Christian churches that share a common basis of faith and practice. It is also referred to as "Eastern

Orthodoxy" (reflecting a simpler time in Christian antiquity when the "East" was Greek speaking, as opposed to the Latin-speaking West). So, while Eastern Orthodoxy is a clearer designation, the terminology is problematic today, when major communities of "Eastern" Orthodox live in Oceania and the Americas.

Divisions within the Orthodox Churches

The Orthodox world itself suffered a division in the fifth century, following a crisis over the reception of one of the early Christological councils (Chalcedon 451). The churches of ancient Syria, Egypt, Armenia, and Ethiopia did not accept this council as definitive of the faith and were thus regarded as "un-Orthodox" by the other churches of the Romano-Byzantine world that did accept it; that is, the majority of both the Greek- and Latin-speaking communities. Thus the Eastern Orthodox Church means today largely those Eastern Christian communities that accept the Seven Ecumenical Councils and the ancient pattern of the honorary "precedence" of episcopal sees (the system of patriarchates and autocephalous churches that was established in antiquity and adapted across the centuries).

There is little (apart from the issue of the acceptance of the number of ecumenical councils) that separates all the churches of the East, which are bound together by a massive coherence of liturgical and spiritual traditions, as well as by major conformity in most areas of doctrine. However, the Byzantine tradition (followed in this by the Western churches, too) regards the non-Chalcedonians as the "Oriental Orthodox" and themselves as simply "the Orthodox." Needless to say, the Oriental Orthodox regard themselves as the Orthodox, and the Byzantines as "heterodox." The Eastern Orthodox Church however, in the main, is regarded as the communion of the Greek, Russian, Bulgarian, Romanian, Serbian, Slovakian, Albanian, and Polish churches (although Poland is also home to a large number of Roman Catholics) and those other churches derived from them through historical missions (such as the Orthodox Church in America that rose to independence from the Russian Orthodox communities in the United States).

The patriarch of Constantinople (Istanbul) is regarded as the honorary senior bishop of the Orthodox Churches, who all hold one another "in communion," despite following national practices of their own in terms of governance structures and liturgical languages (though Byzantine Greek and Old Slavonic are still the major liturgical vehicles). In antiquity the five greatest cities of the Roman Empire were afforded a system of honor and precedence, by the acclamation of their bishop with the title of "patriarch." After the medieval Great Schism between the East and West, the Patriarch of Rome was separated from the list of the five popes, and now the Orthodox world recognizes only the four ancient patriarchal sees of Constantinople, Alexandria, Antioch, and Jerusalem, along with some other patriarchates that were developed to acknowledge the rise to nationhood of great states after the late Middle Ages, such as Russia, Serbia, and Romania.

In the year 2000 the Eastern Orthodox Church comprised about 215 million adherents throughout the world, 15 million of whom are Greek speaking. The Russian Orthodox Church remains the single largest communion in Eastern Orthodoxy with 74 million faithful. The Romanian Church has approximately 20 million adherents. The Greek Orthodox Church (independent from Constantinople since the nineteenth century) totals 10 million. Today the patriarch of Constantinople has very few members of his church in Turkey (once the heartland of the Byzantine empire) but presides over extensive numbers of the Greek Orthodox faithful in Australia, America, and Europe and has always served as a central figure of reference for world Orthodoxy, despite having simply a precedence of honor rather than a juridical power over other bishops.

JOHN ANTHONY MCGUCKIN

See also Catholicism

Further Reading

Meyendorff, J. (1978). *Living tradition: Orthodox witness in the contemporary world.* Crestwood, NY: St. Vladimir's Seminary Press.
Meyendorff, J. (1981). *Orthodox church: Its past and its role in the world today* (3rd ed.). Crestwood, NY: St. Vladimir's Seminary Press.
Meyendorff, J. (1983). *Byzantine theology: Historical trends and doctrinal themes.* New York: Fordham University Press.
Simon, M. (1979). From Greek *haeresis* to Christian heresy. In W. R. Schoedel & R. L. Wilken (Eds.), *Early Christian literature and the classical intellectual tradition* (pp. 101–116). Paris: Éditions Beauchesne.
Ware, T. (1963). *The Orthodox Church.* Baltimore and London: Penguin Books.

Paintings

From the earliest pictorial works of Paleolithic peoples, painting has been a form of religious communication. Around thirty thousand years ago, artists ventured into the deep interiors of uninhabited caves, where, illuminated by animal-fat lamps, they mixed saliva with charcoal to create the first painted images that link human and supernatural realms. The deftly rendered horses, bison, and mammoths remain the tangible evidence of a magic ritual observed over successive years to guarantee successful hunting. Since those days of nomadic hunters, painting has been at the forefront of establishing the visual language of religious communication.

Painting comes from the Latin word *pingere*, to paint with pigments or colored powders. Pigments are organic substances, such as plant and animal matter, or inorganic matter, such as minerals and stones. When mixed with a medium or binder, such as saliva, water, egg, oil, or hot wax, the pigments will adhere to a support. Walls, papyrus, wood panels, fabric, calfskin, and even bark have served as supports for painted imagery in religious contexts.

Paintings communicate religious ideas in several different manners. First, paintings serve as a form of communication from humankind to God. In these instances, painted images honor deities, saints, or holy events in recognition of a supernatural power beyond human comprehension. Sometimes these paintings are considered sacred. Second, paintings serve to convey information about God from human to human. Artists have created paintings that promulgate the essential religious message of a particular belief and have brought together patrons, painters, and viewers. Finally, painting is an act that allows artists to emulate the divine creator. Accordingly, the creative activity of painters mirrors the making of heaven and Earth by God.

Differing Forms

Religious paintings come in various forms, depending on the needs of the patrons and viewers. Grand altarpieces serve as liturgical aids in churches, hand-held manuscript illuminations are used for private devotions, icons are carried in religious processions, scrolls serve as personal acts of meditation, and the walls of tombs are decorated as a means of soothing the transition from an earthly life to the spiritual realm. Religious paintings can be representational or abstract. They can tell a story or present a symbol. Throughout history, they have served as instructive or expressive means of communication. Especially rich and abundant pictorial examples appeared in Christian Europe; in India, where both Buddhism and Hinduism began; in the Zen monasteries of China and Japan; and in Persia during the Islamic age. In these places and elsewhere, humankind's earliest paintings advanced the objectives of religion.

Before monotheism dominated world religions, the polytheism of both the Egyptians and the Aegeans inspired powerful imagery in frescoes or wall paintings. Egyptian tomb paintings depict the myriad gods and goddesses of the underworld and scenes of daily life to ensure a safe journey to the afterlife and an enjoyable place of eternal repose for the deceased. Anonymous Egyptian painters created encyclopedic scenes to surround the mummified body in a sealed tomb. Like the cave paintings of Paleolithic nomads, these images existed for the supernatural world far from living viewers.

On the other hand, the Aegean culture produced paintings in public venues, such as the vast palace complexes on the island of Crete. These contemporary scenes articulated the religious rituals of the active Cretan community. Although Minoan religious beliefs remain obscure, the richly colored, engaging scenes of lively figures, such as the acrobatic bull jumpers from the palace at the Minoan capital of Knossos, seem to celebrate physical accomplishments for a divine audience. Puzzling depictions of ceremonies and processions allude to the goddesses worshipped in this matriarchal society.

The Greeks and Romans also painted on walls, but ceramic vessels provide a more thorough record of mythological narratives. Abundant extant painted pottery with the gods and goddesses identified by action and attribute confirms the significance of myth in the everyday religious beliefs of the first great secular societies. Somewhat more unusual is the well-known scene of a cultic initiation ritual found in a villa in Pompeii. This image presents a ceremony associated with one of the many mystery sects that infiltrated Rome during the early years of the Empire. Here, painting confirmed the patron's religious beliefs and served as a probable teaching tool for interested communicants.

Painting as a Means of Communication

Among the many sects competing for believers in the Roman Empire, Christianity would soon prove unassailable. With the ascendancy of monotheism, particularly Christianity, but also Judaism, the role of painting as a means of communication grew in significance. Although the second of the Ten Commandments, "You shall not make for yourself a graven image [idol], or any likeness of anything that is in heaven above, or that is in the earth below, or that is in the water under the earth," seems to prohibit the making of images, both Jewish and Christian communities depended on paintings to promote religious beliefs. For example, illustrated Jewish texts exist, and frescoed walls of Old Testament imagery from the mid-third century have been discovered at a synagogue at Dura Europos in Syria. These depictions of Jewish history and law, focusing on Old Testament leaders, set forth the important doctrines of the Jewish faith for the congregation in a region rife with competing religious sects.

From the earliest days, Christians used painting to tell the message of Christ's birth, ministries and miracles, sacrifice and Resurrection. In the underground burial passages outside the walls of Rome, early Christians painted imagery to educate and fortify the faithful. Both symbolic depictions, such as the fish, and narrative representations, such as stories from the Old Testament and the New Testament, conveyed the message that faith brings salvation in the context of death.

A significant feature of the enduring spirit of the Christian faith after the fall of the Roman Empire is the manuscript illuminations or hand-decorated pages of text. These copies of the Gospel spread the Good News from the medieval scriptoria to the growing Christian community of believers. The intricate illustrations, with brilliant pigments including gold, literally and figuratively illuminated the sacred text. Scribes used compasses and rulers, mixed pigments with water and egg, and applied the paint to vellum. Of the hundreds of pages in the Book of Kells from the early ninth century, the Incarnation page from the Gospel of St. Matthew demonstrates the power of painted ornamentation to convey the message of Christ. The first three letters of Christ's name (XPI) boldly dominate the page with a swirl of dizzying, delicate interlace.

Icons of the Eastern Orthodox Christians

Meanwhile, the Orthodox Christian communities of the Eastern Byzantine world developed a peculiar form of painted religious communication. Used during religious services to decorate churches, an icon is a consecrated religious painting that displays a holy person or event and is a vehicle to communicate with the spiritual world. For believers, the more famous icons are divine and have miraculous powers. Painted in encaustic, where pigments are bound with hot wax, icons follow traditional formats that remained unchanged for centuries. Icon painters performed a creative act of devotion in making images that closely resembled the original prototype that dated to the time of Christ. Following a period of iconoclasm in the eighth and ninth centuries, when many images were damaged or destroyed, icons once again decorated the sanctuaries of churches along the iconostasis, or screen, separating the congregation from the priest, and also in devotional areas of private homes.

Roman Catholic Altarpieces

The Roman Catholic devotional altarpieces in Western Europe from the fourteenth to the seventeenth centuries also served both the public and private religious realms. Painted on wood or canvas, large paintings of Christ's life, the lives of the saints, or other important scenes from the Bible embellished altars in churches throughout Christendom. Smaller, more intimate versions adorned the private devotional spaces of domestic settings. When panels were doubled and hinged, the resulting diptych could be closed to protect the inner image or opened and set up for prayer. While diptychs became the standard form for the home, three-panel triptychs commonly appeared at church altars. When closed, the outside of the wings protect and hide the interior. When opened, the inside of the wings with portraits of the patrons flank the primary image of the central panel.

Elaborate multipaneled altarpieces called polyptychs include the well-known *Ghent Altarpiece* by Jan van Eyck and the *Isenheim Altarpiece* by Matthias Grünewald. The *Ghent Altarpiece* presents an elaborate celebration of God's sacrifice of his only son, Christ, as the mystic lamb before an array of human and holy witnesses. As a stunning educational and devotional tool for the Flemish viewers of Ghent, the painting encourages the faithful through meticulously convincing realism and brilliant colors. The *Isenheim Altarpiece* reveals another function for religious painting. It was a healing vehicle for the patients in an Alsatian hospital. Sufferers of ergotism found solace in the graphic presentation of the crucified Christ, whose physical torments paralleled their own afflictions.

Frescoes

Altarpieces could be moved, and panels could be opened and closed; however, some medieval, Renaissance, and Baroque artists worked on immovable walls, creating painted frescoes. From Giotto's *Scrovegni Chapel*, through Masaccio's *Brancacci Chapel*, to the famous work of Michelangelo in the Sistine Chapel, frescoes glorified the creation of the world by God, the sacrifice and teachings of Christ, and the role of the saints, especially the revered Mother of God, Mary, in ceilings and walls that also honored the patrons. Narrative scenes, didactic passages, and symbolic presentations occurred in large-scale, enveloping paintings that served as the setting for the most important Christian ritual, the Eucharist, where earthly materials become divine during the Roman Catholic mass.

The Roman Catholic Church depended on the traditional use of images during the Counter Reformation when paintings became a form of fervent propaganda against the northern Protestants who challenged the Roman Catholic domination of European Christianity. Paintings with overtly dynamic, emotional scenes of martyrdom and conversion by Caravaggio and Rubens,

among others, expressed the confident state of the proselytizing and reinvigorated Roman Catholic Church. By recounting dramatic events from the Bible, the paintings encouraged deeper faith among devout Catholics and invited Protestants to return to the Roman Catholic fold.

Modern Examples

The interest in paintings to create an emotional, powerful environment for reflection, contemplation, and connection to God continues today. Important modern examples include the color-field paintings of Mark Rothko in Houston and the mostly black-and-white paintings of Barnett Newman's *Stations of the Cross* in the National Gallery, Washington, D.C. In these cases, abstract or nonobjective paintings of pure pigment with no specific representation invite religious introspection for people of all religious beliefs. More recently, Thomas Kinkade has created popular paintings that speak directly to an American Fundamentalist-Christian community. His colorful pictures of tranquil landscapes with Biblical verses imbedded in the grass, bushes, and walkways assuage believers in an unsure world. Kinkade's global production of imagery brings together the desire to communicate religious sentiments with commercial prosperity for the maker.

Islamic Alternatives to Idolatry

The modern American canvases of unadulterated color of Rothko and Newman resemble much of the Islamic religious arts in the rejection of imagery. The teaching of the prophet Muhammad forbade idolatry, and the Qur'an condemns the figurative representation of Allah or his prophets. Therefore, the finest examples of religious Islamic art are the text-based manuscripts decorated with abstract geometric and floral patterns. To create these painted carpet pages, the artist engaged in an act of piety and devotion by copying the Qur'an in the art of calligraphy. Complex designs join the graceful lines of the Arabic handwriting as an inducement to contemplate the infinite nature of Allah.

Hindu and Buddhist Religious Art

Muslim patrons of religious art and the artists who satisfied the manuscript commissions lived in urban and rural locations from Morocco to Indonesia and from Central Asia to Africa. At the same time, both Buddhism and Hinduism encouraged the production of painting as a form of religious communication in India.

Paintings

In Hinduism, a high point of religious painting occurred during the eighteenth century, when painters moved from the Muslim Mughal capitals to the Hindu courts of the northwest. Local princes commissioned paintings to illustrate Hindu texts, such as the *Ramayana* and the *Bhagavad Gita*, and Hindu poetry, especially narrative scenes about the love of the god Vishnu for human beings. In depictions of the blue-skinned Krishna and his lover, Radha, everyday scenes speak directly to the believer of an intimate, personal relationship with the Hindu deities.

Another manifestation of painting as religious communication in the Hindu culture of India are the mandana, or floor designs, that Indian women paint at the threshold, on the walls, or in the inner rooms of their houses. Carefully prescribed and handed down through generations, these precise drawings are spiritual acts of visual prayer to secure blessings on the household.

Along India's Himalayan border, Buddhism developed in Tibetan monasteries. Here, monks painted traditional magical paintings called *thangkas*, which are portable religious paintings on cloth. Depicting Buddha, a Buddhist deity, or a mandala, *thangkas* are framed in rich, colorful silk brocades to create a presentation of the entire universe for meditation. Rules strictly govern the representation, creation, and use of *thangka* painting. Traditionally, religious patrons commissioned *thangkas* for private meditation; today, however, some *thangkas* are produced in bulk for tourist markets.

Buddhism further developed in China and Japan, where Zen Buddhism became prominent in the fifteenth and sixteenth centuries. In hopes of achieving enlightenment, the samurai class adopted the requirements of prolonged, private meditation (Zen means meditation). Zen priest painters created free, expressive images of teachers, plants, animals, and nature, especially landscape depictions of water, mountains, and clouds, with the rough, simple brushstrokes of black ink on hanging scrolls. By focusing on the spontaneous images, believers focused on the transience of the spirit and of life, the unity of all things, and the spiritual identity of all things as a means of achieving enlightenment.

Australia's Aboriginal Painting Tradition

Humankind's desire to connect with the spiritual realm perseveres in the painting tradition of the aboriginal people of Australia. Paintings of the Dreamtime refer to a past before memory or experience, to a time of the creators and other supernatural beings. By depicting the Rainbow Serpent, for example, aboriginal artists create a link with the spirits of the past that continues today.

In both public arenas, predominately in Christian settings, and in private spheres, as in the Zen monasteries, painting has been and continues to be an important means of religious communication.

VALERIE LIND HEDQUIST

See also Art

Further Reading

Addiss, S. (1989). *The art of Zen: Painting and calligraphy by Japanese monks, 1600–1925*. New York: Abrams.

Baxendall, M. (1972). *Painting and experience in fifteenth-century Italy: A primer in the social history of pictorial style*. Oxford, UK: Clarendon.

Blair, S. S., & Brown, J. M. (1994). *The art and architecture of Islam 1250–1800*. New Haven, CT: Yale University Press.

Blurton, T. R. (1993). *Hindu art*. Cambridge, MA: Harvard University Press.

Farr, C. (1994). *The Book of Kells: Its function and audience*. London: British Museum.

Hayum, A. (1989). *The Isenheim altarpiece: God's medicine and the painter's vision* (Princeton essays on the arts). Princeton, NJ: Princeton University Press.

Lane, B. G. (1984). *The altar and the altarpiece: Sacramental themes in early Netherlandish painting*. New York: Harper & Row.

Martin, L. (2002). *Sacred doorways: A beginner's guide to icons*. Orleans, MA: Paraclete Press.

Minor, V. H. (1999). *Baroque and rococo: Art & culture*. New York: Abrams.

Weidner, M. (Ed.). (1994). *Latter days of the law: Images of Chinese Buddhism, 850–1850*. Lawrence: Spencer Museum of Art, University of Kansas.

Pamphlets

Brief printed texts, published on inexpensive paper and produced in successive runs as the market warranted their reissue, have been a mainstay of print publication in Europe since the late fifteenth century. The precise form of pamphlets is difficult to define, since the format varies while the purpose remains the same: providing readers with texts that can be produced quickly at little cost, and delivering opinion, argument, or amusement to suit current interest. Pamphlets have been among the most powerful genres of print for shaping public discourse on political matters, religion, and science.

The undeniable attraction of pamphlets for authors and producers has always been their low expense and expediency. Whereas periodical publications such as journals and newspapers require a sustained capital outlay and a constant stream of information, pamphlets are able to respond to particular issues and demand, and therefore quickly recoup investment by delivering to a targeted audience. Pamphlet production did not require subscription but appealed to the trade of the hawker or peddler, the street vendor who acted as intermediary and in whose interest it was to sell product promptly. The low cost of production relied on the brevity of the text (allowing printers to keep type set or to quickly reassemble type for subsequent editions), the use of low-quality paper, and cheaply produced woodcuts.

Pamphlets easily changed hands among readers, and thrived on public readings in taverns, homes, and clubs. Because they were low-technology productions, pamphlets were easily illustrated with block prints or metal-plate engravings on separate plates that were stitched in after printing. Illustrations typically appear on the first page or cover page of pamphlets to enhance sales by attracting passersby, to illustrate the content of the pamphlet, and to assist in teaching if the pamphlet was used as an instructional device, as it often was.

"Tract" is a term that has often been used to refer to brief, ephemeral items such as four- or eight-page religious tracts. But in the seventeenth and eighteenth centuries the term also referred to treatises of much greater length on a variety of topics, ranging from philosophy and natural science to political discourses and theological disquisitions. Pamphlets, however, have more consistently been the brief, quickly produced, and inexpensive items that relied on a ready market of readers. Therefore, while the terms can be synonymous, the use of the word "pamphlet" should not be reduced to "tract" but understood as a subcategory of the larger classification of tracts.

This essay will treat the pamphlet as a print artifact engaged in a mass-culture reception and will follow historical lines and focus on Christianity in Europe and North America and the mission efforts of Protestants in Asia. It is important to acknowledge, however, that brief printed texts are both far more pervasive and far older outside the Christian West. Korean, Chinese, and Japanese use of block-printed texts of sacred and literary character were used many centuries before Gutenberg enabled the explosion of print in Western Europe. But pamphlets are defined here in terms of a brief format derived from the Latin codex; in other words, a booklet produced via a moveable-type printing process, designed for mass circulation and consumption, and keyed as a print commodity to the currency of controversy and persuasion, the enduring market for devotional classics and instruction, or the growing desire for literary entertainment.

Reformation

The history of Christianity since the early church is a history of theological debate and controversy. The Protestant Reformation was no different in respect of trenchant disagreement over matters of doctrine and ecclesiastical practice than the preceding millennium. But the political alignments, the emergence of nation-states, and the use of the press augmented the Reformation into a controversy of seismic proportions. Cheaply printed texts, published in the vernacular language (local dialects of German, English, or French and a host of other European languages) as well as the learned languages (Greek and Latin), and widely distributed among popular audiences took the recondite matters of theology to the street and public house, where print acquired the unprecedented role of mediating public opinion. Free cities and the domains of princes and dukes in the German territories, for instance, looked to the circulation of printed texts to sway popular opinion on behalf of the Catholic or the Lutheran party.

The increasing power of public opinion would have been inconceivable without pamphlet publications. Although probably less than half of the population could read, pamphlets were read aloud and passed from hand to hand, informing public discourse, spawning virulent replies from opponents, and sparking "paper wars" that generated public heroes and celebrated clashes among the representatives of the papacy and the Evangelical party. Quite often pamphlets, broadsides, and chapbooks were illustrated with the image of Luther or other popular preachers and antagonists on both sides of the religious debates of the day.

Theological Polemics

Whether or not the early Reformation truly produced a robust public sphere—a discourse in which free agents defined themselves and practiced a freedom of choice and self-determination by relying on the printed circulation of thought—is a matter of debate among scholars of the Reformation. It may be that the primary effect of print and printed imagery was to solidify and maintain group loyalties among those who had already made up their minds. Certainly this seems to be the case among Protestant polemicists during the seventeenth and eighteenth centuries on the Continent and in England. Already in the 1530s, pamphlets, books, broadsides, and sermons poured forth without end to address issues like antinomianism, the Trinity, and the authority of the Scriptures. Issues built around the subtle distinction of theological doctrines invited print as a public manner of clarifying differences. The fact that such distinctions mattered because they held considerable implications for the political patronage and social order of the Reformation only intensified the amount and significance of print.

Other debates that relied fundamentally on the press were free will and predestination, especially as it was waged in England between Wesleyans and orthodox Calvinists. Such paper wars typically attended and articulated struggles between ecclesiastical rivals. Pamphlets appeared in close reply to one another from opposing parties. Once again, if rather few were persuaded to change their views by the flurry of print, the exchange served to clarify differences and publicize loyalties.

As a form of mass media, polemical pamphlets focused debate, organized opposing parties, cultivated relationships among adherents, and sorted out leaders and followers among writers and readers. In other words, the primary function of printed polemics was the structuring of discourse, from which emerged related forms of cultural organization.

Amusement and Instruction

In the turbulence of attack and retaliation, it is easy to overlook entirely different uses of pamphlets—uses that were no less important for the social meanings and cultural work of print. At the same time that Protestants and Catholics were deploying pamphlets to shore up opposition and support for their partisan concerns, printers and booksellers were busy developing alternative forms of print commerce. Primers, especially illustrated primers, were developed in the seventeenth century in Europe and in North America for the instruction of children. As brief as twelve or eighteen pages, these pamphlets provided model sentences and taught the alphabet by linking letter to image and to rhyming sentence. Short children's books appeared with increasing frequency in the late eighteenth century in North America and boomed in the first half of the nineteenth.

As Tessa Watt (1991) and Margaret Spufford (1982) have noted, by the end of the seventeenth century in England, the "chapbook" or small book or pamphlet of tales or religious subjects (circa 24 pages) began to replace the ballad as the most pervasive form of inexpensive print commodity (Watt 1991, 259), a development which closely followed the rise of literacy rates. Narratives based on romances about King Arthur, ballads on Robin Hood, merry tales, and books of riddles were among the inexpensive literary products in the form of pamphlets capitalizing on the expansion of nonelite readers. In seventeenth-century France, inventories indicate a comparable range of genres in popular print (Chartier 1987, 175–178). Religious books and tracts competed in this market and enjoyed the steady success of classics, which were increasingly excerpted in shorter editions for wider consumption. Pamphlets were commonly generated as more marketable abbreviations of longer originals.

Systematic Benevolence and Global Missions

In late eighteenth-century England, Evangelical Protestants combined the strengths of print in instruction, entertainment, and commerce to produce on an unprecedented scale books and pamphlets for children in the new institution of the Sunday school, as well as short tracts or pamphlets for distribution in public, as a means of evangelization. Evangelicals considered the secular print trade to be their primary rival and the principal venue of vice. Inexpensive and short tracts were developed as the means of competing head to head with secular print. In addition to endorsing parliamentary measures to ban Sunday newspapers (an initiative that many Church of England clergy also supported), Evangelicals deliberately sought to displace their competitors by selling their tracts to hawkers at lower rates and by producing tracts and handbills specially intended for consumption on the streets among children and the unchurched.

The Religious Tract Society, formed in London in 1799, quickly developed a highly articulated range of tracts that were targeted at diverse groups such as drunkards, backsliders, infidels, swearers, Catholics, laborers, prisoners, and soldiers. Supporters were encouraged to carry tracts with them at all times and offer an appropriate one to individuals they encountered. Urban groups considered problematic by middle-class moralists and clergy—immigrants, laboring classes, youth, the poor—were the special targets of tract distribution.

The short religious tract was praised by the Tract Society for its ability to go where preachers and evangelists could not; to "speak" in their stead; to lie dormant until such time as it could deliver its message; and to pass from hand to hand until it met with the reader or hearer for whom it was providentially intended. The medium was ideally adapted to its purpose and message. The preached Word of God was effectively translated into sacred information that could be piped out across the countryside, nation, and world by the emerging communication networks and by the new Evangelical institutions that made special use of tracts.

The same group of British Evangelicals that formed the Religious Tract Society had also founded the London Missionary Society (1795) and shortly after established the British and Foreign Bible Society (1804). Print was a fundamental investment for this group, which very successfully exported its organizations and commitment to print to North America, where the American Tract Society was formed in 1825 and operated on the template provided by the British organization.

Moreover, both British and American tract and Bible producers wasted no time in translating their publications into a growing host of languages and sending them to mission fields. Tracts or pamphlets allowed missionaries to tailor evangelism to certain language groups and to reach beyond the limits faced by evangelists, such as facility with languages or the physical restrictions placed on missionaries by local rulers. Therefore, the tract became a fundamental tool in global missions. Baptist missionary Adoniram Judson never entered the temple district in Rangoon, Burma, without a stack of tracts to distribute among Burmese Buddhists as he preached. In a letter of 1831 to his printer, Judson stated that he gave away between forty and fifty tracts each day (Wayland 1854, 1:552). Evangelical tracts also helped fuel messianic revolution in nineteenth-century China (Spence 1996, 18–22).

The suitability of the pamphlet to the Evangelical ideology of print, in which the spoken word passed seamlessly into the printed text for purpose of mass production and universal dissemination, has kept the genre in use to the present day. Such mainstays of tract production as the American Tract Society and the Society for the Promoting of Christian Knowledge still exist, and tracts are still produced by the American Bible Society, as well as a large number of independent religious organizations. The medium's durability has even suggested itself to adaptation in radio and television advertisements and short narratives, and it has recently crossed over to the Internet.

David Morgan

See also Journalism; Media

Further Reading

Chartier, R. (1987). *The cultural uses of print in early modern France* (L.G. Cochrane, Trans.). Princeton, NJ: Princeton University Press.

Edwards, M. U., Jr. (1994). *Printing, propaganda, and Martin Luther*. Berkeley: University of California Press.

Ford, P. L. (Ed.). (1897). *The New England primer: A history of its origins and development.* New York: Dodd, Mead.

Gaustad, E. S. (Ed.). (1972). *American Tract Society documents 1824–1925.* New York: Arno Press.

Lowther Clarke, W. K. (1959). *The history of the S.P.C.K.* London: SPCK.

Morgan, D. (1999). *Protestants and pictures: Religion, visual culture, and the age of American mass production.* New York: Oxford University Press.

Nord, D. (1984). The Evangelical origins of mass media in America. *Journalism Monographs,* 1–30.

Religious Tract Society. (1820). *Proceedings of the first twenty years of the Religious Tract Society.* London: Printed for the Society by Benjamin Bensley.

Schantz, M. (1997). Religious tracts, Evangelical religion, and the market revolution in antebellum America. *Journal of the Early Republic, 17*(3), 425–466.

Scribner, R. W. (1994). *For the sake of simple folk: Popular propaganda for the German Reformation.* Oxford, UK: Clarendon Press.

Spence, J. (1996). *God's Chinese son: The Taiping heavenly kingdom of Hong Xiuquan.* New York: Norton.

Spufford, M. (1982). *Small books and pleasant histories: Popular fiction and its readership in seventeenth-century England.* Athens: University of Georgia Press.

Sweet, L. (Ed.). (1993). *Communication and change in American religious history.* Grand Rapids, MI: Eerdmans.

Watt, T. (1991). *Cheap print and popular piety, 1550–1640.* Cambridge, UK: Cambridge University Press.

Wayland, F. (1854). *A memoir of the life and labors of the Rev. Adoniram Judson, D.D.* 2 vols. Boston: Phillips, Sampson; London: Nisbet.

Papyrus

Growing in shallow lakes or marshes, particularly near the Nile River in Egypt, the papyrus plant reached a height of 12–16 feet. Its stalk was long and without joints, with a thickness of up to six inches in circumference. Over the millennia Egyptians employed this plant in a variety of ways: for sandals, ropes, sails, mats, light boats, and baskets. Tradition even claims that when the baby Moses was placed in the Nile River, he was put into a basket made from papyrus. For purposes of communication, however, the papyrus plant was important because it was the source of a writing material so significant that the English word *paper* is etymologically related to it. Although papyrus was used from as early as 2600 BCE, it was particularly important for ancient Christianity, standing as the most important

medium for the transmission of the earliest manuscripts of the New Testament.

Production and Characteristics of Papyrus Scrolls

Because papyrus was so light and durable, it is not surprising that it was Egypt's greatest export. In the first century CE the ancient historian Pliny the Elder valued written sources so much that he referred to papyrus as that upon which "the immortality of human beings depends." In *Natural History* XIII (Warmington 1968, 68–83), Pliny described how papyrus was prepared and used for writing material. Thin strips were cut from the white pith of the stalk of the papyrus plant; they were laid next to each other vertically, and then another layer of the same was placed horizontally on top (i.e., at right angles to the first). These layers were pressed, pounded, and crushed together, and after they dried in the sun, they were then smoothed with ivory or shell.

A papyrus sheet was approximately the same size as a standard piece of typing paper, 10 by 7 inches, but could be as large as 13 by 9 inches. Pliny notes that twenty such sheets would be glued together for a typical 15-foot book roll (Latin, *volumen,* from the Latin word *volvere,* meaning "to roll"). Rolls could be as large as 35 feet in length, but there are some much longer. The reign of Rameses II is described in the longest extant roll: the 133-foot-long Harris Papyrus in the British Museum.

Because the outside of the papyrus could be damaged when unrolled, writing was generally only on the inside of a scroll, on the horizontal side of the papyrus. The text was arranged in columns and separated by blank spaces: The same layout that is followed in most modern books. At the same time, opisthographs, scrolls with writing on both sides, are described both in Christian texts, such as Revelation 5:1, and in pagan literature, such as the writings of Pliny in which he describes how he left his nephew 160 opisthographs.

As a writing substance, papyrus was not as durable as parchment (animal skin) and could not be used repeatedly. Unlike parchment, however, it would not become puckered and uneven, nor—as Galen the ancient physician noted—would papyrus strain the eyes as much as shiny parchment.

Preservation of Papyri

Papyrus came into widespread use from the time of Alexander of Macedon (the mid-fourth century BCE) on, although it had been used for millennia up until that time. Cheap coffins frequently were made of discarded sheets of papyrus covered with plaster (like papier-mâché), and a number of papyri have survived in that form. Although most texts in Egyptian religion were inscribed on tomb walls or *stelae*, the funerary text known as *The Book of the Dead* was preserved and beautifully decorated on papyrus. This book—consisting largely of magical spells and formulas—was written in cursive hieroglyphs on rolls of papyrus that were buried in the coffin with the deceased.

Although there is evidence that papyrus use was widespread throughout the Near East, few of the extant documents have been found outside of Egypt. Papyrus was durable, but it was weakened by both excessive moisture and dryness, so most papyrus documents have been destroyed by natural conditions. Only in Upper Egypt have a significant number been preserved. Some papyri survived because they were buried in coffins or stored in clay jars. Other papyri have been preserved through their being buried in trash piles. Similarly, some of the Dead Sea Scrolls were preserved when covered accidentally under layers of bat dung.

The great majority of the extant papyri—thousands of them—are documentary papyri, or writings from everyday life: Private letters, deeds, wills, and invitations are some typical genres. The discovery of these papyri, particularly within the past 150 years, has been of great help to scholars in illuminating unusual grammar and syntax challenges within the New Testament. These papyri also tell about ancient life and social history and they give depth of understanding to the sorts of individuals described in the New Testament. These papyri have also highlighted that the koine Greek used in the New Testament was not a unique form of the language but was a style characteristic of everyday language.

In addition to documentary papyri, there are over 3,000 literary papyri and over 600 biblical and patristic papyri. The oldest New Testament manuscript extant today is the Rylands Papyrus, found in Egypt and dated to around 125 CE. This fragment—part of a papyrus codex—contains John 18:31–33 and 37–38.

Significance of Papyrus Codices for Christianity

In *Empire and Communications*, Harold Innis argues that empires are shaped by the media which they find normative. The ancient empires which relied on stone and clay (or other media which are difficult to transport)

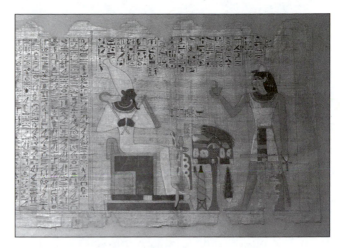

Egyptian papyrus with images.
Courtesy of Four by Three Interactive/istockphoto.com.

tended to be rigid and tradition-oriented. When papyrus came to be more widely used, this allowed for the expansive nature of the Roman Empire. As a result, tradition-based religions came to find themselves competing with more portable religions, like Mithraism and Christianity. Furthermore, as the large number of Greek magical papyri indicates, mysticism, magic, and religious practices which had been socially ostracized came to have a new life. In addition, as religious perspectives spread throughout the empire, syncretism shaped old religious practices and created new ones, bringing together Greek religions, Egyptian religions, and Judaism.

Throughout the Roman Empire, the portability of papyrus benefited the outreach of no religion more than that of Christianity. Even though papyrus scrolls were more transportable than previous media, once Christians came to use papyrus codices, they were able to share their scripture in more efficient and effective ways while traveling.

By the first century BCE, the codex had developed. Like our modern books, codices were composed of folded sheets of papyrus or parchment bound together on one edge. Codices were frequently seen as less expensive than scrolls, more efficient (with writing on both sides of the page), more convenient (with their being held in one hand and with no rolling required), more compact (for people who traveled), and—perhaps—easier to reference. Codices allowed longer texts to be easily kept in one volume and they allowed a number of shorter texts to be stored together. Papyrus 46, for instance, contains all of Paul's letters, though the letters would have taken up at least two rolls if they had been in scroll form.

The papyrus codex was characteristic of early Christianity. Of those biblical manuscripts that came before Constantine (c. 311 CE), about 85 percent were written on papyrus, with the rest on parchment. About a dozen were on rolls—the typical book form of Judaism and classical antiquity—and around ninety had the form of a codex. What makes those latter numbers significant is their contrast with Greek books. Almost all of the Christian books in the first two centuries were in the form of a codex. However, during that same time period, more than 98 percent of the Greek books were scrolls.

Jews transmitted their scripture in parchment or leather scrolls. Pagans used papyrus scrolls. Perhaps because of convenience or because of an interest in a distinctive self-identity, Christians steered away from the use of scrolls and, by using the medium of papyrus codices, asserted the importance of the form of the modern-day book. As mentioned above, Pliny the Elder described papyrus as that upon which the "the immortality of human beings depends." Although he meant the phrase rhetorically, theologically the first Christians could well have agreed.

CRAIG WANSINK

Further Reading

Bagnall, R. S. (1995). *Reading papyri, writing ancient history.* New York: Routledge.

DeHamel, C. (2001). *The book: A history of the Bible.* New York: Phaidon Press.

Innis, H. (1950). *Empire and Communications.* Toronto: University of Toronto Press.

Judge, E. A. (1990). Papyri. In E. Ferguson (Ed.), *Encyclopedia of early Christianity* (pp. 686–691). New York: Garland.

Lightfoot, N. (2003). *How we got the Bible* (3rd ed.). Grand Rapids, MI: Baker Books.

Metzger, B. M. (1968). *The text of the New Testament: Its transmission, corruption, and restoration* (2nd ed.). New York: Oxford University Press.

Metzger, B. M. (2003). *The New Testament: Its background, growth, & content* (3rd ed.). Nashville, TN: Abingdon Press.

Parkinson, R. B., et al. (1995). *Papyrus.* Austin: University of Texas Press.

Pestman, P. W. (1994). *The new papyrological primer* (revised). Leiden, The Netherlands: E. J. Brill.

Reynolds, L. D., & Wilson, N. G. (1974). *Scribes and scholars: A guide to the transmission of Greek and Latin literature* (2nd ed.). New York: Oxford University Press.

Turner, E. G. (1980). *Greek papyri: An introduction* (revised). Oxford, U.K.: Clarendon Press.

Persuasion

Persuasion is a mode of communication by which speakers or writers act as advocates or critics of a point of view or an opinion. The persuader develops a strategy of argument of either a positive or negative nature in order to convince listeners or readers of either the truthfulness or the falsity of premises advanced. The issues of urgency, clarity, or possible consequences may be an integral part of the presentation. The objective may be wholly or partly intellectual, or may press a course of action or seek to dissuade one from such. People see persuasion pervading every area of life—all the way from formal debate, political speeches, and religious discourse to ad hoc conversation on any issue. Everyone is a persuader.

The three great monotheistic religions are all champions of persuasion with respect to their founding documents. On Fridays in the Muslim mosque, the prayer leader shares a *khutbah* (sermon) in which he discourses on necessary responses to the Qur'an, often inciting and arousing the passions of the faithful. It is not difficult to see the roots of Islam in Judaism and Christianity.

In Judaism the rabbi or teacher stands in the tradition of Moses giving his great hortatory declamations in his farewell discourse, as found in Deuteronomy; of Joshua as he pled with Israel, "Choose this day who it is you will serve" (24:15, NIV); or of the prophet Elijah when on Mount Carmel he strongly urged the people, "How long will you waver between two opinions? If the Lord is God, follow him; but if Baal is God, follow him" (2 Kings 18:21, NIV).

As the foundation of its discourse, Christianity also draws on the alleged historical facts on which Christian doctrine and communication are based. Early Christianity was quick to adopt Greek and Roman rhetoric as the vehicle for the transmission of its convictions and its theology.

Greek and Roman Contributions to Persuasion

The ancient Greeks were more self-consciously reflective on the nature of persuasive discourse than perhaps any other people. While Greek rhetoric and oratory have their roots in Homer, it was the rise of the city-states that gave new importance to skills in communication and persuasion. Suasion technique is always critical in a democratic or egalitarian society.

Both Socrates and Plato, with their elitist and monarchical inclinations, generally disdain rhetoric and persuasion. Plato, indeed, dismisses them as "flattery." In *Phaedrus* he analyzes the three ways in which language affects people. However, he is not alone in expressing considerable reservation about the widespread abuse and misuse of persuasion (*Phaedrus* 1952, 260–63).

Aristotle in his *Rhetoric* takes the position that "rhetorical study, in its strict sense, is concerned with the modes of persuasion. Persuasion is clearly a sort of demonstration, since we are most fully persuaded when we consider a thing to be demonstrated" (1.1). In fact Aristotle defines rhetoric as "the faculty of discovering in the particular case what are the available means of persuasion." Aristotle says the persuader uses three avenues of approach to his auditors (1.2):

1. Argument for the intellect (i.e., the skilled marshaling of facts and logic). The communicator must beware of vague generalities, unsupported assertions, and faulty reasoning. General statements need to be advanced and extrapolated with accurate inferences.

2. Appeal to the emotions (i.e., the inescapable necessity of confronting the reality of feeling, mood, and predisposition). Aristotle identifies a dozen significant emotions.

3. Assurance of character. Fascinatingly, this approach is the most indispensable for Aristotle, who argues that people believe good men more fully and readily than others.

Christian Convictions and Persuasion

Jesus Christ, the source of Christianity, is, as presented in the four Gospels, a consummate persuader. He argued that the Holy Spirit would, after His departure, "convict the world of sin, righteousness and judgment" (John 16:8ff, NIV). Burton L. Mack and Vernon K. Robbins argue persuasively for the relevance of Hellenistic rhetorical theory for compositional analysis of the Gospel logia (Mack and Robbins 1989). One would not have to subscribe to every nuance of their position to feel the force of their view that New Testament scholars Martin Dibelius and Rudolf Bultmann went too far in ignoring Greco-Roman education and rhetoric. Every aspect of the reporting of Jesus and His words seems intentional, including the identification of the audience in ninety percent of the logia (the words attributed to Christ).

The apostle Paul wrote insightfully about rhetorical style, with a pronounced preference for the plain style. It was said of him that "he persuaded men" (Acts 18:13, NIV), and he clearly intended to persuade his hearers (2 Corinthians 5:11, NIV). Repeatedly in the Acts of the Apostles the Greek word *peitho* (meaning to move or induce to take action) is used. So, Paul and Barnabas "urged them to continue" (Acts 13:43, NIV); Paul reasoned "trying to persuade Jews and Greeks" (Acts 18:4, NIV); Paul argued "persuasively about the kingdom of God" (Acts 19:8, NIV); Agrippa asked Paul, "Do you think in such a short time you can persuade me?" (Acts 26:28, NIV); Paul declared the Gospel, "trying to convince them about Jesus" (Acts 28:23, NIV). Persuasion was of the essence in early Christian discourse.

St. Augustine's (354–430) *On Christian Doctrine* (327) is an early effort to analyze the relationship between Christian teaching and the Greco-Roman rhetorical system. On the whole, Augustine, who did not read Greek but read Aristotle through Cicero's Latin translation, highly valued diverse styles in presentation and gave priority to careful interpretation of the Scriptural data. Of all speech, he urged that communicators aim for "perspicuity (clarity), beauty and persuasiveness" (Augustine 1952, IV.26.56). Persuasive force was a critical factor, although the work of the Holy Spirit was seen to be determinative in gaining compliance with the Christian truth claim.

While a small cadre have inveighed against any dependence on extra-Biblical rhetoric (such as Francois de Fenelon (1651–1715), the French rhetorician; Peter Ramus (1515–1572), so influential on the Puritans; and Edwin Hatch (1829–1889), who argued in *The Influence of Greek Ideas and Usages on the Christian Church* that Greek rhetoric had killed the Christian sermon), successive generations of Christian communicators have essentially embraced a classical rhetorical theory, with persuasion looming large in their thinking. Dutch humanist Desiderius Erasmus (1467–1536) is a case in point, and Philip Melanchthon (1497–1560), systematician to Martin Luther (1483–1546), used Cicero as his model. Richard Whately (1787–1863), scholar of logic who greatly influenced both Cardinal John Henry Newman (1801–1890) and the Anglican master-preacher F. W. Robertson (1816–1853), sought persuasive testimony along with reasonable and logical proof in his assault upon unbelief in Great Britain. Clergyman John Witherspoon (1723–1794) was active in both colonial politics and in teaching rhetoric and persuasion at what became Princeton University. John Quincy Adams (1767–1848), sixth president of the United States, launched his career as Harvard College's first professor of Rhetoric and Oratory with forty lectures articulating

Persuasion in the New Testament

Acts 13:43, Paul and Barnabas urged them to continue in the grace of God.

Acts 18:4, Paul reasoned, trying to persuade Jews and Greeks.

Acts 19:8, Paul argued persuasively about the kingdom of God.

Acts 26:28, Agrippa asked Paul, Do you think in such a short time you can persuade me?

Acts 28:23, Paul declared the gospel, trying to convince them about Jesus.

2 Corinthians 5:11, Paul said, Since we know what it is to fear God, we persuade men.

the primacy of persuasive discourse. The history of persuasion is striking.

Ethical Concerns about Persuasion

Agrippa does not stand alone as one somewhat skeptical of the Christian communicator's efforts to persuade (Acts 26:28, NIV). An increasingly pervasive skepticism in modern life about persuasion sees it as essentially seduction and trickery. The cynic feels "had" and sees the skilled debater as a manipulator, an enemy of the truth. Yet seeking to change someone's mind on an issue is legitimate. "Preaching without convincing is like cooking a meal which no one eats" (Berkley 1986, 10). Trust is absolutely critical in communication. A strategy of building bridges of appeal and understanding to the audience is essential. The communicator speaks for a verdict, seeking to move men and women to a decision. Application of the truth as the communicator sees it necessitates persuasive speech.

The persuasive communicator must seek to make her or his case, even though the corrosion of traditional morality, the disparagement of virtue, and the erosion of language makes the task more difficult. What a twenty-first century observer describes as "the waning of cultural vitality" is all too apparent. The sense of obligation has been reduced, and the deferral of gratification is unappealing. A utilitarian morality of self-interest predominates. But there are limits to be observed, and the communicator must be aware of the line between persuasion and manipulation and avoid crossing it. Em Griffin has gone right to the heart of the matter when he insists that "any persuasive effort which restricts another's freedom to choose...is wrong" (1976, 136). Three safeguards must be considered:

1. Fairness and honesty must control the communicator's use of materials. Professor of speech Otis M. Walter suggests that this safeguard includes "statistics, hypothetical examples, analogies, summaries, testimonies and visual aids." (Walter 1982, 17–33)

2. The communicator must watch her or his motives. Embellishment and elaboration are perilous. An obsession with results may lead to exaggeration. The end does not justify the means.

3. The communicator must guard her or his use of methods. Coercion and too heavy-handed an approach constitute assault. The communicator must deplore the demagogue who will not take "no" for an answer. To bulldoze free moral agency is reprehensible. Everett L. Shostrom, communications educator, pleads for honesty and transparency rather than deception and phoniness (Shostrom 1967, 50–51). Tunnel vision and concealment lead only to cynicism and distrust.

Donald R. Sunukjian, a professor of preaching, well argues that while competence is an important factor in perceived credibility, even more important is the conviction that the speaker has the hearer's best interests at heart. A blend of assertiveness, softness, and reasonableness seem desirable; warm facial gestures and pleasant tones help. The listener knows if the speaker really cares and speaks because he or she loves him or her. It is perceived the speaker loves the listener too much to use him or her. Vance Packard, popular social critic of the 1950s and 1960s, gave the classic demonstration of the great dangers in persuasion. Everyone has been persuaded to do regrettable and irrational things. Persuasion is thus in a sense both terrifying and exciting to one moving into the marketplace of ideas and seeking to counter false ideology and the tyranny of lies with what is understood to be the truth.

The Canons of Persuasion

The basis of persuasion is the possession and mastery of factual data. Yet persuasion involves more than the stating of facts. Emotion and motivation are strong movers. The communicator's good humor can relax and gain rapport with the listener. Robert Cialdin (1984), professor of speech, conducted a study on influence that suggests these rules of persuasion:

1. The rule of reciprocation. The communicator creates a sense of obligation that causes the listener to want to repay a favor.

2. The rule of consistency and commitment. People are bound to past decisions.

3. The law of social proof. Most people tend to imitate rather than to initiate.

4. The rule of liking. People are more easily persuaded in a warm atmosphere.

5. The rule of authority. Titles and the trappings of power move people to compliance.

6. The rule of scarcity. The limited-number technique always gets customers.

If these rules describe human vulnerabilities, to what degree should religious communicators cater to these weaknesses in the interest of getting commitments for their messages?

The apostle Paul became "all things to all men that he might by all means save some," but at the same time he was deeply concerned not to adulterate or dilute the Gospel which he preached (1 Corinthians 9: 22, 16, NIV). Is there a line religious communicators should not cross in adapting modern marketing and advertising techniques? At what point must the wisdom of this world be challenged? When is the shrewdness of the people of the world acceptable as a model?

The PBS series *The Persuaders* (2004) showed how consumers want to be entertained. Adaptation of these "meant-to-be-subtle strategies" can be seen in the political scene and in religion. How valid is entertainment evangelism? To what extent is entertainment evangelism an oxymoron, especially when considering what is used to win listeners with is what communicators win listeners to? Serious doubts certainly arise.

The Christian communicator is well advised to diversify her or his appeal. The skilled practitioner will have in mind the various conditions among the hearers and regularly distribute the appeal. Psychologist and philosopher William James held that "what holds attention tends to determine action." The false prophet tells the listeners what they want to hear; there can be no growth. The authentic prophet tells the people what they need to hear, but carefully and skillfully; they then can grow.

Persuasion and the Conversion Controversy

A persistent and nagging issue in relation to the use of persuasion in religious discourse has to do with the legitimacy of seeking conversion. Judaism generally processes converts but does not actively seek them. Islam seeks converts but not primarily by persuasion. Many in the mainline denominations disparage any effort to proselytize through any kind of persuasion. Originally, as Lawrence A. Uzzell points out, the term "proselytize" had a positive connotation, as when Gentile converts to Judaism were described as witnesses to the miracle on the Day of Pentecost (Acts 2:11, NIV) and when an early deacon in the church was first a convert from paganism to Judaism and then to Christianity (Acts 6:5, NIV).

Uzzell trenchantly observes: "We live in an age of persuasion, in which we are bombarded by political and commercial messages designed to change our thoughts and actions. The unfavorable term 'proselytism' is reserved for religious persuaders. Phrases such as 'feminist proselytism' or 'environmentalist proselytism' are unknown; it is considered natural, even laudable, for adherents of those secular belief systems to seek converts all over the world, even in cultures where their beliefs are profoundly alien" (2004, October, 14). Some countries have outlawed it, and broad ecumenism sees proselytism as a corruption of the Christian witness. Any effort to gain converts by misrepresentation or coercion is clearly unacceptable. As Uzzell insists, this means of proselytism would be improper persuasion or evangelism.

Religious conservatives would argue that the increasingly imprecise use of the term proselytism can lead to unsound concessions to the religious pluralism and relativism of the twenty-first century by turning society into "a religion-free zone" which is "undisturbed by prophets or saints or even by the memory of them" (Uzzell 2004, October, 15). Believers are to avoid offending unbelievers, but there is little reciprocal obligation for unbelievers. As Uzzell puts it, "In effect the relativists seek selective protectionism in the marketplace of ideas, while continuing to depict themselves as defenders of robust freedom." The issue becomes, Shall religious communicators bend their efforts to suppress persuasion or shall they seek to be more persuasive?

Many Christians feel under the strong mandate of their Lord "to make disciples of all the nations" as well as feel the compulsion of Christian love to share their faith with an appropriate and respectful invitation to respond. Acceptable persuasion can never use an unscrupulous methodology or anything fraudulent or contrived. Advocates of authentic persuasion in a free society must constantly brace themselves against all kinds of exploitation but dedicate themselves to legitimate persuasion in its best and classical sense.

DAVID L. LARSEN

See also Advertising; Public Relations

Further Reading

Aristotle (1952). *Rhetoric*. Chicago: Great Books of the Western World.

Augustine (1952). *On Christian doctrine*. Chicago: Great Books of the Western World.

Berkley, J. D. (Ed.). (1986). *Preaching to convince*. Waco, TX: Word.

Cialdini, R. B. (1984). *Influence: How and why people agree to do things*. New York: Morrow.

Griffin, E. (1976). *The mind changers: The art of Christian persuasion*. Wheaton, IL: Tyndale House.

Hatch, E. (1901). *The influence of Greek ideas and usages on the Christian church*. London: Williams and Norgate.

Larsen, D. L. (1989). *The anatomy of preaching: Identifying the issues in preaching today*. Grand Rapids, MI: Baker.

Mack, B. L. & Robbins, V. K. (1989). *Patterns of persuasion in the Gospels*. Sonoma, CA: Polebridge Press.

Packard, V. O. (1957). *The hidden persuaders*. New York: D. McKay.

Plato (1952). *Phaedrus*. Chicago: Great Books of the Western World.

Shostrom, E. L. (1967). *Man the manipulator: The inner journey from manipulation to actualization*. Nashville, TN: Abingdon.

Sunukjian, D. R. (1982, July–September). The credibility of the preacher. *Bibliotheca Sacra*, 139.

Uzzell, L. A. (2004, October). Don't call it proselytism. *First Things*, 14–16.

Walter, O. M. (1982). *Speaking to inform and persuade* (2nd ed.). New York: Macmillan.

Poetry

Good poetry is like valid prayer: it is pure communication, saying emotionally direct and uncomplicated things in simple and original words, trusting the words will be heard and responded to by the receiver. Certain ways of thinking block pure communication: these may be as various as monolithic myths and symbols from religious dogma, or the pervasive icons of modern advertising. Historically for many believers, the Book of Common Prayer, the Bible, the Torah and the Qur'an were the source texts for poets regarded as holy. In the twentieth century, though, poets had to make themselves famous using media and were forced to compete with music, television, film, and the news industry for public attention. As mass media helped poets assert a public identity, styles in film, photography, and special events shaped modern audience expectations of what constituted poetic form.

Poetry concerned with world religions and universal spiritual themes written for a mass-media audience sought a level of pure communication and a sense of moral proportion. Two aspects of this search for purity and proportion in poetry are themes found in a broad body of classic poetry engaged with ultimate concerns: (1) a search for the beautiful in ordinary, material, everyday objects and (2) a preference for short poetic lines and easy meters and meanings.

The Genesis of Modern Poetry

The genesis of modern and postmodern religious poetry in the West can be traced through movements or schools of writers. They were countercultural, often antimaterialistic and antimilitaristic, concerned about the contradictions between the economy of the material world and the values of the spirit. Among some of the important American groups who wrote poetry with spiritual themes were Imagists (1912–1922), the Harlem Renaissance (1920–1940), Objectivists (1920–1950), and the Beats (1950–1960).

Of course, not all poets worked in schools, and few were "belongers." Most were immersed in their surrounding time and cultures. Many poets wrote as individuals, including G. K. Chesterton (1874–1936), Robert Frost (1874–1963), Robinson Jeffers (1887–1962), Rainer Maria Rilke (1875–1926), Dylan Thomas (1914–1953), Walt Whitman (1819–1892), and William Butler Yeats (1865–1939).

Though there might be a debate as to whether a song lyric ought to be considered a poem, the argument can be made that in modern media songs shape

Selection from *God's Trombones* by James Weldon Johnson

James Weldon Johnson (1871–1938) was an accomplished African-American poet and novelist. Below is an extract from his poem "The Creation," part of his best-known work of poetry: *God's Trombones: Seven Negro Sermons in Verse* (1927).

And God stepped out on space,
And he looked around and said:
I'm lonely—
I'll make me a world.

And far as the eye of God could see
Darkness covered everything,
Blacker than a hundred midnights
Down in a cypress swamp.

Then God smiled,
And the light broke,
And the darkness rolled up on one side,
And the light stood shining on the other,
And God said: That's good!

the audience or readers' ideas about what a poem ought to be, how it should sound more than how it should look. The idea of poetry in the oral tradition spans historical epochs and many religious cultures: the wandering bard who recited poetry was part prophet, part preacher and worked on the social periphery. In contrast, the modern songwriter is located centrally in mainstream consumer culture through the popular music industry.

Printed poems compete with mass-market magazines, news, and advertising culture: poetry rooted in print culture first experimented with graphics and layout of typography in a literary economy of punctuation, capitalization (as in the poems by e. e. cummings, 1894–1962), and how the language looked visually on the page.

Poetry for a Mass Audience

Seventeenth-century "metaphysical" poets (e.g., George Herbert, John Milton, John Donne) were in many cases clergy who wrote for the pious and learned. In the media world of the twentieth century, religious poetry went public and achieved mass-market distribution in print. The mass-media audience between 1890 and 1930 in America thought "poetry" meant the simple rhymes found in advertising jingles, in magazines and newspapers, in radio and film, and on roadside billboards—Burma Shave ads, for instance. The form of poetry, then, has always struggled against "being too highbrow," competing with popular or mass-market culture. Whereas traditional religious poetry had been either autobiographical or for the pious, in the modern era it became both a written mode and a media-driven one; that is, the poem as a product was made popular or sold via publicity and modern marketing savvy.

Poetry, Media, and Industry

The century's first special event using poetry for public relations occurred at the opening of the 1893 Chicago World's Fair, when a chorus of five hundred recited a ceremonial "Ode" written by Harriet Monroe (1860–1936), daughter of a prominent Chicago attorney. She was paid $1,000 for the poem. When the *New York World* published her poem before the event, she sued for violation of copyright, winning $5,000, enough money in 1893 to travel widely. When Harriet returned to Chicago, magazines such as *Ladies' Home Journal* and *The Atlantic*, who were paying $75 per poem, rejected her verse. So she started *Poetry* magazine, which is still in continuous publication today, representing "democracy" in poetry by publishing a broad spectrum of contributors with uneven talents and a religious pluralism suited to a democracy.

Monroe herself was not a very good poet (she is not included in the *Norton Anthology of Modern Poetry*), but her ability to use media to reach an audience and to use PR to market poetry as a civic art launched the medium in the twentieth century. By 1919, nearly twenty-five hundred poems from four to five hundred people arrived in her magazine's office each month. At a time of great awareness of world religions, poems by the Hindu poet Rabindranath Tagore (1861–1941) often were printed, along with the pious sentiments of many people who never wrote a poem before.

Seeing Is Believing

With Harriet Monroe publishing in Chicago; Amy Lowell (1874–1925) working from Boston; and Ezra Pound (1885–1972), an American expatriate, writing in London, a pseudomovement called Imagism began, using media to create a public identity for a few poets who could not get published. Imagists treated photographic scenes constructed through the mind's eye as sacred experiences. Traditionally, epic poetry celebrated the heroic. But Imagists saw "heaven in a grain of sand": looking through the metaphoric lens of the photographer, poets found spiritual substance and poetic meaning in light, color, and juxtaposition of ordinary objects.

Imagism was a way of thinking about how the world should be seen and about how words were arranged as printed objects on a page. Imagist poems resembled the Japanese haiku or the Zen koan (the penetrating question-riddle traditionally posed by the Buddhist monk to the student). For example, the best-known imagist poem is William Carlos Williams's (1883–1962) "The Red Wheelbarrow." It is religious without shouting about belief; rather, the juxtaposition of things in the barnyard illustrate the poet's idea of the holy and the religious intensity placed on objective form that made things seem sacred, like icons.

so much depends
upon
a red wheel
barrow
glazed with rain
water
beside the white
chickens.

What "depends" is the reader's ability to answer the Zen-like riddle. Williams, an East Coast physician, echoed the earlier song style of the Brooklyn newspaperman Walt Whitman in his *Leaves of Grass*, and the short haiku-like verse with a pointed philosophical edge resembled the line length of poems by Emily Dickinson (1830–1886). Poetry is more like a painting than it is like news. The reader is invited to enter the world of the poet and make the imaginary world real by seeing it in a new way.

Monroe claimed she invented Imagism, but Vachel Lindsay (1879–1931), author of "The Gospel of Beauty" and "Johnny Appleseed's Hymn to the Sun," challenged that. He said his poetry was about the "healing of the cities," rather than the healing of individuals, and distributed pamphlets of his "Gospel" poem, walking from Florida to Kentucky in 1906, from New York to Ohio in 1908, and from Illinois to New Mexico in 1912.

Simultaneously, Harlem Renaissance poets drew on the powerful tradition of the Negro spiritual and the experience of the black church: much of the century's most significant spiritual poetry emerged in this community, including James Weldon Johnson's (1871–1938) "The Creation" and "Go Down Death"; Langston Hughes's (1902–1967) "Christ in Alabama"; Countee Cullen's (1903–1946) book, *The Black Christ and Other Poems* (1929); and poetry by Jean Toomer (1894–1967).

Sacred Objects

The Objectivists were another group that stripped poetry down to its barest essentials and animated objects with a sacred voice. The best known were Charles Olson (1910–1970) and Louis Zukofsky (1904–1978). A childlike sense of awe about the holy that is found in the natural world and rhythm arranged musically rather than logically resulted in this style, as in this poem by Zukofsky:

I'm a mosquito
May I bite your big toe? Here's ten dollars
Use it
As you know.

Objectivists looked through a lens with Zen-like concentration on emptiness synonymous with the eternal, tried to locate the human, the finite, within a still shot. They did this while their intended audience was glued to the then-new invention of television, and comic film stars were moving at fast-forward speed.

The Beat Generation

In the West, the Beat Generation poets of the 1950s were the most media savvy of poets, who resisted the cultural assumptions and values of commercial materialism they thought corrupted the American spirit. Though their language was often raw, their quest for purity engaged them with many religions. Among the Beats whose poems were religious were Lawrence Ferlinghetti (1919) and Allen Ginsberg (1926–1997) ("Kaddish," "Howl," and "Supermarket in California)." Each man infused his work with a blend of Hinduism, Hare Krishna, Zen, and self-absorption; women in this group were mostly acolytes.

In a Kentucky Trappist monastery thousands of miles from San Francisco's City Lights bookstore and café that was associated with the Beats, a monk named Thomas Merton (1915–1968), a graduate of Columbia University, wrote that in religious poetry there were two types of poets: those who constructed cathedrals, as in the work of the Italian poet Dante, and those who created movies through poetry, so they evoked the cinema. The poet had to make the audience see the meaning through scenes or clip frames containing memorable characters, locations, and things.

Merton wrote "Cables to the Ace" in 1966–1967, an epic poem about the media: it uses techniques from the Imagists, Objectivists, and Beats. As Merton wrote the longest poem of his career, he wanted to reach the heights of earlier poets such as Homer, Dante, Milton, and also the long poems of T. S. Eliot ("Love Song of J. Alfred Prufrock"), Walt Whitman (*Leaves of Grass*), Allen Ginsberg ("Howl" and *Kaddish*) and Louis Zukovfsky ("A," which was written over a fifty-year period).

He also was thinking of other religious poetry classics such as John Berryman's "Homage to Mistress Bradstreet," William Carlos Williams's "Patterson," Robert Lowell's *Lord Weary's Castle,* and other classic long works of modern poetry expressing the themes of the age: resistance to materialism, a search for the worth of the individual in mass culture, and pure communication with the Divine power or Mystery.

The Effect of the Global Media

The problem of modern mass culture and religious art is that media made it possible for the audiences around the globe to know the same brand names and to think in similar if not identical ways about commercial production. Commercial culture made advertising into a type of global language of brand icons in which there was an economy of beliefs. Poetry never had great audiences; even when schools or movements formed around a philosophy of letters, the group's work was usually short-lived. *Poetry* magazine is the single most enduring cultural product of the era; it consistently exercised inclusiveness without regard for either strict dogma about poetic form or about "correct" thinking about denominational beliefs. The homogenization of global commercial culture through advertising made it increasingly difficult to put original thoughts into new words, making the production at once more difficult, rare, and, because of scarcity, the most privately religious of written media forms.

CLAIRE BADARACCO

See also Literature, Religious; Literature, Sacred

Further Reading

Badaracco, C. (1995). *Trading words: Poetry, typography and illustrated books in the modern literary economy*. Baltimore: The Johns Hopkins University Press.

Harper, M. S. & Walton, A. (2000). *The Vintage book of African American poetry*. New York: Vintage.

Parisi, J. & Young, S. (Eds.). (2002). *The* Poetry *anthology, ninety years of America's most distinguished verse magazine*. Chicago: Ivan R. Dee.

Trapp, J. (Ed.). (1964). *Modern religious poetry*. New York: Harper & Row.

Political Communication

Et tu, Brute? This is perhaps the most famous line of political communication in history. Penned by William Shakespeare in his tragedy *Julius Caesar,* it is what Caesar says to Marcus Brutus after he's been fatally stabbed by conspirators, and it captures much of the essence of the debate over political communication as it has emerged in the United States since the 1980s. It does this in two ways. First, it was a pithy question. In an age of sound-bite journalism, its impact seems ever more contemporary. It joins "Where's the beef?," "There you go again," "Read my lips. No new taxes," "It depends on what the definition of *is* is," and "I voted for it, before I voted against it" as an exemplar of the defining moment. Second, it carries in it the poignancy of betrayal. Much of the political angst of the increasingly partisan nature of American politics is rooted in this sense of inconstancy.

Extracts from Abortion and the Supreme Court: Advancing the Culture of Death

National Conference of Catholic Bishops, November 15, 2000

In 1973, the U.S. Supreme Court decisions *Roe v. Wade* and *Doe v. Bolton* ushered in legalized abortion on request nationwide. By denying protection to unborn children throughout pregnancy, these rulings dealt a devastating blow to the most fundamental human right—the right to life.

In its 1992 *Casey* decision the Court could not muster a majority for the view that *Roe* and *Doe* were rightly decided. Yet the controlling opinion insisted that even if these decisions were wrong, they must stand because Americans have now fashioned their way of life on the availability of abortion.

No more damning indictment of the coarsening effects of Roe on our national character can be imagined. This ruling has helped to create an abortion culture: in which many Americans turn to the destruction of innocent life as an answer to personal, social and economic problems; which encourages many young men to feel no sense of responsibility to take care of the children they helped to create and no loyalty to their child's mother; in which men who do feel responsibility for their children are left helpless to protect them; whose casualties include not only the unborn but the countless thousands of women who have suffered physically, emotionally and spiritually from the deadly effects of abortion; in which fathers, grandparents, siblings, indeed entire families suffer and are forever changed by the loss of a child.

[. . .]

Ultimately this issue is not about "when life begins," or even exclusively about abortion. Modern medicine has brought us face-to-face with the continuum of human life from conception onwards, and the inescapable reality of human life in the womb. Yet our legal system, and thus our national culture, is being pressed to declare that human life has no inherent worth, that the value of human life can be assigned by the powerful and that the protection of the vulnerable is subject to the arbitrary choice of others. The lives of all who are marginalized by our society are endangered by such a trend.

As religious leaders, we know that human life is our first gift from a loving Father and the condition for all other earthly goods. We know that no human government can legitimately deny the right to life or restrict it to certain classes of human beings. Therefore the Court's abortion decisions deserve only to be condemned, repudiated and ultimately reversed.

Building a culture of life in our society will also require efforts reaching beyond legal reform. We rededicate our Church to education, public policy advocacy, pastoral care, and fervent prayer for the cause of human life, as articulated in our *Pastoral Plan for Pro-Life Activities*. In so doing, we hope to help bring an end to the abortion culture in our society. In the words of Pope John Paul II, we hope and pray "that our time, marked by all too many signs of death, may at last witness the establishment of a new culture of life, the fruit of the culture of truth and of love" (*The Gospel of Life*, 77).

Source: United States Conference of Catholic Bishops. (2000). Retrieved December 14, 2005, from http://www.usccb.org/prolife/issues/abortion/culture.htm

When religion is added to the equation (pithiness + poignancy = political points), it complicates matters enormously. Religion is a wild card. There are two reasons. First, there are several religions to be considered, and none of them in the contemporary world are above reproach when it comes to politics. Second, it is extraordinarily difficult to untangle the religious from the political when it comes to determining the actual focus of a message. Groups often use religious cloaks to hide political agendas, and different religions define the relationship between religion and politics in incompatible ways. The question, then, of whether a particular communiqué delivered to an audience is a political claim or manifesto, or whether it is a religious tract or justification, is often in the eyes of the beholder. The rise of the so-called religious right under the influence of Reverend Pat Robertson's Christian Coalition for America, founded in 1989, is perhaps the most well-known example of the amalgamation of politics and religion. The Coalition's original President, Ralph Reed, pioneered the use of direct mail to appeal to Evangelical Christians with its conservative political agenda. During the 2004 election conservative Republican direct mail campaigns were pitted against more liberal Internet-based fund-raising strategies.

At its most basic level, political communication is merely communication about politics. It is easy, seen at this level, to imagine that such communication has been going on from before recorded history. The apostle Paul's simple statement that he was a Roman citizen was even a form of political communication. This declaration triggered political protections that altered the nature of jurisprudence applied to Paul's case before Jewish authority. However, there was little to no sustained attention given to political communication, per se, prior to World War II. Most modern scholars trace the beginning of political communication back only as far as 1960 when the first televised presidential debates were aired. The research around this series of debates between John F. Kennedy and Richard M. Nixon led to the development of political communication as a field of study because of the differences in public perception that emerged between those who saw the first debate on television and those who had only heard it on radio.

In the years following this debate Marshall McLuhan penned his famous aphorism—the medium is the message—which seemed to certify the significance of this perceptual difference. Although there was not another televised debate between presidential contenders until 1976, the aftermath of this debate, the publication of Joe McGinnis's book (*The Selling of the President 1968*) claiming that Nixon's return to the national scene that year had been engineered much like the marketing of soap powder, the voting rights and civil rights movement, the coverage of the 1968 Democratic National Convention in Chicago and especially the antiwar protests against then-President Johnson, and the 1968 riots in the wake of Bobby Kennedy's assassination all contributed to the notion that communication about politics had reached a new level of political impact. It thus seemed appropriate for more scholars to give more sustained attention to what became known as political communication.

As this field of study has matured, scholars have gradually expanded their inquiries to encompass several major questions. Although some of these questions were a matter for examination prior to the development of political communication as a discrete area of inquiry, all of these would now be subsumed under this general rubric. The amount of attention given to each of these areas is subject to ebbs and flows depending on the election cycle and other significant events that attract attention—such as the war on terrorism or international negotiations (such as those concerned with trade or global warming).

Political Communication Issues and the Press

Two main issues have occupied researchers insofar as the press is concerned. These are the questions of whether reporters and the press are guilty of biased reporting on political campaigns and their issues and whether the press sets people's agendas when it comes to considering these issues and deciding for whom to vote in an election. The first of these issues has attracted as much ideologically based debate as it has serious academic work, while the second has largely been an issue for serious scholars of the political process.

However, these two main issues have not captured the entirety of the more popular concerns with political communication. Particularly during the elections in 2000 and 2004 the validity of exit polls as the basis for coverage of election results was raised. In 2004 early exit polls indicated that John Kerry might win the election, but these early polls clearly were not fully representative of voters' sentiments, as George Bush went on to win the presidency. Related to this issue is that of what has been referred to as "horse race" journalism, which is reporting during the campaign season as though it were a horse race. In such a race one candidate or the other will be ahead at particular points of the race, but the leading candidate may not be able to continue his advantage to actually win the race. As journalism has come to rely on the variety of polls taken during the campaign—by such organizations as Roper, Zogby, *USA Today* and other major newspapers, as well as by the broadcasting networks and the candidates own in-house pollsters—the question of whether or not reliance on polls actually replaces more substantive and useful reporting has emerged as a major issue. The horse-race aspect of reporting campaigns has also migrated downward, at first only applied to the race for president, but gradually percolating down to races for state offices.

Political Campaigns and Political Communication

Several issues revolve around the conduct of political campaigns. Many of these issues are associated with these campaigns' use of television and the development of polling organizations. The issues are the role of spin and "spin doctors" in the creation of campaign themes and responses to positions on issues or criticisms emerging from opponents, the crafting of campaign rhetoric, including debate strategies, pithy rejoinders, and political advertising; employment of polling organizations and the use of polls to determine campaign expenditures to manage an election; and the systematic distortion of opponents' views to appeal to voters' fears.

Campaign Contributions and External Advertising

In the United States several attempts have been made since the passage of the Federal Election Campaign Act of 1971 to control the flow of money into the campaign coffers of individual candidates and their sponsoring national committees (Democratic and Republican National Committees, primarily, but also ad hoc organizations such as Richard Nixon's 1972 Committee to Re-Elect the President [CREEP in the parlance of the Watergate scandal]). Each effort has resulted in the discovery of a new loophole that would allow different organizations to spend money to promote or oppose particular candidates. The latest effort, the Bipartisan Campaign Reform Act of 2002 (the so-called McCain-Feingold law) did set stricter limits on the role of political action committees (PACs) in elections, but a new phenomenon, the Section 527 organizations (named for a section of the Internal Revenue Code), arose to challenge both candidates—Kerry by the Vietnam Veterans for Truth that challenged his war record and Bush by MoveOn.org and others that questioned the accomplishments of his first term as president.

Both presidential campaigns claimed that they did not control, or necessarily endorse, the activities of these groups. Their existence, along with the more traditional PACs, labor unions, and business groups, has made it increasingly difficult to control campaign-related advertising. In the 2004 election, advertisements put together by the campaigns themselves carried an official approval from the candidates. The requirements placed on campaigns by campaign finance laws, which stipulate conditions to be met to receive matching funds generated by the Campaign Fund Act, decreased in significance, however, as an increasing amount of money spent on behalf of candidates was raised and spent by organizations external to the major parties and their nominated candidates.

Religion and Political Communication

Religious differences can contribute to the volatility of politics. In Islamic countries many people do not see any difference between the practice of religion and the practice of politics. The *sharia*, based on the Qur'an, contains the rules by which a Muslim society is organized and governed, and it provides the means to resolve conflicts among individuals and between the individual and the state. The use of *sharia* law as one of the mechanisms of governance is taken for granted, just as the invocation of God in the American Pledge of Allegiance or on U.S. currency is taken for granted. In countries where there are significant religious differences, such as in Nigeria, some parts of the country may be governed by *sharia* law while other parts are governed by secular statutes.

In such cases religion makes at least an indirect contribution to the nature of political communication. In the United States religion and politics are perhaps more intertwined than in most other developed countries. Europeans are highly secularized, as are Canadians, Australians, New Zealanders, and the Japanese. The country most like the U. S. in its religious practices is South Korea, but the political activities of the Christian Church there are minimal compared to the United States.

The Pew Forum on Religion & Public Life reports that, in the American case, religion is a critical factor in how the public thinks about contentious policies and political issues. Americans, according to the forum, have increasingly come to think of Islam as a religion encouraging violence, for instance, and they are increasingly comfortable with political leaders declaring their faith—which is largely unthinkable in the European context. The rise of social issues and the role of "values" in presidential politics, too, has increased the attention given to religion. Many religious leaders, even while steering clear of politics, per se, have had much to say about gay rights and marriage, abortion, and stem cell research, all of which have become divisive political issues. The Pew Research Center indicates that the faith of politicians is an issue for many Americas, with 38 percent saying they would not vote for a

Muslim presidential candidate, 50 percent that they would not vote for an atheist candidate, and 15 percent concerned about voting for a qualified Evangelical Christian. In the center's 2004 report on the American political landscape, it concluded that since about 1990 "religion and religious faith have become more strongly aligned with partisan and ideological identification" (Pew Research Center 2003). Although this phenomenon has hit both parties, the center says, the gap between those expressing this belief who are members of the Republican Party and those who are Democrats has begun to widen. The United States Conference of Catholic Bishops took a position during the 2004 election cycle that because human life is sacred, abortion is "intrinsically evil," and that the U. S. Supreme Court had sinned against justice in its 1973 Roe v. Wade decision. Although it did not, as a group, choose to deny Catholics in political life the right to take communion if they publicly supported abortion on demand, it did leave this decision up to individual bishops (U. S. Conference of Catholic Bishops, 2004). The decision made for difficult moments for Senator John Kerry, who was such a practicing Catholic.

Philosophical Issues Raised by These Activities

The United States' Constitution guarantees the rights of free speech, assembly, religion, and freedom of the press. When certain elements of society consider that the press is not doing an adequate job of providing unbiased information concerning public issues—particularly social issues—the question of whether this guarantee is sensible or not becomes an issue of public debate. The trust that people—particularly more politically and socially conservative people—place in the media erodes. Journalists do not enjoy the same status as they did in the 1960s, for instance, when Walter Cronkite, then anchor of CBS news, was the most trusted man in America. Of course the American population is more than twice as large as it was then, and far more fragmented and politicized. Although the antiwar and civil rights movements of the 1960s had polarized Americans, there were clear majorities of citizens who supported the status quo—even if it had regressive qualities. That is no longer true, with presidential elections turning on just a few votes in a few key states with large numbers of votes in the Electoral College, both major political parties split into factions, and various claims made about the centers of these parties having shifted either far right (Republicans) or far left (Democrats).

The Internet has provided new outlets for political communication that have responded to this lack of trust. During the Clinton presidency political talk radio emerged, providing commentators such as Rush Limbaugh, G. Gordon Liddy (one of those indicted in the Watergate investigation), and Colonel Oliver North (of the Iran–Contra scandal) the opportunity to carry on political conversations with the "like-minded" (Limbaugh's listeners were sometimes referred to as "dittoheads"). Matt Drudge also began his *Drudge Report* to provide an alternative to the mainstream media (www .drudgereport.com), providing information that became notorious during the Clinton–Lewinsky scandal, investigations by a special prosecutor, and efforts to impeach Clinton. During the first Bush administration the Internet saw the rise of "blogs," in which people could carry on conversations on a variety of topics set up by an owner who set the agenda by publishing a web-log, or web-based diary. Many of these blogs became a new form of political communication. All of these activities have increased the flow of information about politics and thus contributed to calls for increased regulation of political talk. When a television station that supported George Bush's reelection bid in 2004 announced plans to run a documentary about John Kerry close to the election, Kerry's campaign argued that this provided in-kind advertising to Bush in contravention of campaign finance laws.

Terrorism as Political Communication

Although scholars have written about various liberation movements', terrorist cells', and criminals' use of the media as a tool for legitimation or justification of their actions, in the post–September 11, 2001 environment, terrorism has become a sophisticated—although brutal—form of political communication. For instance, a 1979 conference at the Jonathan Institute in Jerusalem defined terrorism as the "deliberate and systematic murder, maiming, and menacing of the innocent to inspire fear for political ends" (quoted by Gueli 2003). The hostage-taking and beheadings that became common in Iraq during 2004 sent shivers of fear through the international-aid and reconstruction-contractor communities working in that country, causing many of them (including the United Nations) to withdraw their personnel. Assassinations of new security-force personnel likewise impeded the establishment of a peaceful environment for elections and reconstruction.

On the coalition side, demands that communication stay "on message" affected the work of organizations such as Radio Sawa, Radio Free Iraq, and the Voice of America broadcasting into Iraq. Whether news should follow the traditional Western model of balance and fairness in presentation, or whether it should be more propagandistic in tone to support the coalition efforts became a crucial question in budget discussions on Capitol Hill.

Political Communication Issues in Other Countries

The United States remains the country with the greatest amount of scholarly attention paid to political communication. Partly this is due to the quantitative orientation of many American academics and the ease with which quantitative methods can be applied to the political decision-making process. It is also partly due to the wide-open style of American politics and the enormous role played by television-based campaigns, including campaign advertising and news coverage of political events. Increasingly, however, academic studies on political communication in other countries have begun to appear. Political communication study is most advanced in the United Kingdom, where scholars have concentrated on historical studies of political movements and on the role of the media in facilitating or impeding such movements. There are also political-bias studies in the United Kingdom. In addition, Jürgen Habermas has written extensively about the development of political communication in Britain, France, and Germany as part of his work on what he calls the public sphere. Political-campaign studies have also begun to appear in both Canada and Australia, and the role of media as agents of propaganda and legitimation in the genocides of Bosnia and Kosovo in central Europe and Rwanda in central Africa have received the attention of international tribunals. These studies build on the extensive scholarship on propaganda that developed following World War II.

Outlook

Although the future is notoriously difficult to predict, the indications are, at this point, that as media develop around the world, they will take on an ever greater role in political communication. But this does not mean necessarily that "big media" will increase their influence. The democratization of political discourse based on various applications of the Internet, including blogging, vlogging (video logging), podcasting (audio de-

livered to MP3 devices) and the like, and the cell phone (especially texting), will also spread with these technologies. The role of media gatekeepers may actually decline and that of propagandists, publicists and a new breed of muckrakers increase as people invent new ways to express themselves in the political arena.

ROBERT S. FORTNER

Further Reading

Alterman, E. (2003). *What liberal media? The truth about bias and the news*. Cambridge, MA: Basic Books.

Crouse, T. (1973). *The boys on the bus: Riding with the campaign press corps*. New York: Random House.

Federal Election Commission website. Retrieved July 25, 2005 from www.fec.gov/law/feca/feca.shtml

Freedman, E., & Fico, F. (2004). Whither the experts? Newspaper use of horse race and issue experts in the coverage of open governors' races in 2002. *Journalism & Mass Communication Quarterly, 81*(3), 498–510.

Gitlin, T. (1980). *The whole world is watching: Mass media in the making and unmaking of the new left*. Los Angeles: University of California Press.

Goldberg, B. (2003). *BIAS: A CBS insider exposes how the media distort the media*. New York: HarperCollins.

Goldberg, B. (2004). *Arrogance: Rescuing America from the media elite*. New York: Warner Books.

Gueli, R. (2003). Bin Laden and Al-Qaeda: Challenging the assumptions of international terrorism. *Strategic Review for Southern Africa*. Center for Military Studies. Stellenbosch, South Africa: University of Stellenbosch.

Habermas, J. (1991). *The structural transformation of the public sphere: An inquiry into a category of bourgeois society*. Cambridge, MA: MIT Press.

Hofstetter, R. (1974). *The political impact of mass media*. Beverly Hills, CA: Sage.

Kamalipour, Y., & Snow, N. (Eds.). (2004). *War, media, and propaganda: A global perspective*. New York: Rowan & Littlefield.

McGinniss, J. (1969). *The selling of the president 1968*. New York: Trident Press.

Mernissi, F. (1992). *Islam and democracy: Fear of the modern world* (2nd ed.). (M. J. Lakeland, Trans.). Cambridge, MA: Perseus.

Parry-Giles, S. J., & Parry-Giles, T. (2001). Reassessing the state of political communication in the United States. *Argumentation and Advocacy, 37*(3), 158.

Patterson, T. E. (1980). *The mass media election: How Americans choose their president*. New York: Praeger.

Patterson, T. E. (1994). *Out of order*. New York: Vintage Books.

Patterson, T. E., & McClure, R. D. (1976). *The unseeing eye: The myth of television power in national elections.* New York: G. B. Putnam's Sons.

The Pew Forum on Religion & Public Life. *Religion and politics: Contention and consensus.* Retrieved July 25, 2005 from http://pewforum.org/docs/.

The Pew Research Center for the People & the Press. *Evenly divided and increasingly polarized: 2004 political landscape.* Retrieved July 25, 2005 from http://people-press.org/reports/display.php3?ReportID=196.

Robinson, M. J., & Sheehan, M. A. (1983). *Over the wire and on TV: CBS and UPI in campaign '80.* New York: Russell Sage Foundation.

Sabato, L. J. (1981). *The rise of political consultants: New ways of winning elections.* New York: Basic Books.

U. S. Conference of Catholic Bishops. (2004) *Catholics in political life.* Retrieved July 25, 2005 from www.usccb.org/bishops/catholicsinpoliticallife.shtml

Popular Culture

Popular culture has been defined variously as mass culture, folk culture, nonelite culture, and even more vaguely as culture well-liked by many. While its definition is debated, there is no question that popular culture is the most important arena in which to examine the modern interactions between religion, media, and communication. The contemporary study of popular culture began in the 1950s and 1960s United Kingdom with works like Richard Hoggart's *The Uses of Literacy*, Raymond Williams's *The Long Revolution*, and—in terms of religion—E. P. Thompson's *The Making of the English Working Class*. These early studies focused on working class popular culture and proved influential in fomenting later 1970s studies coming out of the Birmingham Centre for Contemporary Cultural Studies. Works such as Stuart Hall and Tony Jefferson's *Resistance Through Rituals* and Dick Hebdige's *Subculture: The Meaning of Style* focused on working-class British youth subcultures. Today the contemporary study of popular culture spans continents and continues to be an interdisciplinary endeavor grounded in fields like cultural studies, American studies, communication, history, comparative literature, sociology, and religious studies.

Defining Popular Culture

Any examination of popular-culture definitions must begin with John Storey's dictum that "popular culture is in effect an empty cultural category, one which can be filled in a wide variety of often conflicting ways depending on the context of use" (Storey 1993, 1). Using Storey's work as a starting point, one can distill four common ways of defining popular culture—two of which are useful for the study of religion, communication, and media. The first two, less helpful, definitions see popular culture as (1) cultural artifacts, materials, and objects that are well-liked by many in the society and (2) cultural items that are defined in juxtaposition to "high" or "elite" culture. Both of these definitions are problematic. In defining popular culture as something liked by a large percentage of the population, the question arises of how one can quantify such judgments. Indeed, even the most popular musicians, movies, and television programs in the contemporary United States garner only a small niche market of the country. Add to this that much popular-culture scholarship has traditionally focused on subcultures that nourish unique, countercultural styles and interests, and one can begin to see the folly of defining popular culture as something well liked.

Defining popular culture by juxtaposing it against a supposed high or elite culture is also an extremely problematic move. As noted by scholars such as John Hall, proposing objective definitional categories like "popular" and "elite" serves more to legitimize one social group's culture as superior to another's than it does to clarify what we might mean by popular culture. Simply put, individuals and groups within any one society may have different cultural preferences based on a variety of conscious and unconscious influences. To call one elite and another popular is to make a subjective judgment call. In addition, scholars such as Bonnie Erickson and Ann Swidler have shown that rather than utilizing only high or popular culture, individuals of various class and status backgrounds use and consume multiple and often contradictory cultural artifacts from a variety of sources.

Two other common definitions of popular culture are useful for the study of religion, media, and communication because they suggest sites where one may examine popular culture and its interactions with religion and media. The first way of defining popular culture as a site is mass culture. In other words, popular culture includes all mass-produced, commercial culture. In this view, popular culture is the historical product of industrial and consumer capitalism, urbanization, and the development of mass media technologies like printing presses, radio, television, and the Internet. The second way of defining popular culture as a site initially appears contradictory to identifying it with mass culture.

In this understanding, popular culture is "folk" culture, those artifacts, materials, and objects not mass-produced, but created and circulated on a small scale and shared by ethnic, regional, and other subcultural groups within the larger society. These two definitions are not incommensurable if understood as two possible sites producing popular culture. In other words, popular culture might be usefully defined as both mass-produced and more localized subcultural artifacts, materials, and objects. The study of religion, media, and popular culture, then, examines both mass-produced, consumer capitalist culture and local, regional, and folk culture. This includes best-selling novels, compact discs, television, film, and Internet websites, but it also includes local and subcultural customs, behaviors, objects, and stories.

Religion and Popular Culture: Currents and Controversies

The academic study of religion and popular culture has become increasingly visible since the mid-1990s. The largest scholarly association for the study of religion in the world, the nine-thousand member American Academy of Religion, started featuring well-attended religion and popular culture sessions at its annual meeting at the turn of the twenty-first century. In addition, scholarly journals like the *Journal of Religion and Popular Culture* and the *Journal of Religion and Film* are devoted to the emerging field of study. The methodological approaches to the subject vary widely, ranging from textual criticism and analysis of religious themes in magazines, films, and television to fieldwork studies of devout celebrity fandoms, like those of Elvis Presley or James Dean. In addition to the variety of methods, scholars have offered a number of frameworks for understanding how popular culture and religion interact in contemporary cultures. Conrad Ostwalt, for example, suggests that secularization in the contemporary United States moves religion and popular culture to interact in two ways. First, as religion loses public authority in society, religious institutions increasingly emulate secular styles. This trend is visible in contemporary Evangelical Protestant co-optations of popular culture. In the United States, the Evangelical subculture offers a mirror image of products found in the larger society. For example, every musical style—including hip hop, punk, and metal—could be found in the Christian music industry by the late 1990s. Evangelicals have also produced their own children's cartoons, glossy magazines, and romance novels. The 1990s growth of Evangelical "seeker

churches" provides an even more focused example. These churches, the most prominent being the Willow Creek Association, strive to attract members by muting explicit religious messages and symbolism and adopting the self-help language, office park architecture, and easy-listening pop music styles of suburban America.

Second, Ostwalt suggests that religious concepts and functions are increasingly finding expression in popular culture. In other words, modern popular-culture materials like music, film, and television appear to have explicit and hidden religious symbols, themes, and meanings embedded within them. At the same time, people in contemporary consumer capitalist societies increasingly seek in popular culture the meanings, identity, and community they once found in religion. Erika Doss, for example, has argued that fans of Elvis Presley display beliefs and practices that supplement or replace their religious ones. She argues that "Elvis fan activities can become religious if they affect a transcendent and all-powerful order that can influence human affairs and is not inherently apprehensible" (Doss 1999, 76). Other studies of what Sean McCloud has dubbed "dead celebrity fandom"— including those of Princess Diana, actor James Dean, and racing driver Dale Earnhardt—offer parallels to Doss's findings.

The idea that popular culture sometimes looks like religion in substance and function has led to some minor debate in the field over whether popular culture can, in effect, be a religion for some people. The unique subject matter of religion and popular culture studies fronts the questions of what the definitional parameters of religion and the topical parameters of religious studies may be. On one side of the debate are scholars who argue that sometimes popular culture functions as religion. In *Film as Religion: Myths, Morals, and Rituals*, John Lyden suggests that movies might be considered religious because "what we have always called 'religion' is identified by its function in society, and that this function can be met even by cultural phenomena not normally called 'religions'" (Lyden 2003, 3). Similarly, Robin Sylvan argues that music subcultures like hip hop, metal, rave, and Grateful Dead fandom are religious because they provide "a powerful religious experience, an encounter with the numinous that is the core of all religions" (Sylvan 2002, 4). On the other side of the debate are scholars such as Steve Bruce who caution against broad functionalist definitions of religion and extrapolating sameness from religion and popular culture parallels.

Regardless of one's position in the debate, most scholars of religion and popular culture agree that there are similarities between the two, as well as common approaches to their study. First, both religion and popular culture involve the intricate details of people's everyday lives. Second, both religion and popular culture help people create and infuse their lives with meaning, identity, community, memory, tradition, and power through the use of various cultural items. Third, what looks religious in popular culture is both explicit and hidden. It may be identified by either descriptive (i.e., rituals, myths, symbols, etc.) or functionalist (how popular culture works in people's lives) definitions of religion.

Research Directions

The study of interactions between contemporary religion and popular culture is foremost the study of mass media forms and communication. Whether examining depictions of religion on television, the parallels between popular culture fandoms and religious movements, or the influence of technologies like the Internet on religious practice and belief, mass media is the conduit linking religion and popular culture. Religion and media studies examining the multiple connections between religious ideas, practices, and institutions and mass communication forms like television, film, radio, print, and electronic media have grown significantly in the 2000s, forming a significant subfield in religion and popular culture studies.

Research on religion, media, and popular culture currently follows two currents that will likely continue in the future. The first approach consists of examining how a particular religious group or religion in general appears and is depicted in various mass media. A plethora of works on religious themes in movies fits into this category. Margaret Miles's *Seeing and Believing: Religion and Values in the Movies* and Joel Martin and Conrad Ostwalt's edited volume, *Screening the Sacred: Religion, Myth, and Ideology in Popular American Film* are just two examples. In addition to film, scholars have written extensively about how religion and religions are portrayed in newspaper, newsmagazine, and other print media outlets. Mark Silk's 1995 work, *Secular Media: Making News of Religion in America*, is one of the earliest book-length studies, followed by works like Mark Hulsether's *Building a Protestant Left: Christianity and Crisis Magazine, 1941–93* and Sean McCloud's *Making the American Religious Fringe: Exotics, Subversives, and Journalists, 1955–1993*. The *Journal of Media and Religion* provides an outlet for article-length studies on media depictions of religion.

A second and growing current in research on religion, media, and popular culture focuses on how religion and media practices interact and influence each other in both larger cultural and smaller individual contexts. For example, in *Haunted Media: Electronic Presence From Telegraphy to Television*, Jeffrey Sconce suggests that the development of media technologies coincided with new ways of imagining the supernatural in American culture. He links such things as the telegraph and the growth of Spiritualism in the nineteenth century to illustrate how mass-media technologies can sometimes offer new religious vocabulary and conceptions into society. Works such as Brenda Brasher's *Give Me That Online Religion* similarly suggest that recent computer and Internet technologies alter our religious conceptions of time, space, and identity. In addition to these broad, culturally focused studies is the growth in the 2000s of fieldwork-based examinations, such as Lynn Shofield Clark's *From Angels to Aliens: Teenagers, the Media, and the Supernatural*. Such works examine how people variously interpret and sometimes incorporate mass-media representations of religion and the supernatural into their personal religious beliefs and practices. This area of research, concurrent with a broader "ethnographic turn" in religious studies, suggests a future trend toward more audience reception–centered studies of religion, media, and popular culture.

SEAN MCCLOUD

See also Film; Music Videos; Radio, Television

Further Reading

Brasher, B. (2001). *Give me that online religion*. San Francisco: Jossey-Bass.

Bruce, S. (2002). *God is dead: Secularization in the West*. Malden, MA: Blackwell.

Clark, L. (2003). *From angels to aliens: Teenagers, the media, and the supernatural*. New York: Oxford University Press.

Doss, E. (1999). *Elvis culture: Fans, faith, and image*. Lawrence: University Press of Kansas.

Erickson, B. (1996). Culture, class, and connections. *American Journal of Sociology 102*, 217–251.

Fiske, J. (1989). *Understanding popular culture*. New York: Routledge.

Forbes, B. & Mahan, J. (Eds.). (2000). *Religion and popular culture in America*. Berkeley: University of California Press.

Hall, J. (1992). The capital(s) of cultures: A nonholistic approach to status situations, class, gender, and ethnicity. In M. Lamont & M. Fournier (Eds.), *Cultivating differences: Symbolic boundaries and the making of inequality.* Chicago: University of Chicago Press.

Hall, S., & Jefferson, T. (Eds.). (1976). *Resistance through rituals: Youth subcultures in postwar Britain.* New York: Routledge.

Hebdige, D. (1979). *Subculture: The meaning of style.* New York: Routledge.

Hendershot, H. (2004). *Shaking the world for Jesus: Media and conservative Evangelical culture.* Chicago: University of Chicago Press.

Hoggart, R. (1958). *The uses of literacy.* Harmondsworth, U.K.: Penguin.

Hulsether, M. (1999). *Building a Protestant left: Christianity and Crisis Magazine, 1941–1993.* Knoxville: University of Tennessee Press.

Lyden, J. (2003). *Film as religion: Myths, morals, and rituals.* New York: New York University Press.

Martin, J., & Ostwalt, C. (Eds.). (1996). *Screening the sacred: Religion, myth, and ideology in popular American film.* Boulder, CO: Westview Press.

Mazur, E., & McCarthy, K. (Eds.) (2001). *God in the details: American religion in popular culture.* New York: Routledge.

McCloud, S. (2003). Popular culture fandoms, the boundaries of religious studies, and the project of the self. *Culture and Religion 4*(2), 187–206.

McCloud, S. (2004). *Making the American religious fringe: Exotics, subversives, and journalists, 1955–1993.* Chapel Hill: University of North Carolina Press.

McDannell, C. (1995). *Material Christianity: Religion and popular culture in America.* New Haven, CT: Yale University Press.

Miles, M. (1996). *Seeing and believing: Religion and values at the movies.* Boston: Beacon Press.

Moore, R. (1994). *Selling God: American religion in the marketplace of culture.* New York: Oxford University Press.

Ostwalt, C. (2003). *Secular steeples: Popular culture and the religious imagination.* Harrisburg: Trinity Press.

Sargeant, K. (2000). *Seeker churches: Promoting traditional religion in a nontraditional way.* New Brunswick, NJ: Rutgers University Press.

Sconce, J. (2000). *Haunted media: Electronic presence from telegraphy to television.* Durham, NC: Duke University Press.

Silk, M. (1995). *Unsecular media: Making news of religion in America.* Urbana: University of Illinois Press.

Storey, J. (1993). *An introductory guide to cultural theory and popular culture.* Athens: University of Georgia Press.

Swidler, A. (2001). *Talk of love: How culture matters.* Chicago: University of Chicago Press.

Sylvan, R. (2002). *Traces of the spirit: The religious dimensions of popular music.* New York: New York University Press.

Thompson, E. P. (1963). *The making of the English working class.* London: Victor Gollancz.

Williams, R. (1963). *Culture and society, 1780–1950.* Harmondsworth, U.K.: Penguin.

Williams, R. (1965). *The long revolution.* Harmondsworth, U.K.: Penguin.

Pornography

Attempts to define pornography have been problematic at best, due to the host of social, moral, political, and other connotations associated with the term. Further complicating these attempts is the frequency with which various scholars, critics, and commentators interchangeably use the labels pornographic, obscene, indecent, erotic, X-rated, sexually explicit, and the like. Where one draws the boundaries of what constitutes pornography is a function of a multitude of factors, including one's own views on sexuality, morality, and perhaps most tellingly, the intent behind one's effort to define it at all.

Some critics make the distinction between *erotica*, defined as the depiction of "mutually pleasurable, sexual expression between people who have enough power to be there by positive choice," and *pornography*, which constitutes any message that features "violence, dominance, and conquest" (Steinem 1980, 37). Moreover, many social scientists choose to avoid using the term *pornography* and rely instead on the more neutral term *sexually explicit materials*. Other scholars distinguish between *erotica*, standard *sexually explicit fare*, and more *hard-core materials* that dwell upon the sexually violent themes of sadomasochism, bondage, rape, as well as exotic themes such as bestiality.

Finding a viable legal definition of pornography is no less difficult. Perhaps former U.S. Supreme Court Justice Potter Stewart best illustrated this challenge when he uttered the oft-quoted phrase, "I know it when I see it" (*Jacobellis v. Ohio* 1964). Statutory attempts to define pornography have been met with legal challenges. The reigning decision regarding the First Amendment protection of sexually explicit materials comes from the case of *Roth v. United States* (1957), when the Supreme Court conspicuously avoided defining pornography and instead elected to set a standard for obscenity. For any material to be judged obscene (and therefore not warrant constitutional protection), the average person, applying contemporary community standards must find that the material, taken as a whole, appeals to prurient interest. The court later modified this definition in *Miller v. California* (1973), adding that the work must depict or describe, in a patently offensive way, sexual conduct specifically defined by the applicable state law, and that the work, taken as a whole, must lack serious artistic, political, or scientific value. Although this legal jurisprudence set a precedent for what is and is not constitutionally protected, the interpretation of this law remains highly subjective.

Many of those opposed to sexually explicit materials on moral grounds are far more inclusive in their definition of pornography. Noted televangelist Jerry Falwell labeled as pornographic any material that is designed to elicit sexual arousal among consumers. Likewise, founder of the American Family Association, Donald Wildmon, in attacking sexual content and obscenity on American television, argued for relying upon personal judgment to identify what materials merited inclusion. Obviously, such broad, subjective definitions greatly expand the realm of pornography to include much of contemporary television programming, as well as a preponderance of advertising content as well.

What Place Religion?

Organized religion has traditionally been critical of pornography and those who produce it. Religious organizations' opposition to sexually explicit materials flourished beginning in the late 1970s, as various denominations became more active in combating pornography. High-profile campaigns such as the Christian Coalition's "Contract with the American Family" encouraged lawmakers to enact tighter restrictions regarding access to sexually explicit materials. In addition, the American Family Association continues to wage grassroots campaigns encouraging boycotts against numerous corporations and media giants such as Books-A-Million, 7-Eleven, Movie Gallery, and MTV, all aimed at limiting access to sexual content.

The reasons religious groups and denominations have opposed pornography are manifold. Some have decried the highly graphic and explicit depictions of sexual behavior displayed in pornography, whereas others have argued that pornography undermines basic human dignity. I. L. Reiss noted that St. Augustine of Rome (354–430 CE) and his interpretation of the story of Adam and Eve "tied the Gordian knot that links sexuality to sin," which continues to this day (1990, 193). St. Augustine believed that humans were powerless to control their sexual urges, and therefore, strict rules must be in place to govern sexuality. Reiss

stated that modern-day scandals such as Jim Bakker's infamous fall from grace perpetuated this notion of sex as powerful and dangerous.

Some observers have argued that what ultimately lies at the heart of this conflict is the opposition between the celebration of human sexuality espoused by religion and the debasement of human dignity embodied in pornography. After all, sex, in the proper context, is biblically ordained and not sinful. Those seeking proof of this argument need look no further than Genesis 2:24, which states that husband and wife will "become one flesh," or to the entirety of Song of Solomon in the Old Testament.

Values in Pornography

Sexually explicit materials come in many shapes and sizes. In addition, sexually explicit materials are now delivered through an ever-increasing number of channels, from traditional media, such as magazines and cable television, to high-tech virtual sex, cybersex, and "teledildonics" made possible via interactive DVDs and the Internet. Despite this seemingly infinite variety, the majority of all sexually explicit content conveys the same theme: women are sexually insatiable creatures longing for male domination. Although "researchers have shown more interest in studying the impact of pornography than in analyzing its contents" (Brown and Bryant 1989, 22), select studies reveal that, by and large, most pornography is produced for male consumption and features depictions of sexual organs and activities such as fellatio, cunnilingus, and coition. In most material containing both males and females, males are depicted as dominating over their partners whereas women are both highly submissive and willing to entertain virtually every male desire. Moreover, the sexual acts depicted tend to deemphasize friendship and love, and marriage, emotional involvement, and commitment.

Although research regarding pornography on the Internet remains in its infancy, early research has shown that these thematic trends extend into cyberspace. Heider and Harp analyzed the content of more than 200 pornographic websites and found that female submissiveness was a dominant theme. Moreover, the presentation of "ideal" beauty was common, as was a focus on youthfulness, illustrated by the frequent use of the word "teen" on many sites. In addition, "niche" sites exist to entertain almost any fantasy possible, including rape sites that dwell on female victimization, pain, and suffering. Given the prevalence of sexually explicit content on the Internet, further research is

Extract from "Pornography and Violence in the Communications Media: A Pastoral Response"

On 7 May 1989 the Vatican's Pontifical Council for Social Communications issued a 32-point response to "the widespread increase of pornography and wanton violence in the media." Below is an excerpt from the response.

13. It has even been said that there can be a psychological link between pornography and sadistic violence, and some pornography is itself overtly violent in theme and content. Those who view or read such material run the risk of carrying over such attitudes and behaviour into their own relationships and can come to lack reverence and respect for others as precious children of God and as brothers and sisters in the same human family. Such a link between pornography and sadistic violence has particular implications for those suffering from certain forms of mental illness.

14. Even so called "soft core" pornography can have a progressively desensitizing effect, gradually rendering individuals morally numb and personally insensitive to the rights and dignity of others. Exposure to pornography can also be - like exposure to narcotics - habit-forming and can lead individuals to seek increasingly "hard core" and perverse material. The likelihood of anti-social behaviour can grow as this process continues.

15. Pornography can foster unhealthy preoccupations in fantasy and behaviour. It can interfere with personal moral growth and the development of healthy and mature relationships, especially in marriage and family life, where mutual trust and openness and personal moral integrity in thought and in action are so important.

16. Indeed, pornography can militate against the family character of true human sexual expression. The more sexual activity is considered as a continuing frenzied search for personal gratification rather than as an expression of enduring love in marriage, the more pornography can be considered as a factor contributing to the undermining of wholesome family life.

17. In the worst cases, pornography can act as an inciting or reinforcing agent, a kind of accomplice, in the behaviour of dangerous sex offenders - child molesters, rapists and killers.

18. A fundamental message of pornography and violence is disdain, the consideration of others as objects rather than as persons. Thus, pornography and violence can eat away at tenderness and compassion and can foster insensitivity and even brutality.

Source: Pontifical Council for Social Communications. (1989). "Pornography and Violence in the Communications Media: A Pastoral Response." Retrieved December 14, 2005, from http://www.vatican.va/roman_curia/pontifical_councils/pccs/documents/rc_pc_pccs_doc_07051989_pornography_en.html

needed to determine how, if at all, pornographic materials delivered via the Internet differ from more traditional forms of sexually explicit materials.

Effects of Pornography on Perception

Religious leaders' concerns regarding the dangers of pornography are not without merit, as a wealth of compelling research evidence exists regarding the potential negative effects of consuming sexually explicit material. Research has shown that prolonged, massive exposure to typical sexually explicit fare can significantly impact research participants' views regarding sexual behavior and the offensiveness of pornography. Zillmann and Bryant exposed participants to a substantial amount (four hours and forty-eight minutes over a six-week period) of common, nonviolent sexually explicit films featuring sexual acts such as oral/genital contact, heterosexual intercourse, and anal intercourse. When compared with participants who viewed no sexually explicit films, participants who viewed the sexually explicit films reported significantly higher estimates of the frequency with which the general population engaged in various common sexual activities. Moreover, the participants who viewed substantial amounts of sexually explicit films also grossly overestimated the frequency with which people engaged in less-typical sexual practices such as sadomasochism, bestiality, and sexual activity with multiple partners. Again, this finding is particularly noteworthy given that participants viewed no films depicting such lower-frequency sexual practices.

Substantial exposure to pornography was also found to weaken participants' arousal responses to sexually explicit fare, resulting in an overall desensitization effect. In addition, three weeks after the viewing period had ended, participants reported being less offended by pornography and rated sexually explicit fare as less pornographic. Zillmann and Bryant provided further evidence for this habituation hypothesis. In one portion of the study, participants were told that a technical problem had caused a delay in the experimental procedures. Participants were then ushered to another room and given the opportunity to watch a number of videotapes while the problem was ostensibly corrected. The tapes included materials ranging from an innocuous G-rated film to R-rated films containing sexual content to triple-X films depicting sadomasochism, bondage, or bestiality. When compared to those who had viewed no sexually explicit films in the recent past, participants who had been heavily exposed to pornography watched significantly more of the hardcore triple-X films depicting nonstandard sexual practices. In essence, the results suggest that the participants exposed to large quantities of standard sexually explicit fare had "graduated" to selecting more uncommon forms of pornography.

The prolonged exposure to sexually explicit material also resulted in significantly greater sexual callousness toward women and to trivialization of rape. Participants were presented with a mock-rape trial scenario and asked to recommend a sentence. For both males and females, participants who had viewed massive amounts of sexually explicit material recommended significantly shorter sentences for the convicted rapist. In addition, participants showed significantly less support for the women's rights movement. Other scholars have also found that in addition to standard sexually explicit materials, exposure to sexually violent pornography also leads to a trivialization of rape and stronger endorsement of rape myths.

Obviously, ethical standards prevent replication of these findings regarding exposure to pornography with younger research participants. However, extant research on seemingly more innocuous (but more widely consumed) sexually themed media content has demonstrated similarly potent results. Numerous content analyses have found that sexual content of varying degrees of explicitness permeate the media, and in general, the messages conveyed by this content are believed to be distorted and potentially harmful. Bryant and Rockwell examined the impact of common sexual content found on prime-time broadcast television programming on teens' moral values. The authors regularly exposed participants to either prime-time programs depicting sexual relations between unmarried partners, sexual relations between married partners, or nonsexual relations between adults. Participants later viewed segments depicting either sexual transgressions or nonsexual transgressions and were asked to rate how morally wrong the transgressions were, how severely injured the victims were, as well as how much the victims had suffered. The findings showed that participants who viewed programs depicting sexual relations between unmarried couples later found the sexual transgressions to be less bad than participants who viewed other types of programming. The authors concluded that the programs had indeed produced a shift in the participants' moral judgment. Similar effects on teens from viewing more explicit pornographic materials can only be hypothesized. However, given that 29 percent of boys cite pornography as the most important source of sexual information, the potential danger that sexually explicit materials can pose for younger consumers is obvious.

Pornography and Family Values

Religious leaders have frequently attacked pornography on the grounds that such material may be harmful not only to individuals, but also to the family as a social institution. Again, research shows that these fears are well founded. Zillmann and Bryant found that massive exposure to common sexually explicit films prompted research participants to show greater tolerance for promiscuity and nonexclusivity in sexual relationships. In addition, participants were more inclined to believe that the repression of sexual urges could be harmful and posed health risks. Both male and female participants who viewed the pornographic films also showed less desire to have children, providing further evidence that participants adopted the message in pornography that sexual relations are best enjoyed without emotional or familial commitments. But perhaps most relevant to this discussion, participants who viewed a substantial amount of pornography reported an overall lower evaluation of the institution of marriage when compared with participants who viewed no pornographic films.

Later research also revealed how pornography can be harmful to the family. Participants who viewed large quantities of pornography reported less satisfaction with their real-life intimate partners, particularly in regard to their physical appearance, sexual curiosity, their affection, and their sexual performance. The authors suggested that these results indicate that those who viewed the pornographic films made comparisons between the presentation of "ideal" sexual relations and beauty presented in the films and their own sexual history. Ultimately, their own experiences paled in comparison to the hyper-sexual behavior depicted in these films. Moreover, previous research provides further evidence that this effect is not limited to highly explicit pornographic materials. In short, "Any pinup—whether nude or in a bathing suit—will do" (Zillmann and Bryant 1988b, 452).

Concerns over the effects of exposure to pornography have been renewed due to the growing phenomenon of Internet pornography and pornography addiction. Likewise, scholars have begun to empirically assess the effects of exposure to this relatively new form of sexually explicit material. Sexual addiction among religious leaders is also drawing increased attention. It is clear that the final word on pornography and religion has not been uttered.

JENNINGS BRYANT AND R. GLENN CUMMINS

See also Culture Wars; Free Speech; Profanity (Taboo)

Further Reading

Binik, Y. M. (Ed.). (2001). Sexuality and the Internet [Special issue]. *Journal of Sex Research, 38*(4).

Brown, D., & Bryant, J. (1989). The manifest content of pornography. In D. Zillmann & J. Bryant (Eds.), *Pornography: Research advances and policy considerations* (pp. 3–24). Hillsdale, NJ: Lawrence Erlbaum Associates.

Bryant, J., & Rockwell, S. C. (1994). Effects of massive exposure to sexually oriented primetime television programming on adolescents' moral judgments. In D. Zillmann, J. Bryant, & A. Huston (Eds.), *Media, children, and the family: Social scientific, psychodynamic, and clinical perspectives* (pp. 183–195). Hillsdale, NJ: Lawrence Erlbaum Associates.

Bryant, J., & Zillmann, D. (2001). Pornography: Models of (effects on sexual deviancy). In C. D. Bryant (Ed.), *Encyclopedia of criminology and deviant behavior* (Vol. 3, pp. 241–244). Oxford, UK: Brunner/Routledge.

Check, J. V. P. (1995). Teenage training: The effects of pornography on adolescent males. In L. Lederer and R. Delgado (Eds.), *The price we pay: The case against racist speech, hate propaganda, and pornography* (pp. 89–91). New York: Hill and Wang.

DelMonaco, D. L. (Ed.). (2003). Cybersex [Special issue]. *Sexual and Relationship Therapy, 18*(3).

Donnerstein, E., Linz, D., & Penrod, S. (1987). *The question of pornography: Research findings and policy implications.* New York: The Free Press.

Dworkin, A. (1981). *Pornography: Men possessing women.* New York: Perigee Books.

Falwell, J. (1980). *Listen America.* Garden City, NY: Doubleday.

Gardner, C. J. (2001, March 5). Tangled in the worst of the Web. *Christianity Today, 45*(4), 42–49.

Harris, R. J., & Scott, C. L. (2002). Effects of sex in the media. In J. Bryant & D. Zillmann (Eds.), *Media Effects: Advances in theory and research* (2nd ed., pp. 307–332). Mahwah, NJ: Lawrence Erlbaum Associates.

Heider, D., & Harp, D. (2002). New hope or old power: Democracy, pornography and the Internet. *Howard Journal of Communication, 13*, 285–299.

Jacobellis v. Ohio, 378 U.S. 184 (1964).

Lederer, L. (Ed.). (1980). *Take back the night: Women on pornography.* New York: Morrow.

Malamuth, N. M., & Donnerstein, E. (Eds.). (1984). *Pornography and sexual aggression.* Orlando, FL: Academic Press.

Mendenhall, R. R. (2002). Responses to television from the new Christian right: The Donald Wildmon Organizations' fight against sexual content. In D. S. Claussen (Ed.), *Sex, religion, media* (pp. 101–114). Lanham, MD: Rowman and Littlefield Publishers.

Miller v. California, 413 U.S. 15 (1973).

Paul, P. (2004, January 19). The porn factor. *Time, 163*(3), 99–101.

Pellauer, M. (1987). Pornography: An agenda for the churches. *Christian Century, 104*, 651–655.

Reiss, I. L. (1990). *An end to shame: Shaping our next sexual revolution.* Buffalo, NY: Prometheus Books.

Ross, M. E. (1990). Censorship or education? Feminist views on pornography. *Christian Century, 107*, 244–246.

Roth v. United States, 354 U.S. 476 (1957).

Stein, J. (2000, June 19). Will cybersex be better than real sex? *Time, 155*(25), 62.

Steinem, G. (1980). Erotica and pornography: A clear and present difference. In L. Lederer (Ed.), *Take back the night: Women on pornography.* New York: Morrow.

U.S. Department of Justice. (1986, July). *Attorney General's Commission on Pornography: Final Report.* Washington, DC: U.S. Government Printing Office.

Zillmann, D., & Bryant, J. (1982). Pornography, sexual callousness, and the trivialization of rape. *Journal of Communication, 32*(4), 10–21.

Zillmann, D., & Bryant, J. (1984). Effects of massive

exposure to pornography. In N. M. Malamuth & E. Donnerstein (Eds.), *Pornography and sexual aggression* (pp. 115–138). New York: Academic Press.

Zillmann, D., & Bryant, J. (1986). Shifting preferences in pornography consumption. *Communication Research, 13*, 560–578.

Zillmann, D., & Bryant, J. (1988a). The effects of prolonged exposure to pornography on family values. *Journal of Family Issues, 9*, 518–544.

Zillmann, D., & Bryant, J. (1988b). Pornography's impact on sexual satisfaction. *Journal of Applied Social Psychology, 18*, 438–453.

Zillmann, D., & Bryant, J. (Eds.). (1989). *Pornography: Research advances and policy considerations.* Hillsdale, NJ: Lawrence Erlbaum Associates.

Priests

The title of *priest* has been associated with religion since early pre-Christian times. The first priest mentioned in the Bible was Melchizedek, who makes a brief and mysterious appearance to bestow a blessing on Abraham in a valley near Jerusalem. "Melchizedek king of Salem brought bread and wine; he was a priest of God Most High" (Genesis 14:18, New Jerusalem Bible). In gratitude, Abraham gave Melchizedek a tenth of all his goods.

The tale of this meeting accomplishes three major purposes in Judeo-Christianity: it establishes the concept of "tithing" to the church, foreshadows the Eucharist and the Eucharistic sacrifice in the bread and wine offered to Abraham, and positions Melchizedek as the first in a long and distinguished line of priests who have presided over numerous religions throughout human history.

The word *priest* originates from the Greek word *presbyteros* and the Latin word *presbyter*, which mean *elder*. In ancient Greece and Rome, priests were responsible for the preservation and repair of the temples of the gods. Indian society developed four main castes, the highest of which was called the Brahman. It presided over sacrifices and performed the most essential religious duties. As part of Hinduism, which is the only major non-Christian religion to still have priests, modern Brahman priests read aloud the ancient scriptures, which are written in Sanskrit. They perform religious ceremonies, maintain a diary of prayer requests, and promote goodwill among followers.

In the Old Testament, priests came from the tribe of Levi, through Aaron. They offered sacrifices and preserved the temple, living on the tithes of the people. As Moses told the Israelites, it was the Levites' responsibility to "stand in the presence of Yahweh, to serve Him and to bless in His name, as they still do today" (Deuteronomy 10:8). After Jesus' death and the destruction of the temple thirty-seven years later, sacrifices—and thus priests—became nonexistent in Judaism. Today the only Jewish religious leaders are rabbis (teachers).

History of Priests in Christianity

St. Paul's letter to the Hebrews distinguishes between two types of priests: levitical and sacrificial. Paul taught that Christ Himself—who was not from the tribe of Levi, but rather from the tribe of Judah—is the only "sacrificial priest" for Christians. As Paul noted, "He has no need to offer sacrifices every day, as the high priests do, first for their own sins and only then for those of the people; this He did once and for all by offering Himself" (Hebrews 7:27).

The term *priest* is still used in several Christian faiths, including Greek Orthodox, Episcopalian, Eastern Rite Catholic, and Roman Catholic. In these faiths, priests are commonly called "father," and have been associated with fatherhood throughout the Bible. Micah asked a traveling Levite to remain with him and "be my father and priest" (Judges 17:10). Later, the same Levite was recruited by the clan of the Danites to "become our father and priest" (Judges 18:19). Jesus' early apostles likewise considered themselves fathers to their congregations. Paul reminded the Corinthians, "It was I who fathered you in Christ Jesus, by the gospel" (1 Corinthians 4:15), told the Thessalonians he "treated every one of you as a father treats his children" (1 Thessalonians 2:11), and, along with John, addressed followers as "my children" (Galatians 4:19, 1 John 2:1).

There are several parallels between the spiritual fatherhood of priests and the physical fatherhood of human parents:

1. Priests give birth to Christians spiritually through the waters of baptism.

2. They provide nourishment with the Body and Blood of Christ in the Eucharist.

3. They provide care and comfort through the healing sacraments of baptism, reconciliation, and anointing of the sick.

4. They shepherd their flocks with love and concern.

Communication Strategies of Priests

Priests have traditionally used three major forms of communication to guide their congregations. The first, and most common, is preaching. Priests offer sermons during church services that instruct on and amplify Biblical passages. Pope John XXIII noted in 1959 that preaching is "a parish priest's first and greatest duty."

The second major form is direct conversation. Priests engage in considerable discussion when leading Bible-study groups, hearing confessions, and offering counsel and spiritual direction. Pope John Paul II wrote in 1984 that administering the sacrament of penance "is, without a doubt, the most difficult and delicate, the most exhausting and demanding, but also one of the most beautiful and consoling ministries of the priest." In the Roman Catholic faith, priests take seriously the secrecy of the confessional and can be excommunicated if they breach this confidentiality. The Code of Canon Law asserts "The sacramental seal is the strict and inviolable obligation of keeping secret all matters that have been related to the confessor for the purpose of obtaining absolution, the revelation of which would render the sacrament odious and onerous" (Coriden 1985, 927).

Priests' third major form of communicating has involved the written word. One of the integral figures in the history of the preservation and transmission of the Bible was St. Jerome. Perhaps the most learned man of the fourth century, Jerome was a monastic priest who translated the Old Testament from Hebrew to Latin, the common language of the western Roman Empire.

He later translated the New Testament Gospels from Greek to Latin and improved the Latin translation of the New Testament epistles. Jerome's "Vulgate" (common-language) Bible has been the source of subsequent translations of the Bible to other languages, including English and German.

In more recent centuries, the priestly use of the written word has been aided by printing and other communication technologies. Priests have utilized such mass media as books, pamphlets, newspapers, radio, television and the Internet to instruct, unite, and encourage.

Priestly Mass Communication in the United States

In 1809 Father Gabriel Richard became the first American priest to use the press by making possible the publication of the first American Catholic periodical. While visiting Baltimore, Father Richard bought a printing press and type. He arranged for these to be transported to Detroit, then a remote outpost in the Old Northwest populated by several hundred French-Canadian refugees. Entrusting the printing duties to layman James M. Miller, Father Richard founded the *Michigan Essay, or Impartial Observer* on 31 August 1809. This four-page newspaper was mostly in English, with one-and-a-half columns of news in French. Intended to be a weekly, it apparently never survived beyond its first issue. From this press Richard also produced religious books and catechisms. These, like the single-issue newspaper, were the first publications in Michigan.

On another frontier, Padre Antonio José Martinez introduced printing to New Mexico in 1834, when it was still a Mexican province. Under Martinez's direction, printer Ramon Abreu published four issues of *El Crepusculo de la Libertad* (The Dawn of Liberty) in Santa Fe before the newspaper folded.

Besides using the press to unite the faithful in remote places, priests have employed it to defend the Catholic faith from prejudicial attacks. Under the editorship of Reverend Dr. Charles Constantine Pise, the first Catholic magazine, *The Metropolitan*, was published in January 1830. Its purpose, Father Pise noted in the inaugural statement, was to be "a magazine through which interesting and useful instruction might be conveyed to the inquiring mind and a medium afforded of defending ourselves against the attacks and misrepresentations of the malevolent and the ignorant." The monthly magazine published forty pages each issue and focused on theological subjects. Its essays included "The Divinity of Christ," "Reason and Faith," and "St. Peter at Rome."

Use of the Airwaves

Other priests embraced the airwaves to communicate their messages. Father Charles Coughlin used radio as a tool to promote social activism and reform. Known simply as "the radio priest," Coughlin began on CBS in 1930. When he was dropped in 1931, he established his own chain of stations and created his own organization, the National Union for Social Justice. He criticized socialism, communism, capitalism, and Judaism, marshaling a nationwide listenership of forty million until he was formally silenced by his bishop in 1942.

A few priests embraced the new medium of television to communicate their messages. Fulton J. Sheen was the most successful. Sheen worked as a parish priest in Peoria, Illinois, before becoming a professor at the Catholic University of America. A dynamic lecturer, he was chosen to host *The Catholic Hour* on NBC Radio in 1928. The program became a success, and Sheen eventually had an estimated audience of seven million listeners. In 1951 the Dumont network offered Sheen a half-hour slot on the new medium of television. Sheen's *Life Is Worth Living* program was a success, and ABC lured him away. His program aired on 170 stations in the U.S., reaching approximately twenty-five million people. It ended in 1957. "Radio is like the Old Testament, for it is the hearing of the Word without the seeing," Sheen noted. "Television is like the New Testament, for the Word is seen as it becomes flesh and dwells among us" (Sheen 1980, 63). Sheen's nearly thirty years on the airwaves gave him a unique opportunity to communicate with a vast audience, which Sheen noted he did not anticipate in the early years of his priesthood. "Little did I know in those days that it would be given me through radio and television to address a greater audience in half an hour than Paul in all the years of his missionary life," Sheen marveled (Sheen 1980, 128). His former diocese of Peoria is seeking to have Sheen declared a saint.

Use of Other Mass Media

One priest who has been elevated to sainthood partly for his work in the mass media is St. Maximilian Kolbe. He published large-circulation religious magazines and newspapers in Poland and Japan, and operated a radio station, before being executed by Nazis at Auschwitz in 1941.

More recently, Father Ellwood "Bud" Kieser communicated the teachings of Jesus through the entertainment media. Kieser founded a film company called Paulist Productions in 1968 and produced a weekly dramatic anthology series called *Insight*. He also produced such films as *Romero*, the story of the martyred archbishop of San Salvador; *Entertaining Angels: The Dorothy Day Story*, about the American social activist; and *The Fourth Wise Man*, a fictional tale set during Jesus' lifetime.

Familiarity with and participation in the mass media has been a major priority of the Roman Catholic Church since the Second Vatican Council. "As representatives of the Church, bishops, priests, religious, and laity are increasingly asked to write in the press, or appear on radio and television, or to collaborate in filming," the Council noted. "They are warmly encouraged to undertake this work, which has consequences that are far more important than is usually imagined" (Flannery 1992, 327).

The Future

All religions are made up of sinners, and priests are no exception. Throughout Christian history, the Church has survived and flourished despite scandals. Both the Catholic and Episcopalian priesthoods are facing contemporary crises because of scandals in their priesthoods. In the Episcopalian denomination, Eugene Robinson became the first openly homosexual bishop in the history of Christendom when he was named bishop of New Hampshire in 2003.

In Catholicism, a small percentage of priests have exhibited sexual disorders and abused youths, usually of the same sex. There has also been diminished accountability on the part of priests and bishops, thereby allowing these crimes to be committed. Another indirect effect is the apparent shortage of men today willing to become priests due to the lack of papal fidelity in some seminaries and dioceses.

These scandals have been attributed by many to the gradual distortion of the Church's teachings, especially in matters of sexuality, and to the ineffectiveness of seminary preparation.

Some propose to fix these problems by accepting avowed homosexuals into the priesthood, allowing women to become Catholic priests, and permitting Catholic priests to be married. Episcopalianism, with two million followers in the United States and about seventy-five million worldwide in what is called the Anglican Communion, is facing a rift between those who approve of homosexual priests and those who do not. Catholicism has rejected priestly homosexuality, preferring instead to reform its seminaries and make priests more accountable.

Sexual scandals have shaken the confidence of some followers, who are already coping with a dwindling number of priests. Sexual controversies and diminishing ranks represent serious problems for Christianity. These are challenges that will affect—and define—Christianity throughout the twenty-first century.

RALPH FRASCA

Further Reading

Bleichner, H. (2004). *View from the altar: Reflections on the rapidly changing Catholic priesthood*. New York: Crossroad.

Coriden, J. A. (Ed.). (1985). *The code of Canon Law: A text and commentary*. Mahwah, NJ: Paulist Press.

Flannery, A. (1992). *Vatican Council II: The conciliar and post-conciliar documents*. (Rev. Ed.). Northport, NY: Costello.

St. Jerome. (1999). *On illustrious men* (T. P. Halton, Trans.). Washington, DC: Catholic University of America Press.

John Paul II. (1984). *Reconciliatio et Paenitentia*. Retrieved from http://www.cin.org/jp2ency/reconcil.html

John XXIII. (1959). *Sacerdotii Nostri Primordia*. Retrieved from http://www.adoremus.org/JohnXXIII-Priesthood.html

Kelly, J. N. D. (1975). *Jerome: His life, writings, and controversies*. London: Duckworth.

Ladd, G. J. (2001). *Archbishop Fulton J. Sheen: A man for all media*. Fort Collins, CO: Ignatius Press.

Lynch, C. (1998). *Selling Catholicism: Bishop Sheen and the power of television*. Lexington: University Press of Kentucky.

Marcus, S. (1973). *Father Coughlin: The tumultuous life of the priest of the Little Flower*. Boston: Little, Brown.

Millar, W. R. (2001). *Priesthood in ancient Israel*. St. Louis, MO: Chalice.

Ogles, R. M., & Howard, H. H. (1984). Father Coughlin in the periodical press, 1931–1942. *Journalism Quarterly 61*, 280–286, 363.

Osborne, K. (1989). *Priesthood: A history of ordained ministry in the Roman Catholic Church*. Mahwah, NJ: Paulist Press.

Roberts, N. (1984). *Dorothy Day and the Catholic worker*. Albany: State University of New York Press.

Sheen, F. J. (1980). *Treasure in clay: The autobiography of Fulton J. Sheen*. Fort Collins, CO: Ignatius Press.

Terwilliger, R. E., & Homes, U. T. (1975). *To be a priest*. New York: Seabury Press.

Tull, C. J. (1965). *Father Coughlin and the New Deal*. Syracuse, NY: Syracuse University Press.

Profane Communication

Ever since humans learned to communicate, certain words, phrases, and gestures have been considered profane. As cultures advanced and language evolved, what was considered profane also changed. However, despite the fact that every age has deemed certain phrases inappropriate to speak or write, profanity itself has remained a permanent fixture in communication repertoires. Are profane expressions just as essential to human communication as sacred expressions?

Definition

In its original form, *profanity* referred to anything that was blasphemous, sacrilegious, or that took God's name in vain. Blasphemous or sacrilegious expressions could be singular idioms like "damn you" and "to hell with you" or descriptions that characterized another human being as anything other than a child of God. For instance, calling someone a "whore," "bitch," or "bastard" would have been deemed "insolent communication." Combining profane and sacred language was considered a dangerous, if not deadly, action.

Taking God's name in vain has always been the ultimate verbal sin that could result in eternal damnation. Since the early thirteenth century religious people have argued that simply by saying "God damn it" a person is sinning by telling God what to do as well as by placing God's name next to a profanity. However, a more progressive and liberal definition sees the taking of God's name in vain as the act of turning away from God and, in a clear mind and with knowledge of the Creator, claiming not to need God for anything. It is, in essence, the idea of knowing there is God but saying human beings are the ultimate measure of all things.

A more moderate form of swearing is known as "minced oaths." Prior to the Victorian era, Puritans and Protestant reformers were particularly strict about profane expressions, doling out exceptionally harsh discipline to those who dared to break the ban on such language. As a result, commoners created a method of swearing that did not directly desecrate holy or sacred places or names. Instead, similar-sounding phrases or idioms were adopted that expressed the same sentiments in limited, peculiar, and less offensive forms so as not to bring on the wrath of the church. Many minced oaths are still commonly used today—for example, jumping Jehoshaphat (for jumping Jesus); son of a gun (son of a bitch); Gadzooks (God's hooks (referring to the nails in Jesus on the cross); drat (God rot it); for crying out loud (for Christ's sake); and tarnation (damnation).

Over time, profane communication accumulated a list of synonyms: vulgarity, swearing, cursing, cussing, blasphemy, sacrilege, obscenity, expletives, and (an American favorite) "the four-letter word." As the list of synonyms has grown, so too has the number of things people consider profane. These now include crude humor about excrement or its function; racist, sexist, homophobic, or demeaning expressions; and insults to the disabled. Expressions of vanity ("I'm beautiful; she is ugly") or statements that crassly express discontent ("your idea sucks") have also been deemed rude, crude, and socially unacceptable.

The Problem of a Singular Definition

Sacred communication is the expression of ideas oriented toward meaning and truth; it provides an axis around which words and actions can be justified. But if profane communication is defined as the opposite, as useless expressions or irrational communication, then defining the exact nature of communication may become problematic, if not impossible. This raises the question of what the purpose of language actually is. At a rudimentary level, communication is an attempt to transfer information or emotions from one person to another. That being the case, any word that can help this transmittal will have both purpose and usefulness. The fact that some people choose vulgar expressions rather than more accepted words shows that profane communication is useful in some circumstances; in fact, research has revealed that profane expressions bring on pleasant feelings of relief from pain and stress. There is a growing consensus that profanity is a useful form of communication.

Tertiary Meanings

According to some observers, people frequently deem words bad or offensive without ever considering their original meaning. Children grow up thinking that some expressions are terrible, sinful, and never to be spoken, yet they cannot articulate why they believe that some words are innately bad. They haven't yet recognized that some words are profane or offensive in one context but completely acceptable in another. For example, it is acceptable to say "Jesus Christ" zealously in a church but not in other public places. It is fine to use the word *broad* to describe a person with a wide girth or chest but not to refer to a woman.

What is considered profane also changes with time and differs among cultures. For example, in early translations of the King James Bible the word *piss* is used, but in modern translations this has been changed to *urinate* (see 2 Kings 18:27; Isaiah 36:12; 1 Sam 25:22, 25:34; 1 Kings 14:10, 16:11, 21:21; 2 Kings 9:8). In Quebec, profanity often uses words from Catholic religion and liturgy. A very strong way to express anger or frustration is to yell the words *tabarnak* (tabernacle), *sacrament* (sacrament), or *câlice* (chalice of Christ's blood).

Modern Definitions of Profanity

Actor Geoffrey Hughes argues in his 1991 book that the words that constitute modern profanity are those that reference the genital or anal area. He finds that the most highly charged and least acceptable words are those that reference activities or functions closest to the genitalia. Other commentators have noted that people are averse to discussing the traits they have in common with animals, specifically sex, sexual organs, and excrement. Verbal standards in place today include specific words that are forbidden on public airwaves. In

December 2000, the British Broadcasting Standards Commission, the Independent Television Commission, the BBC, and the Advertising Standards Authority issued a list of words generally considered the most offensive. The study and findings were aptly named *Delete Expletives* (www.asa.org.uk). In early 2004, the Federal Communications Commission ruled that profane speech is "any speech that is grossly offensive, whether or not it has anything to do with sex or excretion"(www.fcc.gov).

This ruling is a further extension of the FCC's 1973 ruling on George Carlin's comedy routine, which used several "offensive" words on prime-time television. The *Seven Words You Can Never Say on Television* ruling argued that such language could not be broadcast at times of the day when there is a risk children might hear the words.

History

Profanity has always been a primary concern of the Church. In the early thirteenth and fourteenth centuries, Catholic monks were often harshly disciplined when speaking, even humorously, about any part of Jesus' life or of Church matters. In the late fourteenth century, cleric Nicolas Eymerich argued that there was a direct connection between the way people spoke and their consciousness; he claimed that people who cursed were spiritually sick and that spontaneous utterances could reveal a rotting soul and a propensity for religious infidelity and heresy. By the late fifteenth and early sixteenth centuries, Church authorities were arguing that cursing was among the greatest challenges facing the purity of the Church. If words carried the sanctity of law, they reasoned, then profane communication carried the power to offend the heavens and God, to provoke divine wrath on entire communities, and to trigger epidemic diseases, pestilence, and flooding. Therefore, councils were convened and people were charged and punished for speaking profanely. Among the forms of punishment meted out were flogging, banishment, branding the lips with a hot iron, mutilating the tongue, muzzling the mouth like a dog, and being forced to ride backward on a donkey through a city (to demonstrate that profane speakers were no better than the ass that carried them).

Profanity appears to have premiered in written form around the mid-sixteenth century, particularly in the works of William Shakespeare. It was not unusual for Shakespeare's plays to be full of sex, violence, crime, racism, religious satire, profanity, and politics. Literary scholars argue that the popularity of Shakespeare's plays is directly linked to the fact that they are full of religious curses. Religious curses and racy content were Shakespeare's way of challenging taboos against dirty talk and injustice. Nonetheless, Shakespeare found his plays censored quite frequently in order, as the censors claimed, to protect young minds from corrupting thoughts and ideas.

Censorship and the Church's intense concern with profanity led to the growth of arguments that were skeptical of the Church and its ways. Secular apologists and church theologians alike began to explain that profanity is not always wicked. While it may sometimes be aggressive or abusive, vulgarity can also provide harmless, nondirective humor and relief from anger and personal distress; it may be an involuntary response to pain, happiness, or frustration; or it may be used strategically to encourage sexual arousal or emotional action. The neuro-psycho-social theory of cursing argues that language is as much a mode of action as a physical move or gesture. Many social scientists have argued that it is better that people curse than act out their aggressive fantasies.

Future

Speech is the animator of the imagination. There is no doubt that the human mind can create both sacred and profane words, symbols, and actions. Another piece in the puzzle of the complex evolution of religious communication, profane communication helps us understand how ill-mannered speech came to be a primary concern for Church and society. Profane and sacred communication exist side by side, one helping to define the other, and it appears that the future role of profane communication will resemble its role in the past.

MATTHEW NELSON DRUMHELLER

See also Culture Wars; Free Speech; Idolatry; Pornography; Profanity (Taboo)

Further Reading

Burchfield, R. (1972). *Unlocking the English language*. London: Faber.

Guerlac, S. (1997). *Literary polemics*. Stanford, CA: Stanford University Press.

Hughes, G. (1991). *Swearing: A social history of foul language, oaths and profanity in English*. Oxford: Blackwell.

Jay, T. (2000). *Why we curse: A neuro-psycho-social theory of speech*. Amsterdam and Philadelphia: Benjamins.

Montagu, A. (1973). *The anatomy of swearing*. London and New York: Macmillan and Collier.

Partridge, E. (1960). *Slang* (3rd ed.). London: Routledge and Kegan Paul.

Rawson, H. (1989). *Wicked words*. New York: Crown Publishers.

Ullmann, S. (1951). *Words and their use*. London: Frederick Muller.

Profanity (Taboo)

The anthropological concept of *taboo* was originally used by Polynesian cultures to label those practices restricted to kings, priests, or chiefs. Commoners, or just a particular class, were forbidden to eat certain foods, enter certain structures, or perform certain actions. The more modern connotation of the taboo refers to any prohibited behavior considered unacceptable in a particular community or society. For instance, many cultures consider the act of cannibalism to be fundamentally unacceptable, and sexual relations with close blood relatives (incest) are almost universally labeled as immoral. Taboo language imposes a similar restriction on common use. *Profanity* refers to any vocabulary or phrase considered to be blasphemous, vulgar, obscene, or otherwise socially unacceptable. In more common terms, profane speech is synonymous with swearing or cursing. The heated use of expletives is as old as spoken language itself, with examples dating back to the most ancient written records. Such taboo language can be divided into two main categories: words referencing God and religious beliefs (blasphemy, which includes oath making and cursing) and words that deal inappropriately with race, sex, and certain base bodily functions (vulgarity, which includes slurs and swearing). The first set of words offends deity; the second, society.

With the exception of psychological afflictions such as Tourette's syndrome, profanity is usually intentional. The speaker may be reacting to the effects of stress, attempting to illicit a strong emotional reaction, or embracing a cultural dialect. Regardless of the motivation behind such speech, profane language is often received with shock and offense. If such a reaction is intended, the vocabulary has accomplished its purpose. If not, the speaker has created a hostile barrier to communication. In the public sphere, this can be disastrous.

Because profane language is essentially offensive, both organized religions and various institutions of mass communication have a number of rules and regulations that control or otherwise curtail the application of such vocabulary. Most religions share the general concept of blasphemy, and devout worshippers are expected to maintain a certain level of semantic propriety—particularly when making reference to deity. In the public sphere, organizations like the Federal Communications Commission impose rating systems, content regulations, and fines on media companies that use or abuse vulgar language. Yet in spite of such taboos, profanity remains an important part of most languages.

Establishing the Origins of Profanity

According to Ashley Montagu (*The Anatomy of Swearing*, 1967), profane speech dates back to the very first primitive utterances. Early humans would have used grunts or angry growls to express displeasure, pain, and annoyance. Many nonliterate cultures today have similar verbal equivalents, usually invectives used to insult a person's sexuality or physical anatomy. Literate cultures are even more prolific, and evidence of a profane vocabulary is found in most ancient cultures.

The Egyptians had a complex pantheon of Great Powers to call upon for both oaths and curses. In addition, a frank threat of forced sodomy was considered one of the worst threats in that ancient culture. Most Judeo-Christian cultures trace the codification of profane language back to the Ten Commandments. According to the stone tablets born by Moses, "Thou shalt not take the name of the Lord thy God in vain; for the Lord will not hold him guiltless that taketh his name in vain" (Exodus 20:7). Such blasphemy was considered a capital offense, as is rather explicitly illustrated in Leviticus 24.

In the New Testament, Jesus Christ shifted the focus of blasphemy from God to the Holy Ghost: "Wherefore I say unto you, All manner of sin and blasphemy shall be forgiven unto men: but the blasphemy against the Holy Ghost shall not be forgiven unto men" (Matthew 12:31). The Holy Ghost is generally seen as a representation of God's spirit and love; therefore, this admonition redefines blasphemy as the denial of faith itself. This concept is akin to the Muslim sin of *kufr*, which means "disbelief" or "lack of faith."

Offending God: Understanding Blasphemy

In the religious sphere, the broadest definition of the profane refers to anything unconsecrated, secular, or civil. The term can be applied to people and things as well as words and general language. In terms of verbal profanity, however, blasphemy customarily refers to disregard or contempt of the sacred, specifically the taking of God's name in vain or attempting to usurp

His power (to curse another). A more universal application includes slander, evil speaking, and defamation of others.

The admonition to not take the name of God in vain applies to using the name of deity as an exclamation, using the Lord's name to consecrate an inappropriate oath or promise, or to invoke the spirit of God without just cause. While Christianity usually limits this prohibition to unnecessary vocal utterances of "God" or "Jesus Christ," the Jewish tradition honors the written word as well—the letters YHVH (Yahweh or Jehovah) are not to be written frivolously or treated lightly (the literal word itself is a manifestation of God).

Jesus Christ revised the Law of Moses to prohibit all forms of oath making: "But I say unto you, Swear not at all; neither by heaven; for it is God's throne: Nor by the earth; for it is his footstool: neither by Jerusalem; for it is the city of the great King. Neither shalt thou swear by thy head, because thou canst not make one hair white or black" (Matthew 5:34-36). Christians are admonished to keep their speech plain and simple, avoiding the unnecessary invocation of either God or His creations.

Muslims are given somewhat greater freedom in both direct references to Allah and oath making; the sin of blasphemy lies in the failure to honor those references or to realize those oaths. The failure to be thankful for and obedient to God is more serious than taking God's name lightly. Nevertheless, those who vocally express contempt for Allah Himself or His laws, commands, prohibitions, or prophets are considered the most grievous of blasphemers. In addition, unbelievers who live in Islamic communities are forbidden to disrespect Allah or publicly testify to the divine nature of Jesus Christ.

Jews are to reverence the literal name of the almighty, Christians are to love God and follow Jesus Christ's example, and Muslims are required to be constantly thankful for and obedient to Allah. However, in addition to respecting the very name of God—be that Elohim, Jesus Christ, or Allah—one is also forbidden to speak *for* God. Using God's name to evoke a curse without the proper authority is a grievous sin, for it attempts to usurp God's authority. The simplest manifestation of this form of blasphemy is the words *damn*, *hell*, and the more inflammatory *Goddamn it*.

In addition to these more literal manifestations of the profane, where the invocation of deity marks the transgression, all faiths emphasize the need for the pious to be kind and generous to one another. Speaking harshly, slandering someone's good name, or using cruel invectives all demean and belittle others. Such language is hurtful, spiteful, and considered un-God-like, which makes it literally profane and vulgar.

Offending Others: Understanding Vulgarity

Vulgar or otherwise coarse language is used in common speech to a variety of ends. Like the term *profane*, *vulgar* refers to anything common, ordinary, or base. In reference to general language, the vulgar (or vulgate) is the common tongue—the vernacular. It is not considered "proper speech" but it is well known and used nonetheless. Such vocabulary is generally used to insult someone on a personal level, to debase both gender and sex, or to make crude and inappropriate references to other biological functions.

Some of the most offensive and hateful terms in regular use today attack a person's race, parentage, or gender. Racial slurs are one of the oldest forms of invectives: most races, cultures, and nations possess a diverse vocabulary to reference other peoples. Words that openly question someone's birth or social standing are similarly offensive, specifically those accusing one of being a bastard or a "son of a bitch." Some of the most offensive terms, however, use sexual references to belittle and categorize someone's gender.

Crude or base versions of sexual organs are used synecdochically to degrade or humiliate others. For instance, terms like *dick* or *cock* have both a denotative reference to the penis and connotative pejorative meanings. In addition, vulgar references to the sex act itself are often used as both verbs and adjectives, to either convey a sexual threat like sodomy or rape or to add a particularly base modification to an otherwise innocuous term. Such phrases can be as harmless as "screwing around" or as socially taboo as the f-word.

When treated with coarse language, intercourse becomes vulgar and intentionally offensive. Similarly, crude references to digestion and excrement are popular forms of swearing. The terms *arse* and *shit* call attention to the base realities of life, the former used regularly as a noun and the latter as a verb or adjective. All of these terms are often used out of literal context, the emotional impact becoming more important than the actual meaning. For instance, a farmer might casually refer to "horse shit" where no offense is intended, but one who admonishes another to "Get your shit together" is using a vulgar term to elicit an emotional response.

Regardless of the origins or denotative references of such terminology, the words themselves become vulgar or inappropriate because of societal conventions and connotation. When used to express emotional frustration and hostility, almost any word can be considered a curse. Nevertheless, modern society has codified a number of these terms, and those are the ones prohibited and regulated in the media.

Regulating Speech in the Media

With the advent of publicly broadcast radio, television, and film, many agencies have been created to monitor and control media content. Because some argue that such media are imposed upon a listening and viewing public (hearing and seeing are more involuntary than reading), the use of profanity must be carefully controlled to protect children and the innocent public. Although scholars like Matthew Spitzer (*Seven Dirty Words and Six Other Stories*, 1986) challenge this generalization, the United States government seems to agree, for organizations like the Federal Communications Commission exist to filter the obscene out of the public sphere.

Censorship and content regulation of the media in the United States trace their roots back to the Comstock Act of 1873, which was intended to suppress the trade and circulation of obscene and immoral literature. In 1934, the FCC was established by the Communications Act to regulate radio and later television transmissions. In both print and on the airwaves, the government has attempted to balance issues of free speech with the suppression of the obscene and vulgar. This potential conflict came to a possible resolution in 1957 when the Supreme Court ruled in *Roth v. United States* that obscene speech and content was not protected by the second Amendment because of its total lack or redeeming social importance.

The issue of censorship returned in the late 1970s when comedian George Carlin presented his now famous "Filthy Words" monologue. The routine heavily featured seven vulgar and prohibited words (although curiously none of them are blasphemous) and openly mocked the puritanical nature of American broadcasting. A New York radio station aired the routine and was summarily sued by the FCC. In *FCC v. Pacifica Foundation*, Justice Stevens of the Supreme Court ruled that radio stations could be punished and fined for airing indecent material. This precedent has since been extended to television, cable, and satellite transmissions.

Although premium television networks with paying subscribers generally circumvent such strict regulations, the content of radio and basic cable is carefully monitored. "Shock jocks" like Howard Stern test the boundaries of the FCC, but they generally find themselves subject to heavy fines and censorship. Prime time television allows certain profane references like *damn* and *God* but continues to prohibit others, like *shit* and *Jesus*. Shows on basic cable channels like FX have pushed the envelope even further, and programming on premium channels such as HBO and Showtime have virtually no limits.

Predicting the Future of Profane Language

As society becomes more secularized, blasphemous references will cease to offend or even be noticed. Even now the utterance "Oh my God" is treated as commonplace and acceptable, and words like *ass*, *bitch*, and *bastard* are regularly heard during prime time. Although the more vulgar references to sex are limited to adult programming, shows like HBO's *Deadwood* are transcending any conception of propriety and modesty. As the public becomes more desensitized to vulgarity, the use of profanity will become more commonplace.

KYLE WILLIAM BISHOP

See also Pornography

Further Reading

Claussen, D. (Ed.). (2002). *Sex, religion, media.* Lanham, MD: Rowman & Littlefield.

Dooling, R. (1996). *Blue streak: Swearing, free speech, and sexual harassment.* New York: Random House.

Hastings, J. (Ed.). (1955). Blasphemy. In *Encyclopaedia of religion and ethics* (Vol. 2, pp. 669–72). New York: Charles Scribner's Sons.

Hughes, G. (1991). *Swearing: A social history of foul language, oaths and profanity in English.* Cambridge, MA: Blackwell.

Jay, T. (2000). *Why we curse: A neuro-psycho-social theory of speech.* Philadelphia: John Benjamins.

Levi-Strauss, C. (1974). *Structural anthropology.* New York: Basic Books.

Middleton, K. R., Lee, W. E., & Chamberlin, B. F. (2004). *The law of public communication.* New York: Allyn & Bacon.

Montagu, A. (1967). *The anatomy of swearing.* New York: Collier Books.

Post, R. C. (Ed.). (1998). *Censorship and silencing.* Los Angeles: Getty Research Institute.

Spitzer, M. L. (1986). *Seven dirty words and six other stories: Controlling the content of print and broadcast.* New Haven, CT: Yale University Press.

Valenti, J. (2000, December). *How it all began.* Motion Picture Association of America. Retrieved March 14, 2005, from http://www.mpaa.org/movieratings/about/index.htm

Wolfson, N. (1997). *Hate speech, sex speech, free speech.* Westport, CT: Praeger.

Prophets

A prophet is an exceptionally gifted person with spiritual insights who communicates divine revelations. Prophets typically claim divine inspiration for their actions, especially when such actions affect a large group of people who subscribe to the claims of the prophet. Characteristically, prophets not only foretell the future, but they also speak to immediate situations that demand religious, social, and political responses. The medium of communication is the spoken word, which prophets claim they were inspired to use by God and through encounters with the supernatural. In most religions of the world, prophets are regarded as messengers of divine messages. A prophet may carry out a specific divine mandate and thereafter return to ordinary life. On the other hand, a prophet may gather followers and thereby sustain a religious movement that survives after his or her death.

The Prophetic Office

Almost every prophet undergoes a divine encounter or has an experience of the supernatural, often in dreams and visions, which invests him or her with a sense of divine obligation or mission. For example, Moses in the Hebrew Bible encountered the supernatural when a voice attributed to God called out from a burning bush and commissioned him to deliver the Israelites from bondage. Usually the call to prophesy is followed by a period of personal crises when prophets have to change their personality and behavior and assume the responsibility of communicating a divine message to a particular people. The ecstatic experience has often been associated with prophets, and unlike priests, who are official religious functionaries with institutionalized roles, prophets are forceful personalities who do not fit into any existing social or religious order. Quite often, miracles of various kinds are credited to prophets by their followers as part of the confirmation of a divine call.

Prophets typically function in situations of rapid social change or where the future looks bleak. In such situations, it is the task of prophets to call attention to the need to correct certain religious perversions, to demand total devotion to gods or God, or to call for a renewal of neglected social and religious obligations. In addition, prophets may challenge the ruling elite against misgovernance or try to advance social actions to better the society. Prophets demonstrate the relevance of their revelatory knowledge when they speak convincingly about the future. However, in many cases, the majority, who are contented with the status quo, rejects the prophetic message. At some point in their ministry, prophets usually face rejection from the larger society because their messages are considered too novel or radical.

Since prophets operate through verbal communication, their messages may be either direct or couched in a symbolism that requires reflection and interpretation to understand. For example, the prophet Nathan in the Hebrew Bible (II Samuel 12:1–15) told the story of a rich man who, in order to satisfy his selfish desire, oppressed and exploited his poor neighbor as an indirect way of communicating to King David the gravity of his wicked actions of plotting the death of one of his soldiers, Uriah, and then taking the latter's wife.

The prophetic tradition allows prophets to undertake actions that are uncommon or which ordinary people cannot undertake. Among these is the prerogative to rebuke royalties and political officials, to ridicule actions taken by highly placed officials, and to challenge the commitment of people toward a particular course of action. Authoritarian rulers are frequently disdainful of prophets and their prophecies because such prophecies usually challenge royal prerogatives and run counter to the expectations of the people.

Prophets speak not only against the conditions of nations but also against the moral and religious failures of individuals, particularly royalty, though such bold speech may meet with dire consequences. For example, John the Baptist, a first-century prophet in Israel, was imprisoned and later beheaded for preaching against the moral inconsistency of Herod Antipas (4 BCE–39 CE). Even those who are not arrested or killed may have to find refuge far from the reach of the law.

Prophets in Ancient Israel

Prophesying is a common phenomenon, especially in monotheistic religions. For example, many prophets tried to communicate God's message to the ancient Israelites. Although Moses is regarded as the first prophet who addressed both the social and religious conditions of Israelites while they were in servitude in Egypt, it was from the time of Samuel that the prophetic tradition became common and institutionalized. Before Samuel some prophets, such as Deborah and Gideon, also performed certain secular political activities and were therefore referred to as "judges" in the Hebrew Bible.

Between the eighth and ninth centuries BCE, when the nations of Judah and Israel were facing social and political crises, prophetic messages became common

and prominent, and the prophets addressed their messages to these situations. While some prophets, like Hosea and Jeremiah, rebuked the Israelites for abandoning the worship of Yahweh and predicted national calamity, others, such as Amos and Malachi, called for renewed commitment to Yahweh and the upholding of social responsibilities to fellow Israelites, particularly to the poor and the oppressed. Isaiah and Ezekiel and other prophets proclaimed messages of hope, restoration, and divine intervention to bring succor to a people in search of deliverance.

The manner of communicating the messages varied from one prophet to another. Some were dramatic and demonstrated their messages through activities; others just proclaimed their messages verbally. For example, the prophet Jeremiah, despite the doom situation of being imprisoned and the Babylonians laying siege on Jerusalem in 586 BCE, still proceeded to conclude an economic transaction with a future maturity to demonstrate that there was hope of renewed life for the people of Judah.

Although Jesus was regarded as a prophet in the Scriptures, it was his messianic attributes, which fitted the expectation of the Jews and around which his teaching centered, that were emphasized by the early Christians. By the first century CE, prophets featured less frequently in the Jewish religion. However, they have continued to inspire many generations, in part because most of their activities were preserved in the Hebrew Bible.

Prophets in Islam

Prophesy is recognized in Islam, and Muhammad is accepted as a great prophet with the seal of the prophets. About 610 CE, Muhammad received messages from Allah through the angel Gabriel while meditating in a cave. These revelations signified his call to prophesy, and thereafter he challenged the Meccans to forsake idolatry. Having been rejected and persecuted, he fled from Mecca to Medina, a historical event that Muslims celebrate as *hijrah*, the beginning of the Islamic calendar. Symbolically, it means the movement from idolatry to the true knowledge of Allah. It was only in 629 CE that Muhammad was able to conquer the Meccans in a war and to impose his monotheistic belief on them.

The claim that there are other prophets after Muhammad has been a principal cause of disagreement between orthodox Islam and the Ahmadīyya, an Islamic sect originating in the early twentieth century in Pakistan, which regards Ghulam Ahmad (1835–1908) as a prophet similar to Muhammad. However, unlike

Muhammad, who promoted a monotheistic belief in Allah against the erstwhile idolatry of the people, Ghulam's teaching aimed at revitalizing Islam in the face of contending religions of the time.

Although many *mahdi* (reformers) in Islam may have the attributes of a prophet, they do not fit into the prophetic model because they usually do not lay claim to continuous revelation from the supernatural; more often, their central action is to mobilize the collective to participate in certain revolutionary political actions.

Prophets in other Religions

New religious movements are often inspired by prophetic figures, and the sustenance of such movements depends largely on the message brought by the prophets and on their charisma as mediums through which the divine communicates messages. Some founders of new religious movements claim to be prophets or invite their followers to treat them as prophets. Some millennial movements had leaders who engaged in coercion and brainwashing to keep a group together. For example, David Koresh of the Branch Dravidians in Waco, Texas, styled himself a prophet. He was fascinated with End-Times prophecies and interpreted certain passages of the Christian Scriptures as part of God's demand on the group; he finally submitted to the grim apocalyptic vision that led to the military encounters in April and May of 1993.

Prophecy was at a low ebb in Christianity after the prophetic and ecstatic experiences of the Montanists in the second and third century CE until it was revived by the activities of African healer-prophets. By the beginning of the twentieth century, prophets had become a common feature of the new Christian expression in Africa. Fostered by the pressures of colonialism, racial discrimination, and nationalism, these prophets, most of whom had ecstatic experiences in addition to divine revelations, responded to the situations of their times by proclaiming new messages that were suited to the African quest for freedom and deliverance from social and political oppression

With highly successful healing ministries, many of these prophets won thousands of converts to Christianity and eventually established their own churches free from any connection to Western-mission Christianity. These churches, generally called African Independent Churches, became a major social and religious movement. Their first prophet was Isaiah Shembe, who founded the Church of the Nazarites in Natal, South Africa, in 1911. At the same time, in West Africa, William Wade Harris from Liberia carried out an extensive evangelistic activities in present day Côte d'Ivoire and western Ghana, which resulted in the founding of the Harrist churches after his death. In Congo, Central Africa, there was Simon Kimbangu, whose prophetic and healing activities resulted in the establishment of the Church of Jesus Christ on Earth in 1956.

In Nigeria, Joseph Ayo Babalola and Josiah Ositelu were among the foremost prophets of the Aladura revival in the 1930s. Ositelu founded the Church of the Lord (Aladura), and Babalola's activities and other events brought into being the Christ Apostolic Church in the early 1940s. While certain practices of these prophets were consonant with mainline Pentecostal tradition, some practices, such as healing and divination, which were rooted in traditional African cosmology, were viewed as syncretistic and labeled separatist by early Western missionaries and scholars. However, new scholarship in the 1960s has led to a more favorable view of these churches and their prophets. While Babalola and Ositelu promoted the ecstatic experience, healing and foretelling of the future, contemporary Pentecostal preachers expected a spiritual and social empowerment of Christians through the religious experience often described as "baptism of the Holy Spirit."

Social Functions of Prophets

Because prophets are agents of change, they have been responsible for significant social and religious movements. Prophetic movements serve as mechanisms for sustaining transitions from rural to urban life, from the traditional to the modern, and from the local to the global. Furthermore, prophets offer hope to despairing people, and their predictions about the future have inspired social change. They are often regarded also as moral persuaders, and their prescriptions and predictions, which often form the basis of the religious expressions of the faithful, have and resulted in diverse religious movements.

Religious adherents commonly seek to distinguish between true and false prophets by measuring their conformity or deviation from existing religious traditions, the fulfillment or otherwise of the prophecies they proclaimed, or by judging the prophet's lifestyle. However, some of those labeled false prophets have won millions of adherents and formed lasting religious organizations. Indeed, oratory and charisma have enabled prophets to convince many to accept their teaching, despite widespread oppositions. A good example is Joseph Smith, the founder of the Church of Jesus of the Latter Day Saints, who inspired a religious and social movement that led to the founding of the state of

A photo-based mix media collage with prophetic symbolism: the sacrificial goat, cryptic writing, and the door to...
Courtesy of Elena Ray/istockphoto.com

other adaptive strategies within their group for survival. The quest to know the future and overcome the perplexities of life continues to make prophets relevant in many societies. Not only do prophets communicate and interpret divine messages, they are also initiators of major religious and social changes.

MATTHEWS A. OJO

Further Reading

Arthur, D. (2001). *A smooth stone: Biblical prophecy in historical perspective*. Lanham, MD: University Press of America.

Aune, D. E. (1983). *Prophecy in early Christianity and the ancient Mediterranean world*. Grand Rapids, MU: Eerdmans.

Blenkinsopp, J. (1996). *A history of prophecy in Israel*. Louisville, KY: Westminster John Knox Press.

Breck, S. (Ed.). (1996). *Prophets and paradigms: Essays in honour of Gene M. Tucker*. Sheffield, UK: Sheffield Academic Press.

Grabbe, L. L., & Haak, R. D. (2003). *Knowing the end from the beginning: The prophetic, the apocalyptic and their relationships*. London and New York: T & T Clark International.

MacGaffey, W. (1983). *Modern Kongo prophets: Religion in a plural society*. Bloomington: Indiana University Press.

McKenna, M. (2001). *Prophets: Words of fire*. Maryknoll, NY: Orbis Books.

de Moor, J. C. (2001). *The elusive prophet: The prophet as a historical person, literary character and anonymous artist*. Leiden: Brill.

Ndiokwere, N. I. (1981). *Prophecy and revolution: The role of prophets in the independent African churches and in Biblical tradition*. London: SPCK.

Nissinen, M., Ritner, R. K., & Machinist, P. (2003). *Prophets and prophecy in the Ancient Near East*. Atlanta, GA: Society of Biblical Literature.

Peel, J. D. Y. (1968). *Aladura: A religious movement among the Yoruba*. London: Oxford.

Robbins, T., & Palmer, S. J. (Eds.). (1997). *Millennium, Messiah, and mayhem: Contemporary apocalyptic movements*. London and New York: Routledge.

Sawyer, J. F A. (1993). *Prophecy and the Biblical Prophets*. Oxford and New York: Oxford.

Stone, J. R. (Ed.). (2000). *Expecting Armageddon, essential readings in failed prophecy*. London and New York: Routledge.

Sundkler, B. G. M. (1961). *Bantu prophets in South Africa* (2nd Ed.). Oxford and New York: Oxford.

Wheeler, B. M. (2002). *Prophets in the Quran: An introduction to the Quran and Muslim exegesis*. London and New York: Continuum.

Zvi, E. B., & Floyd, M. H. (2000). *Writings and speech in Israelite and ancient Near Eastern prophecy*. Atlanta, GA: Society of Biblical Literature.

Utah in 1847. Regarded as a prophet by Mormons, he was derided by many outside the Church. However, the traditions of the Church of the Latter Day Saints accept Joseph Smith as a great prophet, as do almost all his successors who served as presidents of the church.

Some prophets who preach millennial messages become militant and revolutionary when they are violently opposed by the society. Usually societies that have been affected by crises like war, famine, economic hardship, or political uncertainty witness the rise of prophetic figures who try to address some or part of the crisis. The mass mobilization of people by prophets often has political implications, particularly when these prophets attack policies of the secular ruling class.

The Continuing Relevance of Prophets

The failure of prophecies does not bring an end to a religious movement. On the contrary, it may challenge members of the group to heighten their evangelistic activities, to reaffirm their beliefs in such prophecies, to interpret them as delayed fulfillment, or to draw on

Proselytizing

In 2004 an American Airlines pilot flying from Los Angeles to New York made an announcement over the intercom to his passengers. He suggested that the Christian passengers engage the nonbelievers in dialogue. When the airplane landed four and a half hours later, the pilot responded to objections to his intercom idea with a suggestion that he and the passengers have more dialogue about the Lord. For his witness, the pilot was grounded without pay while American Airlines investigated and the airline president issued a public apology.

The Times called the pilot's behavior proselytizing. For Christians, this label is used when one Christian group disapproves of the mission activities of another group and, consequently, suffers a loss in members. In Protestant circles and elsewhere, this activity is known as evangelism but organizations including Catholics, Eastern or Greek Orthodox and mainline denominations abhor it. It can be found in humorous contexts such as T-shirts sporting slogans such as "Jesus is My Homeboy" for Christians and one reportedly worn by American Muslims that reads, "My beard causes national security alerts, what does yours do?" (Stalnaker 2004).

Proselytizing—Its Original Meaning

The idea of proselytizing is fraught with misunderstanding, often a casualty in the process of communication where one person is unaware of another person's cultural assumptions and history. To better understand the concept of proselytizing, it's helpful to examine the meaning of the word and its noble heritage.

The English noun "proselyte," a calque of the Greek *proselutos* and the Latin *proselytus,* suggests the phrase "one who comes over (from one location to another)" (Griffiths 2002, 30). In the Bible the term is used to designate a Jewish convert. Stalnaker develops this idea in some depth and explains that the Hebrew word *ger* means foreigner or sojourner, a person or persons who would attach themselves to the Jews who would offer safety (Isaiah 14:1, KJV). According to Stalnaker, Israel was obligated to treat *ger* with kindness, according to Leviticus 19:34. The *ger* enjoyed the same rights as native Israelites and over time, the *ger* began participating in worship of the Jewish Lord. The expression *ger* came to mean outsiders who came on their own initiative to align themselves with Judaism. Stalnaker goes on to explain that Exodus 19:15–16 re-

calls God telling Israel that it will be a kingdom of priests and a holy nation, set apart with a missionary role to others. This explanation sees proselytism as a natural consequence of Israel's obedience to God where the *ger* would come voluntarily to adopt the worship of Yahweh.

Following the Babylonian exile, Jews demonstrated "an aggressive missionary spirit" (Stalnaker 2002, 343). However, other scholars would argue that the dramatic growth was a natural byproduct of stability. By the Second Temple period, 70 CE, the term "proselyte" took on a new meaning with the Hellenistic Jewish Diaspora (Stalnaker 2002). The Jews worked to convert Romans but by the time of Jesus' ministry, the idea of proselytism as practiced by Pharisees was condemned in Matthew 23:13–33. The difference is that the conversion wasn't from paganism to Judaism but paganism to Pharisaism.

Proselytize could have this negative meaning but used in its proper biblical sense, the term distinguishes between the national group of Jews and the nonbirth Jews. By contrast, evangelism as used in the New Testament meant spreading the Gospel, not enlarging their shared identity for the sake of growth, but the acceptance of the Gospel message meant a change from Judaism to Christianity. For this reason, the action appeared to be the same kind of change the non-Jews experienced when they began associating with Jews and gradually accepted Judaism.

"Proselytizing" in the Twenty-first Century

Despite this distinction in terms, proselytizing continues to be regarded as rude bordering on evil. In the Christian subculture, proselytizing is regarded as aggressive missionary zeal where one group loses members to another group. However, parachurch ministries such as the Billy Graham Evangelistic Association and other groups focused on converting a person to become a believer and follower of Christ regard the sharing of the Gospel not only as legitimate religious activity but activity that is commanded by scriptures such as Matthew 28:19–20 (NIV), "Jesus said, 'Go and make disciples of all nations, baptizing them in the name of the Father and of the Son and of the Holy Spirit, and teaching them to obey everything I have commanded you. And surely I am with you always, to the very end of the age.'"

To counter the loss of membership from one denomination to another denomination or an independent denomination, some ministries encourage converts to remain in their denomination, but with a renewed sense of spiritual interest and participation. Nonetheless, the World Council of Churches and the Middle East Council of Churches, which includes Oriental Orthodox, Eastern Orthodox, Catholic, and Protestant, along with Vatican II challenge the notion of proselytism. The issue for critics is the attitude of the person who shares the Gospel. If the motivation appears selfish and concerned with expanding membership, the act may be panned as proselytizing; however, if the act is grounded in concern for a person's eternal life, the act can be viewed as evangelism.

It's my story, and I'm sticking to it. [Said in response to questions about McPherson's 1926 disappearance, which she claimed was a "kidnapping."]

Aimee Semple McPherson (1890–1944)

The psychological state by definition is an internal one that only the person can know intimately. Part of this internal condition often is a genuine sense of acting in the other person's self-interest. Consider the smoker who no longer indulges the habit and who considers it good for others to abandon the valley of nicotine-addiction for the mountaintop of improved health. Using the concept of *ger*, the smoker would be proselytized as she joined into the company of nonsmokers. The goodwill expressed by the reformed smokers for active smokers can be tempered with mixed emotions that may include the well-being of the community and society as a whole. In this sense, the action of proselytizing can be evaluated as possessing ulterior motives.

Proselytizing as the Moral Way of Being

To complicate matters, the act of proselytizing can be a cognitive exercise involving persuasion or compulsion using violence, the threat of violence or the mandate by a court. Griffiths argues that we can't not proselytize as it is part of the moral order and eventually a person will want to compel another to join the fold, whether it is a parent who wants to bring a child into the family's mores to accept their cultural worldview, or a fan who promotes her cricket team, favorite charity, or summer dessert.

By contrast, the act of toleration usually manifests itself as allowing a person to remain an outsider although the agent may consider her in error. Using the Jewish idea of proselytizing to mean "bring the alien into the fold," the person practicing toleration would leave the person alone and tolerate the person's judgment in error, misguided though it may be. By pairing the concepts, we can say that proselytism is intolerant. The matter gets further complicated when tolerance itself is presented as a way of being and presented as a position that must attract supporters and converts.

According to Griffiths, proselytism is a moral act that is unavoidable and is rooted in a seventeenth-century understanding of tolerance as "putting up with" or "bearing something unpleasant" (Griffiths 2002, 31). He uses the example of his toleration of another's pipe smoking as long as it isn't done within the confines of a closed automobile. By permitting the smoking, the tolerant person is allowing something that is harmful to another to continue in a particular context. In this sense, tolerance is not the act of a person who wants to reform another for his own good. It is an act of acquiescence.

In the twenty-first century, tolerance has come to mean "permitting that which doesn't threaten the society's order." When hatred threatens individuals or society, no one has to endorse that thinking or action in the spirit of toleration. In short, toleration has its limits.

Proselytizing and Conflict

Tolerance notwithstanding, the act of seeking converts is often interpreted as a divisive, even hostile act. By far, the group that is most often accused of proselytizing is Evangelical missionaries from one culture to another culture, typically from one country to another country, which can lead to tensions with the state. For instance, the Orthodox and Coptic Churches traditionally have managed to live with Muslims, but Evangelical Christians sometimes challenge the dominant order. While Evangelicals, a group that is committed to sharing the Gospel with everyone by biblical mandate, are most cited for proselytizing, other groups are panned for aggressive soul winning. In early 2004, the Vatican sent an envoy to Moscow to diffuse accusations of aggressive proselytizing of Russian Orthodox. In Salt Lake City, Utah, it's the Jehovah's Witnesses who are trying to reach the Mormons.

Nonetheless, Evangelical Christians are the ones most often identified with mission work, particularly in hot spots such as Muslim countries. Yet in Middle Eastern countries such as Iraq where its 25 million residents are predominantly Muslim, the act of conversion is forbidden under penalty of death. According to the seminal work for Muslims, *The Pact of Umar* (also known as *The Pact of Omar*), a parent must allow children to convert to Islam if they wish; however, according to the Islamic code, known as *sharia*, converting

Muslims is not allowed and is subject to draconian penalties. Nonetheless, in Iraq, Christians and Muslims have lived side by side for centuries with Christians considered a protected minority. During Saddam Hussein's reign, which ended in May 2003, the deputy prime minister was Tariq Aziz, a Christian.

Founded in the seventh century, Islam is the world's second great missionary faith, behind Christianity, with the key belief that Allah is the only God and that Muhammad is his prophet. By the beginning of the twenty-first century, Islam acknowledged Christians and Jews as "people of the book," but their failure to conform to the confession of Islam makes these two religious groups unbelievers by Islamic standards. For a Muslim, a person becomes a convert by faith and by compiling good deeds according to the pillars of the Qur'an, which includes praying five times a day, alms giving or "Zalat," and the declaration of faith or "Shahada." Much controversy surrounds the Muslim approach to salvation with some arguing that the means of persuasion are like the Jewish notion of *ger*; others insist that Muslims, by command of the Qur'an, must actively seek converts even if the converts are under duress.

Muslims number 1.2 billion people or 19 percent of the world's 6.2 billion people. While authorities disagree on the numbers, according to the U.S. Center for World Mission, the following statistics are accurate for the year 2000, the most recent year available. Christians number approximately 2 billion or 33 percent of the world's population; Hindus, among the most ancient of religions, number 762 million adherents or 13 percent of the world's population; and Jews account for 13 million people, about .2 percent of the world's population. Buddhists number 5.9 percent of the world's population and more than 925 million people identify themselves as possessing no religion. Membership figures are gathered by asking respondents to self-select themselves into a category. Guidelines for membership may vary dramatically depending on the group's strict or general standards on gaining membership.

Passive Proselytizing Through Mass Media

Many faiths use holy books, booklets known as tracts, magazines, online presence, broadcasting, novelty shirts, and so on to spread their messages. Christians may be best known for their liberal use of mass media in evangelistic efforts with more effort focused on film in the early twenty-first century than ever. While the goal of film is to entertain, supporters suggest that audiences become attracted to the faith through the vicar-

ious experience. Actor-director Mel Gibson produced The *Passion of the Christ* in 2003 to an uproar of criticism and accolades. The graphic film angered some in the religious community over suggestions that it was anti-Semitic. The earliest known Jesus movie was ostensibly a film version of the Passion play at Oberammergau in 1898, which was actually staged and filmed on the rooftop of the Grand Central Palace in New York. Among the best-known evangelism films is the *Jesus* movie. Using their own accounting methods, the San Clemente, California-based Jesus Film Project reported that as of July 1, 2004, 5,790,518,762 have viewed this film since it was released in 1979, and 197,298,327 people were converted.

Despite its rich literal and linguistic history, proselytizing as a notion suggests unwanted and aggressive meddling. At its best, however, the act includes acquainting others with traditions and beliefs of faith as an act of giving. The idea of proselytizing from the Jewish idea of *ger* is about others joining a community and adopting their faith without active lobbying from the community. In this sense, proselytizing can be seen as the best form of evangelism where the convert seeks out the community because the group offers a way of being that offers hope in this life and the afterlife. Future research may explore the affective associations with a term such as proselytizing as well as the use of mass media in seeking converts. While persuasion through publishing remains strong, online appeals promise to have an impact in the years ahead.

MICHAEL RAY SMITH

Further Reading

Arave, L. (2004, February 14). Airline chief apologizes for pilot's evangelical remarks. Retrieved July 25, 2005 from www.cnn.com/2004/TRAVEL/02/14/american/

Arave, L. (2004, June 26). Jehovah's Witnesses realign proselytizing. *Deseret Morning News*, p. E1.

Danker, F. W. (1975). Proselyte, proselytism. In E. F. Harrison (Ed.), *Baker's dictionary of theology* (p. 426). Grand Rapids, MI: Baker Books.

Halsall, P. (1979). *Medieval Sourcebook: Pact of Umar, 7th Century* Retrieved February 22, 2005, from www.fordham .edu/halsall/source/pact-umar.html

Elshtain, J. B., & Griffiths, P. J. (2002, November). Proselytizing for tolerance. *First Things: A Monthly Journal of Religion and Public Life, 127*, 30–36.

Guthrie, S. (2002). Doors into Islam. *Christianity Today. 42*(10), 35–52.

Ingram, J. (2004, February 17). Vatican, Orthodox hierarchy talk in Moscow. Associated Press.

McKnight, S. (1991). *A light to Gentiles: Jewish missionary activity in the Second Temple Period.* Minneapolis, MN: Fortress Press.

McKnight, S. (2004, February 12). The proselytizing pilot. *The New York Times*, p. A6.

Rauf, F. A. (2004). *What's right with Islam.* San Francisco: HarperSanFrancisco.

Reinhartz, A. (2004, March 8). Jesus of Hollywood. *The New Republic*, p. 26.

Sachs, S. (2002, Dec. 31). With missionaries spreading, Muslims' anger is following. *The New York Times,* p. A11.

Stalnaker, C. (2002). Proselytism or evangelism? *Evangelical Review of Theology 26*(4).

Stalnaker, C. (2004, July 30). Tony and tacky, shirty spirituality. *The Wall Street Journal*, p. W13.

Witter, W. (1988, March). A monthly letter on evangelism. Publication of World Council of Churches. New York, 10–11.

Witter, W. (1989, January). A monthly letter on evangelism. Publication of World Council of Churches. New York, 12.

Witter, W. (2004, March 21). Christianity in a crucible; in Iraq, seeking converts dangerous for evangelists. *The Washington Times*, p. A1.

Protestantism, Conservative

Conservative Protestants, a variegated group, are a bit of a moving target. This group can loathe the content of mainstream communication, particularly TV and cinema, for casual use of profanity, sexual behavior and needless violence, but often it is among the earliest adopters of communication technology. For instance, when radio broadcasting was introduced in the early part of the twentieth century, Christians were among the first to embrace it with the hope that sermons could be broadcast into homes across America and lead to a reform movement based on a spiritual conversion (Schultze 1990). With each wave of innovation, conservative Protestants sought out these new communication technologies to spread the Gospel, modeling the approach of the United States Information Agency and its use of short-wave radio and other broadcast technologies to promote American values. Short-wave broadcasts are used aggressively by conservative Protestant missionary groups to reach listeners who may not enjoy the freedom of religion that often accompanies repressive governments. Radio stations such as HCJB in Quito, Ecuador, (along with many others) target groups for missionary messages in language of the national and provide follow-up teaching

aids via the mails. International radio broadcasts have proven to be among the most effective approaches used by conservative Protestants to spread the Gospel. Since the presence of a missionary in the field may be against the law, Christian radio broadcasts using short-wave signals or satellites are considered a safe but productive means of presenting a message.

In some cases, conservative Protestants resort to more radical methods such as the use of messages on helium-filled balloons, billboards, T-shirts, bumper stickers, tattoos and fashion apparel with biblical expressions. Television broadcasts of worship services and conservative Protestant messages remain a lively part of the over-the-air and cable networks with some channels dedicated to conservative Protestantism, such as the Texas-based FamilyNet TV. Yet conservative Protestants are among the most critical observers of mass media with regular radio programs such as the Colorado Springs–based Focus on the Family, which regularly castigates mainstream TV and film for disrespecting parental authority and for questioning established government institutions such as the U.S. military and the Supreme Court.

This love-hate tradeoff also can be seen in conservative Protestants' approach to social issues such as the repeal of abortion laws. Tamney (2002) says that this group can unite on some social issues and just as quickly part company over whether the Bible can be read literally or understood as possessing qualities of any literary genre. He notes that the most resilient churches in America are those without strict boundaries between members and nonmembers. Boundaries over visceral topics such as abortion and homosexuality, when blurred, contribute to a more vigorous organization.

Characteristics of Conservative Protestants

Among the shared characteristics of this group of Christians are four identifying markers: a conversion experience, a belief in the authority of the Bible as divine, activism in evangelism, and the redemptive action of the Crucifixion of Jesus Christ. These concepts are among the doctrines of the Fundamentalist movement that gained attention following World War I and the onset of a literary approach to Scripture known as "higher criticism." Conservative Protestants retained a solid following until the 1960s, when social issues, particularly sexual mores, provided a catalyst for renewed adherence to the orthodoxy of the early twentieth century. Conservative Protestants began challenging the liberal shift that paralleled the civil rights movement and called for a return to traditional values. For example, ordination of homosexual clergy is the kind of issue that separates liberal from conservative Protestants, with conservatives rejecting it without qualification.

Political Issues

To be Protestant and conservative is to embrace political as well as religious debates. Among the salient issues is the role of Israel in the fulfillment of biblical prophecy, but even this issue has supporters on many sides. Some conservative Protestants see the issue of God's promises to Israel as fulfilled through the work of Christ in the Church; others think differently and see an outreach to Jewish people to be among the most important evidence of Christian ministry. Another flash point is abortion. The 1973 U.S. Supreme Court decision on *Roe v. Wade* served to galvanize this group on this topic, which became widely known as the pro-life position.

The conservative Protestant label may just as easily be applied to Evangelicals, a group that may account for about 30 percent of American adults (Understanding Evangelicals 2004). In the 1960s, many in this group wanted political power along with orthodoxy. This religious-political force surprised the nation in 1989 by endorsing television preacher Pat Robertson in his bid for president. In addition, this group of political outsiders coalesced into an unofficial political lobby that cannot be dismissed in national politics in the early days of the twenty-first century.

Micklethwait and Woolridge (2005) consider conservatives of whatever political persuasion as crucial at election time but not necessarily in the forging of public policy. He notes that national figures such as Jimmy Carter, who spoke openly of being "born again," and Jerry Falwell's political group, the Moral Majority, along with Robertson and Ralph Reed's Christian Coalition, moved the conservative religious agenda front and center. In the early twenty-first century, many in this same group are withdrawing from the political maelstrom to create a subculture that features bookstores, coffeehouses, restaurants, and the makings of a counterculture based on an objection to the mainstream.

Writers such as Cal Thomas, the most widely syndicated columnist in the United States (more than 400 newspapers carry his conservative Protestant message), once told his readers to abandon politics in favor of their own world, while other leaders predict the formation of a conservative Protestant third political party. For now, the nation's leading Protestant denomination, the Southern Baptist Convention, with nearly 20 million members, continues to exert public-policy influence, particularly on pro-life initiatives.

If conservative Protestantism can be generally equated with Evangelicalism, Noll (2004) sees this group allowing the partisan nature of politics to demonize opponents and excuse friends. Also of interest is the relentless End-Times literature that inundates the Evangelical market. In the wake of the September 11, 2001, World Trade Center attack, religion and politics have blended to defy John Locke's notion that civil government can be separate from religion (Fish 2005, C1).

Areas of Crossover

Politics aside, Noll (2004) sees some crossover among Evangelical Christians and Roman Catholics. Evangelicals value a sense of tradition, while Catholics value the sense of commitment and eagerness that marks many Evangelicals. Others insist that the trend in the early days of the twenty-first century for mainline Protestant denominations in North America is toward liberalism (Johnson 2004).

However, Beyerlein (2004) emphasizes that conservative Protestantism is not a monolithic religious bloc. The group includes Fundamentalists, Pentecostals, and Evangelicals, segments that tend to stress different features when treated separately. For instance, the authority of the Bible, sometimes referred to as biblical inerrancy, is paramount for Fundamentalists, but the outward manifestation of spiritual gifts is crucial to Pentecostals, who value extrabiblical revelation. Evangelicals tend to value the conversion experiences and avoid divisive debates over issues not essential to making a decision to personalize their faith in Jesus. This decision is often called a salvation experience, and it is the basis for an eternal afterlife in heaven.

Nonetheless, Hart (2004) rejects the idea of labels. For him, Evangelicalism is not a religious identity. Terms such as *conservative Protestantism* or *Protestantism, conservative,* may be understood as an attempt to counter the creeping ecumenicalism of mainline Protestant denominations who value unity over division at the expense of theological purity. The phrase with the conservative descriptive "fore" or "aft" suggests a group that values spiritual regeneration as the supreme theological marker.

Hart notes that this movement lacks an institutional center or rigorous tradition. Among the features associated with the more centrist parts of the group is a shared appreciation of music that defies denominational identity. In some cases, Christian popular music serves to unify supporters from a variety of Protestant traditions. In addition, this group often is supportive of parachurch organizations such as the Billy Graham Evangelistic Association or the politically active James Dobson Family Ministries. Among the cultural feature of this movement is the use of celebrity endorsements from entertainers to athletes to rally support for ideas that are often considered good for both God and country.

Since 1970, Hart found, "Evangelical" is equivalent to conservative Christianity without special attention to a recognized creed, liturgy, church structure, or history. Hart's finding is consistent with the notion that culture, including religion, is becoming more deterritorialized (Coleman 1993). Furthermore, Coleman found that North American missions rely on conservative Protestants to fulfill the biblical "Great Commission" of spreading the Gospel worldwide to create a group not bounded by the geography of a nation-state but every bit as politically powerful. Among the attractive associations of missionary outreach is the teaching by some conservative Protestants (such as Kenneth Hagin, Tulsa, Oklahoma; Kenneth and Gloria Copeland, Fort Worth, Texas; and Lester Sumrall, South Bend, Indiana) that the conquering of illness and poverty is part of a spiritual process. While controversial, this message of prosperity both draws followers and repels others.

Guarding Against Secularization

Whether in the United States or overseas, conservative Protestantism can be cautious regarding influences that dilute the teachings of the Bible or contribute to a casual acceptance of lifestyles that deviate from a biblical model. To guard against secularization, followers monitor the systematic education of their children. Some resort to home-school instruction to ensure that the educational content remains consistent with teachings based on the Bible. Others allow private education in a church-run school. Still others opt for public-school instruction with caution.

At the secondary school level, Beyerlein (2004) found, once he teased out the groups associated with conservative Protestants, that Fundamentalist Protestants and Pentecostal Protestants were generally less likely to be college educated compared to other religious groups and nonreligious groups; however, he found that Evangelical Protestants were as likely or more likely to be educated compared to other religious

and nonreligious groups having similar background and demographic factors. Furthermore, Evangelical Protestants were more likely to complete a four-year college education than Catholics.

Beyerlein notes that due to the perceived danger of secular educational advancement and the mandate to avoid worldly behavior, conservative Protestants discourage educational aspirations. The benefit to attending college, whether public or private, is the opportunity to solidify their conservative Protestant faith and to work to redeem fellow students and others.

MICHAEL RAY SMITH

See also Evangelicalism; Fundamentalism; Televanglism

Further Reading

Beyerlein, K. (2004). Specifying the impact of Protestantism on educational attainment. *Journal of Scientific Study of Religion, 43*(3), 505–518.

Coleman, S. (1993). Conservative Protestantism and the world order: The faith movement in the United States and Sweden. *Sociology of Religion, 54*(4), 353–373.

Cowan, D. E. (2003). *The remnant spirit: Conservative reform in mainline Protestantism.* Westport, CT: Praeger.

Craig, R. H. (1992). *Religion and radical politics: An alternative Christian tradition in the United States.* Philadelphia: Temple University Press.

Fish, S. (2005, January 7). One university under God? *The Chronicle of Higher Education,* pp. C1 & C4.

Hart, D. G. (2004). *Deconstructing Evangelicalism: Conservative Protestantism in the age of Billy Graham.* Grand Rapids, MI: Baker Academic.

Johnson, B. (2004). Review of *The remnant spirit: Conservative reform in mainline Protestantism. Contemporary Sociology, 33*(6), 688–689.

Micklethwait, J. & Woolridge, A. (2005). *The right nation: Conservative power in America.* New York: Penguin.

Noll, M. (2004, October). The Evangelical mind today. *First Things: A Monthly Journal of Religion and Public Life, 146,* 34–39.

O'Donovan, O. (2004). *Bonds of imperfection: Christian politics, past and present.* Grand Rapids, MI: Eerdmans Publishing Company.

Richardson, A. (1973). *The political Christ.* Westminster Press.

Sacvan, B. (1978). *The American jeremiad.* Madison: University of Wisconsin Press.

Schall, J.V. (1984). *The politics of heaven and hell: Christian themes from classical, medieval and modern political philosophy.* Lanham, MD: University Press of America.

Schultze, Q. J. (Ed.). (1990). *American Evangelicals and the mass media: Perspectives on the relationship between Ameri-*

can *Evangelicals and the mass media*. Grand Rapids, MI: Zondervan.

Tamney, J. B. (2002). *The resilience of conservative religion: The case of popular, conservative congregations*. Cambridge, UK: Cambridge University Press.

Understanding Evangelicals. (2004, November). *First Things: A Monthly Journal of Religion and Public Life, 147*, 65–66.

Protestantism, Mainline

Mainline Protestants shaped much of the history of the United States. They were presidents, captains of industry, and community leaders. They founded colleges, wrote novels, and preached sermons. They crusaded for abolition, women's suffrage, and civil rights. They were the establishment, and their faith in individual freedom, reason, and democratic governance defined for many people what it means to be Christian in America. Until the 1960s, the seven sisters of mainline Protestantism—today's American Baptist Convention, Disciples of Christ, Episcopal Church, Evangelical Lutheran Church in America, Presbyterian Church (U.S.A.), United Church of Christ, and United Methodist Church—seemed destined to hold the reins of power in American life.

However, membership in the mainline denominations began its continuous erosion in the 1960s. The population of the United States grew steadily, but the mainline denominations shrank by as much as a third by the turn of the twenty-first century. Mainline Protestantism not only lost members, but the proportion of Americans who belonged to mainline Protestant churches reached a historic low. This loss was simultaneously experienced in reduced social prominence and political leadership. To compound matters further, Protestants also lost influence and presence in the media. In fact, the strength of mainline Protestantism has paralleled its place in the media. Mainline Protestantism excelled in the culture of print but largely withdrew from broadcasting, making mainline Protestantism's story in the media one of former glory.

Print

Just as Protestantism arose with the spread of the printing press in Europe, it thrived in America with the aid of the printing press. The bedrock Protestant belief in *sola scriptura*—"scripture alone"—inspired Bible societies, tract societies, and Sunday schools to try to put a Bible in every American home and to make scripture aids eas-

ily available through church libraries. Sermons that had captivated parishioners in the pews were rushed into print in both periodicals and books. Indeed, until the twentieth century, sermons were routinely published in daily newspapers. Primers published to teach children to read were filled with rhymes like "In Adam's fall, we sinned all." The classic exposition on the journey of faith, John Bunyan's *Pilgrim's Progress* (1681), went through a remarkable one hundred sixty editions by the end of the eighteenth century. Protestantism and publishing have always gone hand in hand.

An enterprise exalting the individual's relationship with God, Protestantism early on fragmented into diverse denominations and related organizations. Whether for evangelism of outsiders or edification of members, Protestant organizations have published profusely. In the first quarter of the nineteenth century, for instance, church-owned presses published some eighty five weeklies, monthlies, or quarterlies in addition to devotional books, educational materials, and hymnals. Today mainline Protestant denominations and like-minded faith-based organizations issue thousands of publications for denomination members or contributors to Protestant-sponsored causes. These publications have sometimes reported information that the commercial media have ignored. In the 1980s, Lutheran and Episcopalian publications responded to requests for prayers and assistance by reporting atrocities committed in South Africa's occupation of Namibia before Namibia attracted much press attention. Other times Protestant publications have kept important social issues on the public agenda long after they had run their course in the commercial news agencies. Such has been the case of homelessness in America. Whether these publications were designed to inform, support, or persuade, they have been influential.

With the rising popularity of novels in the nineteenth century, mainline Protestants found another means of communicating with the American public, occasionally with phenomenal success. Congregational minister Charles Sheldon's novel *In His Steps* (1897) captured the public imagination with its simple story that suggested that asking "What Would Jesus Do?" would Christianize the country. *In His Steps* has never gone out of print, and its message, abbreviated as WWJD, continues to inspire believers. Another Congregational minister, Lloyd Douglas, repeated Sheldon's success with two novels. *The Magnificent Obsession* (1929) featured a protagonist who discovers that selflessness is the biblical secret for success. *The Robe* (1942) told the story of a Roman soldier who wins

Jesus' robe at the foot of the cross and ends up as a Christian martyr in the Coliseum. Both of these novels were turned into Hollywood movies in the 1950s.

Film and Broadcasting

The first alternative to the medium of print was film, which became an entertainment mainstay after American audiences were introduced to feature-length movies with sound in the late 1920s. Protestants responded to movies cautiously at first, for at least three reasons. First, church leaders claimed that movies offered frivolous diversions from higher, spiritual concerns, distracting viewers from important matters of faith. They also claimed that movies had the potential to lead their viewers away from biblical truths with messages that were shallow or wrongheaded. Third, they said that movies could make immoral behavior seem attractive and thus seduce viewers from right beliefs and behaviors. Nonetheless, mainline Protestants gradually began to accept movies as expressions of creativity that could be both enjoyable and instructive and eventually began publishing movie reviews in their magazines.

Protestants accepted radio much more quickly than film. Mainline church broadcasting began in 1921 when KDKA in Pittsburgh, Pennsylvania, carried the vespers service of Calvary Episcopal Church. The pattern was set quickly: Church services were broadcast live to the local community. Mainline Protestant plans to broadcast nationally came to fruition in 1928 when the NBC network broadcast programs of the Federal Council of Churches at no charge as a way of meeting federal requirements to broadcast in "the public interest, convenience, and necessity." So-called sustaining-time programs became a mainstay for decades as the other networks followed NBC's lead. Mainline Protestants took turns with the other "national agencies of great religious faiths," Roman Catholicism and Judaism, to broadcast programs that would reach the largest possible audience without offending other faith traditions. This policy excluded Fundamentalist and Evangelical churches, which had to buy the radio time they got, a policy that forced them to broadcast to audiences that would respond with cash donations. Such was the pattern when television emerged in the late 1940s: Mainline Protestants, together with Roman Catholics and Jews, broadcast nonsectarian, nondenominational messages to a national audience at no cost, while Fundamentalist and Evangelical Christians paid to broadcast their programs.

Television continued to follow this same pattern, with mainline Protestants producing such programs as *Davey and Goliath* (ABC), *Lamp Unto My Feet* (CBS), and *Frontiers of Faith* (NBC) for a small, national audience, but a change in federal regulations ended this privileged position. In 1960, the Federal Communications Commission decided that TV stations that sold time for religious broadcasting were serving the public interest just as much as TV stations that donated time, so free time for TV religion vanished quickly. Fundamentalist and Evangelical ministries continued to promise blessings and ask for donations. Mainline churches, however, had to decide whether to pay the high cost of broadcasting they had been receiving for free or to withdraw from television.

The mainline denominations decided not to buy television time. They paid close attention to the findings in the study *The Television-Radio Audience and Religion* (1955), the major social science study of the time. The study pointed out that TV viewers were neither homogeneous nor passive and that church members were the primary audience for religious television. Television was not the powerful means of reaching the unchurched that mainline churches had hoped it would be, the report concluded. Religious messages on television were capable of exploiting a small group of people who were drawn to authoritarian power, but mainline churches were not anxious to attract these audiences. Besides, mainline Protestants claimed, they did not have the money to lavish on television. Also, they considered their liberal theologies too complex for the simple messages television was able to convey.

Thus, mainline churches ceased television broadcasting, and by doing so retreated from an important dimension of America's public sphere. The void would be filled by conservative Protestant ministries. In 1988, mainline churches tried to reverse this outcome by launching the Vision Interfaith Satellite Network (VISN). The success of this enterprise has been modest. Since changing its name to Faith & Values Media in 1992, this interfaith organization has put mainline religious programming on the Hallmark Channel, but primarily on Sunday and in the early morning, with occasional prime-time holiday specials. The mainline Protestant presence on broadcast, cable, and satellite television remains negligible.

Criticism

Mainline denominations largely gave up producing religious programs for commercial television, but they still paid attention to the media. This attention took two forms: civil-rights activism and media-literacy campaigns. Seeing themselves as moral guardians of the culture, mainline denominations adapted their historic roles as critics and educators to the popular media.

The most famous case of civil-rights activism in television involved WLBT in Jackson, Mississippi. The station was notorious. Led by a white supremacist, WLBT sold White Citizens' Council literature in the lobby, used racist epithets on the air, and refused to sell advertising to African-American candidates for political office even though African-Americans comprised nearly half of the Jackson television market. WLBT routinely censored network news coverage by claiming "cable trouble" whenever civil rights stories were reported. To stop such outrageous practices, the United Church of Christ's Office of Communications joined two local African-American activists in 1964 on an FCC petition to revoke the station's license. The FCC resisted, claiming that the United Church of Christ had no legal standing in Jackson. The case finally went to the U.S. Court of Appeals, which ordered the FCC to assign WLBT's broadcast license to a different operator.

Besides political activism, mainline denominations have also engaged in drives for media literacy. Their purpose is to help media consumers better analyze and evaluate the images and information they receive through the ubiquitous mass media. This was the motivation for Television Valuation Month, the campaign launched by the United Methodist Church in 1967. In order to help church members articulate questions about the values and messages broadcast on television, broadcasters were invited to address church groups, and church members visited local television stations. Church members were also encouraged to put their newly raised consciousness to good use by sending evaluation postcards to local broadcasters and to the networks in order to influence programming decisions. Ten years later, the United Methodists joined with other mainline denominations to produce Television Awareness Training, a ten-week adult education program designed to sensitize viewers to what TV is teaching. Units covered such topics as news, advertising, children's viewing, sex, and violence.

Organized mainline media literacy efforts declined in the 1980s, although a steady stream of books on the subject continue to be published. Designed to help churches and families develop critical viewing skills, these books encourage viewers to watch television selectively, critically, and in moderation.

The Future

In the twentieth century, mainline Protestantism went from being a dominant force in American media to becoming a religious niche market. This experience shows that media dominance may be long lasting, but it is never permanent. Of course, presence in the media is partly a matter of choice, and had mainline Protestants decided to invest considerable funds in broadcasting they may have been able to maintain a greater presence in the public square for a longer time, but such presence probably would not have staved off the membership decline. Church involvement is not a simple correlate of media exposure.

Different media call for different types of involvement, so it will be interesting to see how mainline Protestant denominations will adapt to the environment of media convergence. How church communities function, how teaching and worship operate, how members are attracted, and how community ministries are conducted will continue to change as communication systems change. New technologies do not replace old technologies as much as they change how old technologies are used. As the unidirectional media of print and broadcast make room for increasingly interactive and mobile computer technologies, all with enhanced search and storage capabilities, the challenge for mainline denominations will be to maintain the best of tradition while learning to incorporate the best from ongoing innovations.

JOHN P. FERRÉ

Further Reading

Berckman, E. M. (1980). The changing attitudes of Protestant churches to movies and television. *Encounter, 41*(3), 293–306.

Hubbard, B. J. (Ed.). (1990). *Reporting religion: Facts & faith.* Sonoma, CA: Polebridge.

Hutchison, W. R. (Ed.). (1989). *Between the times: The travail of the Protestant establishment in America, 1900–1960.* Cambridge, U.K.: Cambridge University Press.

Nord, D. P. (2004). *Faith in reading: Religious publishing and the birth of mass media in America.* New York: Oxford University Press.

Parker, E. C., Barry, D. W., & Smythe, D. W. (1955). *The television-radio audience and religion.* New York: Harper & Brothers.

Rosenthal, M. (2001). 'This nation under God': The Broadcast and Film Commission of the National Council of Churches and the new medium of television. *The Communication Review, 4*(3), 347–371.

Schultze, Q. J. (2003). *Christianity and the mass media in America: Toward a democratic accommodation.* East Lansing: Michigan State University Press.

Sloan, W. D. (Ed.). (2000). *Media and religion in American history.* Northport, AL: Vision.

Stout, D. A., & Buddenbaum, J. M. (Eds.). (1996). *Religion and mass media: Audiences and adaptations*. Thousand Oaks, CA: Sage.

Underwood, D. (2002). *From Yahweh to Yahoo! The religious roots of the secular press*. Urbana: University of Illinois Press.

Waters, K. (2001). Vibrant, but invisible: A study of contemporary religious periodicals. *Journalism & Mass Communication Quarterly*, 78(2), 307–20.

Public Relations

The nature of public relations has been variously defined as one of persuasion, advocacy, public information, image/reputation management, education, community service, and issues management. More recently, some have considered public relations to be the work of managing relationships built upon "mutual trust, compromise, cooperation" (Hutton 1999, 208) between an institution and its publics. Corporations, schools, and charities are just some of the organizations that use public relations to create goodwill and understanding with a variety of audiences including employees, the media, and the general public. In its broadest sense, public relations crosses the full spectrum of modern society as "all of us, in one way or another, practice public relations daily. For an organization, every phone call, every letter, every face-to-face encounter is a public relations event" (Seitel 1998, 4).

Some have argued that public relations is an age-old concept, "dating from early Egyptian and Mesopotamian civilizations…used in different ways by… governments, religions" (Botan 1992, 153). In this sense, "pyramids, statues, temples, tombs, paintings" are examples of public relations-like practice because they "reflect early efforts at persuasion," and the Epistles written by St. Paul "to encourage membership growth and to boost the morale of the early Christian churches" were really part of a "PR campaign" (Newsom, Turk, and Kruckeberg 2000, 32). Indeed, the Roman Catholic Church celebrates St. Bernardine of Siena, a fifteenth-century Franciscan credited with attracting many to the order and thousands to the faith through his missionary preaching in Italy, as the patron saint of public relations. Others have even said that "Moses pioneered the concept of the top 10 list (a staple of press releases and late night TV)" with the Ten Commandments (Randall 2000, 20), and that the Islamic prophet Muhammad's *suras* (verses), which collectively became the Qur'an, were an early example of "PR's early best sellers" (Newsom, Turk, and Kruckeberg 2000, 32).

Communicating in Good Faith

Whether or not public relations and religion really go that far back in history, it is important for religious institutions—schools, charities, and faith communities—to establish good relationships with their publics if they are to have the trust that is essential to their well-being and success. In particular, religious institutions should

> have a special purpose—or calling—that directs their communication efforts. And that mission ultimately should shape not only the content and direction but the very nature of such communication. Whether reaching out within their communities or to those outside, religious communicators must always model the very highest of ethical standards in their work. The "word enfleshed" in print, on radio or television, or over the Internet, should reflect a faith community's concern for truth, human dignity, and social responsibility. (Tilson 2004b, 111)

As with secular institutions, religious organizations employ various aspects of public relations—community relations, media relations, fundraising, and special events—to reach internal and external publics. A faith group often will use a variety of media—news releases, public service announcements, brochures and pamphlets, advertising, direct mail, the Internet, and so on—to communicate its message. Faith communities—that is, churches, temples, mosques—"may not only want to reach their own active members and those on the inactive list but also the ecumenical and interfaith community as well as the general public" (Tilson 2004b, 83) in order to persuade

- a given audience to change an attitude or behavior;
- its active members to grow in their stewardship;
- its inactive members to worship more regularly and to participate in service projects;
- those who are not part of a faith community to join their congregation;
- the ecumenical or interfaith community to engage in common projects.

In this respect, faith communities can be said to engage in religious devotional-promotional communication, which "may seek to instill great love or loyalty, enthusiasm, or zeal for a particular religious individual, living or deceased, or for a specific religion or faith" (Tilson and Chao 2002, 89). Provided that public relations is practiced in a way that values mutual trust and two-way communication, such efforts can simultaneously build good relationships and help promote the faith community.

Promoting Religious Devotion

Good public relations—like charity—begins at home, and many faith communities rightly focus their communication efforts on encouraging devotion among members of their congregation and their larger faith family. For example, as the number of Asian-Indians in the United States has doubled over the last ten years (to 1.7 million, according to 2000 U.S. Census Bureau data), and Hindus have built an estimated one hundred temples, temple administrators are using communication channels to encourage devotion to Hinduism among their members and to instill a sense of community within the larger Hindu population. The larger Hindu temples, such as the Sri Venkateswara Temple near Pittsburgh and the Sri Maha Vallabha Ganapati Temple (popularly known as the Ganesha Temple) in Flushing, New York, use newsletter mailings, web-sites, and word-of-mouth publicity to communicate with their faithful. Additionally, temples sponsor religious and philosophical discussions and stage plays and musical concerts with religious themes to promote devotion, especially among adults who have immigrated with little exposure to Hinduism and second-generation Asian-Indian youth with limited exposure to, and knowledge of, Hinduism. In keeping with the essence of Hinduism, which is non-Evangelical unlike some religions—Christianity, for example—that use communication to proselytize, temple administrators are not interested in converting general audiences to their faith but only maintaining a good relationship with devotees. However, Hindu temples are not entirely insular, and some use the mass media to reach out to a broader audience; for example, the Ganesha Temple has been featured on local public and network-affiliate television programs about Hinduism in an effort to educate the larger community about Hindu beliefs and Hinduism's solidarity with other religions.

Other faith communities have launched devotional-promotional public relations campaigns using the mass media to reach out to nonbelievers and attract new members to their congregation. In some cases, local faith groups use ready-to-use radio broadcasts made available regionally or nationally from their parent community. For example, the radio ministry of the Evangelical Lutheran Church in the United States, which has been on the air continuously since 1947, produces *Lutheran Vespers*, a weekly program broadcast on two hundred thirty stations in the United States and also overseas. Local Lutheran congregations buy air time on local radio stations to broadcast the half-hour program; in some cases, the station offers free air time for the broadcast. Local congregations usually include a tag line at the end of the broadcast, identifying the local sponsor and inviting listeners to worship with the congregation. Sometimes, too, local devotional-promotional campaigns are adopted nationally. For example, Tennessee United Methodists, with the help of an advertising agency, created a "Catch the Spirit" campaign, complete with newspaper ads, radio commercials, bumper stickers, and billboards to tell the general public in middle Tennessee that United Methodists were in ministry in their local community. The campaign was well received and eventually adopted by the entire denomination.

On a larger scale, to foster devotion among the faithful and also to evangelize, the priests and brothers of the Carmelite order in the United States organized a national tour of the relics of St. Thérèse—the nineteenth-century Roman Catholic French saint known as the Little Flower—in 1999 to 2000. Since her death in 1879, the life and writings of St. Thérèse have "inspired many to devote themselves to God by doing ordinary things with love to glorify God" (Tilson and Chao 2002, 81), and her autobiography, *Story of a Soul*, translated into all the major languages of the world, has sold millions of copies. The U.S. visit followed a world tour from 1995 to 2000 that included Germany, Slovenia, and Russia among other countries. Promoted by a public relations campaign with media kits, a website, toll-free telephone numbers, brochures, and other materials, her relics visited churches and monasteries in one hundred thirty sites from New York and Miami to San Antonio and Honolulu. Host sites publicized the tour with their own congregations through bulletins and announcements from the pulpit and handled local media inquiries. The tour attracted "considerable secular and religious media coverage, both print and TV, at the national and local level" (Tilson and Chao 2002, 98), including CNN and *Newsweek*, and more than 1 million people came to see the relics—including Catholics, non-Catholics, and nonbelievers. After touring the United States, the relics visited Italy, Mexico, Taiwan, and other countries. Carmelite organizers considered the U.S. tour successful as it strengthened the faithful in their devotion, reenergized "fallen away" Catholics, and spiritually moved nonbelievers.

People also make spiritual journeys or pilgrimages to see relics, shrines, and other sacred sites. Such travel has a major socioeconomic impact on communities as government officials partner with faith groups in hosting and promoting religious-spiritual tourism. In Tarpon Springs, Florida, for example, thirty thousand visitors annually attend Epiphany observances (the day on which, according to tradition, John the Baptist baptized Jesus in the Jordan River) organized by city officials and St. Nicholas Greek Orthodox Church. Celebrations include a food festival in the city's park and a procession of Greek choirs, dance groups, clergy, and city officials to a bayou where, after a blessing-of-the-waters liturgy, Greek-American boys dive in to retrieve a Holy Cross. The celebration generates major newspaper and television coverage and "helps the city's . . . economy" with visitors "filling shops and restaurants" (Tilson 2001, 37). In Santiago de Compostela, Spain, Roman Catholic Church and provincial and city officials have promoted devotion to St. James—one of Jesus' inner circle of apostles with Peter and John—with a coordinated campaign for more than eleven hundred years (his relics are entombed in the Cathedral). Nearly 11 million visitors came to Santiago—one of the most important Christian pilgrimage sites in the world—for its Holy Year celebrations in 1999 and spent $280 million. Celebrations included a pan-European gathering of fifty thousand pilgrims for a Youth Rally, a feast day Mass at the Cathedral with King Juan Carlos and other dignitaries attending, and an array of art exhibits and concerts. Planning is already underway for 2010, another Holy Year (when the feast of St. James—July 25—falls on a Sunday).

Building Community Relations

Public relations, however, is more than just organizing devotional-promotional campaigns. Good public relations also means building good community relations. U.S. religious leaders, together with other civic-minded people, are increasingly involved in interfaith dialogue and social-justice projects to counteract hatred, improve mutual understanding, and help those in need irregardless of religious affiliation.

Following the Persian Gulf War, for example, "many Detroit-area students of Jewish, Chaldean [pre-Arab Iraqis, mostly Catholic, numbering more than 100,000 in the area], and Muslim backgrounds . . . were emotionally upset and hurt because they had relatives in Israel, Iraq or in the armed forces either here or in the Middle East" (Tracy 2003, 10). "No accurate flow of information" and "a lot of misunderstanding among the staff and students" soon led to "ill will and tensions" in the public schools, particularly at West Bloomfield High

where 16 percent of the students are Chaldean-American (Tracy 2003, 10). In October 2002, community civic and religious leaders created the West Bloomfield School–Community Mid-East Task Force, a group that included various religions and cultures, the police, local government, and student leaders. Fact sheets explaining each religion were developed and distributed throughout the school and the community, and a series of multiethnic and religious panel discussions were planned. The following year, the Detroit Public Relations Society of America Chapter (PRSA) organized a workshop at the Arab Cultural Center for Economic and Social Services to educate members and the general public about the history and growing influence of Arab-Americans in the city and the role of public relations in a multicultural society. Local civic and business leaders attended the program—organized with the help of public relations students from Eastern Michigan University—and the Detroit Chapter received a National Diversity Award for outstanding leadership at the International PRSA Conference later that year. The Detroit chapter has continued its multicultural programming with roundtable discussions and receptions to bring together diverse faith, ethnic, and cultural communities. With such avenues for dialogue, community tensions can be proactively diffused.

Similarly, the University of Miami's Religious Diversity Week has brought together students, faculty, and administration through panel discussions, art exhibitions, musical performances, candlelight vigils for peace, and other interfaith prayer services that explore and celebrate the campus' variety of faith perspectives and beliefs. In 2001, *Florida Leader* magazine honored the event with a "Best of Florida Schools" award in recognition of its impact on campus relations. The event, "inspired by an interfaith program initiated by public relations professor Rise Samra, at Barry University, originally began as a public relations campaigns' class project (directed by the lead author) for the Greater Miami chapter of the National Conference for Community and Justice (formerly the National Conference for Christians and Jews)" (Tilson and Venkateswaran 2004a, 41).

Other ecumenical efforts across the United States extend to mosques, which participate in interfaith dialogue and programs—66 percent reported doing so over the past twelve months (including 79 percent of majority African-American mosques and 51 percent for mosques of South-Asian descent)—and Hindu temples. For example, in the Monroeville area near Pittsburgh, "an interfaith umbrella organization, the Monroeville Interfaith Ministerium, facilitates interfaith events, including a Thanksgiving interfaith service at a rotating religious venue" (Tilson and Venkateswaran 2004b, 15). In 2002, the Hindu-Jain Temple hosted the event, attended by more than two hundred fifty people. The Ministerium presidency serves on a rotating basis; the current president is Som Sharma, a Hindu. At the Ganesha Temple in Flushing, New York, local schools, colleges and other groups regularly participate in interfaith discussions and programming at the invitation of temple administrators who plan the visits not to evangelize but to foster an ecumenical spirit in the community.

For many faith traditions—Christianity, Judaism, and Islam, for example—charity is a bedrock obligation, and faith communities assist those in need through various social-service projects. Such community-relations efforts, which often are ecumenical in nature, epitomize the very best in public relations practice. For example, the Shiva-Vishnu Temple in Livermore, California, through its Human Services arm—whose motto is "Serving God By Serving Humanity"—notes on its website that it has "the responsibility of serving the communities locally and globally...irrespective of religion, race and cultural identity depending on available funds, on a priority and need basis" (http://www.livermoretemple.org). Human Services offers free basic health-screening advisory services for half a day, twice a month although patients are requested to donate in cash and in-kind. The website adds that, although "the services are meant for visiting devotees and their friends and relatives, they are open to all independent of any restrictions." Sixteen different community service projects—some aimed at the larger community—"are listed on the website including activities with senior centers, support to other nonprofit organizations dedicated to human services, distribution of clothing, blankets and toys in India and the United States, and donations to victims of natural disaster" (Tilson and Venkateswaran 2004b, 16–17). Mosques also are involved in outreach efforts to their members and the surrounding community, providing cash, counseling, prison outreach, and food and clothing assistance. According to one study, 37 percent of mosques nationally participated in an interfaith social-service project (58 percent for majority African-American mosques, 26 percent for majority South-Asian mosques, and 32 percent for majority Arab mosques).

Religion and the Professional Community

While religion has played a central role in U.S. society since the nation's inception, the public relations profession has been slow to focus on its importance. For ex-

ample, the Public Relations Society of America (PRSA), the profession's largest association in the United States, has a variety of professional interests sections—technology, international, education, and so on—but does not have a section on religion. On the other hand, the Association for Education in Journalism and Mass Communication (AEJMC) formed a Religion and Media Interest group in 1996 (and currently has more than two hundred members), but AEJMC's Public Relations Division, the largest organization of public relations educators in the world, has yet to include religion as a topic at its annual conference. Perhaps the best professional association in this regard is the New York-based Religion Communicators Association (RCC), an international, interfaith group with six hundred members who work in print and electronic communication, marketing, and public relations. Annually, the Council honors "those who demonstrate excellence in religious communication and public relations" at its national conference, which features keynote speakers on religious issues (Tilson and Venkateswaran 2004a, 42).

As an area of public relations research, religion also is unexplored territory. In a study of the profession's leading journals—*Public Relations Review, Journal of Public Relations Research*, for example—only one issue of the *Review* featured religion as a topic (1992), and only three articles in the issue focused on the nexus of religion and public relations per se. Other professional journals have published a limited number of articles on the subject, including the first-ever analysis of religious tourism and public relations in the Fall 2001 issue of the *Public Relations Quarterly*, the first full study of a religious devotional-promotional communication public relations campaign in a 2002 issue of the *Journal of Media and Religion*, and the first broad-based examination of religion and public relations in the Summer 2004 issue of the *Public Relations Quarterly*.

The Future

Indications are that "Americans are actively searching for a deeper spirituality in their lives" even as globally "there seems to be a parallel spiritual reawakening [with] the resurgence of Islamic fundamentalism and the rapid growth of evangelical churches in Latin America" (Tilson 2001, 35). Public relations programs that promote greater devotion, interfaith dialogue, and social justice can help societies search for meaning one community at a time. A devotional-promotional approach to communication can create mutual understanding, foster a spirit of cooperation, and advance a community economically and civically. Most important, a good partnership of religion and public relations can renew a people's faith in themselves and their neighbors.

Donn James Tilson

See also Advertising; Persuasion

Further Reading

Bagby, I., Perl, P., & Froehle, B. (2001). *The Mosque in America: A national portrait.* Washington, DC: Council on American-Islamic Relations.

Botan, C. (1992). International public relations: Critique and reformulation. *Public Relations Review, 18*(2), 149–159.

Hutton, J. (1999). The definition, dimensions, and domain of public relations. *Public Relations Review, 25*(2), 199–214.

Newsom, D., Turk, J., & Kruckeberg, D. (2000). *This is PR: The realities of public relations.* Belmont, CA: Wadsworth/ Thomson Learning.

Public Relations Society of America-Detroit Chapter. (2003, October 20). *PRSA-Detroit Chapter Multicultural Efforts.* (Available from Public Relations Society of America, 33 Maiden Lane, 11th floor, New York, NY 10038–5150).

Randall, V. (2000, March). When your client is God. *PRWeek,* pp. 20–21.

Sallott, L., Lyon, L., Acosta-Alzuru, C., & Jones, K. (2003). From aardvark to zebra: A new millennium analysis of theory development in public relations academic journals. *Journal of Public Relations Research, 15*(1), 27–90.

Seitel, F. (1998). *The practice of public relations* (7th ed.). Upper Saddle River, NJ: Prentice Hall.

Tilson, D. (2001). Religious tourism, public relations and church-state partnerships. *Public Relations Quarterly, 46*(3), 35–39.

Tilson, D. (2004a). Religious-spiritual tourism and promotional campaigning: A church-state partnership for St. James and Spain. *Journal of Hospitality and Leisure Marketing, 12*(3), in press.

Tilson, D. (2004b). Strategic communication: Promoting your faith community in good faith. In J. Peck (Ed.), *Speaking faith: The essential handbook for religion communicators* (pp. 83–111) (7th ed.). Dallas, TX: UMR Communications, Inc.

Tilson, D., & Chao, Y. (2002). Saintly campaigning: devotional-promotional communication and the U.S. tour of St. Thérèse's relics. *Journal of Media and Religion, 1*(2), 81–104.

Tilson, D. & Venkateswaran. (2004a). Toward a peaceable kingdom: Public relations and religious diversity in the U.S. *Public Relations Quarterly, 49*(2), 37–44.

Tilson, D. & Venkateswaran. (2004b, September). Hindu faith communities and the "new religious" America: Toward a covenantal model of public relations. Paper presented to the 4th Annual International Conference on Media, Religion and Culture, Louisville, Kentucky.

Tracy, T. (2003, February 9). Chaldeans don't support Saddam, but worry about war ramifications. *Our Sunday Visitor,* p. 10.

Venkataraman, P. (2003). Hindu-Jain temple holds a well-attended interfaith Thanksgiving celebration. *The Pittsburgh Patrika, 8*(2), p.5.

Walsh, M. (Ed.). (1991). *Butler's lives of the saints.* New York, NY: HarperCollins.

Puritanism

The Puritans who settled Massachusetts in the seventeenth century were masters of religious communication. They represented the culmination of the efforts begun by English Puritans to make free discussion of religion a fact in everyday life. Puritans embraced communication, particularly the printing press, more than other people of their era. They used the press to spread the word of God and, just as importantly, to debate what man's proper relationship to God was. In these endeavors, their American press was open to nearly everyone. Of course, the Puritans thought of sermons as the heart of church communications. Sermons were designed to provoke critical self-examination. They often had great effect on listeners and were deeply revered among churchgoers. But the Puritans' particular genius was their open, unfearful attitude toward printing. It left an indelible mark on early America.

The Puritans imported the first press into Anglo-America in 1638, just nine years after the Puritan settlement of Massachusetts and twenty-eight years after the splinter Puritan group called Pilgrims settled in Plymouth. In contrast, other colonies suppressed the press. Governor William Berkeley (1605–1677) of Virginia commented in 1671, sixty-four years after the founding of the first permanent Virginia settlement at Jamestown, "I thank God, there are no free schools nor printing [in Virginia] and I hope we shall not have these hundred years; for *learning* has brought disobedience, and heresy, and sects into the world, and printing has divulged them, and libels against the best governments. God keep us from both!" (Hawke 1988, 68–69).

Berkeley's attitude was typical in the seventeenth century. The Puritans, in practicing the opposite, were intellectual leaders. They felt that communication was the answer to problems, not the cause of them. Puritans embraced the idea that if they could just get the word

out, people would consider it and come to the right conclusions.

For All to Read the Bible

Puritans came by such a feeling as part of their Protestant faith. While Christianity went back to Jesus' time, the Christian Church for years had conducted its business in Latin. The Protestant Reformation gave birth to the idea that religion should be conducted in people's native tongues. Thanks to Johann Gutenberg (c. 1400–1467 or 1468) and his successors, the Bible was translated and printed in German. The idea caught on. In 1535, Miles Coverdale (1488–1569) printed the first complete English Bible. Puritans, being English Protestants, were anxious to read the Bible in their own language. It was very important, in the Puritan way of thinking, for each individual to read and interpret the Bible or other religious texts. Thus, it was critical for everyone to read. As David D. Hall has pointed out, girls were taught to read alongside boys in the Puritan culture. Servants were taught alongside rich men's children. Again, this was contrary to common practice in much of the world.

If the end point of education was the ability to read and interpret the Bible, then to Puritans it was vitally important to own the actual, physical text of the Bible. Not everyone agreed with the Puritans on the necessity of ordinary people owning the Scriptures. The Anglican Church, of which Puritanism was a sect, harassed Puritans and confiscated their Bibles. Such harassment drove Puritans first to Holland and then to America to safeguard the right to own the Bible. The Puritans' fear of persecution was no theoretical notion—it was easily within family memories to recall a time when there was no English Bible and therefore a time when it was impossible to know God. Thus, while the Puritans of Massachusetts looked back to the time of Christ in their religion, in reality their own form of worship dated to only a generation or two earlier with the onset of sacred texts in English. Here, to Puritans, was where the true journey to know God began.

As Puritans fled to Massachusetts, the goal was to be a "*Citty* upon a Hill," as Puritan leader John Winthrop (1588–1649) liked to think of it (excerpt in Gunn 1994, 112). The *citty* was to be a godly example that would help purify the corrupt Anglican Church the Puritans had left behind. That city on a hill would be most visible via the press. Puritans who remained in England and Holland raised the funds to send a press and a printer across the ocean as soon as possible after the Puritans arrived in Massachusetts. With a press, the Massachusetts Puritans could describe what was going on, and the information could be shipped back across the Atlantic to serve as a guide to purifying corrupt religion.

The Puritan press turned out documents in various genres—educational, governmental, but mainly, religious. The lively Puritan religious press vigorously discussed God and man's relationship to Him. Writers churned out tracts that argued many sides of various religious issues. The most prolific Puritan writer in America, Cotton Mather (1663–1728), published some three hundred thirty religious works directed at diverse people who needed to hear God's word. He published writings, for example, directed specifically at sailors, widows, and slaves.

Hearing All Sides

Modern Americans think of the Puritans as oppressive people who tortured witches and persecuted Quakers. Although those things happened occasionally, more typically Puritans did not expect everyone to agree with them on theological issues and treasured the fact that people disagreed. Debates over theology were part of man's quest to understand and come to know God, as Puritans saw it. True, there were outer boundaries of tolerance—the Puritan press would not, for instance, advocate Indian devil worship, nor could Jesuits hire the press. Those religious practices were considered too heretical and their followers were thus barred by the 1647 Massachusetts lawbook from using the press. However, within the large circle of acceptable communication, many clashing religious ideas were put to press in Puritan Massachusetts.

The Puritans went to great lengths to hear various sides of any question, even if it conflicted with church doctrine. Church members feared that by denying access to the press to minority opinions, the majority might accidentally withhold the truth from mankind. In other words, no Puritan was ever so brash as to assume he had a lock on God's truth. Thus, the Puritan press encouraged all sides to publish. For example, in 1662, there was a huge squabble over baptism of children. So many of them died before they reached the traditional age of conversion and baptism that parents were clamoring for infants to be baptized. A practice thus evolved whereby church members could have their babies baptized, and the children, when they were old enough, could achieve conversion and become baptized in the traditional way.

The trouble was, it was no easy process to become a church member. You did not just join. Members had to go through a rigorous conversion experience that sprang from within. Thus, there were many adults who devoutly attended services but who had not yet achieved conversion and thereby gained church membership. The question in 1662 was whether their children could be baptized. Could it be wrong to baptize children of godly but technically unchurched parents?

After much debate, a church synod agreed to let such children be baptized. A vehement minority disagreed. They fired off a pamphlet, *Another essay for the investigation of truth.* The theological arguments were of grave interest in their day, but today the introductory remarks by the Puritan publishing house are key. The publisher felt obliged to explain why the pamphlet was being put to press, even though it directly attacked the synod's decision. As the publisher put it: "Variety of Judgements may stand with Unity of Affections. He that judgeth a Cause before he hath heard both parties speaking, although he should judge rightly, is not a righteous Judge. We are [therefore] willing that the World should see what is here presented" (Williams 1999, 238). In this and many other cases, the Puritans truly opened their press to opposing sides.

Converting Native Americans

Since Puritans felt that it was essential that all people read the Bible, they earnestly sought to convert the Native Americans. As Puritans saw things, the Indians as a people had never had a chance for salvation, because they did not know God. The first order of business for Puritans, then, was to bring the word of God to Indians. The Puritan Reverend John Eliot (1604–1690) spent his career ministering to Indians. He learned their language and set about converting them. He translated and published the Bible in the native Algonquin tongue—the first Bible printed in North America, which was completed in 1663.

The Indian Bible created quite a stir in Europe. The book gave legitimacy to efforts to bring religion to the Indians, for it showed Europeans in a dramatic way that concrete progress was being made to aid the natives. In fact, the Indian Bible galvanized Europeans and helped solidify the idea of America as a land of religious fulfillment. If a minority religious group such as the Puritans could convert Indians, then maybe any offbeat religion could thrive in America. That particular religious characteristic would eventually become part of the American identity.

What Is News?

Another legacy of the Puritans' interaction with the printing press came in the field of news media. Americans owe their general sense of what news is to the Puritans.

Early Americans had long read European newspapers. Americans up and down the coast—Puritans included—hurried to meet ships as they arrived with newspapers bearing "the freshest advices, foreign and domestic," as the saying went in those days.

As time marched on, it seemed obvious that Americans needed their own newspaper, and it was the dynamic, highly charged communication atmosphere in Puritan Boston that gave rise to the first newspaper in the future United States. Benjamin Harris started a monthly newspaper on 25 September 1690. Harris had choices to make in selecting the format for his newspaper. There were no rules as to what a newspaper was. Some English newspapers of the day focused on reports of "occurrences," or events. Others were completely readerdriven. Readers sent in questions on topics from religion to medicine, and the editor answered them.

Harris, a smart businessman, recognized that the majority of the readership in Boston would appreciate the occurrences model. As David Paul Nord has pointed out, Puritans believed that God spoke through occurrences. Thus, by publishing stories of fires, earthquakes, excellent crops, or other occurrences, Puritans felt in touch with what God was thinking. Calamitous events caused much soul-searching and effort for reform. Good news meant God was pleased and invited thanksgiving as well as continuations of the behavior that had pleased the Almighty.

It was no surprise then, that Harris chose the occurrences model. His largely Puritan readership treasured news events as links to God's opinion. Thus, Harris started *Publick Occurrences, both Forreign and Domestic* using news events as the primary type of material in the newspaper. *Publick Occurrences* lasted only one issue, but the first permanent American newspaper, the *Boston News-Letter,* followed in 1704. It also considered occurrences to be of primary importance in a newspaper, for that was the format that meant the most to the Puritan-dominated population of the colony.

Impact of Puritan Communication

Thus, the communication-oriented Puritans set new paths for American communications in general. Puritans embraced the printing press as a necessary part of life, because it was critical to their religion. Related to the intense desire for all to read the Bible was the Puritan model of universal education, one now followed in the country. The Puritans published for Indians, helping establish a religious identity for America that revered the work of minority religions. In developing their philosophy of printing to spread God's word, the Puritans also developed an open press that accepted arguments from many sides and insisted that people read them all before coming to conclusions—a treasured ideal in modern news media. Ultimately, the American newspaper was born in Boston, following a format that the Puritan readership saw as fundamentally important as they strived to understand God. The basic Puritan definition of news as occurrences has stuck throughout time. Truly, the Puritans and their unwavering support of the printed word left a big mark on American communications.

JULIE HEDGEPETH WILLIAMS

See also Free Speech; Profanity (Taboo)

Further Reading

Berthold, A. B. (1970). *American colonial printing as determined by contemporary cultural forces, 1639–1763.* New York: B. Franklin.

Gunn, G. (Ed.). (1994). *Early American writing.* New York: Penguin.

Hall, D. D. (1990). *Worlds of wonder, days of judgment: Popular religious belief in early New England.* Cambridge, MA: Harvard University Press.

Hawke, D. F. (1988). *Everyday life in early America.* New York: Harper & Row.

Miller, P. (1956). *Errand into the wilderness.* New York: Harper Torchbooks.

Morison, S. E. (1965). *The intellectual life of colonial New England.* New York: New York University Press.

Murdock, K. B. (1949). *Literature and theology in colonial New England.* Cambridge, MA: Harvard University Press.

Nord, D. P. (1990). Teleology and the news: The religious roots of American journalism, 1630-1730. *Journal of American History, 77*(1), 9–38.

Sloan, W. D. (Ed.) (2000). *Media and religion in American history.* Northport, AL: Vision Press.

Williams, J. H. (1999). *The significance of the printed word in early America: Colonists' thoughts on the role of the press.* Westport, CT: Greenwood.

Wright, T. G. (1966). *Literary culture in New England, 1620-1730.* New York: Russell & Russell.

R

Radio

Radio is one of the most enduring and popular electronic media in the world. It is listened to in almost every conceivable corner of the inhabited globe. Radios are to be found in kitchens, bedrooms, restrooms, offices, gyms, cars and buildings used for worship. Radio plays a central role in some people's daily lives; it defines the day, awakening us in the morning, accompanying us to work and soothing us to sleep at night. Radio can act as a speaking book for nonreaders, a friend for the lonely, and a guide for those who cannot see. It can be an irritant in shops, cafes, and hairdressers, where it is hard to escape from radio's unwanted noise pollution.

Many listeners shift the sound of radio with ease from the foreground to the background of their consciousness; listening frequently becomes a secondary activity. Eating, driving, studying, running, dancing, kissing, ironing, milking cows, surfing the Internet, and even praying take place with the radio on. Inherently an intimate medium, radio creates an aural backdrop to many people's lives. While it remains a foundational element of today's communicative environment, radio often now goes unnoticed and is only missed when it is switched off. In the United States the average listener (12 years and older) hears over eleven hundred hours of radio each year. In countries where television is less prevalent, listenership figures are much higher. Worldwide during the year 2000, there were approximately 290 million hours of radio programming produced by over 43,700 active radio stations.

Global Religious Radio

The spread of radio around the globe took less than half a century to happen. Religious groups all over the world, especially Protestant Christians, were swift to recognize the potential of radio as a tool for communicating their beliefs. Other faith communities also embraced the radio. Through the advent of the Internet, it is now possible to tune into transmissions expressing different aspects of all the major religions. From non-stop broadcasts of spiritual discourses on Hinduism to Tibetan Buddhist Internet radio to Jewish, Christian, and Muslim stations, confessional radio is flourishing. Its aim is normally twofold: build up the faithful and proselytize. For example, a temple just outside Melbourne, Australia, produces a weekly two-hour Hindu radio program, both in English and Tamil, to help "develop a better understanding of Hinduism amongst the nonbelievers" and to inform and educate "among the believers."

Other stations combine education with social revolutionary purposes, such as those that emerged out of the 1960s liberation-theology movement in Latin America. Alongside confessional stations, numerous state, commercial, community, and public-service broadcasters provide opportunities for religious broadcasting, commentary, and criticism. Religious radio in these contexts often becomes a site of contest. For instance, in Thailand in 2004, a committee was set up to monitor Buddhist monks' broadcast sermons, following an indirect criticism during a radio sermon of government plans to build a casino. Many of the controversies now provoked by the interaction between radio and religion would have been unimaginable at the time of radio's invention over a hundred years ago.

The Birth of Radio

One cannot really say that radio was invented by a single person; it is more accurate to speak of the inventors of radio, particularly as its development was an international phenomenon. The German Heinrich Hertz (1857–1894) detected and measured radio waves in 1888, proving the accuracy of the mathematically based theories of the Englishman James Clerk Maxwell (1831–1879). These discoveries provided the basis for the work of the Serb-American inventor Nicola Tesla (1856–1943), who developed the alternating current, and the Russian Aleksandr Popov (1859–1906), who successfully transmitted radio signals between buildings at the University of St. Petersburg in 1895.

Both Tesla and Popov have been described as a "father of radio," but it is the Italian-born inventor Gugliemo Marconi (1874–1937) who is most widely known as the father of radio. In 1895, on his father's estate near Bologna, Marconi successfully sent wireless signals over a distance of one and a half miles. Then in 1899 he transmitted across the English Channel, and in 1901, with the help of Tesla's oscillator, he was the first to send a radio signal some twenty-one hundred miles across the Atlantic Ocean, between Poldhu, Cornwall, and St. John's, Newfoundland. The message he received was three dots, "S" in Morse code.

In the face of a largely skeptical scientific community, Marconi demonstrated that it was apparently possible to communicate without wires, invisibly, beyond the horizon and around the curvature of the earth. Like most other developments of communication technology, these breakthroughs relied upon earlier discoveries and inventions. Part of Marconi's genius was his ability to adapt, to integrate, and then to market the insights of other scientists. Marconi's skills as a publicist can also be seen at his 1909 Nobel lecture in Sweden, where he declared, "Whatever may be its present shortcomings and defects, there can be no doubt that wireless telegraphy—even over great distances—has come to stay, and will not only stay, but continue to advance" (Marconi 1967, 221).

The Early Days of Radio

The first long-range radio broadcast was partly religious in content. On Christmas Eve, 1906, at Brant Rock, Massachusetts, the Canadian inventor Reginald Fessenden (1866–1932) passed on Christmas greetings, read a passage from the Bible, and then played "O Holy Night" on his violin, to the amazement of wireless operators on board ships sailing several hundred miles outside Boston. His breakthrough relied upon prior discoveries, including a more powerful alternator developed by the Swede Ernst Alexanderson (1878–1975). By using voice and music instead of the dot-dash of telegraph, he not only showed the potential of the wireless to entertain but also how it could be used to broadcast religious material. This capacity remained latent until the quality of reception improved.

Meanwhile, radio's ubiquity increased, heightened by its use in saving lives at sea. The most famous case of all was the Titanic in 1912, where seven hundred "living souls" were rescued from lifeboats, thanks to the *Carpathia*'s picking up the distress calls some fifty-eight miles away. Tragically, only eleven miles away the radio operator of the *Californian* had gone to bed. Soon after this, any ship carrying over fifty people had to have two operators and a permanent radio watch. Marconi was presented with a gold tablet depicting him as Apollo scattering sparks to the winds. "Those who have been saved," Britain's postmaster-general concluded, "have been saved through one man, Mr. Marconi…and his marvelous invention."

However, not everyone was so euphoric about radio. As with the advent of film, television, and the Internet, some religious leaders and groups were deeply suspicious of this new medium.

Early Broadcast Worship Services

The first broadcast religious service came from Pittsburgh's Calvary Episcopal Church on 2 January 1921. It was broadcast by a small radio station, KDKA (Pittsburgh), which had only been operating for two months. As the senior cleric was skeptical of radio, the more junior one preached. The technicians (one Catholic, one a Jew) dressed in choir robes so that the congregation would not be distracted. KDKA soon offered a regular Sunday evening service from Calvary Church. The priest, Edwin Van Ettin, overcoming his initial reluctance, became a regular speaker, with broadcasts from his church continuing until 1962.

In Britain, the BBC broadcast its first service from a well-known central London church, St. Martin's-in-the-Fields, on 6 January 1924. The service was led by the vicar, Dick Sheppard (1880–1937), who had served as a chaplain in trenches in France during the World War I. He received overwhelming support from a wide spectrum of the public for the broadcast, though there were a number of dissenting voices, who were concerned that this machine might take over from the churches.

In the early days of radio, Christianity dominated broadcasts of worship, but in the twenty-first century it is possible to hear almost every religious tradition at worship on the airwaves.

American Radio Preachers

The golden days of American radio (1920s to late 1950s) are sometimes also portrayed as the halcyon days of radio preachers. In the highly commercialized media environment of the United States, many preachers paid money to be allowed to broadcast on what some saw as a magical new medium. Paul Radar (1879–1938) was a regular and successful radio preacher based in Chicago during the 1920s and early 1930s. Often after buying all the broadcasting time on a Sunday, he would fill it with lively broadcast services and imaginative studio-based programs such as *The Shepherd Hour* for young children, *The Sunshine Hour* for shut-ins, *Radio Rangers* and *Aerial Girls' Hour* for teenage boys and girls respectively.

Another popular radio preacher was the Los Angeles–based Aime Semple McPherson (1890–1944), who became both the first woman to preach a radio sermon and the first to be granted a broadcast license by the Federal Communications Commission (FCC), in February 1924. Better resourced than Radar, she was able to produce an even more lively and diverse schedule of programs for her audience. McPherson was one of the first broadcasters to try to use radio for healing: she would put her hand on the transmitter and then encourage sick listeners to reach out and touch the radio as she prayed.

Her flamboyant style stands in sharp contrast to the much more restrained and probably most successful of all radio preachers, Charles Fuller (1887–1968). His sermons were broadcast on stations all over America for more than thirty years. By the end of the World War II, his *Old Fashioned Revival Hour* was, every Sunday, attracting approximately twenty million listeners worldwide. In the second half of the twentieth century, preachers such as Billy Graham would use radio as part of their media ministries. Ever since the 1920s thousands of unknown radio preachers have bought time at their local radio stations to communicate to their neighbors in "radioland," to the extent that the U.S. government soon had to regulate and limit the number of religious stations. Different faith groups in the United States have used radio to express their religious and cultural identity, from the Latter-Day Saints University in Salt Lake City, Utah, which was the first educational institution to receive a broadcasting license in the United States, to the *Jewish Hour*, originally known as the *Yiddish Hour* or the *Joe Tall Hour Radio Show*, which was produced in the Boston area between 1937 and 1976. While the *Lutheran Hour* is still broadcasting, over seventy years since Walter Maier (1893–1950) began it in 1930, most mainline churches and other religious groups were not as successful in making use of radio as the fundamentalist preachers and Evangelical groups who perceived radio as a unique gift from God for the communication of faith.

Wartime Radio Religion

In 1938 radio's power was exemplified by one of the most famous radio broadcasts of all time. The Mercury Theatre Company's rendition of H. G. Wells' *War of the Worlds* (1938) persuaded about one million listeners, an estimated sixth of the total audience, that the world was losing a war with the Martians. Few broadcasts can claim to have frightened listeners into places of worship, but amongst many immediate responses this drama led people to gather in churches and pray in Birmingham, Alabama. By contrast the response to *The Man Born to Be King*, Dorothy L. Sayers's (1893–1957) modern dramatization of the life of Jesus, was far more restrained. The twelve installments (December 1941–October 1942) remain a landmark in religious radio, particularly for their use of colloquial English.

While Edward R. Murrow (1908–1965) broadcast unforgettable descriptions of the Blitz in London to listeners back in America, and Paul Tillich (1886–1995) outlined the evils of the Nazi regime through the Voice of America to his compatriots back in Germany, the BBC's religious broadcasting department produced numerous radio talks. Writers such as C. S. Lewis (1898–1963) and a Scottish chaplain known as "the radio padre," Ronald Selby Wright (1908–1995), attempted to bring words of faith to listeners battered by war. As in many conflict situations, this was a formative time for religious radio, with the postwar period seeing an increased diversity of voices and beliefs on the radio.

The Death of Radio?

With the advent of television in the postwar period, many commentators predicted the demise of radio broadcasting. The coronation of Queen Elizabeth in 1953 and the funeral of President Kennedy in 1963 saw millions turn to television to *see* historic events unfold. These two services were also covered by radio, which still attracted considerable global audiences. While the golden days of radio would never return, radio broadcasting was certainly not extinguished by the advent of television.

In the 1930s radio listening was often a communal activity; families listened together, gathering around the wireless. With the development of transistors in the 1960s radio became a more individualized phenomenon. Radios were cheaper, smaller, and therefore portable, making it more common to see listeners on the move or lounging while listening to their radios.

"Video Killed the Radio Star" may have been the title of the first song played on MTV in 1981, but radio did not die; it changed. Broadcasting style has become more informal, evolving from proclamatory to more conversational forms, with talk-back or phone-in programs increasing in popularity around the world. Radio is becoming clearer, with digital (DAB) broadcasting, and easier to use than ever before. The invention of the clockwork radio has ensured wider usage in countries where batteries are prohibitively expensive, and the emergence of hundreds of new online radio stations in the last decade has allowed more and more diverse religious perspectives to be heard on air.

The Misuse of Radio

Radio remains the dominant form of mass communication in countries where television has proved too expensive. In Rwanda, central Africa, one radio station, RTLM, became notorious in 1993–1994 for the way in which it reinforced ethnic divides, played upon listeners' anxieties, and generally contributed to poisoning the communicative environment in the run-up to the genocide that claimed over 800,000 lives. In what is supposedly one of the most Catholic countries in Africa, the station's broadcasters used religious language as one of many propagandistic devices to exacerbate their Hutu listeners' fear and hatred for their Tutsi neighbors. During the killing frenzy that lasted little more than one hundred days, the radio station both encouraged "the work" and directed the killers to target specific churches and a mosque where many Rwandans had gone in search of sanctuary.

Hate radio has a long history that includes the likes of the popular broadcaster Father Charles Coughlin's (1891–1979) anti-Semitism in the 1930s, anti-Muslim and anti-Jewish broadcasting in the Middle East, white-supremacist broadcasts in the United States, and Radio Pretoria's continued pro-apartheid broadcasting in South Africa, which developed during the 1990s. More recently governments and faith-based groups have in-

vested resources into peaceful radio stations, as one attempt to counter the misuse of radio.

Beyond Reithian Radio Religion

John Reith (1889–1971) was the BBC's first director general. The son of a Scottish Presbyterian minister, Reith strongly believed that radio should work with all the churches, in a nondivisive fashion, to help make Britain a more Christian country. He believed that radio could be like a chaplain to the nation, promoting a robust form of Christianity. His approach toward radio and religious broadcasting has had a significant impact upon the ways many other broadcasters round the world initially handled religion. It was not until the 1960s that this vision was recognized as unsustainable, and the BBC redefined its religious remit to reflect the diverse faith and religious practices of the nation and the wider world.

The sheer number and diversity of radio stations covering or promoting different religious perspectives today has ensured that radio's overall output now reflects a highly fragmented culture of divergent beliefs. In a multireligious and multicultural world, one of the challenges facing radio broadcasters is how to ensure that violent speech and attitudes are overwhelmed by more peaceful patterns of discourse between different faith groups, so that "nation can speak peace unto nation."

JOLYON MITCHELL

Further Reading

Briggs, A. (1995). *The history of broadcasting in the United Kingdom: The birth of broadcasting, 1896–1927* (Vol. I). Oxford, UK: Oxford University Press.

Briggs, A. (1995). *The history of broadcasting in the United Kingdom: The golden age of wireless, 1927–1939* (Vol. II). Oxford, UK: Oxford University Press.

Dorgan, H. (1993). *The airwaves of Zion: Radio and religion in Appalachia*. Knoxville: University of Tennessee Press.

Hangen, T. J. (2002). *Redeeming the dial: Radio, religion and popular culture in America*. Chapel Hill: University of North Carolina Press.

Lowery, S. A., & DeFleur, M. L. (1995). *Milestones in mass communication research: Media effects* (3rd ed., pp. 45–67). White Plains, NY: Longman.

Marconi, G. (1967). Nobel lecture. In *Nobel Lectures. Physics 1901–1921*. Amsterdam: Elsevier Publishing Company, Amsterdam.

Matelski, M. J. (1995). *Vatican radio: Propagation by the airwaves*. Westport, CT: Praeger.

McIntyre, I. (1993). *The expense of glory: A life of John Reith*. London: HarperCollins.

Mitchell, J. P. (1999). *Visually speaking: Radio and the renaissance of preaching*. Edinburgh, UK: T & T Clark.

Mitchell, J. P. (2006). *Media and Christian ethics*. Cambridge, UK: Cambridge University Press.

Mitchell, J. P., & Marriage, S. (Eds.). (2003). *Mediating religion: Conversations in media, religion and culture*. Edinburgh, UK: T & T Clark.

Sayers, D. L. (1943). *The man born to be king: A play-cycle on the life of our Lord and Saviour*. London: Victor Gollancz.

Scannell, P. (1996). *Radio, television & modern life: A phenomenological approach*. Oxford, UK: Blackwell.

Schultze, Q. J. (Ed.). (1990). *American evangelicals and the mass media—Perspectives on the relationship between American evangelicals and the mass media*. Grand Rapids, MI: Zondervan.

Stone, R. H. & Weather, M. L. (Eds.). (1998). *Against the Third Reich: Paul Tillich's wartime radio broadcasts in Germany*. Louisville, KY: WJKP.

Sweet, L. I. (Ed.). (1993). *Communication and change in American religious history*. Grand Rapids, MI: Eerdmans.

Vigil, J. I. L. (1994). *Rebel radio: The story of El Salvador's radio venceremos*. Willimantic, CT: Curbstone Press.

Warren, D. (1996). *Father Coughlin: The father of hate radio*. New York: Free Press.

Wolfe, K. (1984). *The churches and the British Broadcasting Corporation 1922–1956*. London: SCM.

Relics

As supernaturally powerful human remains or objects associated with sacred figures, kept and revered over time by the faithful, relics are most often associated with Western religious traditions, particularly those within the Roman Catholic and Eastern Orthodox Churches. The terms *relic* and *reliquary* (a receptacle, such as a box or shrine, for housing relics) call to mind medieval European cathedrals and Christian saints. Relics, however, can be found throughout the world in a wide range of religions and historical contexts, from Buddhism to the religions of the pre-Columbian world. In these and other locales, relics provide believers with a tangible link to saints, martyrs, and prominent ancestors. The miraculous powers of relics, stemming from the remains or accoutrements of these hallowed individuals, often play an integral role in public festivals and private rituals as a means of communicating with and tapping into the power of the supernatural realm.

Illustrious History

Despite their association with medieval Europe, holy relics have a long and illustrious history in Western civilization, predating the Church and figuring prominently in antiquity and the Old Testament. In classical Greece (500–323 BCE), for example, the supposed remains of the legendary hero Theseus appear to have been the focus of a religious cult. Though at the birth of the first millennium CE attitudes toward death were decidedly different, as pagan Romans considered the dead body an abhorrent thing, a former vessel that needed to be placated through prayer but remain outside city walls, the growth of Christianity, as well as the rise of martyrs and saints, paved the way for attitudes toward death that again included relics. Certain exalted figures could be buried within churches and basilicas, their remains emblematizing "places as effectively as household gods" (Binski 1996, 12). In the medieval era, such relics became religiously required components of churches and shrines, codified by church law.

Sacralizing Influences

In addition to their sacralizing influences on the churches of the medieval world, European relics were characterized by both supernatural and divisible properties. As physical proof of a life that had unequivocally gained access to heaven and its virtues, the bodies of sainted figures were believed to house the healing or protective powers borne of heaven. Whole corpses or personal effects were unnecessary, for even the smallest remnant of a body represented the saint in his or her entirety. This concept of *pars pro toto*, combined with the power of relics to heal, protect, or consecrate specific locations, led to the rise of religious pilgrimages as well as church competition for the relics of prominent saints. Relics of antiquity and the medieval era became material as well as spiritual resources for the Church, and continue to inspire the faithful in the modern era. Even during the Age of Secularization, as the nineteenth century in Europe has often been considered, relics such as the Holy Tunic inspired a reinvigoration in the culture of pilgrimages and belief in 1840s Germany.

Similar ideas toward relics can be found in Asia, Africa, and the Americas. In modern-day Buddhism, for example, the divisible remains of the Buddha and other

prominent holy figures serve as foundations for temple complexes and pilgrimage centers in places like India, Thailand, and Sri Lanka. Certain expressions of Buddhism, moreover, have historically emphasized the supernaturally powerful and politically expedient aspects of relics, as in the use of wish-fulfilling Buddha relics in imperial Japan during the Heian period (794–1185 CE). In Africa, groups like the Fang of Gabon place key ele-

ments of ancestors (such as mandibles, cranial fragments, or other bones) within wooden boxes (*byéri*) decorated with ancestral images and house them inside specialized structures. These objects—as full, venerated representatives of the ancestors—can reinforce community identity and law, travel with living lineage members to new settlements, protect their guardians, or assist in agricultural pursuits. Examples from the

Americas, particularly from within Mesoamerica and the Andes, strongly parallel practices in Africa with respect to ideas about lineage ancestors, powerful relics, partible or portable human remains, and the use of the dead to define territorial boundaries and locations.

The Maya of sixteenth-century Mexico are a case in point. According to Fray Diego de Landa, images of the deceased were kept in effigy boxes within the villages of Yucatán. The cranial ashes and bones of lineage heads were placed within hollow clay statues and kept below temples, while those belonging to certain elites were placed within a receptacle in the head of a wooden statue and revered.

Like the European example, such figures were tangible links with the divine or supernatural realm. Outside the sixteenth century, the archaeologist A. M. Tozzer observed curated cranial bones and wooden effigies among the nineteenth-century Lacandon Maya, and there is emerging evidence to suggest similar activities in pre-Columbian times. Given the use of ancestral shrines and the importance of ancestral bones—as supernaturally powerful artifacts—throughout Maya history, it seems likely that many of the same considerations employed in the care and usage of relics in other parts of the world apply to Mesoamerica.

Communicative Functions

Relics often connect individuals to saints and, in non-Western societies, can be used to facilitate communication with ancestors. The latter function can be seen in the Andes among the sixteenth-century Incas, whose royal mummies were used in ceremonies of state and served as sacred surrogates for deceased lords in public affairs. Items like royal mummies (*huacas*) provided tangible links with the divine Inca lineage and thereby the gods of the Inca pantheon. Fingernails and hair from dead emperors could be interred within statues (*bultos*) and represented the whole individual in rites of communication and worship in the sociopolitical world of the Inca empire. Although the physical care of such portable relics (pieces of the sacred dead) has dwindled in the Americas since the Conquest, the veneration of ancestors continues as a practice in many areas, particularly within Mesoamerica. Newer relics, largely of Christian inspiration, continue to transform the religious landscape, blending with indigenous traditions and inspiring devotion and pilgrimage throughout the New World.

JAMES L. FITZSIMMONS AND REBECCA A. BENNETTE

See also Material Culture; Museums

Further Reading

Anonymous (2003). *Holy Bible, King James 1611 edition.* Peabody, MA: Hendrickson.

Bacquart, J.-B. (2002). *The tribal arts of Africa.* London: Thames and Hudson.

Binski, P. (1996). *Medieval death: Ritual and representation.* Ithaca, NY: Cornell University Press.

Brown, P. *The cult of the saints: Its rise and function in Latin Christianity.* Chicago: University of Chicago Press.

Byles, C. E. (1907). *Greek lives from Plutarch.* London: E. Arnold.

D'Altroy, T. (2002). *The Incas.* Oxford, UK: Blackwell Publishers.

Fitzsimmons, J. L. (n.d.). *Death and the Classic Maya kings.* Contracted manuscript under review by the University of Texas Press, Austin.

Gombrich, R. F. (1981). *Buddhist precept and practice: Traditional Buddhism in the rural highlands of Ceylon.* Delhi, India: Motilal Banarsidass Publishers.

Hooper, S. (1997). *Robert and Lisa Sainsbury collection: Catalogue in three volumes.* New Haven, CT: Yale University Press.

Landa, Fray Diego de. (1941). *Landa's relación de las cosas de Yucatan: a translation* (A.M. Tozzer, Trans.). Cambridge, MA: Harvard University Press.

McAnany, P. (1995). *Living with the ancestors: Kinship and kingship in ancient Maya society.* Austin: University of Texas Press.

Moseley, M. (1992). *The Incas and their ancestors.* London: Thames and Hudson.

Nash, J. (1970). *In the eyes of the ancestors: Belief and behavior in a Maya community.* New Haven, CT: Yale University Press.

Perrois, L., & Delage, M. S. (1990). *The art of equatorial Guinea: The Fang tribes.* New York: Rizzoli International Publications.

Schieder, W. (1974). Kirche und Revolution: Sozialgeschichtliche Aspekte der Trierer Wallfahrt von 1844. *Archiv für Sozialgeschichte, 14,* 419–454.

Tozzer, A. M. (1907). Survivals of ancient forms of culture among the Mayas of Yucatan and the Lacandones of Chiapas. In *Proceedings of the International Congress of Americanists* (15 Session, Quebec, 1906), Vol. 2, pp. 283–288. Quebec: International Congress of Americanists.

Vogt, E. (1969). *Zinacantan: A Maya community in the highlands of Chiapas.* Cambridge, MA: Belknap Press.

Religious Marketplace

In late modernity, with the ongoing progress of changing relations between religion and social life, what individuals do to make their own religious meaning is as important as their relationship to received doctrines or theologies. This new approach to understanding religion has been called a "new paradigm" in an influential statement. Whereas we once would have thought of the influence of religious belief as flowing from history, doctrine, and clerical and institutional authority to the behavioral sets of adherents, today it is more common to think of religion in terms of what people do to make their own religious and spiritual meanings.

Religion has always depended on the availability of shared symbols, practices, and languages. Even in the historical past, religious expression and experience at the tribal or village level depended on means of symbolic articulation. Cave painting, talismans and other sacred objects, song, movement, dance, and story all depended upon the existence and ongoing development of languages useful to these expressions and interactions. Our received ideas about religious history hold these codes and modes of communication to be authentically related to experience and expression in that they are thought to be organically rooted in practice.

Religion has changed with the onrush of history. It is no longer integrated into the warp and woof of daily life in the way that it once was. What Ferdinand Tönnies described as a transition from the *gemeinschaft* (society) of traditional cultural and social life to the *gesellschaft* (communities) of modernity has within it the gradual erosion of the traditional integration of modes of life that included what we now think of as "religion." This change in the nature of religion, whether we think of it as a broad-scale secularization or not, entailed change as well in the level of the power of religious tradition and doctrine to explain the nature of reality or to legitimate social action of various kinds.

"Quest" Culture

Important recent works in the sociology of religion have identified this new way of doing religion as focusing on "seeking" instead of "dwelling" as modes of faith, to use terms popularized by sociologist Robert Wuthnow. The "dwelling" mode of religion stresses sacred places, while the "seeking" mode stresses sacred moments, which can be transitory and are less connected with space. Further, the religious "seeker" negotiates between "complex and often confusing meanings of spirituality" (Wuthnow 1998, 4). Wade Clark Roof, another major sociological voice in the study of contemporary religion, connects these practices in what he calls "quest" culture rather directly to the media and the provision by the media of a range of symbolic and practical resources for these processes of

"seeking" and "questing." He has noted that the religion sections in bookstores are no longer there, having been replaced by "an expanded, diversified space—beginning with angels and running through the Bible, gurus, prophecy, Buddhism, Catholicism, magic, paganism, Mary, Pentecostalism, eco-spirituality, feminist theology and spirituality, and esoterica right on down to Zoroastrianism" (Roof 1997). This is only part of the picture, though, as a range of popular media now openly deal with spiritual themes, according to Roof.

Role of Media in Quest Culture

What this means is that in late modernity, in the industrialized West, at least, "the media" and "religion" are converging in a fundamental way. At the same time that people are finding ways of being religious and spiritual that involve active seeking and appropriation of symbolic resources in unconventional places (most of which are mediated places), the media sphere is undergoing a transformation that has brought about an increasing diversity of channels and sources and therefore symbolic resources. This convergence raises important questions about the nature of contemporary religion, particularly about the authenticity of these practices.

Growth of Noninstitutional Religious Movements

While the emergence of the media marketplace as an important site of religious practice may seem new, it in fact has some deep roots. First, it is important to see this development in the context of the history of American religion, in particular. Religion historian Nathan Hatch (1989) has shown that in important ways American Christianity in the nineteenth century evolved a vibrant noninstitutional face. Whereas established religious institutions and clerical authority enjoyed status in the colonial period, in the postcolonial period emergent noninstitutional and nonconformist religious movements began to play a larger and larger role. These movements became significant players in the frontiers of the new nation.

The Wesleyan, Campbellite, and Baptist movements that dominated the frontier in the nineteenth-century United States constituted what Hatch calls a "democratization" of Christianity. By this he means that a number of the characteristics of these movements led to the development of an approach to American religion that was less ecclesiastically bounded than the European and colonial precursors. The pluralism of so many competing movements, along with their increasing accessibility through the efforts of frontier evangelists and publishers, led to a situation in which it became conventional to think of American Christianity as a kind of marketplace of faiths. It could be argued that more and more of the power and autonomy over their own faith therefore resided in the hands of individuals, a condition that came to dominate religion in the late twentieth century.

Communication through Media

The communicational context of this era is significant. Many of these Christian movements stressed printing and publishing—producing and marketing Bibles, tracts, magazines, and other such documents. In a germinal work, David Paul Nord has described the media and religion context of the nineteenth century as a time of the origins of American mass media, rooted in the activities of religious publishers and distributors. The marketing of these objects alongside the vibrant revivalism and evangelism of the period enhanced the democratization process Hatch describes. More important to our considerations here, though, is the fact that publishing was integrated into these movements at such an early stage. It is further significant to note Nord's argument that what we think of today as the "secular" media were in fact rooted in these sectarian contexts and movements. The media of the day left their mark on the movements, and the movements left their mark on the media, it might be argued.

A vibrant material culture of religion thus has been at the base of at least American practice ever since. Laurence Moore has shown that from the earliest days religion and markets have been effectively intertwined. While Moore and most others would argue that this has been more a reality for Protestantism than for other religious traditions, a gradual "Protestantization" of all of religion, including the developments described by Hatch above, have left all religions, in modernity, integrated into markets. Reflecting on the nature of American (and much European) religion today reveals the extent to which this is the case. Most religions actively engage in various enterprises devoted to the promotion of their symbols and values in the broader culture. What used to be a clear divide between a "sacred" organic world of ascetic practice and a "profane" world of material concerns and markets has been erased. If indeed it ever existed.

Material Culture: The Visual

More recent scholarship has demonstrated the extension of these ideas and practices into a variety of spe-

cific fields and contexts. What has come to be referred to as the "material culture" of religion has been shown to exist along a range of practices, objects, locations, and platforms. Of particular interest has been a specific type of material culture: the visual. Pictures have long been problematic for religious institutions and authorities. In Protestantism, for example, it has been common to think of faith that would attach itself to pictures as somehow less mature than faith based on the printed word. The problem of idolatry has also been invoked, based on the assumption that visual images are more likely to be objects of this sort of piety.

The idea that modes of practice such as visual communication have been underrepresented in contemporary formal religious practice are at the root of some of the important waves of religious exploration that we earlier described as "seeking" or "questing." Along with the visual mode, this list could include, for example, objects, invented rituals, the body, music, and "experience" itself. As Roof and others have suggested, the seeming suppression of such practices by "traditional religion" has played an important role in the growth of practices of seeking, where these things are sought outside the formal bounds of religious authority.

Emerging Marketplace

Such sensibilities and motivations are an important element of the emerging market for the resources in the religious marketplace. Roof has explored these trends in great detail and along with them an emerging marketplace that has arisen to serve the less conventionally religious seekers. This obviously connects with trends in what some have called "postmodern" religion. What Roof, Colleen McDannell, and others have described as an emerging commodity marketplace of supply in what we think of as "secular" contexts has arisen in response to this trend. The expansive religious, spiritual, and quasi-religious offerings of the typical bookstore are one example of this. Other examples include the ever-expanding market for "self-help" programs and resources and burgeoning religious and spiritual themes across a range of popular media.

At the same time, however, Moore and Nord would have us remember that a material culture, and particularly a mediated material culture, has always been integrated into American religion. Evangelical Protestantism and Catholicism have contained a prodigious array of material objects (many of these dismissed as "kitsch" by religious authorities). The Christian Booksellers Association (CBA) has become the iconic representation of this religious marketplace; its annual convention attracts hundreds of exhibitors and thousands of participants. The evolution of the CBA from a small association of religious publishers to a major location for the articulation of material ways of doing religion and spirituality is an important indicator of the extent to which religion today is rooted in commodities in a marketplace of supply. There is reason to believe, further, that even for more traditional adherents a kind of "seeking" sensibility holds sway.

Structure of the Media Industries

A further dimension of the religious marketplace is the underlying economic structure of the media industries. The voluble demand for religious and spiritual materials is an emergent phenomenon across the last century. However, its expression through supply has been increasingly enabled by the ongoing concentration and restructuring of the media. Where religious materials were relatively rare in the secular-media marketplace in the first half of the twentieth century, they have recently become more and more common. In television, for example, the "network era" was a time of relatively few sources of and outlets for a variety of programming, religious and otherwise. With the advent of cable television, home video, and satellite services, there has been an explosion of channels and a resultant increase in the market for a range of specialized services and programming. The religious networks that were characterized as "televangelism" are only part of the story. In addition to them, a range of quasi-religious programmers such as the Pax network have been joined by other services that carry programming significant to religious and spiritual quests, including channels such as Hallmark, Lifetime, and Oxygen.

Increasing specialization in magazine and book publishing and marketing, and of course the proliferation of resources available on the World Wide Web, have had a parallel effect in opening up an ever wider and more diverse supply. Concentration in the media industries has added momentum to these trends through the tendency for cross-media and cross-platform marketing and promotion, and the parallel tendency for the development of "crossover" resources such as those found in Contemporary Christian Music.

The Future

These trends remain controversial on a number of levels. There is continuing resistance by some religious authorities to modes of practice that seem overly materialistic and rooted in emotional approaches to faith. More widespread are questions about the overall effects of the commodification of faith and spirituality. Can something be authentic if its provenance is the commercial marketplace? This is an important question. History tells us, though, that it is by no means a new one.

STEWART M. HOOVER

See also Bookstores

Further Reading

Berger, P. (1990). *The sacred canopy: Elements of a sociological theory of religion.* New York: Anchor.

Bruce, S. (2002). *God is dead: Secularization in the West.* Oxford, UK: Blackwell.

Clark, L. S. (Ed.). (Forthcoming). Making money, saving souls: The first 25 years of the Christian Booksellers Association. In *Religion, media, and the marketplace.*

Hatch, N. (1989). *The democratization of American Christianity.* New Haven, CT: Yale University Press.

Hoover, S. M. (1998). *Media scholarship and the question of religion: Evolving theory and method.* Paper delivered to the International Communication Association, Jerusalem. Retrieved June 8, 2005, from http://www.colorado.edu/Journalism/MEDIALYF/analysis/ica98.html

Horton, M. S. (1995). *Made in America: The shaping of modern American evangelicalism.* Grand Rapids: Baker Books.

McDannell, C. (1998). *Material Christianity: Religion and popular culture in America.* New Haven, CT: Yale University Press.

Meyers, K. (1989). *All God's children and blue suede shoes: Christians & popular culture.* Wheaton, IL: Crossway Books.

Moore, R. L. (1994). *Selling God: American religion in the marketplace of culture.* New York: Oxford University Press.

Morgan, D. (1999). *Visual piety.* Berkeley: University of California Press.

Morgan, D., & Promey, S. (Eds.). (2001). *The visual culture of American religions.* Berkeley: University of California Press.

Nord, D. P. (2004). *Faith in reading: Religious publishing and the birth of mass media in America.* New York: Oxford.

Ostling, R. N. (1994). Evangelical publishing and broadcasting. In G. Marsden (Ed.), *Evangelicalism and modern America.* Grand Rapids, MI: Eerdmans.

Promey, S. (1996). Interchangeable art: Warner Sallman and the critics of mass culture. In D. Morgan (Ed.), *Icons of American Protestantism: The art of Warner Sallman.* New Haven, CT: Yale.

Roof, W. C. (1997). *Today's spiritual quests.* Princeton lectures on youth, church, and culture. Princeton, NJ: Princeton Theological Seminary.

Roof, W. C. (1999). *Spiritual marketplace: Baby boomers and the remaking of American religion*. Princeton, NJ: Princeton University Press.

Tönnies, F. (2002). *Community and society* (C. P. Loomis, Trans. & Ed.) (Trans. of 1887 German publication *Gemeinschaft und gesellschaft*. Originally published in 1957 by Harper & Row). Mineola, NY: Dover Publications.

Warner, R. S. (1993). Work in progress toward a new paradigm for the sociological study of religion in the United States. *American Journal of Sociology 98*, 1044–1093.

Wuthnow, R. (1998). *After heaven: Spirituality in America since the 1950s*. Berkeley: University of California Press.

Yamane, D. (1997). Secularization on trial: In defense of a neo-secularization paradigm. *Journal for the Scientific Study of Religion, 36*, 107–120.

S

Sacred Communication

In an important sense, all communication is sacred. Every message requires that the message-maker assume some spiritual orientation, some attitude of the heart—which is a significant part of what Richard Weaver, rhetorician and historian of ideas, meant by his claim that all language is sermonic. But there are recognizably sacred forms of communication that are distinguishable from their secular counterparts. Such forms enable humans to respond to "a call; an address from a transcendent 'subject,' whether that subject be understood as God, nature, an undifferentiated unity, or an aesthetic experience" (Collins 2000, 11). In order to address significant meeting points for the sacred and the communicative, this essay will address five characteristic genres of sacred discourse—preaching, iconography, fellowship, prayer, and ritual—in terms of five traditions of communication theory identified by Robert T. Craig, a researcher in communication theory and discourse analysis—rhetoric, semiotics, phenomenology, social psychology, and sociocultural studies.

The Rhetorical Tradition and Preaching

The Western rhetorical tradition is nearly twenty-five hundred years old, and a good deal of the thinking about public address done down the millennia has centered on maintaining a healthy civic polity. The argument could be made that this tradition had almost wholly secular roots, emerging as it did when the Sophists recognized that Greek democracy needed both legislators and legal advocates. Not until Augustine did a fully theorized form of sacred rhetoric emerge in the West. His *On Christian Doctrine* applied Cicero's rhetorical theory to the art of Christian preaching. Augustine also defended the need for sacred eloquence, much in the way that Aristotle defended civic eloquence: If those who are virtuous are inarticulate, those who are vicious but eloquent may trump the truth.

For Augustine, eloquent homiletics had three registers. First, the plain style, which emphasizes the content rather than the form of public address and is useful for instruction; second, the middle style, which aims at delight, especially for those occasions when "the listener is to be delighted if he is to be retained as a listener" (1958, 136); and, finally, the grand style, which seeks to persuade a congregation to act in such and such a way. This final style emphasizes the claim that the sacred message makes on its listeners.

During the Renaissance, the plain style was privileged as the more serious and effective form of preaching. It was (and in some quarters still is) associated with the philosophical honesty and rigor of Plato's dialectic. The grand style, on the other hand, was associated with Cicero's rhetoric, an association not calculated to make preachers more comfortable with grand public speaking. Some seventeenth-century descendents of the Protestant Reformation, for example, resisted the trend to prettify sermons for the sake of congregational itching ears—a stance athwart the long-standing Ciceronian commitment to adapt the truth to the audience and the situation. Still, as Walter Ong, a Catholic scholar, has pointed out, even the Puritans, who protested the need for rhetorical fineries, could not sidestep the need to be rhetorical. Deborah Shuger, a scholar of the English Renaissance, has persuasively argued that the grand style actually has a theological warrant in the Christian tradition.

Semiotics and the Sacred Icon

Rhetoric is often held to be the oldest strand of the study of communication, but semioticians may beg to differ. Semiotics, or the study of how symbols come to bear meaning, is an ancient line of inquiry, though some of its most famous theorists are moderns. The characteristic problems semiotics addresses—misrepresentation and misunderstanding—are also longstanding concerns of the world's great religions, especially Judaism, Christianity, and Islam. The Qur'an, for example, prohibits sculpture, and Muhammad supposedly forbade painting. Judaic law forbade images of God, just as Western Christianity later had a troubled relationship with sacred images. Christians consented finally to understand pictures of Jesus and of the saints as pointers to the divine rather than as bearers of the divine—a position traceable to Augustine's semiotic in *On Christian Doctrine*. Even some contemporary religionists like the French Calvinist Jacque Ellul evince a profound discomfort with the pervasiveness of visual imagery.

In a way, iconoclasm is akin to the insistence of I. A. Richards and Ogden Nash in their great semiotic work, *The Meaning of Meaning*, that there is no direct (much less magical) connection between symbols and the reality to which they point. Just as semioticians have pondered whether or not humans can actually say what they mean, so some of the world's great religions have questioned or condemned the attempt to symbolically represent God. But in Eastern Orthodox Christianity, the image of the divine is no mere conventional sign of the transcendent:

> Images, or icons, were placed before the worshiper to excite the one praying to love and imitate the one portrayed, that is, to turn away from a worldly love toward a purer love of God. But these images did more than simply recall or represent the reality behind them, as images did in the West; in an important sense they became bearers of this reality. (Dyrness 2001, 35)

Eastern Orthodox thought, then, suggests that to talk about iconography is to address meeting points of the semiotic and the sacramental.

Prayer as Sociopsychological Discourse

A sacrament is a means of grace, a medium of divine presence and provision. To position the sacramental in the realm of media is to suggest an important tie-in between religion and all strands of communication theory, for no tradition in the field of communication is uninterested in mediated communication. A religious rhetorician, for example, might study how a televised sermon brings about conviction, and a semiotician of faith might examine how movies have assumed iconic status. But no branch of communication scholarship is so attentive to the effects of mediated communication as the sociopsychological tradition. The social psychologist is preoccupied neither with how persuasion happens (as is the rhetorician) or how symbols convey meaning (as is the semiotician), but rather with what psychological and social impact a particular interaction has. This tradition's famous sender-receiver model of communication finds a counterpart in literature on prayer as a genre of sacred communication.

Blaise Pascal is remembered for saying that through prayer believers are granted the dignity of being second causes. While no thoughtful believer would reduce prayer to a mere technique for making things happen or getting things done, most people who pray hope that interaction with God will achieve recognizable effects. These effects may not be as marked as making the sun stand still in the sky (as Joshua's prayer did, according to the biblical record). While sociopsychological scholarship focuses on psychological predispositions (including attitudes, emotional states, personality traits, unconscious conflicts, social conflicts, and social cognitions), prayer is often taken up in hopes that interaction with God will have psychological and social effects. Prayer is, in other words, intrapersonal and interpersonal. As for the intrapersonal effects of prayer, George MacDonald, a devout Scottish novelist, admitted that prayer's benefits are even felt by people who do not believe in God. "So needful is prayer to the soul that the mere attitude of it may encourage a good mood" (Lewis 2001, 82). To explore the interpersonal effects of prayer, this essay now turns to another kind of sacred discourse, fellowship, and to another tradition of communication theory, phenomenology.

Phenomenology and Sacred Conversation

Communication scholar Julia Wood explains that in the Buddhist tradition, "To be mindful is to empty one's mind of thoughts, feelings, preoccupations, and so forth—to clear the mind in order to be fully present, in a moment, an experience, a conversation" (2004, 35). Here, the Buddhist concern to be fully engaged with another person merges closely with the phenomenological tradition's concern with dialogue as a means of knowing, respecting, and bridging otherness. The questions scholars of phenomenology raise about absence or inauthenticity quickly converge with the concerns of sacred communication, especially when it comes to the ancient religious practice of edifying conversation, or fellowship. In the Christian tradition, for example, the ascension of Jesus Christ left his disciples with two problems: how to continue learning from an absent master and how to edify each other with the teachings of that master.

One first-century solution to both problems was the New Testament concept of fellowship—communion with the divine through prayer, a practice that takes seriously the phenomenological problem of absence. But fellowship was also of fundamental social importance for early Christians, as they sought to build each other up in virtue and to bear with each other's frailties. In this way, fellowship also speaks to the phenomenological problem of inauthenticity.

Perhaps nothing so intensely challenges edifying discourse as the pervasiveness of the mass media. Church services interrupted by cell phones, pastors communicating by satellite with their congregations, invalids who depend on religious radio ministry— these common situations illustrate the phenomenological problems of absence and inauthenticity. Zulkiple Abd, an Islamic communication scholar, notes the challenges that market-driven media industries raise against the truth, and Craig Gay, a Christian sociologist, noted in a 1999 lecture that "in more and more areas of contemporary social life, common speech has either already devolved or is rapidly devolving into mere sophistry—that is, into purely manipulative speech for the sake of taking control of things." As an alternative to the disembodied and dislocated discourse that the mass media sometimes encourage, sacred communication theorists offer the practice of fellowship as a counterpart to phenomenology's empathetic dialogue.

Sociocultural Communication and Ritual

"The natural *habitat* of truth is found in interpersonal communication," wrote Josef Pieper, a German Catholic philosopher. "Truth lives in dialogue, in discussion, in conversation—it resides, therefore, in language, in the word" (1988, 36). Pieper's emphasis on dialogue accords not only with the phenomenological tradition but also with the constructivist focus of what Craig calls "the sociocultural tradition." For sociocultural theorists, truth lives in dialogue in the sense that truth is constructed in dialogue. James Carey, perhaps the most

A shrine in a village in Hong Kong that the villagers make offerings to during certain times of the year. *Courtesy of Christine Gonsalves/istockphoto.com.*

famous representative of this theoretical school, observes that in opposition to the sociopsychological description of senders who affect receivers by messages in certain channels, communication is more usefully understood in terms of communities that construct and reinforce meaning by means of ritual.

A ritual is a symbolic practice developed and carried out in a community so that practitioners can say to each other, in effect, "Here is how the world is—amen?" In contrast with the characteristic informational emphasis of the Protestant sermon—which can be described in the nonritualist terms of the sender-receiver model—the Catholic placement of the Eucharist at the center of the church service emphasizes the way that groups of people gather, not to hear new information but rather to erect and bolster the meanings they hold dear. For Carey, religious worldviews are "produced, maintained, repaired, and transformed" (1989, 23) by means of sacred communal practices. Carey's concern is epistemological, or (more correctly) antiepistemological: He is interested, not in how communication helps communities to know this or that, but rather in how ritual observance creates and braces what communities take to be knowledge.

It should perhaps be added that Protestant scholar Stephen Webb has developed an "accoustemological" understanding of ritual that allows for a rich understanding of the sermon. Indeed, properly understood, all the practices discussed in this essay—preaching iconography, fellowship, prayer, and partaking of sacred feasts—may become sociocultural performance. The ritual nature of a complete worship service gives tacit importance to specific worship practices as a means of maintaining a community's worldview and helps explain why the practitioners of these rituals may be amusingly unwilling to change even small details of their liturgies.

Further Explorations of Sacred Discourse

Many more analogies to secular forms of communication appear in the realm of religious discourse—for example, cybernetics, which finds a counterpart in the time-honored discourse of catechism, and how speaking the truth to power finds a foil in the jeremiad. What has been established is that for people across faith traditions, and even for people who do not profess a religious faith at all, sacred forms of communication serve as a means of response to a reality greater than the responder.

CRAIG E. MATTSON

See also Confession; Mantra; Prophets; Shaman

Further Reading

Abercrombie, N., & Longhurst, B. (1998). *Audiences*. Thousand Oaks, CA: Sage.

Augustine. (1958). *On Christian doctrine* (D. W. Robertson Jr., Trans.). Upper Saddle River, NJ: Prentice Hall.

Berger, P. (1977). *Facing up to modernity: Excursions in society, politics, and religion*. New York: Basic Books.

Booth, W. C. (1974). *Modern dogma and the rhetoric of assent*. Chicago: University of Chicago Press.

Burke, K. (1970). *The rhetoric of religion*. Berkeley: University of California Press.

Carey, J. (1989). Communication as culture: Essays on media and society. In D. Thorburn (Ed.), *Media and popular culture: A series of critical books*. New York: Routledge.

Collins, K. (2000). Introduction. *Exploring Christian spirituality*. Grand Rapids, MI: Baker.

Craig, R. T. (1999). Communication theory as a field. *Communication Theory*, 119–161.

Darsey, J. (1997). *The prophetic tradition and radical rhetoric in America*. New York: New York University Press.

Dues, M., & Brown, M. (2004). *Boxing Plato's shadow: An introduction to the study of human communication*. New York: McGraw-Hill.

Durant, W. (1950). *The age of faith: A history of medieval civilization—Christian, Islamic, and Judaic—from Constantine to Dante: A. D. 325–1300*. New York: Simon & Schuster.

Dyrness, W. A. (2001). Visual faith: Art, theology, and worship in dialogue. In W. A. Dyrness & R. K. Johnston (Eds.), *Engaging culture*. Grand Rapids, MI: Baker Academic.

Ellul, J. (1985). *The humiliation of the word* (J. Main Hanks, Trans.). Grand Rapids, MI: Eerdmans.

Gay, C. (1999). *Postmodernism and the profanation of communication*. (Cassette Recording No. RG2862). Virginia Beach, VA: Regent College.

Ghani Abd. Z. (2004). "Islamic Values and Ethics in Communication." *Journal of Communication and Religion*, 27(1), 58–62.

Graves, M. (2001). The Quaker tapestry: An artistic attempt to stitch together a diverse religious community. *The Journal of Religion and Communication*, 24, 1–42.

Hunt, Arthur W. III. (2003). The vanishing word: The veneration of visual imagery in the postmodern world. In G. E. Veith Jr. (Ed.), *Focal Point Series*. Wheaton, IL: Crossway.

James, W. (1958). *The varieties of religious experience*. New York: Mentor.

Johannesen, R. L., Strickland, R., & Eubanks, R. T., Eds. (1970). *Language is sermonic: Richard M. Weaver on the nature of rhetoric*. Baton Rouge: Louisiana State University Press.

Kramer, K. (1986). *World scriptures: An introduction to comparative religions*. New York: Paulist Press.

Lewis, C. S. (2001). *George MacDonald: An anthology*. San Francisco, CA: HarperSanFrancisco.

Miller, P. (1954). *The New England mind: The seventeenth century*. Cambridge, MA: Harvard University Press.

Mitchell, J., & Marriage, S. (Eds.). (2003). *Mediating religion: Conversations in media, religion and culture*. New York: T & T Clark.

Ong, W. J. (1982). Orality and literacy: The technologizing of the word. In T. Hawkes (Ed.), *New Accents*. New York: Routledge.

Peters, J. D. (1999). *Speaking into the air*. Chicago: University of Chicago Press.

Pieper, J. (1988). *Abuse of language, abuse of power* (L. Krauth, Trans.). San Francisco: Ignatius.

Postman, N. (1985). *Amusing ourselves to death: Public discourse in the age of show business*. New York: Penguin.

Shuger, D. K. (1988). *Sacred rhetoric: The Christian grand style in the English Renaissance*. Princeton, NJ: Princeton University Press.

Webb, S. H. (2004). *The divine voice: Christian proclamation and the theology of sound*. Grand Rapids, MI: Brazos.

Wilder, A. N. (1971). *Early Christian rhetoric: The language of the Gospel*. Peabody, MA: Hendrickson.

Wood, J. (2004). Buddhist influences on teaching and scholarship. *Journal of Communication and Religion, 27*(1), 32–39.

Wuthnow, R. (1992). *Rediscovering the sacred: Perspectives on religion in contemporary society*. Grand Rapids, MI: Eerdmans.

Satellite Communication

Satellite transmission of television, radio, and telephony communications occurs between space-based platforms and Earth-bound antennae. The idea of using artificial satellites for communications was first proposed in 1945 by British science fiction writer Arthur Charles Clarke, who correctly predicted that three satellites positioned 22,300 miles above the equator could relay signals to all points of Earth. At that altitude, satellites travel the same speed as Earth's rotation, making them appear from the ground to be stationary, a phenomenon known as *geosynchronous orbit*. The Soviet Union first put a satellite into orbit around Earth when it launched *Sputnik* in 1957; the United States followed the next year. It was not until 1962, when *Telstar I* debuted, that a satellite was used to transmit television signals between the United States and Europe, thus inaugurating a new age in mass communications.

Religious organizations had used radio and television to preach and proselytize for as long as those media had existed. As broadcast historian J. Harold Ellens noted, it was not insignificant that the first voice broadcast—Reginald Fessenden's Christmas Eve broadcast of a violin solo of "O Holy Night"—was a religious celebration (Ellens 1974, 16). Well-known religious figures such as William (Billy) F. Graham and Rex Humbard made early use of electronic media. However, it was not until the latter decades of the twentieth century that satellites were used extensively to extend religious messages to wider audiences. Initially, C-band satellites were used to distribute religious content to broadcast outlets and cable television systems. In addition, some churches used *direct to home* (DTH) satellite distribution to disseminate worship services and otherwise build religious communities. However, viewers were required to install large and expensive satellite dishes, or *television receive only* (TVRO) earth stations. By the late 1990s, more powerful Ku-band satellites and advances in digital video compression resulted in smaller and less expensive receivers, and the potential for larger DTH audiences.

Evangelizing by Satellite Television

Just as they were among the first religious organizations to utilize radio broadcasting, Fundamentalist Christians in the United States first recognized the potential of satellite broadcasting. This circumstance was influenced in part by early U.S. broadcast policy: Because of radio broadcasters' desire to avoid controversy, mainstream Catholic and Protestant leaders were given free or *sustaining* airtime, to the exclusion of Fundamentalist Christian preachers and controversial figures such as Father Charles E. Coughlin of Detroit, who were left only with the option of buying time from broadcasters. As a result of this long-held practice of buying broadcast time, it ultimately became more economical for religious broadcasters to buy broadcast licenses. Such was the case for Pat Robertson, who purchased a UHF television station in Portsmouth, Virginia, in 1960, and subsequently used satellite technology to transform it into the Christian Broadcasting Network (CBN). In 1977 Robertson constructed a satellite earth station in order to transmit CBN programs to commercial television stations around the country from which he had bought time. The move was meant to save Robertson distribution costs, but he later reached wider audiences by following the lead of Home Box Office (HBO) and offering CBN to cable operators who were starved for content. By 1986, CBN was attracting a large, educated, and affluent audience, and was pulling in more than $139 million a year in donations. Robertson was not alone—other evangelists, such as Oral Roberts, Jim Bakker, and Jimmy Swaggart also became widely known through their satellite broadcasts—but Robertson did not confine CBN to religious programs. The network's flagship program, *The 700 Club*, built on Robertson's early success at raising $7,000 monthly from a "club" of seven hundred telethon contributors, combined news, interviews, and commentary with prayer and viewer participation. Other CBN programs focused on family entertainment and programs in harmony with Christian ideals. Renamed The Family Channel in 1988, the network had become so successful that in order to protect its tax-exempt status, Robertson's ministry was forced to spin CBN into a separate entity, International Family Entertainment, which was subsequently sold to Fox in

1997, then to Disney in 2001. The channel is now known as the ABC Family Channel and it continues to carry *The 700 Club.*

Even larger than CBN is the Trinity Broadcasting Network (TBN), led by Paul Crouch. Like Robertson, Crouch started small, purchasing a UHF television station in Southern California in 1973. During the 1980s, Crouch purchased nearly one hundred television stations, converting each of them to full-time Christian broadcast outlets. Satellite technology facilitated TBN's development after Crouch claimed to have had a vision of "beams of light going out and hitting the major metropolitan areas of America…little pencil threads of light emanating from them, and forming little dots of light until the whole country became like a blaze, a network of light all over" (Melton, Lucas, and Stone 1997, 357). Crouch said when he asked the Lord for the meaning of his vision he was answered with a single word: satellite. The vision led Crouch to lease transponders on RCA satellites, reaching 750 television stations and nearly 28 million cable subscribers by the mid-1990s. Crouch anchors TBN's flagship program, the *Praise the Lord* show, which consists of interviews and musical performances. The network also used satellite technology to broadcast live remote events. In the early 1980s TBN built a portable satellite transmitting facility in an 18-wheel truck, dubbed "The Holy Beamer." Crouch has been a controversial figure, enduring accusations of age and sex discrimination and unfair labor practices in 1989, and of allegations in 2004 of conspicuous consumption and attempting to cover up a homosexual affair with a former employee.

Perhaps the most controversial figure in religious broadcasting, Jim Bakker, worked for Robertson in the 1960s, then Crouch in the 1970s, before starting his own satellite-based television network, the PTL Club. The network drew viewer donations estimated to be in excess of $1 million per week. Bakker resigned from PTL in 1987 after it was revealed that he had paid $265,000 to keep a secretary from revealing their sexual relationship. In 1989 he was sentenced to forty-five years in prison for fraud; he served five years in prison.

Building Religious Communities

In addition to evangelizing, religious organizations have used satellite broadcasts for community building and faith-promoting activities. Such efforts range from individual denominations transmitting meetings, talks, and training sessions, to multiple denominations coming together to create an ecumenical channel.

Foreseeing the potential of satellite communication, United States Catholic dioceses operated the National Catholic Telecommunications Network of America (CTNA) beginning in 1983. Originally seen as a means of saving costs for internal communications and for delivering meetings and training conferences, the CTNA satellite network was used for teleconferencing and distributing programs to cable outlets and dioceses that had satellite dishes and paid the yearly $5,000 fee. Catholic bishops invested approximately $13 million before abandoning the project in 1995.

Similarly, the Church of Jesus Christ of Latter-day Saints (LDS) began building its own satellite distribution system in 1982. The church leased transponder capacity from the Public Broadcasting Service, built uplink facilities at its Salt Lake City headquarters, and installed satellite-receiving dishes at its stake centers throughout North America. By 2004, the LDS church had expanded its satellite network to include approximately 4,500 of its facilities worldwide—transmitting to Europe beginning in 1992 and Latin America, Africa, and the Caribbean in 2000. Initially, the system was used to distribute the church's twice-yearly conference. However, the church gradually added broadcasts of other church activities, such as fireside talks and special meetings. In 2001, the church began using the satellite to broadcast educational programs for its members and training sessions to its lay priesthood leaders throughout the world. Many broadcasts are transmitted in high-definition (HDTV) format and in as many as twenty-four languages. Broadcasts are transmitted in both encoded and open formats, depending on whether the church's intended audience is public or private.

In 1988, the National Interfaith Cable Coalition (NICC), a consortium of seventy Christian and Jewish organizations, founded the Vision Interfaith Satellite Network (VISN). NICC member organizations subsidized the operation of VISN and produced programming for distribution over the network. The network, which was made available to cable systems, transmitted programs by and about Protestant, Evangelical, Catholic, Eastern Orthodox, LDS, and Jewish congregations. In 1992, VISN merged with the Southern Baptist American Christian Television System (ACTS) and was renamed the Faith and Values Channel. Soon afterward, Liberty Media invested in the Faith and Values Channel and it was renamed the Odyssey Channel. Odyssey retained its interfaith mission until 1998, when Hallmark Entertainment and the Jim Hensen Company invested in it and reduced religious programming from forty to fourteen hours per week in order to emphasize family programs. The channel was renamed the Hallmark Channel in 2001. It continues to air some programs produced by Faith and Values Media, the consortium that originally created VISN.

Going Directly to the Viewers

By 1979, some homeowners had installed TVRO earth stations to intercept television transmissions meant for television networks and cable companies. The dishes were large and expensive, however, meaning only the wealthy and those living beyond the reach of terrestrial and cable television signals invested in them. Furthermore, broadcasters objected to dish owners intercepting their programs and ultimately scrambled their satellite signals. Nevertheless, the idea of a DTH satellite system took hold. Such systems were first successful in countries that did not already have a cable television infrastructure. By 1994, new high-powered satellites and digital video compression schemes made it possible to sell small satellite dishes to U.S. homeowners for around $200.

Among the first to recognize the potential of direct broadcast satellite (DBS) for religious broadcasting was Robert Johnson, who applied for a high-power DBS license in 1981. However, it would not be until 1996 that Johnson launched Sky Angel, a multichannel television and radio DBS service. Florida-based Sky Angel has thirty six channels and carries programs from one hunred fifty Christian ministries. Channels specialize in everything from children's programs to music videos. Subscribers must obtain satellite-receiving equipment used by the Dish Network in order to receive the Sky Angel channels. Johnson was able to launch Sky Angel by entering into an agreement with Dish's parent company, EchoStar, in 1994. Johnson's company, Dominion Video Satellite, agreed to use transponders on EchoStar's satellite in exchange for EchoStar using frequencies for which Dominon was licensed. The agreement also stipulated that EchoStar would not carry other religious channels on its Dish service, while Dominion would confine its Sky Angel service to only religious programming. Dominion sued EchoStar in 2004, claiming breach of contract, when Dish added two religious channels, the DayStar Television network and the Southern Baptist Convention's FamilyNet. EchoStar was ordered to pay damages to Dominion and continued to carry Daystar and FamilyNet.

The LDS Church also maintains a satellite channel that is not solely religious in nature. Originating from Brigham Young University in Utah, BYU Television provides educational and religious programs to viewers of the Dish Network and DirecTV, as well as to numerous cable outlets throughout the United States.

Muslims, too, are using satellite technology to promote their religion. Satellite Channel 1 of Saudi Arabia, and al-Manar, run by the Hezbollah Party of Lebanon, both broadcast mostly religious television programming in the Middle East. Channel Islam International, based in South Africa, provides religious radio programming to more than sixty countries. One channel not yet in operation, Makkah Satellite, aims to give a moderating view of Islam in multiple languages. Meanwhile, several Christian satellite channels operate in the Middle East specifically to counter the messages of the Muslim channels. Middle East Television, a Lebanon-based broadcast outlet owned by Pat Robertson, uses satellite technology to uplink programs to viewers in Saudi Arabia, Syria, Iran, Iraq, Egypt, and Kuwait, while Reza F. Safa, a Shiite Muslim who converted to Christianity, airs programming in Persian via satellite into Iran.

Building Faith Through Space

Satellite technology has enabled religious organizations to communicate with their own congregants and with the unconverted. Originally useful for distributing religious programming to television stations and cable outlets, satellite transmissions have also been used for churches to include adherents in long-distance meetings, religious services, and training sessions. The latest satellite technology allows religious organizations to communicate directly to television viewers in their homes, through direct broadcast satellite.

DALE CRESSMAN

Further Reading

Ellens, J. H. (1974). *Models of religious broadcasting*. Grand Rapids, MI: Eerdmans.

Ferré, J. (1990). *Channels of belief: Religion and American commercial television*. Ames: Iowa State University Press.

Gunther, B., & Viney, R. (1994). *Seeing is believing: Religion and television in the 1990's*. London: John Libbey.

Howell, W. J. (1986). *World broadcasting in the age of the satellite*. Norwood, NJ: Ablex Publishing Corporation.

Melton, J., Lucas, P., & Stone, J. (1997). *Prime-time religion: An encyclopedia of religious broadcasting*. Phoenix, AZ: Oryx Press.

Negrine, R. (Ed.). (1988). *Satellite broadcasting: The politics and implications of the new media*. London: Routledge.

Smith, F. L., Wright, J. W., & Ostroff, D. H. (1998). *Perspectives on radio and television: Telecommunications in the United States.* Mahwah, NJ: Lawrence Erlbaum Associates, Publishers.

Wood, J. (1992). *History of international broadcasting.* London: Peter Peregrinus.

Scientology

Communication rules in Scientology are very strict, and a brief overview of them helps to explain a great deal about the organization's interaction with its members and its exchanges with critics. As a concept, communication is a technical term in Scientology, meaning (among other definitions) "the study and practice of interchanging ideas, individual to individual, individual to group, group to individual, and group to group" (Hubbard 1976, 93). It is among the three components of what Scientologists call ARC, which stands for "Affinity, Reality, and Communication, [and] which together equate to understanding" (Hubbard 1976, 27).

Communication Course

An entry-level Scientology course, which the organization sees as a recruitment tool, is called the Success Through Communication Course. In it participants undergo a series of exercises (called training routines or TRs) ostensibly designed to improve interpersonal communication (Church of Scientology International 1994, 145–197) but which begin patterns of compliance to commands of obedience from higher-ranking Scientologists (Lamont 1986, 40–41). For example, one TR involves giving commands to another in a firm, direct voice, which becomes a component of "hard sell" techniques. Scientologists use these hard-sell techniques when attempting to pressure members into taking courses. As Scientology's founder, L. Ron Hubbard (1911–1986) wrote, "Hard sell means insistence that people buy. It means caring about the person and not being reasonable about stops or barriers but caring enough to get him through the stops or barriers to get the service that's going to rehabilitate him" (Hubbard 1991a, 207).

Publishing Negative Material

As the "hard sell" technique suggests, the practice of communication by Scientology is highly restrictive, with its primary purpose being the furtherance of the organization's goals. Those goals involve "clearing the planet," which is a Scientology phrase with a dual meaning. On the one hand, it means helping people apply Scientology techniques to their lives in ways that reputedly eliminate their barriers to success. On the other hand, it means eliminating all opposition to, or even disinterest about, Scientology in the world. Toward this twofold end, all Scientology publications only include "theta," which is material and perspectives favorable to Scientology (Hubbard Association of Scientologists 1953). Scientologists who express "entheta" (negative information) in any circumstances receive harsh punishment (Hubbard 1970).

"Positioning" its Founder

Scientology communicates its message to members and outsiders through an extensive array of magazines, newsletters, newspapers, advertisements, videos, and numerous marketing strategies (including a hot air balloon and a race car). Important in its image-creation efforts are celebrities who also are Scientologists. Because of the media attention that they generate, many of these celebrity members have official titles within the organization as "LRH [L. Ron Hubbard] Honorary Public Relations Officers." The organization assigns the "Public Relations Officers" to "help make LRH's accomplishments and technology known to the public" through a variety of high-profile activities, including meetings with public officials, media appearances, letters to editors, talk shows, testimonies at government hearings, and others (International Association of Scientologists 1990; Kent 2002).

A particular publication, *Hotline*, provides celebrities with images of Hubbard in relation to "broad general matters of world concern" so that they can attempt to position him favorably in relation to these issues. Once *Hotline*'s editors identify those broad general matters, this "positioning" involves designing their communications to celebrities by answering seven questions:

1. How does LRH fit into this?

2. What has LRH done with regard to it?

3. What has LRH produced to resolve it or aid it?

4. What LRH works are the authorities neglecting concerning this?

5. What quotable statement has LRH made about it?

6. What opinion leaders or groups has he befriended or worked with, to bring about a betterment of conditions on the subject?

7. What official recognition or indisputable public recognition has LRH received for his work in this sphere? (Hubbard 1983, 471).

All of Scientology's other official publications reflect similar attention to the way in which they promote and "position" its founder and his goals.

Discrediting Opponents

Toward opponents, however, Scientology developed communication strategies designed to discredit persons and/or organizations whom the leadership believes are attempting to hinder the group's progress. Scientology identifies these opponents as "Suppressive Persons" or "SPs," because they commit "crimes" against the organization according to its own judicial system. Hubbard felt at war with these critics and opponents, so in 1969 he produced a Policy Letter entitled, "Battle Tactics," in which he argued (in the face of critical attacks) that now "warfare is waged in the press and public in the form of ideas." "A good general," Hubbard claimed, "cuts off enemy communications, funds, connections." These and other tactics in the communication war with critics lead to success: "The prize is 'public opinion' where press is concerned. The only safe public opinion to head for is they love us and are in a frenzy against the enemy, this moans [sic: means] standard wartime propaganda is what one is doing; complete with atrocity, war crimes, trials, the lot" (Hubbard 1969, 2).

When in a battle with opponents, key communications strategies were to "always find or manufacture enough threat against them to cause them to sue for peace.…Don't ever defend. Always attack" (Hubbard 1974, 484). A particular "trick" (as Hubbard called it) that was useful in attacking opponents involved "propaganda by redefinition of words," which was "done by associating different emotions and symbols with the word than were intended" (Hubbard 1991c, 42). Hubbard illustrated how this propaganda technique worked using the profession that he hated: "'Psychiatry' and 'psychiatrist' are easily redefined to mean 'antisocial enemy of the people'" (Hubbard 1991c, 42: see Kent 1998, 148–150).

Redefining words within attacks against enemies was part of "black propaganda," which, according to Hubbard, "is the term used to destroy reputation or public belief in persons, companies, or nations." Used when "seeking to destroy real or fancied enemies," black propaganda "seeks to bring a reputation so low that the person, company or nation is denied any rights whatsoever by 'general agreement.' It is then possible

to destroy the person, company, or nation with a minor attack if the black propaganda itself has not already accomplished this" (Hubbard 1991b, 77). An effective way to destroy opponents is to "dead agent" them, which involves disproving (supposedly) false statements with documents or other solid proofs, which will have the effect of discrediting those opponents by ruining their credibility (Hubbard 1991b, 82).

Contradictions

Scientology's founder, L. Ron Hubbard, paid careful attention to issues about communication, attempting to advance his agenda for the organization that he created. Always mindful of his own image, he developed communication strategies that presented positive images of himself and the group to its members, and mobilized celebrity members to propagate public relations material. At the same time, he responded harshly and aggressively toward critics, devising communication strategies that intended to silence them and destroy their credibility. While many of Hubbard's writings regarding communications are decades old, they still direct the basic policies of the organization. Scientology's official creed states "that all men have inalienable rights to think freely, to talk freely, to write freely their own opinions and to counter or utter or write upon the opinions of others" (Church of Scientology International 1992, 579), but the communications restrictions on its own members belie these claims.

STEPHEN A. KENT

See also Free Speech

Further Reading

Church of Scientology International. (1992). *What is Scientology?* Los Angeles: Bridge Publications.
Church of Scientology International. (1994). *The Scientology handbook.* Los Angeles: Bridge Publications.
Hubbard Association of Scientologists. (1953). Editorial. *Journal of the Hubbard Association of Scientologists, Inc., 2.*
Hubbard, L. R. (1969). Battle tactics. *Hubbard Communications Office Policy Letter* (16 February).
Hubbard, L. R. (1970). Entheta letters and the dead file, handling of. *Hubbard Communications Office Policy Letter* (7 June 1965). *The Organization Executive Course* (Vol. 1, pp. 415–421). Copenhagen, Denmark: Scientology Publications Organization.
Hubbard, L. R. (1974). Dept of govt affairs. *Hubbard Communications Policy Letter* (15 August 1960). *The Organization Executive Course* (Vol. 7, pp. 483–485). Los Angeles: Church of Scientology of California.

Hubbard, L. R. (1976). *Modern management technology defined*. Copenhagen, Denmark: New Era Publications.

Hubbard, L. R. (1983). "Hotline," policy of. *Hubbard Communication Policy Letter* (25 September 1979). *The Management Series* (Vol. 2, pp. 470–473). Los Angeles: Bridge Publications.

Hubbard, L. R. (1991a). Copywriting. *Hubbard Communications Office Policy Letter* (26 September 1979). *The Management Series* (Vol. 3, pp. 204–207). Los Angeles: Bridge Publications.

Hubbard, L. R. (1991b). How to handle black propaganda. *Hubbard Communications Office Policy Letter* (21 November 1972). *The Management Series* (Vol. 3, pp. 77–88). Los Angeles: Bridge Publications, Inc.

Hubbard, L. R. (1991c). Propaganda by redefinition of words. *Hubbard Communications Office Policy Letter* (5 October 1971). *The Management Series* (Vol. 3, pp. 42–44). Los Angeles: Bridge Publications, Inc.

International Association of Scientologists. (1990). *What to do*. [Pamphlet].

Kent, S. A. (1998). The globalization of Scientology: Influence, control and opposition in transnational markets. *Religion, 29*, 147–169.

Kent, S. A. (2002). Hollywood's celebrity-lobbyists and the Clinton administration's American foreign policy toward German Scientology. *Journal of Religion and Popular Culture, 1*. Retrieved on October 10, 2002 from http://www.usask.ca/relst/jrpc/scientologyprint.html

Lamont, S. (1986). *Religion inc.: The church of Scientology*. London: Harrap.

Sculpture

From the great early civilizations to contemporary times, sculpture has served as a means of religious communication. A sculptor transforms material into an object in space. Sculptors carve subtractively from wood or stone or model additively with clay or wax. Sculpture in the round is finished on all sides and as a freestanding object is viewed from many different vantage points. Relief sculpture resembles two-dimensional painting in that figures and forms are united with a background and project slightly, as in low or bas-relief, or dramatically, as in high-relief works. Many different forms of sculpture have served the expressive needs of the world's religions.

Early History

Sculptural works illustrate a story, depict a god or worshipper, or function in a liturgical context or ritual. Sometimes the location of the sculptural work contributes to its religious function. For example, the cylindrical figures of men and women found at the Square Temple Eshnunna at Tell Asmar in Iraq (c. 2900–2600 BCE) clasp vessels or pray while wide-open eyes stare forward in an act of worship to a deity, perhaps Abu, the god of vegetation. At the same time as these Sumerian votive statues, Egyptian funerary sculpture was produced for the pyramids. The rigid, cubic figures of Egyptian kings and queens served as eternal homes for the *ka*, or spirit, that lived on after death, according to the religious beliefs of the Egyptian people. As eternal stone surrogates for living humans, Mesopotamian and Egyptian religious sculpture joins this world with the next. The sculptors of these early works are anonymous; however, later artists achieved fame by creating works that served religious functions.

Among the earliest-named sculptors, Pheidias, Polycleitos, and Praxiteles created the great figures of ancient religious sculpture during the Greek classical era of the fifth and fourth centuries BCE. In Greece, monumental cult statues dominated the interiors of temples. For example, at Olympia worshippers could climb a spiral staircase to see the forty-two-foot stone, bronze, and chryselephantine (ivory and gold) statue of Zeus that dominated the inner *cella*. On the exterior of the Greek temple, where ritual animal sacrifices occurred, figures appeared in the pediments and in the metopes and friezes that surround the four sides of the classical temple structures. Typically, these idealized works narrated the heroic exploits of the gods and goddesses to whom the temples were dedicated; at the Parthenon, for example, the east pediment shows the birth of Athena. Although today the extant classical figures are starkly white, at the time of their creation they were highly colored with brilliant applications of red, blue, and yellow.

It is likely that gilded metal also ornamented the sculpted deities of classical Greece. The rich embellishment of these depictions underscores the gratitude of the Greek worshippers for the gifts of the gods. In addition to the narrative reliefs, numerous idealized nude male figures and clothed female figures from the period stood as votive figures at temples and shrines or were used as grave markers. Votive offerings were physical expressions of thanks on the part of individual worshippers. As in Sumerian and Egyptian examples, Greek votive figures united the living to the dead and the divine.

Judeo-Christian Uses of Sculpture

In the Judeo-Christian tradition, the connection between humans and a monotheistic god is exemplified by the act of sculpting as stated in the book of Genesis:

"And the LORD God formed man of the dust of the ground, and breathed into his nostrils the breath of life; and man became a living soul" (Genesis 2:7). As monotheism, particularly Christianity but also Judaism, began to dominate the Mediterranean world, however, the role of sculpture as a means of religious communication was strongly debated. Although painting soon evolved as a means of conveying the central tenets of Christianity, figural sculpture remained closely linked with the idols of paganism, such as the cult statues of Zeus and Athena. Periods of iconoclasm, or image breaking, erupted during the early Christian period and in subsequent eras when the admonition against making "graven things" from the book of Exodus raised questions about the rightness of religious sculpture. This aniconic attitude initially limited sculptural art in the Christian church, but by the fourth century, perhaps in a continuation of Roman practices, symbolic and figural relief sculpture appears on Christian sarcophagi. The Chi-Rho symbol, a monogram of X and P, the first two letters of the Greek word for Christ, frequently adorns early Christian sarcophagi, and narratives highlighting the life of Jesus Christ appear somewhat later. Together, carved symbol and story express the Christian beliefs of the deceased on a timeless stone memorial housing human remains.

Growth of Christianity Affects Sculptural Use

As Christianity grew and spread, the use of sculpture also changed and expanded. Relief and freestanding sculpture appears on the entrance portals and in the interiors of churches on the capitals of columns, as altarpieces, and as liturgical objects. Sculpted reliquaries housed the remains of Jesus, Mary, and the saints and served as objects of devotion for Christian believers. Reliquaries were placed on altars, paraded in processions, or worshipped during important feast days.

Miraculous powers were attributed to relics, which were preserved in ornate sculpted containers. The large statue of Ste. Foi from the late tenth century at Conques is one of the first figures worked in the round since classical antiquity. The sculpted core is covered with gold and gemstones. Monumental crucifixes sculpted in wood and fitted with receptacles for relics also date from this period. The six-foot tall crucifix of Archbishop Gero, sculpted from oak and painted with brilliant colors, shows the lifelike, suffering figure of Christ on the cross. The Gero crucifix stored the consecrated host in an area at the back of the head and was hung above the altar where the sacrament of the Eucharist was celebrated.

By 1300, Christian believers contemplated events from the life of Christ, the Virgin, or the saints, as if they had been present at such events. Sculptural works presented these scenes as tangible events to worshippers who participated in the mass at church or during private prayers at home. Groups of the Virgin and Child and scenes from Christ's Passion were among the most popular images for devotion.

A prevalent form of devotional sculpture that began during the medieval period is the *Vesperbild* or Pietà. The earliest representations of the Pietà are found in thirteenth-century Germany, often in the form of polychromed wood sculpture. These devotional images, known as an *Andachtsbilder*, emphasized the expressionistic, graphic depictions of the sufferings of Christ and the sorrows of his mother. During contemplation before the sculpted Pietà, the worshipper focused on Christ's sacrifice and the Virgin's acceptance of His death for the salvation of humankind. These large, often life-size sculptures were typically placed by altars in churches where the faithful communicated directly with the Savior and His mother.

Perhaps the most famous Christian sculptural work is a Pietà made by the famous Italian sculptor Michelangelo in 1499. Considered a youthful masterpiece, the large marble sculpture was completed for the funerary chapel of a French cardinal in the basilica of St. Peter in Rome. Michelangelo's highly polished marble sculpture offers a striking contrast to northern polychromed wood depictions. Michelangelo presents Christ and Mary as idealized, classically inspired figures in a balanced, pyramidal composition. This sculptural group is the only work signed by Michelangelo as he proudly proclaimed his authorship of the visual manifestation of the Virgin's role as the mother of God's son.

Sculpture that satisfied the demands of Christianity reached an apex during the Counter or Catholic Reformation, when the Roman Catholic Church looked to art as a form of propaganda against the northern Protestants. The renowned Gian Lorenzo Bernini sculpted masterpieces of Baroque art that convey the doctrines of the rejuvenated Roman Catholic Church by celebrating the lives of early Christian martyrs and recent mystic saints. Bernini's *St. Theresa in Ecstasy*, commissioned by the Cornaro family for a chapel in Santa Maria della Vittoria in Rome, exemplifies the success of carved marble to communicate the physical power of Christ's love as experienced by the barefoot Carmelite nun, St. Theresa, who was canonized by Pope Gregory XV in 1622. At the same time, Stefano Maderno carved a moving depiction of the early Christian martyr, St. Cecilia, based on firsthand observation of her uncorrupted body, discovered

A religious sculpture adorning the bridge into Rottweil, Germany. *Michael Blackburn/istockphoto.com.*

in 1599. The touching depiction of the recumbent martyred saint reminded contemporary worshippers of the dedication and sacrifice of early believers.

Uses of Sculpture by Other Religions

Sculpture served other world religions, too. In India, the birthplace of Hinduism and Buddhism, sculptural representations of numerous deities are found in temples and shrines. Hindus worship individually and treat the sculptural figures of gods and goddesses as living human beings who are washed, dressed, and fed. The animated sculptural forms make the deities actually present to the worshipper. Among the leading figures in the Hindu pantheon are the Great Goddess, Brahma the Creator, Vishnu the Preserver, and Siva the Destroyer. These figures are identified by their attributes. In popular depictions of Siva, the god dances in a flaming circle while presenting established gestures and symbolic objects, such as the drum of creation and

the fire of destruction, that communicate his role in the Hindu pantheon.

Early Buddhist sculpture in India depicted symbols and narratives that promulgated the beliefs of a young religion. At this time, Buddhist art was aniconic; that is, the Buddha was not depicted. When pilgrims approached the Great Stupa at Sanchi, they entered through monumental entrance gateways heavily carved with symbols, such as the Wheel of Law, lions, and trees, which allude to the Buddha's life and desire for enlightenment. By walking the continuous ambulatory around the stupa or mound, the worshipper circled a large physical symbol of nirvana or enlightenment.

The iconic representation of the Buddha soon developed as a static, frontal seated or standing figure of calm meditation. The hand gestures, or mudras, communicate the Buddha's state of mind. For example, the Buddha may reassure the viewer with a gesture of raising the exposed palm to the shoulder or the Buddha may signal his meditative condition by resting both hands on his thighs, palms up with finger tips touching. Buddha wears a simple monastic habit; his long earlobes show that he no longer wears the extravagant earrings of royalty. He frequently has a dot, the *urna*, on his forehead and a knot of hair, the *ushnisha*. Behind the Buddha's head radiates a halo. By the Gupta period of the fourth and fifth centuries CE, sculptural presentations of the Buddha become fully developed. The seated Buddha becomes an elegantly seated, smiling figure with eyes closed in an eternal presentation of peace and repose.

As Buddhism spread, the sculptural representations responded to the demands of new followers. On the island of Java, at the temple of Borobudur, pilgrims could follow 1,460 sculpted relief narratives while walking a path upward, retracing the steps of the bodhisattvas who attained enlightenment by successfully passing through all ten stages of existence. The ten miles of stone relief carvings and over four hundred freestanding Buddha statues led the pilgrim through an array of illustrations and meditative stops toward the stupa at the top of the mound.

In Japan and China, sculptural works of Buddha multiply and are altered by the cultural demands of location. In Japan, in the Golden Hall, or *kondo*, of the Horyuji complex from the seventh century, the main gilded statue shows Buddha in the *abhaya* mudra of reassurance. Seated on a lotus throne, this Buddha is part of a grand program of statues and paintings that replicate the spiritual realm of enlightenment on earth. Moreover, the figure is sculpted by Tori Busshi, whose family emigrated to Japan from Korea and China.

Effects of Iconoclasm

Perhaps no better example of the power of religious sculpture exists than the destruction by the Taliban of the Buddhas of Bamiyan. These two monumental statues of standing Buddhas were carved during the fifth and sixth centuries directly into the side of a stone cliff in central Afghanistan. Muslim iconoclasts had begun the destruction of the figures hundreds of years earlier, but in March 2001, the Islamist Taliban government decreed that the statues were idolatrous and destroyed them. The two largest Buddhas were demolished after almost a month of intensive bombardment. During the destruction, the Taliban information minister lamented that "this work of destruction is not as easy as people might think. You can't knock down the statues by shelling as both are carved into a cliff; they are firmly attached to the mountain."

Many sculptural works show the ravages of iconoclasm; however, the rejection of three-dimensional statuary by Islamic Fundamentalists is a modern example of intolerance. Fortunately, a great deal of stone, bronze, and wood sculpture representing the world's religions has survived and reveals the power of imagery to communicate the most profound beliefs about the human relationship to the divine.

VALERIE HEDQUIST

Further Reading

Apostolos-Cappadona, D. (2005). *Religion and art.* Grove Art Online: Oxford University Press.

Bazin, G. (1968). *The history of world sculpture.* Greenwich, CT: New York Graphic Society, Ltd.

Elgood, H. (1999). *Hinduism and the religious arts.* New York: Cassell PLC.

Hibbard, H. (1966). *Masterpieces of Western sculpture: From Medieval to Modern.* New York: HarperCollins.

Lee, S. E. (1998). *China, 5000 years: Innovation and transformation in the arts.* New York: Solomon R. Guggenheim Museum.

Menzies, J. (Ed.). (2003). *Buddha: Radiant awakening.* New Haven, CT: Yale University Press.

Snyder, J. (1989). *Medieval art: Painting, sculpture, architecture, 4th–14th century.* New York: Prentice Hall.

Weston-Lewis, A. & Clifford, T. (1998). *Effigies & ecstasies: Roman baroque sculpture and design in the age of Bernini.* Edinburgh: National Galleries of Scotland.

Sermons

A sermon is a powerful center of a religious community's life where divine and human speech merge; it negotiates an alliance between rhetoric and ritual. It is where text and context strive to make sense of God and the world at a specific time, at a specific place, and for a specific group of people. The sermon is usually an oral interpretation of scripture or a message within the framework of a community. Its raison d'être is to persuade people to lead a new life. The goal of preachers, therefore, is to do more than inform and educate their audiences. Their ultimate objective is to move the will. Religious communities acknowledge and utilize other forms of official speech (for example, legal verdicts, papal announcements, liturgical rites, and eulogies), but the sermon serves as an important central event that defines the life of the community.

History

Although the early practice of Christian preaching is difficult to reconstruct, two influences can be cited: the Jewish synagogue and Greco-Roman rhetoric. As Christianity achieved a privileged status in the Roman Empire in the late fourth century, the sermon was transformed. During this period, bishops were often chosen from the ranks of those who had been trained as rhetoricians. John Chrysostom is generally regarded as the greatest preacher of the early church; Pope Pius X referred to him as the patron saint of Christian preachers. Despite the many different forms and functions of the sermon during these early years, the sermon was regarded as an oral interpretation of scripture for the life of the community, usually within worship.

Sermons have had different characters and served different purposes in different historical periods. However, few periods compare with the late Middle Ages for the outpouring of preaching and sermonic materials. In the thirteenth and fourteenth centuries the quantity of sermons, the enthusiasm with which they were heard, and the sheer volume of "sermon helps" that were produced, were impressive. With the mendicant preachers of this time, the sermon was taken from the church directly to the people.

Humanists broke with medieval preaching in the sixteenth century. They were known as "humanists" because of their concern for the humanities—that is, for the liberal arts of grammar, rhetoric, poetry, history, and moral philosophy. Of these, none was more influential than classical rhetoric. Since the sermon was the main form of public speaking in this period, sermons

"The Divine Light" by Jonathan Edwards

Jonathan Edwards (1703–1758) was one of the leading theologians and preachers of colonial America. He is credited with fomenting the "Great Awakening" religious revival of 1734–1735. The excerpt below is from a sermon originally titled "True Grace Distinguished from the Experience of Devils."

A sense of the beauty of Christ is the beginning of true saving faith in the life of a true convert. This is quite different from any vague feeling that Christ loves him or died for him. These sort of fuzzy feelings can cause a sort of love and joy, because the person feels a gratitude for escaping the punishment of their sin. In actual fact, these feelings are based on self-love, and not on a love for Christ at all. It is a sad thing that so many people are deluded by this false faith. On the other hand, a glimpse of the glory of God in the face of Jesus Christ causes in the heart a *supreme genuine love for God.* This is because the divine light shows the excellent loveliness of God's nature. A love based on this is far, far above anything coming from self-love, which demons can have as well as men. The true love of God which comes from this sight of His beauty causes a spiritual and holy joy in the soul; a joy in God, and exulting in Him. There is no rejoicing in ourselves, but rather in God alone.

The sight of the beauty of divine things will cause true desires after the things of God. These desires are different from the longings of demons, which happen because the demons know their doom awaits them, and they wish it could somehow be otherwise. The desires that come from this sight of Christ's beauty are natural free desires, like a baby desiring milk. Because these desires are so different from their counterfeits, they help to distinguish genuine experiences of God's grace from the false.

immediately began to reflect the rediscovery of "eloquence." The *Ecclesiastes* of Desiderius Erasmus has been called a great watershed in the history of sacred rhetoric.

The Reformation preaching of Martin Luther, John Calvin, and Ulrich Zwingli continued this break with medieval preaching. Although Luther's sermons in particular have shaped Protestant preaching until the present, the homiletical forms devised by his trusted colleague Philip Melanchthon had more influence on Lutheran and Protestant preaching. Melanchthon's polished rhetorical forms, which reflected humanistic consciousness and taste, often eclipsed the eschatological battles that marked Luther's sermons.

Although sermons have always been influenced by rhetoric, this was never truer than in Great Britain from the end of the seventeenth century through the middle of the nineteenth century. English education has always paid attention to what makes oral communication effective, and this period was marked by dramatic movements toward this end. Neoclassicism, the *belles lettres* movement, the elocutionary movement, the epistemologists (John Locke and David Hume), and the great preaching of John Henry Newman and Frederick W.

Robertson all impacted the form and function of the British sermon.

American preaching since World War II reflects as many changes in the basic understanding and practice of sermonizing than in the previous two centuries. Before World War II, puritan, evangelistic, rationalistic-moralistic, and social gospel preaching were common trends. The changes after World War II reflect the increasing pluralism of Western—particularly American—culture and religion. Various movements left their impact on American pulpits: the Great Awakenings, revivalism, the biblical theology movement, the social gospel movement, the liturgical movement, the pastoral care movement, and the Evangelical and Pentecostal movements. African-American sermons, which go back to the second Great Awakening, are influential and widely loved by all ethnic communities. Women have been preaching in the United States since the seventeenth century, and a growing body of evidence demonstrates their important role in shaping the form, function, and content of the American sermon.

Technology has also had a dramatic impact on the shape and content of the American sermon. Digital information—from sources like video clips, television, and the Web—is creating and enhancing the form and content of new sermonic forms. Sermons are becoming media events that touch all the senses. Television, in particular, has created a new intimacy between the preacher and the viewer. Research on the rise of electronic media, especially television and the Web, suggests that these technologies are challenging the old print-dominated Enlightenment culture. The postmodern emphasis on personal experience, cultural pluralism, and nonrational discourse thrives through the new media delivery systems for sermons.

Christian Preaching

There are at least three genres of Christian preaching observable in every epoch and place: missionary or evangelistic, catechetical, and liturgical or homiletical. Many have sought a blueprint for the perfect sermon form in the rules of rhetoric or in the psychological or anthropological principles of their day. However, most people resist saying that all sermons must be of one form—for example, narrative, inductive, with three points, or with at least six illustrations. How a sermon is shaped by the exigencies of a text and a worship situation and how its central idea is expressed cannot be legislated. A sermon may serve many purposes—for example, proclamation (*kerygma*), call to conversion, teaching (*didache*), blessing, comfort, wisdom, remembrance, prophecy, parable, and exhortation.

To a large extent, this purpose will determine the form of a sermon. There are many popular forms, including narrative, argument, funeral discourse, catechetical instruction, homily, the examination of a biblical text, meditation on an image, dialectical discourse, and answering a question. The sermon may be delivered by radio, digital media, or in book format.

H. Grady Davis, a researcher who took a progressive approach to homiletics, found in 1958 that among teachers of homiletics across a wide theological spectrum there was a noticeable uniformity of assumptions about the preaching event. He reported his findings in the following six propositions about the preaching event (Davis 1958):

1. True preaching is a form of the Word of God.

2. True preaching is biblical in the sense of making the Bible a truly living document.

3. True preaching centers on Jesus Christ as God's redemptive act, the restoration of broken humanity.

4. True preaching is itself, contemporaneously, part of the divine redemptive event.

5. The message of preaching is in collision with the thought, cultural habits, and concerns of the times.

6. Preaching is a unique kind of speaking, a special language, a dialogical interaction between God and hearers.

Approaching the sermon from the perspective of communication theory means taking these theological affirmations seriously and integrating them with knowledge of communication. It does not entail the dualistic assumption that divides all knowledge between science and revelation, facts and values. At no time does the transcendent render the scientific superfluous, and vice versa. From the point of view of communication theory, a typical sermon has five dimensions:

1. the creation and delivery of the message;

2. a description of the goal of the of sermon (for example, persuasion, conversion, information);

3. an awareness of the relationship between the act of communication and the community's ritual gathering (for example, a worship service, a revival meeting, or a television event);

4. a desire to maintain the community (for example, an acknowledgment of the pastoral care dimensions of the sermon); and

5. the cultivation of a worldview.

Whereas the earliest attempts to apply insights about communication to preaching consisted largely of pragmatic efforts to apply the new knowledge to the construction and delivery of sermons, communication approaches in more recent years have been used to integrate preaching with other dimensions (for example, to form community or enhance theological and ritual dimensions). The sermon is the place where these dynamics come together in complex ways.

Non-Christian Preaching

Christian preaching, which was born out of the ancient Jewish preaching tradition, has in turn influenced the history and character of the Jewish sermon, especially in the United States. Jewish preaching was born out of the destruction of the kingdom of Judah, its capital Jerusalem, and the ancient Temple, in 586 BCE. After this destruction, Jewish religious leaders felt that their faith in the Torah could best be preserved by combining prayer with instruction. Hence, worship services soon began to include sermons that served to instruct.

The sermonic tradition, however, was not a part of the normal Sabbath or holiday services among early American Jews. Those Jews who migrated to America in the 1700s came from a European tradition that did not include sermons as a part of normal services. It was not until 1830 that Isaac Lesser, of Mikveh Israel Congregation in Philadelphia, began to deliver sermons on a regular basis during normal Sabbath services; these sermons were a response to religious and political pressures. The pressures on Jews at this time in American history were great. The sermon allowed the gatherings at the synagogue to speak formally, directly and religiously to their situation. It was a new and powerful tool of community formation by a minority religious group within a new world. This became true later of Jews initiating Sunday school into their weekly observances to assist with the spiritual formation of children. Sunday school, like sermons, had both apologetic and community-building dimensions. The sermon provided a counterforce and an effective tool for building up their communities both spiritually and sociologically. However, the introduction of vernacular sermons into the Sabbath service was not an occasion for great controversy in the United States, as it had been in Europe. Within thirty years of Lesser's pioneering efforts, English-language sermons had become commonplace in American Jewish services.

Like their Christian counterparts, Jewish preachers use a wide variety of rhetorical, media, and cultural resources to speak upon a wide spectrum of personal, ethical, and moral issues as well as on a vast number of national concerns. The patterns of the Jewish sermon reflect Christian patterns but contain unique characteristics and dynamics. This is also true of the sermonic forms developed by other religious minorities in the United States, including Muslims, Hindus, Jains, and Buddhists.

Contemporary Homiletics

The influence of both classical and popular forms of oratory upon the Christian sermon has been enormous. Sermons are often dominated more by the science of communication than by a theological rationale: The how of sermons can eclipse the why. The patristic image of the ministry shows remarkable similarities to that of the classical orator described by Cicero. Despite its early rejection of so much of the classical heritage, Christianity held to its heart a tradition, that of the or-

ator, because the Church realized its value to preaching. In spite of this, the church has periodically attempted to reform its preaching, often by discarding what Puritans called "the airy dews of effeminate Rhetoric" and returning to the power of Biblical preaching, and contemporary American homiletics no longer speaks of eloquence and rhetoric. Nevertheless, its preoccupation with the formal characteristics of the sermon is a continuation of the rhetorical tradition.

RICHARD H. BLIESE

Further Reading

Brilioth, Y. (1965). *A brief history of preaching* (K. E. Matson, Trans.) Philadelphia: Fortress Press.

Davis, H. G. (1958). *Design for Preaching*. Philadelphia: Muhlenberg.

Forde, G. (1990). *Theology is for proclamation*. Minneapolis, MN: Fortress Press.

Frei, H. W. (1974). *The eclipse of Biblical narrative: A study in eighteen- and nineteenth-century hermeneutics*. New Haven, CT: Yale University Press.

Kennedy, G. A. (1980). *Classical rhetoric and its Christian and secular tradition from ancient to modern times*. Chapel Hill: University of North Carolina at Chapel Hill Press.

Lischer, R. A. (1992). *Theology of preaching*. Durham, NC: Labyrinth Press.

Mitchell, H. H. (1979). *Black preaching*. Nashville, TN: Abingdon Press.

Smyth, C. (1940). *The Art of preaching: A practical survey of preaching in the Church of England, 747–1939*. London: n.p.

Willimon, W. H., & Lischer, R. (Eds.). (1995). *Concise encyclopedia of preaching*. Louisville, KY: Westminster/John Knox Press.

Shaman

A shaman is a traditional healer who employs a variety of diagnostic, healing, and protective ceremonies, which include communication with spirits. Shamans can be male or female, and they are found in cultures worldwide, though the ancient magical-religious belief system of shamanism is strongest in Siberia and Asia.

Prehistoric Origins

The term *shaman* is derived from the Tungus-Mongol noun *saman*, which is constructed from the Indo-European root *sa*, meaning "to know." Shamans may have served prehistoric humans. Paleolithic drawings in the

Lascaux cave in the Dordogne region of southwest France appear to show a shaman with a wounded bison, perhaps indicating the shaman's assistance for a successful hunt. However, the archaeological evidence of shamanistic activity is not absolutely clear. A few archaeological finds indicate that shamanism existed in northern Asia and China about 3000 BCE. Numerous medieval European and Asian records indicate that shamans were common, but documents show that they were only one of many groups of religious specialists. Only in small, scattered societies do shamans consistently occupy a premier position. Shamanism in other cultures began experiencing renewed popularity beginning in the late twentieth century.

Becoming a Shaman

The requirements to become a shaman differ according to culture. Some cultures believe that only those with shaman ancestors can become shamans. All cultures believe that the spirits must select a shaman. Spirits may indicate their choice by wrapping an umbilical cord around a baby at birth, by giving a person an extra finger or toe, by creating gender confusion in an adolescent, or by causing some type of illness. The Uzbeks believe that a shaman's career begins with a special disease, often madness, caused by the spirits. In Central Asia the "shamanic disease" sometimes is manifested not as a mental but as a physical illness. Such ailments might strike not only the shaman but also members of his or her family.

The nature of the shamanic disease is determined by the traditions of the given society and its culture. Most cultures agree that a refusal to become a shaman after being chosen by the spirits leads to great mental suffering. *Kamidari* occurs among Japanese shamans. It includes a wide range of states: psychosis, various hallucinations, and somatic complains, which are often combined with such daily difficulties as economic hardship or conflicts among the family members. The only cure for *kamidari* is worship. Shamans do not choose to become shamans but are instead forced into the position as a means of relieving personal suffering.

The shaman must attain his or her position through a spontaneous trance, visions of dismemberment, and a journey of the soul to the Otherworld. All these states are reached through the spirits and not through study or the application of specific knowledge. A typical example is that of an Uzbek woman who was haunted by spirits, went mad, and finally, on the advice of a Muslim holy person, became a shaman.

Later she was visited several times and instructed in divination and healing by a helping spirit that appeared in the form of an old man.

Duties of a Shaman

As healers, shamans employ various methods to see the cure of a disease and to predict the future. If a member of the community dies, a shaman will guide the soul of the dead to the spiritual realm, thereby making sure that the spirit of the deceased does not become lost in the universal vastness. The Chinese have both male and female shamans, but only a woman can become a *siyang tung*. This type of shaman differs from the other Chinese shamans in her apprenticeship, duties, prayers, and ceremonies that she performs to treat illness.

Shamans do not merely cure disease. Through their rituals, they confirm and reinforce the patterns of traditional religions. They combat not only demons but also black magicians. They also harmonize social and natural dysfunctions and imbalances by opening windows to worlds occupied by gods and spirits. Hunting creates an imbalance through the killing of a being with a soul. To aid hunters, shamans use hunting magic to forge a relationship with the Master of the Animals or an equivalent figure so as to assure a consistent bounty for their people.

Ritual Behavior

To call on the spirits, a shaman must attain an altered and heightened state of consciousness. As a rule, the shaman calls on the spirits at night, often around a fire inside a tent. Musical sounds serve as a transporting technique. Drum playing, dancing, chanting, and singing bring the shaman closer to a mystical journey. The shaman will gradually speed up the drumming pattern and then slow it down as part of a strategy to disorientate the ordinary consciousness in preparation for the flight to other realms. When the shaman has entered a trance, he or she makes the journey. In Turkish and Mongolian mythology, totem animals such as wolves and deer function as mounts for the shaman, while dogs and ravens are the shaman's helping spirits.

The shaman's ritual behavior is the mode for direct contact with spirits and must follow a prescribed pattern. Some shamans wear animal and bird masks as part of a ritual to establish bonds with nature. In Korea, shamans use costumes, role-playing, and feats of wonder to dramatize a spirit's presence and strengthen believers' faith in a spirit's words as transmitted by the healer.

Resurgence in Shamanism

The basic assumption that underlies shamanism is that humans and animals are similar in spirit and essence. It is this belief that has led to conflict with religions that are based on human divinity. Religious persecution over the centuries erased much shamanism; however, a rise in religious toleration has led to renewed interest in shamanistic activity. The ability of shamans to bring healing and meaning into life while creating accord with nature has made them into honored members of many communities.

CARYN E. NEUMANN

Further Reading

Asatchaq, T., & Lowenstein, T. (1992). *The things that were said of them: Shaman stories from Tikigaq.* Berkeley: University of California Press.

Drury, N. (1989). *The elements of shamanism.* Shaftesbury, UK: Element Books.

Eliade, M. (1972). *Shamanism: Archaic techniques of ecstasy.* Princeton, NJ: Princeton University Press.

Lommel, A. (1967). *Shamanism: The beginnings of art.* New York: McGraw-Hill.

Noel, D. L C. (1997). *The soul of shamanism: Western fantasies, imaginal realities.* New York: Continuum.

Pinchbeck, D. (2002). *Breaking open the head: A psychedelic journey into the heart of contemporary shamanism.* New York: Broadway Books.

Ripinsky-Naxon, M. (1993). *The nature of shamanism: Substance and function of a religious metaphor.* Albany: State University of New York Press.

Sansonese, J. N. (1994). *The body of myth: Mythology, shamanic trance, and the sacred geography of the body.* Rochester, VT: Inner Traditions International.

Tucker, M. (1992). *Dreaming with open eyes: The shamanic spirit in twentieth-century art and culture.* London: Aquarian.

Signage

The image of an institution, especially a faith-based institution, is reflected in its signage, both interior and exterior. Religious signage is a subset of processes known in marketing as the "marketing mix." The traditional marketing mix comprises (1) making product decisions, (2) deciding on a distribution process (place), (3) the incorporation of various promotion decisions to create awareness for a product or service, and (4) pricing decisions. When studied together these four areas are known as the four Ps: product, place, promotion, and price. Religious signage in particular can be placed within a marketing subset traditionally associated with outdoor advertising. Included in this marketing subset are both traditional and nontraditional religious signs, either on a religious building or on its property, roadside billboards, posters in terminals, and transit advertising such as that found on the sides of buses and on the insides of trains.

Characteristics of Effective Signage

The very nature of religious signage in America is extraordinary. From crude hand painted signboards affixed to the front of church buildings to more intricate freestanding signs representing the latest in technology placed in front of churches, religious signage seeks not merely to identify and inform but to persuade, mostly through the use of captions and homilies.

In addition to exterior signage, religious signage is also most commonly found on the inside of church walls, usually incorporating bits of scripture or on banners incorporating religious symbols appropriate to a particular religion and a particular season. Outdoor murals are also used but are considerably less common. Most religious murals tend to be Protestant, rarely Jewish, and hardly ever Eastern Orthodox, Islamic, or Buddhist.

In his book, *Why We Buy* (1999), cultural anthropologist Paco Underhill identifies several characteristics that are common to all forms of signage, many of which relate directly to religious signage. First and foremost, signs in general must be able to be read in an instant, since in most cases the viewer or receiver of the intended message has only two to three seconds to see the sign, read it, and comprehend its message. The best signs, including billboards and roadside signs, are those that can be read quickly and are positioned as close to the road as local zoning laws allow. This is an important factor in the signage process, since zoning laws can vary significantly from city to city and from town to town.

It is also important that the sign can be easily read using a minimum number of words while the reader is moving either by foot or in a vehicle. If vehicles are moving past a sign at thirty to forty miles per hour, ten to twelve words are usually more than enough in most cases to communicate an effective message. Effective

signs use no extra words that can create clutter or confusion. Individuals passing a religious institution need to be able to take notice of a particular sign within a period of a very few seconds and in that time be able to read and understand what the institution is and how it can be of service to them. Within this context an effective sign is one that provides a link among a specific religious institution, members of a given community, and the passing public.

Religious signage also becomes a critical link to effective communication between the institution and its community. These signs traditionally use large lettering, incorporating as well good lighting and good positioning as allowed by appropriate zoning laws.

Traditional Religious Signage

As the need for additional religious services and their associated programs continues to increase and megachurches gain in popularity, the use of religious signage becomes increasingly important. This type of signage, however, remains a distant cousin when compared to other forms of marketing, including television, newspapers, magazines, and cable and satellite television delivery systems, as well as the increasing use of direct mail.

Over the years religious signage has evolved into more than just a message board. It not only strives to attract new members but at the same time serves to provide public service announcements as well as social commentary. Religious signage therefore becomes a critical link to effective communication among the institution, its members, and the communities they serve.

With a growing emphasis on historic preservation, many religious institutions are installing custom-built signs to enhance the traditional appearance of their buildings. Much of the religious signage being used is either nondescript or too wordy, which does not help them stand out from other signs. In most instances people will tend to judge a given religious institution by what they can see from the outside—usually the signage. If it is not attractive and inviting, the assumption will be that the religious institution and its members are equally uninviting. In addition, well-thought-out and well-placed religious signage can communicate both inspirational messages and event announcements to members of the community and passersby.

In a compilation of articles by the *New York Times* in 1977, two in particular pinpoint the development of the use of religious signage, specifically billboards. As early as 1912, religious signage began to make an impact on the American religious landscape. Prior to this, religious signage was usually found on the side of the road or attached to the side of a religious building, usually Protestant but sometimes Jewish as well.

Religious signage can typically be found positioned on the street in front or to the side of the religious institution; in parking lots; on the exterior of the building; as graphics on windows, including stained-glass windows; in the entrance area of religious buildings; and as guides for locating classrooms and the nursery/child care area, recreation hall, and information board.

In what was one of the first uses of a billboard in the promotion of church attendance, three New York communities—New Rochelle, Larchmont, and the Pelhams—joined with twenty Protestant churches—six Episcopal, three Methodist, three Baptist, three Lutheran, one African, and four Presbyterian—in the creation of a marketing campaign aimed at increasing attendance during the Lenten season.

In 1920, the United Methodist Episcopal Church in New York City, located just off Broadway, erected what was considered at the time to be the largest electrical sign in the United States. Constructed at a cost of three thousand dollars, a considerable sum in 1920, the twenty-five-foot-high sign was topped by a brilliant illuminated cross six feet tall and four feet wide.

Exterior Signs

The construction of an exterior religious sign requires consideration of several factors. The sign should incorporate appropriate symbols, type styles, words, and colors in order to create strong name identification. An appropriate denominational symbol acts as a logo, to quickly identify the organization to passersby, who have limited time to process what they are seeing. With exterior signage all illumination should be internal, to protect it from weather and vandalism. The lighting should also radiate a warm, welcoming quality.

Outdoor religious signage typically announces the name and address of the particular church, synagogue, or mosque along with the days and times that services are conducted. Also included is the name of the priest, minister, rabbi, or imam. In many Protestant denominations the title of the weekly sermon is also included. As is the case when using any communication medium, religious signage works best when its message is clear and informative. It is the first impression made to visitors and a means of easy identification for those attempting to locate a particular house of worship. It is also a means of evangelizing and for increasing awareness of a house of worship throughout the community.

As highlighted in www.gcoutreach.org, the general church outreach Web page, effective religious signage needs to be visible, readable, and clear and should incorporate bold colors whenever applicable. Other variables need to be considered. Is the lighting adequate for the sign to be easily read in the evening? Is the sign easily changed for different events? Has it been placed at a correct angle relative to the road or street it faces? Does it incorporate moveable type? Does the community allow signs to be placed a few blocks away pointing to and identifying the religious institution?

Due to the high cost of incorporating large billboards into an advertising/promotion budget, most religious organizations tend not to use them. In instances when they have been used, they are typically a component of a particular project such as those promoting a specific religious celebration; for instance, Christmas in the Christian faith or Passover in the Jewish faith. They have also been used to attract potential worshipers to a specific place of worship, such as the nation's growing number of megachurches. Billboards situated on or near a busy highway or interstate can attract the attention of upwards of one hundred thousand vehicles per day or nearly four million per month. They can also cost a religious organization many thousands of dollars. In addition, there is no way to judge their effectiveness. This is not to say that it is never done, but it is rare.

Exterior religious signage can also include signs identifying other ancillary businesses such as Christian book and gift shops, stores for Islamic and Jewish products, and stores specializing in African-American gospel music.

Uses of Interior Signs

Churches, synagogues, and mosques are dynamic places used throughout the day and evening hours. Once people have arrived at a religious institution, they need to have a way of locating where they need to go. Interior signage can assist the worshiper in locating classrooms, restrooms, library, meeting rooms, and a nursery if one is provided. Room identification signage, directional signs, and overhead signs are also included in this category. The important factor is that all signage, both interior and exterior, needs to be consistent. The ability to quickly and easily change messages is a critical component for interior signs; as a consequence, LED signage and magnetic changeable letter boards have become more popular than the more traditional black-felt boards with the white tabbed letters.

The High-tech Era

Digital signage represents the latest trend and is rapidly being incorporated into both indoor and outdoor signs. It is increasingly used by large numbers of religious institutions, as they continue to move toward a more upscale look, in both interior and exterior signs.

Digital signage is especially popular with contemporary-style religious institutions interested in presenting a high-tech image that clearly shows they are not old fashioned.

Digital signage consists of TVs, LCD panels, and the latest thing in religious signage—plasma monitors and projectors that can change images automatically every five to ten seconds or as needed. LCD technology, in particular, is especially popular because the messages can be changed from the inside.

These relatively new technologies are used to make announcements by the various ministries within a religious organization, such as the times of various meetings and upcoming events. They are usually located in the main lobby but are also used to project an image of the religious leader leading the service onto large projection screens in many of the nation's rapidly growing megachurches, those with memberships in excess of ten thousand members. It should be noted that this new technology is not intended to replace the person-to-person contact that is a staple of religious institutions; the purpose of such technology is to gain the attention of the member and nonmember alike.

A Tool for Evangelism

Religious signage provides an opportunity for Christian religious institutions with evangelistic outreach programs to become 24-hour-per-day witnesses to the Gospel. Likewise, it can be used as an evangelism tool for getting a congregation known within its community. With many religious institutions sharing their facilities with other religious groups, lettering in several languages, including on directional signs, has become commonplace.

PETER A. MARESCO

Further Reading

Compton, M. K., & Compton, D. (2001). *Forbidden fruit creates many jams*. New York: New American Library.

Compton, M. K., & Compton, D. (2003). *Life is short, pray hard*. New York: New American Library.

Cooksey, J. (2003). Selecting an exterior sign. *Religious Product News*. Retrieved from http://www.religiousproductnews.com/Articles/2003/11/sign.htm

Glusenkamp, R. T. (1998). *Signs for these times: Church signs that work*. New York: Concordia Publishing House.

Long, C. H. (1986). *Significations: Signs, symbols, and images in the interpretation of religion*. Philadelphia: Fortress Press.

Miller, V. (2004). *Consuming religion*. New York: Continuum.

Moore, L. R. (1994). *Selling God: American religion in the marketplace of culture*. New York: Oxford University Press.

The New York Times Company. (1977). *Religion in America*. New York: Arno Press.

Rabb, T., & Davies, D. (2001). *The proverbial marquee: Words to drive by*. New York: CCS Publishing Company.

Underhill, P. (1999). *Why we buy*. New York: Simon & Schuster.

Verbrugge, V. D. (1999). *Your church sign*. New York: Zondervan Publishing Company.

Wuthnow, R. (1994). *Producing the sacred: An essay on public religion*. Urbana: University of Illinois Press.

Zelinsky, W. (2003, July). The uniqueness of the American religious landscape. *The Geographical Review, 93*, 565–583.

Zepp, I. G., Jr. (1986). *The new religious image of urban America: The shopping mall as ceremonial center*. Westminster, MD: Christian Classics, Inc.

Sikhism

Sikh religious tradition begins with Guru Nanak (1469–1539). He used the medium of devotional religious songs to spread his message of personal love for God and the universal brotherhood of mankind. These songs of simplicity, clarity, and rustic beauty comprise the founding-stones of sikh religious tradition, binding the faith and its followers together into a community (*panth*). Other gurus followed this tradition of devotional literature, instruction, and didacticism. When growth of these materials raised concerns about access and authenticity, Amar Das, the third guru (1552–1574), produced a single collection of approved works. This two-volume collection, known as the *Goindval pothis*, included the works of the first three gurus and those of the bhakti poets. Compiled by Sahansram, the Amar Das's grandson, the *Goindval pothis* remained in the possession of the guru's elder son, Mohan, and unavailable and inaccessible to the panth. When the fourth guru, Ram Das, died in 1581 he was not succeeded by his eldest son, Prithi Chand, but by his youngest son, Arjan. This transposition precipitated a succession dispute and controversy over the *Goindval pothis*, which had passed from Mohan to Ram Das. Doubts about the authenticity of the written compositions arose when Arjan's rival, Prithi Chand, circulated competing compositions.

Arjan, the fifth guru (1581–1606), at the request of his followers, instructed his disciple, Bhai Gurdas, to compose an authorized and authenticated version of Sikh tradition relying on the original *Goindval pothis*, to

403

which Arjan had access. Completed in 1604 (and now in the possession of the *Sodhis* of Kartarpur, and known variously as the Kartarpur version, the Bhai Gurdas version, or the *Adi Bir*), it bore the guru's signature. For the first time, simple believers could rely on a widely available and trustworthy text comprising the devotional songs of all five gurus. In this early text, Sikhism secured the preservation of its fundamental works in an authenticated form. This version could be relied upon to imbue the status of *Gurudom*, and was the ultimate source of religious authority when the succession of ten personal gurus came to an end in 1708. Today, this text of Sikh scriptures (comprising the *Adi Granth*, or the *Guru Granth Sahib*) is the primary source of religious communication in Sikhism. Consisting of 5,894 holy verses in 1,430 pages, the *Granth* contains the sacred and divinely inspired word (*shabad*) of the guru. When a Sikh is born, his name is chosen from the *Granth*. When he prays he takes his daily morning and evening prayers from the *Granth*. When he attends to anything important, from going to work to embarking on a new venture, he takes guidance from the *Granth*. When he marries he circumambulates the *Granth* and not the sacred fire. When he dies he is cremated after recitations from the *Granth*. In fact, all Sikhs must, whenever possible, seek daily guidance from the *Granth* by opening it at random and reading the composition at the top of the left-hand page.

A second set of Sikh scriptures is the *Dasam Granth* (*dasam* meaning "tenth"). There is controversy as to whether they are so-called because they comprise the writings of the tenth guru, Gobind Singh, or whether they are so-called because they form the surviving tenth part of a much larger body of works which was lost during the troubled period of Guru Gobind Singh. The *Dasam Granth* is different in content and style from the *Adi Granth*. Whereas the latter emphasizes the attainment of religious emancipation through meditation on the divine name (*nam*), the former contains legends from the Hindu Puranas and observations unconnected with religious belief. It is written mainly in Braj Bhasha, with some Persian, Punjabi, and Khar Boli, rendering it difficult to access by the common man. Its divisions fall into four classes. There are two autobiographical works: *Vichitar Natak* (or "Wondrous Drama") refers to Guru Gobind's previous incarnation as an ascetic in the Himalayas; the *Zafarnama* is the epistle of victory defiantly addressed to the Mogul emperor Aurangzeb during the tenth guru's most difficult time, when his Sikhs were undergoing a period of relentless religious persecution under the Moguls. Both works are in seventy-three pages. There are four devotional compositions expressing militant piety, which became the hallmark of the tenth guru: *Jap sahib, Akal Ustat, Gian Prabodh*, and the *Sabad Hazare* (all four comprising sixty-eight pages). There are miscellaneous works (filling ninety-six pages): the *Savaiyye* (or *Panegyrics*) and the *Saster Nam-mala* (or "Inventory of Weapons"). Finally, there are lengthy compositions of legend and anecdote on the mother goddess Chandhi and the Hindu avatar (savior) Krishna: *Chandhi Charitr, Chandhi ki Var*, the *Chaubis Avatar*, and the *Tria Charitr*.

The compositions comprise 1,185 pages. The autobiographical and devotional compositions are probably the guru's own works, but the larger remainder almost certainly comprises the writings of other poets at his court, with all works being collected after his death. The *Dasam Granth* ranks well below the *Adi Granth* as a purveyor of Sikh religious tradition. Its language is beyond the understanding of most Punjabi Sikhs today, some of its portions are of dubious provenance, and what remains influential are the *Jap, Bachitra Natak, Akal Ustat,* and aspects of *Savayye, Chandhi ki Var,* and the *Zafarnama.*

Sikhism also has the supplementary scripture of the *vars* (heroic ode or ballad) of Bhai Gurdas and Bhai Nand Lal. The former was related to the third guru, Amar Das, and remained closely associated with him. Bhai Gurdas became known as a missionary, steward, and the first and greatest theologian to emerge from the panth. It was he who acted as scribe for the *Adi Granth* at the behest of Guru Arjan. The *vars* of Bhai Gurdas consist of 39 lengthy poems in Punjabi and a collection of 556 shorter works in Braj Bhasha called *Kabitts.* Sikhs today acquire an understanding of Sikhism through the reading and recital in *sangat* (i.e., congregations) of the *vars.* They are in the vernacular Punjabi and they relate in narrative form episodes from the lives of the gurus. Some are doctrinal and some exegetical. In all, they provide Sikhs with a considerable understanding of what the gurus taught. The writings of Bhai Nand Lal are less influential for two reasons. First, they are all in Persian and were hence accessible to only a small number of educated elite. Second, whilst they relate to the period of Guru Gobind Singh, with whom he was associated (being a poet from his court), they lack the militant spirit of the times, being overly philosophical, and so have been excluded from the *Dasam Granth.* The style in the *Divan* (a collection of 61 ghazels, or odes) and the *Zindagi-nama* (a series of 510 couplets) is in the spirit of the *Adi Granth,* stressing interior devotion and meditation as a means of deliverance.

In Sikhism, the *Janam-Sakhis* (literally "birth-testimony") also exert powerful influence, providing hagiographic accounts of Guru Nanak's life. Guru Nanak spoke of the route to salvation. His disciples bore witness to his message. The disciples recited the anecdotes relating to the guru's activities, thus providing evidence of his divinity. For Sikhs, the *sakhis* are a key source for the understanding of devotional literature. They emphasize the divine quality of the Nanak's calling and describe his feats and endeavors. They expound Sikh belief and social practice in a broad sense.

They are profoundly concerned with bringing Hindus and Muslims together and finding common ground between them. This association is a central motif of the *Janam-Sakhis:* from the joint welcome at Guru Nanak's birth at the beginning, to the joint dispute over the disposition of his dead body at the end. The *Janam-Sakhis* represent Guru Nanak as a Hindu to Hindus and a Muslim to Muslims. He is dressed as a *bairagi* (a Hindu renunciant) and as a *fakir* (a Muslim renunciant). In setting out to achieve this task, the tales focus mostly on his childhood in the village of Talvandi and his wide-ranging travels to outside Punjab. Some consist of simple wonder stories; others provide a moral. Many contain quotes from his works. The narrative often sets the scene for a particular hymn, which is quoted from his works. The theological exposition is then allowed to develop.

The way the *sakhis* developed was incremental. An oral tradition had developed during the time of Guru Nanak. Isolated stories or groups of stories had come into vogue and these comprised the first stage of the *Janam-Sakhis* tradition. The anecdotal *Janam-Sakhis* are modeled on Sufi examples. Other types are drawn from the Hindu epics and Puranas. Where there is an actual authentic incident, it is often based on Sikh tradition. The second stage arose about a hundred years later when these stories were gradually committed to the written form. They refer to isolated instances of hagiological events, and the only chronological schema is in relation to the birth, childhood, manhood, and death of the guru. The third stage occurred when the *sakhis* were set to an orderly chronological format. Guru Nanak's travels were given a specific itinerary in a particular location with a particular travel narrative. The fourth stage arose when the *sakhis* moved away from the narrative or wonder-story to a theological exegesis. The different events or occurrences are used as a context for lengthy expositions of devotional Sikh scripture. The *sakhi* will start with a particular incident. Someone will then ask a question. The guru will then reply with a religious verse. Finally, the writer will provide a detailed exegetic account of the incident. In this way, the popularity of the *Janam-Sakhis* increased as a growing number of religious teachers began to use it for pedagogic purposes. The *sakhis* are the first Punjabi prose form. They were only superseded after the emergence of the twentieth century Punjabi novel. In the late sixteenth and seventeenth centuries a number of different *Janam-Sakhis* genres appeared. The prominent ones are the *Puratan* tradition, the *Bala* tradition, the *Miharban* tradition, the *Adhi Sakhis,* and the *Mahima Prakash* (The Light of Glory). Whereas the other traditions comprise narrative forms, the *Miharban* tradition comprises discourse and exegesis. The eighteenth century so-called *B40 Janam-Sakhis* is the most famous combining all different traditions and styles. Today *Janam-Sakhis* remain popular with Sikh congregations. They may not be sacred scripture, but they form part of the belief-system of the panth. Their robust and appealing prose style is easily adaptable for oral delivery and thus accessible to all adherents.

Finally, the Sikh faith is also propagated by a person's initiation into the Khalsa panth (Order of the Pure) that requires the person to go through a ceremony known as *Amrit Sanskar*. He or she will drink *amrit* (nectar of immortality), which is sweetened water stirred with a short two-edged sword. Sometimes the ceremony is referred to as *Khande di Pahul* (Initiation with the Two-edged Sword). All who partake in such a ceremony are given a "code of conduct," or *rahit-nama*, by the master of the ceremony and thenceforth the initiated must obey that code. A *rahit-nama* (*rahit* meaning "code of belief"; *nama* meaning the manuals that promulgate the *rahit*) sets out how Sikhs should live in a manner consonant with their faith. They are commanded to observe the "Five Ks" (*panj kakar*), so-called for the five items (all of which begin with a *K*) that they must carry on their person, namely, uncut hair (*kes*), a comb (*kangha*), a sword, (*kirpan*), a steel wrist bangle (*kara*), and shorts (*kacha*). In addition, the *rahit-nama* requires them to regularly practice *nam simran* (reciting the name of God) and abstain from smoking, narcotics, and alcohol. *Rahit-namas* are said to date from the time of the tenth guru, Guru Gobind Singh, but the earliest extant version is the *Chaupa Singh rahit-nama*, dating from the 1740s. The proliferation of *rahit-namas* meant that by the end of the nineteenth century the Singh *sabha* reformist movement had emerged from within the panth. After issuing manuals that met with limited success in 1915 and 1931, a final version appeared in 1950 under the title *Sikh Rahit Maryada*, which is now the definitive statement of the *rahit* in Sikhism.

SATVINDER SINGH JUSS

Further Reading

McLeod, H. (1976). *The evolution of the Sikh community*. Oxford, UK: Oxford University Press.

McLeod, H. (1984). *Textual sources for the study of Sikhism*. Chicago: Chicago University Press.

McLeod, H. (1997). *Sikhism*. London: Penguin Paperbacks.

Juss, S. S. (1995). The constitution and Sikhs in Britain. *Brigham Young University Law Review, 2*, 481–533.

Silence

The importance of words and speech to religion is obvious. Many religions are grounded in sacred texts, practiced in verbal rituals, and communicated through articulate expression. Religious writings are central to the identities of Jewish, Christian, and Islamic communities—not only the foundational texts of the Hebrew Bible, the New Testament, and the Qur'an, but also generations of textual interpretation, legal discourse, and doctrinal dispute. Religious writings play an important role in Hinduism as well, and the oral communication of sacred stories continues to be vital to several Native American traditions. Add to this the roles of chanting, singing, praying, and preaching and it seems that religion is squarely located in the province of the word. Aside from traditions such as Buddhism and Quakerism, in which practices of silence are prominent, the importance of silence in religion can be easy to overlook.

However, silence is an important element of many religious traditions, including the most text-dependent. For example, while one of the Creation stories contained in the book of Genesis links the emergence of the created universe with the primary utterance of God, this very account of the significance of speech can be seen to imply that silence, even prior to creative speech, might be closer still to the reality of the divine. A similar dynamic can be seen in Hinduism, in which Aum, the seed syllable of the universe, triggers the unfolding of the manifest world. In symbolizing the absolute, Aum also always indicates that which remains unmanifest. Silence, while often less obvious than speech, is nonetheless an important element in many religious traditions.

Silence, Speech, and Meaning

While silence is perhaps most commonly considered to be the absence of speech or of sound, in religious contexts silence takes on various meanings and multiple roles. Adherents of several different traditions describe religious experiences in which silence figures prominently and denotes more than a pause in verbal communication. For example, in accounts of illumination or adoration, silence can indicate a communion between humans and the holy in which the boundaries of articulation are surpassed. Silence is the terrain of the mystic, who knows or experiences the holy with an intimacy that words cannot obtain.

Similarly, silence can be an acknowledgement of the incapacities of speech, an appropriate response of awe and wonder when all attempts at articulating religious truths are found to be necessarily lacking. Silence speaks of mystery. It acknowledges its own limitations, refraining from the attempt to circumscribe a subject in language. In religious contexts, silence can thus gesture toward that which cannot be snared in the web of language, that which cannot be grasped fully by the human mind and therefore cannot be uttered by the human tongue. That which is holy is ineffable—it cannot be spoken.

Silence, therefore, cannot be best understood as the opposite of speech. It can be many things, including: the necessary prior condition of speech, an element of discourse vital to the meaning-making processes of speech, an indication of the inadequacies of speech to capture or communicate reality, and the pinnacle of speech in which communication becomes communion.

Intentional Religious Practices of Silence

As many religions are concerned with that which is seen to transcend or underlie mundane existence, silence can be an appropriate element of religious practices and discourse by pointing beyond the din of everyday concerns toward that which cannot be comprehended in language. Clearing away the clutter of worldly distractions can help make space in which a deeper sense of reality can emerge—a space to hear the breath of the Spirit, an emptiness that erodes the distorted significance of personal concerns, or an attunement to that which is not manifest in the world around us.

People of many different religious traditions engage in intentional practices of silence, such as silent prayer, meditation, and contemplation. There are significant similarities in the understanding of the importance of silence in different religious traditions. For example, there is a shared perception that the discipline of remaining quiet is of value. Keeping silence has spiritual benefits. Furthermore, the discipline of silence can help persons to achieve a greater capacity and quality of attention, allowing them to see themselves and the world around them with greater clarity. Also, there is a sense that greater truth can be known in silence than in words. As language is inadequate to the task of conveying the deepest truths, such truths can be found only in silence.

Given these similarities, it is also important to note the differences between how practices of silence figure in different traditions. As an example, consider Christianity and Buddhism, two traditions (each containing many variations) that include monastic communities in which silence figures prominently. Perhaps the biggest

difference between how silence functions in these two religions is that in Buddhism, silence is understood in terms of emptiness and is valued precisely as such, whereas in most of Christianity, silence is explicitly understood to be filled with the presence of God. John Chryssavgis, writing about Christian monasticism in third and fourth century Egypt, states, "Silence is fullness, not emptiness; it is not an absence, but the awareness of a presence" (Chryssavgis 2003, 46). The kinds of truth obtained by such practices of silence differ likewise. A Christian might sit in silence while holding an intense internal conversation, bringing questions to God and expecting response, either through the Spirit or through the Bible. In contrast, a Buddhist might sit in silence, in which all internal dialogue is stilled and the mind is quieted, and the experience of such silence then grants new perspective on any questions the person encounters.

Painful Silences

Meditation and contemplation are not the only kinds of silence that occur within religious communities. It is also the case that many people have been and are silenced by religious power, authority, and traditions. This takes place in numerous ways, ranging from prohibitions to religious warfare to subtle cultural marginalization. Silencing can be specific and individual or vast and communal. Within Roman Catholicism, the teaching office of the Church can impose restrictions on theologians whose understanding of doctrine is found threatening or deemed inaccurate, thereby silencing dissenting voices. Within several traditions, women have been excluded from positions of leadership and power, thereby ensuring the voices that shape and maintain the faith are the voices of men, leaving women—even noisy ones—unheard. Judith Plaskow, a Jewish feminist theologian, writes, "The need for a feminist Judaism begins with hearing silence. It begins with noting the absence of women's history and experience as shaping forces in the Jewish traditions" (Plaskow 1991, 1).

The institutional structures and cultural biases of religious communities lead some stories to be valued while others are left untold, unheard, or ignored. Often the factors that allow one group to speak for and shape a tradition also prevent other groups from doing the same. This silencing, while sometimes not as intentional as religious practices of meditation, contemplation, and prayer, is nonetheless an important element in the identities of many religious communities.

407

A related form of religious silence is the refusal to speak out against injustice. At several crucial times, many religious communities have chosen to remain silent in response to the oppression of others. Examples would include the silence of many Christian churches regarding the persecution of Jews during World War II, and the silence of many religious groups in response to the AIDS crisis when it began in the 1980s and as it has continued. This silence, too, shapes the identity of religious communities.

For many people who believe in a powerful deity who could intervene in human affairs, the refusal to speak out against injustice finds its most painful reality in God's apparent silence in the face of human suffering. Many Jews and Christians experienced God as standing silently by while the atrocities of World War II went unchecked. A perception of God as silent in response to evil and in response to fervent prayers for help is a significant challenge to the faith of many.

The ineffability of the holy has been mentioned as one reason why silence has an important role to play in many religious traditions. However, there is another form of ineffability that concerns silence and religion. This is the ineffability of the truly horrendous. After the Shoah (Holocaust), many survivors found themselves unable to talk about the realities of the concentration and death camps. Their silence stemmed, in part, from the fact that no words could contain the truth of the suffering experienced there, that the events that took place were so extreme that language—in its assumption of a bare minimum of human civilization—crumbled in any attempt at description. Language itself had been violated and defiled. Also, people receiving such accounts often found the horrors too much to grasp, incomprehensible, impossible to hear.

Functions of Silence and Speech

Struggling with the ineffability of horror along with a need to witness to the events of the Shoah, some survivors have found that the only discourse that can begin to function is one of words and silence together, in a new relationship. Elie Wiesel, a survivor and prominent Jewish author, writes, "We cannot avoid the silence, we must not. What we can do is somehow charge words with silence" (Abrahamson 1985, 57).

An imperative element to the relationship between speech and silence is also acknowledged in other religious contexts. Within Buddhism, practices of silence are connected to cultivating compassionate speech. Christian theologian Gustavo Gutierrez asserts that the realities of suffering and injustice require Christians to

speak out. At the same time, such speech should be nourished by listening to the poor and oppressed and by a life of prayer, contemplation, and struggle for justice. In this way, theology can become "speech that has been enriched by silence" (Gutierrez 1987, xiv).

Speech and silence are always in relationship with one another, but this relationship cannot be simplified into mere opposition. An awareness of the many ways in which silence functions within religious discourse opens up possibilities for crafting the dynamic between speech and silence in new ways. While silence can be a tool in constructing communal identity by excluding the voices of others, it can also be a posture of openness to the world, to other people, and to the divine. Speech formed from within a posture of silence might possess different characteristics and potentials for communication than speech formed elsewhere.

Future Directions

In the United States, silence has become a form of religious communication or observance without specified content. As such, it is seen as compatible with a secular system of government and a pluralistic population. Particularly in times of sadness or loss, when some sort of religious statement seems necessary, communities in which individuals adhere to different faiths or no faith at all can join together for a moment of silence. Hearkening back to observances to honor the dead of World War I and to traditions of Armistice Day, moments of communal silence serve as secular rituals of respect. Such rituals can be seen as vacuous attempts to fulfill some need for communal religion without offending anyone, or as legitimate opportunities for those of different faiths to join together, or as a bit of both. Given that silence figures in so many different religions, most often in ways that defy strict definition and therefore do not invite dogmatic disputes, silence may have a vital role to play in how increasingly pluralistic societies negotiate respect for differences and the need for communal rituals.

Silence performs many different functions within religious communities. It is a spiritual practice, an element of worship, and an opportunity for communication that transcends language. Silence also characterizes the reality of people whose voices are unheard, the refusal to speak out to help another, the possibility of an absent or uncaring God, and the dissolution of language in the face of horror. Insofar as silence can denote recognition of mystery, acknowledgement of limitation, and a posture of openness, it can be a profound element of religious speech. In all of these ways and many others, silence is part of how religious individuals and communities define themselves.

SHANNON CRAIGO-SNELL

See also Orality

Further Reading

Abrahamson, I. (Ed.). (1985). Introductory essay. *Against silence: The voice and vision of Elie Wiesel* (Vol. 1, pp. 9–74). New York: Holocaust Library.

Chryssavgis, J. (2003). *In the heart of the desert: The spirituality of the desert fathers and mothers*. China: World Wisdom, Inc.

Danielou, A. (1985). *The myths and gods of India*. Rochester, VT: Inner Traditions International, Ltd.

Ettin, A. V. (1994). *Speaking silences: Stillness and voice in modern thought and Jewish tradition*. Charlottesville: University Press of Virginia.

Gutierrez, G. (1987). *On Job: God-talk and the suffering of the innocent*. Maryknoll, NY: Orbis Books.

Merton, T. (1957). *The silent life*. New York: The Noonday Press.

Neher, A. (1981). *The exile of the word: From the silence of the Bible to the silence of Auschwitz* (D. Maisel, Trans.). Philadelphia: The Jewish Publication Society of America.

Panikkar, R. (1989). *The Silence of God: The Answer of the Buddha* (R. R. Barr, Trans.). Maryknoll, NY: Orbis Books.

Picard, M. (1952). *World of silence* (S. Godman, Trans.). Chicago: Henry Regnery Co.

Plaskow, J. (1991). *Standing again at Sinai: Judaism from a feminist perspective*. San Francisco: HarperSanFrancisco.

Rahner, K. (1965). *Encounters with silence* (J. M. Demske, Trans.). Westminster, MD: Newman Press.

Sibelman, S. (1995). *Silence in the novels of Elie Wiesel*. New York: St. Martin's Press.

Steiner, G. (1970). *Language and silence: Essays on language, literature, and the inhuman*. New York: Atheneum.

Sports

With the explosion in media coverage throughout the latter half of the twentieth century, the popularity of sport has risen exponentially. From the constant coverage of sporting events, leagues, and teams on cable and free-to-air television, radio, newspapers, and specialist magazines, through to the Internet with the widespread popularity of fantasy leagues, the public has never had more opportunities to engage with sport. The unwavering devotion that some fans exhibit toward their teams, the emotional distress at defeat, the reverent regard for athletes, as well as the ritualized and superstitious practices that accompany spectating, have led some popular commentators to conclude that sport is a modern religion, the contemporary "opiate of the masses." This religion has its own sacred spaces, cathedrals in the form of sports stadia; its own pantheon of gods, the athletes who assume the role of deity; and its own set of rituals that distinguish it from other religious communities. Of course, not all agree that these structural similarities are sufficient to declare sport a new religion, particularly as, contrary to traditional faiths, sport does not purport to provide any explanations for life's mysteries. This is, however, not to say that sport and religion are completely independent.

Sport and religion have had a significant influence on one another. Among ancient societies there is significant evidence that physical activities were integrated into a range of religious and ritualized practices. The ancient Greek Olympic Games were added to the religious festival in honor of Zeus, while the Heran Games were held to glorify the goddess Hera. The Isthmian Games praised Poseidon, and the Delphian and Nemean Games were held in honor of Apollo. The ancient Mayan ball games were organized and officiated by priests on grounds that adjoined their temples. The Japanese sport of sumo drew heavily on Shinto rituals and religious practices in an effort to legitimate the activity and gain political acceptance.

While there is increasing interest in the role of sport in Eastern, African, and other indigenous religions, it is important to recognize that "modern sport" is a peculiarly Western institution that embodies many of the principles of industrial capitalism. Consequently, there has been a closer structural affinity between Christianity and sport than with other religions, and as a religion of conversion, Christianity has sought the alliance of other cultural institutions in its mission to win new adherents. In other, primarily Eastern, societies, movement activities have been incorporated into devotional and ritualized practices; however, these activities are not competitive, rationalized, or quantified activities in the same way that modern sport is. In addition, many of those religions that rely on a personal transcendence of the material world find little value in the dedicated pursuit of physical accomplishment as an end in itself. The influence of the Christian church on the practice, structure, and philosophy of sport has had a lengthy and profound history.

Sport and Christianity

Sport has not always been valued by the Christian church. The changing conception of the mind/body relationship has influenced the church's interpretation of sport and its suitability as a leisure activity. While the early Catholic Church encouraged the inclusion of a range of physical activities, including ball games, in their religious festivals during the medieval age, the emergence of early Puritan tendencies gave rise to debates about the nature of the Sabbath and its strict observance. Across Europe, various laws and decrees legislated a Sunday rest, which curbed the peasants' ability to engage in many physical recreations. The 1388 laws introduced by King Richard II expressly prohibited servants and laborers from playing games such as tennis on Sundays, though archery was to remain a lawful activity.

Church Denunciation of Physical Contests

Gradually, the church started to denounce festivals during which physical contests and animal sports were conducted. These gatherings were often an occasion for the lower classes to drink, while the various sporting events themselves promoted gambling. The church argued that these amusements threatened morality and had the potential to incite riot and rebellion. The staunchly Protestant English monarch, Queen Elizabeth I, reinforced these principles in 1559, insisting that the Sabbath be set aside for holy reflection, with the exception of the harvest time when labor was permitted. She confirmed her position in 1579 when she prohibited "pipers and minstrels playing, making and frequenting bear-baiting and bull-baiting on the Sabbath days, or upon any other days in time of divine service; and also against superstitious ringing of bells, wakes and common feasts, drunkenness, gaming and other vicious and unprofitably pursuits" (Govett 1890, 25).

The rise of Puritanism in the sixteenth and seventeenth centuries heralded greater restrictions on physical labor and recreational activities on the Sabbath and other religious occasions. With the reduction in the number of lawful activities permitted on a Sunday and with the rest of the week given over to work, there were soon few opportunities for the commoners to gather together in recreation. Despite their popular depictions as a fun-loathing, dour group, the Puritans were nevertheless supportive of recreation that had some kind of preparatory or utilitarian purpose. Popular amusements merely for the sake of personal enjoyment or gambling were, however, considered sinful, while any secular activities that took place on the Sabbath were similarly reviled. The Puritans feared these activities would tempt men away from more pious undertakings and corrupt not just their bodies but their souls as well.

Book of Sports

To curb the Puritan influence, King James I, in response to complaints concerning the lack of opportunity for public gatherings, produced the *Book of Sports* in 1618 in which he listed a range of sporting activities, including dancing, archery, and other "harmless recreations," that were to be considered lawful on a Sunday after divine services were concluded. Significantly, these activities were only permissible for those citizens who had first attended church. This publication was, however, withdrawn in 1620 after the British Parliament passed a bill reasserting the strict observance of the Sabbath, though it was later reissued by King Charles I in 1633. The conflict between sport and Sabbatarianism plagued sport throughout the ensuing centuries and with the resurgence in Christian sports evangelism in the twentieth and twenty-first centuries, it remains a point of conflict.

Muscular Christianity

Until the nineteenth century, sports and physical recreation were regarded primarily as a corporeal activity with little utility in the accomplishment of higher moral objectives. Indeed, in many areas, the pursuit of physical activities was thought to be in direct contrast to religious and classical education. Nevertheless, the emerging popularity of recreational sport was soon harnessed by educational institutions seeking ways to channel the youthful energy of their charges into appropriate activities.

British Combination of Physical and Moral Fitness

An important shift in the relationship between the Protestant Christian church and sport emerged during the mid-nineteenth century and was characterized by efforts to transform young British men into physically and morally fit leaders, imbued with a Christian morality and sensibility. The religious education of boys in the English public school system was thus complemented by physical education in the form of organized games. Initiated by Dr. Thomas Arnold at Rugby School, the focus on both moral and physical education was to produce in the boys a kind of "Muscular Christianity" that would prepare the young men for service in the British Empire. Muscular Christianity was inextricably linked to emerging ideas of masculinity and

"Vitaï Lampada" (1897) by Sir Henry Newbolt

THERE'S a breathless hush in the Close to-night—
Ten to make and the match to win—
A bumping pitch and a blinding light,
An hour to play and the last man in.
And it's not for the sake of a ribboned coat,
Or the selfish hope of a season's fame,
But his Captain's hand on his shoulder smote
"Play up! play up! and play the game!"

The sand of the desert is sodden red,—
Red with the wreck of a square that broke;—
The Gatling's jammed and the colonel dead,
And the regiment blind with dust and smoke.
The river of death has brimmed his banks,
And England's far, and Honor a name,
But the voice of schoolboy rallies the ranks,
"Play up! play up! and play the game!"

This is the word that year by year
While in her place the School is set
Every one of her sons must hear,
And none that hears it dare forget.
This they all with a joyful mind
Bear through life like a torch in flame,
And falling fling to the host behind—
"Play up! play up! and play the game!"

Source: Newbolt, H. (1897). "Vitaï Lampada." Retrieved December 14, 2005, from http://www.theotherpages.org/poems

empire and held that the moral behavior and character training learned on the playing field would transfer to other areas of life. As such, Muscular Christianity provided sport with an ethical and moral basis that remains the foundation of sport and was the forerunner to the concept of amateurism.

Just as English public schools began to focus more on the body than the soul, other religious organizations started to regard sport as a means to other, more virtuous ends. The Young Men's Christian Association (YMCA), founded in 1844 in England, was designed to provide alternative, rational activities to members of the industrial working classes. Bible study and healthy living were encouraged instead of popular urban recreational activities, including gambling and drinking. With the increase in sport's popularity over the ensuing decades, the YMCA started to offer a range of exercises and physical activities in additional to their outreach work, and their mission expanded to include improving the physical as well as the spiritual health of their members. The Jewish equivalent, the Young Men's Hebrew Association, had a similar purpose to use sporting activities as a way to engage young boys in particular and later young girls with the advent of the Young Women's Hebrew Association, to appreciate their cultural and religious heritage whilst simultaneously learning to integrate into a new national culture, the "American way of life." For both Christian and Jewish organizations, participation in sport was an important mechanism for developing a worthy moral character.

The Muscular Christian ideal slowly diffused throughout the British Empire, transmitted by graduates of

English public schools and Oxbridge, visitors to Great Britain, and Christian athletic missionaries, who used sports in their evangelism. These missionaries converted indigenous communities across the Empire to Christianity specifically and to a British sense of civilization more broadly. Sport, in particular cricket, was one of the chief tools of this "civilizing process," and the ability to play became a marker of British civility and culture. The Muscular Christian ethos was circulated through the British Empire and beyond in the writings of Charles Kingsley, Matthew Arnold, and, most famously, in Thomas Hughes's *Tom Brown's Schooldays* (1857), as well as in a range of magazines targeting young boys. These publications promoted not only a love of and regard for British sports but also a dedication to the moral foundation of these activities. Poems, such as Henry Newbolt's "Vitaï Lampada," explicitly linked sport and militarism, highlighting the belief that the strength of character gained in athletics was the best preparation for military discipline and leadership.

Sport Evangelism

The use of sport as a means to evangelize has not been relegated to an imperial past but is an increasingly popular way to convert new adherents to Christianity. During the latter part of the twentieth century, there has been an explosion in "sports evangelism," as well as in the number of organizations, such the Fellowship of Christian Athletes (founded in 1954), which utilize sport as a means to convert or reinforce Christian identity. This form of evangelism is unique to the Christian church and is particularly apparent in the United States, where church-organized and -sponsored sporting leagues are widespread. At both the community and professional levels, incorporating devotional prayers before, during, and after sporting events is increasing, while the halftime entertainment has become an opportunity to preach to spectators. In schools and universities, there is some resistance to this trend as efforts are made to remove sports-related prayer from public educational institutions.

Sport Used to Strengthen Communities

In addition to Christian denominations, other religious groups have used sport in the service of their community and identity. Rather than using sport as a direct means to proselytize and convert, many religious groups use sport to strengthen their communities, just as they rely on a variety of cultural practices to reproduce their faith and identity by providing social as well as spiritual occasions for their members to interact. This is particularly appar-

ent among minority religions that struggle to maintain their distinctive identity. Research on Islamic communities in South Africa and France, for example, suggest that participation in sports may contribute to the maintenance of their religious and community identity, even though sporting activities are not directly utilized as opportunities to evangelize. In addition, there are a number of religions for which competitive, performance-oriented sport is antithetical to their philosophical foundations, though religious experiences may be embedded in traditional movement activities.

Sport as Religion?

The relationship between sport and religion is multifaceted and is the product of a lengthy historical tradition. Debates about the structural similarities of sport have dominated discussions of the two institutions, with some arguing that sport is a religion, while others categorically reject this assertion. It is clear, however, that religious authorities, particularly the Christian Church in all its guises, have had a significant impact on the structure and function of sport. Historically, Christianity has provided a philosophical and moral foundation for sport, while simultaneously serving as a tool to acculturate indigenous populations into British conceptions of civilization. More recently, sport has been revived as a contemporary means of evangelizing, as Christian athletes have organized. While most research has focused on the influence of Christianity on modern sport, there is much to be learned about the role of the body and movement activities in other religions across the world.

TARA MAGDALINSKI

Further Reading

Govett, L. A. (1890). *The king's book of sports: A history of the declarations of King James I and King Charles I as to the use of lawful sports on Sundays.* London: Elliot Stock.
Hoffman, S. (Ed.). (1992). *Sport and religion.* Champaign, IL: Human Kinetics.
Magdalinski, T., & Chandler, T. (Eds.). (2002). *With God on their side: Sport in the service of religion.* London: Routledge.
Novak, N. (1976). *The joy of sports.* New York: Basic Books.

Stereotyping

The term *stereotype* was used in eighteenth century wood-block printing to describe a metal typeface from which any number of exact copies could be made. It combines the Greek term *stereos* (fixed, solid, or permanent) with the late Latin word *typus* (impression). In this way the word itself accurately describes the two most significant attributes of the term in contemporary usage—namely, to describe a *fixed impression* or *copy*. Since its original allocation, the term *stereotype* has been conceptualized by a number of academic disciplines, most noticeably sociology and psychology, and has become part of everyday speech. Today we might define a *stereotype* as an overgeneralization of certain characteristics attributed to an entire social group or to an individual belonging to the group. Any social collective can be stereotyped, but most research has focused on ethnic, gender, age, and class stereotypes.

Stereotypes may be negative or positive, although many researchers have found that even the use of positive stereotypes has negative consequences because it limits the group or individual being stereotyped. For example, one "positive" stereotype of the African-American male—that he excels in sports—may prevent African-American males from seeking alternative avenues of opportunity, for example, those that depend upon academic ability.

Major Works on Stereotypes

American essayist Walter Lippmann is generally credited as the first scholar to explore the concept of stereotyping in its contemporary form. In his book *Public Opinion* (1922, 1949), Lippmann suggests that stereotypes are the "pictures in our heads" that we associate with a social group or an individual who belongs to that group. Lippmann recognized the negative impact of stereotypes and stereotyping, but he also saw the categorizing (and simplifying) of people and groups as an inevitability; he argued that generalizing was a defense against the complexity of a social world that can never be fully comprehended by its inhabitants. Lippmann writes:

> For the real environment is altogether too big, too complex, and too fleeting for direct acquaintance. We are not equipped to deal with so much subtlety, so much variety, so many permutations and combinations. And although we have to act in that environment, we have to reconstruct it on a simpler model before we can manage it. (1922, 16)

In the early thirties, two sociologists, Daniel Katz and Kenneth Braly, provided one of the first social scientific studies on stereotyping. Seeking to measure the degree of stereotypical thinking displayed by a subject group of college students, they designed a study in which participants were asked choose from a list of positive and negative traits the traits that best described the characteristics of various ethnic groups. The results showed that a disproportionate number of positive adjectives were chosen to describe *American*, while the categories of *German*, *Italian*, *Black*, *Jew*, and *Chinese* received a disproportionate number of negative adjectives. Although their work, especially their methodology, came in for a fair amount of criticism over the years, their early research into the phenomenon of stereotyping is still often cited.

Since the work of Lippmann, Katz, and Braly, stereotyping has been the focus of many studies in the social sciences. Sociologist Arthur G. Miller has found that these studies take one of three main approaches. First, he noted that stereotypes fall within the domain of sociology because stereotypic views, beliefs, and perceptions usually precede the individual and are transmitted through agents of socialization—for example, family, peers, and media. He pointed out that although stereotypes may hold some truth, they have a damaging effect on the target group; many sociologists have linked stereotyping with incidences of prejudice and discrimination.

The second approach defined by Miller emphasizes the psychological aspect of stereotyping and regards the process as a product of the stereotyper's need to manage external social stimuli. This approach, which echoes Lippmann's work, incorporates ideas from projection and scapegoat theories along with notions of defective or faulty processes of perception and judgment. The third approach discussed by Miller also focuses on cognition, but it challenges the notion that stereotyping is the product of defective mental processes. This view, while it recognizes the potential destructive power of stereotypes, regards their formation as a necessary cognitive function that enables human beings to organize their social world along manageable lines.

A consensus has not yet been established on the correct definition of stereotyping, but there is a general agreement that stereotypes can and do distort the reality of a group or of a member of that group. Researchers also agree that such distortions create an advantage for those who stereotype and lead to inequities for those who are stereotyped.

Religious Stereotyping in the Media

Religions, religious groups, and the religious practices of groups are stereotyped by both the mainstream secular media and the religious media. In fact, religious

Humor in Stereotypes

Jokes are one form of communication that set forth and perpetuate stereotypes. Here are several "light bulb" jokes that stereotype different Christian denominations.

How many Calvinists does it take to change a light bulb?

Calvinists do not change light bulbs. They simply read out the instructions and pray the light bulb will decide to change itself.

How many Pentecostals does it take to change a light bulb?

Ten. One to change the bulb and nine to pray against the spirit of darkness.

How many Episcopalians does it take to change a light bulb?

Ten. One to call the electrician, and nine to say how much they liked the old one better.

How many Amish does it take to change a light bulb?

What's a light bulb?

How many Mormons does it take to change a light bulb?

Five. One man to change bulb and four wives to tell him how to do it.

organizations themselves project and reinforce stereotypical images.

The secular mass media, particularly popular films and television, is one of the major disseminators of stereotypical imagery. Characters often exhibit culturally accepted stereotypical traits which then reinforce the assumptions and prejudices of viewers—for example, gender stereotypes will be reinforced if the main protagonist of a film is a male who rescues a weaker, less competent female. This oft-repeated imagery reinforces the centrality of men in a patriarchal society. Ethnic stereotypes in film and television have been prominent throughout the history of the medium. However, although extreme forms of prejudicial stereotypes (for instance, those in D. W. Griffith's 1915 film, *The Birth of a Nation*) are no longer acceptable, ethnic stereotypes are still prevalent, albeit more subtle.

There is often considerable overlap between ethnic and religious stereotypes in media portrayals, particularly when they depict nationalities or cultures in which religion plays a central role. A recent target group for Hollywood has been Muslims. In feature films (predominantly action and war films), Arabs are often portrayed as fanatical terrorists set on waging jihad against the West. Although negative stereotypes of groups may not be viewed as accurate by the audience, they may lead to very real and very negative consequences. Even before the September 11 World Trade Center attacks, the number of hate crimes against Muslims in the United States had increased; and although the correlation between hate crimes and media stereotyping is complex, much research suggests that negative imagery can be a significant contributing factor.

Within the United States, the proliferation of religious television ministries (predominantly Christian) and their related enterprises has been striking. Not only do religious programs provide a means of evangelism (the initial reason for their formation) but they also provide a host of alternative viewing options for the Christian community. Studies have shown that the propensity to draw on, and therefore reinforce, traditional stereotypes is as common in religious television and film as in the secular media. For example, religious programming typically projects the prominence and power of males over females, and portrays the majority status of Caucasians and the minority status of African-Americans and other minority groups.

Stereotyping remains a topic of concern in the social sciences and in cultural studies departments. Although there is no clear consensus regarding the definition, function, and consequences of stereotyping, evidence indicates that by reinforcing the status quo of power and status, stereotypes help a society to maintain its inequities.

MALCOLM GOLD

Further Reading

Abelman, R., & Neuendorf, K. (1983). *Religion in broadcasting: Demographics.* Cleveland, OH: Cleveland State University.

Adorno, T. W., Frenkel-Brunswik, E., Levinson, D. J., & Sanford, R. N. (1950). *The authoritarian personality.* New York: Harper & Row.

Eitzen, D. S. (1999). *Fair and foul: Beyond myths and paradoxes of sport.* Lanham, MD: Rowen & Littlefield.

Gerbner, G., Gross, L., Hoover, S., Morgan, M., Signorielli, N., Cotugno, H. E., et al. (1984). *Religion on television and in the lives of viewers.* (Report prepared for the Ad Hoc Committee on Religious Television Research). New York: National Council for Churches of Christ.

Katz, D., & Braly, K. (1933). Racial prejudice and racial stereotypes. *Journal of Abnormal and Social Psychology, 30,* 175–193.

Knepler, H., Knepler, A., Knepler, E., & Knepler, M. (Eds.). (1998). *Crossing cultures: Readings for composition.* Boston: Allyn and Bacon.

Lippmann, W. (1949). *Public Opinion.* New York: The Free Press. (Original work published 1922)

Miller, A. G. (Ed.). (1982). *In The eye of the beholder: Contemporary issues in stereotyping.* New York: Praeger.

Monk, R. C. (Ed.). (2000). *Are Arabs and other Muslims portrayed unfairly in American films? Taking sides: Clashing views on controversial issues in race and ethnicity.* Guildford, CT: Dushkin/McGraw-Hill.

Shaheen, J. G. (1988). The media's image of Arabs. In H. W. Knepler et al. (Eds.). *Crossing cultures: Readings for composition.* Boston: Allyn and Bacon.

Shaheen, J. G. (2001). *Reel bad Arabs: How Hollywood vilifies a people.* New York: Olive Branch Press.

Signorelli, N. (Ed.) (1985). *Role portrayal and stereotyping on television: An annotated bibliography of studies relating to women, minorities, aging, sexual behavior, health, and handicaps.* Westport, CT: Greenwood Press.

Symbolism (Semiotics)

I. A. Richards once insisted that semiotics, or the study of symbols, is a mystery that "goes down as deep as the nature of life itself" (Richards 1965, 34–35). Exploring how words relate to objects and ideas confronts the semiotician with many intersections between symbolism and the sacred. The following discussion examines one such meeting point by searching out how beliefs about the nature of reality can inform semiotics. In brief, some semioticians consider spiritual reality to be prior to physical reality, others give material reality preeminence over spiritual reality, and still others understand spiritual and material reality in union.

Symbols and the Spiritual World

The decline of Rome and the rise of Christendom in the fifth century CE compelled Aurelius Augustine, as a rhetorician and a church bishop, to stand athwart the city of man and the city of God. He managed to do this in his treatise *On Christian Doctrine*, where he brought the rhetorical insights of the pagan Cicero to bear on the practice of Christian homiletics. Before he could get to rhetoric, though, he had to broach semiotics.

All teaching, explained Augustine, can be reduced to a discussion of signs or things. "Things" are entities that do not refer to or replace anything else. "Signs," on the other hand, "are things used to signify something" (Augustine 1958, 8). Sometimes signs can be both things and signs, as when the biblical figure Moses threw a stick into bitter water to render it drinkable. The stick was not only a miraculous thing, but also an anticipatory sign of the cross of Christ. For Augustine, then, signs had to be things, but things did not have to be signs. "And thus in distinction between things and signs, when we speak of things, we shall so to speak that, although some of them may be used to signify something else, this fact shall not disturb the arrangement we have made to speak of things as such first and of signs later" (Augustine 1958, 9). This explanation of how semiotics begins with objects that may or may not become symbolic may seem, at first glance, as overly obvious. But Augustine parsed his subject very closely because of his convictions about the relationship between the spiritual and material worlds. He was willing to appropriate pagan theories of rhetoric, as the Hebrews plundered Egypt for gold, as long as his readers remember that skill with symbols must always be treated as skill with any other thing—for utility and not for pleasure. "To enjoy something is to cling to it with love for its own sake. To use something, however, is to employ it in obtaining that which you love, provided that it is worthy of love" (Augustine 1958, 9). Signs must be used for spiritual benefit, not for material satisfaction.

To demonstrate the priority of spiritual over material reality, Augustine developed an analogy between the Incarnation and symbolic exchange. God became flesh in Jesus Christ, which would prove to be a kind of symbolic act on the grandest scale. Similarly, every time humans communicate with one another, their words incarnate thought. "In order that what we are thinking may reach the mind of the listener through the fleshly ears, that which we have in mind is expressed in words and is called speech" (Augustine 1958, 14). The thought becomes word and dwells among us. Significantly, just as Christ's deity was not altered by His enfleshment, so symbolic meaning is not altered by its material vehicle. This constancy of the spiritual thought in contrast with the changefulness of the fleshly word makes clear that although Augustine, at least while writing this particular work, considered the symbol as an indispensable material component in communication, he valued the spiritual meaning as finally important.

Symbols and the Material World

One of Augustine's twentieth-century descendants in the study of symbols, I. A. Richards, liked to tell the story of his days in the classroom of the great and nearly incomprehensible G. E. Moore, who insisted that humans could not mean what they say. "I was silently persuaded," wrote Richards, "that they could not possibly *say* what they *meant*" (1991, 6). According to his own account of things, Richards never understood anything of Moore's lectures, and it was partially this confusion that convinced Richards of the importance of semiotics to rhetorical theory, which he thought should be "a study of misunderstanding and its remedies" (1965, 3).

But unlike Augustine, Richards developed a semiotic theory that assumed the material to be primary and the spiritual to be secondary, or even insignificant. In order to understand how he said a word comes to stand for something else, it is useful to explore the psychology informing Richards's thought. Although later in life he tried to disassociate himself from behaviorism (the school of thought that considers all human action explainable in terms of a response to stimulus), the influences of this psychology are still apparent in *The Meaning of Meaning*, which he coauthored with C. K. Ogden. In this work, Richards and Ogden declare the mind to be a passive recipient of impressions called "engrams," each of which is "the residual trace of an adaptation made by the organism to a stimulus" (Ogden & Richards 1956, 53). And when any event, or any part of that event, recurs, the signs of that event call forth in a person's thinking the engram associated with that sign. Ogden and Richards call the occasion for this recurrence a "sign-situation" (Ogden & Richards 1956, 48, 53–54, 56).

To illustrate, Richards used the act of striking a match. When a person rubs a kitchen match along the side of a matchbox, there occurs a familiar series of signs: the scraping sound, the flare, the heat. The person

would not know what these signs are apart from past experiences with matches. But the scrape of the match immediately stirs up engrams that enable the person to interpret the signs of the act of match striking.

It is important to note that the sign-situation, the context, precedes the sign. The sound of the scraping match does not precede a person's past experience of hearing and seeing and feeling the lighting of a match. "This theorem alleges that meanings, from the very beginning, have a primordial generality and abstractness" (Richards 1965, 31). So, in communication, a word is a sign that is actually a part of an original context. In the sentence, "I lit a match," the word "match" is actually a part of the whole context of a person's striking of a small stick dipped in chlorate against a strip of phosphorus. For the recipient of this declaration, the word "match" must evoke engrams from past personal experience, if the word is to make any sense. Therefore, a sign is not an immediate, isolatable sensation of an event bearing independent meaning but is instead a synecdoche of similar contexts in the past. "When this abridgment happens, what the sign or word—the item with these delegated powers—means is the missing parts of the context" (Richards 1965, 34).

This materialistic explanation of symbolism nonetheless betrays spiritual urges. The great fear driving Richards's semiotics was that one mind locked in a body should be unable to convey ideas to another body-locked mind. The work of semiotics was to transfer something immaterial across material space. Whereas Augustine gave primacy to the spiritual without being able to dispense with the material, Richards privileged the material without quite slipping the claims of the spiritual. A more perfect integration of flesh and spirit in semiotics would emerge in the writings of Suzanne Langer.

Symbols in Union with the Spiritual and Material

Walker Percy, a novelist and semiotician, once observed that an alien visiting our planet would be first struck by the fact that however else people resemble other creatures, the human species is inevitably distinguished by its talkativeness. This needless talk contradicts the basic assumption behind behaviorist semiotics: that all human action is response to physical needs. Because of a preoccupation with science, behaviorist semiotics has tended to focus on how symbols get things done, how they meet needs. But as Percy was wont to point out, humans have a peculiar habit of being happy in the middle of a hurricane and sad just after dinner on a sunny afternoon. In other words, humans often act like poorly evolved animals oblivious to their most basic needs. They treat art seriously, dream prodigiously, and practice religious rituals—none of which actions is calculated to improve human survival. Not only do such practices fail to provide for individual material needs, they do not always manage to contribute to the survival of the tribe as a whole. What turns people to such practices, Suzanne Langer explained, is not a misconception of causality—as if such and such a sacrifice will bring the autumn rains—but a deeper need to symbolize for which no cause-and-effect explanation is adequate.

What turns semioticians to materialistic explanations, however, is the elusiveness of the meaning of meaning. So many different senses of the word "meaning" exist that it seems decreasingly likely that all of them may be subsumed under a single term. But this is only a difficulty if meaning is assumed to have an essential quality, a substance. But if meaning has no substance, no essential property, then the concept becomes definable as a relation. Think of a constellation of stars. The meaning of the constellation—its name—is only apparent by looking at the pattern that the stars form. Similarly, as Langer explained, meaning emerges only as "a pattern viewed with reference to one special term round which it centers" (Langer 1960, 55). To say what "charity" or "courage" means is not to identify the component parts of these virtues, but to attend to patterns of ideas, objects, and habits that take shape around each of these terms.

A meaningful pattern can be simple or complex. Smoke, for instance, is a simple pattern of events that generally indicates the presence of fire. Smoke never signifies that a cow is ready to be milked. In Langer's semiotic theory, when the correlation between a term and what it means is immediate, then the term is referred to as a sign. A sign indicates or predicts a scientifically explainable series of events. But meaningful patterns are often more complicated than a one-to-one correlation in which a sign substitutes for another object. When a meaningful pattern elicits a response that has no immediate relation to a referred-to object, then what is at work according to Langer is not a sign, but a symbol. If a person mentions the word "ball" to her dog—a creature generally accustomed to sign usage—Fido will look around for the ball. If a person utters the same word to her father, the man will probably say, "What about it?"—a clear illustration of the human tendency to use symbols, not to react to symbols as indicators of an object's immediate presence or as predictors of an action of that object, but rather to create

Apples and honey which symbolize sweetness to Jews at the New Year. *Courtesy of Kelly Cline/istockphoto.com.*

conceptions of things. As Langer put it, "Behavior toward conceptions is what words normally evoke; this is the typical process of thinking" (Langer 1960, 61).

Of course, symbols may be used as signs, but only with some indicator that they are so used—an inclined head, a raised eyebrow, a pointed finger. Generally, however, signs indicate, whereas symbols evoke thought. In this bringing together of word and conception and referred-to object occurs the semiotic union of the spiritual and the material. No wonder, then, that in religious symbolism to hold aloft the sacramental chalice or to touch fire to the sacrificial offering is not merely an instrumental, but rather a meaningful act that orders or reorders personal or public life. In Langer's words, such rituals "may be called *symbolic transformation of experiences*" (Langer 1960, 44).

Semiotics and Religion

Semiotic theory and application has an impossible-to-predict trajectory. More recent semiotic theorists, such as Umberto Eco, have explored the role of abductive logic in symbolism. Communication scholar Sandra

Moriarty insists that semiotics is basic to understanding the rhetoric of visual imagery. And the philosopher David Naugle holds that the concept of worldview should be understood semiotically. But whatever the ideas behind or the applications before semiotics, the study is likely to retain the concerns of spiritual and physical reality, or what Thomas Merton identified as the sacramental aspect of symbolism: the bringing together of the seen and the unseen.

CRAIG E. MATTSON

Further Reading

Augustine. (1958). *On Christian doctrine.* (D. W. Robertson, Jr., Trans.). Upper Saddle River, NJ: Prentice Hall.

Barthes, R. (1964). *Elements of semiology.* (A. Lavers & C. Smith, Trans.). New York: Hill & Wang.

Buber, M. (1970). *I and thou.* (W. Kaufmann, Trans.). New York: Scribner's.

Eco, U. (1984). Semiotics and the philosophy of language. In T. A. Sebeok (Ed.), *Advances in semiotics* (pp. 14–45). Bloomington: Indiana University Press.

Griffin, E. (2003). *A first look at communication theory* (5th ed.). Boston: McGraw-Hill Higher Education.

Langer, S. (1960). *Philosophy in a new key* (3rd ed.). Cambridge, MA: Harvard University Press.

Littlejohn, S. W. (1999). *Theories of human communication* (6th ed.). Belmont, CA: Wadsworth.

Mechling, E. W., & Mechling, J. (1981). The sale of two cities: A semiotic comparison of Disneyland with Marriott's Great America. *Journal of Popular Culture, 15,* 166–179.

Merton, T. (1977). *Loving and living.* (N. Burton Stone & P. Hart, Eds.). New York: Bantam.

Moriarty, S. E. (1996). Abduction: A theory of visual interpretation. *Communication Theory, 6*(2), 167–187.

Morris, C. (1946). *Signs, language, and behavior.* New York: Prentice Hall.

Naugle, D. (2002). *Worldview: The history of the concept.* Grand Rapids, MI: Eerdmans.

Ogden, C. K., & Richards, I. A. (1956). *The meaning of meaning: A study of the influence of language upon thought and of the science of symbolism* (8th ed.). New York: Harcourt, Brace & Company.

Ong, W. J. (1982). Orality and literacy: The technologizing of the word. In T. Hawkes (Ed.), *New accents.* New York: Routledge.

Percy, W. (1975). *The message in the bottle.* New York: Noonday.

Percy, W. (1983). *Lost in the cosmos: The last self-help book.* New York: Picador.

Peters, J. D. (1999). *Speaking into the air.* Chicago: University of Chicago Press.

Pierce, D. L. (2003). *Rhetorical criticism and theory in practice.* Boston: McGraw-Hill.

Polanyi, M., & Prosch, H. (1975). *Meaning.* Chicago: University of Chicago Press.

Richards, I. A. (1942). *How to read a page: A course in efficient reading with an introduction to a hundred great words.* New York: Norton.

Richards, I. A. (1965). *The philosophy of rhetoric.* (Mary Flexner Lectures on the Humanities 3). London: Oxford University Press.

Richards, I. A. (1991). Beginnings and transitions: I. A. Richards interviewed by Reuben Brower. (1991). In A. E. Berthoff, *Selected essays (1928–1974).* New York: Oxford University Press, 3-22.

T

Technology

In this technological age, communication technologies are strategic and necessary. Government, banking, education and science, the military, medicine, and religious institutions, all depend for their very existence on electronic communication systems. Online networks coordinate terrorist organizations across national boundaries. Fiber optics, supercomputer data, satellite technology, and the Internet are increasingly global, but other technologies invade our home life—television, DVDs, video games, and cellular telephones. Media systems need examination, and religious perspectives on communications technology can deepen our understanding of them beyond the technical.

Ritual View

James Carey (1989, 14–23) distinguishes transmission and ritual views of communication. Transmission is the standard model, defined by the transportation of signals or messages over space. In the ritual view, communication is the process of constructing and maintaining a meaningful human world.

In the transmission view, communication technologies are neutral. They are tools, things apart from values. Technologies are independent, we are told; they can be used to support completely different cultures and lifestyles. The same video player shows pornography and *National Geographic* specials. Television technology can promote salvation rather than commerce. The prevailing opinion that technology is neutral focuses on hardware. In these terms, technology is the province of engineers, manufacturers, and consumers.

In the ritual view, technology is a human creation that is value laden throughout. From this perspective, valuing permeates all technological activity, from the processes of design and fabrication, to manufacturing and use. When technology is understood this way, students of media and religion can make a major contribution.

Religious Thinkers

Religious perspectives help free the field from the narrow, technical view of neutral technology. Engineers design a global media system using the principle of efficiency, but religion as a symbolic universe of ultimate concern emphasizes human wholeness and moral imperatives.

Marshall McLuhan

Marshall McLuhan (1911–1980) is one example of important theorists of communication technology who are deeply religious (cf. Marchessault 2005). He was converted to Catholicism at age twenty-six and became a devout church member attending mass daily. For McLuhan, technologies are extensions of the human being—radio of the ear, television of the eye, the wheel extending the foot. This philosophy was influenced by the Jesuit philosopher Pierre Teilhard de Chardin, who argued that the use of electricity extends the central nervous system. De Chardin was McLuhan's source of divine insight for his theories of global electric culture in *The Gutenberg Galaxy* (1962), and through his influence McLuhan sometimes assumed that electronic civilization was a spiritual leap forward.

For McLuhan, the medium is the message, as described in his most famous book *Understanding Media:*

The Extensions of Man (1964). Debates over media content, such as sex and violence, miss the point. The medium transforms human life more than its programs do. McLuhan's predecessor at the University of Toronto, Harold Innis, argued that the history of communications is central to the history of civilization. Profound social and psychological changes occur from changes in the medium. For example, we think in linear patterns with print and grasp the whole visually with electronic media such as television. For McLuhan, television is cool and print is hot. "Hot" refers to media that are rich in information and require little involvement from users. Radio magnifies and standardizes human speech, reducing the amount of interpretation needed to understand it. Television, on the other hand, is a low-resolution technology requiring viewers' mental participation.

On the social level, in the electronic age we live in a global village of universal harmony, an idea reflecting both the impact of the electronic media and McLuhan's religion, where the mystical unity of humanity is like a Christian Pentecost. In the Canadian communication theory that he represents, the challenge is to identify the distinguishing properties of particular media technologies, from cuneiform writing to today's fiber optics and the Internet.

Jacques Ellul

Jacques Ellul (1912–1994) of the University of Bordeaux is another example of a religious perspective focused on technology, writing as he did with sociology and religion in counterpoint. Ellul became a Marxist at the age of nineteen, with Marx's *Das Capital* explaining for him the economic upheaval and cruel injustice in the world. Then at age twenty-two while a student at Bordeaux he was converted to Christianity, and both commitments inspired him until his death, even though he could not reconcile them. "My thinking can be explained by starting with this contradiction" (Ellul 1982, 16). Ellul became a member of the Reformed Church of France, and the theologian Karl Barth influenced his Protestant thinking the most.

Ellul (1964) was concerned about instrumentalism in technological societies. Technique and moral values are mutually exclusive. We specialize in means and not ends; we ignore ethics for technological prowess. In previous eras, tools were held in check within a larger complex of social values. However, in industrial societies today, the pervasiveness and sophistication of technology leads us to make sacred the genius behind machines and organize our institutions to conform to their efficiency.

Ellul's religious tradition gave him a framework for raising substantive questions about technology. In his thinking, people are created beings who create cultures and are responsible to God for them. Culture stands distinct from nature as a human achievement, and communication is the driving force in cultural formation. As brokers of human life and culture, the media need to be shaped to reflect human values rather than follow the imperatives of the machine.

For Ellul (1965), the media are agents of covert propaganda. Propaganda since World War I has meant a deliberate attempt to deceive or manipulate. However, in addition to this overt, political propaganda, Ellul is concerned about a subtle, sociological understanding of it as molding people into conformity. Modern communication technologies for him are not merely informational stimuli, but subtly stitch humans into an efficiency-dominated culture. Manipulation through the media by governments or advertising is a serious problem, but not as long-term and revolutionary as the mass media's in-depth molding of people into a technicalized conception of life.

Walter Ong

Walter Ong, S. J. (1913–2003) was a professor of humanities and of English at St. Louis University and a professor of humanities in psychiatry at the Saint Louis University School of Medicine. He was trained in philosophy and theology in addition to literature, and Marshall McLuhan was his M.A. thesis advisor. With his work always organized historically, he divided media technologies into oral, literate, and electronic stages (Ong 1967), with digital media the dominant mode at present. New forms of communication build on older forms, but the effect on human interaction was always the central question for him.

Orality and Literacy (2002) is Ong's most famous treatment of words written and spoken. Its subtitle, *The Technologizing of the Word*, indicates that humans use technology to preserve and extend the word. Oral communication dominated Western societies until the printing revolution of early modern Europe. During typographical culture, the oral-aural is reduced to a minimum. With the advent of electronic communications, oral forms reappear in radio and television, in intercom systems and voice recordings. But it is a secondary orality, showing some of the psychodynamics of orality and its patterns of rhythm and formulas; oral cultures dwell fully in sound. Computer-based communication depends on an exchange of meanings through a common set of symbols, and the immediacy of electronics gives

The Swinside stone circle situated in the Southern Lake District National Park, England. This stone circle dates back to the early Bronze age and nestles in the rugged windswept Cumbria hills. Although fairly complete this circle is rarely visited due to lack of parking nearby. *Courtesy of Chris Crafter/istockphoto.com.*

participants proximity to events and overcomes distance. However, this mediation through a textual code results in immediacy and relations that are artificial. With information storage and retrieval transformed, the centrality of human memory is altered and historical consciousness is ruptured. In each of these stages, as words are changed, human consciousness is restructured—from human bondedness and participation in oral culture to distance and precision in the age of literacy, for example. Through all the technological transformations of the word, the oral-aural center of human life is irrevocable.

Ivan Illich

Ivan Illich (1926–2002) was a Catholic priest, philosopher, historian, theologian, social critic, and activist who opened a center in Cuernavaca, Mexico, in 1961 to train missionaries, educators, and development workers for Latin America. Eventually it was called the Center for Intercultural Documentation (CICOC) and openly fought imperialism and neocolonialism in the church and in North American politics. After disputes with the Church over CICOC's "subversive" activities, Illich resigned from the priesthood in 1969.

Speaker of a dozen languages, he taught regularly in European universities and for more than a decade in North America. During the 1970s and until his death, he wrote radical critiques of the industrial order, of education (*Deschooling Society*), of medicine (*Medical Nemesis*), of technology (*Tools for Conviviality*), and of the professions (*Disabling Professions*). He also documented how ideas, necessities, and needs that we consider true and inevitable had an origin in history and can be changed (for example, *Shadow Work, H20 and the Waters of Forgetfulness, ABC: The Alphabetization of the Popular Mind*). For him, the story of institutions, habits of thought, and ways of life are best told as the story of evolving forms of communication. Human consciousness and culture throughout history are dominated linguistically by those in power, and therefore transformations in language and culture are the centerpiece of both the past and the present.

In technological societies, what is at stake fundamentally are the human relationships, the ways of living together (*con-vivio*) that tools make possible (Illich 1973). Convivial tools are open to all, easily used, and freely chosen. Convivial technology needs little specialized training to operate and emphasizes personal satisfaction. Through convivial tools we can act directly in the world, rather than letting industrial technologies dictate our way of life. In communications, such tools as the telephone, the library, community radio, videocassettes, minicams, and independent film are convivial. The standard for technological development and proper use of tools is cultural continuity. The overall pattern is cultural formation rather than the blind progress of technological change that ignores continuity. Because communication technologies are important in themselves, reordering their size and shape is an imperative for social change.

Other

Jewish and Muslim scholars have not concentrated on media technologies per se. Islamists emphasize moral decadence portrayed in the media; that mass media—television, film, Internet, radio, newspapers, magazines—bring about moral decline, particularly among Muslim teenagers (Hoover and Clark 2002). Jewish concerns with ethnic-national identity focus primarily on the way religious minorities are represented in the secular media (Hoover and Clark 2002).

Digital Technology

Mass media technologies are converging into digital formats. The World Wide Web, e-mail, chat rooms, MUDs (multiuser domains), web-based production, and the ability to hyperlink through computer-mediated systems bring new forms of interaction and social structure. Internet technology gives people a voice and connects users directly without professionals or gatekeepers in between. Digital technologies are democratic tools in principle that serve people's everyday needs, rather than those of special interest groups or the market's. Computer-based systems present social researchers with new opportunities. These promising attributes of the Internet spawn the optimist view that it is an ideal technology for social improvement.

Three books illustrate how digital technology is treated in religious terms. Rex Miller's *The Millennium Matrix* (2004) uses a historical perspective to demonstrate how the church, born in oral culture, adapted first to print, then to broadcasting, and today faces the challenges of the digital media. Quentin Schultze in *Habits of the High-Tech Heart* (2002) challenges us to work on the basic issues of personal and collective responsibility in the age of cyber technology. Heidi Campbell's *Exploring Religious Community Online* (2005) studies the formation of religious online communities and analyzes them through the sociology of religion and religious ethics. In the process of demonstrating how digital tools can be analyzed effectively, these authors remind us of the larger picture that creative imagination and broad learning are always indispensable.

Applications

Several questions and issues in media technology are of particular concern to religion.

First, for global media empires, the centerpiece of religious ethics is justice. Religious traditions advocate a thick theory of justice based on need in contrast to justice as a thin and static fairness. When justice is understood in terms of essential needs, the basic issue for communication technologies is accessibility. With media increasingly necessary in industrialized societies, technologies ought to be allocated to everyone regardless of income or geography. Scholars with a religious perspective are concerned that we will continue to divide the world into the technologically elite and those without adequate means to participate, unless we follow the principle of distributive justice.

Second, what is the best framework for understanding cyberspace? The mainline view puts the issues in epistemological terms: What is the character of knowledge in the digital world; what is reality in the minds of cyber-users? While also working on the issue of the real and unreal, religious thinkers focus primarily on the human question. Is submersion in digital technology empowering of our humanness? Who do we engage in cyberspace? What do agency and identity mean? What is a person in a world of cyborgs and beyond them? This approach is the most daring intellectually and potentially the most powerful.

Third, can television be redemptive? Rather than using television to evangelize the world quickly and cheaply, how can this technology be brought to maturity? All media have their own character and potential, and television as an artistic form still needs further development. Television is a primary medium of acculturation; how can this technological transformation of energy present aesthetic realism and holistic humans? Television is a distinctive technology, not small-screen film or picture radio or electronic book. Assisting this medium in becoming self-consciously mature is a worthy enterprise for the religious community.

These are three illustrations of the way religious thinking is involved in media technology. They and other initiatives reflect the long-term and overriding issue of the sacredness of life in competition with technology's instrumentalism. Hardware and software tend to follow the technical dynamics of the machine. Religious thinkers live out of a non-instrumental, humanistic worldview instead. For them reverence for human life is paramount, and the challenge is to promote these values effectively as an alternative.

Clifford G. Christians

See also Satellite Communication

Further Reading

Campbell, H. (2005). *Exploring religious community online.* New York: Peter Lang.

Carey, J. W. (1989). *Communication as culture.* Boston: Unwin Hyman.

Ellul, J. (1964). *The technological society.* (J. Wilkinson, Trans.). New York: Vintage.

Ellul, J. (1965). *Propaganda: The formation of men's attitudes.* (K. Kellen, Trans.). New York: Alfred A. Knopf.

Ellul, J. (1982). *In season and out of season: An introduction to the thought of Jacques Ellul.* New York: Harper and Row.

Gronbeck, B. E., Farrell, T. J., & Soukup, P. S. (Eds.). (1991). *Media, consciousness, and culture: Explorations of Walter Ong's thought.* Newbury Park, CA: Sage.

Hoover, S. M., & Clark, L. S. (Eds.). (2002). *Practicing religion in the age of the media.* New York: Columbia University Press.

Illich, I. (1973). *Tools for conviviality.* New York: Harper and Row.

Marchessault, J. (2005). *Marshall McLuhan.* Thousand Oaks, CA: Sage.

McLuhan, M. (1962). *The Gutenberg galaxy: The making of typographic man.* Toronto, Canada: University of Toronto Press.

McLuhan, M. (1964). *Understanding media: The extensions of man.* New York: McGraw Hill.

Miller, M. R. (2004). *The millennium matrix: Reclaiming the past, reframing the future of the church.* San Francisco: Jossey-Bass.

Ong, W. (1967). *The presence of the word: Some prolegomena for cultural and religious history.* New Haven, CT: Yale University Press.

Ong, W. (2002). *Orality and literacy: The technologizing of the word.* Florence, KY: Taylor and Francis Books. (Original work published 1982)

Schultze, Q. J. (2002). *Habits of the high-tech heart: Living virtuously in the information age.* Grand Rapids, MI: Baker Academic.

Televangelism

Nearly two thousand years ago, Jesus Christ initiated what would become a worldwide proselytizing effort with the following instruction, known as "The Great Commission":

> Go ye, therefore, and teach all nations, baptizing them in the name of the Father, and of the Son, and of the Holy Ghost: Teaching them to observe all things whatsoever I have commanded you: and lo, I am with you always, even unto the end of the world. Amen. (Matthew 28:19, 20)

Subsequently, most manifestations of Christianity have been missionary minded, resulting in some two billion people, or about 34 percent of the current world population, estimated to be Christian. In the United States and Canada, however, the rate is much higher; 75 percent of the adults in North America describe themselves as Christians.

It is clear that the potential audience for televised Christian outreach, or televangelism, in North America is impressive. One recent estimate placed the number of Americans who regularly watch televangelists at about thirteen million, but other estimates claim that as many as sixty million Americans may be reached each week by some form of religious media. Finally, a national survey of television viewers found that 43 percent of American adults had seen Christian programming during the previous month. Though the reach of televangelists and other forms of Christian programming would seem to be impressive, additional research is needed to establish more precisely how many Americans are watching which types of Christian programming.

The "Good News" of the Christian Gospel

The Greek word *evangelos* means "bringing good news," and that is what Christian clergy and lay missionaries have traditionally seen themselves as doing as they have preached the "good news" of the Gospel of Jesus Christ. Many engaged in Christian outreach are Evangelical Christians. Evangelical Christians have, historically, been conservative and Protestant, no matter their specific denominational affiliation. Generally, Evangelicals share a belief in the Bible as inerrant, take a strict literal approach to Biblical interpretation, conceive of the Godhead as triune in nature, and place a strong emphasis on faith and grace rather than on good works in receiving salvation. Additionally, Evangelical Christians tend to be conservative in their lifestyles, in their toleration of deviations from biblical injunctions, and in the political philosophies they support. It is estimated that as many as one in four Americans affiliate with churches considered to be evangelical in nature.

While it is true that a disproportionately large number of televangelists come from this strand of Christianity, virtually any religionist with a message for a television viewer, no matter his or her religious background or the format of the program, can be said to be engaging in televangelism. A very general definition of televangelism, which removes the creed component, reads, "The use of broadcast airwaves as an alternative way to preach a ministry/religion" (www .pearsoncustom.com/link/televangelism.html).

Traditionally, religious television programming has been limited to a few prominent formats, most usually with the featured televangelist preaching a sermon. Typically, the sermon, usually based on a biblical reference, has been accompanied by uplifting music, offers of services or products often available for a specific cash gift, and perhaps a testimonial or two. Variations include discussion formats, sometimes interspersed with world and national news and accompanying Christian-oriented commentary, interviews with celebrities and others having conversion stories to tell, reports on aid programs sponsored by the ministry, and so on. At times, an actual worship service is aired. Of late, newer formats like Christian-themed comedy and game shows have begun to emerge.

Some successful televangelists have been women, including, for example, Mother Angelica, Kathryn Kuhlman, Aimee Semple McPherson, Tammy Faye Bakker Messner, Joyce Meyer, Elizabeth Clare Prophet, and Rexella Van Impy. However, the American electronic pulpit remains a mostly male stronghold. John Ankerberg, Herbert and Garner Ted Armstrong, Morris Cerullo, Kenneth Copeland, James Dobson, Jerry Falwell, Billy Graham, Benny Hinn, Rex Humbard, D. James Kennedy, Oral Roberts, Pat Robertson, James Robison, Robert Schuller, Charles Stanley, Robert Tilton, Jack Van Impy, and dozens of others have enjoyed successful television ministries.

Many televangelists place their shows on established religious networks such as the Inspirational Network (INSP), formerly PTL; the Christian Broadcasting Network (CBN); and the Trinity Broadcasting Network (TBN), but many air their shows via syndication on individual stations.

Needs Addressed by Televangelism

Termed "transmitted unction" (Erickson 1992, ix) by an early participant, various theories have been advanced in an attempt to explain televangelism's role in society. For example, some theorize that televangelists are successful because they appeal to viewers' worst fears about the world and help create a worldview that is full of anxiety, fear, and distrust. Implicit in this approach is the message that if viewers will financially support a television ministry, the televangelist will provide the information and encouragement needed to cope with a world perceived as evil, threatening, dangerous, and immoral. Sometimes a cash gift is suggested in return for the information, prayers, or advice proffered on behalf of viewers.

Others argue that televangelism serves another purpose. That is, it helps uplift viewers, through their participation in the weekly, mediated worship rituals, by separating them from the world and legitimating their beliefs. The "us against them" or "God versus Satan" struggle is reconfirmed each week in the minds of viewers, who take heart in the fact that they are not alone in the struggle. Viewers are frequently reassured that they are special people, indeed, God's people, and this message, apparently, provides the hope they need to cope with secular society week after week.

Radio Sets the Stage

With the advent of radio in the early twentieth century, the Christian Gospel could, theoretically, be spread more widely, quickly, efficiently, and effectively than ever before. Seeing the potential in the electronic pulpit early on, an army of what would become a predominantly Evangelical Christian clergy and a few others took to the airwaves to spread the word. Beginning with a radio broadcast in early 1921 of the worship service of the Calvary Episcopal Church in Pittsburgh, the race to electronically evangelize the populace was on. These pioneer electronic preachers would be joined by Catholics, Latter-Day Saints, Seventh-day Adventists, and a host of other religionists with doctrines, causes, and lifestyles to espouse.

As radio's influence grew and evangelists eagerly sought airtime, a number of influential, mainline religious organizations attempted to limit access to the airwaves by the more conservative, Fundamentalist, and Evangelical religious groups. These efforts were spearheaded by the Federal Council of Churches (now, National Council of Churches), its member organizations, and the Institute of Education for Radio. Their stance was based solely on the fact that they disapproved of the more conservative, often more rigid, positions advocated by Evangelical Christian and like-minded groups and individuals.

Limiting access was accomplished by urging broadcasters to refuse to sell airtime to religious organizations and individuals, unless they had been approved by the more establishment-type official organizations. Instead, the networks provided free or "sustaining" time to religious organizations passing muster with the networks and their religious advisers. This policy allowed the networks to demonstrate that they were attempting to air programs in the "public interest." This approach worked for radio and was initially successful in restricting television access by the more conservative religious organizations in the short term.

However, beginning with its creation in 1942, the National Association of Evangelicals (NAE) lobbied to change the policy. Eventually, through its efforts, as well as those of the National Religious Broadcasters, created by the NAE in 1944, and the efforts of other groups, along with a ruling by the Federal Communication Commission that, essentially, gave equal weight to both sustaining and sold time in demonstrating "public interest" programming, the policy was abandoned. Perhaps an even stronger factor contributing to the policy's demise was the expanding need for programming as television networks and stations proliferated, accompanied by the willingness by all types of religious organizations to pay for airtime.

Challenges

Clearly, there are some for whom televangelism evokes unsavory connotations. Perhaps negative perceptions have been caused, at least in part, by the many unflattering television shows and motion-picture-industry portrayals of mediated religious outreach. Frequently, such depictions of televangelists are based on stereotypical caricatures whose goals seem to be fortune and self-aggrandizement, rather than converting their audiences to religious devotion. For example, in many treatments of the subject, Sinclair Lewis's popular 1927 novel and the subsequent movie describing the excesses of traveling tent revivalist Elmer Gantry are mentioned. Only occasionally is the reader reminded that, although the story may have been partially based on a number of perhaps isolated snapshots of reality, it is still, nevertheless, fiction. Unfortunately, the Elmer Gantry depiction and its numerous derivatives are what many Americans suspect is all too true of televangelism.

Contributing to this view of televangelism, or the "electronic church," as it is sometimes called, and perhaps adding credibility to the despicable Gantry stereotype, have been a number of scandals. The transgressions of, for example, Jimmy Swaggart and Jim and Tammy Faye Bakker in the 1980s garnered extensive media coverage. The popular and successful Swaggart was caught on videotape consorting with prostitutes on more than one occasion, despite his religion's proscription of such conduct. Obviously, such hypocritical behavior can only contribute to the distaste some have for televangelists.

In Jim Bakker's case, a sexual tryst with church secretary Jessica Hahn, allegations of homosexual activity, financial fraud charges, along with an extravagant lifestyle, supported by viewer donations to the PTL Club, doomed the Bakkers. The subsequent, widely reported, embarrassing circus atmosphere created by the mismanagement failures of a series of other Evangelical ministers brought in to run the ministry, including the Bakkers' Heritage USA Christian theme park, saddled the industry with an even more negative image.

Although not traditionally scandalous like the cases above, nevertheless, Oral Roberts' reputation suffered when he closeted himself in his university's prayer tower in 1980 in Tulsa, Oklahoma, claiming that the "Lord would take him home" if millions of dollars in donations were not received by a certain date in support of his on-campus hospital. Roberts's behavior followed his claim to have seen a vision of a nine-hundred-foot-tall Jesus. This type of tactic has been termed "creating crisis" (Schultze 1991, 170) and has been suspected by critics of being deliberately used to increase revenue to financially strapped television ministries. The too-frequent use of the "creating crisis" technique runs the risk of alienating viewers and can contribute to the negative perception that some have of televangelism. It is likely that crisis-creating abuses along with the earlier-mentioned scandals have been significant factors in the estimated 75 percent drop in viewers and financial support for television ministries since the 1980s.

Although televangelism has, at times, been buffeted by these kinds of unfortunate episodes, the majority of televangelists seem to be sincere in their efforts to share the Christian Gospel, as they variously interpret it. Perhaps one indicator of genuine religious intent is if a televangelist belongs to, for example, the National Religious Broadcasters (and subscribes to its Ethics and Financial Integrity Commission) and similar organizations where financial accountability is a condition of membership. Although quite a few televangelists subscribe to such financial codes and conditions, many, perhaps the majority, do not. Consequently, one of the criticisms of televangelism is that it is entirely self-regulated. Therefore, if a televangelist decides not to subject his or her ministry to, for example, the oversight of the National Religious Broadcasters or a similar organization and their financial accountability standards, then there is no accountability, and the particular televangelist could, conceivably, abuse viewers' trust and engage in fraudulent use of donated monies.

Other Voices

Although the vast majority of American religious television programming has been produced by Evangelical Christians, other efforts have not been insignificant. For example, weekly radio and subsequent television broadcasts by Bishop Fulton J. Sheen were warmly received by Catholics and many non-Catholics alike. Beginning with his *Catholic Hour* radio program in 1930, Sheen later began showcasing Catholicism's teachings via television in an interesting and effective way in 1952 with his *Life Is Worth Living* program. Following that show's successful six-year run, Sheen hosted *The Bishop Sheen Program* from 1961 to 1968. Both programs benefited from Bishop Sheen's warm personality, his somewhat theatrical presentation style, his storytelling skills, and his always pleasant and engaging manner. Sheen's shows attracted strong followings and won many friends for the church. Today, the successful Eternal Word Television Network (EWTN), established in 1981 by Mother Angelica, with its dignified and low-key discussions, prayers, feel-good stories, reruns of Bishop Sheen's *Life Is Worth Living* show, and instructional sessions explicating Roman Catholic doctrine, reaches a huge audience both in the United States and abroad. EWTN's programming is offered free to numerous cable and satellite systems.

The Mormons can claim the longest nationally broadcast, continuously running religious program in *Music and the Spoken Word*, featuring the highly acclaimed Mormon Tabernacle Choir and a short, nonsectarian message each Sunday morning. Beginning in 1929 on radio, the half hour *Music and the Spoken Word* has also been available on television for a number of years. The Church of Jesus Christ of Latter-Day Saints (nicknames are Mormon or LDS Church) has recently expanded its programming with BYU Television (BYUTV), which features everything from Mormon Church–owned Brigham Young University (BYU) sporting events and BYU religion faculty discussing the Scriptures to LDS Church General Authorities addressing the membership in semiannual General Conferences and self-help-type programs. BYUTV is increasingly available on cable networks as well as the DISH Network and DirecTV satellite systems.

Islam, Hinduism, Buddhism, and other major non-Christian religions do not, thus far, have a significant presence in American religious television programming.

Although there are some local programs and religious associations with technology committees, these and most other non-Christian groups do not benefit from large national audiences like Christian broadcasters do. However, as immigration, especially among Muslims, continues, this situation will no doubt change, since Islam is a proselytizing religion as well.

Interestingly, the only national telecasts with Jewish principals are those mounted by Jews who have converted to Christianity, like Zola Levitt. The absence of Judaism from televangelism is understandable, since Judaism has not traditionally sought converts.

Issues

There have been fears voiced that, along with other factors, the success of televangelism has helped create a vast "unchurched" population among professing Christians in America. Research has revealed that some 75 million Americans do not attend church regularly, although many of these so-called un-churched persons may be reached by televangelists weekly. The concern is that, instead of supporting local churches financially, socially, in community outreach and service, and so forth, many spiritually minded Americans are getting religion from televangelists and, in turn, sending money to TV preachers at the expense of the local churches and their community initiatives. Although Pat Robertson's *The 700 Club* and the Billy Graham Evangelistic Association, for example, urge their viewers to become involved with their local churches, many televangelists do not partner with or even encourage involvement with local congregations.

There have also been concerns voiced about the attempts of some televangelists to influence American political campaigns. Jerry Falwell and his Moral Majority organization and *The 700 Club*'s Pat Robertson seeking the 1988 Republican presidential nomination are two prominent examples. It is impossible to precisely measure the impact of the political stances of these persons and their followers on the electorate, but successes have been claimed by these groups, especially in getting more conservative Christians involved in the political process. The argument against outright religious involvement in politics revolves around the doctrine of separation of church and state and the tax-exempt status of churches and other religious organizations.

Another development has seen the 1,350-member National Religious Broadcasters (NRB) parting ways with the National Association of Evangelicals (NAE) in 2001, even though the NAE established the NRB in 1944 as its radio and television arm. It is thought that the breakup came because the NAE had been conducting a dialogue with the more liberal National Council of Churches (NCC) and had dropped its bylaw prohibiting affiliate groups from also holding membership in the NCC. Apparently, the NRB saw such actions as consorting with the enemy. It remains to be seen what, if any, effect this parting of the ways will have on American televangelism. Before the divorce of the NRB and the NAE in 2001, it had been estimated that up to 75 percent of American religious broadcasting was produced by NRB members.

New Directions

As noted in the "Good News" section, a recent development has seen Christian televangelism, in some cases, taking the form of game and comedy shows. It is doubtful that the newer forms will entirely replace the featured televangelist preaching the gospel for at least part of the program, but the innovations are interesting and indicate that some in the field are thinking about newer ways of sharing the "good news" of the Christian gospel. Further, at this writing, two different groups are set to launch Christian music video networks designed to compete with the secular MTV- and VH1-type offerings. It remains to be seen if these endeavors will take their place as successful religious television and if they can be characterized as televangelism, which seems to be their intent.

The Future

Televangelism has been an integral part of American television for more than fifty years. Although televangelism's reach and impact have ebbed and flowed due, in part, to scandals, changing national demographics and what conservative religionists would call the ascension of secularism, it remains a force to be reckoned with. Any religious group with the desire and financial means can obtain access to American airwaves to broadcast their message. One of the distinguishing characteristics of a democratic society is the free and open expression of ideas, and religious ideas have always been part of that landscape and, now, the airwaves of America. There is every reason to believe that the place of religion in the electronic town hall of America is secure.

RICHARD N. ARMSTRONG

Further Reading

Abelman, R., & Hoover, S. M. (Eds.). (1990). *Religious television: Controversies and conclusions*. Norwood, NJ: Ablex Publishing Corporation.

Barna Group, The. (2005). Retrieved June 8, 2005, from http://www.barna.org

Bruce, S. (1990). *Pray TV: Televangelism in America*. London and New York: Routledge.

Cardwell, J. D. (1984). *Mass media Christianity: Televangelism and the great commission*. Boston: University Press of America.

de Vries, H., & Weber, S. (Eds.) (2001). *Religion and media*. Stanford, CA: Stanford University Press.

Ellens, J. H. (1974). *Models of religious broadcasting*. New York: William Eerdmans.

Erickson, H. (1992). *Religious radio and television in the United States, 1921–1991: The programs and personalities*. Jefferson, NC: McFarland & Company, Inc., Publishers.

Foege, A. (1996). *The empire God built: Inside Pat Robertson's media machine*. New York: John Wiley & Sons.

Frankl, R. (1987). *Televangelism: The marketing of popular religion*. Carbondale and Edwardsville: Southern Illinois University Press.

Hadden, J. K., & Shupe, A. (1988). *Televangelism: Power and politics on God's frontier*. New York: Henry Holt and Company.

Hadden, J. K., & Swann, C. E. (1981). *Prime time preachers: The rising power of televangelism*. Reading, MA: Addison-Wesley Publishing Company.

Hoover, S. M. (1988). *Mass media religion: The social sources of the electronic church*. Thousand Oaks, CA: Sage Publications.

Hoover, S. M., & Clark, L. S. (Eds.). (2002). *Practicing religion in the age of media: Explorations in media, religion, and culture*. New York: Columbia University Press.

Hoover, S. M., & Lundby, K. (1997). *Rethinking media, religion and culture*. Thousand Oaks, CA: Sage Publications.

Horsfield, P. G. (1984). *Religious television: The American experience*. New York: Longman.

Howley, K. (2001). Prey TV televangelism and interpellation. *Journal of Film & Video, 53*(2/3), 23–38.

Melton, J. G., Lucas, P. C., & Stone, J. R. (1997). *Prime-time religion: An encyclopedia of religious broadcasting*. Phoenix, AZ: Oryx Press.

Newman, J. (1996). *Religion vs. television: Competitors in cultural context*. Westport, CT: Praeger.

Noll, M. A. (2000). *American Evangelical Christianity: An introduction*. Malden, MA: Blackwell Publishers.

Peck, J. (1993). *The gods of televangelism*. Cresskill, NJ: Hampton Press, Inc.

Peck, J. (1993). Selling goods and selling God: Advertising, televangelism and the commodity form. *Journal of Communication Inquiry, 17*, 5–25.

Schultze, Q. J. (1991). *Televangelism and American culture: The business of popular religion*. Grand Rapids, MI: Baker Book House.

Winzenburg, S. (2001). Televangelist report card. *Christianity Today*, 45(13), 88–92.

Television

Television and its role in religious institutions, culture, and daily life encompasses not only the traditional broadcast medium and the dissemination of institutional worship services, but also the newer technologies of cable, satellite and digital broadcast, and home video/DVD technologies employed to convey a myriad of religious messages. Paralleling the breadth of technology and programming relevant to religion and television is also a range of agents creating programming from media-savvy ministries, traditional churches, individuals, corporations, and governments. While televangelism is certainly the most well known intersection of religion and television, it is by no means the only or even the solely dominant form of programming.

Caveat

While the American experience of both broadcasting and religious culture has been documented heavily and dominates the research discussion on this topic and will form the core of this article, readers must understand that the American experience of both is quite idiosyncratic and may not be terribly generalizable to international experiences. International research on this topic does, in fact, point up the multiple instances in which the American experience is not representative, but taken together, they do provide interesting points of comparison.

Governmental Control or Market Control

Two major themes dominate the intersection of religion and television: free expression and the free market. The evidence of these two concepts is dependent on the national environment of both religion and media in a given state. In nations that exert governmental control and provide governmental support for their media (and despite the global nature of communication, broadcast and electronic media are still heavily constrained by national laws), much of the discussion of religious activities on television take the form of the use of television to both promote the national religion or to document the use of the medium to express disagreement with the religious preferences of the state. A significant example of this is in the Muslim countries of Iran and Taliban-controlled Afghanistan. Newspaper accounts of Iranian television document complaints by more liberal Muslim clerics that conservative clerics in the government control access to the airwaves; in Taliban-controlled Afghanistan, conservative Muslim clerics in 1998 ruled that all television sets, videocassette recorders, videotapes, and satellite dishes must be removed from homes and claimed that such media were the cause of moral corruption.

Conversely, the American experience of religion and television has centered on a market approach and access to the airwaves has largely been a matter of finding an audience and someone to finance the production and airtime. While U.S. political leaders such as Ronald Reagan and George W. Bush both encouraged Evangelical broadcasters during their presidencies, political leaders have had little ability to directly influence either access or content. While the experiences of Iran and Afghanistan and the United States certainly exhibit the two ends on the spectrum between full government control/limited free expression and marginal government control/significant market control, most nations fall somewhere in the middle.

Much of the rest of the world, notably the United Kingdom, Western Europe, and many African countries, has a mixture of state-sponsored channels and programming and an influx of independently produced programming from outside, either through satellite television or media ministries. This mixture of state-controlled and independently created programming provides ample opportunity to compare the different funding mechanisms, programming styles, and distribution networks along with the distinct religious or service impulses behind the programming.

American Television and Religion

Although, as mentioned above, the American experience is not representative internationally in terms of either technological dissemination or religious history and culture, research on American television and religion is significant and can be a useful foil for examining other national experiences. Key to understanding both religious culture and television in the United States is grasping the nature of religious disestablishment and limited media regulation. The lack of a state church and the enshrined freedom of religion created a religious marketplace in which competition by sects for adherents was a necessity. Because a denomination couldn't count on support from the state or a certain number of de facto members given the number of people in the nation, individual religious groups had to actively seek members. Similarly, at the advent of television in the United States, broadcast regulation followed the same technological, but not content-related strictures on programming as had governed radio. Early broadcast stations were given a specified frequency and told to provide certain kinds of programming (educational, religious, public affairs) in order to serve the public interest, but they were not required to get programming approved by the government or to air government programming. Because of the market orientations of both television and religion and the limited nature of government interference, this intersection was poised for robust development that was not only unique to the United States but would also directly influence other national media and religious systems.

While American religious programming was exempt from government interference, this does not mean it was exempt from control and critique from religious denominations and other organizations. The first notable example of this is in the very establishment of religious broadcast programming in which control was given to the National Council of Churches, which was dominated by mainline denominations. These denominations were loathe to provide time to Evangelical sects and were equally opposed to creating programming more creative than televised worship services. Evangelicals were forced to find ways to pay for airtime and were, thus, required to create programming that viewers would want to support with donations; this created the sort of televangelism usually associated with religious television. As broadcasters' requirements to provide free airtime to churches was decreased and eliminated by regulators, mainline churches found themselves ill prepared to sponsor their own programming and ultimately ceded the airwaves to Evangelicals.

With the growth in cable as a means of providing additional channels, religious programmers were eager to fill available time and this led to additional types of programming beyond televised worship, calls to conversion, and Gospel shows. Current-affairs programs such as *The 700 Club* developed, as did channels devoted to programming friendly to a conservative Christian audience, such as the Family Channel and the PAX network, both of which featured reruns of shows such as *The Waltons*. It is important to note, however, that in the current media landscape, the Family Channel and PAX are no longer independent and no longer provide much in the way of identifiably religious fare.

In addition to cable, the home videocassette recorder (VCR) and the current dissemination of DVD technology have provided additional sources of religious television. Two notable examples of home video for the Christian audience are the Adventures in Odyssey series by Focus on the Family, a conservative media ministry, and the Veggie Tales series by Big Idea, Inc., a formerly independent Christian-oriented video company now owned by Classic Media. While Christians certainly dominate American religious television, home video has also been a point of interest for Jewish media creators who have developed the Shalom Sesame series and the Alef Bet Blast-off! series that provide basic information about Jewish and Israeli culture in a manner accessible to children without the proselytizing tone inherent in most Christian media. Both Christian and Jewish series are heavily influenced by the commercial children's video genre and make creative use of animation, music, and rapid video editing techniques in order to get and keep kids' attention.

Religious Television Within Distinct National Systems

As noted in the discussion of governmental control versus market control, the shape of religion on television and the relationship between organized religion and television is largely determined by the amount and kind of state control exerted over both religion and media. One system undergoing transition in this area is Russia where the influence of religion has grown dramatically since the breakup of the former Soviet Union; the reemergence of religion has allowed for the broadcast of church services for the first time. A second example of transition is taking place in the United Kingdom in which the national system of government-sponsored programming is being challenged by international satellite channels and the demographic makeup of the country is challenging traditional notions of what British religion looks like. A report on these issues found that government-sponsored programming should take into account the religious programming provided by the commercial section and seek audiences not served by the predominantly conservative Christian fare. Another evolution of internationalized television has taken place in Côte d'Ivoire in which the state has allowed Sunday morning use of the airwave by Christian churches, Catholic and Protestant, and Thursday evening broadcasts of *Allahu Akbar!* for Muslim viewers. But because there are few established Muslim organizations that have credibility with the government for the purposes of creating or sanctioning programming, additional

Muslim programming is dominated by Saudi-trained clerics who have extensive television training that contrasts with native clerics who tend toward a more extemporaneous style of sermon that is not conducive to the restrictions of the medium.

Critiques of Religious Television and Religion on Television

As alluded to in the example of religious broadcasting in Côte d'Ivoire, televising religious experience necessarily changes its nature. Sermons need to conform to time restrictions not present in most face-to-face services and the worship leader isn't able to respond directly to the disconnected television audience. The notion of a sermon as a leading of the Spirit, as indeed a presence of the Spirit, is significantly challenged by the intrusive production elements inherent in television. Some religious groups are troubled by most representations of religion on television as a watering-down or a misrepresentation of faith and these debates over representation ultimately boil down to how and who defines religion. American television shows such as *Joan of Arcadia*, in which a teenage girl talks to a higher power, are lauded for their sensitive and unchallenging representation of faith, but other shows such as *Buffy the Vampire Slayer* and *Charmed* are castigated for promoting subversive religious belief. Evangelical groups such as the American Family Association and Focus on the Family have been outspoken critics of commercial television's use of religious themes and these critiques join the longstanding concerns of the U.S. Catholic Bishop's Office for Film and Broadcasting. In addition, groups such as the Southern Baptist Convention have attempted boycotts as a way of trying to achieve an effect on media programming, but the recent 1998 boycott by Southern Baptists of the Walt Disney Corporation was largely ineffective to the financial standing of the corporation.

Challenges

Challenges facing religious television and treatment of religion by television are considerable but they should be seen as early marks of evolution in this area, not decline. The first such is the increased competition in the mission field between the Catholic Church, charismatic and Evangelical Protestantism, and Islam for believers and the use of television to reach potential converts. Just as Saudi Arabia is active in providing training and programming useful to Muslim believers and potential converts in Africa, Focus on the Family is heavily invested in providing Christian programming to the region as well. Similarly, the Catholic Church is increasing its investments in Latin American television as a way of stemming the tide of converts to Protestantism. It is not surprising that competition in the mission field would lead to competition on the airwaves.

Finally, as commercial television programmers, as opposed to government-sponsored or ministry-sponsored programmers, control more and more of the material seen by the viewing audience, there may be a reshaping of religious content toward that which is seen as most profitable: the messages that target the most attractive demographic for advertisers. The proliferation of television channels afforded by digital cable, satellite, and digital broadcast technologies offers new opportunities for groups to find niche audiences, however, these opportunities, at least in the United States, will still be limited to those who can afford the technology. In fact, as the country transitions away from the analog spectrum to the digital spectrum it is estimated that small religious broadcasters will encounter significant difficulties in affording the new equipment required. This proliferation of channels may also have a negative effect in terms of the ability of audience members to avoid messages that they find disturbing or challenging, preferring to live in a media universe in which they agree with what they see, but limit opportunities for new ideas and information.

HILLARY WARREN

See also Radio; Televangelism

Further Reading

Afghan religious police ban television, girls' schools. (1998). *Church & State, 51*(8), 21.

Birman L., & Lehmann, P. (1999). Religion and the media for idealogical [sic] hegemony: The Universal Church of the Kingdom of God and TV Globo in Brazil. *Bulletin of Latin American Research, 18*(2), 145–165.

Dubov, I. G. (2003). Level of religious commitment and the influence of religious precepts on Russian citizens' attitudes toward political leaders. *Russian Social Science Review, 44*(6) 82–108.

Hadden, J. K. (1993). The rise and fall of American televangelism. *Annals of the American Academy of Political and Social Science, 527.*

Hadden, J. K. (1994). Policing the religious airwaves: A case of market place regulation. *BYU Journal of Public Law, 8*(2), 393–417.

Launay, R. (1997). Spirit media: The electronic media and Islam among the Dyula of Northern Côte D'Ivoire. *Africa, 67*(3), 441–453.

Meyer, B. (2003). Editorial. *Journal of Religion in Africa, 33*(2), 125–128.

Sciolino, E. (1998). Iran's alternative voices now demand to be heard. *New York Times, 147*(51223), 8.

Serbin, K. (1995). Bishops to expand TV network. *National Catholic Reporter, 32*(1), 7.

Viney, R. (1999). Religious broadcasting on UK television: Policy, public perception and programmes. *Cultural Trends, 9*(36), 1–28.

Temples

Temples are highly institutionalized sacred places. Temples fulfill two complementary functions: They act as residences for the gods and as social centers of political, cultural, and economic importance. Most temples are composed of a man-made structure that encloses a sacred site. These structures are often decorated with designs that reveal the meaning of that sacred site and provide facilities for a priestly class that guides ritual and oversees behavior at the site.

The origin of the term is Latin: *Templa* were rectangular open areas, delineated and consecrated by Roman priests to serve as sites for sacrifice. In a later stage in their development, structures were added in order to house the god's image and to store the implements required for worship or the worshippers' offerings. Temples constituted primary centers of worship for several Near Eastern civilizations, including the Sumerians, Hittites, Babylonians, Phoenicians, Egyptians, Israelites, and Greeks. These impressive stone edifices served as homes for their gods and locations where priests served the needs of the deity, often represented by a statue, through ritual, sacrifice, and festivals. Where the king acted as the chief priest, temples doubled as political centers that provided a variety of social functions, ranging from the housing of orphans to the manufacture of food and supplies for the priestly class. Though markedly different in architecture and style, temples fulfilled similar religious and social roles among South American civilizations. In Aztec and Maya religions, though not in Inca practice, these temples also functioned as the primary locus for human sacrifices.

The English term has been extended to describe the most sacred shrines in which contemporary Buddhists, Hindus, Sikhs and adherents of Japanese religions worship. The members of several Western movements, in turn, refer to their local houses of worship as temples, even in the absence of a residing deity or an underlying sacred space, in order to explicitly or implicitly stress an affinity in design, function or lineage between themselves and a preceding religious movement. This use of the term is common among the members of several Western Jewish movements, Mormons, Masons, and various New Age religions.

Instability of Sacred Space

At the physical and historical core of the temple lies a sacred place. Sacred spaces are religious centers at which the heavenly and earthly meet, a means of access between the human and the divine world. The sanctity of the place may be communicated by the gods through a special sign or the location may become holy because a religiously significant event took place there. It may have been imbued with sanctity because of the presence of relics or because its shape hints at the link that it establishes between the mundane and the divine. Rivers, mountains, forests, and lakes are often venerated because they reach toward, or reflect, the realm of the gods.

Sacred places fulfill three primary functions. They are places of communication with divinity through prayer, movement, or visual contact with an image of the divine; they are places of divine presence, often promising healing, success or salvation; and they provide meaning to the faithful by metaphorically reflecting the underlying order of the world. These three characteristics combine to turn the sacred space into a religious center for the believer, spiritually or even geographically.

At sacred sites the experience of the holy is at its purest and most unmediated. This primordial expression of the sacred in space is highly unstable, just like its two parallels, sacred time and charismatic authority. The German sociologist Max Weber has discussed the difficulties associated with charismatic authority and the manner in which processes of legalization and rationalization imbue institutions with a permanence that is not subject to instabilities. In Weber, charismatic authority gains permanence through transformation to traditional authority and finally legal authority. Weber's analytical framework can be extended to sacred space to shed light on the manner in which such space is transformed first into a temple and then into a local house of worship.

Unlike charismatic authority, the danger to unmediated sacred space is not in the problem of succession but in the risk of desecration. The distinct status of sacred space requires restrictions in access and behavior that are prohibitively difficult to enforce. By virtue of divine presence, access to sacred space must be restricted to the initiated. Often, only believers, members of a particular gender or class, or none but select individuals may

A shrine in an Asian garden. *Courtesy of istockphoto.com.*

enter the sacred space, in part or in whole. This restriction, in turn, requires a precise definition of the boundaries of the sacred place and supervision over entrance to that place. In the absence of such delineation and oversight, the site will suffer desecration. Desecration will also occur if worshippers fail to undergo the elaborate rites of purification and the precise gestures of approach required upon entering the site, such as covering or revealing the head in Judaism, Sikhism, and Christianity; removing shoes in Islam; or washing the mouth in Shintoism. The participation of worshippers in rituals at the sacred site is governed by a similarly complex series of rules. These rites require supervision and constant reinterpretation as worship is adapted to changing circumstances.

From Sacred Space to Shrine

Given the complex rules associated with access to and behavior at sacred sites and the extreme dangers associated with desecration, sacred places are likely to undergo a transition from site to shrine. This transition, a parallel of the process of legalization that occurs as charismatic authority is replaced with what Weber termed traditional authority, involves two changes in particular: the construction of a permanent structure and the establishment of a priestly class that is responsible for managing the sacred site.

Aside from preventing erosion to the underlying site, the construction of a permanent edifice over the sacred site has the purpose of reflecting, in outward appearance, inner design and detailed ornamentation, the meaning of the sacred site. Its outward appearance is aimed primarily at those prohibited from access to the site. It is likely to represent the host religion at its most splendiferous, all the while hinting at mysteries within that must remain inaccessible to the uninitiated observer. In the design of the shrine, architecture is employed to represent the rules governing behavior and access. The structure channels and constrains movement around the sacred site by means of barriers, gateways and passageways. It also creates the necessary spaces and facilities for performing rituals such as group worship, ablution, baptism, confession or sacrifice. The ornate symbols that decorate the shrine recall the founding miracle of the underlying site, retell the movement's myths, and represent its core principles, leaders, and events. Decorations also act as guides to behavior and ritual by designating areas in the shrine according to function or by representing appropriate and prohibited behavior.

In addition to the appearance of a permanent structure, the shift from sacred place to shrine is also accompanied by the formalized presence of religious actors at the site. As public presence and worship take on a permanence, such actors are required to control access, supervise behavior, and assist in the performance of ritual. Where believers expect divine favor in exchange for sacrifice, for example, priests collect, administer, and apportion the offering. The shrine structure provides the priestly class with the facilities required for performing their tasks, including chambers for storing the implements of ritual or sacred artifacts, sites required for priestly rites, and locations at which these actors can communicate with worshippers or from which they can supervise and guide their behavior.

From Shrine to Temple

The increase in the religious centrality of a sacred shrine sets off a series of self-reinforcing mechanisms. As the number of worshippers attending the site grows in size, priests will require and demand increasingly elaborate facilities. Increased public attendance will contribute to the expansion and embellishment of the shrine structure, that, in turn, will enhance the shrine's attraction to worshippers. Once the shrine has superseded competing sacred sites in importance, priestly classes are likely to make it their permanent site of activity or even residence. Shrines that occupy a prominent place in a society's religious landscape are likely to assume a central position in its social, cultural, and even economic and political sphere. Political and economic entrepreneurs drawn to the shrine will strive to associate themselves with the site, contribute to its expansion and decoration, construct their own centers of activity at the site or in its vicinity and, in so doing, will underscore the centrality of the shrine to the community.

Indeed, once the shrine has been suitably prepared, the gods themselves may choose to make their home in it. Unlike a simple shrine, the construction of which might be initiated and completed by the worshippers themselves, the erection of a divine residence requires levels of planning, supervision, and even execution that can only be performed by religious actors, inspired by divine guidance.

The product of this process is the temple, a shrine that has expanded to become a social, religious and political center. Temples and urban population centers are thus symbiotic, the former often lying at the heart of, giving rise to, and at the same time requiring the existence of the latter. Temples serve their cities of residence by drawing local worshippers, pilgrims, and powerful actors who wish to incur the favor of the priestly classes or control their activities. The city, in turn, draws in its design on the layout of the temple, derives significant financial and political clout from the presence of the sacred site in its midst, and utilizes the temple for a variety of social activities. Temples have doubled as courts, schools, marketplaces, and royal residences.

From Temple to House of Worship

Temples are institutionalized sacred places, comparable to legalized charismatic authority. Neither of these two forms, however, brings the process of rationalization to its logical conclusion because neither institution is entirely stable. Whereas traditional authority, such as leadership based on patrimony, may degenerate into corruption, temples are susceptible to a more physical vulnerability: the dangers of foreign conquest and destruction. Indeed, the concentration of religious, political, and economic resources at or near temples creates significant temptations for violence. Wars to control or annihilate temples, initiated by secular actors or religious competitors, go a long way toward explaining the destruction of so many ancient temples, from Delphi to Preah Vihear. One study of temples in India, for example, counted eighty recorded incidents of temple desecration between 1193 and 1729. Such incidents have disastrous consequences for societies that organize around these religious institutions, as exemplified by the fate of the Jewish people after the destruction of their temple in Jerusalem.

Whether in anticipation of or in response to such catastrophes, or where the temple has become inaccessible for some other reason, religious entrepreneurs have initiated the reproduction of temples into local shrines, mosques, churches, or synagogues. The resulting mirror sites, a "bureaucratization" of the original, reflect the designs of their source temple yet are significantly more enduring. In the absence of an underlying sacred place, the likelihood and risks accompanying desecration are reduced. As a consequence, the rules that govern access to and behavior at these shrines can be partially relaxed and the need for direct priestly supervision is diminished. The multiplicity of small and localized houses of worship poses a far less attractive target for outsiders intent on targeting the community core.

Though in appearance and daily administration these houses of worship retain but a faint echo of the original, they continuously invoke the temple that inspired their construction. The mirror site may face towards the temple or its layout and physical components may represent the abstracted design of the temple. The symbols that adorn the house of worship will emulate either the form of the temple, the shape of ritual objects located in the temple or the very symbols that adorned the temple. Rites performed in the house of worship are stylized variations on rituals performed in the temple, conducted at parallel points in the religious calendar. The link between the two sites is constantly underscored in prayers, rituals, and invocations. In all these, the modern house of prayer constantly conjures up the image of the primordial temple.

RON E. HASSNER

Further Reading

Brereton, J. P. (1987). Sacred space. In M. Eliade (Ed.), *The encyclopedia of religion* (Vol. 12, pp. 526–535). New York: Macmillan.

Eaton, R. M. (2000). Temple desecration in pre-modern India. *Frontline* 17, no. 25 and 26, 22 December 2000 and 5 January 2001.

Eliade, M. (1958). *Patterns in comparative religion*. New York: Sheed & Ward.

Hassner, R. E. (2003). To halve and to hold: Conflicts over sacred space and the problem of indivisibility. *Security Studies*, 12(4), 1–33.

Holm J. (Ed.). (1994). *Sacred places*. London: Pinter.

Weber, M. (1958). *From Max Weber, essays in sociology.* (H. H. Gerth, & C. Wright Mills, Eds.). New York: Oxford University Press.

Tolerance

Tolerance is an ambiguous term. Still, many would insist that tolerance is a virtue. In one context it is an intentional virtue, in another it appears more as a reflex of human nature at its best. It may also refer to a grudging and incomplete willingness to "bear" as moral burdens those who should change their minds. Surely, however, tolerance is a preferred attitude in any or all religious traditions, though it often seems an ideal honored more in theory than in practice. Its contrary, intolerance, may become public at times when ordinary mortals confront other ordinary mortals whose worldview or rhetoric does not correspond to their own expectations.

There may in fact be circumstances in which tolerance is compromised by questions of personal identity, when one person worries that another's behavior and beliefs seem to threaten just who he or she is. Intolerance then may overshadow the presumed virtue of tolerance. Because personal identity is always formed by reference to and distinction from others, tolerance may not be an easy response when one person meets another. Unless taken under deliberate control, the impulse to protect one's identity may tempt one to assume intolerant attitudes and behavior toward others from whom one feels separate. So, even if intolerance is neither necessary nor appropriate, it may often be an inevitable byproduct of immediate human experience.

Even when we shift our attention from the realm of human psychology to the realm of human religion, tolerance still does not escape the trap of paradox. In monotheistic traditions especially, we are exhorted to love our neighbors and even our enemies. Such "love" is surely at least a cousin of "tolerance." Those same traditions, however, are often built on the presumption that their truths are revealed and hence not subject to doubt or variation. The stage is set for a myriad array of intolerance toward others, ranging from indifference to hostility, from disdain to inquisition, from resentment to crusade. In such circumstances an exclusionary ethic is the reflex of dogmatic certainty—itself a function of historical conflict and contention. Belief in the "one true religion" is a temptation foisted on the best among us. That belief, of course, has exacted (and continues to exact) a high price among human communities.

Contradictions

How shall we make sense of this contradiction? Even a casual glance at the contemporary scene reveals not merely the limits of tolerance, but indeed its virtual abandonment. But such a judgment may obscure a deeper paradox. The intolerance of indiscriminate tolerance may be claimed as a virtue. The truth must be maintained against all those who refuse to acknowledge it. The other side of that conceptual coin is a dilemma: One's own truth-claims subjectively seem self-validating. What I believe is true is true because I *believe* it is true—and a superordinate reality or my undeniable personal experience has authenticated it. Individuals can entertain such a conviction because, despite the transportation and communications revolutions, most of us still live in religious isolation.

It seems that we know very little about the beliefs, practices, or experiences of others who are involved in religious communities different from our own. The reasons for such a condition are legion; the fact is singular. Many of us are reluctant to extend the courtesy of understanding to those on other paths. Even the notion of a "religious path" may confuse certain of us. Our "religion" is a fixed place on which we take a stand rather than a journey whose direction and purpose we are unsure of, no matter our inherited certainties. Even if the "path" is an acceptable metaphor, we prefer to act as though the highway that we follow is the only one with a significant destination.

Still, most seriously religious persons are likely to admit that tolerance is a virtue. That tolerance may lose its shine, however, when we begin to compare our own persuasions to those belonging to people of whom we have been tolerant. Then we may retreat to a defensive position where we begin to protect ourselves by attacking, ignoring or at least belittling others.

Paradoxically, then, it is the ignorance brought on by isolation that may tempt us to be tolerant. On the other hand, the desire to understand may reveal for us unexpected differences that strain credulity and threaten our previously safe identity. We face here a serious dilemma: Even if understanding is a moral good, as it surely is, it can still lead to a failure of goodwill within the human community. Tolerance, on the other hand, even though an acknowledged virtue, may rest on ignorance that can hardly be called moral in any ordinary sense of the word.

Article 18 of the Universal Declaration of Human Rights

Everyone has the right to freedom of thought, conscience and religion; this right includes freedom to change his religion or belief, and freedom, either alone or in community with others and in public or private, to manifest his religion or belief in teaching, practice, worship and observance.

The uncertainties of religious tolerance, however, are even more intricate than we have seen so far. The very notion of "tolerance" is ambiguous, even if tolerant behavior is a virtue. There are forms of tolerance that range from an affirmation of others as an honest invitation to dialogue to hesitant acquiescence that may imperfectly cover up a disdain slipping precariously into hostility.

Limits to Tolerance

The human community is a fragile construct indeed. It can be broken and divided in myriad ways. The opportunities for intolerance and hostility that plague the human species have elicited remarkable ingenuity among us. On the intrahuman level, variations of gender, color, ethnicity, age, size, and intelligence inflict upon each of us suspicion of others. Class, nationality, and religion are some of the gross differences that turn us against one another. Tolerance, it seems, is not one of our spontaneous virtues. But, again, there is a paradox.

The divine presence loves what it has created—or so most religious folks believe. Thereby, love becomes a virtue of the divine and so a divine virtue. Surely ordinary piety should do no less than imitate that virtue. Human beings, overwhelmed by absolute love, must find it in themselves to love one another, even in face of the differences that divide and distinguish them from each other. The divine itself, after all, must be able to "see beyond" the mere humanity it has created. It must be able to override the virtually endless diversity that distinguishes the human order.

On the other hand, we seem unable or unwilling to practice the virtue that we so often attribute to the divine. Though God "bears" us, we may not find it in our human selves to bear each other as happy burdens. That, after all, is what "tolerance" implies. The word is derived from the Latin verb that means to pick up, to carry some object. Presumably, under divine command, or doing what the truth demands, we should

gladly "bear the burden" of human variety. But who among us will actually do so without at least some reservation, without begrudging the differences that create the marvelous kaleidoscope of humanity? Tolerance has its limits.

The paradox is disarming. By a strange logic that scrambles the universal and the particular, as well as divine virtue and merely human morality, our inclusive vision excludes. Secure in our parochial versions of the truth of universal love, we discover intolerance to be the shadow of tolerance; exclusion the reciprocal of inclusion; the insistence on conformity, the reflex of a love that should be able to dissolve differences but often does not. And, again, we must conclude that tolerance has its limits—despite the habitual presumption that it is a virtue, pure and simple.

Should we believe, then, that we can discover those limits? An even more challenging question is "Where should we look?" Here we face an authentic conundrum. Shall we explore specific *religious* traditions or shall we conjure some presumed generic, a historical reality called "religion?" Are the limits of tolerance to be searched out in the behavior of religious individuals, embedded in institutional communities? Or, tempted by the contemporary interest in "spirituality" shall we try to excavate beneath beliefs and practices to uncover the obscure origins of intolerance in the psychological impulses of the human person?

We may explore the history of religion to find traditions in which this dilemma is embedded. There are surely many traditions to excavate, but Judaism is an obvious example. We can discover the roots of intolerance in that community that has itself born the brunt of intolerance through so many centuries. The Jewish claim that there is only one God entails distrust of, even hostility to, those who cannot countenance that claim. Hence those who determine to obey the divine law as though it had been revealed exclusively to them may eventually be diverted by a temptation to intolerance. The logic of social history becomes clear: Theological arrogance draws abuse to those who practice it; intolerance perpetuates itself and comes to prey on the intolerant. The rabbis, however, express the logical necessity of religious tolerance when they declare, "God will uproot from the world everyone who hates his fellow man."

But even those who are moved by monotheism to despise others who may have missed its presumptive truth are able to reflect that they had also been victims of intolerance. Torah reminds Jews that "You should not oppress a stranger; you know the heart of a stranger, for you were strangers in the land of Egypt" (Exodus 23:9).

So, again, where are the limits of religious tolerance? Are they coextensive with our humanity? Then surely the limits are narrow and we may not be able to avoid much longer the self-destructive impulses that haunt our personal and communal lives. Do we then find ourselves trapped in a web of our own devising? But if religious people are servants of another truth, then the limits are set beyond even our imagining. If that is the case, however, how shall we know who we are and what we are? For our identity as human beings depends on living within recognizable limits defined in part by others whose beliefs we cannot countenance.

Religious Paradox

In practical terms, for many the boundaries that define them are the religious traditions that claim them—or to which they claim allegiance. What if those very traditions force on them an identity that elicits intolerance? The dilemma is acute. What often may bind us to the universe and to each other is the very sense that makes us hostile to each other. We are burdened by the claim that persuades us that we have been especially chosen by the universe to protect the truth that passes understanding.

Hypnotized by that paradox, stunned by that irony, what can we do? What should we do? It is this two-edged sword that hangs over ethical discourse. Where can we locate the limits of religious tolerance? Must responsible and moral persons necessarily feel constraints on their will to tolerance? Or is tolerance only an illusion behind which a particular human person harbors a grudge against vagrant and benighted others?

If we seek no reprieve from candor, we ask whether the limits of tolerance are drawn indelibly for the monotheist and obliterated for the atheist. Do not all religious traditions, perhaps paradoxically, set limits to a tolerance within which the committed must live? No matter where in the historical course of religious traditions we look we are almost certain to find both a will

to include and to exclude. But who of us can tolerate the unresolved dilemma forever: It is as adherents of a universal truth that we ourselves are privileged to practice exclusion. Thereby we set the limits of religious tolerance perilously close to the borders of our own egos.

At the center of this conversation we find not so much a categorical imperative as a question: "If our particular version of truth is not Truth, then religious faith becomes relative. If we find there the Truth, how do we accommodate those who hold otherwise?" The dangers of this dilemma are all too apparent. Within the realm of ethical discourse, some will argue that intolerance of other religious persuasions is "sinful." Others will argue that religious tolerance may compromise the integrity of particular religious convictions—and hence is no virtue at all. Is the limit of religious tolerance a theological or a psychological question? Must we purchase peace in the body social by giving up the "peace that passes understanding"? Does the intolerance we impute to other religious folks really reflect our own intolerance embedded in irresistible "habits of the heart"? The questions proliferate, and we may wonder whether it is God or we who beat our heads against the limits of our humanity.

However moral one's intentions, the rhetoric of freedom, liberty and justice may conceal the dilemma that haunts those who would practice the virtue of tolerance. In the Vatican II Declaration of Religious Freedom (*Dignitatis Humanae*), we read the following:

> The Vatican Council declares that the human person has a right to religious freedom. Freedom of this kind means that all men should be immune from coercion on the part of individuals, social groups and every human power so that, within due limits, nobody is forced to act against his convictions nor is anyone to be restrained from acting in accordance with his convictions in religious matters in private or in public, alone or in associations with others.

If we assume that the "immunity from coercion" clearly implies that the Church takes tolerance to be a positive virtue, then this declaration should be the basis of personal as well as individual behaviors that are responsive to others and consistent with the Church's teaching.

However:

> Council further declares that the right to religious freedom is based on the very dignity of the human person as known through the revealed word of God

and by reason itself. This right of the human person to religious freedom must be given such recognition in the constitutional order of society as will make it a civil right.

The evocation of the "dignity of the human persons" surely reinforces the virtue of tolerance that is implied in the earlier statement. But, if affirming this "dignity" requires subscribing to the proposition that it is "known through the revealed word of God," then the tolerance may not be felt as authentic. Of course, it is also "reason itself" that guarantees one's dignity and hence one's deserving tolerance. Or must we also ask: Does an affirmation of one "revealed" truth possibly compromise the Council's generous statement? Or does the shadow of one absolute—revealed—Truth obscure and at the same time define the limits of religious tolerance?

Louis J. Hammann

See also Culture Wars, Free Speech; Pornography; Profane Communication

Further Reading

Boyle, K., & Sheen, J. (Eds.). (1997). *Freedom of religion and belief: A world report*. New York: Routledge.

Hammann, L. J., & Buck, H. M. (Eds.). (1988). *Religious traditions and the limits of tolerance*. New York: Columbia University Press.

Translation

The word *translation* comes from Latin and literally means, "to carry across." Translations seek to carry meaning across from one context to another. Because all acts of communication are acts of translation, and all acts of translation involve interpretation, the stakes of translation are particularly high when "eternal meaning" linked to God, religion, or scripture is carried across into a new context.

Why Is Translation Challenging?

The process of translating a language is not a mechanical one. In some contexts, for instance, the German word *Gesundheit* could be translated as "God bless you," even though the word itself literally means "health." In English, the word *fast* could refer to speed or to a person deliberately choosing not to eat. It could refer to tightness (when referring to something that

holds fast). There is no one-to-one correspondence between languages.

Because words have a host of connotations from within the culture in which they are used, because word-plays, irony, and idioms do not readily transfer from one language to another, because the meaning of a word frequently is based on its context within a sentence, translating *from* a language can be a challenging task. Because people react to words differently, because the meanings of words change over time, because cultural concepts also change over time, translating *into* a language also is a challenging task. As the prologue to Ecclesiasticus (The Wisdom of Ben Sirach) exhorts its readers, "What was originally expressed in Hebrew does not have exactly the same sense when translated into another language" (RSV). Translation necessarily involves evaluation, interpretation, and choice on the part of the translator.

Translation Challenges for Religions

Translations themselves pose a variety of challenges for religions that seek to communicate clearly through their scripture. Four examples show some of the breadth of concerns.

1. Because translation involves interpretation, and because Arabic itself is seen as the language chosen by Allah to communicate his message, Orthodox Muslims see the Qur'an as untranslatable. As A. J. Arberry notes in the preface to *The Koran Interpreted*, "The rhetoric and rhythm of the Arabic of the Koran are so characteristic, so powerful, so highly emotive, that any version whatsoever is bound in the nature of things to be but a poor copy of the glittering splendour of the original." (1955, 24)

2. Direct translations are not always seen as appropriate within a religion. In the book of Exodus, when Moses looks into the burning bush and asks for the divine name, the response that God gives consists of four Hebrew letters—yod, heh, vav, heh—and is referred to as the tetragrammaton (i.e., "the four letters"). Although the name is not a four-letter word in the sense in which people use that term today, like four-letter words today, that name is not to be said out loud. Instead, out of respect and deference to God, that word is translated with all sorts of circumlocutions.

3. Sometimes a translation of a religious text functions to obfuscate the meaning of the text rather than illuminate it. In Richard Burton's translation

of the Kamasutra, the Hindu concept of Kama recognizably could have caused consternation among readers with Victorian sensibilities. As a result, Burton started the tradition of using the words "lingam" and "yoni"—direct transliterations of Hindi words—to refer to male and female genitalia, rather than using the English words themselves. What is particularly peculiar, however, is that the Kamasutra itself rarely uses the Hindi words "lingam" and "yoni"; it uses other Hindu words to refer to genitalia. The net effect of avoiding sexually provocative language was that the translation was much less jarring than it might otherwise have been, but also less accurate.

4. Within Christianity, scholars of the historical Jesus recognize that one challenge they face is that the New Testament was written in Greek, the lingua franca of the day. As a result, if Jesus spoke Aramaic—as many assume he did—scholars need to engage in a kind of retroreconstructive translation into Aramaic if they are to identify the ipsissima verba ("actual words") of Jesus.

Religious Justifications for Translation

In other instances, religions have recognized the necessity of translation, regardless of the challenges posed. Early Buddhists, Martin Luther, and the Second Vatican Council each saw the liturgies of their day as having become ossified through the persistent use of a language that was no longer used by the laity. Each of the three emphasized the importance of translating liturgical language into the vernacular. Translation, in these cases, was seen as making the Scripture or liturgy more relevant to worshippers.

Apprehension about the value of translations likely is what lies behind the traditions and stories surrounding the Greek translation of the Hebrew Bible. The creation of the Septuagint is seen as one of the most significant events in religious history because it represents the first wholesale attempt to translate religious narrative and theological concepts from one language (Hebrew) into another (Greek). This Greek Old Testament came to be known as the Septuagint, abbreviated by the Roman numeral LXX, as traditions say that seventy (or seventy-two) scholars were involved in its translation. Since their translations were identical, the process itself is presented as inspired and the results trustworthy.

Translating the Bible: Key Historical Events

Because the Bible is the most widely translated book in the world, key developments in the translation of the Bible particularly illuminate the challenges of communicating in different languages and cultures.

The Septuagint

Most modern theories surrounding the translation of the Septuagint focus on how Greek-speaking Jews in Egypt had a need for a Greek translation of the Hebrew Scriptures. The Epistle of Aristeas highlights the process through which the Pentateuch was translated in the third century BCE. Some would say that the Septuagint is the most significant translation in history, not only because of the scale of the translation itself but also because of the ways in which the first Christians used this translation. The Septuagint provided an example for how to appropriate and think about Hebrew concepts and was used by the first Christians as Scripture: They did not quote from the Hebrew Scriptures; they quoted from the Septuagint. Scholars also have said that Isaiah 7:14b represents one of the most significant translation challenges in history. A direct translation of the Hebrew into English can be seen in the Revised Standard Version, which says, "Behold, a young woman shall conceive and bear a son, and shall call his name Immanuel." When the Hebrew word *almah* (which generally meant "young woman") came to be translated in the LXX with the Greek word *parthenos* (meaning "virgin"), this verse came to be seen not in light of an historical incident in the past, but in light of Christian prophecy about the Messiah.

The Vulgate

For almost 1000 years the Latin Vulgate was the standard version of Scripture used throughout western Europe. Because of a proliferation of diverse Latin translations, in the year 383 CE Pope Damascus asked Jerome—the foremost Christian scholar of his day—to create a dependable Latin text. From 383 to 404 CE Jerome developed his "common" (i.e., Vulgate) translation by translating Hebrew and Greek manuscripts and by revising existing Latin manuscripts. The Vulgate had tremendous influence on the development of Romance languages such as Spanish, French, and Portuguese and on the development of the Church and its theology. Words like *justification, sanctification,* and *propitiation* took on new meanings in light of Jerome's translation.

From the Prologue to Ecclessiasticus (RSV)

You are urged therefore to read with good will and attention, and to be indulgent in cases where, despite our diligent labor in translating, we may seem to have rendered some phrases imperfectly. For what was originally expressed in Hebrew does not have exactly the same sense when translated into another language. Not only this work, but even the law itself, the prophecies, and the rest of the books differ not a little as originally expressed.

Key Translations through the 16th Century

In the 730s the Venerable Bede, a Benedictine monk and historian of Anglo-Saxon England, became the first person to be credited with translating Scripture into one of the new European languages (in this case, English). At the end of the 1300s John Wycliffe's influence ensured that that both the Old and New Testaments were translated into English from Latin, although the Wycliffe Bible soon came to be condemned by the Pope and throughout England. From 1522 to 1534 Martin Luther—working in German—created the first Bible translation based not on the Latin Vulgate, but on the original Hebrew and Greek. Concurrently, William Tyndale created the first English translation from the Hebrew and Greek. Although his work would greatly influence and shape the wording of subsequent English translations, his act was seen as heretical. To avoid persecution, Tyndale fled to Germany. In 1535–1536, however, he was betrayed, tried for heresy, and burned at the stake.

The King James Version

Since 1611 the most widely used English translation has been the King James Version (KJV), or "Authorized Version" (i.e., for use in the Church of England). In 1604 King James I called for a conference on religious toleration at Hampton Court. One reason for the conference was the tension among various Christians that had resulted from the variety of English translations of the Bible. Although that tension was not resolved, King James I became convinced of the inadequacies of all of the English translations, and so he commissioned a new one. The KJV was completed by around fifty scholars, has language characteristics similar to Shakespearean English, and is generally considered to be a literary masterpiece. In the preface of the KJV, the translators

describe how, recognizing that no one English word could embrace all of the meanings, nuances, and connotations of any Hebrew or Greek word, they used a variety of English words for certain Hebrew and Greek ones. This strength—the choosing of precise words—is also a weakness, in part because it is difficult in the KJV to recognize when the ancient authors deliberately repeat a word. One example frequently cited is the Greek verb *katargeo*, which occurs twenty-seven times in the New Testament and is translated eighteen different ways (e.g., "abolish," "deliver," "fail," "loose") in the KJV. Although the passing of time requires new translations for general usage, the language of the KJV continues to be actively used within liturgies, and within the language of the public square.

Subsequent History

Scholars, increasingly concerned that the KJV (and especially its New Testament) was based upon an errant Greek text, continued to develop new translations, such as the British Revised Version (1881–1885) and the American Standard Version (1901). As more and more ancient secular Greek texts were found, scholars recognized that the Greek used in the New Testament was the same Koine Greek that was used in everyday life. As a result, more translations in the twentieth century focused on use of informal, colloquial, or readily understandable English. The latter part of the twentieth century resulted in a remarkable number of translations. From 1952 (when the Revised Standard Version was completed) to 1990 (when the New Revised Standard Version was published), twenty-seven English translations of the Bible were published, with an additional twenty-eight versions of the New Testament alone. In 1966 The Jerusalem Bible was published, the first complete Roman Catholic translation of the Scriptures from the original Hebrew and Greek. Jewish scholars also sought to make their Scriptures more accessible. In 1917 the Jewish Publication Society of America issued *The Holy Scriptures according to the Masoretic Text*, a translation very similar to the KJV. Recognizing the need to make the English translation more contemporary, the Jewish Publication Society issued the Tanakh in 1985.

The Controversy of Translations

Although new translations intend to provide clarity, reduce archaic words or concepts, and avoid ambiguities, rarely do they appear without controversy. Jerome defended his Vulgate translation by referring to detractors as "two-legged asses," who "think that ignorance is identical with holiness." When the KJV was first published, Dr. Hugh Broughton—a scholar in the Church of England—said of it: "I had rather be rent in pieces with wild horses, than any such translation, by my consent, should be urged upon poor churches." When the Revised Standard Version was first published in 1952, some detractors referred to it as a Communist Bible. Others ripped out pages with what they saw as inappropriate translations (e.g., "young woman" instead of "virgin" in Isaiah 7:14), burned the pages, and sent the ashes to the general editor of the translation.

Translation issues continue to be important within the use of religious language in American public life. At the beginning of the twenty-first century, as courts and individuals debate the appropriateness of posting the Ten Commandments in public schools or government facilities, one concern frequently raised has to do with which translation of the Ten Commandments should be posted. Whereas Evangelical Christians tend to favor—for traditional and aesthetic reasons—the "Thou shalt not kill" language of the King James Version, many Jews tend to favor "You shall not murder," which they see as a more literal translation of the Hebrew. Regardless of the preferred translation, readers must be aware that translation is not a mechanical process. Rather it demands evaluation, interpretation, and choice.

CRAIG WANSINK

Further Reading

Ali, A. Y. (2001). *The Qur'an: Text, translation, and commentary*. Elmhurst, NY: Tahrike Tarsile Qur'an, Inc.

Arberry, A. J. (1955). *The Koran interpreted*. New York: Macmillan.

Biguenet, J., & Schulte, R. (Eds.). (1989). *The craft of translation*. Chicago: The University of Chicago Press.

Bobrick, B. (2001). *Wide as the waters: The story of the English Bible and the revolution it inspired*. New York: Simon & Schuster.

Daniell, D. (2001). *William Tyndale*. New Haven, CT: Yale University Press.

Daniell, D. (2003). *The Bible in English: Its history and influence*. New Haven, CT: Yale University Press.

DeHamel, C. (2001). *The book: A history of the Bible*. New York: Phaidon Press.

Gutjahr, P. C. (1999). *An American Bible: A history of the good book in the United States, 1777–1880*. Stanford, CA: Stanford University Press.

Lightfoot, N. (2003). *How we got the Bible* (3rd ed.). Grand Rapids, MI: Baker Books.

Mallanaga, V. (2002). *Kamasutra*. (W. Doniger & S. Kakar, Trans.). New York: Oxford University Press.

McGrath, A. (2002). *In the beginning: The story of the King James Bible and how it changed a nation, a language, and a culture*. Garden City, NY: Anchor.

Metzger, B. M. (1968). *The text of the New Testament: Its transmission, corruption, and restoration* (2nd ed.). New York: Oxford University Press.

Metzger, B. M. (2001). *The Bible in translation: Ancient and English versions*. Grand Rapids, MI: Baker House.

Metzger, B. M. (2003). *The New Testament: Its background, growth, and content* (3rd ed.). Nashville, TN: Abingdon Press.

Nicolson, A. (2003). *God's secretaries: The making of the King James Bible*. San Francisco: HarperCollins.

Ryken, L. (2003). *The word of God in English: Criteria for excellence in Bible translation*. Wheaton, IL: Crossway Books.

Youngblood, R. F., Strauss, M. L., Voth, S. M., & Scorgie, G. G. (2003). *The challenge of Bible translation*. Grand Rapids, MI: Zondervan.

W

Wicca

Wicca is a contemporary religion within the larger religious movement known as neopaganism. There are a number of Wicca "religions" that share a number of common characteristics including a predominately female membership, use of witchcraft symbolism, organization as covens, worship of nature, and an emphasis on personal happiness and growth. Wicca is just over fifty years old, as its start can be traced to the publication of Gerald B. Gardner's (1884–1964) *Witchcraft Today* in 1954. Gardner provided a new interpretation of witchcraft in medieval Europe as an ancient fertility belief system centered on the worship of a goddess of the moon and a lesser male god. Wiccan theology and practice is flexible and allows for different groups to worship different goddesses, gods not at all, and to include worship of different goddesses in the same rituals. Despite the association with witchcraft, Wiccans are not witches and do not seek to harm others, nor do they worship the devil. Quite to the contrary, their central ethical principle is to "harm none."

Communication is important to Wiccans for several reasons. First, Wiccans communicate with the supernatural world through worship and rituals to seek help both for themselves and the wider community. Second, in pursuit of personal growth and development, Wiccans place much emphasis on effective and open communication among themselves. And, third, Wiccans seek to communicate their religion to non-Wiccans, especially to attract adherents and to correct misperceptions about witchcraft and black magic.

Ritual Communication

Wiccans usually worship in covens, groups ranging from three to thirteen believers that meet regularly to perform rituals. Each coven is led by a high priestess, who may be assisted by a high priest. Esbats and sabbats are the two primary forms of Wiccan ritual. Esbats are held more or less monthly in harmony with the full moon and also by some covens at the time of the new moon. Adherents come together in covens to worship, study, and conduct business. Rituals are performed to help those in need, and at this time, individuals may ask for help with personal issues. New members may be initiated at esbats, especially during the period between 1 February and 21 June.

Sabbats are larger rituals which can attract hundreds or even thousands of Wiccans. Sabbats are held eight times a year and are tied to "the Wheel of the Year," the Wiccan annual cycle. The Samhain ritual marks the beginning and end of the Wiccan annual cycle and typically also involves ritual behavior to honor and communicate with the dead. Altars are decorated with photographs, flowers, candles, and mementos of deceased loved ones and at the "dumb supper," the souls of dead relatives are invited to commune with their living descendants who eat in silence. Many Wiccan rituals are initiation rites through which initiates join the coven and learn its customs. These rituals are usually secret ceremonies that cannot be shared with outsiders.

Much communication in the rituals take place through dancing in a circle and chanting. Some participants may enter into alternate states of consciousness

Movies and Television Shows with Witchcraft Themes

Movies
Bewitched (2005)
Blair Witch Project (1999)
The Chronicles of Narnia: The Lion, the Witch, and the Wardrobe (2005)
The Craft (1996)
The Mists of Avalon (2001)
Practical Magic (1998)
Witches of Eastwick (1987)
The Wizard of Oz (1939)

Television Shows
Bewitched (1964–1972)
Charmed (1998–2006)
Sabrina, the Teenage Witch (1996–2003)

during which they commune with the deities and receive personal messages or divine healing.

Spells

Wiccans use spells, although very carefully and with much forethought and planning. This is because the use of spells must adhere to the Three-Fold Law: "All that a person does to another returns three fold in this life; harm is also returned three-fold." This means that a spell may not be used to harm, dominate, or manipulate another person. Many Wiccan spells involve love and the desire for a romantic relationship with another person. The spell cannot be used to make another person fall in love with the Wiccan nor even to be more open to a romantic relationship. But, a spell can be used to make the Wiccan more open to a love relationship.

Spells vary widely from full rituals to ones with only a few phrases. One spell handbook suggests that spells include four steps: knowing what one seeks to accomplish, having the will, daring to change, and silence. Spells are open to individual interpretation, and most Wiccans adapt them to fit their mood, needs, and personal situation. Here is an example of a spell used to make contact with a lost friend:

Materials

White candle	Glass or cup of water
Sandalwood oil and incense	Sea salt
Photograph of person	

Instructions

Cast a circle in your usual manner. Light incense and anoint candle with sandalwood oil. Place the photo of the person you wish to have contact you on your altar. If you have no photo, write their name on a piece of paper. Take a small handful of salt in your right hand, and let it trickle into the cup of water. While the salt falls, repeat the words "contact me," and concentrate on your friend getting in touch with you. Place the salt water on your altar and leave the candle to burn out. Your friend should make contact with you before the water evaporates from the cup.

Wicca on the Internet

Not surprisingly, a number of websites exist as forums for Wiccan information and sales venues for Wiccan merchandise. For example, WICA.com is the website for the Witchcraft Information Centre and Archive, offering courses in Wicca and witchcraft, as well as books, T-shirts, jewelry, and mugs. Other sites feature "virtual covens," and some even offer buttons and bumper stickers with slogans like "Goddess Bless Us" and "Thank Goddess."

David Levinson

Further Reading

Adler, M. (1986). *Drawing down the moon: Witches, druids, goddess-worshippers, and other pagans in America today.* Boston: Beacon Press. (Original work published 1979)

Berger, H. (1999). *A community of witches. Contemporary neo-paganism and witchcraft in the United States.* Columbia: University of South Carolina Press.

Budapest, Z. (1991). *Grandmother Moon: Lunar magic in our lives—spells, rituals, goddesses, legends and emotions.* San Francisco: HarperSanFrancisco.

Farrar, J., & Farrar, St. (1990). *Spells and how they work.* Blaine, WA: Phoenix Publishing.

Gardner, G. B. (1973). *Witchcraft today.* Seacaucus, NJ: Citadel Press. (Original work published 1954)

Hutton, R. (2000). *Triumph of the moon: A history of modern pagan witchcraft.* Oxford, UK: Oxford University Press.

Ravenwolf, S. H. (1998). *American folk magick: charms, spells & herbals.* Woodbury, MN: Llewellyn Publications.

Youth Culture

The concept of youth culture usually refers to forms of culture produced for or by young people. The concept is quite similar to subculture, referring to a group centered around particular cultural expressions, often a musical genre, as well as to popular culture—forms of culture considered to focus primarily on commercial success rather than aesthetic qualities and therefore understood as being in opposition to elite culture. Some of the central cultural products involved are comic books, films and television programs, role-playing games, computer games, and music. To a large extent these cultural products are made by adults and marketed to youth.

Religion relates to youth culture in several ways. The media content central to a particular youth culture may be influenced by religion, or youth culture can serve as a functional equivalent to religion. Youth culture sometimes serves as a challenge to established religion, and the religious establishment may be critical to some aspects of youth culture, for example, media content that is considered contrary to religious beliefs and values.

It is generally considered that even if forms of youth culture existed previously, the importance of youth culture increased greatly after World War II, particularly during the 1960s, with the rise of subcultures such as mods, skinheads, and hippies. The increase of economic means for young people led to a growing interest in youth as a market segment, and the products marketed to young people were and still are to a great extent products related to leisure and entertainment. It is, however, important to note that entertainment is a matter to be taken seriously to the extent that it functions as a sphere for production of meaning, belonging, and identity, as often is the case within youth culture.

The importance of youth culture in the identity formation process must be linked to the processes of modernization and secularization. The weakening of common traditions concerning areas such as gender, class, family patterns, and religion has increased individuals' opportunities—or requirements—to make lifestyle choices and to find out for themselves who they are and what they want to believe in. This development has been apparent not least among young people, on whom the weakening of common traditions has had dramatic effects.

Among all the authorities affected by these changes, religion may be the one that has been affected the most. Since religion is one of the most powerful tools we have to create order and a sense of direction and meaning in our lives, the decline of Christianity has led to many problems for the individual. The absence of a source of reliable answers to existential questions leads to a state of deficiency in a number of fundamental existential areas, in particular for young people in the Western world.

Religion in Non-Christian Youth Cultures

Religion in non-Christian youth cultures is a phenomenon that has been observed and discussed at least since the days of the hippie, or countercultural movements of the late sixties and early seventies. The religious beliefs evident in these youth cultures are almost exclusively centered around questions and problems concerning the here and now. Issues concerning the individual life and the inner self are also central. Young people do not try to build large belief systems around morals and ethics. Instead, they focus on pure existential here-and-now problems: the world must be saved; the rain forests must be saved; the survival of the individual must be made secure; meaning, structure, goals, and hope must be brought back to life. Questions concerning beliefs in gods and goddesses are given less weight. Worship of deities is of secondary importance among many non-Christian youth cultures.

Most, if not all, youth cultures share a struggle to create a sense of hope and meaning in a seemingly ever-changing society. Youth cultures that use religion in an overt way often strive to reinvent a sense of unity in life. For example, within Scandinavian black-metal culture—a subgenre of heavy metal, where Satanism and different forms of paganism are common features—there is a declared effort to rid the community of foreign elements, especially Christianity, and create unity within what is perceived as a pure pagan community. Another example is the psychedelic-trance culture, which is a subgenre of the rave culture, where hippie ideals are mixed with New Age, shamanism, and Eastern religions. Here the goal of unity is perceived as a gathering of all the peoples of the world into one tribe living in close connection with the spirits of nature and the universe.

Religion in non-Christian youth cultures is best described as postmodern bricolages. The individuals pick up pieces from different belief systems (rituals, conceptions) and build their own worldview from these. Often these conceptions and rituals are taken not from actual religions, but from mass media products of popular culture. Movies, books, and games in the genres of science fiction, fantasy, and horror are all important sources for the religion of youth culture. Most religions in these types of cultures are invisible private religions. Religion is not primarily something that is expressed and talked about but rather something to be kept in the private sphere of the individual.

Religion in youth culture is to a large extent taken from and inspired by mass media popular culture, and when religion is expressed in youth culture it is also most commonly done with the help of different media. The medium where young people primarily have an opportunity to express their religion is popular music. Different popular music subcultures are arenas where a lot of young people express their thoughts on the existential questions. This is done not only through the music itself, but also with specific lifestyles, clothing styles, body adornments, pictures, and lyrics closely connected to the music.

Religion, Music, and Youth Culture

There are five main ways to describe the use and attitudes of religion in popular music culture. The first of these is as *a religion without belief*. There is a tendency among young people to describe music in itself as something holy and spiritual and as something associated with religion. In the musical events—for example concerts, rave parties, or home stereo listening—young people have what they describe as religious experiences. It has, for example, been argued that what we were witnessing in the American counterculture was the birth of a new religious lifestyle in which religious experience was precisely analogous to the esthetic experience of music. This new religious lifestyle was based only on strong and shared musical experiences and was made possible not in spite of, but because of, the total lack of doctrines and truth claims.

The second way in which we meet religion in popular music culture is in a tendency to *spiritualize or deify a popular artist*. Most commonly this tendency is involves charismatic and often spiritually interested artists who died young, for example, Jim Morrison, Janis Joplin, and Bob Marley. A well-known example of this, maybe more concerning adults than youngsters, is the religious conceptions surrounding Elvis Presley and the emerging Elvis religion.

The third way is *a connection of religious concepts to a musical style*. In this case music comes first. Young people make strong musical experiences, but do not settle for a religion without belief. Instead, in interaction with others of the same subculture, they start to connect religious concepts and beliefs to their music. Good examples of this are the above-mentioned black-metal and psychedelic-trance cultures.

The fourth way is *a connection of a musical style to a religion*. This is quite similar to the previous way, but in this case religion comes first. One good example of this is the connection of Rastafarianism and reggae music. Rastafarianism existed for several decades as a more or less isolated Jamaican phenomenon. During the early seventies, however, there was a Rasta revival among young people in Jamaica. This new youth-based Rasta cult found its foremost expression in reggae music, and leading reggae artists like Bob Marley, who made an international breakthrough during the early seventies, helped spread the Rasta message all over the world. Since then Rastafarianism is more than anything connected with reggae and has become a vital part of Western youth culture.

The fifth and last way is *the use by religious movements of different types of popular music to express and spread their beliefs and religion.* The Hare Krishna movement's use of music is one well-known example of this, but most of all this is connected to Christianity and especially to the Evangelical churches that use almost any kind of music, including death metal and hardcore punk music, to spread the gospel.

Christian Youth Culture

The Christian youth culture can be understood as an example of the use of particular media to communicate a Christian message to nonbelievers. As most of the consumers of these media are active Christians, it is more relevant to talk of a subculture of Christian youth. As in other forms of youth culture, Christian youth culture is to a large extent centered around music, but it must also be noted that, for example, festivals of contemporary Christian music also function as focal points for many other aspects of Christian youth culture. One such aspect is the sale and use of various artifacts, such as T-shirts with religious messages or bracelets with the letters "WWJD," an abbreviation of the ethical principle "What Would Jesus Do?"

Another important feature of the Christian youth culture is the number of parachurch-type organizations, often focusing on evangelizing among young people or involving youth in missionary work, such as Campus Crusade for Christ or Youth with a Mission. Some of these organizations trace their roots to the most obvious example of a Christian parallel to the subcultures of the 1960s and 1970s, the Jesus Movement. Another kind of movement is the True Love Waits campaign, started in the mid 1990s, which promotes a message of sexual abstinence to Christian youth.

State of Research

There is a clear lack of reference to religion in most studies of youth subcultures conducted, for example, within the cultural studies paradigm. The main exceptions have been studies of the youth culture of minorities, for example, West Indian immigrants or Muslims.

Within religious studies, and particularly within some branches of theological research, there has been a great increase in the research on popular culture. Some

of these studies focus on youth, for example, in studies on the role of religion in the identity formation of young people. There are continuous efforts to combine an interest in religion and the insights from cultural studies, and this seems to be a promising development for future research in religion and youth culture.

THOMAS BOSSIUS AND ANDREAS HÄGER

See also Music Videos

Further Reading

Bauman, Z. (2001). *The individualized society*. Malden, MA: Polity Press.
Beaudoin, T. (2000). *Virtual faith: The irreverent spiritual quest of generation X*. San Francisco: Jossey-Bass.
Beck, U. (1999). *World risk society*. Cambridge, MA: Polity Press.
Bossius, T. (2003). *Med framtiden i backspegeln: Black metal-och transkulturen. Ungdomar, musik och religion i en senmodern värld. (The Future in the rear-view mirror: black metal and trance culture. youth, music, and religion in a late modern world.)* Göteborg: Daidalos.
Brake, M. (1980). *The sociology of youth culture and youth subcultures*. London: Routledge & Kegan Paul.
Forbes, B. D., & Mahan, J. H. (Eds.). (2000). *Religion and popular culture in America*. Berkeley & Los Angeles: University of California Press.
Fornäs, J. (1995). *Cultural theory and late modernity*. London: Sage.
Fornäs, J., & Bolin, G. (Eds.). (1995). *Youth culture in late modernity*. London: Sage.
Giddens, A. (1991). *Modernity and self-identity: Self and society in the late modern age*. Cambridge, MA: Polity Press.
Hebdige, D. (1979). *Subculture: the meaning of style*. London: Methuen.
Howard, J. R., & Streck, J. M. (1999). *Apostles of rock: the splintered world of contemporary Christian music*. Lexington: The University Press of Kentucky.
Martin, B. (1981). *A sociology of contemporary cultural change*. New York: St. Martins.
Schofield Clark, L. (2003). *From angels to aliens: teenagers, the media, and the supernatural*. New York: Oxford University Press.
Shepherd, W. C. (1972). Religion and the counter culture: a new religiosity. *Sociological Inquiry, 42*.
Ziehe, T. (1975). *Pubertät und Narzissmus*. Köln: Europäische Verlagsanstalt.
Ziehe, T. (1982). *Plädoyer für ungewöhnliches Lernen. Ideen zur Jugendsituation*. Reinbek: Rowohlt.

Ziehe, T. (1992). Cultural modernity and individualization. In J. Fornäs & G. Bolin (Eds.), *Moves in modernity*. Stockholm: Almqvist & Wiksell International.

Ziehe, T. (1996). How to cope with contingency: Youth cultures facing the "normality" of modernization. In *Education of teachers and social educators facing youth culture and subculture* (Ed. National Institute for Social Educators). Copenhagen: Højvangseminariet.

Index

Note: Main encyclopedia entries are indicated by **bold** type

Index